APPLICATIONS

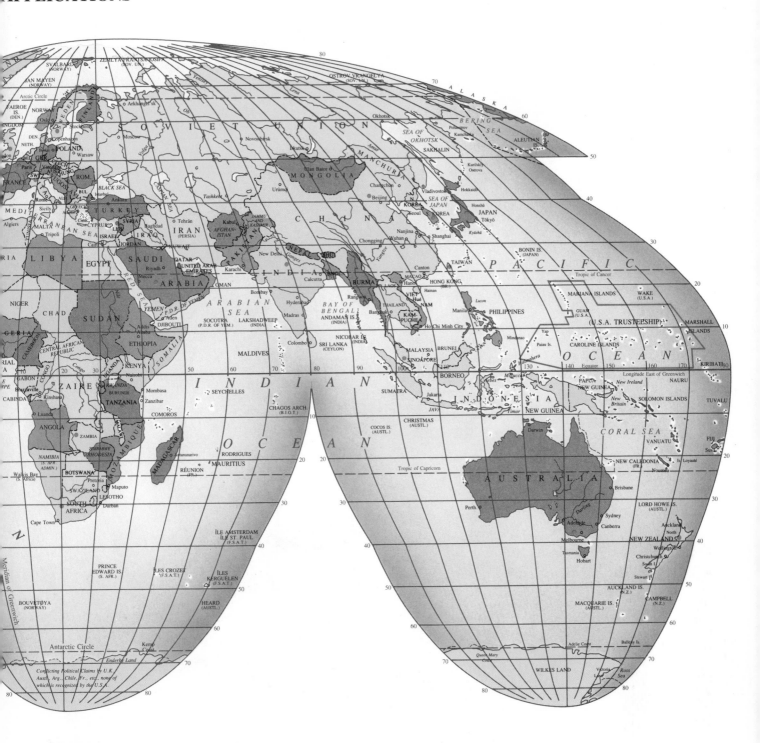

THIRD EDITION

MANGEMENT

Stephen P. Robbins

San Diego State University

PRENTICE HALL
Englewood Cliffs, New Jersey

Library of Congress Cataloging-in-Publication Data

Robbins, Stephen P.,
    Management / Stephen P. Robbins.—3rd ed.
        p.   cm.
    Includes index.
    ISBN 0-13-556655-X
    1. Management.   I. Title.
HD31.R5647   1991
658—dc20   90-42718
                                                       CIP

© 1991, 1988, 1984 by Prentice-Hall, Inc.
A Division of Simon & Schuster
Englewood Cliffs, New Jersey 07632

Editorial/production supervision: *York Production Services*
Interior and cover design: *York Production Services*
Manufacturing buyers: *Trudy Pisciotti/Robert Anderson*
Photo research: *Teri Stratford*

Printed in the United States of America
10 9 8 7 6 5 4 3 2

ISBN 0-13-556655-X

Prentice-Hall International (UK) Limited, *London*
Prentice-Hall of Australia Pty. Limited, *Sydney*
Prentice-Hall Canada Inc., *Toronto*
Prentice-Hall Hispanoamericana, S.A., *Mexico*
Prentice-Hall of India Private Limited, *New Delhi*
Prentice-Hall of Japan, Inc., *Tokyo*
Simon & Schuster Asia Pte. Ltd., *Singapore*
Editora Prentice-Hall do Brasil, Ltda., *Rio de Janeiro*

This book is dedicated to those unsung heroes without whose sugar and caffeine products this revision could never have been completed:

Coca-Cola Corp.
Godiva Division of Pillsbury
Gourmet Coffee To Go
Hershey Foods
Mars, Inc.
Mrs. Fields
Sara Lee Corp.

ABOUT THE AUTHOR

STEPHEN P. ROBBINS is Professor of Management at San Diego State University. Before receiving his Ph. D. from the University of Arizona, he worked for the Shell Oil Company and Reynolds Metals Company. Since completing his doctorate, Professor Robbins has taught at the University of Nebraska at Omaha and the Sir George Williams campus of Concordia University in Montreal. He has also held visiting appointments at the University of Baltimore and Southern Illinois University at Edwardsville.

Professor Robbins' research interests have focused on conflict, power, and politics in organizations, as well as the development of effective interpersonal skills. His articles on these and other topics have appeared in such journals as *Business Horizons,* the *California Management Review, Business and Economic Perspectives, International Management, Management Review, Organizational Behavior Teaching Review,* and the *Canadian Personnel and Industrial Relations Journal.* In recent years, Professor Robbins has been spending most of his time writing textbooks. He currently has eight books in print, several of which have been translated into foreign languages and made into Canadian and Australian editions. Professor Robbins' books are currently used in more than 500 U.S. colleges and universities.

BRIEF CONTENTS

•

CONTENTS

●

PART TWO

DEFINING THE MANAGER'S TERRAIN

CHAPTER

ORGANIZATIONAL CULTURE AND ENVIRONMENT: THE CONSTRAINTS 67

CHAPTER

INTERNATIONAL MANAGEMENT: RESPONDING TO A GLOBAL ENVIRONMENT 93

CHAPTER

SOCIAL RESPONSIBILITY AND MANAGERIAL ETHICS 117

CHAPTER 6

DECISION MAKING: THE ESSENCE OF
THE MANAGER'S JOB 151

PART THREE

PLANNING

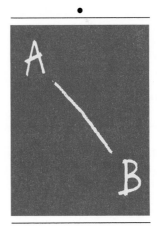

CHAPTER 7

FOUNDATIONS OF PLANNING 189

CHAPTER

STRATEGIC PLANNING AND
MANAGEMENT 215

CHAPTER

PLANNING TOOLS AND
TECHNIQUES 245

PART FOUR

ORGANIZING

•

CHAPTER **10**
•

FOUNDATIONS OF ORGANIZING 283

CHAPTER **11**
•

ORGANIZATION AND JOB DESIGN OPTIONS 313

CHAPTER 12

HUMAN RESOURCE MANAGEMENT 349

PART FIVE

LEADING

CHAPTER 13

FOUNDATIONS OF INDIVIDUAL AND GROUP BEHAVIOR 397

PART SIX

CONTROLLING

CHAPTER 18

FOUNDATIONS OF CONTROL 563

CHAPTER 17

MANAGING CHANGE 527

CHAPTER 19

INFORMATION CONTROL SYSTEMS
591

CHAPTER 20

OPERATIONS MANAGEMENT 625

PREFACE TO THE STUDENT

•

•

A preface should provide answers to certain key questions. I have specifically identified six: (1) What assumptions have guided the development of this book? (2) Is the content up-to-date? (3) How does the book itself facilitate learning for the reader? (4) Who else, besides the person whose name is on the front cover, helped to create this book? Let me try now to answer each of these questions.

ASSUMPTIONS

Every author who sits down to write a book has a set of assumptions—either explicit or implied—that guide what is included and what is excluded. I want to state mine upfront.

Management is an exciting field. The subject matter encompassed in an introductory management book is inherently exciting. We're not talking about esoteric theories here. We're talking about the real world. We're talking about why Honda and Toyota are beating the pants off General Motors; how, in less than half a dozen years, Walt Disney Co. went from mediocre performance to being one of the best managed, most profitable entertainment organizations in the world; how to cut waste and control costs in hospitals; and techniques that can make your state motor vehicle department more efficient and responsive to clients.

A good management text should capture this excitement. Nowhere is it written that a textbook *has* to be dry and boring! If its subject matter is exciting, the text should reflect that fact. It should include lots of examples and photographs to make concepts come alive, capture the excitement of the field, and convey this excitement to the reader.

Management should not be studied solely from the perspective of "top management" or "billion-dollar

corporations." The subject matter in management encompasses everyone from the lowest supervisor to the chief executive officer. The content should give as much attention to the challenges and opportunities in supervising fifteen clerical workers as those in directing a cadre of MBA-educated executive vice presidents. Similarly, not everyone wants to work for a *Fortune* 500 company. Readers who are interested in working in small businesses or not-for-profit organizations should find the descriptions of management concepts applicable to their needs.

Content should emphasize relevance. Before an author commits something to paper and includes it in his or her text, it should meet the "So what?" test. Why would someone need to know this fact or that? If the relevance isn't overtly clear, either the item should be omitted or its relevance should be directly explained.

Content should be timely. We live in dynamic times. Changes are taking place at an unprecedented pace. A textbook in a dynamic field like management must reflect this fact by including the latest concepts and practices.

UP-TO-DATE CONTENT

Management is a dynamic field and a management text should reflect this fact. The following is a partial list of some of the more significant changes and additions made in this revision to keep the text up to date (specific page numbers are provided for quick references):

- Luthan's research on effective versus successful managers (p. 12)
- Deming on improved production efficiency (pp. 52 and 629)
- The European Community, maquiladoras, and other

regional cooperative arrangements (pp. 100–04)
- Three different views on ethics (pp. 132–33)
- Significantly expanded coverage of strategic frameworks (pp. 225–35)
- Totally revamped presentation of basic organization design concepts (pp. 286–99)
- New and improved model for understanding group behavior (pp. 417–20)
- New model that integrates the major motivation theories (pp. 442–44)
- Charismatic leadership (pp. 477–79)
- New material on interpersonal skills (pp. 499–520)
- "Calm-water" versus "white-water rapids" metaphors of change (pp. 532–33)
- Use of information systems to gain a competitive advantage (pp. 612–15)
- Technology and product development (pp. 648)
- Speed in operations management as a competitive advantage (pp. 654)

IN-TEXT LEARNING AIDS

A good textbook should teach as well as present ideas. Toward that end, I've tried to make this book an effective learning tool. Let me specifically point out some pedagogical features that are designed to help readers better assimilate the material presented.

Chapter objectives. Before you start a trip, it's valuable to know where you're headed. That way, you can minimize detours. The same holds true in reading a text. To make your learning more efficient, each chapter of this book opens with a list of learning objectives that describe what you should be able to do after reading the chapter. These objectives are designed to focus your attention on the major issues within each chapter.

Chapter summaries. Just as objectives clarify where one is going, chapter summaries remind you where you've been. Each chapter of this book concludes with a concise summary organized around the opening learning objectives.

Key terms. Every chapter includes a number of key terms that you'll need to know. These terms are highlighted in bold print when they first appear and are defined at that time in the adjoining margin. These same terms are also grouped together at the end of the book in the Glossary.

Review questions. Every chapter in this book ends with a set of ten review questions. If you have read and understood the contents of a chapter, you should be able to answer these questions. They are drawn directly from the material in the chapter.

Discussion questions. In addition to the review questions, each chapter also has five discussion questions that go beyond the content of the chapter. They require you to integrate, synthesize, or apply management concepts. The discussion questions allow you to demonstrate that you not only know the facts in the chapter but also can use those facts to deal with more complex issues.

ACKNOWLEDGMENTS

Every author relies on the comments of reviewers, and mine were particularly helpful. I want to thank the following people for their comments and suggestions:

Professor Alan L. Carsrud, *University of Southern California*

Professor Patricia Feltes, *Southwest Missouri State University*

Professor Roger Volkema, *American University in Washington*

Professor Carleton S. (Pete) Everett, *Des Moines Area Community College*

Professor Diane L. Ferry, *University of Delaware*

Professor Jack Maroun, *Herkimer City Community College*

Professor Roy A. Cook, *Fort Lewis College*

Professor Robert S. Bulls, *J. Sargeant Reynolds College*

Professor David G. Williams, *West Virginia University*

Professor Robert A. Figler, *University of Akron*

Professor Donald G. Muston, *Elizabethtown College*

Professor Victor G. Panico, *California State University, Fresno*

Professor Dixon G. Stevens, *College of Saint Rose*

Professor James Horsford, *Northeastern Junior College*

Professor Judson C. Faurer, *Metro State College*

Professor Milan Savan, *Walsh College*

Professor John A. Hornaday, *Daniel Webster College*

Professor Anne C. Cowden, *California State University—Sacramento*

Professor Deborah Wells, *Creighton University*

Professor Linda Wicander, *Central Michigan University*

Professor Doris P. McConnell, *Northern Virginia Community College*

Professor Donald Baynham, *Eastfield College*

Professor Phyllis G. Holland, *Valdosta State College*

Professor Douglas Jones, *Jacksonville University*

Professor Dale Feinauer, *University of Wisconsin*

Professor Taggart Ford Frost, *University of Northern Iowa*

Professor Bernard L. Hinton, *California State University, Chico*

In addition, I want to thank my colleague at San Diego State, F. Neil Brady, for his ideas and comments on the "Ethical Dilemmas in Management" features. A number of the dilemmas used in these features are direct applications of ideas that Neil suggested.

As I stated in the second edition, a book is not a book without a publisher. Mine is Prentice-Hall. There isn't enough room for me to name all the P-H people, past and present, to whom I'm indebted. However, the following made major contributions to this text: Alison Reeves, Dennis Hogan, Jenny Kletzin, Caroline Ruddle, Lori Morris-Nantz, and Lioux Brun.

To all the people at Prentice Hall: Thanks!

Finally, this book was designed and produced by a highly competent team of people at York Production Services. They brought new meaning, to me, to the term "fast turnaround." I thank you for an outstanding job.

Stephen P. Robbins
Del Mar, California

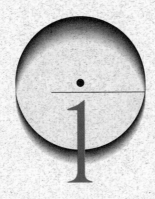

MANAGERS
AND
MANAGEMENT

LEARNING OBJECTIVES

After Reading This Chapter, You Should Be Able To:

1. Differentiate managers from operatives.
2. Define management.
3. Distinguish between effectiveness and efficiency.
4. Identify the roles performed by managers.
5. Differentiate the activities of successful managers from effective ones.
6. Explain whether the manager's job is generic.
7. Explain the value of studying management.

Alice Illchman is an academic administrator. As president of Sarah Lawrence College in Bronxville, New York, she presides over a small but highly regarded liberal arts college. For the past month, she has been spending a good deal of her time developing the first draft of the college's five-year plan.

WMNE are the call letters for a radio station in Portland, Maine. Stan Kivett is WMNE's general manager. One of Stan's responsibilities is to review the monthly sales report. He does this on the first Monday of every month, analyzing the data from the preceding month. He compares the station's actual sales figures against the estimates he and the station's sales manager had prepared six months earlier; he notes important deviations and then discusses these deviations with the sales manager.

Marva Johnson is a supervisor in the claims department at Mutual of Omaha. One of her major tasks is scheduling work for the twelve clerks who report to her. On the Monday morning we observed her, she reviewed her department's work load for that week, prepared schedules for each of her employees, and called each in individually to discuss her performance expectations for the coming week and any problems that her clerks should be on the lookout for.

EC-Audiotronics of Austin, Texas, is a relatively new company—less than a year old—but business is booming. The firm manufactures several electronic components that are used in compact disc players. The company already employs fifteen people, and its owner, Joe Hernandez, thinks that sales, profits, and his labor force will triple during the next twelve months. The morning we observed Joe in action, he spent most of his time interviewing candidates for several newly created positions as design engineers.

It was a typical busy day in the life of Maureen O'Connor, mayor of San Diego. During the early morning, she attended several meetings. Later, she reprimanded one of her assistants for being late with a report that the assistant and his staff were completing on the effectiveness of the city's fire department. Lunch was spent with a group of Republican fund-raisers. The mayor worked most of the afternoon on a speech she would give later in the week on her position concerning population growth and building restrictions in the City of San Diego. In the speech, she would present her arguments for specific controls on the development of new housing projects.

All the individuals named above have something in common. While they work in widely different organizations—profit and not-for-profit, small and large, some at the top and some near the bottom, in a variety of locations—the one thing they have in common is that they are all managers. The activities we have described are some of the activities associated with management.

This book is about people like Alice Illchman, Stan Kivett, Marva Johnson, Joe Hernandez, Maureen O'Connor, and millions more like them and about the jobs they do. This book is about managers and management. In this chapter, we want to introduce you to managers and management by answering, or at least beginning to answer, these questions: *Who* are managers? *What* is management and *what* do managers do? And *why* should you spend your time studying management?

WHO ARE MANAGERS?

organization
A systematic arrangement of people to accomplish some specific purpose.

Managers work in a place we call an organization. Therefore, before we can identify who managers are, it is important to clarify what we mean by the term *organization*.

An **organization** is a systematic arrangement of people to accomplish some specific purpose. Your college or university is an organization. So are fraternities, government agencies, churches, the Xerox Corporation, your neighborhood gas station, the American Medical Association, the New York Yankees baseball team, and the United Way. These are all organizations because they all have three common characteristics.

First, each has a distinct purpose. This purpose is typically expressed in terms of a goal or set of goals. Second, each is composed of people. Third, all organizations develop a systematic structure that defines and limits the behavior of its members. This would include, for example, creating rules and regulations, identifying some members as "bosses" and giving them authority over other members, or writing up job descriptions so that members know what they are supposed to do. The term *organization* therefore refers to an entity that has a distinct purpose, includes people or members, and has a systematic structure.

operatives
People who work directly on a job or task and have no responsibility for overseeing the work of others.

managers
Individuals in an organization who direct the activities of others.

Managers work in organizations, but not everyone in an organization is a manager. For simplicity's sake, we can divide organizational members into two categories: operatives or managers. **Operatives** are people who work directly on a job or task and have *no* responsibility for overseeing the work of others. The people who attach fenders in an automobile assembly line, cook your hamburger at McDonald's, or process your license renewal application at the state motor vehicles office are all operatives. In contrast, **managers** direct the activities of other people. They are shown in the colored areas in Figure 1–1. Managers may also have some operative responsibilities; for example, a typing pool supervisor may also have basic typing responsibilities in addition to overseeing the activities of the other typists in the pool. However, our definition presumes that a manager has subordinates. Also, as shown in Figure 1–1, we typically classify managers as either first-line, middle, or top.

Identifying exactly who the managers are in an organization is not a difficult task, although you should be aware that managers come packaged in a variety of titles.

FIGURE 1–1
Organizational Levels

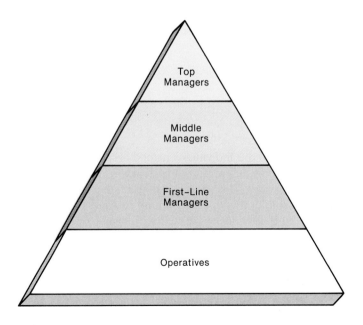

first-line managers
Supervisors; the lowest level of management.

First-line managers are usually called supervisors. In a manufacturing plant, the first-line (or lowest level) manager may be called a foreman. On an athletic team, this job carries the title of coach. Middle managers may have titles such as department or agency head, project leader, unit chief, district manager, dean, bishop, or division manager. At or near the top of an organization, managers typically have titles such as vice president, president, chancellor, managing director, chief operating officer, chief executive officer, or chairman of the board. In a manufacturing company, a twenty-five-year managerial career might include the following sequence of job titles: production foreman, shift foreman, scheduling manager, assistant plant superintendent, plant superintendent, plant manager, district operations manager, eastern regional manufacturing manager, and vice president of manufacturing. In a large metropolitan school district, a twenty-five-year journey up the managerial ladder might include titles such as department head, principal, assistant superintendent for administrative affairs, and district superintendent.

WHAT IS MANAGEMENT AND WHAT DO MANAGERS DO?

Just as organizations have common characteristics, so do managers. In spite of the fact that their titles vary widely, there are common characteristics to their jobs—regardless of whether the manager is a $25,000-a-year supervisor in the mailroom at Hershey Foods who oversees a staff of five or the $1.2 million-a-year chairman of the board of AT&T responsible for coordinating an organization with 300,000 employees and with an annual sales total of $35 billion. In this section, we define management, present the classical functions of management, review recent research on managerial roles, and consider the universal applicability of managerial concepts.

Defining Management

management
The process of getting activities completed efficiently with and through other people.

efficiency
The relationship between inputs and outputs; seeks to minimize resource costs.

effectiveness
Goal attainment.

The term **management** refers to the process of getting activities completed efficiently with and through other people.

The *process* represents the functions or primary activities engaged in by managers. These functions are typically labeled planning, organizing, leading, and controlling. We elaborate on these functions in the next section.

Efficiency is a vital part of management. It refers to the relationship between inputs and outputs. If you get more output for a given input, you have increased efficiency. Similarly, if you can get the same output from less input, you again increase efficiency. Since managers deal with input resources that are scarce—money, people, equipment—they are concerned with the efficient use of these resources. Management, therefore, is concerned with minimizing resource costs.

It is not enough simply to be efficient. Management is also concerned with getting activities completed; that is, it seeks **effectiveness.** When managers achieve their organization's goals, we say they are effective. So efficiency is concerned with means and effectiveness with ends. (See Figure 1–2.)

Efficiency and effectiveness are interrelated. For instance, it is easier to be effective if one ignores efficiency. Seiko could produce more accurate and attractive timepieces if it disregarded labor and material input costs. Some federal agencies have been regularly attacked on the ground that they are reasonably effective but extremely inefficient; that is, they get their job done but at a very high cost. Management is therefore concerned not only with getting activities completed (effectiveness), but also with doing so as efficiently as possible.

FIGURE 1–2
Management Seeks Efficiency and Effectiveness

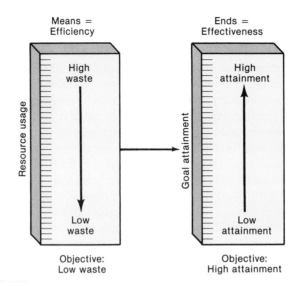

Can organizations be efficient and yet not be effective? Yes, by doing the wrong things well! A number of colleges have become highly efficient in processing students. Through the use of computer-assisted learning, large classes, and heavy reliance on part-time faculty, the administrators have significantly cut the cost of educating each student. Yet some of these colleges have been criticized by students, alumni, and accrediting agencies for failing to educate their students properly. Of course, high efficiency is associated more typically with high effectiveness. And poor management is most often due to both inefficiency and ineffectiveness or to effectiveness achieved through inefficiency.

Large classes are *efficient.* They allow instructors to teach more students. But are large classes *effective*? That has been an issue of some debate.

Management Functions

In the early part of this century, a French industrialist by the name of Henri Fayol wrote that all managers perform five management functions: They plan, organize, command, coordinate, and control.[1] In the mid-1950s, two professors at UCLA used the functions of planning, organizing, staffing, directing, and controlling as the framework for a textbook on management that for twenty years was unquestionably the most widely sold text on the subject.[2] The most popular textbooks (and this one is no exception) still continue to be organized around **management functions,** though these have generally been condensed down to the basic four: planning, organizing, leading, and controlling. (See Figure 1–3.) Let's briefly define what each of these functions encompasses.

If you don't have any particular destination in mind, any road will get you there. Since organizations exist to achieve some purpose, someone has to define that purpose and the means for its achievement. Management is that someone. The **planning** function encompasses defining an organization's goals, establishing an overall strategy for achieving these goals, and developing a comprehensive hierarchy of plans to integrate and coordinate activities.

Managers are also responsible for designing an organization's structure. We call this function **organizing.** It includes the determination of what tasks are to be done, who is to do them, how the tasks are to be grouped, who reports to whom, and where decisions are to be made.

Every organization contains people, and it is management's job to direct and coordinate these people. This is the **leading** function. When managers motivate subordinates, direct the activities of others, select the most effective communication channel, or resolve conflicts among members, they are engaging in leading.

The final function managers perform is **controlling.** After the goals are set; the plans formulated; the structural arrangements delineated; and the people hired, trained, and motivated, something may still go amiss. To ensure that things are going as they should, management must monitor the organization's performance. Actual performance must be compared with the previously set goals. If there are any significant deviations, it is management's job to get the organization back on track. This process of monitoring, comparing, and correcting is what we mean when we refer to the controlling function.

The continued popularity of the functional approach is a tribute to its clarity and simplicity. But it is an accurate description of what managers actually do?[3] Following the functional approach, it is easy to answer the question, What do managers do? They plan, organize, lead, and control. But is this really true of all managers? Fayol's original

management functions
Planning, organizing, leading, and controlling.

planning
Includes defining goals, establishing strategy, and developing plans to coordinate activities.

organizing
Determining what tasks are to be done, who is to do them, how the tasks are to be grouped, who reports to whom, and where decisions are to be made.

leading
Includes motivating subordinates, directing others, selecting the most effective communication channels, and resolving conflicts.

controlling
Monitoring activities to ensure that they are being accomplished as planned and correcting any significant deviations.

FIGURE 1–3
Management Functions

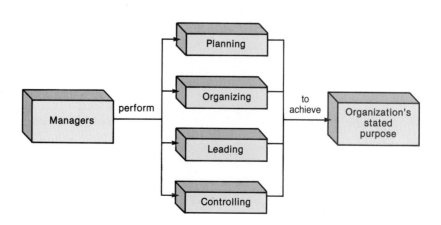

Mintzberg found that managers prefer verbal communications that can be accessed quickly—such as telephone calls, unscheduled meetings, and informal encounters—rather than well-documented reports.

functions were not derived from a careful survey of thousands of managers in hundreds of organizations. Rather, they merely represented observations based on his experience in the French mining industry.

Management Roles

In the late 1960s, Henry Mintzberg undertook a careful study of five executives at work.[4] What he discovered challenged several long-held notions about the manager's job. For instance, in contrast to the predominant views at the time that managers were reflective thinkers who carefully and systematically processed information before making decisions, Mintzberg found that his managers engaged in a large number of varied, unpatterned, and short-duration activities. There was little time for reflective thinking because the managers encountered constant interruptions. Half of these managers' activities lasted less than nine minutes. But in addition to these insights, Mintzberg provided a categorization scheme for defining what managers do based on actual managers on the job.

management roles
Behaviors attributable to a job or position.

Mintzberg concluded that managers perform ten different but highly interrelated roles. The term **management roles** refers to behaviors attributable to a job or position. As shown in Table 1–1, these ten roles can be grouped as those primarily concerned with interpersonal relationships, those with the transfer of information, and those with decision making.

TABLE 1–1   Mintzberg's Managerial Roles

Role	Description	Identifiable Activities
Interpersonal		
Figurehead	Symbolic head; obliged to perform a number of routine duties of a legal or social nature	Ceremony, status requests, solicitations
Leader	Responsible for the motivation and activation of subordinates; responsible for staffing, training, and associated duties	Virtually all managerial activities involving subordinates
Liaison	Maintains self-developed network of outside contacts and informers who provide favors and information	Acknowledgements of mail; external board work; other activities involving outsiders

Role	Description	Identifiable Activities
Informational		
Monitor	Seeks and receives wide variety of special information (much of it current) to develop thorough understanding of organization and environment; emerges as nerve center of internal and external information of the organization	Handling all mail and contacts categorized as concerned primarily with receiving information (e.g., periodical news, observational tours)
Disseminator	Transmits information received from outsiders or from other subordinates to members of the organization; some information factual, some involving interpretation and integration of diverse value positions of organizational influencers	Forwarding mail into organization for informational purposes, verbal contacts involving information flow to subordinates (e.g., review sessions, instant communication flows)
Spokesperson	Transmits information to outsiders on organization's plans, policies, actions, results, etc.; serves as expert on organization's industry	Board meetings; handling mail and contacts involving transmission of information to outsiders
Decisional		
Entrepreneur	Searches organization and its environment for opportunities and initiates "improvement projects" to bring about change; supervises design of certain projects as well	Strategy and review sessions involving initiation or design of improvement projects
Disturbance handler	Responsible for corrective action when organization faces important, unexpected disturbances	Strategy and review sessions involving disturbances and crises
Resource allocator	Responsible for the allocation of organizational resources of all kinds—in effect, the making or approval of all significant organizational decisions	Scheduling; requests for authorization; any activity involving budgeting and the programming of subordinates' work
Negotiator	Responsible for representing the organization at major negotiations	Negotiation

Source: Henry Mintzberg, _The Nature of Managerial Work_ (New York: Harper & Row, 1973), pp. 93–94. Copyright © 1973 by Henry Mintzberg. Reprinted by permission of Harper & Row, Publishers, Inc.

interpersonal roles
Roles that include figurehead, leadership, and liaison activities.

Interpersonal Roles   All managers are required to perform duties that are ceremonial and symbolic in nature. When the president of a college hands out diplomas at commencement or a factory supervisor gives a group of high school students a tour of the plant, he or she is acting in a _figurehead_ role. All managers have a _leadership_ role.

This role includes hiring, training, motivating, and disciplining employees. The third role within the interpersonal grouping is the *liaison* role. Mintzberg described this activity as contacting outsiders who provide the manager with information. These may be individuals or groups inside or outside the organization. The sales manager who obtains information from the personnel manager in his or her same company has an internal liaison relationship. When that sales manager has contacts with other sales executives through a marketing trade association, he or she has an outside liaison relationship.

informational roles
Roles that include monitoring, disseminating, and spokesperson activities.

Informational Roles   All managers will, to some degree, receive and collect information from organizations and institutions outside their own. Typically, this is done through reading magazines and talking with others to learn of changes in the public's tastes, what competitors may be planning, and the like. Mintzberg called this the *monitor* role. Managers also act as a conduit to transmit information to organizational members. This is the *disseminator* role. Managers also perform a *spokesperson* role when they represent the organization to outsiders.

decisional roles
Roles that include those of entrepreneur, disturbance handler, resource allocator, and negotiator.

Decisional Roles   Finally, Mintzberg identified four roles that revolve around the making of choices. In the *entrepreneur* role, managers initiate and oversee new projects that will improve their organization's performance. As *disturbance handlers,* managers take corrective action in response to previously unforeseen problems. As *resource allocators,* managers are responsible for allocating human, physical, and monetary resources. Last, managers perform a *negotiator* role, in which they discuss and bargain with other units to gain advantages for their own unit.

An Evaluation   A number of follow-up studies have tested the validity of Mintzberg's role categories across different types of organizations and at different levels within given organizations.[5] The evidence generally supports the idea that managers—regardless of the type of organization or level in the organization—perform similar roles. However, the emphasis that managers give to the various roles seems to change with hierarchical level.[6] Specifically, the roles of disseminator, figurehead, negotiator, liaison, and spokesperson are more important at the higher levels than at the lower ones. Conversely, the leader role is more important for lower-level managers than it is for either middle- or top-level managers.

Have these ten roles, which are derived from actual observations of managerial work, invalidated the more traditional functions of planning, organizing, leading, and controlling? No!

First, the functional approach still represents the most useful way of conceptualizing the manager's job. "The classical functions provide clear and discrete methods of classifying the thousands of activities that managers carry out and the techniques they use in terms of the functions they perform for the achievement of organizational goals."[7] Second, although Mintzberg may offer a more detailed and elaborate classification scheme of what managers do, these roles are substantially reconcilable with the four functions.[8] Many of Mintzberg's roles align smoothly with one or more of the functions. Resource allocation is part of planning, as is the entrepreneurial role. All three of the interpersonal roles are part of the leading function. Most of the other roles fit into one or more of the four functions. But not all of them do. The difference is substantially explained by Mintzberg's intermixing management activities and pure managerial work.[9]

All managers do *some* work that is not purely managerial. The fact that Mintzberg's executives spent time in public relations or raising money attests to the precision of Mintzberg's observational methods, but not everything a manager does is necessarily an essential part of the manager's job. This may have resulted in some activities being included in Mintzberg's schema that should not have been.

Do the comments above mean that Mintzberg's role categories are invalid? Not at all! Mintzberg has clearly offered new insights into what managers do. The attention his work has received is evidence of the importance attributed to defining management roles. But, as we will point out in the next chapter, management is a young discipline that is still evolving. Future research comparing and integrating Mintzberg's roles with the four functions will continue to expand our understanding of the manager's job.

ETHICAL DILEMMAS IN MANAGEMENT

Is it Wrong to Tell a Lie?

An instructor might not be able to change moral standards in a college classroom, but he or she can teach students how to analyze questions so that they can bring to bear whatever moral standards they have when they make decisions.

If you haven't already done so, there is no better time than now to develop a rule or set of rules against which you can measure the "rightness" or "wrongness" of your decisions and actions. It may be nothing more provocative than "Do unto others as you would have them do unto you." Or it might be a question or set of questions that you consistently ask: How would I feel about explaining what I did to my parents or children? How would I feel if the action I took was described, in detail, on the front page of my local newspaper? Have I avoided even the appearance that there might be a conflict of interest in my decision? Would my action infringe on the liberty or constitutional rights of others?

Let's begin our look at ethical dilemmas in management by asking: Is it wrong to tell a lie?

Mintzberg found that managers play a number of roles, one of which is to act as a spokesperson. In this specific role, a manager transmits information to people outside the organization. Occasionally, the facts that the manager must transmit and explain aren't particularly flattering to the organization. This presents the dilemma of whether or not it is unethical to tell a lie.

For example, a senior manager is reviewing her company's financial performance for the previous year at the annual stockholders' meeting. The news is not good. Sales dropped 30 percent, and profits are down 50 percent. A stockholder asks the manager, "What caused this drastic decline and has it been corrected?" The manager knows that the primary cause of the decline was a series of poor top-management decisions made over the past several years, but she also knows that's not what her management colleagues want her to say. Further, she personally believes that the decline is far from over, but she recognizes that's not what the stockholders want to hear.

Should this manager lie? Is lying always wrong, or is it acceptable under certain circumstances? What, if any, would those circumstances be? What do *you* think?

Are Effective Managers Also Successful Managers?

Fred Luthans and his associates looked at the issue of what managers do from a somewhat different perspective.[10] They asked the question: Do managers who move up most quickly in an organization do the same activities and with the same emphasis as those managers who do the best job? You would tend to think that those managers who were the most effective in their jobs would also be the ones who were promoted fastest. But that's not what appears to happen.

Luthans and his associates studied more than 450 managers. What they found was that these managers all engaged in four managerial activities:

1. *Traditional management:* Decision-making, planning, and controlling
2. *Communication:* Exchanging routine information and processing paperwork
3. *Human resource management:* Motivating, disciplining, managing conflict, staffing, and training
4. *Networking:* Socializing, politicking, and interacting with outsiders

The "average" manager studied spent 32 percent of his or her time in traditional management activities, 29 percent communicating, 20 percent in human resource management activities, and 19 percent networking. However, the amount of time and effort that different managers spent on these four activities varied a great deal. Specifically, as shown in Table 1–2, managers who were *successful* (defined in terms of the speed of promotion within their organization) had a very different emphasis than managers who were *effective* (defined in terms of the quantity and quality of their performance and the satisfaction and commitment of their subordinates). Networking makes the biggest relative contribution to manager success, while human resource management activities made the least relative contribution. Among effective managers, communication made the largest relative contribution and networking the least.

This study adds important insights to our knowledge of what managers do. On average, managers spend approximately 20 to 30 percent of their time on each of the four activities of traditional management, communication, human resource management, and networking. However, successful managers don't give the same emphasis to activities as do effective managers. In fact, they do almost the opposite. This challenges the historical assumption that promotions are based on performance, vividly illustrating the importance that social and political skills play in getting ahead in organizations.

TABLE 1–2   Allocation of Activities by Time

Activity	Average Managers	Successful Managers	Effective Managers
Traditional management	32	13	19
Communication	29	28	44
Human resource management	20	11	26
Networking	19	48	11

Based on Fred Luthans, Richard M. Hodgetts, and Stuart A. Rosenkrantz, *Real Managers* (Cambridge, Mass.: Ballinger Publishing, 1988).

Is the Manager's Job Universal?

We have previously mentioned the universal application of management. To this point, we have discussed management as if it were generic; that is, a *manager* is a *manager* regardless of where he or she manages. If management is truly a generic discipline, then what a manager does should be essentially the same regardless of whether he or she is a top-level executive or low-level supervisor; in a business firm or a government agency; in a large corporation or small business; or located in Paris, France, or Paris, Texas. Let's take a closer look at the generic issue.

Organizational Level   We have already acknowledged that the importance of managerial roles varies depending on the manager's level in the organization. But the fact that a supervisor in a research laboratory at Dow Chemical doesn't do exactly the same things that the president of Dow Chemical does should not be interpreted to mean that their jobs are inherently different. The differences are of degree and emphasis, but not of function.

The type of planning that top managers do is different from that performed by lower-level managers. The senior manager on the top is engaged in long-term planning, while the supervisor below is reviewing a daily production schedule for his department.

FIGURE 1–4
Distribution of Time per
Function by Organizational
Level

Source: Adapted from T. A. Mahoney, T. H.
Jerdee, and S. J. Carroll, "The Job(s) of
Management," *Industrial Relations,* vol. 4,
no. 2 (1965), p. 103.

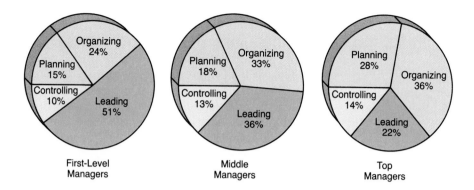

In functional terms, as managers move up the organization, they do more planning and less direct supervising. This is visually depicted in Figure 1–4. All managers, regardless of level, make decisions. They perform planning, organizing, leading, and controlling functions. But the amount of time they give to each function is not necessarily constant. Additionally, the content of the managerial functions changes with the manager's level. For example, as we'll demonstrate in Chapter 11, top managers are concerned with designing the overall organization, while lower-level managers focus on designing the jobs of individuals and work groups.

Organizational Type   Does a manager who works for the Internal Revenue Service or a public library do the same things that a manager in a business firm does? Put another way, is the manager's job the same in both profit and not-for-profit organizations? The answer is: For the most part, yes.[11]

First, let's dispense with a few myths that surround the manager's job in public organizations.

Myth #1: Decisions in public organizations emphasize political priorities, while decisions in business organizations are rational and apolitical. *Truth:* Decisions in all organizations are influenced by political considerations. We'll discuss this fact in Chapter 6.

Myth #2: Public decision makers, in contrast to their business counterparts, are constrained by administrative procedures that limit managerial authority and autonomy. *Truth:* As we'll show in Chapter 3, almost all managers find that significant constraints have been placed on their managerial discretion.

Myth #3: It's hard to get high performance out of government employees because, compared to their business counterparts, they're lazy, more security oriented, and less motivated. *Truth:* The evidence indicates that there is no significant difference in the motivational needs between public and business employees.[12]

Regardless of the type of organization a manager works in, there are commonalities to his or her job. All make decisions, set objectives, create workable organization structures, hire and motivate employees, seek efficiency, secure legitimacy for their organization's existence, and develop internal political support in order to implement programs.

Of course, there are some noteworthy differences. The most important is measuring performance. Profit, or "the bottom line," acts as an unambiguous measure of the effectiveness of a business organization. There is no such universal measure in not-for-profit organizations. Measuring the performance of schools, museums, government agencies, or charitable organizations, therefore, is made considerably more difficult. Managers in these organizations generally don't face the market test for performance.

MANAGERS WHO MADE A DIFFERENCE

General W. L. Creech of the U.S. Tactical Air Command

Good management practices are as relevant to managing a military unit as they are to an automobile factory. General W. L. Creech demonstrated that when he became commander of the U.S. Tactical Air Command (TAC) in 1978.[13]

Creech took over an organization in complete disarray. TAC had more than 115,000 full-time employees, 150 installations around the world, and a multi-billion-dollar budget. But its effectiveness—that is, its ability to defend U.S. interests in the skies anywhere in the world—had become a joke. In 1978, half of TAC's $25 billion aircraft fleet was not battle ready. More than 200 planes were grounded for weeks on end for lack of spare parts or maintenance. The average plane, which had flown 23 missions a month in 1969, was down to flying only 11 by 1978. Morale of pilots, mechanics, and technicians was at a devastatingly low level. The best of these people were deserting the organization in droves. Worst of all, a soaring accident rate was resulting in tragic deaths of TAC pilots and the unnecessary loss of expensive aircraft. For every 100,000 hours flown, seven planes were crashing. Investigators were blaming many of these crashes on faulty maintenance.

The major source of these problems, as Creech saw it, was that TAC decision making had become too centralized. Senior management didn't trust or respect the ability of TAC personnel to make the key decisions that affected their work. The overbearing, centralized control imposed from the top had robbed personnel of their spirit and initiative. Creech was determined to change all that. In the next half-dozen years, he completely revamped the TAC organization to emphasize motivation, competition, delegation, and employee accountability. Just a few of the changes that Creech instituted were restructuring commands into much smaller units, setting up maintenance teams that were assigned to specific planes, and allowing squadron commanders to design their own flying schedules.

The results from Creech's changes were nothing short of miraculous. Only a handful of planes were no longer battle ready. The average missions per plane were up to 21 a month. Orders for parts that had previously taken hours were now being filled in minutes. Morale and pride were up, as evidenced by reenlistment rates that were nearly double the rate that existed the year before Creech's arrival. The all-important accident rate had been slashed from one crash for every 13,000 flying hours to one for every 50,000, and crashes traced to faulty maintenance nearly vanished. Interestingly, these improvements in TAC effectiveness were achieved with no more money, no more planes, and no more personnel than were in place when Creech accepted the command.

Photo courtesy of General W. L. Creech.

Our conclusion is that, while there are distinctions between the management of profit and not-for-profit organizations, the two are far more alike than they are different. Both are similarly concerned with studying the role of decision makers as they plan, organize, lead, and control.

Organizational Size   Is the manager's job any different in a small organization than in a large one? This question is best answered by looking at the job of managers in small business firms and comparing them to our previous discussion of managerial roles. First, however, let's define *small business* and the part it plays in our society.

There is no commonly agreed-upon definition of a small business because of different criteria used to define "small"—for example, number of employees, annual sales, or total assets. For our purposes, we'll call a **small business** any independently owned and operated, profit-seeking enterprise that has fewer than 100 employees and annual sales of less than $5 million and that offers its product or service in a limited geographical area. This description is consistent with most authoritative definitions.

Small businesses may be little in size, but they have a very large impact on our society. Statistics tell us that small businesses comprise about 97 percent of all non-farm businesses in the United States; they employ over 60 percent of the private work force; they dominate industries like retailing and construction; and they will generate half of all new jobs during the next decade.[14]

Now to the question at hand: Is the job of managing a small business different from that of managing a large one? A study comparing the two found that the importance of roles differed significantly.[15] As illustrated in Figure 1–5, the small-business manager's most important role is that of spokesperson. The small-business manager spends a large amount of time doing outwardly directed things like meeting with customers, arranging financing with bankers, searching for new opportunities, and stimulating change. In contrast, the most important concerns of a manager in a large organization are directed internally—toward deciding which organizational units get what available resources and how much of them. According to this study, the entrepreneurial role—looking for business opportunities and planning activities for performance improvement—is least important to managers in large firms.

small business
An independently owned and operated profit-seeking enterprise having fewer than 100 employees and annual sales of less than $5 million and offering its product or service in a limited geographical area.

FIGURE 1–5

Managerial Roles in Small and Large Firms

Source: Adapted from Joseph G. P. Paolillo, "The Manager's Self-Assessments of Managerial Roles: Small vs. Large Firms," *American Journal of Small Business,* January–March 1984, pp. 61–62.

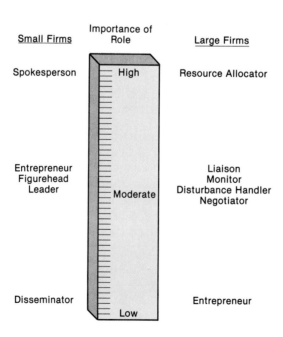

Giant firms like IBM and General Motors may dominate the headlines, but the majority of business managers work—and are likely to work in the future—in small firms like this retail computer store.

Compared to a manager in a large organization, a small-business manager is more likely to be a generalist. His or her job will combine the activities of a large corporation's chief executive with many of the day-to-day activities undertaken by a first-line supervisor. Moreover, the structure and formality that characterize a manager's job in a large organization tend to give way to informality in small firms. Planning is less likely to be a carefully orchestrated ritual, the organization's design will be less complex and structured, and control in the small business will rely more on direct observation than on sophisticated computerized monitoring systems.[16]

Again, as with organizational level, we see differences in degree and emphasis, but not in function. Managers in both small and large organizations perform essentially the same activities; only how they go about them and the proportion of time they spend on each are different.

Cross-national Transferability   The last generic issue concerns whether management concepts are transferable across national borders. If managerial concepts were completely generic, they would apply universally, regardless of economic, social, political, or cultural differences. Studies that have compared preferred managerial practices between countries have not generally supported the universality of management concepts. In Chapter 4, we'll examine specifically some differences between countries. At this point, it is sufficient to say that most of the concepts we'll be discussing in future chapters apply to the United States, Canada, Great Britain, Australia, and other English-speaking democracies. However, we would have to modify these concepts if we wanted to apply them in India, Yugoslavia, Chile, or any other country whose economic, political, social, or cultural environment differs greatly from that of the so-called free-market democracies.

THE VALUE THE MARKETPLACE PUTS ON MANAGERS

Good managers can turn straw to gold. Poor managers can do the reverse. This realization has not been lost on those who design compensation systems for organizations. Managers tend to be more highly paid than operatives. As a manager's authority and responsibility expand, so typically does his or her pay. Moreover, many organizations

RJR Nabisco recently gave
Louis Gerstner, Jr. a $10 million
signing bonus, a $2.3 million
first-year salary, and a lucrative
incentive package to entice him
away from the presidency of
American Express.

willingly offer extremely lucrative compensation packages to get and keep good managers.

If you were privy to the compensation paid employees at large public accounting firms like Price Waterhouse and Arthur Andersen, you would discover an interesting fact. The best accounting specialists rarely earn more than $75,000 a year. In contrast, the annual income of senior managing partners is rarely less than $125,000 and, in some cases, may exceed $750,000. The fact that these firms pay their managers considerably more than their nonmanagers is a measure of the importance placed on effective management skills. What is true at these accounting firms is true in most organizations. Good managerial skills are a scarce commodity, and compensation packages are one measure of the value that organizations place on them.

Do all managers make six-figure incomes? No! Such salaries are usually reserved for senior executives. What could you expect to make as a manager? The answer to this

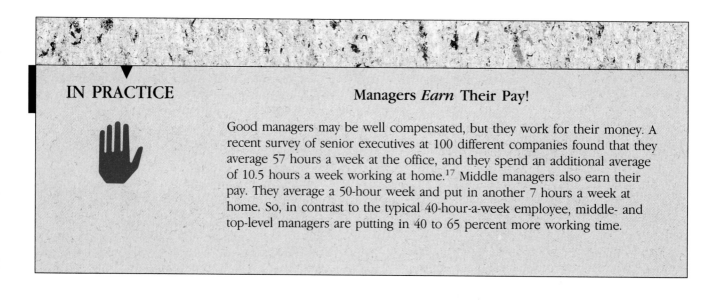

IN PRACTICE   **Managers *Earn* Their Pay!**

Good managers may be well compensated, but they work for their money. A recent survey of senior executives at 100 different companies found that they average 57 hours a week at the office, and they spend an additional average of 10.5 hours a week working at home.[17] Middle managers also earn their pay. They average a 50-hour week and put in another 7 hours a week at home. So, in contrast to the typical 40-hour-a-week employee, middle- and top-level managers are putting in 40 to 65 percent more working time.

question depends on your level in the organization, your education and experience, the type of business the organization is in, comparable pay standards in the community, and how effective a manager you are. Most first-line supervisors earn between $20,000 and $40,000 a year. Middle managers start in the low 30s and top out at around $90,000. Senior managers in large corporations can earn $1 million a year or more. In 1987, for instance, the average cash compensation (salary plus annual bonus) for chief executives at the 25 largest industrial companies was $1.38 million.[18] In many cases, this was enhanced by stock options. In one recent year, Jack Welsh earned $2 million as head of General Electric. He made another $10.5 million from cashing in previously granted stock options.

Management salaries reflect the market forces of supply and demand. Management superstars, like superstar athletes in professional sports, are wooed with signing bonuses, interest-free loans, performance incentive packages, and guaranteed contracts.

WHY STUDY MANAGEMENT?

The 1980s saw a dramatic increase in the public's interest in management. It is not unusual now to find management books at the top of the *New York Times*'s best-seller list along with romance novels and books on dieting.

People in all walks of life have come to recognize the important role good management plays in our society. You don't have to be a student of management, for instance, to recognize that U.S. organizations are under strong pressure to reduce costs and increase quality in order to stay even with foreign competitors such as the Japanese and the South Koreans. You read about these challenges to business firms every day in the newspapers. But the quest for good management goes beyond just profit-seeking firms. We expect effective and efficient management in not-for-profit organizations, too. As taxpayers, we want decision makers in the Department of Defense to develop a strong military without wasting our tax dollars. We're angered when we hear about the Pentagon spending $700 for a hammer or $1,500 for a toilet seat. That's inefficiency, and we want it eliminated. Similarly, we want our public schools to teach students the basic skills to make them productive citizens. When we learn that high school graduates are reading on a fourth-grade level, we expect school administrators to explain how they are going to improve their organizations' effectiveness. One reason for studying management, therefore, is its importance in our society today. Organizations that are well managed will sustain a loyal constituency, grow, and prosper. Those that are poorly managed will find their continued existence threatened.

The second reason for studying management is the reality that once you graduate from college and begin your career, you will either *manage* or *be managed*. It would be naive to assume that everyone who studies management is planning a career in management. A course in management may only be a requirement for a degree you want. But that needn't make the study of management irrelevant. Assuming that you will have to work for a living and recognizing that you will almost certainly work in an organization, you will be a manager and/or work for a manager. If you plan on working for a manager, you can gain a great deal of insight into the way your boss behaves and into the internal workings of organizations by studying management. The point is that you needn't aspire to be a manager to gain something valuable from a course in management.

SUMMARY

This summary is organized by the chapter-opening learning objectives found on page 1.

1. Managers are individuals in an organization who direct the activities of others. They have titles like supervisor, department head, dean, division manager, vice president, president, and chief executive officer. Operatives are nonmanagerial personnel. They work directly on a job or task and have no responsibility for overseeing the work of others.

2. Management refers to the process of getting activities completed efficiently with and through other people. The process represents the functions or primary activities of planning, organizing, leading, and controlling.

3. Effectiveness is concerned with getting activities completed—that is, goal attainment. Efficiency is concerned with minimizing resource costs in the completion of those activities.

4. Henry Mintzberg concluded from his study of five chief executives that managers perform ten different roles or behaviors. He classified them into three sets. One set is concerned with interpersonal relationships (figurehead, leader, liaison). The second set relates to the transfer of information (monitor, disseminator, spokesperson). The third set deals with decision making (entrepreneur, disturbance handler, resource allocator, negotiator).

5. Fred Luthans and his associates found that successful managers—those who got promoted most quickly—emphasized networking activities. In contrast, effective managers—those who performed best—emphasized communication. This suggests the importance of social and political skills in getting ahead in organizations.

6. Management has several generic properties. Regardless of level in an organization, all managers perform the same four functions; however, the emphasis given to each function varies with the manager's position in the hierarchy. Similarly, for the most part, the manager's job is the same regardless of the type of organization he or she is in. The generic properties of management are found mainly in the world's English-speaking democracies, and it is therefore dangerous to assume that they are universally transferable outside so-called free-market democracies.

7. People in all walks of life have come to recognize the important role that good management plays in our society. The study of management, for those who aspire to managerial positions, provides the body of knowledge that will help them to be more effective managers. For those who do not plan on careers in management, the study of management can give them a great deal of insight into the way their bosses behave and into the internal activities of organizations.

REVIEW QUESTIONS

1. What is an organization? Why are managers important to an organization's success?

2. Are all effective organizations also efficient? Discuss.

3. What common functions do all managers perform? Briefly describe them.

4. Contrast the four functions with Mintzberg's ten roles.

5. What are the four managerial activities identified by Luthans? Contrast the emphasis placed on these four activities by average, successful, and effective managers.

6. How does a manager's job change with his or her level in the organization?

7. In what ways would the mayor's job in a large city and the president's job in a large corporation be similar? In what ways would they be different?

8. How might the job of an owner-manager of a small business compare with the job of president of a large corporation?

9. How would a large corporation justify paying its senior executives high six-figure or even seven-figure annual compensation packages?

10. How might the study of management benefit an accounting major who plans on (a) working for a large accounting firm or (b) starting his or her own small accounting firm?

DISCUSSION QUESTIONS

1. Would you describe management as a profession?

2. Is your college instructor a manager?

3. The most senior executive in almost every one of the 100 largest U.S. corporations makes more than the President of the United States. Why?

4. Some people in organizations are called managers, but they have no subordinates to oversee. Are they actually managers?

5. What factors might limit the transferability of management concepts across national boundaries?

SELF-ASSESSMENT EXERCISE

How Do You (Or Would You) Rate as a Manager?

The following questionnaire evaluates five dimensions of management: style, planning, information/communication, time management, and delegation. It was originally designed for individuals who have had management experience. If you haven't, complete it anyway, refocusing the questions from "Do I . . . ?" to "Would I . . . ?"

For each question listed, rate yourself as follows: Definite strength: 10–9, Moderately effective: 8–7, Average performance: 6–5, Rarely effective: 4–3, Definite weakness: 2–1

1. Management style

1. Am I sensitive to the influence my actions have on my subordinates? _____

2. Do I understand their reactions to my actions? _____

3. Do I find an appropriate balance between encouragement and pressure?

   _____

4. Do I allow subordinates to express ideas and opinions? _____

5. Am I effective at motivating subordinates? _____

6. Am I able to resolve conflicts in a constructive way? _____

7. Have I developed a spirit of teamwork among my subordinates? _____

8. Do I have a clear understanding of my role in the organization? _____

9. Am I tactful in disciplining an employee? _____

10. Do I have a personal plan for self-improvement? _____

Section total _____

2. Planning

1. Are the operations of my organization balanced so that the pace of change is neither too routine nor too disruptive? _____

2. Do I sufficiently analyze the impact of particular changes on the future of my organization? _____

3. Am I sufficiently well informed to pass judgment on the proposals that my employees make? _____

4. Do I schedule my meetings appropriately? _____

5. Are my meetings planned in advance? _____

6. Do I have a clear vision of direction for my organization? _____

7. Are these plans in written form to guide me as well as others? _____

8. Do I make them explicit in order to better guide the decisions of others in the organization? _____

9. Are they flexible enough to be changed, if necessary, to meet the changing needs of the organization? _____

10. Does the day-to-day work in my organization run smoothly? _____

Section total _____

3. Information/communication

1. Do I have good sources of information and methods for obtaining information? _____

2. Is my information organized so that it is easy to locate and use? _____

3. Do I have other people do some of my scanning for me? _____

4. Do I make good use of my contacts to get information? _____

5. Do I balance the collection of information with action? _____

6. Do my people have the information they need when they need it? _____

7. Do I put it in writing so that my employees are not at an informational disadvantage? _____

8. Do I use interoffice communication media appropriately? _____

9. Do I make the most of meetings for which I am responsible? _____

10. Do I spend enough time visiting other areas in the office to observe firsthand the results accomplished? _____

Section total _____

4. Time management

1. Do I have a time-scheduling system? _____

2. Do I avoid reacting to the pressures of the moment? _____

3. Do I avoid concentrating on one particular function or one type of problem just because I find it uninteresting? _____

4. Do I schedule particular kinds of work at special times of the day or week to take advantage of my own energy/effectiveness levels? _____

5. Am I in control of the amount of fragmentation and interruption of my work? _____

6. Do I balance current, tangible activities with time for reflection and planning? _____

7. Do key problems/priorities receive the attention they deserve? _____

8. Do I make use of time-saving devices such as dictating machines and PCs? _____

9. Do I have my priorities clearly in mind most of the time? _____

10. Do I have the necessary information available to me at the right time to meet my deadlines? _____

Section total _____

5. Delegation

1. Do my employees understand our objectives and know what is to be done, when, and by whom? _____

2. Do I know which of my responsibilities I must meet myself and which I can delegate? _____

3. Do I encourage initiative in the people I supervise? _____

4. Do I leave the final decision to my employees often enough? _____

5. Do I avoid doing my employees' work? _____

6. Do I show genuine interest in my employees' work? _____

7. Am I confident that my subordinates can handle the work I give them? _____

8. Do I give employees the guidance, training, and authority they need to make decisions independently? _____

9. Do I regularly assess the quality of my work and that of my employees? _____

10. Do I use delegation to help my employees gain new skills and grow in the organization? _____

Section total _____

Turn to page 669 for scoring directions and key.

Source: Roger Fritz, "How Do You Rate as a Manager?," *Management Solutions,* February 1988, pp. 28–32. With permission.

CASE APPLICATION 1A

Bob Crandall and American Airlines

Some say that you can't argue with results. If that's true, then you can't disagree with Bob Crandall, the chief executive officer and chairman of American Airlines and its parent company, AMR Corp. Since taking over in 1980, Crandall has turned American into the most profitable airline in the United States. His strategy has focused on internal growth, adding new hubs, increasing market share, getting workers more involved in company decision making, and developing a partnership with his unionized employees that provides job security and profit sharing in return for higher productivity and accepting more market-competitive starting salaries.[19]

Between 1982 and 1988, American virtually doubled the size of its fleet, doubled the number of its flights, opened three new hubs, and moved into the California market with the acquisition of AirCal, Inc. In 1989, the company placed orders and options worth $7.5 billion to acquire 160 new jetliners. Crandall decided to use his company's strong financial position to put distance between American and its competitors. He views this investment as a way to reduce maintenance problems. Some outside analysts add that this is also an innovative marketing strategy to soothe the flying public's concerns about the safety of old planes.

In 1986, American opened a new hub in Nashville. This was followed in 1987 with a new hub in Raleigh-Durham. This expansion did not come painlessly. The startup costs for these hubs caused operating expenses to rise faster than revenues, and profits dropped in both 1986 and 1987. But Crandall argues that he's playing the game for the long term. He is willing to sacrifice short-term profits to grow to the size he feels is necessary to compete nationwide.

Crandall relies on a consensus-building management style. He lets managers act on their own, and he has pushed authority down into the worker ranks. For example, ticket agents at airport gates have the authority to settle problems on the spot and issue a refund to a customer or provide a free hotel room when there are flight problems. Crandall also encourages both management and workers to submit their ideas. Suggestions from his management team are discussed at the early Monday morning meetings he holds with all his senior vice presidents. If an idea merits attention, the group sets up a task force to recommend a course of action.

American Airlines' average compensation per employee is now lower than all but one or two of its competitors. But getting American's labor costs competitive was no easy task for Crandall. In 1983, he successfully persuaded mechanics and baggage clerks, pilots and flight attendants to change unproductive, outdated work rules and to accept a new lower-scale "market rate" for new hires. In 1987, the two pay schedules were merged into a single elongated wage scale in which employees take four times longer to reach the top. In exchange for these concessions, Crandall promised the workers no layoffs, wage reductions, or benefit cuts; gave a large percentage of workers lifetime job security; and launched a corporate-wide profit-sharing plan. He also promised to invest in new aircraft and new facilities and to expand in the Southeast and California to create more jobs and more opportunities for union members to move up the ranks. Moreover, Crandall has installed a new management philosophy that places an increased importance on employees. He wants all managers to understand that the active participation and full commitment of every employee are essential ingredients for the company's success. Crandall believes that most people don't need supervision to do a good job. As he puts it, management is "not out there to tell people what to do. We must teach, coach, counsel, and get the best ideas from people."

Questions

1. Is American Airlines effective? Is it efficient? On what basis did you reach your conclusion?

2. Both General Creech at the TAC and Crandall reorganized to get their workers more involved. Do you think this is the way most organizations are managed today? Discuss. What drawbacks, if any, do you see with this management approach?

3. Go through Mintzberg's ten managerial roles and give a specific example of an activity that Crandall, as CEO at American, might engage in for each.

CASE APPLICATION 1B

Stephens Auto Parts

Jan Stephens was four years out of college when her father died suddenly from a heart attack. As an only child, she responded to her ailing mother's request; she quit her job as assistant manager of home furnishings for a large department store chain in order to run the family business, Stephens Auto Parts.

Jan's father started the business in 1955, and it had grown and prospered ever since. In 1990, Stephens Auto Parts had three stores and employed twenty-three full-time people and another twenty part-time. Annual sales exceeded $3.5 million, and pretax profits were close to 20 percent.

Each store had its own manager and assistant manager, but all important decisions had been made by Jan's father. As a result, none of the firm's current managers were really capable of running the business. Jan's mother inherited everything and knew she needed Jan to run things. Her proposition to Jan: "If you take over running the business, you can draw a $50,000 salary to begin with and I'll give you 50 percent of the profits. After I'm gone, the business is all yours."

Jan had worked for her dad during summer and Christmas vacations all through high school and college. She knew the business in a very superficial way. But she had no day-to-day experience in auto parts. As Jan went into work on that first day as head of Stephens Auto Parts, she hoped her work experience and college degree in business administration had prepared her for what was to come.

Questions

1. What management problems do you think Jan will face?

2. Is her prior experience valuable? Explain.

3. If you were Jan, what things would you focus on during the first month?

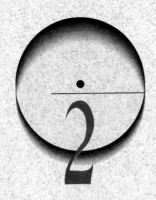

THE EVOLUTION OF MANAGEMENT THOUGHT

Current management theory and practices did not pop out of thin air. They evolved over many years. If you were to walk into any organization today, you would find examples of management practices, the origins of which can be traced back 30, 40, 50, or more years. To illustrate this point, let's take a brief tour of the facilities of three organizations. The ones we will look at happen to be located in Atlanta, Georgia, but you could perform this exercise in almost any community.

The first place we enter is a manufacturing plant operated by the Missile Systems Division of Rockwell International. This plant fabricates electronic components. People are working on assembly lines. Each person on the line has a specific task to perform, and he or she does it over and over again in a very uniform and standardized way. Industrial engineers have analyzed each job on the assembly line and, through careful time-and-motion studies, have determined the precise steps each worker should go through and the speed at which the conveyor belt should move. Over on the far side of the manufacturing floor is a separate, glass-enclosed room where the plant's central computers are located. One computer handles administrative functions; it holds personnel data, computes payroll expenditures, and the like. The other computer collects and analyzes production data. For instance, on the basis of decision criteria determined by top management and given to the computer programmers, the computer controls the speed of the various assembly lines, monitors the supply of raw materials necessary to make the electronic components, schedules orders, and determines the optimum level of finished-goods inventory the plant should carry.

Just down the street from Rockwell is a plant run by Scientific-Atlanta. It produces satellite earth stations. As we enter the plant, we notice a number of people in the personnel office. When we walk into that office, we find job candidates filling out application forms and taking a set of employment tests. Moving into the plant, we find no assembly lines but, instead, teams of employees assembling satellite station components, working in groups of four or five. The tasks these workers are doing seem to be much broader and more varied than those done on the assembly line at Rockwell. Each worker appears to know the others' jobs, and workers rotate activities so that no one person does the same thing all the time. These assembly teams have a daily quota to meet, but the team members themselves participate in setting the quota. In contrast to the Rockwell assembly line, furthermore, there is no separate inspector at Scientific-Atlanta to check over the finished products. The Scientific-Atlanta assembly teams inspect their own work, and when an assembly unit is complete, they stamp a number on the bottom of it to identify which team assembled it.

Our third visit moves us downtown to Coca-Cola's world headquarters. Nothing is being manufactured here. This headquarters operation houses marketing and sales offices, research and development laboratories, clerks, secretaries, and managers. The first thing that strikes our attention is that the 500 or so people who work here are scattered over the ten floors in the building and that there seems to be an obvious status hierarchy. The person at the information desk on the ground floor confirms our suspicions. She tells us that clerks responsible for accounting, personnel, insurance, and franchise licensing occupy the first four floors. Marketing and research offices dominate the middle floors. The top two floors are reserved for the company's top management. The woman at the information desk then pulls out an organization chart. It shows many boxes arranged in a pyramid with a name and title in each box, and it defines the hierarchy of who reports to whom at the Coca-Cola Company. When asked whether there is any other document that can tell us about Coca-Cola, she produces a large manual from under her desk. She says that this contains the organization's policies and regulations, descriptions of key jobs, and even details of the benefit programs provided for all Coca-Cola employees.

What we have just seen at Rockwell, Scientific-Atlanta, and Coca-Cola are examples of practices whose origins can be traced by reviewing the evolution of management thought. In the pages just ahead, you will learn that the notion of dividing workers' jobs into narrowly defined, specialized, and repetitive steps to achieve high productivity is far from new. It dates back more than 200 years to the writings of Adam Smith. Designing jobs through time-and-motion techniques came out of the work in scientific management at the turn of this century. The quantitative decision models used in Rockwell International's computer are a product of transferring problem-solving techniques used in World War II to industrial applications.

Management researchers discovered long ago that having employees perform narrow, repetitive tasks is not always the best way to get things done. Using teams, having employees participate in decisions that affect them, and allowing employees to inspect and evaluate their own work are practices derived from behavioral science. Psychologists, sociologists, and other behavioral scientists have been increasing our knowledge of organizational behavior and have significantly influenced the way in which managers have designed jobs, selected employees, arranged compensation and benefit programs, and chosen leadership styles.

Authority hierarchies, like the one depicted in Coca-Cola's organization chart, are also far from being new ideas. They can be traced back to ancient times. Roman military generals, for instance, created a well-defined authority structure in their organization—from generals and officers down through troop divisions.

The purpose of this chapter should now be clear: A knowledge of management history can help you understand theory and practice as they are today. This chapter will introduce you to the origins of many contemporary management concepts and demonstrate how they have evolved to reflect the changing needs of organizations and society as a whole. You will also see how the management field has grown by linking together ideas and research findings from many diverse specializations. Because the body of management knowledge is relatively young, you will realize that the field is *still evolving*. Specific theories are being tested regularly. When limitations are found, modifications are made and new theories proposed. Through theory development, testing, modification, retesting, and so on, we are continuing to build a comprehensive body of knowledge for the practicing manager.

HISTORICAL BACKGROUND

Organized endeavors that are overseen by people responsible for planning, organizing, leading, and controlling activities have existed for thousands of years. The Egyptian Pyramids and the Great Wall of China are current evidence that projects of tremendous scope, employing tens of thousands of people, were undertaken well before

The largest of the Pyramids contained more than two million stone blocks, each weighing several tons. The quarries from which the blocks came were many miles from the sites where the Pyramids were constructed. Someone had to design the structure, find a stone quarry, and arrange for the stones to be cut and moved—probably over land and by water—to the construction site.

modern times. The Pyramids are a particularly interesting example. The construction of a single Pyramid occupied over 100,000 people for twenty years.[1] Who told each worker what he or she was supposed to do? Who ensured that there would be enough stones at the site to keep workers busy? The answer to questions such as these is Management. Regardless of what managers were called at the time, someone had to plan what was to be done, organize people and materials to do it, lead and direct the workers, and impose some controls to ensure that everything was done as planned.

Even the Bible refers to management concepts. For instance, the following quotation dramatizes the need for a manager to delegate authority in a large organization and to review only the unusual or exceptional cases that cannot be resolved by lower-level managers. Moses' father-in-law is speaking to Moses:

> The thing that thou doest is not good. Thou wilt surely wear away, both thou, and this people that is with thee: for this thing is too heavy for thee; thou art not able to perform it thyself alone. Hearken now unto my voice, I will give thee counsel. . . . Moreover thou shalt provide out of all the people able men . . . and place such over them, to be rulers of thousands, and rulers of hundreds, rulers of fifties, and rulers of tens. And let them judge the people at all seasons: and it shall be, that every great matter they shall bring unto thee, but every small matter they shall judge: so shall it be easier for thyself, and they shall bear the burden with thee. If thou shalt do this thing, and God command thee so, then thou shalt be able to endure, and all this people shall go to their place in peace.[2]

The Roman Catholic Church also represents an interesting example of the practice of management. The current structure of the Church was essentially established in the second century A.D. At that time, its objectives and doctrines were more rigorously

FIGURE 2–1
Hierarchy of the Roman
Catholic Church

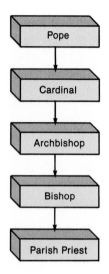

defined. Final authority was centralized in Rome. A simple authority hierarchy was created, as shown in Figure 2–1, which has remained basically unchanged for nearly 2,000 years.

These examples from the past demonstrate that organizations have been with us for thousands of years and that management has been practiced for an equivalent period. However, it has been only in the past several hundred years, particularly in the last century, that management has undergone systematic investigation, acquired a common body of knowledge, and become a formal discipline for study.

Earlier, we mentioned Adam Smith. He is more typically cited in economics courses for his contributions to classical economic doctrine, but his discussion in *The Wealth of Nations,* published in 1776, included a brilliant argument on the economic advantages that organizations and society would reap from the **division of labor.** He used the pin-manufacturing industry for his examples. Smith noted that ten individuals, each doing a specialized task, could produce about 48,000 pins a day among them. He proposed, however, that if each were working separately and independently, the ten workers would be lucky to make 200, or even 10, pins combined in one day. If each had to draw the wire, straighten it, cut it, pound heads for each pin, sharpen the point, and solder the head and pin shaft, it would be quite a feat to produce 10 pins a day!

Smith concluded that division of labor increased productivity by increasing each worker's skill and dexterity, saving time that is commonly lost in changing tasks, and by the creation of labor-saving inventions and machinery. The wide popularity today of job specialization—in service jobs like teaching as well as on assembly lines such as that at Rockwell—is undoubtedly due to the economic advantages cited over 200 years ago by Adam Smith.

Possibly the most important pre-twentieth-century influence on management was the **Industrial Revolution.** Begun in the eighteenth century in Great Britain, the Revolution had crossed the Atlantic to America by the end of the Civil War. Machine power was rapidly being substituted for human power. This, in turn, made it more economical to manufacture goods in factories. For instance, before the Industrial Revolution, an item such as a blanket was made by one person, typically at home. The worker would shear wool from his or her sheep, twist the wool into yarn, dye the yarn, weave the blanket manually on a home loom, and then sell the finished product to merchants who would travel to farms buying merchandise, which then would be sold at regional fairs or markets. The introduction of machine power made it possible to combine division of labor with power-driven equipment. A blanket factory with 100

division of labor
The breakdown of jobs into narrow, repetitive tasks.

Industrial Revolution
The advent of machine power, mass production, and efficient transportation.

people doing specialized tasks—some making wool into yarn, some dyeing, others working on the looms—could manufacture large numbers of blankets at a fraction of their previous cost. But these factories required managerial skills. Managers were needed to forecast demand, ensure that enough wool was on hand to make the yarn, assign tasks to people, direct daily activities, coordinate the various tasks, ensure that the machines were kept in good working order and that output standards were maintained, find markets for the finished blankets, and so forth. When blankets were made individually at home, there was little concern with efficiency. Suddenly, however, when the factory owner had 100 people working for him or her and a regular payroll to meet, the owner wanted to be sure that workers were kept busy. Planning, organizing, leading, and controlling became necessary.

The advent of machine power, mass production, reduced transportation costs with the rapid expansion of the railroads, and almost no governmental regulation also fostered the development of big organizations. Rockefeller was putting together the Standard Oil monopoly, Carnegie was gaining control of two-thirds of the steel industry, and similar entrepreneurs were creating other large businesses that would require formalized management practices. The need had arrived for a formal theory to guide managers in running their organizations. However, it was not until the early 1900s that the first major step toward developing such a theory occurred.

THE PERIOD OF DIVERSITY

The first half of this century was a period of diversity in management thought. Scientific management looked at the field from the perspective of how to improve the productivity of operative personnel. The general administrative theorists were concerned with the overall organization and how to make it more effective. One group of writers and researchers emphasized the human resources or "people side" of management, while another group focused on developing and applying quantitative models.

In this section we present the contributions of these four approaches. Keep in mind that each is concerned with the same "animal"; the differences reflect the backgrounds and interests of the writers. A relevant analogy is the classic fable of the blind men and the elephant. The first man touches the side of the elephant and declares that an elephant is like a wall. The second touches the trunk and says the elephant is like a snake. The third feels one of the elephant's tusks and believes the elephant to be like a spear. The fourth grabs a leg and says that an elephant is like a tree. The fifth touches the elephant's tail and concludes that the animal is like a rope. Each of these blind men is encountering the same elephant, but what they "see" depends on where they stand. Similarly, each of the following perspectives is correct and makes an important contribution to our understanding of management. But each is also a limited view of a larger "animal."

Scientific Management

scientific management
The use of the scientific method to define the "one best way" for a job to be done.

If one had to pinpoint the year that modern management theory was born, one could make a strong case for 1911. This was the year that Frederick Winslow Taylor's *Principles of Scientific Management* was published. Its contents would become widely accepted by managers throughout the world. The book described the theory of **scientific management**—the use of the scientific method to define the "one best way" for a job to be done. The studies conducted before and after the book's publication would establish Taylor as the father of scientific management.

Frederick Taylor Frederick Taylor did most of his work at the Midvale and Bethlehem Steel companies in Pennsylvania. As a mechanical engineer with a Quaker-Puritan background, he was consistently appalled at the inefficiency of workers. Employees used vastly different techniques to do the same job. They were prone to "taking it easy" on the job. Taylor believed that worker output was only about one-third of what was possible. Therefore, he set out to correct the situation by applying the scientific method to jobs on the shop floor. He spent more than two decades pursuing with a passion the "one best way" for each job to be done. In this section, we will describe the typical work environment before the development of scientific management, define Taylor's principles of management, and illustrate how he went about practicing scientific management.

It's important to understand what Taylor saw at Midvale Steel that aroused his determination to improve the way things were done in the plant. At the time, there were no clear concepts of worker and management responsibilities. Virtually no effective work standards existed. Workers purposely worked at a slow pace. Management decisions were of the "seat-of-the-pants" nature, based on hunch and intuition. Workers were placed on jobs with little or no concern for matching their abilities and aptitudes with the tasks they were required to do. Most important, management and workers considered themselves to be in continual conflict. Rather than cooperating to their mutual benefit, they perceived their relationship as a zero-sum game—any gain by one would be at the expense of the other.

Taylor sought to create a mental revolution among both the workers and management by defining clear guidelines for improving production efficiency. He defined four principles of management, listed in Table 2–1; he argued that following these principles would result in the prosperity of both management and workers. Workers would earn more pay, and management more profits.

Probably the most widely cited example of scientific management has been Taylor's pig iron experiment. The average daily output of 92-pound pigs loaded onto rail cars was 12.5 tons per worker. Taylor believed that by scientifically analyzing the job to determine the one best way to load pig iron, the output could be increased to between 47 and 48 tons per day.

Taylor began his experiment by looking for a physically strong subject who placed a high value on the dollar. The individual Taylor chose was a big, strong, Dutch immigrant, whom he called Schmidt. Schmidt, like the other loaders, earned $1.15 a day, which even at the turn of the century, was barely enough for a person to survive on. As the following quotation from Taylor's book demonstrates, Taylor used money—the opportunity to make $1.85 a day—as the primary means to get workers like

TABLE 2–1
Taylor's Four Principles of Management

1. Develop a science for each element of an individual's work, which replaces the old rule-of-thumb method.

2. Scientifically select and then train, teach, and develop the worker. (Previously, workers chose their own work and trained themselves as best they could.)

3. Heartily cooperate with the workers so as to ensure that all work is done in accordance with the principles of the science that has been developed.

4. Divide work and responsibility almost equally between management and workers. Management takes over all work for which it is better fitted than the workers. (Previously, almost all the work and the greater part of the responsibility were thrown upon the workers.)

Schmidt to do exactly as they were told:

> "Schmidt, are you a high-priced man?" "Vell, I don't know vat you mean." "Oh, yes you do. What I want to know is whether you are a high-priced man or not." "Vell, I don't know vat you mean." "Oh, come now, you answer my questions. What I want to find out is whether you are a high-priced man or one of these cheap fellows here. What I want to know is whether you want to earn $1.85 a day or whether you are satisfied with $1.15, just the same as all those cheap fellows are getting." "Did I vant $1.85 a day? Vas dot a high-priced man? Vell, yes. I vas a high-priced man."[3]

Using money to motivate Schmidt, Taylor went about having him load the pig irons, alternating various job factors to see what impact the changes had on Schmidt's daily output. For instance, on some days Schmidt would lift the pig irons by bending his knees, whereas on other days he would keep his legs straight and use his back. He experimented with rest periods, walking speed, carrying positions, and other variables. After a long period of scientifically trying various combinations of procedures, techniques, and tools, Taylor succeeded in obtaining the level of productivity he thought possible. By putting the right person on the job with the correct tools and equipment, by having the worker follow his instructions exactly, and by motivating the worker through the economic incentive of a significantly higher daily wage, Taylor was able to reach his 48-ton objective.

Another Taylor experiment dealt with shovel sizes. Taylor noticed that every worker in the plant used the same-size shovel, regardless of the material he was moving. This made no sense to Taylor. If there was an optimum weight that would maximize a worker's shoveling output over an entire day, then Taylor thought the size of the shovel should vary depending on the weight of the material being moved. After extensive experimentation, Taylor found that 21 pounds was the optimum shovel capacity. To achieve this optimum weight, heavy material like iron ore would be moved with a small-faced shovel and light material like coke with a large-faced shovel. Based on Taylor's findings, supervisors would no longer merely tell a worker to "shovel that pile over there." Depending on the material to be moved, the supervisor would now have to determine the appropriate shovel size and assign that size to the worker. The result, of course, was again significant increases in worker output.

Using similar approaches in other jobs, Taylor was able to define the one best way for doing each job. He could then, after selecting the right people for the job, train them to do it precisely in this one best way. To motivate workers, he favored incentive wage plans. Overall, Taylor achieved consistent improvements in productivity in the range of 200 percent or more. He reaffirmed the role of managers to plan and control and that of workers to perform as they were instructed. The *Principles of Scientific Management,* as well as other papers that Taylor wrote and presented, spread his ideas not only in the United States, but also in France, Germany, Russia, and Japan. One of the biggest boosts in interest in scientific management in the United States came during a 1910 hearing on railroad rates before the Interstate Commerce Commission. Appearing before the commission, an efficiency expert claimed that railroads could save a million dollars a day (equivalent to about $13 million a day in 1991 dollars) through the application of scientific management! The early acceptance of scientific management techniques by U.S. manufacturing companies, in fact, gave them a comparative advantage over foreign firms that made U.S. manufacturing efficiency the envy of the world—at least for fifty years or so!

Frank and Lillian Gilbreth   Taylor's ideas inspired others to study and develop methods of scientific management. His most prominent disciples were Frank and Lillian Gilbreth.

A construction contractor by background, Frank Gilbreth gave up his contracting career in 1912 to study scientific management after hearing Taylor speak at a professional meeting. Along with his wife Lillian, a psychologist, he studied work arrangements to eliminate wasteful hand-and-body motions. The Gilbreths also experimented in the design and use of the proper tools and equipment for optimizing work performance.[4] Frank Gilbreth is probably best known for his experiments in reducing the number of motions in bricklaying.

By carefully analyzing the bricklayer's job, he reduced the number of motions in the laying of exterior brick from eighteen to four and one-half. On interior brick, the eighteen motions were reduced to two. He developed a new way to stack bricks, invented the scaffold to reduce bending, and even devised a different mortar consistency that reduced the need for the bricklayer to level the brick by tapping it with a trowel.

The Gilbreths were among the first to use motion picture films to study hand-and-body motions. They devised a microchronometer that recorded time to $\frac{1}{2000}$ second, placed it in the field of study being photographed, and thus determined how long a worker spent enacting each motion. Wasted motions missed by the naked eye could be identified and eliminated. The Gilbreths also devised a classification scheme to label seventeen basic hand motions—such as "search," "select," "grasp," "hold"—which they called **therbligs** ("Gilbreth" spelled backward with the "th" transposed). This allowed the Gilbreths a more precise way of analyzing the exact elements of any worker's hand movements.

therbligs
A classification scheme for labeling seventeen basic hand motions.

Henry L. Gantt A close associate of Taylor at Midvale and Bethlehem Steel was a young engineer named Henry L. Gantt. Like Taylor and the Gilbreths, Gantt sought to increase worker efficiency through scientific investigation. But he extended some of Taylor's original ideas and added a few of his own. For instance, Gantt devised an incentive system that gave workers a bonus for completing their jobs in less time than the allowed standard. He also introduced a bonus for foremen to be paid for each worker who made the standard plus an extra bonus if all the workers under the foreman made it. In so doing, Gantt expanded the scope of scientific management to encompass the work of managers as well as that of operatives.

However, Gantt is probably most noted for creating a graphic bar chart that could be used by managers as a scheduling device for planning and controlling work. The **Gantt chart** showed the relationship between work planned and completed on one axis and time elapsed on the other. Revolutionary for its day, the Gantt chart allowed management to see how plans were progressing and to take the necessary action to keep projects on time. The Gantt chart and modern variations of it are still widely used in organizations as a method for scheduling work.

Gantt chart
A graphic bar chart that shows the relationship between work planned and completed on one axis and time elapsed on the other.

Putting Scientific Management into Perspective Why did scientific management receive so much attention? What was it about scientific management that made Taylor such a heroic figure in management literature? Certainly, many of his and others' guidelines for improving production efficiency appear to us today to be common sense. For instance, one can say that it should have been obvious to managers in those days that workers should be carefully screened, selected, and trained before being put into a job.

To understand the importance of scientific management, you have to consider the times in which Taylor, the Gilbreths, and Gantt lived. The standard of living was low. Production was highly labor intensive. Midvale Steel, at the turn of the century, may have employed twenty or thirty workers who did nothing but load pig iron onto rail cars. Today, their entire daily tonnage could probably be done in several hours by one person and a hydraulic lift truck. But they didn't have such mechanical devices. Similarly, the breakthroughs Frank Gilbreth achieved in bricklaying are meaningful only

Henry Kaiser used principles of scientific management during World War II to build liberty ships on an assembly line. In 1940, the standard time to build one of these ships was six months. At the peak of the wartime effort, Kaiser's ship-yards were putting out one ship every day and a half.

when you recognize that most quality buildings at that time were constructed of brick, that land was cheap, and that the major cost of a plant or home was the cost of the materials (bricks) and the labor cost to lay them.

To illustrate the point, if 30 percent of the cost of a $20,000 building represented the labor of bricklayers and if bricklayer productivity could be improved by 300 percent, the cost of that building would be reduced to $16,000. At the lower price, more buildings could be built because more people could afford them. Scientific management was important, therefore, because it could raise the standard of living of entire countries. Additionally, spending six months or more studying one job—as Taylor did in the pig iron experiment—made sense only for labor-intensive proce-dures in which many workers performed the same tasks.

General Administrative Theorists

general administrative theorists
Writers who developed general theories of what managers do and what constitutes good man-agement practice.

classical theorists
A group that includes writers on scientific management and gen-eral administrative theory.

Another group of writers looked at the subject of management but focused on the entire organization. We call them the **general administrative theorists.** The follow-ing contributors are important for developing more general theories of what manag-ers do and what constitutes good management practice. Because their writings set the framework for many of our contemporary ideas on management and organization, this group, along with the scientific management contributors, is frequently referred to as the **classical theorists.** The most prominent of these general administrative theorists were Henri Fayol and Max Weber.

Henri Fayol   We mentioned Henri Fayol in the previous chapter for having desig-nated management as a universal set of functions, specifically planning, organizing, commanding, coordinating, and controlling. Because his writings were important, let's take a more careful look at what he had to say.[5]

Fayol wrote during the same time as Taylor. However, whereas Taylor was con-cerned with management at the shop level (or what we today would describe as the job of a supervisor) and used the scientific method, Fayol's attention was directed at the activities of *all* managers, and he wrote from personal experience. Taylor was a scientist. Fayol, the managing director of a large French coal-mining firm, was a practitioner.

Fayol described the practice of management as something distinct from accounting, finance, production, distribution, and other typical business functions. He argued that management was an activity common to all human undertakings in business, in government, and even in the home. He then proceeded to state fourteen **principles of management**—that is, fundamental or universal truths—that could be taught in schools and universities. These principles are shown in Table 2–2.

Max Weber Max Weber (pronounced *Vay-ber*) was a German sociologist. Writing in the early part of this century, Weber developed a theory of authority structures and described organizational activity based on authority relations.[6] He described an ideal type of organization that he called a **bureaucracy.** It was a system characterized by division of labor, a clearly defined hierarchy, detailed rules and regulations, and impersonal relationships. Weber recognized that this "ideal bureaucracy" didn't exist in reality but, rather, represented a selective reconstruction of the real world. He meant it as a basis for theorizing about work and how work could be done in large

principles of management
Universal truths of management that can be taught.

bureaucracy
A form of organization marked by division of labor, hierarchy, rules and regulations, and impersonal relationships.

TABLE 2–2   Fayol's Fourteen Principles of Management

1. *Division of Work.* This principle is the same as Adam Smith's "division of labor." Specialization increases output by making employees more efficient.

2. *Authority.* Managers must be able to give orders. Authority gives them this right. Along with authority, however, goes responsibility. Wherever authority is exercised, responsibility arises.

3. *Discipline.* Employees must obey and respect the rules that govern the organization. Good discipline is the result of effective leadership, a clear understanding between management and workers regarding the organization's rules, and the judicious use of penalties for infractions of the rules.

4. *Unity of Command.* Every employee should receive orders from only *one* superior.

5. *Unity of Direction.* Each group of organizational activities that have the same objective should be directed by one manager using one plan.

6. *Subordination of Individual Interests to the General Interests.* The interests of any one employee or group of employees should not take precedence over the interests of the organization as a whole.

7. *Remuneration.* Workers must be paid a fair wage for their services.

8. *Centralization.* Centralization refers to the degree to which subordinates are involved in decision making. Whether decision making is centralized (to management) or decentralized (to subordinates) is a question of proper proportion. The problem is to find the optimum degree of centralization for each situation.

9. *Scalar Chain.* The line of authority from top management to the lowest ranks represents the scalar chain. Communications should follow this chain. However, if following the chain creates delays, cross-communications can be allowed if agreed to by all parties and superiors are kept informed.

10. *Order.* People and materials should be in the right place at the right time.

11. *Equity.* Managers should be kind and fair to their subordinates.

12. *Stability of Tenure of Personnel.* High employee turnover is inefficient. Management should provide orderly personnel planning and ensure that replacements are available to fill vacancies.

13. *Initiative.* Employees who are allowed to originate and carry out plans will exert high levels of effort.

14. *Esprit de Corps.* Promoting team spirit will build harmony and unity within the organization.

IN PRACTICE

The Rise of the Professional Manager

professional managers
Managers who have no significant ownership in their organization.

At about the same time that Taylor and Fayol were writing down their principles of management, an important phenomenon was taking place in business organizations. It was the creation of the professional manager.

The senior executives of most large companies today rarely own a significant part of their organizations. For example, a recent study found that only 77 of the CEOs of the 1,000 largest U.S. corporations owned 10 percent or more of their companies. In fact, the average shareownership of these 1,000 CEOs was worth less than $260,000.[7] This, however, is a relatively recent phenomenon. Before the turn of this century, organizations were run by owner-managers. **Professional managers**—those who make managerial decisions but have no significant ownership in the organization—held lower-level positions, but the top slots were filled by the owner and his or her family. You can now aspire to head a major corporation some day, without any significant financial stake in that firm and without being a member of the founder's family. Such aspirations were not very realistic a century ago.

The rise of the professional manager has had an important impact on management practice. How? The owner-manager's interest and the organization's interest are one and the same; but those of professional managers and their organizations are not necessarily so. The professional manager's ambitions, loyalties, career rewards, and motivations might not align with the best interests of the organization. As you'll see in Chapter 6, this can lead to a different focus in decision making—particularly toward short-term considerations and minimizing risk.

groups. His theory became the design prototype for almost all of today's large organizations. The detailed features of Weber's ideal bureaucratic structure are outlined in Table 2–3.

TABLE 2–3   Weber's Ideal Bureaucracy

1. *Division of Labor.* Jobs are broken down into simple, routine, and well-defined tasks.

2. *Authority Hierarchy.* Offices or positions are organized in a hierarchy, each lower one being controlled and supervised by a higher one.

3. *Formal Selection.* All organizational members are to be selected on the basis of technical qualifications demonstrated by training, education, or formal examination.

4. *Formal Rules and Regulations.* To ensure uniformity and to regulate the actions of employees, managers must depend heavily on formal organizational rules.

5. *Impersonality.* Rules and controls are applied uniformly, avoiding involvement with personalities and personal preferences of employees.

6. *Career Orientation.* Managers are professional officials rather than owners of the units they manage. They work for fixed salaries and pursue their careers within the organization.

Bureaucracy, as described by Weber, is not unlike scientific management in its ideology. Both emphasize rationality, predictability, impersonality, technical competence, and authoritarianism. While Weber's writings were less operational than Taylor's, the fact that his "ideal type" describes most contemporary organizations, such as Coca-Cola's head office described at the beginning of the chapter, attests to the importance of his work.

Putting the General Administrative Theorists into Perspective A number of our current ideas and practices in management can be directly traced to the contributions of the general administrative theorists. For instance, the functional view of the manager's job owes its origin to Henri Fayol. Also, while many of his principles may not be universally applicable to the wide variety of organizations that exist today, they became a frame of reference against which many current concepts have evolved.

Weber's bureaucracy was an attempt to formulate an ideal model around which organizations could be designed. It was a response to the abuses that Weber saw going on within organizations. Weber believed that his model could remove the ambiguity, inefficiencies, and patronage that characterized most organizations at that time. It has become *the* most popular model around which large organizations are designed.

The Human Resources Approach

Managers get things done by working with people. This explains why some writers and researchers have chosen to look at management by focusing on the organization's human resources. Much of what currently makes up the field of personnel management, as well as contemporary views on motivation and leadership, has come out of the work of those we have categorized as being part of the **human resources approach** to management.

Early Advocates While there were undoubtedly a number of people in the nineteenth and early part of the twentieth century who recognized the importance of the human factor to an organization's success, four individuals are consistently singled out as early advocates of the human resources approach. They were Robert Owen, Hugo Münsterberg, Mary Parker Follett, and Chester Barnard.

Robert Owen was a successful Scottish businessman who bought his first factory in 1789, at the age of 18. Repulsed by the harsh practices he saw in factories across Scotland—such as the employment of young children (many under the age of 10), thirteen-hour work days, and miserable working conditions—Owen became a reformer. He chided factory owners for treating their equipment better than their employees. He said that they would buy the best machines, but then buy the cheapest labor to run them. Owen argued that money spent on improving labor was one of the best investments that business executives could make. He claimed that showing concern for employees both was highly profitable for management and would relieve human misery.

Owen proposed a utopian workplace. As one author noted, Owen is not remembered in management history for his successes, but rather for his courage and commitment to reducing the suffering of the working class.[8] He was more than a hundred years ahead of his time when he argued, in 1825, for regulated hours of work for all, child labor laws, public education, company-furnished meals at work, and business involvement in community projects.[9]

Hugo Münsterberg created the field of industrial psychology. His text, *Psychology and Industrial Efficiency*, was published in 1913. In it, he argued for the scientific study of human behavior to identify general patterns and to explain individual differences. Interestingly, he saw a link between scientific management and industrial psychology. Both sought increased efficiency through scientific work analyses and

human resources approach
The study of management that focuses on human behavior.

through better alignment of individual skills and abilities with the demands of various jobs.

Münsterberg suggested the use of psychological tests to improve employee selection, the value of learning theory in the development of training methods, and the study of human behavior in order to understand what techniques are most effective for motivating workers. Much of our current knowledge of selection techniques, employee training, job design, and motivation is built on the work of Münsterberg.

One of the earliest writers to recognize that organizations could be viewed from the perspective of individual and group behavior was Mary Parker Follett.[10] A transitionalist writing in the time of scientific management but proposing more people-oriented ideas, Ms. Follett was a social philosopher. But her ideas had clear implications for management practice. Follett thought organizations should be based on a group ethic rather than individualism. Individual potential, she argued, remained only potential until released through group association. The manager's job was to harmonize and coordinate group efforts. Managers and workers should view themselves as partners—as part of a common group. As such, managers should rely more on their expertise and knowledge to lead subordinates than on the formal authority of their position. Her humanistic ideas influenced the way we look at motivation, leadership, power, and authority. In fact, Japanese organization and management styles, which are currently receiving a lot of attention in North America, have long followed Follett's ideas. They place a heavy emphasis on group togetherness and team effort.

Also a transitionalist, Chester Barnard's ideas bridged classical and human resources viewpoints. Like Fayol, Barnard was a practitioner. He was president of New Jersey Bell Telephone Company. He had read Weber and was influenced by his writings. But unlike Weber, who had a mechanistic and impersonal view of organizations, Barnard saw organizations as social systems that require human cooperation. He expressed his views in his book, *The Functions of the Executive,*[11] published in 1938.

Barnard viewed organizations as being made up of people who have interacting social relationships. The managers' major roles were to communicate and to stimulate subordinates to high levels of effort. A major part of an organization's success, as Barnard saw it, depended on obtaining cooperation from its personnel. Barnard also argued that success depended on maintaining good relations with people and institutions outside the organization with whom the organization regularly interacted. By recognizing the organization's dependence on investors, suppliers, customers, and other external constituencies, Barnard introduced the idea that managers had to examine the environment and then adjust the organization to maintain a state of equilibrium. Regardless of how efficient an organization's production might be, if management failed to ensure a continuous input of materials and supplies or to find markets for its outputs, then the organization's survival would be threatened.

traditional view of authority
The view that authority comes from above.

acceptance view of authority
The theory that authority comes from the willingness of subordinates to accept it.

Barnard is also important for his enlightened ideas on authority. The dominant or **traditional view of authority** at the time he wrote was that a superior's right to exact compliance from subordinates develops at the top and moves down through an organization. The ultimate source of a manager's authority, in the traditional view, was the society that allows the creation of social institutions. Barnard offered a contrasting position, arguing that authority comes from below. The **acceptance view of authority** proposed that authority comes from the willingness of subordinates to accept it. According to Barnard, there can be no such thing as persons of authority, but only persons to whom authority is addressed. Should an employee disobey a superior's directive, the disobedience is a denial of the directive's authority over the employee. Of course, superiors may be able to punish subordinates who don't comply; nevertheless, the superior's directive has not been complied with.

Hawthorne studies
A series of studies during the 1920s and 1930s that provided new insights into group norms and behavior.

The Hawthorne Studies   Without question, the most important contribution to the human resources approach to management came out of the **Hawthorne studies** undertaken at the Western Electric Company's Hawthorne Works in Cicero, Illinois.

The Hawthorne studies dramatized that a worker was not a
machine, and scientific management's "one best way"
approach had to be tempered
to recognize the effects of
group behavior.

These studies, originally begun in 1924 but eventually expanded and carried on through the early 1930s, were initially devised by Western Electric industrial engineers to examine the effect of various illumination levels on worker productivity. Control and experimental groups were established. The experimental group was presented with varying illumination intensities, while the control group worked under a constant intensity. The engineers had expected individual output to be directly related to the intensity of light. However, they found that as the light level was increased in the experimental group, output for both groups rose. To the surprise of the engineers, as the light level was dropped in the experimental group, productivity continued to increase in both groups. In fact, a productivity decrease was observed in the experimental group only when the light intensity had been reduced to that of moonlight. The engineers concluded that illumination intensity was not directly related to group productivity, but they could not explain the behavior they had witnessed.

The Western Electric engineers asked Harvard professor Elton Mayo and his associates in 1927 to join the study as consultants. Thus began a relationship that would last through 1932 and encompass numerous experiments covering the redesign of jobs, changes in the length of the workday and workweek, introduction of rest periods, and individual versus group wage plans.[12] For example, one experiment was designed to evaluate the effect of a group piecework incentive pay system on group productivity. The results indicated that the incentive plan had less effect on a worker's output than did group pressure and acceptance and the concomitant security. Social norms or standards of the group, therefore, were concluded to be the key determinants of individual work behavior.

Scholars generally agree that the Hawthorne studies had a dramatic impact on the direction of management thought. Mayo's conclusions were that behavior and sentiments were closely related, that group influences significantly affected individual behavior, that group standards established individual worker output, and that money was less a factor in determining output than were group standards, group sentiments, and security. These conclusions led to a new emphasis on the human factor in the functioning of organizations and the attainment of their goals. They also led to increased paternalism by management.

The Hawthorne studies have not been without critics. Attacks have been made on procedures, analyses of the findings, and the conclusions drawn.[13] However, from an historical standpoint, it is of little importance whether the studies were academically sound or their conclusions justified. What is important is that they stimulated an interest in human factors. The Hawthorne studies went a long way in changing the dominant view at the time that people were no different than machines; that is, you put them on the shop floor, cranked in the inputs, and they produced a known quantity of outputs.

human relations movement
The belief, for the most part unsubstantiated by research, that a satisfied worker will be productive.

The Human Relations Movement   Another group within the human resources approach is important to management history for its unflinching commitment to remaking management practices in a more humane way. Members of the **human relations movement** uniformly believed in the importance of employee satisfaction—a satisfied worker was believed to be a productive worker. For the most part, names associated with this movement—Dale Carnegie, Abraham Maslow, and Douglas McGregor—were individuals whose views were shaped more by their personal philosophies than by substantive research evidence.

Dale Carnegie is often overlooked by management scholars, but his ideas and teachings have had an enormous effect on management practice. His book, *How to Win Friends and Influence People,*[14] was read by millions in the 1930s, 1940s, and 1950s. In addition, during this same period, tens of thousands of managers and aspiring managers attended his management speeches and seminars.

What was the theme of Carnegie's book and lectures? Essentially, he said that the way to success was through winning the cooperation of others. Carnegie advised that the path to success resided in (1) making others feel important through a sincere appreciation of their efforts; (2) making a good first impression; (3) winning people to your way of thinking by letting others do the talking, being sympathetic, and "never telling a man he is wrong"; and (4) changing people by praising of good traits and giving the offender the opportunity to save face.[15]

Few students of college age have not been exposed to the ideas of Abraham Maslow. A humanistic psychologist, Maslow proposed a theoretical hierarchy of five needs: physiological, safety, love, esteem, and self-actualization.[16] From a motivation standpoint, Maslow argued that each step in the hierarchy must be satisfied before the next can be activated and that once a need was substantially satisfied, it no longer motivated behavior. Moreover, Maslow believed that self-actualization—that is, achieving one's full potential—was the summit of a human being's existence. Managers who accepted Maslow's hierarchy attempted to alter their organizations and management practices to reduce barriers that stood in the way of employees being able to self-actualize. In Chapter 14, we'll discuss and evaluate Maslow's need hierarchy in detail.

Douglas McGregor is best known for his formulation of two sets of assumptions—Theory X and Theory Y—about human nature.[17] We will also discuss these assumptions more fully in Chapter 14. Briefly, Theory X presents an essentially negative view of people. It assumes that they have little ambition, dislike work, want to avoid responsibility, and need to be closely directed to work effectively. On the other hand, Theory Y offers a positive view. It assumes that people can exercise self-direction, accept responsibility, and consider work to be as natural as rest or play. McGregor believed that Theory Y assumptions best captured the true nature of workers and should guide management practice.

The common thread that united human relations supporters like Carnegie, Maslow, and McGregor was an unshakeable optimism about people's capabilities. They believed strongly in their cause and were inflexible in their beliefs, even when faced with contradictory evidence. McGregor, for instance, taught for a dozen years at the Massachusetts Institute of Technology. Then he became the president of Antioch College. After six years at Antioch, he decided to return to his professorship at M.I.T. In his farewell address at Antioch, McGregor seemed to recognize that his philosophy had failed to cope with the realities of organizational life:

I believed, for example, that a leader could operate successfully as a kind of adviser to his organization. I thought I could avoid being a "boss." Unconsciously, I suspect, I hoped to duck the unpleasant necessity of making difficult decisions, of taking the responsibility for one course of action, among many uncertain alternatives, of making mistakes and taking the consequences. I thought that maybe I could operate so that everyone would like me—that "good human relations" would eliminate all discord and disagreement.

I couldn't have been more wrong. It took a couple of years, but I finally began to realize that a leader cannot avoid the exercise of authority any more than he can avoid responsibility for what happens to his organization.[18]

The irony in McGregor's case was that he went back to M.I.T. and began preaching his humanistic doctrine again. He continued doing so until his death. The point is that people like McGregor, Maslow, and Carnegie were deeply committed to their beliefs about people, and no amount of contrary experience or research evidence would alter their views. Of course, in spite of this lack of objectivity, advocates of the human relations movement had a definite influence on management theory and practice.

Behavioral Science Theorists   Our final category within the human resources approach encompasses a group of psychologists and sociologists who relied on the scientific method for the studying of organizational behavior. Unlike individuals in the human relations movement, the **behavioral science theorists** engaged in *objective* research of human behavior in organizations. They carefully attempted to keep their personal beliefs out of their work. They sought to develop rigorous research designs that could be replicated by other behavioral scientists. In so doing, they hoped to build a science of organizational behavior.

behavioral science theorists
Psychologists and sociologists who relied on the scientific method for the study of organizational behavior.

Psychologists like Fred Fiedler, Victor Vroom, Frederick Herzberg, Edwin Locke, David McClelland, and Richard Hackman have made important contributions to our current understanding of leadership, employee motivation, and the design of jobs. Researchers with a sociological perspective, too, have made significant advances toward our understanding of organizational behavior. For instance, Jeffrey Pfeffer, Kenneth Thomas, and Charles Perrow have added important insights to our understanding of power, conflict, and organization design. The contributions of each of these behavioral science theorists will be detailed in later chapters.

Putting the Human Resources Contributors into Perspective   Both scientific management and the general administrative theorists viewed organizations as machines. As such, managers were the engineers. They ensured that the inputs were available and that the machine was properly maintained. Any failure by the employee to generate the desired output was viewed as an engineering problem: It was time to redesign the job or grease the "machine" by offering the employee an incentive wage plan. After all, who wouldn't work harder for a few more dollars? Contributors to the human resources approach forced a reassessment of this simplistic machine-model view.

In Chapters 3 and 8, we consider how the survival of an organization depends on how effectively it interacts with its environment. This concept clearly originated in Barnard's work. Barnard should also be recognized for emphasizing the need for managers to understand organizational communications and group behavior.

Much of the content of Chapters 13 through 17 in this book has evolved from the human resources approach. For instance, Owen, Münsterberg, Follett, the Hawthorne studies, McClelland, Fiedler, and Vroom provided the foundation for our current understanding of motivation, group dynamics, leadership, and communication. Moreover, much of the current interest in humanizing the workplace to increase productivity and improve employee job satisfaction can be traced to the work of Maslow, McGregor, and Herzberg.

The Quantitative Approach

We close our discussion of the period of diversity with a review of quantitative contributions to the study of management. This approach has also been labeled as *operations research* or *management science.*

The quantitative approach to management evolved out of the development of mathematical and statistical solutions to military problems during World War II. For instance, when the British confronted the problem of how to get the maximum effectiveness from their limited aircraft capability against the massive forces of the Germans, they turned to their mathematicians to devise an optimum allocation model. Similarly, U.S. antisubmarine warfare teams used operations research techniques to improve the odds of survival for Allied convoys crossing the North Atlantic and for selecting the optimal depth-charge patterns for aircraft and surface vessel attacks on German U-boats.

After the war, many of the quantitative techniques that had been applied to military problems were moved into the business sector. One group of military officers labeled the "Whiz Kids" joined Ford Motor Company in the mid-1940s and immediately began

ETHICAL DILEMMAS IN MANAGEMENT

Were Early Corporate Tycoons Benefactors or "Robber Barons"?

Management practices at the turn of the century were not always conducted with the highest of integrity. People like Cornelius Vanderbilt and John D. Rockefeller built immensely successful railroads and oil companies by engaging in activities that some have described as unethical and irresponsible.

Vanderbilt gained control of the New York and Harlem railroad lines by bribing the New York state legislature and by stock manipulation. Rockefeller conspired with the railroads to extract rebates on his freight and obtained kickbacks on the oil that his rivals shipped. Rockefeller also engaged in ruthless competition, driving his competitors out of business and then buying their assets at a fraction of their value.

In spite of their unsavory practices, these early tycoons built companies that created tens of thousands of jobs and provided the industrial base for U.S. manufacturing preeminence during the first 60 years of this century. At one point, for instance, Vanderbilt employed more people than anyone in the United States. Some of these tycoons also returned a large portion of the profits they made back to society through their philanthropic efforts. Rockefeller, for instance, endowed the University of Chicago, gave millions to educate southern blacks, and established the Rockefeller Foundation, which continues to give away tens of millions of dollars each year.

Were business tycoons like Vanderbilt and Rockefeller benefactors or exploiters of society? Did they act unethically? What do *you* think?

using statistical devices to improve decision making at Ford. Two of the most famous Whiz Kids were Robert McNamara and Charles "Tex" Thornton. McNamara rose to the presidency of Ford and then became U.S. Secretary of Defense. At the Department of Defense, he sought to quantify resource allocation decisions in the Pentagon through cost-benefit analyses. He concluded his career as head of the World Bank. Tex Thornton founded the billion-dollar conglomerate Litton Industries, again relying on quantitative techniques to make acquisition and allocation decisions.

What are these quantitative techniques, and how have they contributed to current management practice?

quantitative approach
The use of quantitative techniques to improve decision making.

The **quantitative approach** to management includes applications of statistics, optimization models, information models, and computer simulations. Linear programming, for instance, is a technique that managers can use to improve resource allocation choices. Work scheduling can be made more efficient as a result of critical-path scheduling analysis. Decisions on determining the optimum inventory levels a firm should maintain have been significantly influenced by the economic order quantity model.

The quantitative approach has contributed most directly to management decision making, particularly to planning and control decisions. Not to denigrate the contribution of the quantitative approach, but it should be noted that it has never gained the influence on management practice that the human resources approach has. This is undoubtedly due to a number of factors: Many managers are unfamiliar with the quantitative tools; behavioral problems are more widespread and visible; and most students and managers can relate better to real, day-to-day people problems in organizations, such as motivating subordinates and reducing conflicts, than to the more abstract activity of constructing quantitative models.

RECENT YEARS: TOWARD INTEGRATION

The previous discussion depicted four perspectives on management: the view of the foreman or supervisor, the whole organization, the manager as guiding and directing human resources, and the manager as developing quantitative models to make optimizing decisions. Each perspective has validity, but no single approach is a panacea. Though not mentioned before, occasional sporadic efforts were made during the period of diversity to synthesize the major writings of the time. For instance, in the early 1940s, Lyndall Urwick published *The Elements of Administration,* in which he noted numerous similarities in thought and terminology between scientific management and the general administrative theorists.[19] But these were exceptions. Concern with developing a unifying framework for management began in earnest only in the early 1960s. Like most fields of study, management, in its maturity, has moved toward integration.

The Process Approach

process approach
Management performs the functions of planning, organizing, leading, and controlling.

In December 1961, Professor Harold Koontz published an article in which he carefully detailed the diversity of approaches to the study of management and concluded that there existed a "management theory jungle."[20] Koontz conceded that each of the diverse approaches had something to offer management theory but then proceeded to demonstrate that (1) the human resources and quantitative approaches were not equivalent to the field of management, but rather were tools to be used by managers, and (2) a process approach could encompass and synthesize the diversity of the day. The **process approach,** originally introduced by Henri Fayol, views management as a

FIGURE 2–2
The Process Approach

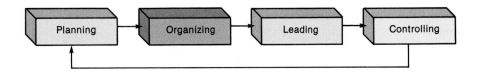

process of getting things done through and with people operating in organized groups. As depicted in Figure 2–2, managers are seen as performing the four functions of planning, organizing, leading, and controlling. The process is circular; the arrow from controlling back to planning indicates that the process is continuous. The control function ensures that the organization is actually attaining the planned objectives.

Koontz's article stimulated considerable debate. In 1962, Koontz played host to a group of distinguished management teachers and practitioners. They came to review the diverse approaches and to determine whether there could be a synthesis for a general theory. Koontz's idea of a general theory, however, was acceptance of the process approach.

A review of the papers presented at that meeting indicates that the conference participants left as entrenched in their individual perspectives as when they arrived.[21] But Koontz had made a mark. He gave high visibility to the process approach and forcefully argued that it offered a path out of "the jungle." The fact that the most popular current management textbooks follow the process orientation is evidence that the process approach continues to be a viable integrative framework.

The Systems Approach

The mid-1960s began a decade in which the idea that organizations could be analyzed in a systems framework gained a strong following. The **systems approach** defines a system as a set of interrelated and interdependent parts arranged in a manner that produces a unified whole. Societies are systems, and so too are automobiles, animals, and human bodies. The systems perspective, for instance, has been used by physiologists to explain how animals maintain an equilibrium state by taking in inputs and generating outputs.

There are two basic types of systems: closed systems and open systems. **Closed systems** are not influenced by and do not interact with their environment. Frederick Taylor's machine view of people and organizations was essentially a closed systems perspective. In contrast, an **open systems** approach recognizes the dynamic interaction of the system with its environment. While Barnard fostered the idea that organizations are open systems in the 1930s, widespread acceptance of the notion took another thirty years. Today, when we talk of organizations as systems, we mean open systems; that is, we acknowledge the organization's constant interaction with its environment.

Figure 2–3 shows a diagram of an organization from an open systems perspective. For a business firm, inputs would be material, labor, and capital. The transformation process would turn these inputs into finished products or services. The system's success depends on successful interactions with its environment, that is, those groups or institutions upon which it is dependent. These might include suppliers, labor unions, financial institutions, government agencies, and customers. The sale of outputs generates revenue, which can be used to pay wages and taxes, buy inputs, repay loans, and generate profits for stockholders. If revenues are not large enough to satisfy environmental demands, the organization shrinks or dies.

How can the systems perspective be used to integrate the diverse approaches to management? Systems advocates envision the organization as being made up of "interdependent factors, including individuals, groups, attitudes, motives, formal

systems approach
A theory that sees an organization as a set of interrelated and interdependent parts.

closed systems
Systems that neither are influenced by nor interact with their environment.

open systems
Dynamic systems that interact with and respond to their environment.

FIGURE 2–3
The Systems Approach

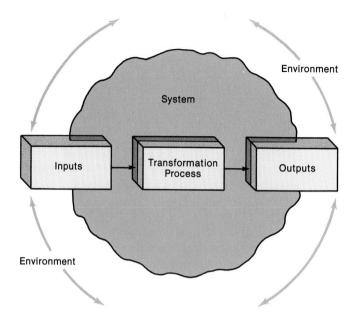

structure, interactions, goals, status, and authority."[22] The job of a manager is to ensure that all parts of the organization are coordinated internally so that the organization's goals can be achieved. A systems view of management, for instance, would recognize that, regardless of how efficient the production department might be, if the marketing department does not anticipate changes in consumer tastes and work with the product development department in creating what consumers want, the organization's overall performance will be hampered. Similarly, if the purchasing department fails to acquire the right quantity and quality of inputs, the production department will not be able to do its job effectively. So the systems approach recognizes the interdependence of the various activities within the organization.

Additionally, the open systems approach recognizes that organizations are not self-contained. They rely on their environment for life-sustaining inputs and as sources to absorb their outputs. No organization can survive for long if it ignores government regulations, supplier relations, or the myriad of external constituencies upon which the organization depends. As we discuss in the next chapter, management must understand its environment and the constraints that that environment imposes.

In later chapters, we'll introduce topics such as international management, social responsibility, strategy formation, and selecting the proper organization structure. All contemporary discussions on these issues build on the awareness that organizations are open systems. For instance, effective strategy formation requires that management analyze its organization's environment, assess the organization's strengths and weaknesses, and then identify opportunities or niches in that environment where the organization could have a competitive advantage.

The Contingency Approach

Management, like life itself, is not based on simplistic principles. You know that everyone who likes quality cars doesn't necessarily like Ferraris. Factors such as age, sex, marital status, income, and the importance placed on performance are *contingencies* that influence this preference. Baseball fans know that a batter doesn't always try for a

FIGURE 2–4
The Principles Approach

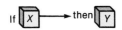

contingency approach
The development of situational variables that moderate "if X, then Y" statements of causation.

home run. It depends on the score, the inning, whether runners are on base, and similar *contingency* variables. Similarly, you can't say that students always learn more in small classes than in large ones. An extensive body of research tells us that *contingency* factors such as course content and the teaching style of the instructor influence the relationship between class size and learning effectiveness. It's not just a coincidence that college courses in introductory psychology are often taught in mass lectures; the course content lends itself well to the straight lecture format. The **contingency approach** (also sometimes called the situational approach) has been used in recent years to replace simplistic principles of management and to integrate much of management theory.[23]

Early management contributors like Taylor, Fayol, and Weber gave us principles of management and organization that they generally assumed to be universally applicable. Later research, however, has found exceptions to many of their principles. Division of labor, for example, is undoubtedly valuable in many situations, but jobs can also become *too* specialized. There are conditions—and we discuss them later in this book—in which employee productivity has been shown to increase by expanding rather than by narrowing job tasks. Bureaucracy, as a structural form, is desirable in many situations, but there are places where other structural designs are *more* effective. Allowing employees to participate in decision making is sometimes a preferred leadership style, but not *all* the time. There are conditions under which leaders should autocratically make their decision and then tell their employees what it is.

Figure 2–4 illustrates the simple principles' statement: "If X, then Y." *If* you want higher productivity, *then* institute division of labor. *If* you want more productive workers, *then* make them happy. But as we noted, these types of principles don't work in *all* situations. The contingency approach has attempted to deal with this reality by integrating management concepts into a situational framework. Figure 2–5 represents the contingency thesis: "If X, then Y, but only under conditions identified in Z." In the contingency approach, Z is the contingency variable. Recent efforts in contingency theory have tried to isolate "the Z variable," or situational determinant.

A contingency approach to the study of management is intuitively logical. Since organizations are diverse—in size, objectives, tasks being done, and the like—it would be surprising to find that there would be universally applicable principles that would work in *all* situations. But, of course, it is one thing to say, *"It all depends"* and another to say *what* it depends upon. Management researchers, therefore, have been trying to identify these "what" variables. Table 2–4 describes four popular contingency variables. This list is not comprehensive—there are at least 100 different variables that have been identified—but it represents those most widely in use and gives you an idea of what we mean by the term *contingency variable.*

FIGURE 2–5
The Contingency Approach

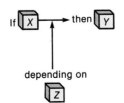

TABLE 2—4   Popular Contingency Variables

Organization Size. The number of people in an organization is a major influence on what managers do. As size increases, so do the problems of coordination. For instance, the type of organization structure appropriate for an organization of 50,000 employees is likely to be inefficient for an organization of 50 employees.

Routineness of Task Technology. In order for an organization to achieve its purpose, it uses technology; that is, it engages in the process of transforming inputs into outputs. Routine technologies require organizational structures, leadership styles, and control systems that differ from those required by customized or nonroutine technologies.

Environmental Uncertainty. The degree of uncertainty caused by political, technological, sociocultural, and economic changes influences the management process. What works best in a stable and predictable environment may be totally inappropriate in a rapidly changing and unpredictable environment.

Individual Differences. Individuals differ in terms of their desire for growth, autonomy, tolerance for ambiguity, and expectations. These and other individual differences are particularly important when managers select motivation techniques, leadership styles, and job designs.

WHERE ARE WE TODAY?

Current management concepts and practices reflect their historical origins. For example, this text is basically designed around the process approach. Chapters 7 through 20 cover the four functions of planning, organizing, leading, and controlling. But organizations depend on their environment for survival. In the next chapter, we demonstrate a basic tenet of the systems approach: The environment acts to constrain managerial discretion.

The contingency approach, too, has not been overlooked. It is integrated throughout this book. When we talk about plans, we'll identify those conditions under which they should be specific and those under which they should be more flexible and directional. We'll also identify the contingency variables that affect choices regarding organization structures, job designs, motivational techniques, leadership styles, conflict management, and control systems. What works best, and when, depends on contingency variables.

Have we discarded the early ideas of the scientific management or general administrative theorists? Not at all. Much of the discussion of operations management in Chapter 20 is directly traceable to the work of Taylor and Gilbreth. The basics of planning and organization design presented in Chapters 7 and 10 were originally articulated by Fayol and Weber. Similarly, the human resources approach has strongly influenced current personnel and employee relations practices, while the complex decision-making models that some managers use were developed by contributors to the quantitative approach.

Figure 2–6 summarizes the approaches introduced in this chapter, when they began, and their primary period of influence.

FIGURE 2–6
Summary of Modern Management Approaches

Approach	Central Theme	Approximate Time Period
		1910 1920 1930 1940 1950 1960 1970 1980 1990 →
Scientific management	Search for the "one best way" for performing any given task	
General administrative theorists	What managers do and what constitutes good management practice	
Human resources	Understanding employee behavior is the key to effective management	
Quantitative	Decision quality can be improved by quantifying decision variables	
Process	Managers perform discrete functions	
Systems	"It's all interrelated"	
Contingency	"It all depends"	

RECENT TRENDS

Most of us are vividly aware of the changing environment in which many managers have to operate today. Environmental forces such as government deregulation of the airline, trucking, and telecommunications industries; corporate raiders; and aggressive foreign competition are putting a premium on good management.

We conclude this chapter by briefly discussing two recent trends that are responses to this changing environment: the spread of Japanese-style management practices and the concern for stimulating innovation and change in organizations. Both are currently receiving a great deal of attention from practicing managers and are having a major influence on management theory.

Japanese-Style Management Practices

Japan's productive capability was almost completely destroyed by the end of World War II. Yet in less than 40 years, the Japanese had turned themselves into the dominant manufacturing power in the world. How did they do it? They introduced a comprehensive management system developed by an American consultant named W. Edwards Deming.

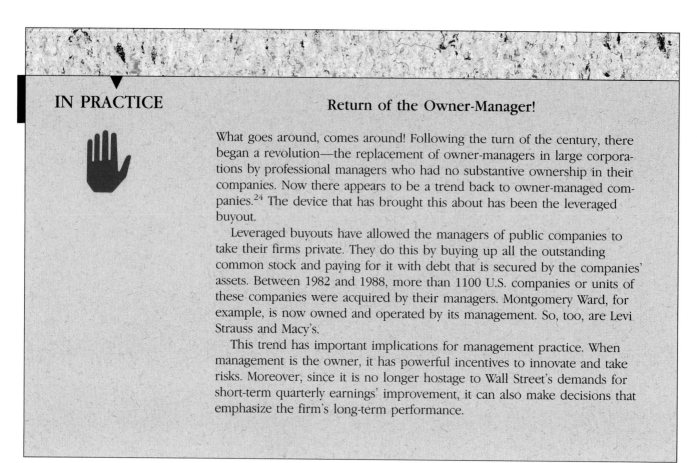

IN PRACTICE   **Return of the Owner-Manager!**

What goes around, comes around! Following the turn of the century, there began a revolution—the replacement of owner-managers in large corporations by professional managers who had no substantive ownership in their companies. Now there appears to be a trend back to owner-managed companies.[24] The device that has brought this about has been the leveraged buyout.

Leveraged buyouts have allowed the managers of public companies to take their firms private. They do this by buying up all the outstanding common stock and paying for it with debt that is secured by the companies' assets. Between 1982 and 1988, more than 1100 U.S. companies or units of these companies were acquired by their managers. Montgomery Ward, for example, is now owned and operated by its management. So, too, are Levi Strauss and Macy's.

This trend has important implications for management practice. When management is the owner, it has powerful incentives to innovate and take risks. Moreover, since it is no longer hostage to Wall Street's demands for short-term quarterly earnings' improvement, it can also make decisions that emphasize the firm's long-term performance.

In 1950, Deming went to Japan and spoke to many top Japanese managers on how to improve their production effectiveness. Central to his management methods was the use of statistics to analyze variability in production processes. A well-managed organization, according to Deming, was one in which statistical control reduced variability and resulted in uniform quality and predictable quantity of output.[25] Deming developed a fourteen-point program for transforming organizations. We review this program in detail in Chapter 20 when we discuss operations management.

Deming's influence has spread well beyond the borders of Japan, and his methods have been widely adopted throughout the world. Efforts to impose rigorous quality standards on the initial design of products, seeking constant and ongoing improvements in production and service operations, developing close long-term relationships with suppliers, and providing thorough training for employees are examples of practices that are gaining in popularity around the world. However, they have long been part of Deming's distinctive approach to management.

In the early 1980s, Professor William Ouchi of UCLA noted that a number of U.S. companies—IBM, Procter & Gamble, Hewlett-Packard—had developed management systems that have many of the characteristics evident in successful Japanese firms. He created the term *Theory Z* to describe their management practices.[26] While most U.S. firms emphasized employee specialization and individualized decision making and routinely fired people when business slowed, Theory Z firms were taking a different path. They developed a close and trusting relationship with their employees. They made long-term employment commitments to new hires. They developed their employees' talents and did those things that fostered teamwork. This included extensive lateral job rotation and collective decision making. Ouchi's book on Theory Z became a best-seller. Along with his articles and lectures on Theory Z, Ouchi served to further spread the word of the value of Japanese-style management practices.

Later in the book we'll discuss concepts such as quality circles, just-in-time inventory systems, and team-based job design. Like Theory Z, the seeds of these concepts lie in practices originally developed and perfected in Japan.

Stimulating Innovation and Change

"The organizations that are going to grow and prosper in the 1990s and beyond are the ones that foster innovation and master the art of change." That theme began to develop in the late 1970s and has had a major influence on the structure and design of organizations. Two people have played the major role in awakening management to the importance of managing change. These are Professor Rosabeth Moss Kanter of Harvard and consultant and lecturer Tom Peters.

In Kanter's best-selling book, *The Change Masters,*[27] she presents the results of her research in over 100 U.S. companies. She describes the potential for a U.S. corporate renaissance among people and organizations that are adept at the art of anticipating the need for, and of leading, productive change.

Tom Peters takes a far more aggressive stand, arguing that past guidelines for managing no longer apply.[28] These guidelines worked in a relatively stable and predictable world, but that world no longer exists. Managers now confront an environment in which change is taking place at an unprecedented rate; new competitors spring up overnight and old ones disappear through mergers, acquisitions, or just failing to keep up with the changing marketplace. Constant innovations in computer and telecommunications technologies combined with the globalization of product

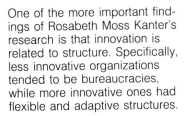

One of the more important findings of Rosabeth Moss Kanter's research is that innovation is related to structure. Specifically, less innovative organizations tended to be bureaucracies, while more innovative ones had flexible and adaptive structures.

Tom Peters concludes that managers must create organizations that can constantly change.

and financial markets have created chaos. According to Peters, only organizations that learn to cherish impermanence and thrive on chaos will survive as winners. He blends ideas offered by Deming and Kanter when he states that successful organizations must change and emphasize world-class quality and service, improved responsiveness through greatly enhanced flexibility, and continuous innovation and improvement aimed at creating new markets for both new and mature products and services. The success of Peters' books and his high visibility on the lecture circuit have carried his ideas to millions of managers. Peters has been a major impetus to such current management trends as self-managing teams, organizationwide incentive pay plans, and simplified organization structures.

SUMMARY

This summary is organized by the chapter-opening learning objectives found on page 27.

1. Studying management history helps you to understand theory and practice as they are today. It also helps you to see how current management concepts have evolved over time. Current management concepts are the result of continual development, testing, modification, retesting, and so on.

2. Important pre-twentieth-century contributions to management included the building of the Egyptian Pyramids, Adam Smith's writings on division of labor, and the Industrial Revolution. The building of the Pyramids was a monstrous project requiring the coordination of tens of thousands of workers. Clearly, this

demanded management skills. Smith's writings on the manufacturing of pins vividly illustrated the dramatic economies that could be achieved through division of labor. The Industrial Revolution made it more economical to manufacture goods in factories, which, in turn, significantly increased the need for applying management techniques to production operations.

3. The first half of the twentieth century was a period of diversity in management thought. Scientific management sought production efficiencies by searching for "the one best way" to do each job. The general administrative theorists sought principles of management that applied to the entire organization. The human resources approach focused on the management of people. The quantitative approach used mathematical and statistical techniques to improve resource allocation decisions.

4. Frederick Taylor proposed four principles of management: (1) developing a science for each element of an individual's work, (2) scientifically selecting and training workers, (3) management-worker cooperation, and (4) allocating responsibility to both management and workers.

5. Scientific management made possible dramatic increases—300 percent and more—in productivity. The application of its principles moved management from being a "seat-of-the-pants" practice to a serious, scientific discipline.

6. Henri Fayol was the first to define management as a universal set of functions: planning, organizing, commanding, coordinating, and controlling. He argued that management was an activity common to all human undertakings, and he identified fourteen principles of management that could be taught in schools and universities.

7. Max Weber defined the ideal bureaucracy as having division of labor, a clearly defined hierarchy, detailed rules and regulations, and impersonal relationships.

8. The Hawthorne studies led to a new emphasis on the human factor in the functioning of organizations and provided new insights into group norms and behavior. Management actively began to seek increased employee job satisfaction and higher morale.

9. Human relations advocates held strong personal convictions about people at work. They believed in the capability of people and argued for management practices that would increase employee satisfaction. In contrast, the behavioral science theorists engaged in objective research on human behavior in organizations. They carefully attempted to keep their personal beliefs out of their scientific research. A number of the behavioral science theorists objectively reached some of the same conclusions that the human relations advocates had earlier argued for and recommended similar management practices.

10. A unifying framework for management began in earnest in the early 1960s. The process approach was proposed as a way to synthesize the diversity. Managers plan, organize, lead, and control according to the process approach. The systems approach recognizes the interdependency of internal activities in the organization and between the organization and its external environment. The contingency approach isolates situational variables that affect managerial actions and organizational performance.

11. W. Edwards Deming introduced a comprehensive system that became the model for what we now think of as Japanese-style management practices. Central to his system was the use of statistics to analyze variability in production processes and to improve product quality.

12. Tom Peters argues that today's organizations face highly dynamic and changing environments. He believes that only organizations that can thrive on chaos will

survive. He argues that the management of successful organizations will emphasize quality, flexibility, and innovation.

REVIEW QUESTIONS

1. Describe how the construction of the Egyptian Pyramids would have required management skills.
2. Explain the advantages of using division of labor in an organization.
3. How did the Industrial Revolution increase the need for a formal theory of management?
4. Explain scientific management's contribution to management thought.
5. Identify six of Fayol's principles of management. How do they compare with Taylor's?
6. What is the historical importance of the Hawthorne studies?
7. How is the process approach integrative?
8. Explain how practicing managers can benefit by using the contingency approach.
9. How might ownership affect managerial practice?
10. What is a Theory Z organization?

DISCUSSION QUESTIONS

1. "The development of management thought has been determined by times and conditions." Do you agree or disagree with this statement? Discuss.
2. "Since management is discussed in the Bible, it was one of the first academic disciplines, preceding physics, biology, mathematics, or chemistry." Do you agree or disagree with this statement? Discuss.
3. "Everyone wants a challenging job with opportunities for advancement." Analyze this statement and modify it to reflect the contingency approach.
4. "Taylor and Fayol gave us some specific principles of management. The contingency approach says, 'it all depends.' We've gone backward in seventy-five years—from a set of specific principles to a set of vague and ambiguous guidelines." Do you agree or disagree with this statement? Discuss.
5. It has been said that those who cannot remember the past are condemned to relive it. Analyze this statement by demonstrating how the history of management thought could help you be a better manager today.

SELF-ASSESSMENT EXERCISE

Are You the Quantitative Type?

Instructions: Do numbers make you nervous? Do you suffer from math anxiety? To find out, score each of the following situations with the figure that corresponds to the intensity of your reaction:

Relaxed (1)
A little tense (2)
Tense (3)
Very tense (4)

How Do You Feel When You Are Called on to:

---

1. Determine the amount of change you should get back from a purchase involving several items?   1 2 3 4
2. Calculate how much it will cost to buy a product on credit, figuring in the interest rate?   1 2 3 4
3. Total up a dinner bill for which you think you were over-charged?   1 2 3 4
4. Tell the waiter that you think the dinner bill is incorrect, then watch him total it up?   1 2 3 4
5. Estimate the number of words in an article or paper that you are trying to write to a specified length?   1 2 3 4
6. Figure out the number of pages left in a novel you are reading?   1 2 3 4
7. Compute the miles per gallon on your car?   1 2 3 4
8. Read your W-2 form?   1 2 3 4
9. Check over your monthly bank statement?   1 2 3 4
10. Listen to someone describe how to set the shutter speed, film speed, and *f*-stop readings on your new single-lens reflex camera?   1 2 3 4
11. Check someone else's figures in a simple calculation, such as addition or division?   1 2 3 4
12. Play card games, such as bridge or poker, that involve scoring?   1 2 3 4
13. Add 976 and 777 in your head?   1 2 3 4
14. Add 976 and 777 with a pencil and paper?   1 2 3 4
15. Listen to explanations about bank interest rates as you decide on a savings account?   1 2 3 4

Turn to page 669 for scoring directions and key.

Source: Adapted from the *Mathematics Anxiety Rating Scale (MARS),* copyright © 1972 by Richard M. Suinn. All rights reserved. Published by RMBSI, Inc., P.O. Box 1066, Ft. Collins, Colo. 80522.

CASE APPLICATION 2A

The Seattle Consulting Group

The Seattle Consulting Group (SCG) is well known in the Pacific Northwest for the quality of its executive and supervisory development courses. One of its more popular courses is a three-day seminar, restricted to twelve participants, that helps supervisors with high potential think about the problems of middle-management positions and the abilities necessary to succeed in these jobs.

In September 1990, four companies each sent three of their supervisors to the SCG course. The participants flew into Seattle and then took the short ferry ride to SCG's development headquarters on Vashon Island in Puget Sound. They arrived on a late Tuesday afternoon, prepared to begin their course on Wednesday morning.

Marc Stern and John Mather were two participants in the seminar. Marc and John were employed by a major paper and forest products firm headquartered in Oregon. In the few years they had been with the company, both had displayed outstanding abilities and were expected to move quickly into its upper echelons. But the two had distinctly different backgrounds. Marc was an accountant, held a C.P.A. certificate, and was currently a supervisor in the accounting office. John, on the other hand, had a degree in psychology and was a supervisor in the corporate relations group.

The seminar began promptly at 8:00 A.M. on Wednesday morning, and the participants showed no reluctance to talk, share experiences, or disagree with comments made by others. After lunch on the first day, the SCG discussion leader asked the question: "What are the qualities of a good manager?" While no one lacked for an opinion, it was rapidly evident that John and Marc were the most dogmatic and polarized.

John summed up his position curtly: "It's clear to me that a good manager knows the behavioral sciences and can apply their findings. It's obvious that the factors that make or break a manager are things like: Can he communicate effectively? Is he able to lead his employees? Does he know how to motivate employees? These are the issues that the behavioral sciences can help answer. So I'm convinced a good manager understands behavior."

Marc's summary indicated that he couldn't have disagreed more: "You look at the good managers and compare them with the poor ones. What I see is that the good ones know their numbers. They know how to allocate scarce resources. They understand economics. The difference between success and failure lies in the ability to design jobs, identify efficient work methods, know what equipment is necessary, lay out and coordinate work flow, schedule personnel and the work to be completed, and establish and monitor controls over things like the quality and quantity of output and costs."

Questions

1. What evidence can you provide to support John's argument? What negative consequences might result from John's following this view of management?

2. What evidence can you provide to support Marc's argument? What negative consequences might result from Marc's following this view of management?

3. Is one more right than the other? Support your position.

4. Do you think the department in which managers work or their major in college has any bearing on their approach to management? Support your position.

CASE APPLICATION 2B

Lechmere, Inc.

In late 1987, the unemployment rate in Sarasota, Florida, was down to a minuscule 4 percent.[29] This was a disturbing fact for senior executives at Lechmere, Inc., a twenty-seven-store retail chain operated by the Dayton Hudson stores. Lechmere was about to open an outlet in Sarasota, and the supply of qualified job applicants was scarce. Like many retailers, Lechmere's management customarily hired a large number of teenagers and housewives to fill entry-level part-time positions. These people gave management a great deal of flexibility because they could be moved around as needed and their hours scheduled to match demand. But in Sarasota, Lechmere's executives faced a small applicant pool. The low unemployment rate had dried up most of the potential part-time population.

Lechmere's management came up with a creative solution to their problem. They offered the Sarasota workers raises based on the number of jobs they learned to perform. Cashiers were encouraged to sell records and tapes. Sporting goods sales personnel learned to operate forklift trucks. The result? The Sarasota store now has the capability to quickly adjust to shifts in staffing needs simply by deploying existing workers.

The pay incentives, coupled with the prospect of a more varied and interesting workday, proved to be effective lures for recruiting new people. The Sarasota store now has a work force that is 60 percent full-timers. This compares to an average of 30 percent for the rest of the chain. In addition, management claims that the Sarasota store is substantially more productive than the others. Lechmere is now extending the flexible-worker idea to a number of its other stores around the United States.

Questions

1. Compare the labor market conditions that Lechmere faced in Sarasota with the conditions that Taylor likely saw in turn-of-the-century Pennsylvania. What does this suggest about the possible influence of labor supply on management practices?

2. Contrast the flexible-worker idea with the concept of division of labor. How would the former increase productivity? What effect do you think it would have on quality of effort?

3. How might the contingency approach explain why some workers would prefer the flexibility at Lechmere, while others would prefer jobs that are more specialized?

Managerial Roles

PURPOSE

1. To examine the key components of a manager's job.
2. To contrast the job of first-level supervisor with that of a top executive.
3. To apply the role concept to actual jobs.

REQUIRED KNOWLEDGE

1. The functions and roles of a manager's job.
2. The effect of organizational level on a manager's job.

TIME REQUIRED

Approximately 45 minutes.

INSTRUCTIONS

Consider the jobs of (a) supervisor of the painting department at the St. Louis assembly plant of Chrysler Corporation and (b) Chairman of the Board and Chief Executive Officer of Chrysler Corporation.

Table I–A presents a list of roles in which the supervisor and CEO might engage. For each of the above jobs:

1. List any of the roles that would *not* be relevant to the job and explain why.
2. For the remaining roles, give a specific example of something each might do as part of that job.
3. Rank in order, from 1 to *n,* the applicable roles for each job on the basis of the amount of time devoted to each role. (Give the role that demands the most time the number 1, and no ties are allowed.)
4. Form into groups of three to five students. Discuss your individual analyses and, as a group, arrive at a rank order for each job, just as you did in the previous step individually.
5. Each group will appoint a spokesperson to present your group's conclusions and discuss the group decision with the class.

TABLE I—A   Allocation of Time for Chrysler Managers

Managerial Role	Specific Example*	Individual Ranking	Group Ranking
Job: Supervisor of Painting Department			
Figurehead			
Leader			
Liaison			
Monitor			
Disseminator			
Spokesperson			
Entrepreneur			
Disturbance handler			
Resource allocator			
Negotiator			
Job: Chairman of the Board and Chief Executive Officer			
Figurehead			
Leader			
Liaison			
Monitor			
Disseminator			
Spokesperson			
Entrepreneur			
Disturbance handler			
Resource allocator			
Negotiator			

*Write NA if not applicable, then explain why.

The Case
of the
Missing Time

It was 7:30 Tuesday morning when Chet Craig, General Manager of the Norris Company's Central Plant, swung his car out of the driveway of his suburban home and headed to the plant in Midvale, six miles away. The trip to the plant took about twenty minutes and gave Chet an opportunity to think about plant problems without interruption.

The Norris Company operated three printing plants and did a nationwide business in quality color work. It had about 350 employees, nearly half of whom were employed at the Central Plant. (See Figure I-1.) The company's headquarters offices were also located in the Central Plant building.

Chet had started with the Norris Company as an expeditor in its Eastern Plant ten years ago, after his graduation from Ohio State. After three years, he was promoted to Production Supervisor; two years later, he was made assistant to the manager of the Eastern Plant. A year and a half ago, he had been transferred to the Central Plant as assistant to the Plant Manager, and one month later, when the manager retired, Chet was promoted to General Plant Manager.

Chet was in good spirits this morning. Various thoughts occurred to him as he said to himself, "This is going to be the day to really get things done." He thought of the day's work, first one project, then another, trying to establish priorities. He decided that the open-end unit scheduling was probably the most important—certainly the most urgent. He recalled that on Friday the Vice President had casually asked him if he had given the project any further thought. Chet realized that he had not been giving it any attention lately. He had been meaning to get to work on his idea for over three months, but something else always seemed to crop up.

"I haven't had time to really work it out," he said to himself. "I'd better get going and finish it off one of these days." He then began to break down the objectives, procedures, and installation steps in the project. It gave him a feeling of satisfaction as he calculated the anticipated cost savings. "It's high time," he told himself. "This idea should have been completed a long time ago."

Chet had first conceived the open-end unit scheduling idea almost two years ago just prior to leaving the Eastern Plant. He had talked it over with the General Manager of the Eastern Plant, and both agreed that it was a good idea and worth developing. The idea was temporarily shelved when Chet had been transferred to the Central Plant a month later.

His thoughts returned to other plant projects he was determined to get under way. He started to think through a procedure for the simpler transport of dies to and from the Eastern Plant. He thought of the notes on his desk: the inventory analysis he needed to identify and eliminate some of the slow-moving stock items, the packing controls which needed revision, and the need to design a new special order form. He also decided that this was the day to settle on a job printer to do the outside printing of simple office forms. There were a few other projects he could not recall offhand, but he felt sure that he could tend to them some time during the day. Again he said to himself, "This is the day to really get rolling."

When he entered the plant, Chet was met by Al Noren, the stockroom foreman, who appeared troubled. "A great morning, Al," said Chet, cheerfully.

"Well, I don't know, Chet. My new man isn't in this morning," said Noren morosely.

"Have you heard from him?" asked Chet.

"No, I haven't."

"These stock handlers take it for granted that if they're not here, they don't have to call in and report. Better ask Personnel to call him."

Al hesitated a moment. "Okay, Chet," he said, "but can you find me a man? I have two cars to unload today."

Making a note of the incident, Chet headed for his office. He greeted some workers discussing the day's work with Marilyn, the Office Manager. As the meeting broke up, Marilyn took some samples from a clasper and showed them to Chet and asked if they should be shipped that way, or if it would be necessary to inspect them. Before he could answer, Marilyn went on to ask if he could suggest another clerical operator for the

sealing machine to replace the regular operator, who was home ill. She also told him that Gene, the Industrial Engineer, had called and was waiting to hear from Chet.

Chet told Marilyn to ship the samples and made a note of the need for a sealer operator and then called Gene. He agreed to stop by Gene's office before lunch and started on his routine morning tour of the plant. He asked each foreman the volumes and types of orders they were running, the number of people present, how the schedules were coming along, and the orders to be run next; he helped the folding room foreman find temporary storage space for consolidating a carload shipment; discussed quality control with a pressman who had been running poor work; arranged to transfer four people temporarily to different depart-

FIGURE I–1

Norris Company Organization Chart

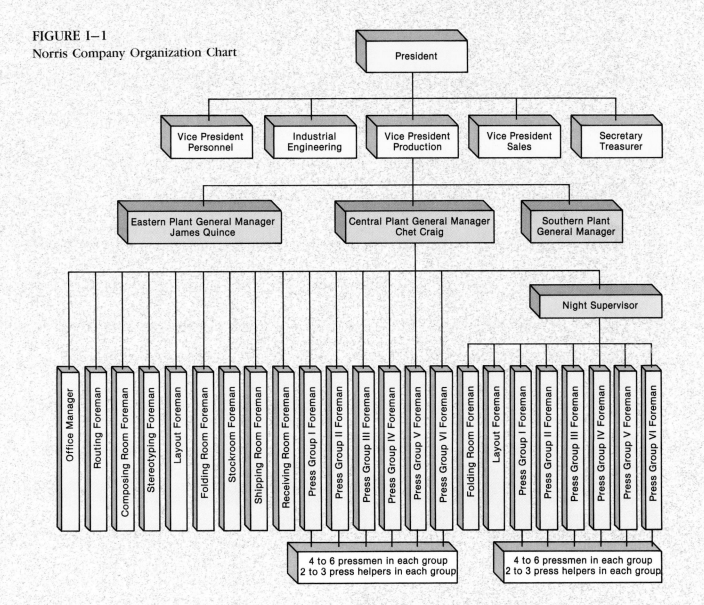

ments, including two for Al in the stockroom; talked to the shipping foreman about pickups and special orders to be delivered that day. As he continued through the plant, he saw to it that reserve stock was moved out of the forward stock area; talked to another pressman about his requested change of vacation schedule; had a "heart-to-heart" talk with a press helper who seemed to need frequent assurance; approved two type and one color okays for different pressmen.

Returning to his office, Chet reviewed the production reports on the larger orders against his initial projections and found that the plant was running slightly behind schedule. He called in the folding room foreman, and together they went over the line-up of machines and made several changes.

During this discussion, the composing room foreman stopped in to cover several type changes, and the routing foreman telephoned for approval of a revised printing schedule. The stockroom foreman called twice—first to inform him that two standard, fast-moving stock items were dangerously low; later to advise him that the paper stock for the urgent Dillon job had finally arrived. Chet telephoned this information to the people concerned.

He then began to put delivery dates on important inquiries received from customers and salesmen. (The routine inquiries were handled by Marilyn.) While he was doing this, he was interrupted twice—once by a sales correspondent calling from the West Coast to ask for a better delivery date than originally scheduled; once by the Vice President, Personnel, asking Chet to set a time when he could hold an initial induction interview with a new employee.

After dating the customer and salesmen inquiries, Chet headed for his morning conference in the executive office. At this meeting he answered the Vice President, Sales's questions in connection with "hot" orders, complaints, the status of large-volume orders and potential new orders. Then he met with the Vice President and General Production Manager to answer "the old man's" questions on several production and personnel problems. Before leaving the executive offices, he stopped at the office of the Purchasing Agent to inquire about the delivery of some cartons, paper, and boxes and to place an order for some new paper.

On the way back to his own office, Chet conferred with Gene about two current engineering projects. When he reached his desk, he lit a cigarette and looked at his watch. It was ten minutes before lunch—just time enough to make a few notes of the details he needed to check in order to answer knotty questions raised by the Vice President, Sales, that morning.

After lunch, Chet started again. He began by checking the previous day's production reports; did some

rescheduling to get out urgent orders; placed delivery dates on new orders and inquiries received that morning; consulted with a foreman on a personal problem. He spent about twenty minutes at the TWX[1] going over mutual problems with the Eastern Plant.

By midafternoon, Chet had made another tour of the plant, after which he met with the Vice President, Personnel, to review with him a touchy personal problem raised by one of the clerical employees, the vacation schedules submitted by his foreman, and the pending job evaluation program. Following this conference, Chet hurried back to his office to complete the special statistical report for Universal Waxing Corporation, one of Norris's biggest customers. When he finished the report, he discovered that it was ten after six and he was the only one left in the office. Chet was tired. He put on his coat and headed for the parking lot. On the way out, he stopped by the night supervisor and the night layout foreman for approval of type and layout changes.

As he drove home, Chet reviewed the day he had just completed. "Busy?" he asked himself. "Too much so—but did I accomplish anything?" The answer seemed to be "Yes, and no—there was the usual routine, the same as any other day. The plant kept going, and it was a good production day. Any creative or special work done?" Chet winced. "I guess not."

With a feeling of guilt, Chet asked himself, "Am I an executive? I'm paid like one, and I have a responsible assignment and the authority to carry it out. My supervisors at headquarters think I'm a good manager. Yet one of the greatest returns a company gets from an executive is his innovative thinking and accomplishments. What have I done about that? Today was just like other days, and I didn't do any creative work. The projects that I was so eager to work on this morning are no further ahead than they were yesterday. What's more, I can't say that tomorrow night or the next night they'll be any closer to completion. This is a real problem, and there must be some answer to it."

"Night work? Yes, sometimes. This is understood. But I've been doing too much night work lately. My wife and family deserve some of my time. After all, they are the people for whom I'm really working. If I spend much more time away from them, I'm not meeting my own personal objectives. I spend a lot of time on church work. Should I eliminate that? I feel I owe that as an obligation. Besides, I feel I'm making a worthwhile contribution in this work. Maybe I can squeeze a little time from my fraternal activities. But where does recreation fit in?"

Chet groped for the solution. "Maybe I'm just rationalizing because I schedule my own work poorly. But I don't think so. I've studied my work habits and I think I plan intelligently and delegate authority. Do I need an assistant? Possibly, but that's a long-term project, and I don't believe I could justify the additional overhead expense. Anyway, I doubt whether it would solve the problem."

By this time, Chet had turned off the highway into the side street leading to his home. "I guess I really don't know the answer," he said to himself as he pulled into his driveway. "This morning everything seemed so simple, but now. . . ."

QUESTIONS

1. Which of Chet's activities on this Tuesday would you describe as managerial? Which aren't?

2. How do Chet's activities compare with Mintzberg's description of managerial roles?

3. Which, if any, of Fayol's principles of management did Chet follow on this Tuesday?

4. Analyze Chet's day in terms of the systems approach to management.

5. What might Chet do to improve his effectiveness as a manager?

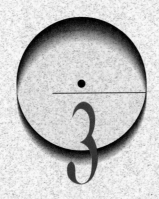

ORGANIZATIONAL CULTURE AND ENVIRONMENT: THE CONSTRAINTS

1. Differentiate the symbolic from the omnipotent view of management.
2. Define organizational culture.
3. Identify the ten characteristics that make up an organization's culture.
4. Describe how culture is created.
5. Explain how culture constrains managers.
6. Define an organization's environment.
7. Distinguish between the general and specific environment.
8. Explain how the environment constrains managers.

To
TYLENOL EXCHANGE
P.O. BOX2000
MAPLE PLAIN
MINN
55438
TYLENOL EXC
MAPLE PL
MINNESOT

In the fall of 1982, eight Chicago-area residents died after taking Extra-Strength Tylenol capsules that had been laced with cyanide. In the winter of 1986, in a similar scenario, a New York woman died from a cyanide-laced Tylenol capsule. In both cases, the management at McNeil Consumer Products, the manufacturer and a division of Johnson & Johnson (J&J), claimed that it was blameless. Thorough investigations proved it right. Both poisonings were clearly the actions of deranged individuals. That fact, however, didn't reduce the devastating impact the poisonings had on Tylenol's sales and J&J's profits.[1]

After the 1982 incident, J&J recalled and destroyed 31 million bottles of Tylenol capsules, resulting in an after-tax write-off of $50 million. The company then spent nearly $300 million more to promote its repackaged "triple-sealed to resist tampering" capsules. It succeeded in restoring public trust in the product and reclaiming its market position. But after the 1986 poisoning, J&J's management decided to abandon the use of capsules in all its over-the-counter drugs and instead market them in the form of solid caplets. Again, the costs were high; approximately $150 million was spent to recall the capsules, reorganize the production process, and promote the new caplets.

J&J's troubles were not of its own making. Incidents such as these raise the question of whether an organization's successes or failures are always directly attributable to management.

> Johnson & Johnson no longer sells Tylenol in capsule form because of two apparently unrelated poisonings. Tylenol is now sold as solid caplets. These poisonings cost J&J a half-billion dollars and significantly hurt the company's financial performance, yet these incidents were something over which management had little control.

THE MANAGER: OMNIPOTENT OR SYMBOLIC?

omnipotent view
The view that managers are directly responsible for the success or failure of an organization.

symbolic view
The view that management has only a limited effect on substantive organizational outcomes owing to the large number of factors outside of management's control.

The dominant view in management theory and in society is that managers are directly responsible for an organization's success or failure. We'll call this perspective the **omnipotent view of management.** In contrast, some observers have argued that managers have little influence on organizational outcomes. Instead, much of an organization's success or failure is said to be due to forces outside management's control. This perspective has been labeled the **symbolic view of management.**[2]

In this section, we want to review each of these positions. Our reason should be obvious. The answer will go a long way in clarifying just how much credit or blame managers should receive for their organization's performance.

The Omnipotent View

In Chapter 1, we said, "Good managers can turn straw to gold. Poor managers can do the reverse." These statements reflect a dominant assumption in management theory: The quality of an organization's managers determines the quality of the organization itself. It's assumed that differences in an organization's effectiveness or efficiency are due to the decisions and actions of its managers. Good managers anticipate change, exploit opportunities, correct poor performance, and lead their organizations toward their objectives (and even change those objectives when necessary). When profits are up, management takes the credit and rewards itself with bonuses, stock options, and the like. When profits are down, the board of directors replaces top management in the belief that new management will bring improved results.

This omnipotent view of managers is consistent with the stereotypical picture of the swashbuckling, take-charge executive who can overcome any obstacle in carrying out the organization's objectives. This omnipotent view is not limited to business organizations. It can, for instance, help to explain the high turnover among college coaches.

College coaches manage their teams. They decide which players to recruit and which players start, select assistant coaches, teach plays to their teams, and select every play during games. Coaches who lose more games than they win are seen as ineffective. They are fired and replaced by new coaches who, it is assumed, will correct the inadequate performance.

Regardless of extenuating circumstances, when organizations perform poorly, someone has to be held accountable. In our society, that role is played by management. Of course, when things go well, management gets the credit (even if it had little to do with causing the positive outcome).

The Symbolic View

In the early 1980s, the board of directors of International Harvester (now called Navistar International) fired the company's chairman and chief executive officer, Archie McCardell. The company was losing tens of millions of dollars a month because farmers, suffering from depressed farm prices, couldn't afford to buy the farm machinery and heavy-duty trucks that International Harvester made. Of course, McCardell hadn't created the farm problem, nor was his firing likely to increase the demand for farm machinery and trucks. He was merely in the wrong place at the wrong time, and he lost his job because of it.

This example illustrates the symbolic view of managers. The symbolic view assumes that a manager's ability to affect outcomes is highly constrained. In this view, it is unreasonable to expect managers to have much of an effect on an organization's performance.

According to the symbolic view, an organization's results are influenced by a number of factors outside the control of management. These include the economy, government policies, competitors' actions, the state of the particular industry, the

When medical findings discovered that whole-grain oats reduce cholesterol and lessen the chance of a heart attack, the sales of all oat and bran cereals increased dramatically. The manager at General Mills, responsible for the Cheerios product line, suddenly found her sales and profits skyrocketing. She, of course, was rewarded with handsome bonuses based on her product line's performance. This is the opposite of Archie McCardell's situation at International Harvester. The General Mills manager happened to be in the *right* place at the *right* time.

FIGURE 3–1
Parameters of Managerial
Discretion

control of proprietary technology, and decisions made by previous managers in the organization.

Following the symbolic view, management has, at best, only a limited effect on *substantive organizational* outcomes. What management does affect greatly are *symbolic* outcomes.[3] Management's role is seen as one of creating meaning out of randomness, confusion, and ambiguity. Management creates the illusion of control for the benefit of stockholders, customers, employees, and the public. When things go right, we need someone to praise. Management plays that role. Similarly, when things go wrong, we need a scapegoat. Management plays that role, too. However, the *actual* part management plays in success or failure is minimal.

Reality Suggests a Synthesis

In reality, managers are neither impotent nor all-powerful. Internal constraints exist within every organization that restrict a manager's decision options. These internal constraints are derived from the organization's culture. In addition, external constraints impinge on the organization and restrict managerial freedom. These external constraints come from the organization's environment.

Figure 3–1 depicts the manager as operating within constraints. The organization's culture and environment press against the manager, restricting his or her options. Yet, in spite of these constraints, managers are not powerless. There still remains an area in which managers can exert a significant amount of influence on an organization's performance—an area in which good managers differentiate themselves from poor ones. In the remainder of this chapter, we'll discuss organizational culture and environment as constraints. But, as we'll also point out later in this book, these constraints need not be regarded as fixed in all situations. For some organizations, in certain circumstances, it may be possible to change and influence their culture and environment and thus expand their management's area of discretion.

THE ORGANIZATION'S CULTURE

We know that every individual has something that psychologists have termed "personality." An individual's personality is made up of a set of relatively permanent and stable traits. When we describe someone as warm, innovative, relaxed, or conservative, we are describing personality traits. An organization, too, has a personality, which we call the organization's *culture*.

What Is Organizational Culture?

Just as tribal cultures have totems and taboos that dictate how each member will act toward fellow members and outsiders, organizations have cultures that govern how members should behave. The culture conveys assumptions and norms governing values, activities, and goals. In doing so, it tells employees how things should be done and what's important. As an example, in organizations whose culture conveys a basic distrust of employees, managers are much more likely to use an authoritarian leadership style than a democratic one. Why? The culture conveys to managers what is appropriate behavior.

organizational culture
A system of shared meaning.

What do we specifically mean by the term **organizational culture?** We use the term to refer to a system of *shared meaning*. In every organization, there are systems or patterns of values, symbols, rituals, myths, and practice that have evolved over time.[4] These shared values determine, in large degree, what managers see and how they respond to their world.[5] When confronted with a problem, the organizational culture restricts what managers can do by suggesting the correct way—"the way we do things here"—to conceptualize, define, analyze, and solve the problem. For example, the president of Honeywell Information Systems recognized the constraining role that culture was playing in his effort to get his managers to be less authoritarian.[6] He noted that his organization's culture would have to become more democratic if it was going to succeed in the marketplace. "He explained that managers' shared beliefs in authoritarian management had to some extent predisposed them to keep information 'very close to the vest,' resulting in situations in which people did not have '*all* the data [they needed] to make decent decisions.'"[7]

Our definition of culture implies several things. First, culture is a perception. But this perception exists in the organization, not in the individual. As a result, individuals with different backgrounds or at different levels in the organization tend to describe the organization's culture in similar terms. That is the *shared* aspect of culture. Second, organizational culture is a descriptive term. It is concerned with how members perceive the organization, not with whether or not they like it. It describes rather than evaluates.

Though we currently have no definitive method for measuring an organization's culture, preliminary research suggests that cultures can be analyzed by assessing how an organization rates on ten characteristics. They have been identified as follows:

1. *Individual initiative:* the degree of responsibility, freedom, and independence that individuals have.

2. *Risk tolerance:* the degree to which employees are encouraged to be aggressive, innovative, and risk-seeking.

3. *Direction:* the degree to which the organization creates clear objectives and performance expectations.

4. *Integration:* the degree to which units within the organization are encouraged to operate in a coordinated manner.

5. *Management support:* the degree to which managers provide clear communication, assistance, and support to their subordinates.

6. *Control:* the number of rules and regulations and the amount of direct supervision that is used to oversee and control employee behavior.

7. *Identity:* the degree to which members identify with the organization as a whole rather than with their particular work group or field of professional expertise.

8. *Reward system:* the degree to which reward allocations (such as salary increases, promotions) are based on employee performance criteria in contrast to seniority, favoritism, and so on.

9. *Conflict tolerance:* the degree to which employees are encouraged to air conflicts and criticisms openly.

10. *Communication patterns:* the degree to which organizational communications are restricted to the formal hierarchy of authority.[8]

The organization's culture is a composite picture formed from these ten characteristics. Table 3–1 demonstrates how these characteristics can be mixed to create highly diverse organizations.

TABLE 3–1   Two Highly Diverse Organizational Cultures

Organization A	Organization B
This organization is a manufacturing firm. There are extensive rules and regulations that employees are required to follow. Every employee has specific objectives to achieve in his or her job. Managers supervise employees closely to ensure that there are no deviations. People are allowed little discretion in doing their jobs. Employees are instructed to bring any unusual problem to their superior, who will then determine the solution. All employees are required to communicate through formal channels. Because management has no confidence in the honesty or integrity of its employees, it imposes tight controls. Managers and employees alike tend to be hired by the organization early in their careers and rotated into and out of various departments on a regular basis. They are generalists rather than specialists. Effort, loyalty, cooperation, and avoidance of errors are highly valued and rewarded.	This organization is also a manufacturing firm. Here, however, there are few rules and regulations. Employees are seen as hard-working and trustworthy, so supervision is loose. Employees are encouraged to solve problems themselves but to feel free to consult with their supervisors when they need assistance. Top management downplays authority differences. Employees are also encouraged to develop their unique specialized skills. Interpersonal and interdepartmental differences are seen as natural occurrences. Managers are evaluated not only on their department's performance but also on how well their department coordinates its activities with other departments in the organization. Promotions and other valuable rewards go to the employees who make the greatest contribution to the organization, even when those employees have strange ideas, unusual personal mannerisms, or unconventional work habits.

The characteristics listed above are relatively stable and permanent over time. Just as an individual's personality is stable and permanent—if you were an extrovert last month, you're likely to be an extrovert next month—an organization's culture is relatively enduring over time and relatively static in its propensity to change.

General Motors has been almost universally described as a cold, formal, risk-aversive firm. It was that way in the 1930s, and it is basically the same today. In contrast, Hewlett-Packard is an informal, loosely structured, and highly humanistic organization. Both General Motors and Hewlett-Packard have been essentially successful over the years. The fact that their cultures are different may or may not contribute to their effectiveness. That is not our point. Rather, these organizations are different, just as Organizations A and B in Table 3–1 are different, and these differences in organizational culture influence management practices. Culture constrains choices by conveying to managers which practices are acceptable in their organization and which are not.

Strong Versus Weak Cultures

strong cultures
Organizations in which the key values are intensely held and widely shared.

While all organizations have cultures, not all cultures have an equal impact on employees. **Strong cultures**—organizations in which the key values are intensely held and widely shared—have a greater influence on employees than do weak cultures. The more that employees accept the organization's key values and the greater their commitment to those values, the stronger the culture is.

Whether an organization's culture is strong, weak, or somewhere in between depends on factors such as the size of the organization, how long it has been around, how much turnover there has been among employees, and the intensity with which the culture was originated. In some organizations, it's unclear what's important and

ETHICAL DILEMMAS IN MANAGEMENT

Whistleblowing
Reporting unethical practices by your employer to outsiders such as the press, government agencies, or public interest groups.

Should Organizations Protect Whistleblowers?

What do you do when you discover that your boss or your entire organization is engaged in unethical practices?

Some organizations have created cultures that encourage free expression of controversial or dissenting views, protect employees with formal grievance procedures, and provide mechanisms whereby employees can anonymously report unethical practices to senior management. Others, however, regard **whistleblowing**—reporting unethical practices to outsiders such as the press, government agencies, or public interest groups—as the ultimate demonstration of disloyalty. Whistleblowing embarrasses managers and erodes their authority. In such organizations, whistleblowing can mean putting one's job or entire career on the line.

On the other hand, does loyalty to an organization require one to ignore unethical or illegal practices? Does an employee have to forgo his or her rights to free speech in order to keep a job? Many states have passed laws to protect whistleblowers. But even where there is legal protection, employees often still fear subtle forms of retaliation if they embarrass their boss, senior management, or the organization. What do *you* think about whistleblowing? Would *you* be willing to blow the whistle if it meant risking your job?

what isn't—a characteristic of weak cultures. In such organizations, culture is less likely to mold or constrain managers. However, most organizations have moderate to strong cultures. There is relatively high agreement on what's important, how "good" employees should behave, what it takes to get ahead, and so forth. We should expect that culture will have an increasing impact on what managers do as it becomes stronger.[9]

The Source of Culture

An organization's culture reflects the vision or mission of the organization's founders. The founders establish the early culture by projecting an image of what the organization should be. They are unconstrained by previous customs or ideologies. The smallness of most new organizations also helps the founders impose their vision on all organizational members. Because the founders have the original idea, they also have biases on how to carry out the idea. An organization's culture, then, results from the interaction between (1) the founders' biases and assumptions and (2) what the first employees learn subsequently from their own experiences.[10]

Thomas Watson at IBM and Frederick Smith at Federal Express are just two examples of individuals who have had an immeasurable influence on shaping their organization's culture. For instance, Watson's views on research and development, product quality, employee attire, and compensation policies are still evident at IBM, although

Wal-Mart's culture is characterized by frugality, simplicity, and
humility. These traits personify
its founder, Sam Walton.
Although a billionaire, he lives
modestly in Bentonville, Arkansas.

he died in 1956. Federal Express's aggressiveness, willingness to take risks, focus on
innovation, and emphasis on service are central themes that founder Smith has articulated since the company's birth.

Influence on Management Practice

An organization's culture is particularly relevant to managers because it establishes
constraints upon what they can and cannot do.

> Culture controls the manager . . . through the automatic filters that bias the
> manager's perceptions, thoughts, and feelings. As culture arises and gains
> strength, it becomes pervasive and influences *everything* the manager does,
> even his own thinking and feeling. This point is especially important because
> most of the elements that the manager views as aspects of "effective" manage-
> ment—setting objectives, measuring, following up, controlling, giving perfor-
> mance feedback, and so on—are themselves culturally biased to an unknown
> degree in any given organization. There is no such thing as a culture-free con-
> cept of management.[11]

These automatic filters or constraints are rarely explicit. They are not written down. It
may even be rare to hear them articulated verbally. But they're there, and all managers
quickly learn "the ropes to skip and the ropes to know" in their organization. To
illustrate, you won't find the following values written down anywhere, but each comes
from a real organization:

Look busy even if you're not.

If you take risks and fail around here, you'll pay dearly for it.

Before you make a decision, run it by your boss so that he or she is never surprised.

TABLE 3–2   The Impact of Culture on Management Functions

Planning
The degree of risk that plans should contain
Whether decisions should emphasize the long or short term
Whether or not employees should have clear, tangible objectives

Organizing
How much authority should be delegated to subordinate managers
How much freedom should be designed into employees' jobs
The degree to which procedures and policies should be enforced

Leading
What motivation techniques should be used
What leadership styles are appropriate
Whether all disagreements—even constructive ones—should be eliminated

Controlling
Whether to allow employees to control their own actions or to impose external controls
What criteria should be emphasized in employee performance evaluations
What repercussions will occur from exceeding one's budget

We make our product only as good as the competition forces us to.

What made us successful in the past will make us successful in the future.

The road to the top here begins in the financial area.

The link between values such as these and managerial behavior is fairly straightforward. Managerial decisions are not made in a vacuum. They reflect the history of the organization and "the way things are done around here." If a business firm's culture supports the belief that profits can be increased by cost cutting and that the company's best interests are served by achieving slow but steady increases in quarterly earnings, managers down the line are unlikely to pursue programs that are innovative, risky, long term, or expansionary.

An organization's culture, especially a strong one, therefore constrains a manager's decision-making options concerning all management functions. As depicted in Table 3–2, the major areas of a manager's job are influenced by the culture in which he or she operates.

THE ENVIRONMENT

The recognition that no organization is an island unto itself was a major contribution of the systems approach to management. Anyone who questions the impact of the external environment on managing should consider the following:

One morning in January 1990, Pan Am executives learned through a trade paper that Delta was cutting the price of a one-way ticket between New York and Miami from $199 to $69. As a competitor to Delta on this route and being determined not to lose market share, Pan Am executives found themselves with no alternative other than to match Delta's cut-rate price.

American Brands is one of the largest cigarette manufacturers in the United States. Management is sporadically jolted by government research reports indicating new evidence linking cigarette smoking to cancer.

The Worker Adjustment and Retraining Notification Act, which went into effect in 1989, requires businesses that have more than 100 employees to give at least 60 days' notice before they are allowed to close down a plant or office.

As these examples show, there are forces in the environment that play a major role in shaping managers' actions. In this section, we will identify some of the critical environmental forces that affect management and demonstrate how they constrain managerial discretion.[12]

Defining the Environment

environment
Outside institutions or forces that affect an organization's performance.

The term **environment** refers to institutions or forces that are outside the organization and affect the organization's performance. As one writer put it, "Just take the universe, subtract from it the subset that represents the organization, and the remainder is environment."[13] But it's really not that simple.

general environment
Everything outside the organization.

General Versus Specific Environment   The **general environment** includes *everything* outside the organization, such as economic factors, political conditions, the social milieu, and technological factors. It encompasses conditions that *may* affect the organization but whose relevance is not clear. The passage of the Gramm-Rudman Act in 1985, which outlined for the federal government specific yearly deficit-reduction targets, is an example of a condition in the general environment of the New York's Museum of Modern Art. Its effect on funding for the arts is unclear, yet its potential impact could be very great. Similarly, the strength of the U.S. dollar against the pound and franc is an environmental force for U.S. companies that operate in Great Britain and France, but its effect is best described as only potentially relevant.

specific environment
The part of the environment that is directly relevant to the achievement of an organization's goals.

The bulk of management's attention is usually given to the organization's specific environment. The **specific environment** is the part of the environment that is directly relevant to the achievement of an organization's goals. It consists of the critical constituencies or components that can positively or negatively influence an organization's effectiveness. The specific environment is unique to each organization and changes with conditions. Typically, it will include suppliers of inputs, clients or customers, competitors, government agencies, and public pressure groups. Lockheed Corporation depends heavily on defense contracts; therefore the U.S. Department of Defense is in its specific environment. Of course, elements in an organization's specific environment can move into its general environment over time and vice versa. An appliance manufacturer that had previously never sold to Sears, Roebuck recently signed a three-year contract to sell Sears 40 percent of its output of washing machines, which are to be sold under the retailer's Kenmore brand. This action moved Sears from the manufacturer's general environment to its specific environment.

An organization's specific environment varies depending on the "niche" that the organization has made for itself with respect to the range of products or services it offers and the markets it serves. Timex and Rolex both make wristwatches, but their specific environments differ because they operate in distinctly different market niches. Miami-Dade Junior College and the University of Michigan are both institutions of higher education, but they do substantially different things and appeal to different segments of the higher-education market. The managers or administrators in these organizations face different constituencies in their specific environments.

A comparison of private colleges and state colleges may make this clearer. Tuition at private colleges is considerably higher than it is at public colleges. The survival of

Burger King is an example of an organization in McDonald's specific environment. Actions that Burger King's management takes regarding concerns such as menu offerings and pricing have a direct effect on McDonald's operations.

private colleges depends on a constant influx of new students who can pay the tuition, alumni donations, and a record of placing their graduates in good jobs and graduate schools. A public college's survival is most dependent on appropriations by the state legislature. The result is that private colleges expend more effort than state colleges on student recruitment, alumni relations, and placement services. State college administrators, on the other hand, spend a lot of their time lobbying in the state capital for increased appropriations. The importance of our point should not be lost: The environmental factors that one organization is dependent upon and that have a critical bearing on its performance may not be relevant to another organization at all, even though they may appear at first glance to be in the same type of business.

Assessing Environmental Uncertainty   The environment is important to managers because not all environments are the same. They differ by what we call their degree of **environmental uncertainty.** Environmental uncertainty, in turn, can be broken down into two dimensions: degree of change and degree of complexity.

environmental uncertainty
The degree of change and complexity in an organization's environment.

If the components in an organization's environment change a lot, we call it a *dynamic* environment. If change is minimal, we call it a *stable* one. A stable environment might be one in which there are no new competitors, no new technological breakthroughs by current competitors, little activity by public pressure groups to influence the organization, and so forth. This might describe, for instance, Smith-Corona's environment in the 1960s.

Smith-Corona had few significant competitors in its market niche: portable typewriters. When kids went off to college in the 1960s or early 1970s, they typically took a new Smith-Corona manual or electric typewriter with them. With the exception of the introduction of the electric portable, the technology was unchanging. But beginning in the mid-to-late 1970s, major alterations began to occur in Smith-Corona's environment because of breakthroughs in technology. Low-cost personal computers could do word processing and other functions in addition to typing. Electronic typewriters could do everything an electric could do but more cheaply because they have far fewer moving parts. Firms such as Apple, IBM, and Canon had superior technical capabilities in this new technology. Smith-Corona saw its market for portable typewriters virtually collapse in less than six years. The degree of change in Smith-Corona's environment went from stable to dynamic.

Similarly, U.S. automakers since the mid-1970s have faced a dynamic environment. In the 1950s and 1960s, for instance, they could predict with extremely high accuracy each year's sales and profits. Then came increased government safety and emission regulations, foreign competition, and escalating gasoline prices. Suddenly, managers in the U.S. auto industry found themselves confronting a radically changed environment.

What about rapid change that is predictable? Retail department stores are a case in point. They typically make a quarter or a third of their sales in December. The drop-off from December to January is precipitous. Does this predictable change in consumer demand make department stores' environment dynamic? No. When we talk about degree of change, we mean change that is unpredictable. If change can be accurately anticipated, it is not an uncertainty with which managers have to deal.

The other dimension of uncertainty relates to the degree of **environmental complexity.** The degree of complexity refers to the number of components in an organization's environment and the extent of knowledge that the organization has about its environmental components. When the washing machine manufacturer signed a contract to sell 40 percent of its output to Sears, it reduced its environmental complexity. It then had fewer customers. The fewer customers, suppliers, competitors, and government agencies that an organization is required to interact with, the less uncertainty there is in its environment.

Complexity is also measured in terms of the knowledge an organization needs to have about its environment. Boeing managers must know a great deal about their suppliers' operations, for instance, if they are to ensure that the jet planes they build will perform without a flaw. Managers of retail grocery stores, in contrast, have a minimal need for sophisticated knowledge about their suppliers.

Environmental uncertainty is presented as a two-by-two matrix in Table 3–3. There are four cells, cell 1 being lowest in environmental uncertainty and cell 4 being

environmental complexity
The number of components in an organization's environment and the extent of an organization's knowledge about its environmental components.

TABLE 3–3   Environmental Uncertainty Matrix

		Degree of Change	
		Stable	*Dynamic*
Degree of Complexity	Simple	**CELL 1** Stable and predictable environment Few components in environment Components are somewhat similar and remain basically the same Minimal need for sophisticated knowledge of components	**CELL 2** Dynamic and unpredictable environment Few components in environment Components are somewhat similar but are in continual process of change Minimal need for sophisticated knowledge of components
	Complex	**CELL 3** Stable and predictable environment Many components in environment Components are not similar to one another and remain basically the same High need for sophisticated knowledge of components	**CELL 4** Dynamic and unpredictable environment Many components in environment Components are not similar to one another and are in continual process of change High need for sophisticated knowledge of components

highest. Management's influence on organizational outcomes is greatest in cell 1 and least in cell 4.

Since uncertainty is a threat to an organization's effectiveness, managers try to minimize it. Given a choice, managers would prefer to operate in environments like those in cell 1. But managers rarely have full control over that choice. For example, managers in firms that produced and marketed computer software in 1989 found themselves in cell 4. Because they chose this particular niche to operate in, they faced a highly dynamic and complex environment. Had they chosen to manufacture standard wire coat hangers, they would probably have found themselves in cell 1.

The Organization and Its Environment   Figure 3–2 summarizes our position that an organization is a system that interacts with and depends upon its specific environment but remains ever mindful of the potential influences of its general environment.

In the following sections we elaborate on the components in both specific and general environments and demonstrate how environments can constrain the choices available to managers.

The Specific Environment

As was noted previously, different organizations face different specific environments. For most organizations, though, suppliers, customers, competitors, governmental agencies, and special-interest pressure groups are external factors that impose uncertainty.

Suppliers   When you think of an organization's suppliers, you typically think of firms that provide materials and equipment. For a building contractor, this includes firms that sell and rent bulldozers and trucks, office supply firms, lumber yards, hardware suppliers, and distributors of brick and concrete. But the term *suppliers* also includes providers of financial and labor inputs. Stockholders, banks, insurance companies, pension funds, and other similar institutions are needed to ensure a continuous supply of capital. Exxon can have rights to an oil field that can generate billions of dollars in profits, but the profits will remain only potential unless management can obtain the funds necessary to drill the wells. Labor unions, occupational associations, and local labor markets are sources of employees. A lack of qualified nurses, for instance, makes it difficult for a hospital to run efficiently.

FIGURE 3–2
The Organization and Its Environment

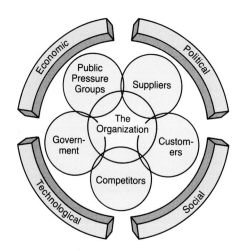

Management seeks to ensure a steady flow of needed inputs at the lowest price possible. Because these inputs represent uncertainties—that is, their unavailability or delay can significantly reduce the organization's effectiveness—management typically goes to great efforts to ensure a steady flow. As you'll see later in this book, the reason most large organizations have departments of purchasing, finance, and personnel is the importance management places on the acquisition of machinery, equipment, capital, and labor inputs.

Customers   Organizations exist to meet the needs of customers. It is the customer or client who absorbs the organization's output. This is true even for government organizations. They exist to provide services, and we are reminded, especially at election time, that we indicate by the way we vote how satisfied we actually are as customers.

Customers obviously represent potential uncertainty to an organization. Customers' tastes can change. They can become dissatisfied with the organization's product or service. Of course, some organizations face considerably more uncertainty as a result of their customers than do others. In general, we would expect customers to represent greater uncertainty for a manager of an upscale restaurant than for a manager of a county hospital.

Competitors   All organizations, even monopolies, have one or more competitors. Macy's has Bloomingdale's. General Motors has Toyota. New York University has Columbia, City University of New York, and a host of others. The U.S. Postal Service has a monopoly on mail service, but it competes against United Parcel, Federal Express, Western Union, and other forms of communication such as the telephone and fax machines.

No management can afford to ignore its competition. When they do, they pay a very serious price. Many problems incurred by the railroads, for instance, have been attributed to their failure to recognize who their competitors were. They believed they were in the railroad business when, in fact, they were in the transportation business. Trucking, shipping, aviation, and bus and private automobile transportation are all competitors of railroads. Fifteen years ago, the three major broadcasting networks—ABC, CBS, and NBC—virtually controlled what you watched on television. If your set was on, the probability was better than 90 percent that you were watching one of the major networks. Today, with the rapid expansion of cable, VCRs, and the syndicated programs sold to local stations, less than half of the average television viewer's time is spent watching programming from the major networks.

These examples illustrate that competitors—in terms of pricing, services offered, new products developed, and the like—represent an important environmental force that management must monitor and be prepared to respond to.

Government   Federal, state, and local governments influence what organizations can and cannot do. Some federal legislation has tremendous impact. For example, consider the following: The Sherman Anti-Trust Act of 1890 sought to stop monopoly practices that resulted in restraint of trade. The National Labor Relations Act of 1935 stipulated that employers are required to recognize a union chosen by the majority of their employees; it also established procedures and rules governing collective bargaining. The Civil Rights Act of 1964 made it unlawful for an employer to discharge, refuse to hire, or discriminate in employment against an individual because of race, color, religion, sex, or national origin. The Occupational Safety and Health Act of 1970 established an extensive list of safety and health standards that employers were required to meet. The Immigration Reform and Control Act of 1986 prohibits employers from knowingly hiring illegal workers and requires employers to verify the immigration status of all workers. To illustrate the impact that federal regulation has had on business firms, Table 3–4 lists a dozen pieces of legislation passed in the last twenty years.

TABLE 3–4   Significant Legislation Regulating Business Since 1970

Economic Stabilization Act of 1970
Fair Credit Reporting Act of 1970
Occupational Safety and Health Act of 1970
Consumer Product Safety Act of 1972
Equal Employment Opportunity Act of 1972
Employee Retirement Income Security Act of 1974
Toxic Substance Control Act of 1976
Pregnancy Discrimination Act of 1978
Airline Deregulation Act of 1978
Immigration Reform and Control Act of 1986
Tax Reform Act of 1986
Americans with Disabilities Act of 1989

Certain organizations, by virtue of their business, are scrutinized by specific government agencies. Organizations in the telecommunications industry—including telephone companies and radio and television stations—are regulated by the Federal Communications Commission. Publicly held companies must abide by the acceptable financial standards and practices as defined by the Securities and Exchange Commission. If your firm manufactures pharmaceuticals, what you can sell is determined by the Food and Drug Administration.

The federal government is not the only source of legal regulations that govern organizations. State and local governmental regulations extend and modify many federal standards.

Organizations spend a great deal of time and money to meet government regulations.[14] But the effects of these regulations go beyond time and money. They also reduce managerial discretion. They limit the choices available to managers.

Consider the decision to dismiss an employee.[15] Historically, employees were free to quit an organization at any time, and employers had the right to fire an employee any time with or without cause. Recent laws and court decisions, however, have put new limits on what employers may do. Employers are increasingly expected to deal with employees by following the principles of good faith and fair dealing. Employees who feel they have been wrongfully discharged can take their case to court. Juries are increasingly deciding what is or is not "fair." This has made it more difficult for managers to fire poor performers or dismiss employees for off-duty conduct. For example, IBM dismissed a female employee for dating a person who worked for a competitor. She sued IBM, arguing that her personal relationship wasn't expressly prohibited by IBM's policies and represented no conflict of interest. She won a $300,000 settlement from IBM.

Whether or not these statutes and court decisions are a proper means to protect the rights of employees is not at issue here. We merely want to demonstrate the constraints that government regulation places on managerial discretion.

Pressure Groups   Managers cannot fail to recognize the special-interest groups that attempt to influence the actions of organizations. Automobile manufacturers, toy makers, and airlines have been visible targets of Ralph Nader's Center for Responsive Law. The managers of several large university endowments, like those at Harvard and the Massachusetts Institute of Technology, have changed some of their decisions as a result of lobbying efforts by people who oppose holding stock in firms that operate or sell in South Africa. Opponents of nuclear power have been successful in slowing the construction of new nuclear plants and in delaying their licensing. As social and politi-

Eli Lilly reports that it fills out more than 27,000 federal forms annually, and Dow Chemical estimates that it spends more than $400 million a year to meet federal regulations.

cal causes change, so too does the power of pressure groups. Managers should be aware of the power that these groups can exert on their decisions.

The General Environment

Now we turn to the general environment. In this section, we discuss economic, political, social, and technological conditions that can affect the management of organizations. In contrast to the specific environment, these factors usually do not have as large an impact on an organization's operations. However, management must take them into account. For instance, cold fusion research has recently received a great deal of attention by chemists and physicists. This research is in its infancy, but if scientists learn to produce controlled nuclear fusion at room temperature, it will offer the prospect of virtually limitless energy. Senior managers at oil companies, automobile firms, and aircraft manufacturers recognize that a major breakthrough in cold fusion research could have far-reaching effects on their organizations' growth and profitability, so they carefully follow its progress.

Economic Conditions   Interest rates, inflation rates, changes in disposable income, stock market indexes, and the general business cycle are some of the economic factors in the general environment that can affect management practices in an organization.

In 1986, executives at a number of banks learned the hard way how closely their fortunes were tied to the economics of the oil business. Many of the largest U.S. banks—such as Citicorp and Chase Manhattan—had previously lent billions of dollars to oil-producing countries such as Mexico, Nigeria, and Venezuela based on the value of their oil reserves. But as oil prices fell as much as 40 percent, the ability of these countries to sell their oil and repay their loans was threatened. A default on these loans would require massive write-offs for the banks. The impact of lower oil prices

In the 1980s, when the price of oil collapsed, dozens of banks, like United Bank in Houston, Texas as well as several savings and loans, were forced out of business or taken over by agencies of the federal government.

also hit many smaller banks in oil-producing states. Houston's First City Bancorp. of Texas, for instance, had to charge off more than $100 million in loans in one quarter alone.[16] Clearly, for banks with large loan exposures in oil-producing countries and firms in the oil industry, changes in the price of oil have drastic implications for their own future performance.

Political Conditions   Political conditions include the general stability of the country in which an organization operates and the specific attitudes that elected government officials hold toward the role of business in society.

In the United States, organizations have generally operated in a stable political environment. But management is a worldwide activity. Moreover, many U.S. firms have operations in countries whose record for stability is quite spotty—for example, El Salvador, Libya, Argentina, Chile, and Iran. The internal aspects of management require that organizations attempt to forecast major political changes in countries in which they operate. In this way, management can better anticipate political conditions, from the devaluation of a country's monetary unit to a dictator's decision to nationalize certain industries and expropriate their assets.

From the mid-1930s through the late 1970s, the political environment in the United States consistently moved toward government playing a larger role in society. Business regulation increased. Belief in capitalism and the free market came under increasing attack. The 1980s, however, saw the election of conservative U.S. Presidents and a shift in the political environment. The Reagan administration, for instance, committed itself to less government support for social programs, more support for business, and increased defense spending. These changes in the political environment had implications for managers in many organizations. This is because changes in the attitudes held by elected political officials presage government legislation. They also indicate changes in government spending and taxing policies. Changes in expenditures for defense, energy development, public housing, space exploration, and state and local grants—to name just a few—can have a wide impact on some organizations and their managers. Similarly, changes in tax policies may alter management decisions in such areas as new investments, program expansions, inventory levels, and the like.

Social Conditions Management must adapt its practices to the changing expectations of the society in which it operates. As values, customs, and tastes change, so too must management. This applies to both their products and service offerings and their internal policies. Recent examples of social conditions that have had a significant impact on the management of certain organizations include the changing career expectations of women, the changing aspirations of young people, and the aging of the work force.

Inflation, the women's movement, and an increased divorce rate have all contributed to a dramatic increase in female labor-participation rates. Today, more than half of all adult women are gainfully employed outside the home. This change has particularly hit hard organizations like Avon Products and Tupperware that traditionally have sold their products to housewives at home. Today's working woman tends to buy her cosmetics and housewares during her lunch hour or after work. Banks, automobile manufacturers, and women's apparel makers have also found their markets changing because of the career expectations of women. Women want expanded credit; they look for cars that are consistent with their new life-styles; and their wardrobe purchases increasingly are business suits rather than casual wear. Management has also had to adjust its internal organizational policies because of the increase in the number of working women. Organizations that fail to offer child care facilities, for instance, may lose in their efforts to hire competent women employees.

Today's young adult is more materialistic than his or her peers of twenty years ago. Making a lot of money and achieving financial security are increasingly important goals for people in their twenties and thirties. Colleges and universities have seen this trend affect the majors that students are selecting. In the mid-1960s, about 14 percent of college students were majoring in business. By the mid-1970s, it was up to 18 percent. Today, one out of every four college students is a business major. Colleges that have no business programs or only small ones have had an increasingly difficult time recruiting students.

In 1970, the median age in the United States was under 28. It is now past 30 and will reach 35 in another decade. Organizations that cater to the needs of seniors will have a larger market. This implies increased demand for health care, homes in the Sunbelt, and golf equipment. It also means that organizations will have to redesign products and services for an aging market. Levi Strauss, for example, now produces fuller-cut jeans designed to fit the middle-aged person's less svelte body. Inside organizations, management can expect to have more employees in their fifties and sixties. This is likely to translate into more experienced workers with needs that differ from those of their younger counterparts. For instance, older workers tend to place greater value on employee benefits like health insurance and pension plans and less value on college-tuition-reimbursement programs and generous moving allowances.

Technological Conditions Our final consideration in the general environment is technology. We live in a technological age. In terms of the four components in the general environment, the most rapid change during the past quarter-century has probably occurred in technology. We now have automated offices, robots in manufacturing, lasers, integrated circuits, microdots, microprocessors, and synthetic fuels. Companies that make the most of technology—such as Apple Computer, 3M, and General Electric—prosper. Similarly, hospitals, universities, airports, police departments, and even military organizations that adapt to major technological advances have a competitive edge over those that do not.

An example of how the technological environment affects management is in the design of offices. Offices have become communication centers. Management can now link its computers, telephones, word processors, photocopiers, fax machines, filing storage, and other office activities into an integrated system. For management of all organizations, this means faster and better decision-making capability. For firms that have historically sold products in only one part of the office market—those offering only typewriters or photocopying equipment, for instance—it means developing comprehensive office systems or being entirely excluded from the market.

Influence on Management Practice

Organizations are not islands unto themselves. They interact with, and are influenced by, their environment. Organizations depend on their environment as a source of inputs and as a recipient of its outputs. Organizations must also abide by the laws of the land and respond to groups who challenge the organization's actions. As such, suppliers, customers, government agencies, public pressure groups, and similar constituencies can exert power over an organization. This power, for instance, is unusually evident among publicly held corporations whose stock is controlled by institutional investors like insurance companies, mutual funds, and pension plans. These institutions control as much as 70 percent of the stock in some companies.[17] As a result, their interests dictate management's interests. These institutions have the power to control boards of directors and indirectly to fire management. The result is that management's options are constrained to reflect the desires of these institutional investors.

A recent survey of 400 chief executives from among the 1000 largest U.S. companies indicates that environmental constituencies have increased their influence on management in recent years.[18] As shown in Table 3–5, except for labor unions, all of

MANAGERS WHO MADE A DIFFERENCE

Marina v.N. Whitman at General Motors

Marina v.N. Whitman is General Motors' guardian of the future.[19] Since joining GM in 1979 as its chief economist, she has risen to vice president and group executive. She oversees the company's staffs in public relations and economics, environmental activities, and industry-government relations.

Whitman deals with those functions that affect how the world sees General Motors and how GM sees the world. As such, she's GM's senior environmental scanner. One of her key functions is ensuring that the company's top executives understand the effects of political and economic policy. For instance, on the basis of her assessment of future monetary policy, she'll project the ultimate effect on car sales. She also scans the economic environment for forces that could affect GM. After the October 1987 stock market crash, many economists believed that a serious recession was just around the corner—but not Whitman. On the basis of her analysis, she cautioned GM executives against cutbacks in production. That proved to be good advice for GM because her prognosis turned out to be correct. The economic expansion continued throughout 1988. With it, auto sales continued strong. GM kept to its pre–market crash production schedules, and the result was record profits for GM in 1988.

Photo courtesy of Dr. Marina v.N. Whitman.

TABLE 3–5   Influence of Forces in the Environment

In September 1987, 400 chief executives were asked, "Compared with five years ago, would you say that the following individuals or institutions have gained, lost, or kept their influence over decisions in companies such as yours?" They responded as follows:

Force in the Environment	Gained Influence	Lost Influence	Kept Influence	Not Sure
Institutions holding big stock blocks	47%	2%	42%	9%
Raiders and potential raiders	58	2	24	16
Investment bankers	46	13	36	5
Stock analysts	48	4	43	5
Government regulators	41	20	34	5
Environmentalists	37	14	40	9
Consumer groups	28	14	49	9
Labor unions	2	54	34	10

Source: "Business Week/Harris Executive Poll," *Business Week,* October 23, 1987, p. 28.

the listed forces in the environment generally expanded their influence between 1982 and 1987. Keep in mind that this survey addressed only *changes* since 1982. These forces were already powerful constraints on managerial decision making in the early 1980s!

Many of these environmental forces are dynamic and create considerable uncertainty for management. Customers' tastes and preferences change. New laws are passed. Suppliers can't meet contractual delivery dates. Competitors introduce new technologies, products, and services. To the degree that these environmental uncertainties cannot be anticipated, they force management to respond in ways that it might not prefer. The greater the environmental uncertainty an organization faces, the more the environment limits management's options and its freedom to determine its own destiny.

SUMMARY

This summary is organized by the chapter-opening learning objectives found on page 67.

1. The omnipotent view is dominant in management theory and in society. It argues that managers are directly responsible for the success or failure of an organization. In contrast, the symbolic view argues that management has only a limited effect on substantive organizational outcomes because of the large number of factors outside of management's control; however, management greatly influences symbolic outcomes.

2. Organizational culture is a system of shared meaning.

3. An organization's culture is composed of ten characteristics: individual initiative, risk tolerance, direction, integration, management support, control, identity, reward system, conflict tolerance, and communication patterns.

4. Culture evolves from the original vision of the organization's founders.

5. Culture constrains managerial choices by conveying which practices are acceptable and which are not.

6. The organization's environment consists of institutions or forces that are outside the organization and affect its performance.

7. The general environment encompasses forces that have the potential to affect the organization but whose relevance is not overtly clear. The specific environment is that part of the environment that is directly relevant to the achievement of the organization's goals. Relevant elements in an organization's specific environment might include suppliers, customers, competitors, government agencies, and public pressure groups.

8. High environmental uncertainty limits management's options and forces it to respond in ways that it might not prefer.

REVIEW QUESTIONS

1. Why does the omnipotent view of management dominate management theory?

2. According to the symbolic view, what is management's role in organizations?

3. Is there a "correct" culture that successful organizations possess? Explain.

4. Contrast strong and weak cultures. Which has the greatest impact on managers? Why?

5. How does culture affect a manager's execution of the four management functions?

6. What individuals or institutions are in a typical organization's specific environment?

7. What defines the degree of an organization's environmental uncertainty?

8. How can federal government regulations constrain managerial discretion?

9. Why do managers try to minimize environmental uncertainty?

10. What effect, if any, does the general environment have on managerial practice?

DISCUSSION QUESTIONS

1. Classrooms have cultures. Describe your class culture. Does it constrain your instructor? If so, how?

2. Define a local grocery store's specific environment. How does it constrain the store manager?

3. Refer to Table 3–1. How would a first-line supervisor's job differ in these two organizations?

4. When a large corporation loses money for several years in a row, the board of directors almost always replaces the corporation's chief executive. Why? What would failure to take such action say about the board?

5. "The President of the United States has little real influence over Congress, the budget process, or the economy. Yet when things go right, he takes the credit for it. When things go wrong, he puts the blame somewhere else." Do you agree or disagree with this statement? Support your position.

SELF-ASSESSMENT EXERCISE

What Kind of Organizational Culture Fits You Best?

Instructions: For each one of the following statements, circle the level of agreement or disagreement that you personally feel:

Strongly Agree (SA)
Agree (A)
Uncertain (U)
Disagree (D)
Strongly Disagree (SD)

I Like a Place to Work Where:

1. I have to wear a suit to work everyday.	SA A U D SD
2. Things are unpredictable.	SA A U D SD
3. People don't break the rules.	SA A U D SD
4. Parking spaces are assigned on the basis of job level.	SA A U D SD
5. I will have high job security.	SA A U D SD
6. People who work for me feel free to disagree with my decisions.	SA A U D SD
7. People who work for me feel free to take their problems over me to my boss.	SA A U D SD
8. Seniority is as important as performance in determining pay increases and promotions.	SA A U D SD
9. Loyalty to the organization is highly rewarded.	SA A U D SD
10. I'm not likely to be asked to work overtime or delay my planned vacation.	SA A U D SD

Turn to page 669 for scoring directions and key.

CASE APPLICATION 3A

International Business Machines

IBM's sales exceed $60 *billion* a year. Its worldwide operations employ almost 400,000 people. IBM's product lines range from $800 electric typewriters to data-processing systems that sell for more than $100 million. It controls 40 percent of the worldwide market for computing equipment. The company is generally acknowledged to be one of the most successful and best-managed corporations in the United States. Of course, it didn't achieve its stature solely by luck. The company obviously does a number of things that work. The following describes a few of the qualities that make IBM the leader in its field.

Employee behavior at IBM is the product of its founder's philosophy. Thomas Watson had rules for almost everything. Dark business suits, white shirts, and striped ties were "the uniform." Drinking alcoholic beverages, even off the job, was prohibited. Employees were expected to accept frequent transfers—insiders liked to say that IBM stood for "I've Been Moved." Today, the rules are a bit less severe, but the conservative image is still there. Male sales personnel are expected to wear suits and ties when meeting customers, but shirts no longer have to be white. When entertaining customers, IBM people are still not allowed to drink alcohol. All employees are also subject to a thirty-two-page code of business ethics.

IBM has always demonstrated a strong commitment to its employees. People get fired, but layoffs are avoided. Redundant employees are retrained and then reassigned. Commitment also has to flow in the opposite direction. IBM carefully screens job candidates to identify those who will grow with the company. New employees are expected to spend their working careers with IBM. Of course, it doesn't always work that way. Many employees leave voluntarily. The computer industry is largely made up of former IBM-ers. They fill senior executive slots at many of its competitors, and former IBM people are frequently the corporate decision makers who choose which computer system will be installed in their company.

Salaries and benefits at IBM are highly competitive. In several communities, IBM has its own country clubs and makes memberships available to employees for $5 a year. It is not surprising that this concern for its employees has led to a strongly committed work force. As a case in point, IBM has never had a union vote in any U.S. facility.

Part of IBM's success is also undoubtedly attributable to its commitment to service. Its sales personnel are the envy of the industry. They are thoroughly trained and highly knowledgeable. Most new employees spend much of their first six weeks in company-run classes. Managers are required to take at least forty hours of additional instruction each year.

Every year, IBM spends more than $500 million on employee education and training. Customers can feel confident that if they have a problem with IBM equipment, its sales and service personnel will be able to solve it.

The commitment to service is strongly customer focused. IBM spends heavily to acquire comprehensive and up-to-date market research data on potential customer needs. In contrast to many of its competitors, which have allowed technology to drive their product line, IBM has sought to let the customers determine what it will produce and sell.

Questions

1. How would you describe IBM's culture?
2. What does IBM do to maintain its culture?
3. How is IBM's culture likely to influence its managers?
4. In what ways might you use the symbolic view of management to describe IBM's success?

CASE APPLICATION 3B

Valley State College

Dr. Wilson Hopkins had spent twenty years building his reputation as an internationally known physicist. At the age of 48, he held an endowed chair at an Ivy League university, served on the board of several prestigious corporations, and was widely regarded as a potential Nobel Prize laureate. But he was becoming restless. Dr. Hopkins was looking for a new challenge outside the research laboratory. So when he was asked to be a candidate for the presidency of Valley State College in the Midwest, he found the idea interesting. In spite of his never having held an administrative post, the college's governing board chose Dr. Hopkins. There were obvious reasons; he had a long academic career, a strong commitment to quality education, and a personal reputation that was sure to enhance Valley State's own academic image. Dr. Hopkins accepted the position. He looked forward to shaping Valley State into a first-class educational institution. As president, he figured he would have the clout to do what was necessary to move Valley State into the ranks of the top state colleges and universities in the country.

Before moving to Valley State, Dr. Hopkins learned that each year an Eastern university offered a free one-week course to new college presidents. Hopkins saw it as a chance to get a head start on some of the challenges he would face on his new job. It would also provide an opportunity to meet some other people in a similar circumstance.

That one-week course presented a number of shocks to Dr. Hopkins. Of the fifteen new presidents in attendance, he was the only one with no prior administrative experience. He quickly came to realize how naive he had been about his ability to change Valley State College. The course content didn't focus on planning, leadership, or other management issues as he had expected. Rather, the instructors spent almost all the time discussing concerns like alumni and donor relations, working with government officials, and collective bargaining.

Questions

1. Describe Valley State's specific environment.
2. How does each element in this environment restrict Dr. Hopkins's managerial discretion?
3. What would Valley State's specific environment be like if it were a private Catholic college instead of a state-supported institution?

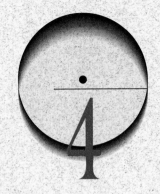

4

INTERNATIONAL MANAGEMENT: RESPONDING TO A GLOBAL ENVIRONMENT

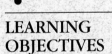

LEARNING OBJECTIVES

After Reading
This Chapter,
You Should
Be Able To:

1. Explain the importance of viewing management from a global perspective.

2. Describe problems created by national parochialism.

3. Explain the growing impact of multinational corporations on world economies.

4. Identify active areas of regional cooperation between countries.

5. List the four dimensions of national culture.

6. Describe the U.S. culture according to the four dimensions.

Nestlé has plants in more than sixty countries, and its products can be found almost everywhere on the globe.

Nestlé was once a lethargic Swiss chocolate maker. In recent years, however, under the leadership of its chief executive, Helmut Maucher, Nestlé has rapidly become the world's largest food company with sales in excess of $27 billion.[1]

The secret to Nestlé's success lies essentially in the effective execution of a global strategy that Maucher created for the company. He has acquired a number of name brands—including Nescafé instant coffee, Carnation Coffee Mate, Stouffer frozen foods, Buitoni pasta, and Friskies pet food—and expanded his product line into worldwide markets. Better than any of its competitors, Nestlé is capitalizing on the globalization of markets. For instance, coffee is sneaking up on tea as the favorite drink in Japan, and U.S.-style gourmet frozen dinners have become a big hit in Europe.

The globalization of Nestlé's operations can be seen in the sources of its revenues. Forty-three percent of its sales come from Europe, 28 percent from North America, 13 percent from Asia, and the rest from operations in Latin America, Africa, and Oceania.

Nestlé's response to the changing global environment may have been more successful than comparable efforts by other companies, but it illustrates an important fact of life for today's managers: They operate in a global economy. The borders around countries, which historically identified their range of operations, are no longer constraints on organizational activities.[2] This is most evident in the automobile industry. The more than 6000 miles that separate the United States from Japan constrain neither trade nor the building of manufacturing facilities. Honda, Toyota, Nissan, Mazda, and Mitsubishi all have plants in the United States. Honda even exports its Accord coupes, which are manufactured in Ohio, back to Japan![3]

Accepting the reality of a global environment means that it is "a whole new ballgame" for managers. This dynamic environment creates both opportunities and threats for managers. With the world as a marketplace and national borders becoming meaningless, the potential for organizations to grow and expand becomes almost unlimited. However, new competitors can suddenly appear anytime, from anywhere. Managers who don't closely monitor changes in their global environment or fail to respond quickly to those changes are likely to find their organization's survival in doubt.

WHO OWNS WHAT?

One way to grasp the changing nature of the global environment is to consider the country of origin for ownership of some familiar companies. Take a look at the following list of companies. Which do you think are U.S.-owned? For the remaining, jot down the country in which you think the primary owners reside.

1. Spaulding (sporting goods)
2. Seagram (liquor and wines)
3. CBS Records (records and videos)

4. Maserati (sports cars)

5. DuPont (chemicals)

6. Firestone Tire & Rubber (tires)

7. Irving Bank & Trust (banking)

8. Miles Laboratories (pharmaceuticals)

9. Macmillan (publishing)

10. Farmers Group (insurance)

11. General Tire (tires)

12. Pillsbury (Burger King, Green Giant)

You'll find the detailed answers in the notes at the end of the book.[4] The U.S.-owned firms on this list, incidentally, are DuPont and Maserati. How well did you score? Were you aware of how many "name" companies that operate in the United States are actually foreign owned?

To further dramatize the international aspects of business today, take a look at Table 4–1. This is a partial list of "U.S." companies that derive half or more of their income from foreign operations.

ATTACKING PAROCHIALISM

It is not unusual for Germans and Italians to speak three or four languages. Most Japanese schoolchildren begin studying English in the early elementary grades. On the other hand, most Americans study only English in school. Americans tend to think of English as the international business language. They don't see a need to study other languages.

parochialism

A selfish, narrow view of the world; an inability to recognize differences between people.

Monolingualism is just one of the signs that Americans suffer from **parochialism,** that is, they view the world solely through their own eyes and perspective.[5] People with a parochial perspective do not recognize that other people have different ways of living and working. Parochialism has become an increasing obstacle for many U.S.

TABLE 4–1   Selected Companies Deriving 50 Percent or More of Revenues from Non-U.S. Operations

Company	Non-U.S. Income as Percent of Total
Exxon	71.6
Gillette	65.1
Colgate-Palmolive	64.4
IBM	57.6
Coca-Cola	55.4
Dow Chemical	55.1
Hewlett-Packard	51.6
Citicorp	51.4
Avon Products	50.6

Source: "The 100 Largest U.S. Multinationals," excerpted by permission of *Forbes* magazine, July 24, 1989, pp. 320–24. © Forbes Inc., 1989.

While few Americans have developed multilingual skills, most Japanese spend many years studying English in school. This gives them important insights into the cultures of English-speaking countries. Japanese managers are also far more likely to read books and periodicals written in English than their U.S. counterparts are to read Japanese publications.

managers. While their counterparts around the world have sought to better understand foreign customs and market differences, U.S. managers have too frequently been guilty of rigidly applying their values and customs to foreign cultures, often with adverse results.

A U.S. manager recently transferred to Saudi Arabia successfully obtained a million-dollar contract from a Saudi manufacturer. The manufacturer's representative had arrived at the meeting several hours late, but the U.S. executive considered it unimportant. The American was certainly surprised and frustrated to learn later that the Saudi had no intention of abiding by the contract. He had signed it only to be polite after showing up late for the appointment.

A U.S. executive operating in Peru was viewed by Peruvian managers as cold and unworthy of trust because, in face-to-face discussions, he kept backing up. He did not understand that, in Peru, the custom is to stand quite close to the person with whom you are speaking.

A U.S. manager in Japan offended a high-ranking Japanese executive by failing to give him the respect his position commanded. The manager was introduced to the Japanese executive in the latter's office. The American manager assumed that the executive was a low-level decision maker and paid him little attention because of the small and sparsely furnished office the executive occupied. He did not realize that the offices of top Japanese executives do not display the status accoutrements that their American counterparts do.

A manager raised in the Dominican Republic and working for a health products firm in the United States was perceived by colleagues as a "time waster." Back home, businesspeople would begin meetings with relaxed chitchat. In the United States, managers view such sociability as an unnecessary and time-consuming diversion.[6]

Successful global management requires enhanced sensitivity to differences in national customs and practices. Management practices that work in Chicago might not be appropriate in Shanghai. Later in this chapter and in theme boxes throughout the rest of this book, you will see how a global perspective on managing requires throwing off parochialism and carefully developing an understanding of cultural differences between countries.

THE CHANGING GLOBAL ENVIRONMENT

A number of forces are reshaping the global environment. In this section we'll discuss a few of the more important of these forces.

The Growing Impact of Multinationals

The names are familiar: IBM, Procter & Gamble, Occidental Petroleum, General Motors, RJR Nabisco. They are companies that maintain significant operations in two or more countries simultaneously. We call them **multinational corporations** (MNCs).

multinational corporation
A company that maintains significant operations in two or more countries simultaneously.

While international businesses have been around for centuries, MNCs are a relatively recent phenomenon. They are the natural outcome of a global economy. For instance, Ford focuses on building a "world car"—a standardized vehicle that can be manufactured and sold around the globe. MNCs use their worldwide operations to develop global strategies. Van Huesen has its shirts manufactured in South Korea to take advantage of low labor costs. Honda, on the other hand, builds factories in the United States to ensure access to the U.S. market regardless of import restrictions or unfavorable fluctuations in the yen.

How big are multinationals? It is hard to overstate their size and impact. If nations and industrial firms are ranked by gross national product (GNP) and total sales, respectively, thirty-seven of the first 100 on the list would be industrial corporations.[7] Exxon's sales, for example, exceed the GNPs of countries such as Indonesia, Nigeria, Argentina, and Denmark.

Managers of multinationals confront a wealth of challenges. They face diverse political systems, laws, and customs. But these differences create both problems and opportunities. It is obviously more difficult to manage an operation that spans 15,000 miles and whose employees speak five different languages than one located under a single roof where a common language is spoken. But differences also create opportunities, and that has been a primary motivation for corporations to expand their worldwide operations.

Coca-Cola, a multinational with one of the world's best known brand names, has sales or bottling facilities in more than 150 countries.

IN PRACTICE

Preparing for Chez Mickey Mouse

Anyone who thinks that cultural differences between countries should be a minor concern in exporting a winning business idea—after all, isn't a better mousetrap a better mousetrap anywhere?—should think again. Take theme parks as an example.[8] Disney has done incredibly well with its parks in California and Florida. Since Mickey Mouse and his friends are known throughout the world, exporting the Disneyland idea to Europe made good sense. In 1992, Euro Disneyland will open twenty miles east of Paris. The cost? $2.5 billion! Will it look and operate exactly like its U.S. counterparts? No! The following facts about the French and their life-style will tell you why:

1. While there have been large amusement parks in West Germany and Belgium since the late 1960s, the French got their first only in 1987, and they don't understand the concept very well. One Frenchman, who didn't understand why he had to pay to get in, asked, "I have to pay to do what?"

2. The French reserve only one day a week—Sunday—for family outings. Going out with the family on a Saturday or a weekday isn't something they're used to doing.

3. The French have long been averse to meeting strangers. The idea of being welcomed by strangers with buoyant smiles and a lighthearted greeting is not appreciated.

4. In the United States, 50 percent of Disney visitors eat fast food at the parks. Most French people, however, don't snack.

5. The French insist on eating lunch at exactly 12:30. They will not eat at 11 A.M. or 3 P.M.

6. The French are very impatient. They are not comfortable waiting in long lines.

7. The French adore their dogs. They take them everywhere—to most French resorts and even fine restaurants. However, dogs have always been banned from Disney parks.

8. Disney employee badges displaying only the employee's first name work well in the United States, where informality is well accepted. Such a practice is an un-French way of doing business.

9. French workers don't like to obey orders. They are not likely to take kindly to management's demands that they not smoke, chew gum, or converse with their co-workers.

As Disney management prepares to open Euro Disneyland, it is carefully studying cultural idiosyncracies that could affect its business. It then plans to make the necessary changes.

Regional Cooperation

Many knowledgeable economists and political scientists argue that global competition in the 1990s will be greatly enhanced by regional cooperative agreements between countries. The most notable will be a European Community made up of twelve West European countries. The United States and Canada have negotiated a free trade agreement that will lessen the traditional importance of their border. In addition, a very active border economy has recently developed between the United States and Mexico, spurred by the low labor costs in Mexican border cities. Finally, it is difficult to ignore recent upheavals in Eastern Europe and the potential economic shifts there.

The European Community   December 31, 1992 is the target date for the creation of a "United States of Europe."[9] There are 320 million people in the twelve nations making up the **European Community.** Separated by borders, they have border controls, border taxes, border subsidies, nationalistic policies, and protected industries. But by the end of 1992, these countries are to become a single market. Gone will be national barriers to travel, employment, investment, and trade. There will be a free flow of money, workers, goods, and services. A driver hauling cargo from Amsterdam to Lisbon will be able to clear four border crossings and five countries by showing a single piece of paper. In 1990, that same driver needed two pounds of documents.

The primary motivation for these twelve nations to unite was to reassert their position against the industrial might of the United States and Japan. As separate countries, creating barriers against one another, European industries were unable to develop the economies of scale enjoyed by the United States and Japan. The new European Community, however, will allow European firms to tap into what will become the world's single richest market.

European Community
The 320 million people living in the following 12 countries: Belgium, Denmark, France, Greece, Ireland, Italy, Luxembourg, Netherlands, Portugal, Spain, the United Kingdom, and West Germany.

•

The twelve nations making up the European Community include Belgium, Denmark, France, Greece, Ireland, Italy, Luxembourg, the Netherlands, Portugal, Spain, the United Kingdom, and West Germany.

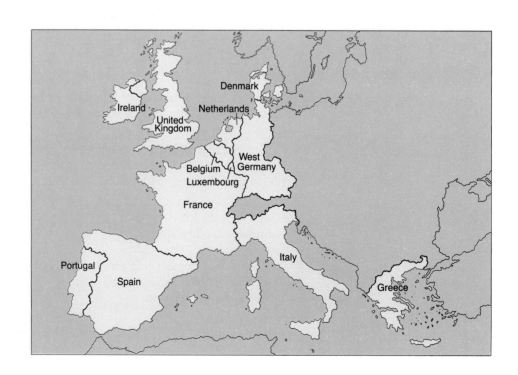

The European Community will further escalate global competition. European multinationals like Siemens of West Germany and Grand Metropolitan of Britain will achieve world-class size through acquisitions and alliances. Non-European multinationals like IBM and Matsushita Electric will need to consolidate their European operations and prepare for an onslaught of competition the like of which they've never seen. U.S. firms in such diverse industries as telecommunications equipment, pharmaceuticals, civilian aerospace, banking, automobiles, computers, electronics, food, and beverages should prepare themselves for vigorous challenges from their European counterparts. For European and non-European firms alike, a united Europe will provide both expanded opportunities and new competitive challenges.

U.S.–Canadian Alliance   Another set of national barriers are coming down between the United States and Canada.[10] These two countries are already the world's largest trading partners—doing at least $150 billion worth of business a year with each other. The recent signing of the U.S.-Canadian Free Trade Agreement only means increased competition for firms in each country.

The Free Trade Agreement, in effect, seeks to create a unified North America. It phases out tariffs on most goods traded between the two countries. It is also initiating a wave of consolidations as Canadian companies merge among themselves or with U.S. companies to form single giant firms.

The U.S.-Canadian Free Trade Agreement has been an economic stimulant to many cities along each country's border. A number of U.S. firms, for instance, have located operations in Buffalo, New York, to gain easy access to Toronto and other Canadian markets.

Canada has traditionally had smaller companies in relatively fragmented industries. The Free Trade Agreement has changed the competitive rules, and Canadian firms are responding. To prepare for the eventual battle for survival when U.S. and Canadian airlines are given unlimited access to the airports of both countries, Canadian Airlines International, which is Number 2 in market share, has bought Number 3 Wardair. To consolidate markets in the Canadian oil industry, Number 1 Imperial Oil has purchased Texaco Canada. Chicago-based packaging giant Stone Container bought Consolidated-Bathurst of Montreal to improve its pulp and paper position in Canada. The second and third largest Canadian breweries, Molson and Carling O'Keefe, are also planning to merge. This will allow them to better compete in Canada against U.S. heavyweights Anheuser-Busch and Miller Brewing and to prepare for a full-scale counterassault on the U.S. market.

U.S.–Mexico Border Zones   They're called **maquiladoras,** and an estimated 1400 firms—including General Motors, GE, Zenith, Honeywell, Hitachi, and Sanyo—are setting them up. Maquiladoras are assembly plants operating along the Mexican side of the border from Texas to California.[11]

The concept of maquiladoras was devised by the Mexican and U.S. governments in 1965 to help develop both sides of the impoverished border region. However, it was the massive devaluation of the peso, which occurred in 1982, that initiated a virtual explosion of maquiladoras. One estimate indicates that these cross-border plants could employ as many as three million workers by the year 2000.

Mexican wages are equal to, or even less than, wages in many countries in Asia. With a Mexican minimum wage of around 40 cents an hour, at current exchange rates, companies producing for North American markets no longer have to go to the Far East to find low-cost labor. As an executive at Fisher-Price Toys commented, "Labor costs 25 percent more in Hong Kong and Taiwan, and we can be to market four weeks ahead of the Far East."[12]

maquiladoras
Non-Mexican companies operating assembly plants along the Mexican side of the U.S.-Mexican border from Texas to California.

Since 1982, the number of maquiladora plants has nearly tripled. They are in Ciudad Juárez, Nogales, Tijuana, Mexicali, and similar northern Mexican cities.

ETHICAL DILEMMAS IN MANAGEMENT

Do Maquiladoras Exploit Mexican Workers?

Do U.S., Japanese, and European corporations take advantage of Mexican workers by operating plants just south of the U.S. border? Are they exporting U.S. jobs?[13]

On one side are those who argue that maquiladoras exploit the large pool of unskilled Mexicans who have migrated north to these border cities to escape the poverty in inner Mexico. These people are desperate for work and are glad to take jobs at wages that are one-tenth those of employees just over the border. U.S. union officials further charge that maquiladoras took 300,000 U.S. jobs during the 1980s and will increasingly siphon off higher-paid jobs. Additionally, many Mexicans claim that the jobs and money come at too high a social cost; that is, northern Mexico is being Americanized. They are upset by the dilution of Mexican culture created by the spreading use of both English and the U.S. dollar.

The other side of the argument proposes that, far from feeling exploited, Mexican workers often find their clean, air-conditioned work surroundings a relief from their humble homes. While the pay is low by U.S. standards, these jobs are in high demand and provide an escape from poverty for hundreds of thousands of Mexicans. Moreover, proponents of maquiladoras stress that economics and global competition demand that production seek its lowest cost level. Firms north of the border that fail to transfer operations to gain cost benefits save jobs in the United States only in the short term. In the long term, competition will drive these firms out of business.

Are corporations that build plants south of the border profiting at the expense of exploited Mexican workers and taking jobs away from U.S. workers? What do *you* think?

What's Next? Eastern Europe! Reforms in Eastern Europe, which began in late 1989, are almost certain to create new cooperative arrangements between Eastern European countries, the European Community, and other western countries.[14]

The combined gross national product of East Germany, Hungary, and Czechoslovakia is larger than that of China. These three countries also have relatively well-trained and reliable workers who earn less than a quarter of their Western counterparts. If these countries gain access to Western capital resources and their developed Western neighbors' markets, these countries could very well become the fastest-growing economies in the world during the 1990s. Additionally, the less developed Eastern European countries such as Poland, Yugoslavia, and Rumania represent tremendous untapped markets.

The future, at this point, is unclear. It is almost certain, however, that West and East Germany will be reunified. Some predict that countries like Hungary, Poland, and East Germany will press for some kind of membership in an even greater European

Community. Regardless, important changes are taking place in Eastern Europe and opportunities will abound. The West is likely to gain new markets as well as the availability of a well-trained and low-cost labor supply.

Global Competition Moves to Services

Through the early 1970s, the United States dominated world manufacturing. It made money by making things—pouring steel, stamping out automobile fenders, assembling television sets. Then the Japanese and dozens of other foreign rivals took many of those manufacturing jobs.[15]

The U.S. economy survived and prospered by refocusing on services. By the late 1980s, 71 percent of U.S. output was in services—shuffling papers; processing data on computer terminals; making bank loans; selling insurance, real estate, and securities; doing accounting; "lawyering"; and the like. Advances in computers and telecommunications and aggressive moves into the U.S. market by foreign firms now make the service industries in the United States vulnerable to the same forces that manufacturing faced only a decade or two ago. The United States lost its edge in manufacturing because managers became preoccupied with short-term profits, didn't pay attention to detail, alienated workers, and emphasized cost savings at the expense of customer service. If U.S. managers in service industries become complacent, they might find U.S. banking, accounting, retailing, and the like becoming dominated by more aggressive foreign competitors.

A few examples illustrate that services have become a major competitive arena in the U.S. market. Blue Arrow of Great Britain has purchased Manpower, Inc. and is now the world's largest employment-services firm. ISS of Denmark employs 16,000 people in the United States to perform janitorial services. A number of Far East multinationals are preparing plans for massive development of retail and specialty stores in the United States.

The other side of global competition in services is the expanded opportunities for U.S. firms to export their businesses into countries around the world. There is no reason, for instance, why U.S. colleges and universities can't take advantage of their

The Japanese are now major players in U.S. banking centers such as New York, San Francisco, and Los Angeles. The Bank of Tokyo is the largest Japanese bank in the United States.

expertise and become the higher educators of the world. Similarly, U.S. food and franchising know-how could allow the likes of McDonald's, Kentucky Fried Chicken, and Domino's to dominate world markets for fast food.

MANAGING IN A FOREIGN ENVIRONMENT

Assume for a moment that you're an American manager who is going to work for a branch of a U.S. multinational in a foreign country. You know that your environment will differ from the one at home, but how? What should you be on the lookout for?

Any manager who finds himself or herself in a strange country faces new challenges. In this section, we will look at these challenges and offer some guidelines for how to respond. Since most readers of this text were raised in the United States, we'll present our discussion through the eyes of an American manager. Of course, our analytical framework could be used by any manager, regardless of national origin, who has to manage in a foreign environment.

MANAGERS WHO MADE A DIFFERENCE

Frederick W. Smith at Federal Express

Frederick Smith founded Federal Express in 1973. In so doing, he almost single-handedly created the overnight-package business.[16] Today, with 45 percent of the U.S. market, Federal Express is the nation's largest overnight carrier. Its annual revenues are nearly $4 billion a year.

In early 1989, Federal Express spent $880 million to buy Tiger International Inc., the world's biggest heavy-cargo airline, best known for its Flying Tiger Line air freight service. The merger takes Federal Express one more step toward its goal of being the largest and best transportation company in the world.

Smith had tried for several years to grow internally and penetrate world markets with his own delivery system. He found that foreign rivals such as DHL Worldwide Express, Australia's TNT, and Japan's Nippon Cargo Airlines had well-established markets. Additionally, onerous foreign regulations made it hard for newcomers like Federal to compete. Between 1985 and 1988, Federal's international business lost approximately $74 million. The purchase of Tiger allows Federal to leapfrog the competition. All at once, Federal has a global network of international routes, long-haul aircraft, and international heavy-freight business that will be tough for its rivals to match.

At a time when Federal is facing intense competition from facsimile machines and price cutting by rivals in its U.S. market, Fred Smith is opening up new markets by positioning Federal Express to become the dominant carrier in overseas freight.

Photo courtesy of Federal Express.

The political environment in Panama over the past half-dozen years has created high uncertainty for managers of organizations in this country. Military coups are not unusual in a number of Latin American countries, while the United States has long had a reputation for high political stability.

The Legal-Political Environment

U.S. managers are accustomed to stable legal and political systems. Changes are slow, and procedures are well established. Elections are held at regular intervals. Even changes in parties after a presidential election do not produce any quick, radical transformations. The stability of laws governing the actions of individuals and institutions allows for very accurate predictions. The same cannot be said for all nations.

Some countries have a history of unstable governments. Some South American and African countries have had six different governments in as many years. With each new government have come new rules. The goal of one government may be to nationalize the country's key industries; the goal of the next may be to stimulate free enterprise. Managers of business firms in these countries face dramatically greater uncertainty as a result of political instability.

The legal-political environment does not have to be unstable or revolutionary to be of concern to managers. Just the fact that a country's social and political system differs from that of the United States is important. Managers need to recognize these differences if they are to understand the constraints under which they operate and the opportunities that exist. For example, Hong Kong imposes few legal constraints on business. France imposes many. Laws differ between nations on industrial spying, restraint of trade, working conditions, the rights of privacy, the rights of workers, and so forth. In Brazil, two-thirds of any company's employees must be local. In Mexico, the requirement is 90 percent.

The Economic Environment

The multinational manager has economic concerns that the manager who operates in a single country does not. Two of the most obvious are fluctuating exchange rates and diverse tax policies.

A multinational firm's profits can alter dramatically, depending on the strength of its home currency and the currencies of the countries in which it operates. For instance, in the summer of 1990, the West German mark stood at 1.70 to the U.S. dollar. Five years earlier, it took 2.84 marks to equal a dollar. A 50-million-mark profit in 1985 by a West German subsidiary of a U.S. multinational converted to $17.6 million in U.S. dollars. The same profit five years later resulted in $29.4 million in U.S. dollars. An investment by a U.S. multinational in 1980 of 100 million Mexican pesos cost approximately $7 million in U.S. dollars. Between 1980 and 1990, the peso went from 14.5 to the dollar to a staggering 2800 to the dollar. If that $7 million investment in Mexico had been reconverted to U.S. dollars in 1990, it would have been worth about $35,000! For multinationals, such fluctuations pose risks not only in production and marketing but also in the value of assets and liabilities.

Similarly, diverse tax policies are a major worry for a multinational manager. Some host countries are more restrictive than the corporation's home country; others are far more lenient. Managers need precise knowledge of the various tax rules in the countries in which they operate to minimize their corporation's overall tax obligations.

The Cultural Environment

The final environmental force is the cultural differences between nations. As we know from Chapter 3, organizations have different internal cultures. Countries have cultures, too, as anthropologists have long been telling us. Like organizational culture, **national culture** is something that is shared by all, or most, inhabitants of a country and that shapes their behavior and the way they see the world.[17]

Does national culture override an organization's culture? For example, is an IBM facility in West Germany more likely to reflect German ethnicity or IBM's corporate culture? Research indicates that national culture has a greater effect on employees than does their organization's culture.[18] German employees at an IBM facility in Munich will be influenced more by German culture than by IBM's culture. This means that as influential as organizational culture is on managerial practice, national culture is even more so.

Legal, political, and economic differences among countries are fairly straightforward. The Japanese manager who finds himself working in the United States or his American counterpart in Japan can obtain information on their new country's laws or tax policies without too much difficulty. However, obtaining information about a new country's cultural differences is a lot more troublesome. The primary reason is that the "natives" are least capable of explaining their culture's unique characteristics to someone else. If you're an American raised in the United States, how would you characterize your culture? Think about it for a moment and then see how many of the points in Table 4–2 you correctly identified.

To date, the most valuable framework to help managers better understand differences between national cultures has been developed by Geert Hofstede.[19] He surveyed 160,000 employees in sixty countries who worked for a single multinational corporation. What did he find? His huge data base indicated that national culture had a major impact on employees' work-related values and attitudes. In fact, it explained more of the differences than did age, sex, profession, or position in the organization. More important, Hofstede found that managers and employees vary on four dimensions of national culture: (1) individualism versus collectivism, (2) power distance, (3) uncertainty avoidance, and (4) masculinity versus femininity.

Individualism Versus Collectivism   **Individualism** refers to a loosely knit social framework in which people are supposed to look after their own interests and those of their immediate family. This is made possible because of the large amount of

national culture
The attitudes and perspectives shared by individuals from a specific country that shape their behavior and the way they see the world.

individualism
A cultural dimension in which people are supposed to look after their own interests and those of their immediate family.

TABLE 4–2   What Are Americans Like?

Americans are *informal.* They don't tend to treat people differently even when there are great differences in age or social standing.

Americans are *direct.* They don't talk around things. To some foreigners, this may appear as abrupt or even rude behavior.

Americans are *competitive.* Some foreigners may find Americans assertive or overbearing.

Americans are *achievers.* They like to keep score, whether at work or play. They emphasize accomplishments.

Americans are *independent and individualistic.* They place a high value on freedom and believe that individuals can shape and control their own destiny.

Americans are *questioners.* They ask a lot of questions, even of someone they have just met. Many of these questions may seem pointless ("How ya doing?") or personal ("What kind of work do you do?").

Americans dislike *silence.* They would rather talk about the weather than deal with silence in a conversation.

Americans value *punctuality.* They keep appointment calendars and live according to schedules and clocks.

Americans value *cleanliness.* They often seem obsessed with bathing, eliminating body odors, and wearing clean clothes.

Source: Based on Margo Ernest, ed., *Predeparture Orientation Handbook: For Foreign Students and Scholars Planning to Study in the United States* (Washington, D.C.: U.S. Information Agency, Bureau of Cultural Affairs, 1984), pp. 103–5; Amanda Bennett, "American Culture Is Often a Puzzle for Foreign Managers in the U.S.," *Wall Street Journal,* February 12, 1986, p. 29; "Don't Think Our Way's the Only Way," *The Pryor Report,* February 1988, p. 9; and Ben J. Wattenberg, "The Attitudes Behind American Exceptionalism," *U.S. News & World Report,* August 7, 1989, p. 25.

collectivism
A cultural dimension in which people expect others in their group to look after them and protect them when they are in trouble.

freedom that such a society allows individuals. Its opposite is **collectivism,** which is characterized by a tight social framework in which people expect others in groups of which they are a part (such as a family or an organization) to look after them and protect them when they are in trouble. In exchange for this, they feel they owe absolute loyalty to the group.

Hofstede found that the degree of individualism in a country is closely related to that country's wealth. Rich countries like the United States, Great Britain, and the Netherlands are very individualistic. Poor countries like Colombia, Pakistan, and Taiwan are very collectivist.

power distance
A cultural measure of the extent to which a society accepts the unequal distribution of power in institutions and organizations.

Power Distance   People naturally vary in terms of physical and intellectual abilities. This, in turn, creates differences in wealth and power. How does a society deal with these inequalities? Hofstede used the term **power distance** as a measure of the extent to which a society accepts the fact that power in institutions and organizations is distributed unequally. A high power distance society accepts wide differences in power in organizations. Employees show a great deal of respect for those in authority. Titles, rank, and status carry a lot of weight. When negotiating in high power distance countries, companies find it helps to send representatives with titles at least as high as those with whom they're bargaining. Countries high in power distance include the Philippines, Venezuela, and India. In contrast, a low power distance society plays down inequalities as much as possible. Superiors still have authority, but employees are not fearful or in awe of the boss. Denmark, Israel, and Austria are examples of countries with low power distance scores.

uncertainty avoidance
A cultural measure of the degree to which people tolerate risk and unconventional behavior.

Uncertainty Avoidance   We live in a world of uncertainty. The future is largely unknown and always will be. Societies respond to this uncertainty in different ways.

Some socialize their members into accepting it with equanimity. People in such societies are more or less comfortable with risks. They're also relatively tolerant of behavior and opinions that differ from their own because they don't feel threatened by them. Hofstede describes such societies as having low **uncertainty avoidance.** That is, people feel relatively secure. Countries that fall into this category include Singapore, Hong Kong, and Denmark.

A society that is high in uncertainty avoidance is characterized by an increased level of anxiety among its people, which manifests itself in greater nervousness, stress, and aggressiveness. Because people feel threatened by uncertainty and ambiguity in these societies, mechanisms are created to provide security and reduce risk. Their organizations are likely to have more formal rules, there will be less tolerance for deviant ideas and behaviors, and members will strive to believe in absolute truths. Not surprisingly, in organizations in countries with high uncertainty avoidance, employees demonstrate relatively low job mobility, and lifetime employment is a widely practiced policy. Countries in this category include Japan, Portugal, and Greece.

Masculinity Versus Femininity   The fourth dimension, like individualism and collectivism, represents a dichotomy. Hofstede called it masculinity versus femininity. Though his choice of terms is unfortunate (as you'll see, he gives them a strong sexist connotation), we'll use his labels to maintain the integrity of his work.

According to Hofstede, some societies allow both men and women to take many different roles. Others insist that people behave according to rigid sex roles. When societies make a sharp division between male and female activities, Hofstede claims, "the distribution is always such that men take more assertive and dominant roles and women the more service-oriented and caring roles."[20] Under the category **masculinity,** he puts societies that emphasize assertiveness and the acquisition of money and material things, while deemphasizing caring for others. Under the category **femininity,** he puts societies that emphasize relationships, concern for others, and the overall quality of life. Where femininity dominates, members put human relationships before money and are concerned with the quality of life, preserving the environment, and helping others.

Hofstede found Japan to be the most masculine country. In Japan, almost all women are expected to stay home and take care of children. At the other extreme, he found the Nordic countries and the Netherlands to be the most feminine. There, it's common to see men staying home while their wives work, and working men are offered paternity leave to take care of newborn children.

Table 4–3 highlights Hofstede's results. It lists the countries that Hofstede found at the extremes on each of the four dimensions.

A Guide for U.S. Managers   Since we used the United States earlier as a point of reference, we'll conclude this section by (1) reviewing how the United States ranked on Hofstede's four dimensions and (2) considering how an American manager, working in another country, might be able to use Hofstede's research findings.

Comparing the sixty countries on the four dimensions, Hofstede found the U.S. culture to be the highest among all countries on individualism, below average on power distance, well below average on uncertainty avoidance, and well above average on masculinity. These conclusions are not inconsistent with the world image of the United States. That is, America is seen as fostering the individualistic ethic, having a representative government with democratic ideals, being relatively free from threats of uncertainty, and having a capitalistic economy that values aggressiveness and material things.

masculinity
A cultural dimension that describes a society that emphasizes assertiveness and the acquisition of money and material things.

femininity
A cultural dimension describing societies that emphasize relationships, concern for others, and the overall quality of life.

TABLE 4–3
Examples of Cultural Differences Among World Nations

Individualism	Collectivism
United States	Colombia
Australia	Venezuela
Great Britain	Pakistan
Canada	Peru

High Power Distance	Low Power Distance
Philippines	Austria
Mexico	Israel
Venezuela	Denmark
Yugoslavia	New Zealand

High Uncertainty Avoidance	Low Uncertainty Avoidance
Greece	Singapore
Portugal	Denmark
Belgium	Sweden
Japan	Hong Kong

Masculinity	Femininity
Japan	Sweden
Austria	Norway
Venezuela	Yugoslavia
Italy	Denmark

Which countries are U.S. managers likely to best fit into? Which are likely to create the biggest adjustment problems? All we have to do is identify those countries that are most and least like the United States on the four dimensions.

The United States is strongly individualistic but low on power distance. This same pattern was exhibited by Great Britain, Australia, Canada, the Netherlands, and New Zealand. Those least similar to the United States on these dimensions were Venezuela, Colombia, Pakistan, Singapore, and the Philippines.

The United States scored low on uncertainty avoidance and high on masculinity. This same pattern was shown by Ireland, Great Britain, the Philippines, Canada, New Zealand, Australia, India, and South Africa. Those least similar to the United States on these dimensions were Chile, Yugoslavia, and Portugal.

These results empirically support part of what many of us suspected—that the American manager transferred to London, Toronto, Melbourne, or a similar Anglo city would have to make the fewest adjustments. In addition, the results further identify the countries in which "culture shock" is likely to be greatest and the need to modify one's managerial style most imperative.

SUMMARY

This summary is organized by the chapter-opening learning objectives found on page 93.

1. Competitors are no longer defined within national borders. New competitors can suddenly appear anytime, from anywhere in the world. Managers must think globally if their organizations are to succeed over the long term.

2. National parochialism prevents people from recognizing that people in other

countries have different ways of living and working. Parochial people rigidly apply their own values and customs to foreign cultures. The result is that they fail to understand foreigners and reduce their ability to effectively work with such people.

3. Multinational corporations have significant operations functioning in two or more countries simultaneously. Their worldwide strategies are having an impact on the economies of every country in the world. The revenues of the largest multinationals are larger than the GNPs of many nations. Many top managers in multinationals have as much power as do heads of state. In a global economy, multinationals will increasingly provide the world's goods and services.

4. Three active areas of regional cooperation are the twelve western European nations making up the European Community, U.S.-Canadian efforts to create a unified North American market, and border zones for assembly and manufacturing on the Mexican side of the U.S.-Mexican border. Eastern Europe offers a potentially active area of regional cooperation.

5. The four primary dimensions in which nations differ are individualism-collectivism, power distance, uncertainty avoidance, and masculinity-femininity.

6. U.S. culture is characterized as high on individualism, below average on power distance, well below average on uncertainty avoidance, and well above average on masculinity.

REVIEW QUESTIONS

1. How does a global economy create both opportunities and threats for managers?
2. Contrast Americans and Europeans in terms of national parochialism.
3. What is a *multinational corporation?* What challenges do they present for their managers?
4. What are the implications of a "United States of Europe" for managers of multinationals?
5. What are *maquiladoras?*
6. What were the primary causes of the decline in U.S. manufacturing domination?
7. Describe opportunities and threats for service firms in a global economy.
8. What countries have a legal-political environment most like that of the United States? Least like that of the United States?
9. What countries have an economic environment most like that of the United States? Least like it?
10. How can an understanding of Hofstede's four dimensions help managers to be more effective?

DISCUSSION QUESTIONS

1. "Multinational corporations provide benefits in each country in which they operate." Build an argument to support this statement. Then negate that argument.
2. Can the framework presented in this chapter be used to manage a hospital in South Korea or a government agency in Peru? Discuss.

3. What political risks does the Ford Motor Company take in operating outside the United States?

4. Research the characteristics of Japanese business organizations. How do they fit the Japanese culture? Are they applicable in the United States?

5. In what ways do you think the global environment has or will change the way in which business firms select and train managers?

SELF-ASSESSMENT EXERCISE

What Are Your Cultural Attitudes?

Instructions: Please indicate the extent to which you agree or disagree with each of the following statements. Respond to each statement by circling the appropriate number; for example, if you strongly agree with a particular statement, you would circle the "5" next to that statement.

5 = Strongly agree
4 = Agree
3 = Neither agree nor disagree
2 = Disagree
1 = Strongly disagree

	Strongly Disagree				Strongly Agree
1. Meetings are usually run more effectively when they are chaired by a man.	1	2	3	4	5
2. It is more important for men to have a professional career than it is for women to have a professional career.	1	2	3	4	5
3. Women do not value recognition and promotion in their work as much as men do.	1	2	3	4	5
4. Women value working in a friendly atmosphere more than men do.	1	2	3	4	5
5. Men usually solve problems with logical analysis; women usually solve problems with intuition.	1	2	3	4	5
6. Solving organizational problems usually requires the active, forcible approach that is typical of men.	1	2	3	4	5
7. It is preferable to have a man in a high-level position rather than a woman.	1	2	3	4	5
8. There are some jobs in which a man can always do better than a woman.	1	2	3	4	5
9. Women are more concerned with the social aspects of their job than they are with getting ahead.	1	2	3	4	5
10. An individual should not pursue his/her own goals without considering the welfare of the group.	1	2	3	4	5
11. It is important for a manager to encourage loyalty and a sense of duty in the group.	1	2	3	4	5
12. Being accepted by the group is more important than working on your own.	1	2	3	4	5
13. Individual rewards are not as important as group welfare.	1	2	3	4	5
14. Group success is more important than individual success.	1	2	3	4	5

	Strongly Disagree				Strongly Agree
15. It is important to have job requirements and instructions spelled out in detail so that people always know what they are expected to do.	1	2	3	4	5
16. Managers expect workers to closely follow instructions and procedures.	1	2	3	4	5
17. Rules and regulations are important because they inform workers what the organization expects of them.	1	2	3	4	5
18. Standard operating procedures are helpful to workers on the job.	1	2	3	4	5
19. Instructions for operations are important for workers on the job.	1	2	3	4	5
20. It is often necessary for a supervisor to emphasize his/her authority and power when dealing with subordinates.	1	2	3	4	5
21. Managers should be careful not to ask the opinions of subordinates too frequently.	1	2	3	4	5
22. A manager should avoid socializing with his/her subordinates off the job.	1	2	3	4	5
23. Subordinates should not disagree with their manager's decisions.	1	2	3	4	5
24. Managers should not delegate difficult and important tasks to his/her subordinates.	1	2	3	4	5
25. Managers should make most decisions without consulting subordinates.	1	2	3	4	5

Turn to page 670 for scoring directions and key.

Source: This questionnaire is part of a larger instrument currently under development by professors Peter W. Dorfman and Jon P. Howell, both of New Mexico State University. Reprinted by permission of the authors.

CASE APPLICATION 4A

3M Company

It began in 1902 with a single product—sandpaper.[21] Today, Minnesota Mining and Manufacturing (better known as 3M) has nearly 50,000 products and sales of $10.5 billion a year. These products cut across virtually every industry from entertainment to health care, construction to chemicals—products as diverse as kitchen scourers, videocassettes, reflective road signs, and surgical masks. You probably know them best for their "Scotch" brand transparent tape and their little yellow "Post-It" notepads.

3M became a global firm in 1951 when it established an international division. Sales from outside the United States now generate 40 percent of the company's worldwide revenues. Of the 82,000 3M employees, 17,000 work at its headquarters in St. Paul, Minnesota, and 35,000 work outside the United States. Of those 35,000, however, only 100 are Americans. 3M's international managers freely cross national boundaries; for instance, a French manager may be running a Korean operation, a Briton managing a subsidiary in Spain, or a Dane managing one in Germany.

3M has an impressive performance record. It generates more than 100 new products every year and has regularly produced a 20 percent return on equity for its investors. It has achieved these results by pursuing a simple strategy against competitors: quality products priced fairly and sold aggressively, with a steady stream of innovations replenishing the market.

The company faces an increasingly dynamic environment. Challenges include inflation, volatile interest rates, regulatory changes, scarcity of key resources, declining demand in some major markets, and increased competition on a worldwide scale in such fields as film and magnetic memory technology, office products, pressure-sensitive tape, and the graphic arts.

Questions

1. What can a firm like 3M do to overcome national parochialism among its headquarters staff?

2. Why do you think 3M has so few Americans in its foreign operations?

3. As a global company, 3M must compete against European firms. How can a company whose headquarters is in Minnesota compete effectively in, say, West Germany against German rivals?

4. How could 3M take advantage of recent trends toward regional cooperation among countries?

CASE APPLICATION 4B

Xerox of Mexico

Paul Hunt grew up in Houston and got his degree in business management from Texas A & M in 1983. Upon graduation, Paul took a job with the Xerox Corporation in Dallas as a personnel specialist. During his first two years, he split his time between recruiting on college campuses and establishing a training program for maintenance engineers. In 1985, Paul was promoted to Assistant Manager for Human Resources—Western Region. The company moved him to the western regional office in Denver.

Paul's annual performance appraisals were consistently high. The company believed that he had strong advancement potential. Though Paul was ambitious and made no attempt to hide his desire to move into higher management, even he was a bit surprised when he was called to Xerox's Connecticut headquarters in April 1989 and offered the position of Director of Human Resources for Xerox of Mexico. If he accepted the position, Paul would oversee a staff of twenty people in Mexico City and be responsible for all human resource activities—hiring, compensation, labor relations, and so on—for the company's Mexican operations. He was told that the combination of his outstanding job performance ratings and ability to speak Spanish (Paul had taken four years of Spanish in high school and another twelve hours of advanced coursework in college) led the company to select him for the promotion.

Paul accepted the offer. Why not? It was an important promotion, meant a large increase in pay, and provided an opportunity to live in a foreign country.

Questions

1. How does Mexico's legal and political environment differ from that of the United States?

2. How does Mexico's economic environment differ from that of the United States?

3. Describe Mexico's national culture.

4. Based on the discussion in Chapter 1 of what managers do, what changes do you think Paul will need to make in his managerial style?

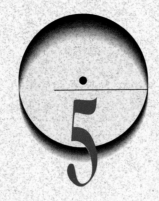

5

SOCIAL RESPONSIBILITY AND MANAGERIAL ETHICS

McDonald's prides itself on being a good corporate citizen. The fast-food chain values its reputation and seeks to behave in a socially responsible manner. It actively seeks minority owners for its franchises. It supports the Ronald McDonald Houses (located in Atlanta, Chicago, Philadelphia, and over sixty other cities), places where parents of hospitalized children can stay free of charge. The company even carefully reviews the television programs it sponsors to screen out undesirable themes. For example, it won't advertise on programs such as *Geraldo* or *A Current Affair* because it finds them incompatible with McDonald's family-oriented image.

In spite of McDonald's efforts to be socially responsible, its actions are not always seen that way.[1] For example, it has been accused of supporting the killing of baby harp seals. Seal supporters claim that Canadian fishermen are battering the seal pups to death. Since McDonald's is the largest single purchaser of Canadian fish, the critics contend that the firm should pressure suppliers to halt the seal hunts. McDonald's has also been criticized by the NAACP in southern California for "keeping blacks and other minorities in the ghetto." The NAACP contends that McDonald's sells franchises to blacks only in minority neighborhoods, where profits are generally lower because the outlets are older and operating costs are higher. The company has even been the target of a recent attack by the American Heart Association, which claims that "hamburgers and fries" are high-fat, high-cholesterol products that contribute to the problem of heart disease in the United States.

At the extreme, one might ask whether it is possible for a company like McDonald's to be socially responsible if its basic products aren't good for people. If fast food contains high levels of saturated fat, cholesterol, and sodium, which have been clearly linked to coronary disease, arteriosclerosis, obesity, and stroke, can any amount of minority ownership, Ronald McDonald Houses, or support of quality television programming make McDonald's a socially responsible organization?

Clearly, a good part of the difficulty of being a socially responsible organization today lies in the definition of social responsibility. What management believes is a socially responsible action may be seen by others as "not good enough" or even "irresponsible."

In this chapter, we'll present a foundation for understanding social responsibility and managerial ethics. We place the discussion of these topics at this point in the text so as to link them to the preceding and following subjects. Specifically, we'll show that social responsibility is a response to a changing environment and that ethical considerations should be an important criterion in managerial decision making (the topic of Chapter 6).

WHAT IS SOCIAL RESPONSIBILITY?

The issue of corporate social responsibility drew little attention before the 1960s. However, the activist movement at that time began to call into question the singular economic objective of business firms. Was Dow Chemical irresponsible for producing napalm used in the Vietnam War, even though it was a profitable product for Dow?

Boeing is Seattle's largest employer. More than 100,000 people work at its plants and offices in the Seattle area. Does Boeing have a greater responsibility to the Seattle community than, say, a firm that employs only 200 people in Seattle? A number of experts think so.

Were large corporations irresponsible because they discriminated against women and minorities, as shown by the obvious absence of female and minority managers at that time? Did Kennecott Copper ignore its social responsibilities by allowing its smelters to pollute the air over hundreds of square miles of Arizona?

Before the 1960s, few people asked such questions. But times have changed. Managers are now regularly confronted with decisions that have a social responsibility dimension—philanthropy, pricing, employee relations, resource conservation, product quality, and operations in countries with oppressive governments are some of the more obvious. To help managers make such decisions, let's begin by defining social responsibility.

Two Opposing Views

Few terms have been defined in as many different ways as *social responsibility*. Some of the more popular meanings include "profit making only," "going beyond profit making," "voluntary activities," "concern for the broader social system," and "social responsiveness."[2] Most of the debate has focused at the extremes. On one side, there is the classical—or purely economic—view that management's only social responsibility is to maximize profits. On the other side stands the socioeconomic position, which holds that management's responsibility goes well beyond making profits to include protecting and improving society's welfare.

classical view
The view that management's only social responsibility is to maximize profits.

The Classical View   The most outspoken advocate of the **classical view** is economist and Nobel laureate Milton Friedman.[3] He argues that most managers today are professional managers, which means that they don't own the businesses they run. They're employees, responsible to the stockholders. Their primary charge is therefore to conduct the business in the interests of the stockholders. And what are those interests? Friedman argues that the stockholders have a single concern: financial return.

According to Friedman, when managers take it upon themselves to spend their organization's resources for the "social good," they undermine the market mechanism. Someone has to pay for this redistribution of assets. If socially responsible actions reduce profits and dividends, stockholders are the losers. If wages and benefits have to be reduced to pay for social action, employees lose. If prices are raised to pay for social actions, consumers lose. If higher prices are rejected by the market and sales drop, the business might not survive—in which case, *all* the organization's constituencies lose. Moreover, Friedman contends that when professional managers pursue anything other than profit, they implicitly appoint themselves as nonelected policymakers. He questions whether managers of business firms have the expertise for deciding how society *should* be. That, Friedman would argue, is what we elect political representatives to decide.

Friedman's argument is probably best understood in terms of microeconomics. If socially responsible acts add to the cost of doing business, those costs have to be either passed on to consumers in higher prices or absorbed by stockholders through a smaller profit margin. In a competitive market, if management raises prices, it will lose sales. In a purely competitive market, given that the competition hasn't also assumed the costs of social responsibility, prices can't be raised without losing the entire market. Such a situation means that the costs have to be absorbed by the business, which results in lower profits.

The classical view would also argue that there are pressures in a competitive market for investment funds to go where they'll get the highest return. If the socially responsible firm can't pass on its higher social costs to consumers and has to absorb them internally, it will generate a lower rate of return. Over time, investment funds will gravitate away from socially responsible firms toward those that aren't, since the latter will provide the higher rate of return. That might even mean that if all the firms in a particular country—such as the United States—incurred additional social costs because management perceived this to be one of business's goals, the survival of entire domestic industries could be threatened by foreign competitors who chose not to incur such social costs.

The Socioeconomic View   The socioeconomic position counters that times have changed and, with them, society's expectations of business. This is best illustrated in the legal formation of corporations. Corporations are chartered by state governments. The same government that creates a charter can take it away. So corporations are not independent entities, responsible only to stockholders. They also have a responsibility to the larger society that creates and sustains them.

socioeconomic view
The view that management's social responsibility goes well beyond the making of profits to include protecting and improving society's welfare.

One author, in supporting the **socioeconomic view,** reminds us that "maximizing profits is a company's second priority, not its first. The first is ensuring its survival."[4]

Take the case of the Manville Corporation. More than forty years ago, its senior management had evidence that one of its products, asbestos, caused fatal lung diseases. As a matter of policy, management decided to conceal the information from affected employees. The reason? Profits! In court testimony, a lawyer recalled how, in the mid-1940s, he had questioned Manville's corporate counsel about the company's policy of concealing chest X-ray results from employees. The lawyer had asked, "Do you mean to tell me you would let them work until they dropped dead?" The reply was, "Yes, we save a lot of money that way."[5] This might have been true in the short term, but certainly not in the long term. The company was forced to file for bankruptcy in 1982 to protect itself against tens of thousands of potential asbestos-related lawsuits. It emerged from bankruptcy in 1988, but with staggering asbestos-related liabilities. To compensate victims, Manville agreed to set up a personal injury settlement trust, funding it with $2.6 billion in cash and bonds and up to 20 percent of the company's annual profits through the year 2015. Here is an example of what can happen when management takes a short-term perspective. Many workers died before their time, the stockholders lost a great deal of money, and a major corporation was forced into reorganization.

A major flaw in the classicists' view, as seen by socioeconomic proponents, is their time frame. Supporters of the socioeconomic view contend that managers should be concerned with maximizing financial returns over the *long run*. To do that, they must accept some social obligations and the costs that go with them. They must protect society's welfare by *not* polluting, *not* discriminating, *not* engaging in deceptive advertising, and the like. They must also play an affirmative role in improving society by involving themselves in their communities and contributing to charitable organizations.

A final point made by proponents of the socioeconomic position is that the classical view flies in the face of reality.[6] Modern business firms are no longer merely economic institutions. They lobby, form political action committees, and engage in other activities to influence the political process for their benefit. Society accepts and even encourages business to become involved in its social, political, and legal environment. That might not have been true thirty or forty years ago, but it is the reality of today.

Arguments For and Against Social Responsibility

What are the specific arguments for and against business assuming social responsibilities? In this section, we'll outline the major points that have been brought forward.[7]

Arguments For   The major arguments supporting the assumption of social responsibilities by business are summarized in Table 5–1.

TABLE 5–1   Arguments For Social Responsibility

 1. Public expectations
 2. Long-run profits
 3. Ethical obligation
 4. Public image
 5. Better environment
 6. Discouragement of further government regulation
 7. Balance of responsibility and power
 8. Stockholder interests
 9. Possession of resources
10. Superiority of prevention over cures

1. *Public expectations.* Social expectations of business have increased dramatically since the 1960s. Public opinion in support of business pursuing social as well as economic goals is now well solidified.

2. *Long-run profits.* Socially responsible businesses tend to have more secure long-run profits. This is the normal result of the better community relations and improved business image that responsible behavior brings.

3. *Ethical obligation.* A business firm can and should have a conscience. Business should be socially responsible because responsible actions are *right* for their own sake.

4. *Public image.* Firms seek to enhance their public image to gain more customers, better employees, access to money markets, and other benefits. Since the public considers social goals to be important, business can create a favorable public image by pursuing social goals.

5. *Better environment.* Involvement by business can solve difficult social problems, thus creating a better quality of life and a more desirable community in which to attract and hold skilled employees.

6. *Discouragement of further government regulation.* Government regulation adds economic costs and restricts management's decision flexibility. By becoming socially responsible, business can expect less government regulation.

7. *Balance of responsibility and power.* Business has a large amount of power in society. An equally large amount of responsibility is required to match it. When power is significantly greater than responsibility, the imbalance encourages irresponsible behavior that works against the public good.

8. *Stockholder interests.* Social responsibility will improve the price of a business's stock in the long run. The stock market will view the socially responsible company as less risky and open to public attack. Therefore, it will award its stock a higher price-earnings ratio.

9. *Possession of resources.* Business has the financial resources, technical experts, and managerial talent to provide support to public and charitable projects that need assistance.

10. *Superiority of prevention over cures.* Social problems must be dealt with at some time. Business should act on them before they become more serious and costly to correct and take management's energy away from accomplishing its goal of producing goods and services.

Arguments Against   The major arguments against business assuming social responsibility are summarized in Table 5–2.

TABLE 5–2   Arguments Against Social Responsibility

1. Violation of profit maximization
2. Dilution of purpose
3. Costs
4. Too much power
5. Lack of skills
6. Lack of accountability
7. Lack of broad public support

1. *Violation of profit maximization.* This is the essence of the classical viewpoint. Business is most socially responsible when it attends strictly to its economic interests and leaves other activities to other institutions.

2. *Dilution of purpose.* The pursuit of social goals dilutes business's primary purpose: economic productivity. Society may suffer as both economic and social goals are poorly accomplished.

3. *Costs.* Many socially responsible activities don't pay their own way. Someone has to pay these costs. Business must absorb these costs or pass them on to consumers in higher prices.

4. *Too much power.* Business is already one of the most powerful institutions in our society. If it pursues social goals, it would have even more power. Society has given business enough power.

5. *Lack of skills.* The outlook and abilities of business leaders are oriented primarily toward economics. Businesspeople are poorly qualified to cope with social issues.

6. *Lack of accountability.* Political representatives pursue social goals and are held accountable for their actions. Such is not the case with business leaders. There are no direct lines of social accountability from the business sector to the public.

7. *Lack of broad public support.* There is no broad mandate from society for business to become involved in social issues. The public is divided on the issue. In fact, it is a topic that rarely fails to generate a heated debate. Actions taken under such divided support are likely to fail.

From Obligations to Responsiveness

social responsibility
A social obligation, beyond that required by the law and economics, for a firm to pursue long-term goals that are good for society.

Now it's time to narrow in on precisely what *we* mean when we talk about **social responsibility.** It is a business firm's social obligation, beyond that required by the law and economics, to pursue long-term goals that are good for society.[8] Note that this definition assumes that business obeys the law and pursues economic interests. We take as a given that all business firms—those that are socially responsible and those that aren't—will obey all laws that society imposes. Also note that this definition views business as a moral agent. In its effort to do *good* for society, it must differentiate between right and wrong.

We can understand social responsibility better if we compare it with two similar concepts: social obligation and social responsiveness.[9] As Figure 5–1 depicts, social obligation is the foundation of business's social involvement. A business has fulfilled

social obligation
The obligation of a business to meet its economic and legal responsibilities.

its **social obligation** when it meets its economic and legal responsibilities and no more. It does the minimum that the law requires. A firm pursues social goals only to the extent that they contribute to its economic goals. In contrast to social obligation, both social responsibility and social responsiveness go beyond merely meeting basic economic and legal standards.

Social responsibility adds an ethical imperative to do those things that make society better and *not* to do anything that could make it worse. **Social responsiveness** refers to the capacity of a firm to respond to social pressures.[10]

social responsiveness
The capacity of a firm to respond to social pressures.

As Table 5–3 describes, social responsibility requires business to determine what is right or wrong and thus seek fundamental ethical truths. Social responsiveness is guided by social norms. The value of social norms is that they can provide managers with a more meaningful guide for decision making. The following makes the distinction clearer.

Suppose, for example, that a multiproduct firm's social responsibility is to produce reasonably safe products. Similarly, the same firm is responsive every time it produces an unsafe product: it withdraws the product from the market as soon as the product is found to be unsafe. After, say, ten recalls, will the firm be

FIGURE 5–1
Evolution of Business's Social Involvement

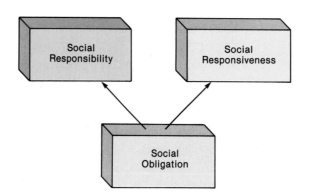

TABLE 5–3   Social Responsibility Versus Social Responsiveness

	Social Responsibility	**Social Responsiveness**
Major consideration	Ethical	Pragmatic
Focus	Ends	Means
Emphasis	Obligation	Responses
Decision framework	Long-term	Medium- and short-term

Source: Adapted from Steven L. Wartick and Philip L. Cochran, "The Evolution of the Corporate Social Performance Model," *Academy of Management Review,* October 1985, p. 766.

recognized as socially responsible? Will the firm be recognized as socially responsive? The likely answers to these questions are No to the first, but Yes to the second.[11]

When a company meets pollution control standards established by the federal government or doesn't discriminate against employees over the age of 40 in promotion decisions, it is meeting its social obligation and nothing more. The reason is that the law says that the company may not pollute or practice age discrimination. In 1990, if a company provided on-site child care facilities for employees or stopped doing business in South Africa, it would have been acting socially responsively. Why? Pressures from working mothers and antiapartheid groups made such practices pragmatic. Of course, if that same company had provided child care or pulled out of South Africa in 1970, it probably would have been more accurately characterized as a socially responsible action.

When Hallmark sponsors Shakespeare plays, operas, and classical music offerings on its *Hallmark Hall of Fame* television program, it is engaging in social responsibility. These shows traditionally get low ratings, but the company is committed to making television better and supporting the arts.

Advocates of social responsiveness believe that the concept replaces philosophical discourse with pragmatism. They see it as a more tangible and achievable objective than social responsibility.[12] Rather than assessing what is good for society in the long term, a socially responsive management identifies the prevailing social norms and then changes its social involvement to respond to changing societal conditions.

Is any one of these three concepts preferable to the others? While some people imply that social responsiveness is an advanced way of thinking about business's social involvement,[13] we should probably consider the three concepts as merely a framework for classifying business's response to the increasing demands for it to pursue social goals.

STRATEGY AND SOCIAL INVOLVEMENT

In a later chapter, we'll argue that every organization needs an overall strategy to guide it. Management develops such a strategy by assessing the organization's environment, evaluating the organization's strengths and weaknesses, and then merging this information to locate an exploitable niche where the organization will have a competitive advantage. Enlightened managers can use a similar strategic framework to make effective social involvement decisions.

As one author has explicitly noted in developing his case for a strategic approach to social involvement: (1) The institution of business does not stand in isolation, nor does it serve a single purpose or a single constituency; and (2) the major threats and opportunities facing business reside in the environment and in the organization's interactions with that environment.[14] Business firms therefore try to find a position in which they can best deal with threats and opportunities. But threats and opportunities arise not only from product, market, technology, and other traditional competitive variables. They also arise from the social and political dimensions of an organization's environment.

Patterns of Strategic Response

Research has disclosed that business firms often pursue one of three strategies when responding to a changing social environment. These strategies have been labeled adaptive, proactive, and interactive.[15]

adaptive strategy
Responding to a changing social environment after the fact.

An **adaptive strategy** is usually adopted *after* the fact. The environment changes, and management reacts to defend itself. Many firms have followed this approach in dealing with the growing public concern over business investments in South Africa.[16] For instance, Bell & Howell sold its profitable audio-visual and mail-sorting operation there in response to the threat of boycotts in the United States, and Citibank has stopped making new loans to both South African government agencies and business firms until progress is made in dismantling apartheid.

proactive strategy
Manipulating a firm's social environment in ways that will work to the firm's advantage.

Firms that follow a **proactive strategy** do more than merely adapt in a reactive manner. They seek to manipulate the environment in ways that will work to their advantage. They might, for instance, make donations to political candidates who will support legislation favorable to them. This approach is widely used by real estate developers who, by supporting local progrowth and development political candidates, attempt to shape the environment to their advantage.

interactive strategy
Anticipating environmental change and adapting a firm's actions to it.

Business firms that anticipate environmental change and adapt their actions accordingly are following an **interactive strategy.** When air and water pollution control laws gained popularity in the late 1960s, most firms responded by installing equipment that reduced their pollutants to the new standards. A few, however, pursued an interactive strategy. They anticipated more stringent regulations in the future and installed more sophisticated technology that was capable of reducing pollution to levels well below those required by laws at the time.

Managers can adapt to, manipulate, or anticipate social and political forces in the environment. Which strategy they choose will depend on how they think business should pursue social goals. Managers who take the classical view that business is only an economic institution are likely to follow an adaptive approach. The interactive strategy, on the other hand, is consistent with the socioeconomic view and the idea of business being socially aggressive.

Social Issues Management

social issues management
Identifying, analyzing, and responding to issues in order to minimize surprises and enforce social policies that benefit the firm.

Some firms, such as Aetna Life and Casualty, are going beyond the adaptive response to the social and political environment. They are acting on their environment through **social issues management.**[17] They identify, analyze, and respond to issues in order to minimize surprises and enforce social policies that benefit the firm. They expand their forecasting to identify political, legal, and social changes in addition to the more traditional concerns such as technology, the economy, and the competition. They try to spot potential changes in the law and social norms early to buffer the organization from shocks. They try to influence the environment by creating a positive public image of the organization and achieving favorable government treatment. They use public relations campaigns (that is, promoting the company's social involvement through advertising and news releases), hire lobbyists to present the company's case directly to legislative decision makers, and provide financial support to elected officials through political action committees.

Aetna Life and Casualty Co., for instance, has four primary external affairs departments, each of which specializes in a different aspect of the company's social environment.[18] Corporate Communications handles public relations and manages all advertising activities. It oversees Aetna's "issues" or advocacy program, which is designed to raise the level of public awareness of problems in society that affect the insurance business. The Government Relations department represents Aetna to local, state, and government agencies and monitors the changing regulatory environment. The Corporate Social Responsibility department addresses the problem of how to institutionalize corporate responsibility. Its major functions include running the company's Affirmative Action program, managing Aetna's minority investment programs, and formulating policy for corporate philanthropy. Finally, the Public Policy Issues Analysis department acts as a clearinghouse for social issues affecting the company, manages the analysis of issues having high impact potential, and facilitates managerial learning about the social environment.

SOCIAL RESPONSIBILITY AND ECONOMIC PERFORMANCE

In this section, we seek to answer the question: Do socially responsible activities lower a company's economic performance?

More than a dozen studies have looked at this question.[19] All have some methodological limitations related to measures of "social responsibility" and "economic performance."[20] Most ascertain a firm's social performance by analyzing the content of annual reports, citations of social actions in articles on the company, or public perception "reputation" indexes. Such criteria certainly have flaws as objective, reliable measures of social responsibility. While measures of economic performance (net income, return on equity, or per share stock prices) are more objective, they suffer from a time problem. Most studies look at short-term financial performance. It may well be that the impact of social responsibility on a firm's profits—either positive or negative—takes a number of years to work itself through. If there is a time lag, then studies that use short-term financial data aren't likely to show valid results.

Given these caveats, what do the research studies find? The majority show a *positive* relationship between corporate social involvement and economic performance. One review of thirteen studies found only one negative association—in this case, the price of socially responsible firms' stocks didn't do as well as national stock indices.[21]

There is, however, another way to look at this issue. Let's examine a set of socially conscious mutual stock funds that have developed in recent years and compare their performance to the average of all mutual funds. Table 5–4 lists six of the largest and most popular funds in the United States that represent themselves as being responsible investors.[22] In recent years, these funds have not invested in companies connected with South Africa, defense weapons, liquor, gambling, tobacco, price fixing, or criminal fraud. As you can see, between 1984 and 1988, all outperformed the average of equity funds as a group.

In aggregate, the evidence suggests that socially responsible activities result in *higher* economic performance. Of course, problems in defining social responsibility and economic performance may taint these results. In addition, the strong performance of socially conscious mutual funds has been attributed largely to the role that small-company stocks played in the 1988 rebound in equity markets.[23] After funds rule out investing in companies linked with South Africa or nuclear power or companies with poor records in hiring and promoting women and minority-group members, in addition to banning stocks related to alcohol, tobacco, gambling, and weapons, what is left tends to be small-company stocks. In the year following the October 1987 market crash, small-company stocks bounced up about 16 percent, compared to only 6 percent for the Standard & Poor's 500 (which is made up of very large firms). Therefore, the strong performance of socially conscious funds might be due more to the size of companies in which they invest than to the companies' social awareness.

Maybe the most meaningful conclusion we can draw is that, at least at present, there is little substantive evidence to say that a company's socially responsible actions significantly reduce its long-term economic performance. Given the current political and social pressures on business to pursue social goals, this may have the greatest significance for managerial decision making.[24]

TABLE 5–4   Average Annual Total Return of Socially Conscious Funds, 1984–1988

Calvert Social Investment	13.2%
Dreyfus Third Century	11.7
Pax World	10.9
Pioneer Fund	11.5
Pioneer II	12.1
Pioneer Three	11.4
All equity funds	10.3

Source: Business Week, February 20, 1989, pp. 80–114.

IS SOCIAL RESPONSIBILITY JUST PROFIT-MAXIMIZING BEHAVIOR?

If social responsibility does not affect economic performance negatively, maybe the whole notion of social responsibility is just a fancy public relations concept that allows corporate management to appear socially conscious while it pursues its profit objectives. That is, socially responsible actions might be nothing more than profit-maximizing actions in disguise. While this line of questioning appears to be cynical, business students, the media, and other groups regularly challenge any implication that business's pursuit of social goals is altruistically motivated.

cause-related marketing
Social actions that are motivated directly by profits.

There is no question that some social actions taken by companies are motivated primarily by profits. In fact, the practice has acquired a name: **cause-related marketing.**[25] Firms such as American Express, Coca-Cola, General Foods, and MasterCard make no apologies for capitalizing on the public's social conscience.[26] As an executive at American Express put it, "Social responsibility is a good marketing hook."[27]

In 1986, American Express sponsored a major share of the restoration of the Statue of Liberty and Ellis Island. It promised to contribute a certain amount of money to the restoration fund each time a consumer was granted a new card, used an existing one, bought American Express traveler's checks, or purchased a travel package over $500. The company claims that cardholder dollar charges rose 30 percent during the campaign. The $4 million spent by American Express to advertise its promise came from its marketing budget.[28]

Coca-Cola put up $5 million in cash and spent more than $2 million for advertising to support its sponsorship of "Hands Across America," a cause that raised money for America's hungry and homeless. Coke's director of public affairs explained at the time that "'Hands Across America' is a natural fit with Coke's brand strategy—a totally unique concept, yet steeped in the American tradition of togetherness, family, the big event."[29]

Ben & Jerry's Homemade Inc.'s management believes in world peace. Their Peace Pop's box and interior wrapper invite consumers to join a political movement called "1% for Peace," which advocates real-locating 1 percent of the U.S. defense budget for peace projects. Ben & Jerry's has found strong public acceptance of the ice cream bars. Said the company's cofounder, "If it happens that doing what we believe in is also good for business, then that is good."

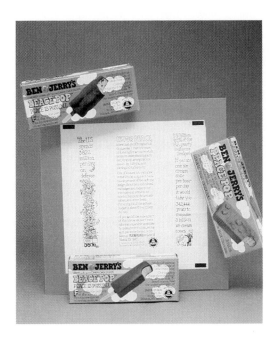

General Foods promoted its Tang breakfast drink mix by sponsoring a march across the United States for Mothers Against Drunk Driving (MADD). General Foods distributed cents-off coupons to consumers and offered to give ten cents to MADD for every Tang proof-of-purchase seal that consumers sent in. During the four-month promotion, shipments of Tang increased 13 percent, and retailers responded by giving Tang back previously lost shelf space. Said the manager of corporate communications at General Foods, "We could have spent the money that went to MADD on discounts to the grocers, but we would never have gotten the same response."[30]

MasterCard's "Choose to Make a Difference" campaign sought to raise $3 million in three months for six major charities. The charities were selected partly on the basis of a consumer popularity poll.[31]

Research indicates that these examples are not atypical. Corporate philanthropy has been found to complement advertising and to be motivated by profit considerations.[32] In fact, *Business Week* recently described cause-related marketing as "the hottest thing going in philanthropy."[33]

So what is our conclusion? Is social responsibility just profit-maximizing behavior? While we can't speak for the motivation of every "social" act by business firms, it is clear that at least some of these actions are profit motivated and consistent with the classical goal of economic maximization. Incidentally, this may explain why so many research studies (cited in the previous section) found a positive relationship between corporate social responsibility and economic performance.

MANAGERS WHO MADE A DIFFERENCE

Laura Scher at Working Assets Funding Service

Laura Scher is a thirty-year-old Harvard MBA with a social conscience. She has found a way to turn that social conscience into a profitable business.[34]

Scher is the chief executive of Working Assets Funding Service, a money management firm that caters to people who have an ethical as well as financial interest in where their cash is invested. Among the more popular products that her firm currently sells are a money market fund that invests in socially responsible companies and a Visa card that automatically donates 5 cents to charity each time it is used. The fund has more than $100 million under management, and in one recent year, revenues from the Visa card generated $32,000, which was donated to such organizations as Amnesty International USA, Greenpeace USA, and the National Coalition for the Homeless.

Scher is not content to rest on her laurels. She sees additional opportunities to develop socially conscious products. For instance, she has recently launched a new credit card, the Working Assets Women's Card, which will generate donations to charities supporting women every time it is used. Scher has also started a travel service that donates a small percentage of ticket sales to charity.

Photo courtesy of Ms. Laura Scher.

A GUIDE THROUGH THE MAZE

stakeholders

Any constituency in the environment that is affected by an organization's decisions and policies.

Is business socially responsible? Should it be? What is even meant by the term *social responsibility?* We have seen a lot of diverse data on these questions. In this section, we'll provide a modest guide through the maze and, in so doing, try to clarify these issues.

The path will become easier to follow if we can identify to whom business managers are responsible. Classicists would say that stockholders or owners are their only legitimate concern. Progressives would respond that managers are responsible to any individual or group that is affected by the organization's decisions and policies. These **stakeholders** are any constituency in an organization's environment: government agencies, unions, employees, customers, suppliers, host communities, and public interest groups.

Figure 5–2 illustrates a four-stage model of an organization whose domain of social responsibility is continually expanding.[35] Stage 1 encompasses only the owners and managers. Stage 2 adds all the employees. Stage 3 includes constituencies in the organization's specific environment. Stage 4 goes farthest by proposing that management is responsible to all of society. What you do as a manager, in terms of pursuing social goals, depends on to whom you believe you're responsible. A stage 1 manager will promote the stockholders' interest by seeking to minimize costs and maximize profits. At stage 2, managers will accept their responsibility to their employees and focus on human resource concerns. Because they'll want to get, keep, and motivate good employees, they'll improve working conditions, expand employee rights, increase job security, and the like.

At stage 3, managers will expand their goals to include fair prices, high-quality products and services, safe products, good supplier relations, and similar practices. Stage 3 managers perceive that they can meet their responsibilities to stockholders only indirectly by meeting the needs of their other constituents.

Finally, stage 4 aligns with the extreme socioeconomic definition of social responsibility. At this stage, managers are responsible to society as a whole. Their business is seen as a public property, and they are responsible for advancing the public good. The acceptance of such responsibility means that managers actively promote social justice, preserve the environment, support social and cultural activities, and take similar stances even if such actions negatively affect profits.

Each stage carries with it an increasing level of managerial discretion. As managers move to the right along the continuum in Figure 5–2, they have to make more judgment calls. At stage 4, they are required to impose their values of right and wrong on society. When is a product, for example, dangerous to society? Is RJR Nabisco doing "right" for society when it markets Oreo cookies but "wrong" when it sells cigarettes? Or perhaps producing cookies with a high sugar content is also wrong? Is a public utility that operates nuclear power plants behaving irresponsibly toward society? Is it wrong for a company to take advantage of all potential tax loopholes, even if this means paying little or no tax on billions of dollars of profits?

FIGURE 5–2
To Whom Is Management Responsible?

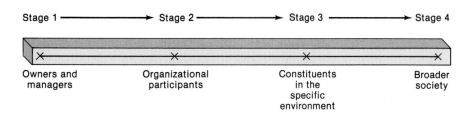

There is no simple right-wrong dichotomy that can help managers to make socially responsible decisions. Clearly, managers of business firms have a basic responsibility to obey the law and make a profit. Failure to achieve either of these goals threatens the organization's survival. Beyond that, managers need to identify to whom they believe they are responsible. We suggest that by focusing on their stakeholders and their expectations of the organization, managers reduce the likelihood that they will ignore their responsibilities to, or alienate, critical constituencies.

MANAGERIAL ETHICS

Is it ethical for a salesperson to offer a bribe to a purchasing agent as an inducement to buy? What if the bribe comes out of the salesperson's commission? Does that make it any different? Is it ethical for someone to understate his or her educational qualifications in order to get a job during hard times if that person would ordinarily be considered overqualified for the job? Is it ethical for someone to use company gasoline for private use? How about using the company telephone for personal long-distance calls? Is it ethical to ask a company secretary to type personal letters?[36]

ethics
The rules and principles that define right and wrong conduct.

Ethics commonly refers to "the rules or principles that define right and wrong conduct."[37] In this section, we want to look at the ethical dimension of managerial decisions. Many decisions that managers make require them to consider who may be affected—in terms of the result as well as the means.[38] We'll present three different views on ethics, look at the factors that influence a manager's ethics, and consider four common rationalizations used to justify unethical behavior. We'll conclude by offering some suggestions for what organizations can do to improve the ethical behavior of employees.

Three Different Views on Ethics

utilitarian view of ethics
Decisions are made solely on the basis of their outcomes or consequences.

There are three different views on ethical standards.[39] The first is the **utilitarian view of ethics,** in which decisions are made solely on the basis of their outcomes or consequences. The goal of utilitarianism is to provide the greatest good for the greatest number. Following the utilitarian view, a manager might conclude that laying off 20 percent of the work force in her plant is justified because it will increase the plant's profitability, improve job security for the remaining 80 percent, and be in the best interest of stockholders.

rights view of ethics
Decisions are concerned with respecting and protecting basic rights of individuals.

Another ethical perspective is the **rights view of ethics.** This position is concerned with respecting and protecting basic rights of individuals such as the rights to free consent, privacy, freedom of conscience, free speech, and due process.[40] In the 1960s, for instance, few organizations had procedures for employees to challenge a disciplinary action taken against them that they felt was unjustified. Today, many organizations have such procedures to guide managers and to offer due process protection for employees.

theory of justice view of ethics
Decision makers seek to impose and enforce rules fairly and impartially.

The final view is the **theory of justice view of ethics.** This calls upon managers to impose and enforce rules fairly and impartially. A theory of justice perspective would be operating when a manager decided to pay a new entry-level employee $1.50 an hour over the minimum wage because she believes that the minimum wage is inadequate to allow employees to meet their basic financial commitments.

It has been found that most businesspeople continue to hold utilitarian attitudes concerning ethical behavior.[41] This shouldn't be totally surprising, since this view is consistent with goals like efficiency, productivity, and high profits. By maximizing profits, for instance, an executive can argue that he or she is securing the greatest good for the greatest number.

That perspective needs to change. Utilitarianism sacrifices the welfare of minorities in the interest of the majority. New trends toward individual rights and social justice mean that managers need ethical standards based on nonutilitarian criteria. This is a solid challenge to today's manager because making decisions using criteria such as individual rights and social justice involves far more ambiguities than using utilitarian criteria such as effects on efficiency and profits. The result, of course, is that managers increasingly find themselves facing ethical dilemmas.

MANAGING FROM A GLOBAL PERSPECTIVE

Ethics in an International Context

In recent years, big-name companies such as Ford, Union Carbide, Motorola, Coca Cola, IBM, and General Motors have decided to end or significantly reduce their presence in South Africa. The reason? The firms oppose the racist policies practiced against South African blacks by the white minority government. These companies intended to place pressure on the South African government to cease its inhuman treatment of black South Africans.

The manager of a Mexican firm bribes several high-ranking government officials in Mexico City to secure a profitable government contract for his firm. Such a practice would be seen as unethical, if not illegal, in the United States, but it's a standard business practice in Mexico.

Should IBM employees in Saudi Arabia adhere to U.S. ethical standards, or should the phrase "When in Rome do as the Romans do" guide them? If Airbus (a European firm) will pay a $10 million "broker's fee" to a middle-man to get a major contract with a Middle Eastern airline, should Boeing or McDonnell Douglas be restricted from doing the same because such practices are considered improper in the United States?

These examples are meant to remind you that social and cultural differences between countries are important environmental factors that define ethical and unethical behavior.

In the case of payments to influence foreign officials or politicians, there is a law to guide U.S. managers. The Foreign Corrupt Practices Act, passed in 1977, makes it illegal for U.S. firms to knowingly corrupt a foreign official. Even this doesn't always reduce ethical problems to black or white. In some Latin American countries, for example, government bureaucrats are paid ridiculously low salaries because custom dictates that they receive small payments from those they serve. These payoffs grease the machinery of government and ensure that things get done. The Foreign Corrupt Practices Act does not expressly outlaw small payoffs to foreign government employees whose duties are primarily ministerial or clerical when such payoffs are an accepted part of a country's business practices.

FIGURE 5–3
Factors Affecting Ethical/Unethical Behavior

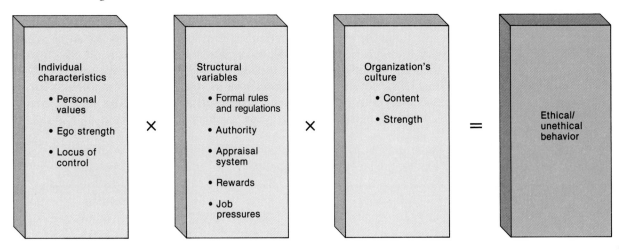

Factors Affecting Managerial Ethics

Whether a manager acts ethically or unethically is the result of a complex interaction between the manager's individual characteristics, the organization's structural design, and the organization's culture.[42] (See Figure 5–3.) People who lack a strong moral sense are much less likely to do wrong things if they are constrained by rules, policies, job descriptions, or strong cultural norms that frown on such behaviors. Conversely, very righteous individuals can be corrupted by an organizational structure and culture that permit or encourage unethical practices.

Individual Characteristics   Every person enters an organization with a relatively entrenched set of **values.** Developed in the early years—from parents, teachers, friends, and others—these values represent basic convictions about what is right and wrong. Thus managers in an organization often possess very different personal values.[43] Two personality variables have also been found to influence an individual's actions according to his or her beliefs about what is right or wrong. They are ego strength and locus of control.

Ego strength is a personality measure of the strength of one's convictions. People who score high on ego strength are likely to resist impulses and follow their convictions more than those who are low on ego strength. That is, individuals high in ego strength are more likely to do what they think is right. We would expect managers with high ego strength to demonstrate more consistency between moral judgment and moral action than those with low ego strength.

Locus of control is a personality attribute that measures the degree to which people believe they are masters of their own fate. People with an internal locus of control believe that they control their own destiny, while those with an external locus believe that what befalls them in life is due to luck or chance. From an ethical perspective, externals are less likely to take personal responsibility for the consequences of their behavior and are more likely to rely on external forces. Internals, on the other hand, are more likely to take responsibility for consequences and rely on their own internal standards of right or wrong to guide their behavior. Managers with an internal locus of control will probably demonstrate more consistency between their moral judgments and moral actions than will "external" managers.

values
Basic convictions about what is right and wrong.

ego strength
A personality characteristic that measures the strength of one's convictions.

locus of control
A personality attribute that measures the degree to which people believe they are masters of their own fate.

Structural Variables   An organization's structural design helps to shape the ethical behavior of managers. Some structures provide strong guidance, while others only create ambiguity for managers. Structural designs that minimize ambiguity and continuously remind managers of what is "ethical" are more likely to encourage ethical behavior.

Formal rules and regulations reduce ambiguity. Job descriptions and written codes of ethics are examples of formal guides that promote consistent behavior. Research continues to indicate that the behavior of superiors is the strongest single influence on an individual's own ethical or unethical behavior.[44] People check to see what those in authority are doing and use that as a bench mark for acceptable practices and what is expected of them. Some performance appraisal systems focus exclusively on outcomes. Others evaluate means as well as ends. Where managers are appraised only on outcomes, there will be increased pressures to do "whatever is necessary" to look good on the outcome variables. Closely associated with the appraisal system is the way rewards are allocated. The more rewards or punishments depend on specific goal outcomes, the more pressure there is on managers to reach those goals and compromise their ethical standards. Structures also differ in the amount of time, competition, cost, and similar pressure they place on job incumbents. The greater the pressure, the more likely that managers will compromise their ethical standards.

Organization's Culture   The content and strength of an organization's culture are the final set of factors that influence ethical behavior.[45]

A culture that is likely to shape high ethical standards is one that is high in risk tolerance, direction, and conflict tolerance. Managers in such a culture will be encouraged to be aggressive and innovative, will have clear objectives and performance expectations to guide them, and will feel free to openly challenge demands or expectations they consider to be unrealistic or personally distasteful.

A strong culture will exert more influence on managers than a weak one. If the culture is strong and supports high ethical standards, it should have a very powerful and positive influence on a manager's ethical behavior. Johnson & Johnson, for example, has a strong culture that has long stressed obligations to customers, employees, the community, and shareholders, in that order. When poisoned Tylenol was found on store shelves, J&J employees across the United States independently pulled the product from these stores. No one had to tell these people what was morally right; they knew what J&J would expect them to do. In a weak culture, however, managers are more likely to rely on subculture norms as a behavioral guide. Work groups and departmental standards will strongly influence ethical behavior in organizations that have weak overall cultures.

Four Common Rationalizations

Saul Gellerman has identified four common rationalizations that, he argues, people have used through the ages to justify questionable conduct.[46] These rationalizations provide some important insights into why managers might make poor ethical choices. They will also help us to understand what organizations can do to reduce unethical practices.

1. "It's Not 'Really' Illegal or Immoral"   Where is the line between being smart and being shady? Between an ingenious decision and an immoral one? Because this line is often ambiguous, people can rationalize that what they've done is not really wrong. As Gellerman notes, if you put enough people in an ill-defined situation, some will conclude that whatever hasn't been labeled specifically wrong must be O.K.—especially if there are rich rewards for attaining certain goals and the organization's appraisal system doesn't look too carefully at how those goals are achieved. The practice of profiting on a stock tip through insider information seems often to fall in this category.

2. "It's in My (or the Organization's) Best Interests"   According to Gellerman, the belief that unethical conduct is in a person's or an organization's best interests nearly always results from a narrow view of what those interests are. Managers can come to believe that it's acceptable to bribe officials if the bribe results in the organization's getting a contract or to falsify financial records if this improves their unit's performance record.[47]

3. "No One Will Find Out"   The third rationalization accepts the wrongdoing but assumes that it will never be uncovered. Philosophers ponder, "If a tree falls in a forest and no one hears it, did it make a noise?" Some managers answer the analogous question, "If an unethical act is committed and no one knows it, is it wrong?" in the negative. This rationalization is often stimulated by inadequate controls, strong pressures to perform, the appraisal of results to the exclusion of assessing how they were achieved, the allocation of big salary increases and promotions to those who achieve these results, and the absence of punishment for those who get caught.

4. "Since It Helps the Organization, the Organization Will Condone It and Protect Me"   Gellerman interprets this response as loyalty gone berserk. Managers come to believe that not only do the organization's interests override the laws and values of society, but also that the organization *expects* its employees to exhibit unqualified loyalty. Even if the manager is caught, he or she believes that the organization will support and reward him or her for showing loyalty. Managers who use this rationalization to justify unethical practices place the organization's good name in jeopardy. In recent years, this seems to be the rationalization that motivated some defense contractor executives to justify labor mischarges, cost duplications, bribery, product substitutions, subcontractor kickbacks, and other contract abuses. While managers should be expected to be loyal to the organization against competitors and detractors, that loyalty shouldn't put the organization above the law, common morality, or society itself.

Toward Improving Ethical Behavior

A number of things can be done if top management seriously wants to reduce unethical practices in its organization. Taken individually, the following suggestions will probably not make much of an impact; but when all or most of them are implemented as part of a comprehensive program, they can greatly improve an organization's ethical climate.

Selection   Given that individuals have different personal value systems and personalities, an organization's employee selection process—interviews, tests, background checks, and the like—should be used to weed out ethically undesirable applicants. This is no easy task. Even under the best of circumstances, individuals with questionable standards of right and wrong will be hired. That, however, is to be expected and needn't be a problem if other controls are imposed. But the selection process should be viewed as an opportunity to learn about an individual's personal values, ego strength, and locus of control. This can then be used to identify individuals whose

Johnson & Johnson corporate credo reads: "Our first responsibility is to the families, doctors, nurses, and patients who use our products everywhere." When the first Tylenol poisoning incident occurred, J&J salespeople were in stores removing Tylenol from the shelves before any formal statement by J&J management. They knew what was right, based on the company's credo.

code of ethics

A formal statement of an organization's primary values and the ethical rules it expects its employees to follow.

ethical standards might be in conflict with those of the organization or who are particularly vulnerable to negative external influences.

Codes of Ethics and Decision Rules   We know, from previously discussed research, that ambiguity about what is ethical can be a problem for employees. Codes of ethics are an increasingly popular response for reducing that ambiguity.[48]

A **code of ethics** is a formal document that states an organization's primary values and the ethical rules it expects its employees to follow. It has been suggested that codes should be specific enough to give employees the spirit in which they're supposed to do things, yet loose enough to allow for freedom of judgment.[49] These suggestions seem to have been applied at McDonnell Douglas, as shown in Figure 5–4.

What do most codes of ethics look like? A survey of eighty-three codes of business ethics including those of such varied firms as Exxon, Sara Lee, DuPont, Bank of Boston, and Wisconsin Electric Power—found that their content tended to fall into three clusters: (1) Be a dependable organizational citizen, (2) do not do anything unlawful or improper that will harm the organization, and (3) be good to customers.[50] Table 5–5 on page 139 lists the variables included in each of these clusters in order of their frequency of mention. However, another study of 202 codes from Fortune 500 corporations suggests that many are not as effective as they might be because they omit important issues.[51] Seventy-five percent, for example, fail to address personal character matters, product safety, environmental affairs, product quality, or civic and community affairs. In contrast, more than three-quarters mentioned issues such as relations with the U.S. government, customer/supplier relations, political contributions, and conflicts of interest. Authors of this study concluded that "codes are really dealing with infractions against the corporation, rather than illegalities on behalf of the corporation."[52] That is, codes tend to give most attention to areas of illegal or unethical conduct that are likely to decrease a company's profits.[53]

FIGURE 5—4

McDonnell Douglas' Code of Ethics

McDonnell Douglas' Code of Ethics

Integrity and ethics exist in the individual or they do not exist at all. They must be upheld by individuals or they are not upheld at all. In order for integrity and ethics to be characteristics of McDonnell Douglas, we who make up the corporation must strive to be:

- Honest and trustworthy in all our relationships.
- Reliable in carrying out assignments and responsibilities.
- Truthful and accurate in what we say and write.
- Cooperative and constructive in all work undertaken.
- Fair and considerate in our treatment of fellow employees, customers, and all other persons.
- Law abiding in all our activities.
- Committed to accomplishing all tasks in a superior way.
- Economical in utilizing company resources.
- Dedicated in service to our company and to improvement of the quality of life in the world in which we live.

Integrity and high standards of ethics require hard work, courage, and difficult choices. Consultation among employees, top management, and the Board of Directors will sometimes be necessary to determine a proper course of action. Integrity and ethics may sometimes require us to forego business opportunities. In the long run, however, we will be better served by doing what is right than what is expedient.

Source: Courtesy of McDonnell Douglas Corporation.

Robert West, Chairman and CEO of Butler Manufacturing, states, "We have a published policy on business conduct. We update it regularly, distribute it to all of our salaried employees, and ask them to sign an acknowledgement that they have read it. Then if there are breaches of that policy, justice is swift and sure. It happens rarely, but we have terminated corporate officers."

TABLE 5–5   Clusters of Variables Found in 83 Corporate Codes of Business Ethics

Cluster 1. Be a Dependable Organizational Citizen.

1. Comply with safety, health, and security regulations.
2. Demonstrate courtesy, respect, honesty, and fairness.
3. Illegal drugs and alcohol at work are prohibited.
4. Manage personal finances well.
5. Exhibit good attendance and punctuality.
6. Follow directives of supervisors.
7. Do not use abusive language.
8. Dress in businesslike attire.
9. Firearms at work are prohibited.

Cluster 2. Do Not Do Anything Unlawful or Improper That Will Harm the Organization.

1. Conduct business in compliance with all laws.
2. Payments for unlawful purposes are prohibited.
3. Bribes are prohibited.
4. Avoid outside activities that impair duties.
5. Maintain confidentiality of records.
6. Comply with all antitrust and trade regulations.
7. Comply with accounting rules and controls.
8. Do not use company property for personal benefit.
9. Employees are personally accountable for company funds.
10. Do not propagate false or misleading information.
11. Make decisions without regard for personal gain.

Cluster 3. Be Good to Customers.

1. Convey true claims in product advertisements.
2. Perform assigned duties to the best of your ability.
3. Provide products and services of the highest quality.

Source: Fred R. David, "An Empirical Study of Codes of Business Ethics: A Strategic Perspective." Paper presented at the 48th Annual Academy of Management Conference. Anaheim, California; August 1988.

In isolation, ethical codes are not likely to be much more than public relations statements. Their effectiveness depends heavily on whether management supports them and how employees who break the codes are treated. When management considers them to be important, regularly reaffirms their content, and publicly reprimands rule breakers, codes can supply a strong foundation for an effective ethics program.

Another approach that uses formal written statements to guide behavior has been suggested by Laura Nash.[54] She proposes twelve questions that act as decision rules to guide managers in handling ethical dimensions in decision making. These questions are listed in Table 5–6.

TABLE 5–6   Twelve Questions for Examining the Ethics of a Business Decision

1. Have you defined the problem accurately?
2. How would you define the problem if you stood on the other side of the fence?
3. How did this situation occur in the first place?
4. To whom and to what do you give your loyalty as a person and as a member of the corporation?
5. What is your intention in making this decision?
6. How does this intention compare with the probable results?
7. Whom could your decision or action injure?
8. Can you discuss the problem with the affected parties before you make the decision?
9. Are you confident that your position will be as valid over a long period of time as it seems now?
10. Could you disclose without qualm your decision or action to your boss, your chief executive officer, the board of directors, your family, society as a whole?
11. What is the symbolic potential of your action if understood? If misunderstood?
12. Under what conditions would you allow exceptions to your stand?

Source: Reprinted by permission of *Harvard Business Review.* An exhibit from "Ethics Without the Sermon" by Laura L. Nash, November–December 1981, p. 81. Copyright © 1981 by the President and Fellows of Harvard College; all rights reserved.

Top Management's Leadership   Codes of ethics require a commitment from top management. Why? Because it's the top managers who set the cultural tone. They are role models in terms of both words and actions—though what they do is probably more important than what they say. If top managers, for example, use company resources for their personal use, inflate their expense accounts, give favored treatment to friends, or conduct similar practices, they imply that such behavior is acceptable for all employees.

Top management also sets the cultural tone by its reward and punishment practices. The choice of who and what are rewarded with pay increases and promotions sends a strong message to employees. The promotion of a manager for achieving impressive results in questionable ways indicates to everyone that those questionable ways are acceptable. When it uncovers wrongdoing, management must not only punish the wrongdoer but publicize the fact and make the outcome visible for all to see. This sends another message: "Doing wrong has a price, and it's *not* in your best interest to act unethically!"

Job Goals   Employees should have tangible and realistic goals. Explicit goals can create ethical problems if they make unrealistic demands on employees. Under the stress of unrealistic goals, otherwise ethical employees will often take the attitude that "anything goes." On the other hand, when goals are clear and realistic, they reduce ambiguity for employees and motivate rather than punish.

Ethics Training   Organizations, especially those that have had previous problems with improper employee conduct, are increasingly setting up seminars, workshops, and similar training programs. As part of Citicorp's comprehensive corporate-ethics training program, for instance, managers participate in a game that allows them to practice their understanding of the company's ethical standards.[55] Players move markers around a game board by correctly answering multiple-choice questions presented

Jack S. Llewellyn, President and CEO of Ocean Spray, believes that the CEO has to be the model for ethical standards. "It's like the Marine Corps: The leader has to be able to do everything the rest of the troops do, and he has to be able to do it better. I don't think written policy statements are worth anything. Managers will treat customers and workers fairly if the CEO does."

on cards. Each card poses an ethical dilemma a bank employee might encounter. As the game progresses, players are "promoted" from entry-level employee to supervisor and eventually to senior manager.

As an example, one question asks: "After successfully completing a complex deal for a Japanese client, he presents you with a vase to express his appreciation. It's an expensive item, and accepting a gift of such value is clearly against Citicorp policy. Yet returning it would insult your client." Would you: (a) return the vase to the client and explain diplomatically that it's against Citicorp policy to accept gifts from clients; (b) accept the gift because you can't risk insulting an important client; (c) accept the gift on behalf of Citicorp, log it with premises management as a furnishing, and display it in a public area of the office; (d) accept the gift and use it as an award for an employee who displays service excellence? (Citicorp, by the way, likes answer "c.") Another question asks: "What if the manager of a competing bank calls to suggest colluding on interest rates?" If the player picks "ask to meet him and discuss it further," that player is "fired for cause" and is out of the game!

Ethical training sessions can provide a number of benefits. They reinforce the organization's standards of conduct. They're a reminder that top management wants participants to consider ethical issues in their decisions. They clarify what practices are and are not permissible. Finally, when managers discuss common concerns among themselves, they become reassured that they aren't alone in facing ethical dilemmas. This can strengthen their confidence when they have to take unpopular but ethically correct stances.

Comprehensive Performance Appraisal   When performance appraisals focus only on economic goal outcomes, ends will begin to justify means. If an organization wants its managers to uphold high ethical standards, it *must* include this dimension in its appraisal process. For example, a manager's annual review might include a point-by-point evaluation of how his or her decisions stacked up against the organization's code of ethics as well as on the more traditional economic criteria. Needless to say, if the manager looks good on the economic criteria but scores poorly on ethical conduct, appropriate penalties need to be enacted.

Independent Social Audits   An important deterrent of unethical behavior is fear of being caught. Independent audits, which evaluate decisions and management practices in terms of the organization's code of ethics, increase the probability of detection. These audits can be routine evaluations, performed on a regular basis as are financial audits, or they can occur at random, with no prior announcement. An effective ethical program should probably include both. To maintain integrity, the auditors should be responsible to, and present their findings directly to, the organization's board of directors. This not only gives the auditors clout but lessens the opportunity for retaliation from those being audited.

Formal Protective Mechanisms   Our last recommendation is for organizations to provide formal mechanisms so that employees who have ethical dilemmas can do something about them without fear of reprimand.

An organization might, for instance, designate ethical advisors. When employees face a dilemma, they could go to an advisor for guidance. The ethical advisor's role would first be as a sounding board, a channel to let employees openly verbalize their ethical problem, what's causing it, and their options. Then, after the options are clear, the advisor might take the role of an advocate who promotes the "right" alternatives. The organization might also create a special appeals process that employees could use without risk to themselves to raise ethical questions or blow the whistle on violators.

A FINAL THOUGHT

If you picked up a twenty-year-old management text, it's almost certain that you would not find a chapter on social responsibility and ethics. If you even found the terms in the text, they wouldn't receive more than a paragraph of attention. What has happened to bring about this evolution?

One line of thinking is that the recent focus on these topics is a response to a *decline* in business's willingness to accept its societal responsibilities and in the ethical standards of managers. For instance, a Gallup poll reported that 65 percent of Americans thought that the overall levels of ethics in society declined between the mid-1970s and mid-1980s.[56] Experts in the role of business in society see it another way.[57] They contend that managers are *more* socially conscious and ethical than their counterparts of a generation ago. What has happened, as illustrated in Figure 5–5, is that the demands on business and expectations of what is considered "proper conduct" have risen faster than the ability of business to raise its standards.

Society's expectations of business have changed. Cornelius Vanderbilt's famous phrase "the public be damned" was accepted by many in the 1890s. It certainly is not acceptable in the 1990s. It was acceptable for Cleveland steel plants to pollute Lake Erie in the 1950s, but not so today.

FIGURE 5–5
Social Responsibility and Ethics Over Time

Source: Reprinted with permission of Macmillan Publishing Company from *Social Responsibility of Management* by Archie B. Carroll. (New York: Macmillan Publishing Company, 1984), p. 14.

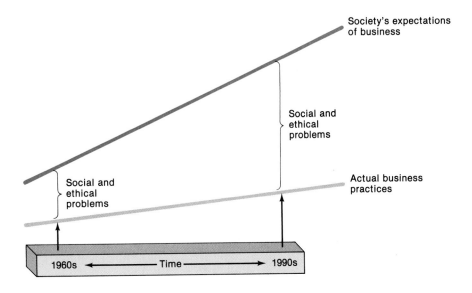

This observation has implications for managers. Since society's expectations of its institutions are regularly undergoing change, managers must continually monitor these expectations. What is ethically acceptable today may be a poor guide for the future.

SUMMARY

This summary is organized by the chapter-opening learning objectives found on page 117.

1. According to the classical view, business's social responsibility is to maximize financial returns for stockholders. The opposing socioeconomic view holds that business has a responsibility to the larger society.

2. The arguments for business being socially responsible include public expectations, long-run profits, ethical obligation, public image, a better environment, discouraging further government regulations, balancing of responsibility and power, stockholder interests, possession of resources, and the superiority of prevention over cures. The arguments against hold that social responsibility violates the profit-maximization objective, dilutes the organization's purpose, costs too much, gives business too much power, requires skills that business doesn't have, lacks accountability, and lacks wide public support.

3. Social responsibility refers to business's pursuit of long-term goals that are good for society. Social responsiveness refers to the capacity of a firm to respond to social pressures. The former requires business to determine what is right or wrong and thus seek fundamental ethical truths, while the latter is guided by social norms.

4. Business firms often pursue one of three strategies in responding to a changing social environment. They can adapt after the fact, manipulate the environment for their advantage, or anticipate environmental change and adapt accordingly.

5. Most research studies show a positive relationship between corporate social involvement and economic performance. The evidence does *not* find that acting in a socially responsible way significantly reduces a corporation's long-term economic performance.

6. To whom is management responsible? That is the critical question in defining management's social responsibilities. By focusing on the organization's stakeholders and their expectations of the organization, management is less likely to ignore its responsibilities to critical constituencies.

7. Ethics refers to the rules or principles that define right and wrong conduct.

8. The utilitarian view seeks to provide the greatest good for the greatest number. The rights view seeks to respect and protect basic rights of individuals. The theory of justice view seeks to achieve fair and impartial outcomes.

9. Whether a manager acts ethically or unethically is the result of a complex interaction between the manager's individual characteristics, the organization's structural design, and the organization's culture.

10. A comprehensive ethical program would include selection to weed out ethically undesirable applicants, a code of ethics and decision rules, a commitment by top management, clear and realistic job goals, ethics training, comprehensive performance appraisals, independent social audits, and formal protective mechanisms.

REVIEW QUESTIONS

1. Why is the social responsibility of business receiving so much more attention today than in the 1940s or 1950s?

2. According to the socioeconomic view of social responsibility, what are the flaws in the classical view?

3. Contrast *social responsibility* and *social responsiveness*. Which is more theoretical? Why?

4. How are social involvement and strategy linked?

5. What is *cause-related marketing?* Is it socially responsible in the classical view?

6. Who are an organization's *stakeholders?*

7. Which of the three views on ethics is most popular among businesspeople? Why?

8. Explain the factors that affect managerial ethics. What can management do to influence each factor?

9. What behaviors are most likely to be mentioned as prohibited by an organization's code of ethics? Which are most likely not to be mentioned?

10. Over the past twenty years, has business become less willing to accept its societal responsibilities? Explain.

DISCUSSION QUESTIONS

1. What does social responsibility mean to you? Do you think business firms should be socially responsible? Why?

2. Discuss this statement: "In the long run, those who do not use power in a way that society considers responsible will tend to lose it."

3. What are some ethical issues that you have faced in college? How did you resolve them?

4. "Companies that promote women are good, but those that exploit women are bad. While Playboy Enterprises has a woman president, its photographs and stories may be regarded as exploitive." What ethical issues are involved in this statement?

5. "The business of business is business." Review this statement from the (a) classical view and (b) socioeconomic view.

SELF-ASSESSMENT EXERCISE

What's Your Ethical Orientation in Decision Making?

Instructions: For each of the following items, circle either answer A or B.

1. Peoples' actions should be described in terms of . . .
   A. good or bad.
   B. right or wrong.

2. When making an ethical decision, one should pay attention to . . .
   A. one's conscience.
   B. others' needs, wants, and desires.

3. Solutions to ethical problems are usually . . .
   A. some shade of grey.
   B. black or white.

4. It is of more value to societies to . . .
   A. follow stable traditions and maintain a distinctive identity.
   B. be responsive and adapt to new conditions as the world changes.

5. When thinking through ethical problems, I prefer to . . .
   A. think up practical, workable alternatives.
   B. make reasonable distinctions and clarifications.

6. When people disagree over ethical matters, I strive for . . .
   A. some point(s) of agreement.
   B. workable compromises.

7. Uttering a falsehood is wrong because . . .
   A. depending on the results, it can lead to further problems.
   B. it wouldn't be right for anyone to lie.

8. Thinking of occupations, I would rather be a . . .
   A. wise judge, applying the law with fairness and impartiality.
   B. benevolent legislator, seeking an improved life for all.

9. I would rather be known as a person who . . .
   A. has accomplished a lot and achieved much.
   B. has integrity and is a person of principle.

10. The aim of science should be . . .
    A. to discover truth.
    B. to solve existing problems.

11. Whether a person is a liar is . . .
    A. a matter of degree.
    B. a question of kind.

12. A nation should pay more attention to . . .
    A. its heritage, its roots.
    B. its future, its potential.

13. It is more important to be . . .
    A. happy.
    B. worthy.

14. Unethical behavior is best described as . . .
    A. violation of principle or law.
    B. causing some degree of harm.

15. The purpose of government should be . . .
    A. to promote the best possible life for its citizens.
    B. to secure justice and fair treatment.

Turn to page 670 for scoring directions and key.

Source: F. Neil Brady and Penny L. Wright, "Testing the Empirical Strength of the Ethical Distinction Between Utilitarians and Formalists." Working paper. San Diego State University, 1988.

CASE APPLICATION 5A

An Ethical Dilemma

Yours is a small service unit of only six people in a large firm, and you all work at top speed to keep up.[58] One of your best employees has indicated that she is eager to move up to a first-level supervisory position, but your boss tells you that because of escalating costs, you will not be able to replace anyone on your staff, no matter how much extra work this puts on the rest of your group.

A week later you hear on the grapevine that a first-line supervisory job is opening in the materials division, and you decide to check with the director of materials. As you enter the reception area outside his office, you hear the voice of the company vice president saying, "Not only is my son a good prospect technically, but it has always been this company's practice to encourage the hiring of employees' relatives." This nepotism might affect your ability to get your employee the job; but complaining about it might hurt you.

Questions

1. What would you do?
2. Why?

CASE APPLICATION 5B

Ben and Jerry's Homemade Inc.

In the summer of 1978, Ben Cohen and Jerry Greenfield opened an ice cream parlor in a renovated Burlington, Vermont gas station.[59] Their goals were to make and sell super-premium ice cream and to have fun doing it. During the next ten years, Ben & Jerry's Homemade Inc. grew into a $45 million a year business with 150 employees. In spite of its success, Ben & Jerry's is not your typical business firm. Some examples help to demonstrate why.

- The company gives 7.5 percent of its pretax income to the Ben & Jerry's Foundation. That money is used for a broad array of causes, including parent-child programs and small business for youth.
- The company provides free ice cream to any nonprofit company in Vermont that requests it.
- No executive can earn more than five times what the lowest-paid employee makes. If senior managers want higher salaries, they have to raise the lowest salaries.
- The company actively hires the handicapped.
- The company provides free therapy sessions—including anonymous drug and alcohol counseling—to any employee who needs it.

- There is a changing table for babies in the men's room as well as in the women's room.
- During a recent occasion, when production employees had to work long overtime hours to meet increased demand, the company hired a masseuse to give workers massages during their breaks.

Questions

1. "Because they produce a product that is a known contributor to heart disease, Ben & Jerry's is inherently an irresponsible firm." Do you agree or disagree? Discuss.
2. Is Ben & Jerry's socially responsible, socially responsive, or something else? Explain.
3. What would Milton Friedman say about Ben & Jerry's business practices?
4. Would you invest your money in their company or would you prefer to invest in another manufacturer of super-premium ice cream that followed more utilitarian practices? Explain.

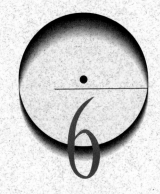

6

DECISION MAKING: THE ESSENCE OF THE MANAGER'S JOB

LEARNING OBJECTIVES

After Reading
This Chapter,
You Should
Be Able To:

1. Outline the steps in the decision-making process.
2. Define the rational decision maker.
3. Explain the limits to rationality.
4. Describe the perfectly rational decision-making process.
5. Describe the boundedly rational decision-making process.
6. State the two types of decision problems.
7. Identify the two types of decisions.
8. Differentiate certainty, risk, and uncertainty decision conditions.
9. Identify the advantages and disadvantages of group decisions.
10. Describe three techniques for improving group decision making.

erb Kelleher, chairman of Southwest Airlines, made the decision to remove the closets at the front of his firm's planes.[1] He didn't do it to gain more seats. Rather, he did it to improve the speed with which passengers board and depart. Since all Southwest planes operate with open seating, the first people on the plane typically went to the closets first and then grabbed the nearest seats. Upon landing, departing passengers were held up while the people in the front rows rummaged through the closets for their bags.

As Kelleher put it, the removal of the closets was just one of "1,000 small decisions, all designed to achieve simplicity." Some of the other decisions he made to achieve this goal of simplicity included no meals, no reserved or first-class seats, the use of reusable boarding passes, and making no connections with other airlines.

Kelleher seems to know what he's doing. Customers like Southwest's low fares and on-time schedules. The airline turns around nearly 85 percent of its flights in fifteen minutes or less and is one of the most profitable major airlines, with a remarkable 16 percent average return on equity over the past eight years.

Herb Kelleher, like all managers, makes a lot of decisions—some small and some large. The one common denominator in these decisions is that they all require making choices. In this chapter, we look at this thing called "decision making."

Since its birth as a tiny Texas commuter airline in 1971, Herb Kelleher has built Southwest Airlines into the ninth-largest airline by devoting enormous attention to thousands of small decisions.

THE DECISION-MAKING PROCESS

decision-making process
A set of eight steps that include formulating a problem, selecting an alternative, and evaluating the decision's effectiveness.

Decision making is typically described as "choosing among alternatives." But this view is overly simplistic. Why? Because decision making is a *process* rather than the simple act of choosing among alternatives.

Figure 6–1 illustrates the **decision-making process** as a set of eight steps that begins with formulating a problem, moves to selecting an alternative that can alleviate the problem, and concludes with evaluating the decision's effectiveness. This process is as applicable to your personal decision about where you're going to take your

FIGURE 6–1
The Decision-Making Process

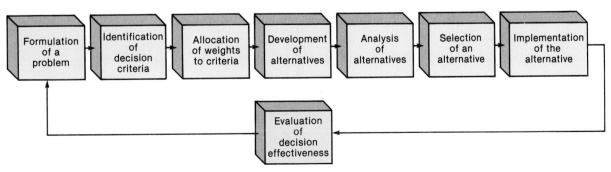

summer vacation as it is to a corporate action such as Hershey Foods' decision to introduce a new candy bar. The process can also be used to describe both individual and group decisions. Let's take a closer look at the process in order to understand what each step encompasses.

Step 1: Formulating a Problem

problem
A discrepancy between an existing and a desired state of affairs.

The decision-making process begins with the existence of a **problem** or, more specifically, a discrepancy between an existing and a desired state of affairs.[2] Let's develop an example that illustrates this point and that we can use throughout this section. For the sake of simplicity, let's make the example something most of us can relate to: the decision to buy a new car. Take the case of the manager of a manufacturing plant whose company car just blew its engine. Again, for simplicity's sake, assume that it's uneconomic to repair the car and that corporate headquarters requires plant managers to buy new cars rather than lease them. So now we have a problem. There is a disparity between the manager's desire to have a car that runs and the fact that his current one doesn't.

Unfortunately, this example doesn't tell us much about how managers identify problems. In the real world, most problems don't come with neon signs identifying them as such. While a blown engine might be a clear signal to the plant manager that he or she needs a new car, few problems are so obvious. Is a 5 percent decline in sales a *problem*? Or are declining sales merely a *symptom* of another problem, such as product obsolescence or an inadequate advertising budget? Also, keep in mind that one manager's "problem" is another manager's "satisfactory state of affairs." Problem identification is a subjective interpretation. Furthermore, the manager who mistakenly solves the *wrong* problem perfectly is likely to perform just as poorly as the manager who fails to identify the *right* problem and does nothing. Problem identification is neither a simple nor an unimportant part of the decision-making process.[3]

Before something can be characterized as a problem, managers have to be aware of the discrepancy, they have to be under pressure to take action, and they must have the necessary resources to take action.[4]

How do managers become aware that they have a discrepancy? They obviously have to make a comparison between their current state of affairs and some standard. What is that standard? It can be past performance, previously set goals, or the performance of some other unit within the organization or in other organizations. In our car-buying example, the standard is a previously set goal: having a car that runs.

But a discrepancy without pressure becomes a problem that can be put off to some future time. To initiate the decision process, then, the problem must be such that it exerts some type of pressure on the manager to act. Pressure might include organizational policies, deadlines, financial crises, expectations from the boss, or an upcoming performance evaluation.

Finally, managers aren't likely to characterize something as a problem if they perceive that they don't have the authority, money, information, or other resources necessary to act on it. When managers perceive a problem and are under pressure to act, but feel they have inadequate resources, they usually describe the situation as one in which unrealistic expectations are being placed upon them.

Step 2: Identifying Decision Criteria

decision criteria
Criteria that define what is relevant in a decision.

Once a manager has identified a problem that needs attention, the **decision criteria** that will be important in solving the problem must be identified. That is, what's relevant in the decision?

TABLE 6–1 Criteria and Weight in Car Replacement Decision

Criteria	Weight
Initial price	10[a]
Interior comfort	8
Durability	5
Repair record	5
Performance	3
Handling	1

[a]In this example, the highest rating for a criterion is 10 points.

In our car-buying example, the plant manager has to assess what factors are relevant in his decision. These might include criteria such a price, model (two-door or four-door), size (compact or intermediate), manufacturer (foreign or domestic), optional equipment (automatic transmission, air conditioning, and so on), and repair records. These criteria reflect what the plant manager thinks is relevant in his decision.

Whether explicitly stated or not, every decision maker has criteria that guide his or her decision. Note that in this step in the decision-making process, what is *not* listed is as important as what *is*. If the plant manager doesn't consider fuel economy to be a criterion, then it will not influence his final choice of car. Thus if a decision maker does not identify a particular criterion in this second step, then it's treated as irrelevant to the decision maker.

Step 3: Allocating Weights to the Criteria

The criteria listed in the previous step are not all equally important. It's necessary, therefore, to weight the items listed in Step 2 in order to give them the correct priority in the decision.

How does the decision maker weight criteria? A simple approach is merely to give *the* most important criterion a weight of ten and then assign weights to the rest against this standard. Thus, in contrast to a criterion that you gave a five, the highest-rated factor would be twice as important. Of course, you could begin by assigning 100 or 1,000 as the highest weight. Nevertheless, the idea is to use your personal preferences to assign a priority to the relevant criteria in your decision as well as to indicate their degree of importance by assigning a weight to each.

Table 6–1 lists the criteria and weights that our plant manager developed for his car replacement decision. Price is the most important criterion in his decision, with factors like performance and handling having low weights.

Step 4: Developing Alternatives

The fourth step requires the decision maker to list the viable alternatives that could succeed in resolving the problem. No attempt is made in this step to appraise these alternatives, only to list them. Let's assume that our plant manager has identified nine cars as viable choices. They are shown in Table 6–2.

When you made your decision on what college to attend, you might have considered factors such as location, size of the school, admission requirements, cost, availability of financial assistance, required courses, male-female ratio, prestige, where your best friend was applying, and the like. But these criteria were not all equally important in your final decision. That is, they might all have been relevant, but some were more relevant than others. For instance, some high school seniors consider cost and availability of financial assistance to be the crucial factors in their decision. They might prefer to go to school away from home, but cost considerations are more compelling.

TABLE 6–2   Alternatives in Car Replacement Decision

Chevrolet Lumina
Eagle Premier LX
Ford Taurus GL
Honda Accord LX
Hyundai Sonata GLS
Mazda 626 DX
Nissan Maxima GXE
Plymouth Acclaim
Volvo 740GL

Step 5: Analyzing Alternatives

Once the alternatives have been identified, the decision maker must critically analyze each one. The strengths and weaknesses of each alternative become evident as they are compared with the criteria and weights established in Steps 2 and 3.

Each alternative is evaluated by appraising it against the criteria. Table 6–3 shows the assessed values that the plant manager put on each of his nine alternatives after he had test-driven each car.

Keep in mind that the ratings given the nine cars shown in Table 6–3 are based on the assessment made by the plant manager. Again, we are using a 1 to 10 scale. Some assessments can be achieved in a relatively objective fashion. For instance, the purchase price represents the best price the manager can get from local dealers, and

TABLE 6–3   Assessment of the Nine Alternatives Against the Decision Criteria

	Criteria					
Alternatives	**Initial Price**	**Interior Comfort**	**Durability**	**Repair Record**	**Performance**	**Handling**
Chevrolet Lumina	7	8	5	6	8	7
Eagle Premier LX	8	8	4	5	6	6
Ford Taurus GL	7	10	5	6	6	8
Honda Accord LX	7	5	9	10	5	7
Hyundai Sonata GLS	8	5	5	4	4	3
Mazda 626 DX	7	4	7	8	7	8
Nissan Maxima GXE	7	5	7	7	10	10
Plymouth Acclaim	10	5	4	3	4	3
Volvo 740GL	5	6	10	10	5	7

consumer magazines report data from owners on frequency of repairs. But the assessment of handling is clearly a personal judgment. The point is that most decisions contain judgments. They are reflected in the criteria chosen in Step 2, the weights given to the criteria, and the evaluation of alternatives. This explains why two car buyers with the same amount of money may look at two totally different sets of alternatives or even look at the same alternatives and rate them so dissimilarly.

Table 6–3 represents only an assessment of the nine alternatives against the decision criteria. It does not reflect the weighting done in Step 3. If one choice had scored 10 on every criterion, you wouldn't need to consider the weights. Similarly, if the weights were all equal, you could evaluate each alternative merely by summing up the appropriate lines in Table 6–3. For instance, the Nissan Maxima would have a score of 46 and the Ford Taurus a score of 42. If you multiply each alternative assessment against its weight, you get Table 6–4. The summation of these scores represents an evaluation of each alternative against the previously established criteria and weights. Notice that, in terms of our example, the weighting of the criteria has significantly changed the ranking of alternatives. The Maxima, for instance, has gone from first to a tie for third. In spite of being first on two of the six criteria, the Maxima scored highest on the criteria that the plant manager placed lowest in importance. Similarly, the Volvo scored highest on two criteria, but its high initial price worked against it.

TABLE 6–4   Assessment of Car Alternatives

	Criteria						
Alternatives	**Initial Price**	**Interior Comfort**	**Durability**	**Repair Record**	**Performance**	**Handling**	**Totals**
Chevrolet Lumina	70	64	25	30	24	7	= 220
Eagle Premier LX	80	64	20	25	18	6	= 213
Ford Taurus GL	70	80	25	30	18	8	= 231
Honda Accord LX	70	40	45	50	15	7	= 227
Hyundai Sonata GLS	80	40	25	20	12	3	= 180
Mazda 626 DX	70	32	35	40	21	8	= 206
Nissan Maxima GXE	70	40	35	35	30	10	= 220
Plymouth Acclaim	100	40	20	15	12	3	= 190
Volvo 740GL	50	48	50	50	15	7	= 220

Step 6: Selecting an Alternative

The sixth step is the critical act of choosing the best alternative from among those enumerated and assessed. Since we have determined all the pertinent factors in the decision, allocated to them an appropriate importance weighting, and identified the viable alternatives, we merely have to choose the alternative that generated the highest score in Step 5. In our car purchase example (Table 6–4), the decision maker would choose the Ford Taurus. On the basis of the criteria identified, the weights given to the criteria, and the decision maker's assessment of each car's achievement on the criteria, the Taurus scored highest and thus became the "best" alternative.

Step 7: Implementing the Alternative

While the choice process is completed in the previous step, the decision may still fail if it is not implemented properly. Therefore, Step 7 is concerned with putting the decision into action.

implementation
Conveying a decision to those affected and getting their commitment to it.

Implementation includes conveying the decision to those affected and getting their commitment to it. As we'll demonstrate later in this chapter, groups or committees can help a manager achieve commitment. If the people who must carry out a decision participate in the process, they are more likely to endorse enthusiastically the outcome. (Parts III through V of this book detail how decisions are implemented by effective planning, organizing, and leading.)

Step 8: Evaluating Decision Effectiveness

The last step in the decision-making process appraises the result of the decision to see whether it has corrected the problem. Did the alternative chosen in Step 6 and implemented in Step 7 accomplish the desired result? The evaluation of such results is detailed in Part VI of this book, where we look at the control function.

What happens if, as a result of this evaluation, the problem is found to still exist? The manager needs then to dissect carefully what went wrong. Was the problem incorrectly defined? Were errors made in the evaluation of the various alternatives? Was the right alternative selected but improperly implemented? Answers to questions like these might send the manager back to one of the earlier steps. It might even require starting the whole decision process anew.

THE PERVASIVENESS OF DECISION MAKING

The importance of decision making to every facet of a manager's job cannot be overstated. As Table 6–5 illustrates, decision making permeates all four managerial functions. In fact, this explains why managers—when they plan, organize, lead, and control—are frequently called *decision makers*. So it is not incorrect to say that decision making is synonymous with managing.[5]

The fact that almost everything a manager does involves decision making does not mean that decisions are always long, involved, or clearly evident to an outside observer. Much of a manager's decision-making activity is of a routine nature. You make a decision every day of the year to deal with the problem of when to eat lunch. It's no big deal. You've made the decision thousands of times before. It offers few problems and can usually be handled quickly. It's the type of decision you almost

TABLE 6–5
Examples of Decisions in the Management Functions

Planning

What are the organization's long-term objectives?
What strategies will best achieve these objectives?
What should the organization's short-term objectives be?
How difficult should individual goals be?

Organizing

How many subordinates should I have report directly to me?
How much centralization should there be in the organization?
How should jobs be designed?
When should the organization implement a different structure?

Leading

How do I handle employees who appear to be low in motivation?
What is the most effective leadership style in a given situation?
How will a specific change affect worker productivity?
When is the right time to stimulate conflict?

Controlling

What activities in the organization need to be controlled?
How should these activities be controlled?
When is a performance deviation significant?
What type of management information system should the organization have?

forget *is* a decision. Managers make dozens of these routine decisions every day. Keep in mind that even though a decision seems easy to make or has been faced by a manager a number of times before, it is nonetheless a decision.

THE RATIONAL DECISION MAKER

rational
Describes choices that are consistent and value-maximizing within specified constraints.

Managerial decision making is assumed to be **rational.** By that we mean that managers make consistent, value-maximizing choices within specified constraints.[6] In this section, we want to take a close look at the underlying assumptions of rationality and then determine how valid these assumptions actually are.

Assumptions of Rationality

A decision maker who was perfectly rational would be fully objective and logical. He or she would define a problem carefully and would have a clear and specific goal. Moreover, the steps in the decision-making process would consistently lead toward selecting the alternative that maximizes that goal. (See Figure 6–2.) The following list summarizes the assumptions of rationality.

Problem clarity. In rational decision making, the problem is clear and unambiguous. The decision maker is assumed to have complete information regarding the decision situation.

FIGURE 6–2
Assumptions of Rationality

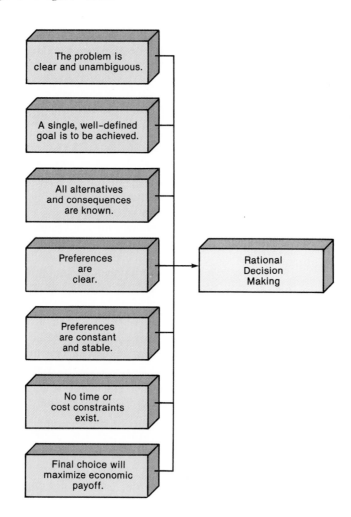

Goal orientation. In rational decision making there is no conflict over the goal. Whether the decision involves purchasing a new car, selecting a college to attend, choosing the proper price for a new product, or picking the right applicant to fill a job vacancy, the decision maker has a single, well-defined goal that he or she is trying to reach.

Known options. It is assumed that the decision maker is creative, can identify all the relevant criteria, and can list all the viable alternatives. Further, the decision maker is aware of all the possible consequences for each alternative.

Clear preferences. Rationality assumes that the criteria and alternatives can be ranked according to their importance.

Constant preferences. In addition to a clear goal and preferences, it is assumed that the specific decision criteria are constant and that the weights assigned to them are stable over time.

No time or cost constraints. The rational decision maker can obtain full information about criteria and alternatives because it is assumed that there are no time or cost constraints.

Maximum payoff. The rational decision maker always chooses the alternative that will yield the maximum economic payoff.

These assumptions of rationality apply to any decision. However, since we're concerned with managerial decision making in an organization, we need to add one further assumption. Rational managerial decision making assumes that decisions are made in the economic best interests of the organization. That is, the decision maker is assumed to be maximizing the *organization's* interests, not the interests of the decision maker.

ETHICAL DILEMMAS IN MANAGEMENT

Should Social Responsibility Play a Factor in the Decision to Relocate a Plant or Headquarters' Office?

In the 1960s, Bethlehem Steel employed 26,000 people in the small town of Lackawanna, New York. Today, it is still the town's largest employer with only 1300 people. In 1979, U.S. Steel (now USX Corp.) employed more than 26,000 in the Monongahela Valley of Western Pennsylvania. After closing three mills, the number of employees is now under 4,000. R.J. Reynolds Tobacco was the dominant employer in Winston-Salem, North Carolina, for much of this century. When the tobacco firm absorbed Nabisco Brands in 1987, the thousands of company headquarters personnel were uprooted from Winston-Salem and moved to Atlanta. In 1989, RJR Nabisco again relocated its corporate headquarters, this time from Atlanta to New York City.

Relocating plants and corporate headquarters can be devastating to small towns and even to large cities if the organization is a major employer.[7] Homestead, Pennsylvania, for instance, is one of the small towns in the Monongahela Valley that has been permanently altered as a result of USX's 1986 decision to close its mammoth Homestead Works plant, which once employed 15,000 steelworkers. Most of the former USX workers in their mid-40s or older who have found work are underemployed in part-time, low-paying jobs. Mental and physical problems are extremely common in the community. Police and other services have been drastically cut as the tax base has disappeared. Most of the stores in town are now closed and boarded up.

Many communities incur very high expenditures to entice and appease large employers. They build roads, schools, and hospitals for corporations and their personnel. They provide police and fire protection. Other businesses, of course, open up to service the needs of the corporation, its workers, and their families. The decision by management to relocate out of such communities—as experienced by places like Lackawanna, Homestead, and Winston-Salem—can bring economic devastation to towns and whole regions.

Management can respond by arguing that it brought more to the relationship than the community gave back—specifically, high-paying jobs that allowed the community to grow and prosper—and that, in today's global economy, hometown loyalties cannot override economic considerations.

Should social responsibility play a factor in management's decision to relocate a plant or headquarters office? What do *you* think?

Limits to Rationality

Managerial decision making *can* follow rational assumptions. If a manager is faced with a simple problem in which the goals are clear and the alternatives few, in which the time pressures are minimal and the cost of searching out and evaluating alternatives is low, for which the organizational culture supports innovation and risk taking, and in which the outcomes are relatively concrete and measurable, the decision process is likely to follow the assumptions of rationality.[8] But most decisions that managers face don't meet all these tests.

Hundreds of studies have sought to improve our understanding of managerial decision making.[9] Individually, these studies often challenge one or more of the assumptions of rationality. Taken together, they suggest that decision making often veers from the logical, consistent, and systematic process that rationality implies. Let us examine some important insights that researchers have uncovered about the decision-making process:

1. There are limits to an individual's information-processing capacity.[10] Most people are able to hold in short-term memory only about seven pieces of information. When decisions become complex, individuals tend to create simple models that allow them to reduce the problem to understandable dimensions.

2. Decision makers tend to intermix solutions with problems.[11] The definition of a problem often includes a rough description of an acceptable solution. This clouds the objectivity of both the alternative-generation stage and the alternative-evaluation stage of the decision process.

3. Perceptual biases can distort problem identification.[12] We know that "except in detective stories, the facts don't speak for themselves; they must be interpreted."[13] The decision maker's background, position in the organization, interests, and past experiences focus his or her attention on certain problems and not others. The organization's culture can also distort a manager's perceptions: "Managers sometimes don't see what they believe can't be there."[14]

4. Many decision makers select information more for its accessibility than for its quality.[15] Important information, therefore, may carry less weight in a decision than information that is easy to get.

5. Decision makers tend to commit themselves prematurely to a specific alternative early in the decision process, thus biasing the process toward choosing that alternative.[16]

6. Evidence that a previous solution is not working does not always generate a search for new alternatives. Instead, it frequently initiates an **escalation of commitment** whereby the decision maker further increases the commitment of resources to the previous course of action in an effort to demonstrate that the initial decision was not wrong.[17]

7. Prior decision precedents constrain current choices.[18] Decisions are rarely simple, discrete events. They are more aptly described as points in a stream of choices. Most decisions are really an accumulation of subdecisions made over long periods of time.

8. Organizations are made up of divergent interests that make it difficult, even impossible, to create a common effort toward a single goal. Decisions are therefore rarely directed toward achieving an overall organizational goal. Instead, there is a constant bargaining among managers, who perceive problems differently and prefer different alternatives.[19] The existence of divergent interests ensures that there will be differences in goals, alternatives, and consequences. Bargaining is needed to achieve compromise and support for implementing the final solution. Consequently, "where you stand depends on where you sit."[20] In ambiguous and

escalation of commitment
An increased commitment to a previous decision in spite of negative information.

contradictory situations, decisions are largely the outcome of power and political influences.[21]

9. Organizations place time and cost constraints on decision makers, which, in turn, limit the amount of search that a manager can undertake.[22] Thus, new alternatives tend to be sought in the neighborhood of old ones.[23]

10. In spite of the potential for diversity, a strong conservative bias exists in most organizational cultures.[24] Most organizational cultures reinforce the status quo, which discourages risk taking and innovation. In such cultures, employees are frequently rewarded for being "team players" and for not "making waves," and wrong choices have more of an impact on a decision maker's career than does the

IN PRACTICE

Looking Forward to *Rocky XXVI*

Critics enjoy attacking the major motion picture studios, television networks, and book publishers for their lack of creativity. They charge that these industries are the great "copycats."

If a movie succeeds, there is never any trouble getting money to produce a sequel. *Jaws* spurred *Jaws II. Star Wars* initiated *Return of the Jedi* and *The Empire Strikes Back. Raiders of the Lost Ark* initiated both imitators and sequels. And don't forget the *Rocky, Superman, Star Trek,* James Bond, *Rambo, Friday the 13th,* and *Police Academy* series.

A successful television show almost always generates new shows of a similar kind. *Dallas* begat *Knots Landing.* The *Cosby Show* begat *A Different World. Donahue* begat *Oprah, Geraldo,* and *Sally Jessy Raphael.*

Watch the list of best-selling books. *In Search of Excellence* opened the door to the publication of dozens of business management books. Lee Iacocca and Chuck Yeager's autobiographies started an onslaught of other autobiographies. Jane Fonda's workout book has spawned at least three dozen imitators. The realities of publishing are such that Stephen King, Danielle Steele, and James Michener get million-dollar advances on new projects even if their books occasionally bomb.

Is this tendency to go with the "tried and proven" a chance occurrence? Of course not! It reflects the risk aversiveness of executives in these industries. The cost of failure is great in any decision to back a new motion picture, television series, or mass-marketed book. There are literally millions of dollars on the line. That risk cannot be avoided. However, by doing spin-offs and rip-offs of what has already proven successful, when the eventual failure comes, the managers who made the decision can always claim, "Look at the previous projects, just like this one, that have succeeded!" Truly creative decisions—going with the unusual or unique project—run counter to the culture of most large entertainment organizations.

development of new ideas. So decision makers spend more effort trying to avoid mistakes than in developing innovative ideas.

Bounded Rationality

Do these limits to rationality mean that managers ignore the eight-step decision process we described at the beginning of this chapter? Not necessarily. Why? Because in spite of the limits to perfect rationality, managers are expected to appear to follow the rational process.[25] Managers know that "good" decision makers are *supposed* to do certain things: identify problems, consider alternatives, gather information, and act decisively but prudently. Managers can thus be expected to exhibit the correct decision-making behaviors. By doing so, managers signal to their superiors, peers, and subordinates that they are competent and that their decisions are the result of intelligent and rational deliberation.

Table 6–6 summarizes how the perfectly rational manager should proceed through the eight-step decision process. It also describes an alternative model: one followed by a manager operating under assumptions of **bounded rationality**.[26] In bounded rationality, managers construct simplified models that extract the essential features from problems without capturing all their complexity. Then, given information-processing limitations and constraints imposed by the organization, managers attempt to behave rationally within the parameters of the simple model. The result is a **satisficing** decision rather than a maximizing one, that is, a decision in which the solution is "good enough."

The implications of bounded rationality on the manager's job cannot be overlooked. In situations in which the assumptions of perfect rationality do not apply (including many of the most important and far-reaching decisions that a manager makes), the details of the decision-making process are strongly influenced by the decision maker's self-interest, the organization's culture, internal politics, and power considerations. As you'll see in future chapters, the disparity between the perfectly rational view of how managers *should* make decisions and the bounded rationality description of how managers *actually* make them often explains the instances when management practice deviates from management theory.

bounded rationality

Behavior that is rational within the parameters of a simplified model that captures the essential features of a problem.

satisficing

Acceptance of solutions that are "good enough."

PROBLEMS AND DECISIONS: A CONTINGENCY APPROACH

The *type* of problem a manager faces in a decision-making situation often determines how that problem is treated. In this section we present a categorization scheme for problems and for types of decisions. Then we show how the type of decision a manager uses should reflect the characteristics of the problem.

Types of Problems

Some problems are straightforward. The goal of the decision maker is clear, the problem familiar, and the information about the problem easily defined and complete. Examples might include a customer wanting to return a purchase to a retail store, a supplier being late with an important delivery, a newspaper having to respond to an unexpected and fast-breaking news event, or a college's handling of a student

TABLE 6–6
Two Views of the Decision-Making Process

Decision-Making Step	Perfect Rationality	Bounded Rationality
1. Problem formulation	An important and relevant organizational problem is identified.	A visible problem that reflects the manager's interests and background is identified.
2. Identification of decision criteria	All criteria are identified.	A limited set of criteria are identified.
3. Allocation of weights to criteria	All criteria are evaluated and rated in terms of their importance to the organization's goal.	A simple model is constructed to evaluate and rate the criteria; the decision maker's self-interest strongly influences the ratings.
4. Development of alternatives	A comprehensive list of all alternatives is developed creatively.	A limited set of similar alternatives is identified.
5. Analysis of alternatives	All alternatives are assessed against the decision criteria and weights; the consequences for each alternative are known.	Beginning with a favored solution, alternatives are assessed, one at a time, against the decision criteria.
6. Selection of an alternative	*Maximizing decision:* the one with the highest economic outcome (in terms of the organization's goal) is chosen.	*Satisficing decision:* the search continues until a solution is found that is satisfactory and sufficient, at which time the search stops.
7. Implementation of alternative	Since the decision maximizes the single, well-defined goal, all organizational members will embrace the solution.	Politics and power considerations will influence the acceptance of, and commitment to, the decision.
8. Evaluation	The decision's outcome is objectively evaluated against the original problem.	Measurement of the decision's results are rarely so objective as to eliminate self-interests of the evaluator; possible escalation of resources to prior commitments in spite of previous failures and strong evidence that allocation of additional resources is not warranted.

well-structured problems
Straightforward, familiar, easily defined problems.

ill-structured problems
New problems in which information is ambiguous or incomplete.

who seeks to drop a class. Such situations are called **well-structured problems.** They align closely with the assumptions underlying perfect rationality.

Many situations faced by managers, however, are **ill-structured problems.** They are new or unusual. Information about such problems is ambiguous or incomplete. The selection of an architect to design a new corporate headquarters building is one example. So too is the decision to invest in a new, unproven technology.

Types of Decisions

Just as problems can be dissected into two categories, so too can decisions. As we will show, *programmed,* or routine, decision making is the most efficient way to handle well-structured problems. However, when problems are ill-structured, managers must rely on *nonprogrammed* decision making in order to develop unique solutions.

programmed decision
A repetitive decision that can be handled by a routine approach.

Programmed Decisions   A waitress in a restaurant spills a drink on a customer's coat. The restaurant manager has an upset customer. What does the manager do? Since such occurrences are not infrequent, there is probably some standardized routine for handling the problem. For example, if it is the waitress's fault, if the damage is significant, and if the customer has asked for a remedy, the manager offers to have the coat cleaned at the restaurant's expense. This is a **programmed decision.**

Decisions are programmed to the extent that they are repetitive and routine and to the extent that a definite approach has been worked out for handling them. Because the problem is well-structured, the manager does not have to go to the trouble and expense of working up an involved decision process. Programmed decision making is relatively simple and tends to rely heavily on previous solutions. The "develop-the-alternatives" stage in the decision-making process is either nonexistent or given little attention. Why? Because once the structured problem is defined, its solution is usually self-evident or at least reduced to very few alternatives that are familiar and that have proven successful in the past. In many cases, programmed decision making becomes decision making by precedent. Managers simply do what they and others have done in the same situation. The spilled drink on the customer's coat does not require the restaurant manager to identify and weigh decision criteria nor develop a long list of possible solutions. Rather, the manager falls back on a systematic procedure, rule, or policy.

procedure
A series of interrelated sequential steps that can be used to respond to a structured problem.

A **procedure** is a series of interrelated sequential steps that a manager can use for responding to a structured problem. The only real difficulty is in identifying the problem. Once the problem is clear, so is the procedure. For instance, a purchasing manager receives a request from accounting for five desktop printing calculators that can perform a certain set of functions. The purchasing manager knows that there is a definite procedure for handling this decision. Has the requisition been properly filled out and approved? If not, send the requisition back with a note explaining what is deficient. If the request is complete, the approximate costs are estimated. If the total exceeds $5,000, three bids must be obtained. If the total is $5,000 or less, only one vendor need be identified and the order placed. The decision-making process in this case is merely the executing of a simple series of sequential steps.

rule
An explicit statement that tells managers what they ought or ought not to do.

A **rule** is an explicit statement that tells a manager what he or she ought or ought not to do. Rules are frequently used by managers when they confront a well-structured problem because they are simple to follow and ensure consistency. In the illustration above, the $5,000 cutoff rule simplifies the purchasing manager's decision about when to use multiple bids. Similarly, rules about lateness and absenteeism permit supervisors to make discipline decisions rapidly and with a relatively high degree of fairness.

policy
A guide that establishes parameters for making decisions.

A third guide for making programmed decisions is a **policy.** It provides guidelines to channel a manager's thinking in a specific direction. In contrast to a rule, a policy establishes parameters for the decision maker rather than specifically stating what should or should not be done. As an analogy, think of the Ten Commandments as rules, whereas the U.S. Constitution is a policy. The latter requires judgment and interpretation; the former do not.

Policies typically contain an ambiguous term that leaves interpretation to the decision maker. For instance, each of the following is a policy statement: "The customer shall always be *satisfied.*" "We promote from within, *whenever possible.*" "Employee wages shall be *competitive* for the community in which our plants are located." Notice that *satisfied, whenever possible,* and *competitive* are terms that require interpretation. The policy to pay competitive wages does not tell a given plant's personnel manager what he or she should pay, but it does give direction to the decision he or she will make. If other firms in the community are paying between $6.70 and $8.50 an hour for unskilled labor, the decision to set hourly rates at $6.40 or $9.00 would clearly not be within the guidelines set by company policy.

Nonprogrammed Decisions   Deciding whether or not to merge with another organization, how to restructure an organization to improve efficiency, or whether to close a money-losing division are examples of **nonprogrammed decisions.** Such decisions are unique and nonrecurring. When a manager confronts an ill-structured problem or one that is novel, there is no cut-and-dried solution. It requires a custom-made response.

The creation of a marketing strategy for a new product represents an example of a nonprogrammed decision. It will be different from previous marketing decisions because the product is new, a different set of competitors exists, and other conditions that may have existed when previous products were introduced years earlier have changed. IBM's introduction in the early 1980s of a personal computer was unlike any other marketing decision the company had previously made. Certainly, IBM had a wealth of experience selling computers. It also had previously sold to small businesses and general consumers through its typewriter division. But it had no substantive experience in mass-marketing relatively low-cost personal computers. It faced aggressive competitors like Apple, Hewlett-Packard, and Digital Equipment. The needs and sophistication of personal computer customers differed from those of buyers who purchased multimillion-dollar systems for their corporate headquarters. The hundreds of decisions that went into IBM's marketing strategy for personal computers had never been made before and thus were clearly of the nonprogrammed variety.

Integration

Figure 6–3 describes the relationship between the types of problems, the types of decisions, and level in the organization. Well-structured problems are responded to with programmed decision making. Ill-structured problems require nonprogrammed decision making. Lower-level managers essentially confront familiar and repetitive problems; therefore, they most typically rely on programmed decisions such as standard operating procedures. However, the problems confronting managers are more likely to become ill-structured as the managers move up the organizational hierarchy. Why? Because lower-level managers handle the routine decisions themselves and pass upward only decisions that they find unique or difficult. Similarly, managers pass down routine decisions to their subordinates in order to spend their time on more problematic issues.

Few managerial decisions in the real world are either fully programmed or nonprogrammed. These are extremes, with most decisions falling somewhere in between.

nonprogrammed decisions
Unique decisions that require a custom-made solution.

FIGURE 6–3
Types of Problems, Types of Decisions, and Level in the Organization

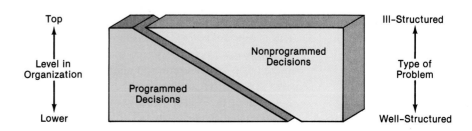

MANAGERS WHO MADE A DIFFERENCE

Jeffrey Jordan of Pepsi-Cola South

Jeffrey Jordan joined Pepsi-Cola in 1987 as a project manager at its corporate headquarters in New York, fresh with his new MBA from Harvard.[27] Only 26 at the time, he served as liaison between a group of Pepsi-Cola bottling plants and corporate headquarters. After a year in New York, he was named production/warehouse manager at Pepsi's Houston plant where he oversees a budget of nearly $30 million. Jordan heads the production of 2-liter, 16-liter, and 20-ounce bottles. Additionally, he is responsible for supplying and overseeing inventory at nine warehouses in Southern Texas.

Among his accomplishments at the Houston plant has been successfully converting the 16-ounce, nonrefillable package line with cardboard cases to 2-inch plastic returnable trays. While this might not sound like a critical job, it was. If his decisions proved faulty, Pepsi could have lost millions of dollars in sales. Jordan had to coordinate the build-up of inventory, decide what products to produce, and how much and when to produce them while the line was down. He also had to coordinate the inventory with satellite warehouses to make sure they didn't run out of soda while the line was being automated.

Jordan proved up to the conversion task. He deftly juggled schedules and switched employees among production lines. He also successfully quelled the fears of workers who were intimidated by the new computerized line.

Photo courtesy of Jeffrey Jordan.

Few programmed decisions are designed to completely eliminate individual judgment. At the other extreme, even the most unique situation requiring a nonprogrammed decision can be helped by programmed routines. It is best to think of decisions as *mainly* programmed or *mainly* nonprogrammed, rather than as fully one or the other.

A last point on this topic is that organizational efficiency is facilitated by the use of programmed decision making, which may explain its wide popularity. Wherever possible, management decisions are likely to be programmed. Obviously, this is not too realistic at the top of the organization, since most of the problems that top management confronts are of a nonrecurring nature. But there are strong economic incentives for top management to create standard operating procedures (SOPs), rules, and policies to guide other managers.

Programmed decisions minimize the need for managers to exercise discretion. This is relevant because discretion costs money. The more nonprogrammed decision making a manager is required to do, the greater the judgment needed. Since sound judgment is an uncommon quality, it costs more to acquire the services of managers who possess this ability.

Consider the following: One multibillion-dollar corporation has controllers (chief accounting managers) at each of its more than three dozen plants throughout the

United States. The controllers typically have three to six supervisors reporting to them and are responsible for staffs of twenty-five to fifty. How much do you think those controllers earn? Would it surprise you to learn that, in 1990, most were earning within a thousand dollars of $35,000 a year? This seems extremely low compensation for such responsibilities, but the company has succeeded in making almost all of the controller's decisions highly programmed. Most of the controllers have only a high school education. They are not exceedingly talented. However, they can follow directions. The company has produced a 4,000-page accounting manual, which is continually updated. The manual tells each controller specifically how almost any problem he or she encounters should be handled. If the problem and the procedure for handling it cannot be found, the controller is instructed to call the head office, which will instruct the controller in what to do. Not surprisingly, calls to the head office concerning new problems are typically followed a month or so later by an addition to the manual to guide other plant controllers who might confront this same problem.

In this corporation, the high-priced talent makes all the nonprogrammed accounting decisions at the head office. When these problems become recurring ones, they write up SOPs and distribute them to all plant controllers. In this way, the company is able to get consistent and competent decision making without having to hire experienced individuals with a college education, possibly a master's degree, and a C.P.A. certificate, who would command an annual salary of $60,000 or more.

It should be mentioned that other areas in this company—purchasing, personnel, quality control—also have plant manuals that are regularly updated by their respective staffs at the head office.

Of course, some organizations try to economize by hiring less-skilled managers without developing programmed decision guides for them to follow. For example, the author is familiar with a small women's clothing store chain whose owner, because he chooses to pay low salaries, hires store managers with little experience and limited ability to make good judgments. This, in itself, needn't be a problem. The trouble is that the owner provides neither training nor explicit rules and procedures to guide the decisions of his store managers. The result has been continuous complaints by customers about things like promotional discounts, processing credit sales, and the handling of returns.

ANALYZING DECISION ALTERNATIVES

One of the more challenging tasks facing a manager is analyzing decision alternatives (Step 5 in the decision-making process). This section discusses approaches for analyzing alternatives under three different conditions: certainty, risk, and uncertainty.

Certainty

certainty
A situation in which a manager can make accurate decisions because the outcome from every alternative is known.

The ideal situation for making decisions is one of **certainty;** that is, the manager is able to make perfectly accurate decisions because the outcome from every alternative is known. As you might expect, this is *not* the situation in which most decisions are made. It is more idealistic than pragmatic.

Risk

risk
Those conditions in which the decision maker has to estimate the likelihood of certain outcomes.

A far more relevant situation is one of **risk.** By risk, we mean those conditions in which the decision maker has to estimate the likelihood of certain alternatives or outcomes. This ability to assign probabilities to outcomes may be the result of personal experience or secondary information. However, under the conditions of risk,

TABLE 6–7   Expected Value for Revenues from the Addition of One Ski Lift

Event	Revenues	×	Probability	=	Expected Value of Each Alternative
Heavy snowfall	$850,000		0.3		$255,000
Normal snowfall	725,000		0.5		362,500
Light snowfall	350,000		0.2		70,000
Expected revenues					$687,500

the manager has historical data that allow him or her to assign probabilities to different alternatives. Let's look at an example.

Suppose that you manage a ski resort in the Colorado Rockies. You are contemplating whether to add another lift to your current facility. Obviously, your decision will be significantly influenced by the amount of additional revenue that the new lift would generate, and this will depend on the level of snowfall. The decision is made somewhat clearer when you are reminded that you have reasonably reliable past data on snowfall levels in your area. The data indicate that during the past ten years, you received three years of heavy snowfall, five years of normal snow, and two years of light snow. Can you use this information to determine the expected future annual revenue if the new lift is added? If you have good information on the amount of revenues for each level of snow, the answer is Yes.

You can create an expected value formulation; that is, you can compute the conditional return from each possible outcome by multiplying expected revenues by probabilities. The result is the average revenue that can be expected over time if the given probabilities hold. As Table 6–7 shows, the expected revenue from adding a new ski lift is $687,500. Of course, whether that justifies a positive or negative decision would depend on the costs involved in generating this revenue—factors such as the cost of erecting the lift, the additional annual maintenance expenses for another lift, the interest rate for borrowing money, and so forth.

uncertainty
A situation in which a decision maker has neither certainty nor reasonable probability estimates available.

Uncertainty

What happens if we have to make a decision when neither certainty nor reasonable probability estimates are available? We call such a condition **uncertainty,** and choice will be influenced by the psychological orientation of the decision maker. The optimistic manager will follow a *maximax* choice (maximizing of the maximum possible payoff), the pessimist will pursue a *maximin* choice (maximizing the minimum possible payoff), while the manager who desires to minimize his maximum "regret" will opt for a *minimax* choice.

Consider the case of the marketing manager at Citibank in New York. He has determined four possible strategies for promoting Citibank's Mastercard throughout the Northeast. But the marketing manager is also aware that his major competitor, Chase Manhattan, has three competitive actions of its own for promoting its Visa card in the same region. In this case, we will assume that the Citibank executive has no previous knowledge that would allow him to place probabilities on the success of any of his four strategies. With these facts, the Citibank manager has formulated the matrix in Table 6–8 to show the various Citibank strategies and the resulting profit to Citibank depending on the competitive action chosen by Chase Manhattan.

In this example, if our Citibank manager is an optimist, he will choose S_4 because that will produce the largest possible gain: $28 million. Note that this choice maximizes the maximum possible gain.

TABLE 6–8   Payoff Matrix (in millions of dollars)

Citibank Marketing Strategies	Chase Manhattan's Response		
	CA_1	CA_2	CA_3
S_1	13	14	11
S_2	9	15	18
S_3	24	21	15
S_4	18	14	28

But if our manager is a pessimist, he will assume that only the worst can occur. The worst outcome for each strategy is as follows: $S_1 = 11$; $S_2 = 9$; $S_3 = 15$; $S_4 = 14$. These are the most pessimistic outcomes from each strategy. Following the maximin choice, he would maximize the minimum payoff; that is, he would select S_3.

The third approach recognizes that once a decision is made, it will not necessarily result in the most favorable payoff. This implies regret of profits forgone on the part of the manager, regret being defined as the payoff for each strategy under every competitive action subtracted from the most favorable payoff that is possible with the occurrence of the particular event. For our Citibank manager, the highest payoff, given that Chase engages in CA_1, CA_2, CA_3, is $24 million, $21 million, and $28 million, respectively (the highest number in each column). Subtracting the payoffs in Table 6–8 from these figures produces the results shown in Table 6–9.

The maximum regrets are: $S_1 = 17$; $S_2 = 15$; $S_3 = 13$; and $S_4 = 7$. Since the minimax choice minimizes the maximum regret, our Citibank manager would choose S_4. By making this choice, he will never have a regret of profits forgone of more than $7 million. This contrasts, for example, with a regret of $15 million had he chosen S_2 and Chase Manhattan taken CA_1. In such a case, he would regret that he had not taken S_3, for then he would have made $24 million.

GROUP DECISION MAKING

Many decisions in organizations, especially important ones that have a far-reaching impact on organizational activities and personnel, are made in groups. It's a rare organization that doesn't, at some time, use committees, task forces, review panels, study teams, and similar groups as vehicles for making decisions. Studies tell us that managers spend up to 40 percent or more of their time in meetings.[28] Undoubtedly, a large portion of that time is involved with formulating problems, arriving at solutions to those problems, and determining the means for implementing solutions. It's possi-

TABLE 6–9   Regret Matrix (in millions of dollars)

Citibank Marketing Strategies	Chase Manhattan's Response		
	CA_1	CA_2	CA_3
S_1	11	7	17
S_2	15	6	10
S_3	0	0	13
S_4	6	7	0

ble, in fact, for groups to be assigned any of the eight steps in the decision-making process.

In this section, we'll look at the advantages and disadvantages of both group and individual decision making, identify when groups should be preferred, and review the more popular techniques for improving group decision making.

Advantages and Disadvantages

Individual and group decisions each have their own set of strengths. Neither is ideal for all situations. Let's begin by reviewing the *advantages* that group decisions have over individual decisions.

1. *Provides more complete information.* There is often truth to the axiom that two heads are better than one. A group will bring a diversity of experience and perspectives to the decision process that an individual, acting alone, cannot.

2. *Generates more alternatives.* Because groups have a greater quantity and diversity of information, they can identify more alternatives than can an individual. This is most evident when group members represent different specialities. For instance, a group made up of representatives from engineering, accounting, production, marketing, and personnel will generate alternatives that reflect their diverse backgrounds. Such a multiplicity of "world views" often yields a greater array of alternatives.

3. *Increases acceptance of a solution.* Many decisions fail after the final choice has been made because people do not accept the solution. However, if the people who will be affected by a certain solution and who will help implement it get to participate in the decision making itself, they will be more likely to accept the decision and to encourage others to accept it. Participation in the process increases the commitment and motivation of those who will carry out the decision. Group members are reluctant to fight or undermine a decision they have helped develop.

4. *Increases legitimacy.* Our society fosters democratic methods. The group decision-making process is consistent with democratic ideals and therefore may be perceived as more legitimate than decisions made by a single person. The fact that the decision maker has complete power and has not consulted others can create a perception that a decision was made autocratically and arbitrarily.

If groups are so good, how did the phrase "A camel is a racehorse put together by a committee" become so popular? The answer, of course, is that group decisions are not without their drawbacks. The major *disadvantages* of group decision making are as follows.

1. *Time consuming.* It takes time to assemble a group. Additionally, the interaction that takes place once the group is in place is frequently inefficient. The result is that groups almost always take more time to reach a solution than an individual making the decision alone.

2. *Minority domination.* Members of a group are never perfectly equal. They may differ in terms of rank in the organization, experience, knowledge about the problem, influence with other members, verbal skills, assertiveness, and the like. This creates the opportunity for one or more members to use their advantages to dominate others in the group. A minority that dominates a group frequently has an undue influence on the final decision.

3. *Pressures to conform.* There are social pressures in groups. The desire of group members to be accepted and considered assets to the group can quash any overt disagreement and encourage conformity among viewpoints.

4. *Ambiguous responsibility.* Group members share responsibility, but who is actually responsible for the final outcome? In an individual decision, it is clear who is responsible. In a group decision, the responsibility of any single member is watered down.

Effectiveness and Efficiency

Whether groups are more effective than individuals depends on the criteria you use for defining effectiveness. In terms of *accuracy,* group decisions tend to be more accurate. The evidence indicates that, on the average, groups make better decisions than individuals.[29] This doesn't mean, of course, that *all* groups outperform *every* individual. Rather, group decisions have been found to be better than those that would have been reached by the average individual in the group. However, they are seldom better than the performance of the best individual.

If decision effectiveness is defined in terms of *speed,* individuals are superior. Group decision processes are characterized by give and take, which consumes time.

Effectiveness may mean the degree to which a solution demonstrates *creativity.* If creativity is important, groups tend to be more effective than individuals. This requires, however, that the forces that foster groupthink be constrained (see "In Practice" box). In the next section, we'll review several remedies for the groupthink ailment.

The final criterion for effectiveness is the degree of *acceptance* the final solution achieves. As was previously noted, because group decisions have input from more people, they are likely to result in solutions that will be more widely accepted.

The effectiveness of group decision making is also influenced by the size of the group. The larger the group, the greater the opportunity for heterogeneous representation. On the other hand, a larger group requires more coordination and more time to allow all members to contribute. What this means is that groups probably should not be too large: a minimum of five to a maximum of about fifteen. Evidence indicates,

Organizations need to consider the advantages and disadvantages to both individual and group decisions. For instance, group decisions generate more information and more alternatives, as well as increasing solution acceptance and legitimizing the final choice. However, they are time consuming, create the opportunity for minority domination, create pressures to conform, and cloud responsibility.

in fact, that groups of five and, to a lesser extent, seven are the most effective.[30] Because five and seven are odd numbers, strict deadlocks are avoided. These groups are large enough for members to shift roles and withdraw from embarrassing positions but still small enough for quieter members to participate actively in discussions.

Effectiveness should not be considered without also assessing efficiency. In terms of efficiency, groups almost always stack up a poor second to the individual decision maker. With few exceptions, group decision making consumes more work hours than does individual decision making. Exceptions occur when, to achieve comparable quantities of diverse input, the individual decision maker must spend a great deal of time reviewing files and talking to people. Because groups can include members from diverse areas, they can spend less time searching for information. However, as we noted, such decisions tend to be the exception. Generally, groups are less efficient than individuals. In deciding whether to use groups, then, primary consideration must be given to assessing whether increases in effectiveness are more than enough to offset the losses in efficiency.

IN PRACTICE   Groupthink

groupthink
The withholding by group members of different views in order to appear in agreement.

Have you ever not understood something in a class but refrained from asking the instructor for clarification because you thought you were the only one who was confused, only to learn later, in discussion with other class members, that they too were confused? You undoubtedly interpreted the silence to mean that everyone understood what the instructor had said. Of course, silence might mean nothing of the kind. In groups, especially when there are strong pressures to give the appearance of agreement, silence is typically interpreted as agreement.

What you experienced is what Irving Janis has called **groupthink**.[31] This is a form of conformity in which group members withhold deviant, minority, or unpopular views in order to give the appearance of agreement. It can undermine critical thinking in the group and eventually the quality of the final decision. The symptoms of groupthink are as likely to be seen in a corporate board meeting as in a classroom.

1. Group members rationalize any resistance to the assumptions they have made. No matter how much the evidence may contradict their basic assumptions, members behave so as to continually reinforce those assumptions.

2. Members directly pressure those who momentarily express doubts about any of the group's shared views or who question the validity of arguments supporting the alternative favored by the majority.

3. Members who have doubts or hold differing points of view seek to avoid deviating from what appears to be group consensus by keeping silent about misgivings and even minimizing to themselves the importance of their doubts.

4. There is an illusion of unanimity. If someone does not speak, it is assumed that he or she is in full accord. In other words, abstention becomes viewed as a "yes" vote.

In brainstorming sessions, one idea stimulates others. Since judgment of even the most bizarre suggestions is withheld until later, this technique encourages group members to "think the unusual."

Techniques for Improving Group Decision Making

When members of a group physically confront and interact with one another, they create the potential for groupthink. They can censor themselves and pressure other group members into agreement. Three ways of making group decision making more creative have been suggested: the brainstorming, nominal group, and Delphi techniques.

brainstorming
An idea-generating process that encourages alternatives while withholding criticism.

Brainstorming **Brainstorming** is a relatively simple technique for overcoming pressures for conformity that retard the development of creative alternatives.[32] It does this by utilizing an idea-generating process that specifically encourages any and all alternatives while withholding any criticism of those alternatives.

In a typical brainstorming session, a half-dozen to a dozen people sit around a table. The group leader states the problem in a clear manner so that it is understood by all participants. Members then "free-wheel" as many alternatives as they can in a given time. No criticism is allowed, and all the alternatives are recorded for later discussion and analysis.

Brainstorming, however, is merely a process for generating ideas. The next two techniques go further by offering ways to arrive at a preferred solution.[33]

nominal group technique
A group decision-making technique in which members are present but operate independently.

Nominal Group Technique The nominal group restricts discussion during the decision-making process, hence the term **nominal group technique.** Group members are all physically present, as in a traditional committee meeting, but the members are required to operate independently. Specifically, the following steps take place:

1. Members meet as a group; but before any discussion takes place, each member independently writes down his or her ideas on the problem.

2. This silent period is followed by each member presenting one idea to the group. Each member takes his or her turn, going around the table, presenting one idea at a time until all ideas have been presented and recorded (typically on a flip chart or chalkboard). No discussion takes place until all ideas have been recorded.

3. The group now discusses the ideas for clarity and evaluates them.

MANAGING FROM A GLOBAL PERSPECTIVE

The Effect of National Culture on Decision-Making Styles

The way decisions are made (whether by group, participatively, or autocratically by an individual manager) and the degree of risk a decision maker is willing to take are just two examples of decision variables that reflect a country's cultural environment. Decision making in Japan, for instance, is much more group-oriented than in the United States, and characteristics of the Japanese national culture can explain why.[34]

The Japanese value conformity and cooperation. One can see this in their schools as well as their business organizations. Before making decisions, Japanese CEOs collect a large amount of information, which is then used in consensus-forming group decisions. Since employees in Japanese organizations have high job security, managerial decisions take a long-term perspective rather than focusing on short-term profits as practiced by most managers in the United States.

Senior managers in other nations—such as France, West Germany, and Sweden—also adapt their decision styles to their country's culture. In France, for instance, autocratic decision making is widely practiced, and managers avoid risks. Managerial styles in West Germany reflect the German culture's concern for structure and order. There are extensive rules and regulations in West German organizations. Managers have well-defined responsibilities and accept that decisions must go through channels. Decision styles of Swedish managers differ considerably from those of their French and German counterparts. Managers in Sweden are more aggressive; they take the initiative with problems and are not afraid to take risks. Senior managers in Sweden also push decisions down in the ranks. They encourage lower-level managers and employees to take part in decisions that affect them.

These examples are meant to remind you that managers need to modify their decision styles to reflect the national culture of the country in which they live as well as to reflect the organizational culture of the firm in which they work.

4. Each group member silently and independently assigns a rank to the ideas. The final decision is determined by the idea with the highest aggregate ranking.

The chief advantage of this technique is that it permits the group to meet formally but does not restrict independent thinking as so often happens in the traditional interacting group.

Delphi technique

A group decision-making technique in which members never meet face to face.

Delphi Technique   A more complex and time-consuming alternative is the **Delphi technique,** which is similar to the nominal group technique except that it does not require the physical presence of the group members. This is because the Delphi technique never allows the group members to meet face to face. The following steps characterize the Delphi technique:

1. The problem is identified, and members are asked to provide potential solutions through a series of carefully designed questionnaires.

2. Each member anonymously and independently completes the first questionnaire.

3. Results of the first questionnaire are compiled at a central location, transcribed, and reproduced.

4. Each member receives a copy of the results.

5. After viewing the results, members are again asked for their solutions. The results typically trigger new solutions or cause changes in the original position.

6. Steps 4 and 5 are repeated as often as necessary until consensus is reached.

Like the nominal group technique, the Delphi technique insulates group members from the undue influence of others. It also does not require the physical presence of the participants. So, for instance, Minolta could use the technique to query its sales managers in Tokyo, Hong Kong, Paris, London, New York, Toronto, Mexico City, and Melbourne as to the best worldwide price for one of the company's new cameras. The cost of bringing the executives together at a central location is avoided, yet input is obtained from Minolta's major markets. Of course, the Delphi technique has its drawbacks. The method is extremely time-consuming. It is frequently not applicable when a speedy decision is necessary. Further, the method might not develop the rich array of alternatives that the interacting or nominal groups do. The ideas that might surface from the heat of face-to-face interaction might never arise.

SUMMARY

This summary is organized by the chapter-opening learning objectives found on page 151.

1. Decision making is an eight-step process: (1) formulation of a problem, (2) identification of decision criteria, (3) allocation of weights to the criteria, (4) development of alternatives, (5) analysis of alternatives, (6) selection of an alternative, (7) implementation of the alternative, and (8) evaluation of decision effectiveness.

2. The rational decision maker is assumed to have a clear problem, have no goal conflict, know all options, have a clear preference ordering, keep all preferences constant, have no time or cost constraints, and select a final choice that maximizes his or her economic payoff.

3. Rationality assumptions don't apply in many situations because (1) an individual's information-processing capacity is limited; (2) decision makers tend to intermix solutions with problems; (3) perceptual biases distort problem identification; (4) information may be selected more for its accessibility than for its quality; (5) decision makers often have favorite alternatives that bias their assessment;

(6) decision makers sometimes increase commitment to a previous choice to confirm its original correctness; (7) prior decision precedents constrain current choices; (8) there is rarely agreement on a single goal; (9) decision makers must face time and cost constraints; and (10) most organizational cultures discourage taking risks and searching for innovative alternatives.

4. In the perfectly rational decision-making process: (1) the problem identified is important and relevant; (2) all criteria are identified; (3) all criteria are evaluated; (4) a comprehensive list of alternatives is generated; (5) all alternatives are assessed against the decision criteria and weights; (6) the decision with the highest economic outcome is chosen; (7) all organizational members embrace the solution chosen; and (8) the decision's outcome is objectively evaluated against the original problem.

5. In the boundedly rational decision-making process: (1) the problem chosen is visible and reflects the manager's interests and background; (2) a limited set of criteria is identified; (3) a simple model is constructed to evaluate criteria; (4) a limited set of similar alternatives is identified; (5) alternatives are assessed one at a time; (6) the search continues until a satisficing solution is found; (7) politics and power influence decision acceptance; and (8) the decision's outcome is evaluated against the self-interests of the evaluator.

6. Managers face two types of problems: well-structured and ill-structured. Well-structured problems are straightforward, familiar, and easily defined. Ill-structured problems are new or unusual, involving ambiguous or incomplete information.

7. Organizations respond with programmed and nonprogrammed decisions. Programmed decisions are used by managers with well-structured problems, and nonprogrammed decisions by managers with ill-structured problems.

8. The ideal situation for making decisions occurs when the manager can make accurate decisions because he or she knows the outcome from every alternative. Such certainty, however, rarely occurs. A far more relevant situation is one of risk, when the decision maker can estimate the likelihood of certain alternatives or outcomes. If neither certainty nor reasonable probability estimates are available, uncertainty exists, and the decision maker's choice will be influenced by his or her psychological orientation.

9. Groups offer certain advantages: more complete information, more alternatives, increased acceptance of a solution, and greater legitimacy. On the other hand, groups are time-consuming, can be dominated by a minority, create pressures to conform, and cloud responsibility.

10. Three ways of improving group decision making are brainstorming, the nominal group technique, and the Delphi technique.

REVIEW QUESTIONS

1. What initiates the decision-making process?
2. What is *rationality?*
3. What is a *satisficing* decision?
4. When should you use programmed decision making? Nonprogrammed decision making?
5. What's the difference between a *rule* and a *policy?*

6. Why would an organization's senior executives favor developing a wide range of programmed decisions for middle- and lower-level managers?

7. Why might a manager use a simplified decision model?

8. Is the order in which alternatives are considered more critical under assumptions of perfect rationality or bounded rationality? Why?

9. What is *groupthink?* What are its implications for decision making?

10. Is group decision making effective?

DISCUSSION QUESTIONS

1. Why would decision making be described as "the essence of a manager's job"?

2. How might an organization's culture influence the way in which managers make decisions?

3. Describe a decision you have made that closely aligns with the assumptions of perfect rationality. Compare this with the process you used to select your college. Is there a deviation? Explain.

4. Why do you think organizations have increased the use of groups for making decisions during the past twenty years?

5. When would you recommend using groups to make decisions?

SELF-ASSESSMENT EXERCISE

How Good Are You at Decision Making?

Instructions: For each statement, respond either Yes or No.

	Yes	No
1. Do you often try to avoid or delay making important decisions and even hope that problems will go away?	_____	_____
2. When required to make a decision fairly promptly, do you become flustered and fail to function at your best?	_____	_____
3. Would you consider it demeaning to consult your subordinates regarding a problem with which they have experience?	_____	_____
4. In deciding a complicated problem in which strong arguments exist for both sides, would you trust your "gut reaction"?	_____	_____
5. Do you often wish that you didn't have to make any decisions?	_____	_____
6. When faced with a serious decision, are your sleep and appetite usually adversely affected?	_____	_____
7. Do you secretly dislike making decisions because you lack self-confidence?	_____	_____
8. Are you uneasy even when required to make unimportant decisions?	_____	_____
9. Would you fire a friend if his continued employment was against the welfare of the enterprise in which you held a high position?	_____	_____
10. When baffled by a problem within your jurisdiction, would you try to pass it off to others?	_____	_____
11. At home, do you participate in all or most of the important decisions?	_____	_____
12. Are you usually edgy both before and after making important decisions?	_____	_____

Turn to page 670 for scoring directions and key.

Source: Adapted from Walter Duckat, "Check Your Decisionmaking Skills," *Supervision* 41 (February 1979), 3. Reprinted with permission from *Supervision.* Copyright © 1979 by The National Research Bureau, Inc., 424 North Third Street, Burlington, Iowa 52601.

CASE APPLICATION 6A

Charles Schwab Corp.

Charles Schwab Corp. is the largest discount brokerage firm in the United States.[35] With about 40 percent of the discount market, it generates approximately $400 million a year in revenues. Yet it is small potatoes in the brokerage industry. Schwab is essentially a big fish in a small pond because discounters, which charge about half of what conventional brokers charge, take in only about 8 percent of all retail commissions. All discounters together, for instance, are smaller than Merrill Lynch alone.

In contrast to the big, full-service brokerage firms—which make a lot of money by buying and selling securities for banks, mutual funds, pension groups, insurance companies, and other institutional investors—Schwab's business comes almost entirely from individual investors. This is the group that has most rejected Wall Street since the market crash in October 1987.

In the first year following the 1987 crash, Schwab's average trading volume dropped 40 percent, and its earnings fell nearly 70 percent. The company wasn't in serious trouble. Its operating cash flow, in fact, was up 50 percent after the crash. Yet the company's founder and chairman, Charles Schwab, was looking at a number of options. The following are a few of these alternatives.

He could become a full service brokerage firm and go after institutional accounts. He could lay off employees and/or reduce broker's pay to cut costs. He could increase the company's commission-fee schedule anywhere from 5 to 20 percent. He could expand internally by opening new offices in the United States and overseas. He could expand externally by buying another discount broker. (Chicago-based Rose & Co., the country's fifth largest discount broker with 200,000 accounts, owned by Chase Manhattan, could be bought for 50 percent over book value.) His company could be sold to a full-service brokerage firm or to a large financial services company seeking to diversify.

Questions

1. What do you see as Charles Schwab's primary problem? Differentiate this problem from its symptoms.

2. Assess Schwab's problem as a decision point in a stream of decisions.

3. Review the strengths and weaknesses of Schwab's options. What other alternatives might be available that he hasn't identified?

4. How would Schwab's decision criteria influence his assessment of options?

CASE APPLICATION 6B

Exxon

On March 24, 1989, the 987-foot supertanker *Exxon Valdez* ran aground in the crystalline waters of Alaska's Prince William Sound. Eleven million gallons of oil spilled into the sound, spreading oil over more than 2500 miles of beaches. Sea life was covered in oil, fisheries were poisoned, the $100 million a year seafood harvest from the sound was decimated, and the livelihoods of thousands of Alaskans were threatened.

The accident was the largest oil spill in North American history. It represented the "worst-case scenario" that environmentalists had feared ever since the Alaskan pipeline was completed in 1977. Experts agreed that, regardless of efforts to clean up the oil spill, it would take years to eradicate the smear and stink it caused. It might be a decade or more before the sound returned to its former pristine conditions. The following briefly summarizes some of the key events that followed the accident and the actions that Exxon and Alyeska Pipeline Service executives took to deal with the problem.[36] Alyeska, an eight-company consortium, operated the Alaskan pipeline and the Valdez oil terminal. It was responsible for mounting the initial defense in case of an oil spill.

- When the supertanker ran aground on the morning of March 24, the ship's captain was in his cabin. This is in violation of Exxon policy, which calls for the captain to keep command until the ship is on the open ocean. The third mate was illegally in command. Upon boarding the ship, Coast Guard authorities believed the captain to be intoxicated. Exxon admits that it knew the captain had gone through an alcohol detoxification program but still put him in command of its largest tanker.
- Alyeska's only containment barge was stripped for repairs at the time of the accident. When it was finally loaded, it was with equipment meant to take oil off the tanker, rather than barrier booms to fight the spill. The barge had to be reloaded, which further delayed action by hours.
- Neither Alyeska nor Exxon had enough booms or chemical dispersants to adequately contain the spill.
- The oil companies weren't ready to test for dispersants for 18 hours.
- The skimmer boats' equipment used to scoop oil out of the sea was so old that it kept breaking down and clogging.
- Both Alyeska and Exxon failed, despite pleas from fishermen, to mobilize squads of private fishing boats poised to rush to the scene.

Exxon and Alyeska's lack of preparedness made a mockery of the 250-page containment plan, approved by the state of Alaska, for how spills in Prince William Sound would be fought. For example, the plan required encirclement of a spill or tanker within five hours. The *Exxon Valdez* wasn't encircled for thirty-five hours.

A week after the accident, Exxon chairman Lawrence Rawl was saying that his company was getting a "bad rap" for the alleged delays. Exxon spent $2 million on the following full-page ad that ran in a number of major newspapers on April 3, 1989.

Within several weeks of the accident, the Federal Bureau of Investigation had opened a criminal probe of the oil spill, a warrant had been issued for the arrest of the tanker's captain, and dozens of lawsuits had been filed against Exxon. Exxon's potential liability from the spill could amount to $1 billion or more. In 1989 alone, Exxon took an $850 million write-off to cover its costs to date for the Alaska oil spill.

An Open Letter to the Public

On March 24, in the early morning hours, a disastrous accident happened in the waters of Prince William Sound, Alaska. By now you all know that our tanker, the Exxon Valdez, hit a submerged reef and lost 240,000 barrels of oil into the waters of the Sound.

We believe that Exxon has moved swiftly and competently to minimize the effect this oil will have on the environment, fish and other wildlife. Further, I hope that you know we have already committed several hundred people to work on the cleanup. We also will meet our obligation to all those who have suffered damage from the spill.

Finally, and most importantly, I want to tell you how sorry I am that this accident took place. We at Exxon are especially sympathetic to the residents of Valdez and the people of the State of Alaska. We cannot, of course, undo what has been done. But I can assure you that since March 24, the accident has been receiving our full attention and will continue to do so.

L.G. Rawl
Chairman

Questions

1. From Rawl's perspective, is this a well-structured or ill-structured problem? Explain.

2. What type of decision does this require?

3. If you had been Exxon's chairman, what decisions would you have made and when?

4. To what do you attribute Exxon's delayed action in responding to the oil spill?

Crime-Severity Decision

PURPOSE

To compare individual and group decision making.

REQUIRED KNOWLEDGE

1. The steps in the decision-making process.
2. Advantages of group decisions over individual decisions.

TIME REQUIRED

Approximately 45 minutes.

INSTRUCTIONS

1. Set up groups of five to ten participants.
2. Each class member will use column 1 in Table II-A to order the following 15 crimes by rank in terms of their severity. Give the most severe a rank of 1, the next severe a 2, and so on. The least severe is ranked 15. Do not talk to others in your group while doing your individual ranking. You have five minutes to complete this step.
3. After the individual rankings are complete, the groups are to arrive at a group ranking (use column 2) by use of consensus. This step is not to exceed 20 minutes in duration.
4. Your instructor will give you the actual rankings. Put these in column 3.
5. Calculate your individual and group error scores (columns 4 and 5) by scoring differences (ignore minus signs).
6. Group members are to compare their group error scores against their individual error scores. Did the performance of the group, as a whole, improve? Group members should then review the quality of discussion during the group decision making. Was there any difference in the quality of discussion in groups that had low group error scores compared to those that had high scores?

Source: Christopher Taylor, "Crimes, Death, and Stress: Three New Consensus Tasks," *Organizational Behavior Teaching Review,* Vol. XII, No. 2, 1987–1988, pp. 115–17.

TABLE II-A

Crime	Your Ranks	Group Ranks	Actual Ranks	Your Error	Group Error
Person kills victim by recklessly driving a car					
Person runs a narcotic ring					
Parent beats young child to death with fists					
Person plants bomb in public building; explosion kills one person					
Wife stabs husband to death					
Man forcibly rapes woman, who dies from injuries					
Legislator takes $10,000 company bribe to support favoring firm					
Man tries to entice minor into car for immoral purposes					
Person runs prostitution ring					
Husband stabs wife to death					
Person smuggles marijuana into country for resale					
Person shoots victim fatally during robbery					
Person commits arson; $500,000 damage					
Person breaks into home and steals $1,000					
Person kidnaps a victim					

Source: Christopher Taylor, "Crimes, Death, and Stress: Three New Consensus Tasks," *Organizational Behavior Teaching Review,* Vol. XII, No. 2, 1987–1988, pp. 115–17.

Adidas Misses
the Fast Track

In the early 1970s, Adidas dominated the running-shoe industry. It had done so for decades. The German company was in the right place at the right time to profit from what would prove to be the biggest surge of popularity any recreational pursuit had ever known: the running craze! Tens of millions of people would take up running or jogging in the 1970s; other millions of nonrunners would buy running shoes for comfort or fashion or to emulate the young and health-conscious.

Did Adidas cash in on this recreational boom? No! It grossly understated the market for running shoes and attire. Even worse, it underestimated the aggressiveness of its U.S. competitors. Most of these competitors were upstart firms that had not even been around in 1970. Adidas got pushed aside during the 1970s by Nike; and both these firms were suffering in 1990 under the onslaught of Reebok and L.A. Gear. But this is the story of Adidas, and the opportunity that got away.

HISTORICAL BACKGROUND

Rudolf and Adolf Dassler began making shoes in what is now West Germany, shortly after World War I. Adolf was the innovator, and Rudolf was the seller of his brother's creations. The brothers achieved only moderate success at first, but then, in 1936, a big breakthrough came. Jesse Owens agreed to wear their shoes in the Olympics and won four Gold Medals. The lucrative association of shoes with a famous athlete triggered a marketing strategy that Adidas—and other athletic shoe manufacturers—practiced from that point on.

In 1949, the brothers had a falling out and, indeed, never spoke to each other again outside of court. Rudolf took half the equipment and left his brother to go to the other side of town and set up the Puma Company. Adolf created Adidas from the existing firm.

Adolf was an experimenter. He tried new materials and techniques to develop stronger and lighter shoes. He introduced kangaroo leather to toughen the sides of shoes, four-spiked running shoes, track shoes with nylon soles, and interchangeable spikes.

Adidas's high quality, innovation, and variety of products resulted in the firm's dominating international competitions through the mid-1970s. For example, at the 1976 Montreal Olympics, Adidas-equipped athletes accounted for 82.8 percent of all individual track-and-field medal winners. This was tremendous publicity for the company, and sales rose to $1 billion worldwide.

But competitors were emerging. Before 1972, Adidas and Puma had practically the entire athletic shoe market to themselves. Although this was changing, Adidas had built up a seemingly insurmountable lead, providing footwear for virtually every type of sporting activity as well as diversifying into other sports-related product lines: shorts, jerseys, leisure wear, and track suits; tennis and swimwear; balls for every kind of sport; tennis racquets and cross-country skis; and the popular sports bag that carried the Adidas name as a prominently displayed status symbol.

THE 1970s RUNNING MARKET

Beginning in the early 1970s, Americans became increasingly concerned with physical fitness. One of the major offshoots of this concern with fitness was the running boom. What started it? No one is certain. The televising of the 1972 Munich Olympics and the victory of the United States' Frank Shorter in the marathon was probably a factor. Kenneth Cooper's book *Aerobics,* which sold millions of copies, argued strongly that running was an easy and inexpensive way to build aerobic capacity. *The Complete Book of Running* by Jim

Fixx was on the best-seller list for months in the mid-1970s. Whatever the cause, the facts could not be denied. By the late 1970s, it was estimated that 25 to 30 million Americans were joggers, while another 10 million wore running shoes for leisure wear. Of course, along with this increase in demand for running shoes came a host of new competitors. Adidas and Puma were joined by Nike, Brooks, New Balance, Tiger, and many others. Likewise, specialty shoe stores such as Foot Locker and Athletic Attic expanded nationwide to capitalize on the public's desire to be able to find variety and expert advice in one location. Anyone interested in running, and those who couldn't care less, even found running periodicals on local magazine racks. *Runner's World,* for example, became a highly successful and profitable magazine.

ENTER: NIKE

While Adidas faced a half-dozen or more competitors in the athletic shoe market, one was to become more aggressive and innovative than the rest. That was Nike. Begun in Oregon by a former University of Oregon miler, Nike shoes made their first competitive appearance during the 1972 Olympic trials in Eugene, Oregon. Marathon runners who had been persuaded to wear the new shoes placed fourth through seventh. Competitors wearing Adidas, however, finished first, second, and third in these trials.

Nike's big breakthrough came in 1975 with the development of the "waffle sole," whose tiny rubber studs made it more springy than those of other shoes then on the market. The popularity of the waffle sole, along with the rapidly expanding market for running shoes, resulted in sales of $14 million for Nike in 1976. This was against only $2 million in 1972. By the late 1970s and early 1980s, demand for Nikes was so great that 60 percent of its 8,000 department store, sporting goods, and shoe store dealers had to give advance orders, often waiting six months for delivery. This gave Nike a big advantage in production scheduling and inventory costs. Because it manufactured most of its shoes in Asia, Nike had low costs; it also had a dominant market share (estimated at approximately 50 percent in 1981).

Nike's success could be traced to its emphasis on (1) research and technological improvement and (2) its variety of styles and models. The company had nearly 100 employees working in research and development.

Its 1981 budget in this area alone was approximately $4 million. Some of these R & D activities include high-speed photographic analyses of the human body in motion, the use of athletes on force plates and treadmills, wear testing with over 300 athletes in an organized program, and continual testing and study of new and modified shoes and materials.

On the marketing side, Nike offered the most comprehensive choice of styles for consumers. It appealed to all kinds of runners and conveyed the image of the most complete running-shoe manufacturer of them all. Furthermore, Nike found that it could tap the widest possible distribution with its breadth of products. It could sell its shoes to conventional retailers such as department stores and shoes stores; and it could continue to do business with specialized running-shoe stores.

THE 1990 MARKET

When the running boom reached a plateau in the early 1980s, Adidas had little success in regaining its market dominance. By the end of the decade, Adidas's market share had fallen to a dismal 4 percent. Nike was the industry leader with a 26 market share. But two relatively new kids on the block—Reebok and L.A. Gear—were making a lot of noise with 22 and 13 percent market shares, respectively.

In 1982, Reebok was doing a paltry $4 million a year in business. By 1986, that figure had boomed to $919 million! This success was essentially due to inventing and persistently exploiting the market for women's aerobic shoes, a shift in the business that Nike had completely missed. Reebok offered shoes in brilliant colors and made of soft leather. Meanwhile, L.A. Gear took Reebok's "shoes as a fashion statement" concept another step forward. L.A. Gear's sales were only $11 million in 1985, but four years later they were doing more than $400 million! L.A. Gear's secret was selling shoes for show rather than sport. Adorned with bright neon trim, buckles, and rhinestones, L.A. Gear's shoes suggested "hardbodies" and Southern California.

Only time will tell whether Reebok and L.A. Gear can maintain their rapidly expanding markets by selling shoes as fashion items. They may well end up as footnotes in the history of athletic footwear. What is clear, however, is that the mid-1970s, when athletic-shoe manufacturers were dubbed "Adidas and the Seven Dwarfs," is a distant memory for executives at Adidas.

QUESTIONS

1. Describe Adidas's environment in (a) 1970, (b) 1980, and (c) 1990.

2. What errors did Adidas make in the early 1970s that led to its significantly reduced market share by 1990?

3. How might Adidas's culture have influenced its decline?

4. How might a committee structure, in which all major decisions are made through a group process, have resulted in a different outcome at Adidas?

5. In what ways does Adidas's current environment constrain its management?

6. Given these constraints, what can Adidas's management do today to exploit opportunities in its environment?

7. Is the athletic-shoe industry a global business? Discuss.

The major part of this case was adapted from Robert F. Hartley, *Management Mistakes*, 2nd ed. (New York: John Wiley & Sons, 1986), pp. 44–51. Reprinted by permission. Updated from Kathleen Kerwin, "L.A. Gear Is Going Where the Boys Are," *Business Week*, June 19, 1989, p. 54; and Barbara Rudolph, "Foot's Paradise," *Time*, August 28, 1989, pp. 54–55.

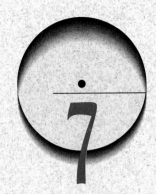

FOUNDATIONS OF PLANNING

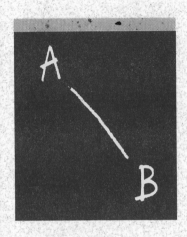

1. Define planning.
2. Explain the potential benefits of planning.
3. Distinguish between strategic and operational plans.
4. State when directional plans are preferred.
5. Identify four contingency factors in planning.
6. Explain how far ahead a manager should plan.
7. Describe why an organization's stated objectives might not be its real objectives.
8. Describe a typical MBO program.
9. Explain how MBO makes goals motivators.
10. Describe the conditions under which MBO is most likely to succeed.

Planning for the end of the world as we know it is not easy, but Weyerhaeuser is one company that's making the effort.[1] The giant lumber and paper firm is closely monitoring the global warming trend known as the greenhouse effect and attempting to assess its impact on Weyerhaeuser's business.

Since the Industrial Revolution, the increased burning of fossil fuels has spewed large volumes of carbon dioxide and other gases into the earth's atmosphere. Many scientists are now predicting that the buildup of these gases will create massive changes in the earth's climate.

A worst-case scenario proposes that the world's temperature could rise as much as 8 degrees Fahrenheit by the year 2050. That might not seem like much—after all, people have been suffering through 110°-plus days in places like Phoenix and Las Vegas since those cities were settled—but such an increase in the earth's temperature would cause enormous changes. Ice caps would melt, the sea level would rise eight to sixteen inches, and coastlines would be reconfigured. Countries like the Netherlands and Bangladesh, which are at or below sea level, could disappear. Interiors of continents would tend to become drier as the coasts got wetter. Cold seasons would shorten, and warm seasons would lengthen. Increased evaporation would lead to drier soils over wide areas. In the United States, the worst-case scenario might be a mid-twenty-first-century in which the Mississippi River had become a narrow stream, the once rich Midwest plains had turned into a dust bowl, and the east and west coasts had become swamp lands.

Weyerhaeuser's management isn't standing by passively watching the greenhouse effect. It is planning ahead. It is actively strengthening its genetics-engineering program to improve its trees' drought resistance and planting more drought-resistant tree varieties in its midwestern forests.

Weyerhaeuser depends on trees that need to grow for thirty to sixty years before they can be harvested. Many of these trees are on nearly two million acres that the company owns in Oklahoma and Arkansas. These trees would be particularly hard hit by the warming, drying trend created by the greenhouse effect.

THE DEFINITION OF PLANNING

If climate scientists' worst-case greenhouse-effect scenario comes true, Weyerhaeuser's planning should pay handsome dividends. But what do we specifically mean by the term *planning*? As we stated in Chapter 1, planning encompasses defining the organization's objectives or goals, establishing an overall strategy for achieving these goals, and developing a comprehensive hierarchy of plans to integrate and coordinate activities. It is concerned, then, with *ends* (what is to be done) as well as with *means* (how it is to be done).

Planning can be further defined in terms of whether it is informal or formal. All managers engage in planning, but it might be only the informal variety. In informal planning, nothing is written down, and there is little or no sharing of objectives with others in the organization. This describes planning in many small businesses; the owner-manager has a vision of where he or she wants to go and how he or she expects to get there. The planning is general and lacks continuity. Of course, informal planning exists in some large organizations, and some small businesses have very sophisticated formal plans.

When we use the term planning, we are implying *formal* planning. Specific objectives are formulated covering a period of years. These objectives are committed to writing and made available to organization members. Finally, specific action programs exist for the achievement of these objectives; that is, management clearly defines the path it wants to take to get from where it is to where it wants to be.

THE PURPOSE OF PLANNING

Why should managers engage in planning? It gives direction, reduces the impact of change, minimizes waste and redundancy, and sets the standards to facilitate control.

Planning establishes coordinated effort. It gives direction to managers and non-managers alike. When all concerned know where the organization is going and what they must contribute to reach the objective, they can begin to coordinate their activities, cooperate with each other, and work in teams. A lack of planning can foster "zigzagging" and thus prevent an organization from moving efficiently toward its objectives.

Planning reduces uncertainty by anticipating change. It also clarifies the consequences of the actions managers might take in response to change. Planning forces managers to look ahead, anticipate change, consider the impact of change, and develop appropriate responses.

Planning also reduces overlapping and wasteful activities. Coordination before the fact is likely to uncover waste and redundancy. Further, when means and ends are clear, inefficiencies become obvious.

Finally, planning establishes objectives or standards that facilitate control. If we are unsure of what we are trying to achieve, how can we determine whether we have achieved it? In planning, we develop the objectives. In the controlling function, we compare actual performance against the objectives, identify any significant deviations, and take the necessary corrective action. Without planning, there can be no control.

PLANNING AND PERFORMANCE

Do managers and organizations that plan outperform those that don't? Intuitively, you would expect the answer to be a resounding Yes. Reviews of the evidence are generally affirmative, but that shouldn't be interpreted as a blanket endorsement of formal planning. We cannot say that organizations that formally plan *always* outperform those that don't.

Dozens of studies have been undertaken to test the relationship between planning and performance.[2] They allow us to draw the following conclusions. First, generally speaking, formal planning is associated with higher profits, higher return on assets, and other positive financial results. Second, the *quality* of the planning process and the appropriate *implementation* of the plans probably contribute more to high performance than does the *extent* of planning. Finally, in those studies in which formal planning hasn't led to higher performance, the environment is typically the culprit. When government regulations, powerful labor unions, and similar environmental forces constrain management's options, planning will have less of an impact on an organization's performance. Why? Because management will have fewer choices for which planning can propose viable alternatives. For example, planning might suggest that a manufacturing firm produce a number of its key parts in Asia in order to compete effectively against low-cost foreign competitors. But if the firm's contract with its labor union specifically forbids transferring work overseas, the value of the firm's planning effort is significantly reduced. Dramatic shocks from the environment can also undermine the best-laid plans. The stock market crash in October 1987 undermined most of the formal plans previously developed by brokerage firms. In conditions of such environmental uncertainty, there is no reason to expect that planners will necessarily outperform nonplanners.

MYTHS ABOUT PLANNING

There is no shortage of myths and misconceptions about planning. The following identifies a few common myths and seeks to clarify the misunderstanding behind them.

1. *Planning that proves inaccurate is a waste of management's time.* The end result of planning is only one of its purposes. The process itself can be valuable even if the results miss the target. Planning requires management to think through what it wants to do and how it is going to do it. This clarification can have significant value in and of itself. Management that does a good job of planning will have direction and purpose, and planning is likely to minimize the misdirection of energy. All this is in spite of missing the objectives being sought.

2. *Planning makes future decisions.* Planning doesn't make future decisions. It is concerned with the impact of current decisions on future events. So while planning is concerned with the future, planning decisions are made in the present.

3. *Planning can eliminate change.* Planning cannot eliminate change. Changes will happen regardless of what management does. Management engages in planning in order to *anticipate* changes and to develop the most effective response to them.

4. *Planning reduces flexibility.* Planning implies commitments, but it is a constraint only if management stops planning after doing it once. Planning is an ongoing activity. The fact that formal plans have been reasoned out and clearly articulated can make them easier to revise than an ambiguous set of assumptions carried

around in some senior executive's head. Some plans, furthermore, can be made to be more flexible than others.

TYPES OF PLANS

strategic plans
Plans that are organizationwide, establish overall objectives, and position an organization in terms of its environment.

operational plans
Plans that specify details on how overall objectives are to be achieved.

short-term plans
Plans that cover less than one year.

long-term plans
Plans that extend beyond five years.

specific plans
Plans that are clearly defined and leave no room for interpretation.

directional plans
Flexible plans that set out general guidelines.

The most popular ways to describe plans is by their breadth (strategic versus operational), time frame (short- versus long-term), and specificity (specific versus directional).

Plans that apply to the entire organization, that establish the organization's overall objectives, and that seek to position the organization in terms of its environment are called **strategic plans.** Plans that specify the details of how the overall objectives are to be achieved are called **operational plans.**

Plans that are referred to as short-term or long-term are classified by time frame. **Short-term plans** are less than one year in length, while **long-term plans** cover a period in excess of five years.

Plans can also be categorized in terms of their specificity. When thinking about planning, most of us envision **specific plans.** These are clearly defined and leave no room for interpretation. But there are times when management prefers to use **directional plans** to facilitate flexibility. We'll consider, in the next section, when directional plans might be preferred.

Table 7–1 lists all these types of plans according to category.

Strategic Versus Operational Plans

Strategic and operational plans differ in their time frame, scope, and whether or not they include a known set of organizational objectives.[3] Operational plans tend to cover shorter periods of time. For instance, an organization's monthly, weekly, and day-to-day plans are almost all operational. Strategic plans tend to include an extended time period—usually five years or more. They also cover a broader area and deal less with specifics. A final distinction concerns objectives. Strategic plans include the formulation of objectives, whereas operational plans assume the existence of objectives. Operational plans offer ways of attaining these objectives.

TABLE 7–1   Plans

Categorized by	Types
Breadth	Strategic
	Operational
Time Frame	Short-term
	Long-term
Specificity	Specific
	Directional

In the late 1980s, many public utilities that had nuclear plants under construction were unable to make specific plans concerning their future power-generation capacity. Federal and local regulations and increasingly stringent safety standards made it impossible to predict with any accuracy when, or if, a new nuclear plant would be fully operating. Even some of the utilities that had completed nuclear plants and had them up and running were unable to develop specific plans because state regulators were not permitting the utilities to recover their construction costs through rate increases. Environmental conditions thus made it very difficult for utilities committed to nuclear power to establish very specific objectives or budgets because of the high degree of uncertainty.

Short-Term Versus Long-Term Plans

Financial analysts traditionally describe investment returns as *short-*, *intermediate-*, and *long-term*. The short term covers less than one year. Any time frame beyond five years is classified as long-term. The intermediate term covers the period in between. Managers have adopted the same terminology to describe plans. For clarity, we'll emphasize the short-term and long-term extremes in future discussions.

Keep in mind that our planning classifications are not independent of one another. For instance, there is a close relationship between the short- and long-term categories and our previous discussion of strategic and operational plans. Because of their character, strategic plans include both long-term and short-term plans. However, their emphasis is on the big picture and the long term. Operational plans, for the most part, are of the short-term variety.

Specific Versus Directional Plans

It seems intuitively correct that specific plans are always preferable to directional, or loosely guided, plans. Specific plans have clearly defined objectives. There is no ambiguity, no problem with misunderstandings. For example, a manager who seeks to increase his or her firm's sales by 20 percent over a given twelve-month period might

FIGURE 7–1
Specific Versus Directional
Plans

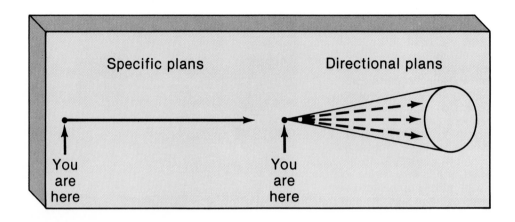

establish specific procedures, budget allocations, and schedules of activities to reach that objective. These represent specific plans.

However, specific plans are not without drawbacks. They require clarity and a sense of predictability that often does not exist. When uncertainty is high, which requires management to maintain flexibility in order to respond to unexpected changes, then it is preferable to use directional plans. (See Figure 7–1.)

Directional plans identify general guidelines. They provide focus but do not lock management into specific objectives or specific courses of action. Instead of a manager following a specific plan to cut costs by 4 percent and increase revenues by 6 percent in the next six months, a directional plan might aim at improving corporate profits by 5 to 10 percent during the next six months. The flexibility inherent in directional plans is obvious. This advantage must be weighed against the loss in clarity provided by specific plans.

CONTINGENCY FACTORS IN PLANNING

Under certain conditions, strategic planning is preferred. In some cases, long-term plans make sense; in others they do not. Similarly, in some situations, directional plans are more effective than specific ones. What are these conditions? In this section, we identify several contingency factors that affect planning.[4]

Level in the Organization

Figure 7–2 illustrates the general relationship between managerial level in an organization and the type of planning that is done. For the most part, operational planning dominates the planning activities of lower-level managers. As managers rise in the hierarchy, their planning role becomes more strategy-oriented. The planning effort by the top executives in large organizations is essentially strategic. In a small business, of course, the owner-manager needs to do both.

FIGURE 7–2

Planning and the Organizational Hierarchy

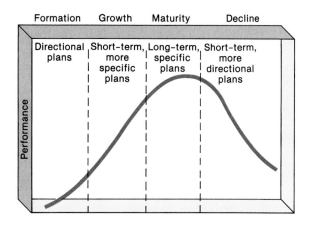

Life Cycle of the Organization

life cycle of the organization
Four stages that organizations go through: formation, growth, maturity, and decline.

Organizations go through a **life cycle.** Beginning with the formative stage, organizations grow, mature, and eventually decline. Planning is not homogeneous across these stages. As Figure 7–3 depicts, the length and specificity of plans should be adjusted at each stage.

If all things were equal, management would undoubtedly benefit most by developing and using specific plans. Not only would this provide the clearest direction, it would also establish the most detailed bench marks against which to compare actual performance. However, all things aren't equal.

When an organization is mature, predictability is greatest. It is at this stage in the life cycle, therefore, when specific plans are most appropriate. Managers should rely more heavily on directional plans in an organization's infancy. It is at precisely this time that high flexibility is desired. Objectives are tentative, resource availability is more uncertain, and the identification of clients or customers is more in doubt. Directional plans, at this stage, allow managers to make changes as necessary. During the growth stage, plans become more specific as objectives become more definite, resources more committed, and loyalty of clients or customers more developed. The pattern reverses itself on the downward swing of the cycle. From maturity to decline, plans need to

FIGURE 7–3

Plans and the Organization's Life Cycle

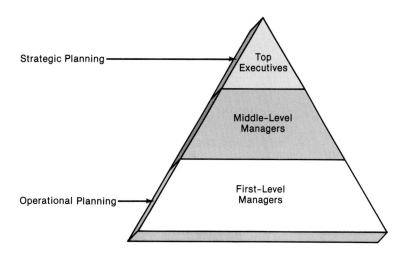

move from the specific to directional as objectives are reconsidered, resources reallocated, and other adjustments made.

The length of planning should also be related to the life cycle. Short-term plans offer the greatest flexibility and should therefore be more prevalent during the formative and decline stages. Maturity is the time when stability is greatest and when long-term plans can pay the biggest dividends.

Degree of Environmental Uncertainty

The greater the environmental uncertainty, the more plans should be directional and emphasis placed on the short term.

If rapid or important technological, social, economic, legal, or other changes are taking place, well-defined and precisely chartered routes are more likely to hinder an organization's performance than aid it. When environmental uncertainty is high, specific plans have to be altered to accommodate the changes—often at high cost and decreased efficiency. For example, in the mid-1980s, when intense rate wars were raging among airlines on major cross-country routes, the airlines should have moved to more directional plans concerning price setting, number and size of aircraft allocated to routes, and operating budgets.

Similarly, in times of high environmental uncertainty, more changes that affect an organization are likely to occur. The greater the change, the less likely plans are to be accurate. For example, one study found that one-year revenue plans tended to achieve 99 percent accuracy in comparison to 84 percent for five-year plans.[5] Therefore, if an organization faces rapidly changing environments, management should seek flexibility. This translates into greater emphasis on short-term plans. Since the farther ahead management's time horizon is, the greater the error, we should expect those organizations that face relatively stable environments to have relatively sophisticated and complex long-term plans, whereas those that face relatively dynamic environments to have plans directed almost exclusively to the short term.

Length of Future Commitments

commitment concept
Plans should extend far enough to see through current commitments.

A final contingency factor again relates to the time frame of plans. The more that current plans affect future commitments, the longer the time frame for which management should plan. This **commitment concept** means that plans should extend far enough to see through those commitments that are made today. Planning for too long or for too short a period is inefficient.

Remember, as we noted in our discussion on myths about planning, managers are not planning for future decisions. Rather, they are planning for the future impact of the decisions that they are currently making. Decisions made today become a commitment to some future action or expenditure. Tenure decisions in colleges and universities provide an excellent illustration of how the commitment concept should work.

When a college gives tenure to a faculty member, it is making a commitment to provide life-long employment for that individual. The tenure decision must therefore reflect an assessment by the college's administration that there will be a need for that faculty member's teaching expertise through his or her lifetime. If a college awards

MANAGING FROM A GLOBAL PERSPECTIVE

Planning Under Extreme Uncertainty

In early 1990, Nicaragua was in the midst of a civil war. In Brazil, inflation was running at a rate of over 1800 percent a year. If you were a manager in Nicaragua or Brazil, would war, hyperinflation, or similar political and economic instabilities affect your planning practices? You bet they would!

In contrast to many parts of the world, managers in North America operate in an incredibly stable environment. While there may be uncertainty, it is relatively low. Elections are predictable and regular, economic policies are reasonably well managed by the federal government, social unrest is minimal, and when changes come, they tend to be evolutionary rather than revolutionary. This stability allows managers to make forecasts and plans that are far more predictable and concise than those of managers in countries like Nicaragua, Brazil, Iran, Iraq, and South Africa.

Our point is not that managers in North America operate in a stable environment, because most don't. Rather the point is that, relative to many parts of the world, managers in North America face a comparatively predictable environment. This, in turn, allows them to develop more comprehensive plans because such plans are likely to be accurate and provide valuable guides for future action. In contrast, in a country like South Africa, which has been struggling for many years with problems created by its apartheid laws, managers in business firms would tend to minimize long-term planning and maintain flexibility by relying on directional plans.

tenure to a thirty-year-old sociology instructor, it should have a plan that covers at least the thirty to forty or more years this instructor could be teaching in that institution. Most important, the plan should demonstrate the need for a permanent sociology instructor through that time period.

Interestingly, the commitment concept was ignored by many college administrators in the late 1960s and early 1970s. They tenured a number of instructors in disciplines that were then popular with students, such as philosophy and religion, without considering whether that popularity would continue throughout the period of commitment. As the demand for courses in these areas has declined, many college administrators have found themselves locked in with tenured faculty in low-demand areas. It will be interesting to see whether college administrators have learned from past mistakes.

Currently, with instructors in business, computer science, and engineering in great demand, many faculty members in these disciplines are being considered for tenure. Administrators who understand the importance of the commitment concept will formulate plans that include forecasts of student demand in these disciplines extending well into the next century.

There is no single objective that characterizes an elementary school. Among its many objectives are transmitting basic reading, writing, and mathematics skills; teaching discipline; fostering the value of achievement; and developing good citizenship behaviors.

OBJECTIVES: THE FOUNDATION OF PLANNING

objectives

Desired outcomes for individuals, groups, or entire organizations.

Objectives are goals. We use the two terms interchangeably. What do these terms mean? They refer to desired outcomes for individuals, groups, or entire organizations.[6] They provide the direction for all management decisions and form the criterion against which actual accomplishments can be measured. It is for these reasons that they are the foundation of planning.

Multiplicity of Objectives

At first glance, it might appear that organizations have a singular objective: for business firms, to make a profit; for nonprofit organizations, to provide a service efficiently. But closer analysis demonstrates that all organizations have multiple objectives. Businesses also seek to increase market share and satisfy employee welfare. A church provides a "road to heaven through absolution," but it also assists the underprivileged in its community and acts as a gathering place for church members to congregate socially. No one measure can evaluate effectively whether an organization is performing successfully. Emphasis on one goal, such as profit, ignores other goals that must also be reached if long-term profits are to be achieved. Moreover, the use of a single objective almost certainly will result in undesirable practices, since managers will ignore important parts of their job in order to look good on the single measure.

Table 7–2 lists the ten most highly rated goals from over eighty of the largest corporations in the United States.[7] The number of goals per company ranged from one to eighteen, the average being five to six. Except for profitability, the goals are applicable to nonprofit as well as business organizations. Notice, too, that although survival is not specifically mentioned by the firms, it is paramount to all organizations. Some of the criteria listed in Table 7–2 contribute directly to profits, but it is obvious that all organizations must survive if other objectives are to be achieved.

TABLE 7–2   Stated Objectives from a Survey of Large Corporations

Objective	Percent Acknowledging the Objective
Profitability	
Absolute dollars of profit or percentage return on invested capital	89
Growth	
Increase in total revenues, number of employees, and the like	82
Market Share	
An organization's percentage share of total industry sales	66
Social Responsibility	
Recognition of the organization's responsibility to the greater society in which it functions to help solve pollution, discrimination, urban, and similar problems	65
Employee Welfare	
Concern for the satisfaction of employees and the quality of their working life	62
Product Quality and Service	
Excellence of the product or service that the organization produces	60
Research and Development	
Success in generating new and innovative products and processes	54
Diversification	
Ability to identify and move into new markets	51
Efficiency	
Ability to convert inputs into outputs at the lowest cost	50
Financial Stability	
Performance on financial criteria void of erratic movements	49

Source: Adapted from Y. K. Shetty, "New Look at Corporate Goals," *California Management Review,* Vol. XVI, No. 2, p. 73. Reprinted by permission of the Regents. © 1978 by the Regents of the University of California.

Real Versus Stated Objectives

Table 7–2 is a list of stated objectives. **Stated objectives** are official statements of what an organization says—and what it wants various publics to believe—are its objectives. However, stated objectives—which can be found in the organization's charter, annual report, public-relations announcements, or in public statements made by managers— are often conflicting and excessively influenced by what society believes organizations *should* do.

stated objectives
Official statements of what an organization says—and what it wants various publics to believe—are its objectives.

The conflict in stated goals exists because organizations respond to a vast array of constituencies. Unfortunately, these constituencies frequently evaluate the organization by different criteria. As a result, management is forced to say different things to different audiences. For example, TWA was recently negotiating to get wage concessions from its flight attendants' union.[8] The union, not wanting to give up anything, was threatening to strike. To the union's representatives, TWA's management was saying, "If you strike, we'll dismantle the airline. By selling off its aircraft and air routes, the company is worth more dead than alive." At the same time, the management was trying to calm the nerves of travel agents and potential passengers by saying the company was determined to fly and survive, even if its flight attendants struck. To support its intention, management said that it was training 1,500 people to step in if its attendants walked out. TWA's management had explicitly presented itself in one way to the union and in another way to the public. Was one true and the other false? No. Both were true, but they were in conflict.

Did you ever read an organization's objectives as they are stated in corporate brochures? The following are not atypical: "To provide products and services of the greatest possible value to our customers"; "To make the organization a coordinated team"; "To encourage employees to do their best"; "To honor our obligations to society by being an economic, intellectual, and social asset to each nation and each community in which we operate." Such statements are, at best, vague and more likely representative of management's public relations skills than meaningful guides to what the organization is actually seeking to accomplish.

It shouldn't be surprising, then, to find that an organization's stated objectives are often quite irrelevant to what actually goes on in that organization.[9] In a corporation, for instance, one statement of objectives is issued to stockholders, another to customers, and still others to employees and the public.[10]

real objectives
Objectives that an organization actually pursues, as defined by the actions of its members.

The overall objectives that top management states should be treated for what they are: "fiction produced by an organization to account for, explain, or rationalize to particular audiences rather than as valid and reliable indications of purpose."[11] The content of objectives is substantially determined by what those audiences want to hear. If you want to know what an organization's **real objectives** are, closely observe what members of the organization actually do. Actions define priorities. The university

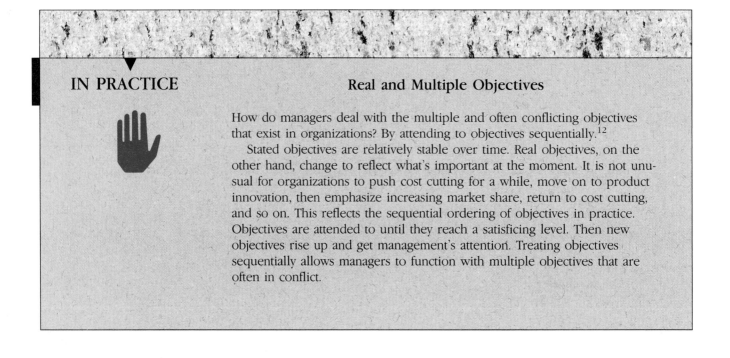

IN PRACTICE   Real and Multiple Objectives

How do managers deal with the multiple and often conflicting objectives that exist in organizations? By attending to objectives sequentially.[12]

Stated objectives are relatively stable over time. Real objectives, on the other hand, change to reflect what's important at the moment. It is not unusual for organizations to push cost cutting for a while, move on to product innovation, then emphasize increasing market share, return to cost cutting, and so on. This reflects the sequential ordering of objectives in practice. Objectives are attended to until they reach a satisficing level. Then new objectives rise up and get management's attention. Treating objectives sequentially allows managers to function with multiple objectives that are often in conflict.

that proclaims the objectives of limiting class size, facilitating close student-faculty relations, and actively involving students in the learning process, and then puts its students into lecture halls of 300 or more, is not unusual. Nor is the automobile service center that promotes fast, low-cost repairs and then gives mediocre service at high prices. An awareness that real and stated objectives can deviate is important, if for no other reason than because it can help you to explain what might otherwise seem like management inconsistencies.

Traditional Objective Setting

The traditional role of objectives is one of control imposed by an organization's top management. The president of a manufacturing firm *tells* the production vice president what he or she expects manufacturing costs to be for the coming year. The president *tells* the marketing vice president what level he or she expects sales to reach for the coming year. The city mayor *tells* his or her chief of police how much the departmental budget will be. Then, at some later point, performance is evaluated to determine whether the assigned objectives have been achieved.

The central theme in **traditional objective setting** is that objectives are set at the top and then broken down into subgoals for each level of an organization. It is a one-way process: The top imposes its standards on everyone below. This traditional perspective assumes that top management knows what's best because only it can see the "big picture."

In addition to being imposed from above, traditional objective setting is often largely nonoperational.[13] If top management defines the organization's objectives in broad terms such as achieving "sufficient profits" or "market leadership," these ambiguities have to be turned into specifics as the objectives filter down through the organization. At each level, managers supply operational meaning to the goals. Specificity is achieved by each manager applying his or her own set of interpretations and biases. The result is that objectives lose clarity and unity as they make their way down from the top. (See Figure 7–4.)

traditional objective setting
Objectives are set at the top and then broken down into subgoals for each level in an organization. The top imposes its standards on everyone below.

FIGURE 7–4
Traditional Objective Setting

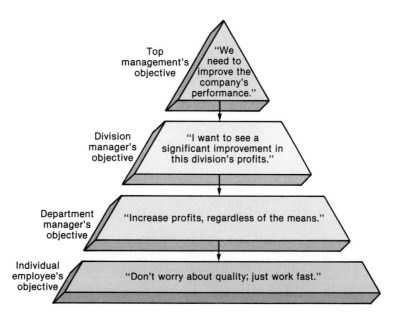

Top management's objective — "We need to improve the company's performance."

Division manager's objective — "I want to see a significant improvement in this division's profits."

Department manager's objective — "Increase profits, regardless of the means."

Individual employee's objective — "Don't worry about quality; just work fast."

Management by Objectives

management by objectives (MBO)

A system in which subordinates jointly determine specific performance objectives with their superiors, progress toward objectives is periodically reviewed, and rewards are allocated on the basis of this progress.

An alternative to the traditional approach is **management by objectives (MBO).** It is a system in which subordinates jointly determine specific performance objectives with their superiors, progress toward objectives is periodically reviewed, and rewards are allocated on the basis of this progress. Rather than using goals to control, MBO uses them to motivate.

What Is MBO?   Management by objectives is not new. The concept goes back more than thirty-five years.[14] Its appeal undoubtedly lies in its emphasis on converting overall objectives into specific objectives for organizational units and individual members.

MBO makes objectives operational by devising a process by which they cascade down through the organization. As depicted in Figure 7–5, the organization's overall objectives are translated into specific objectives for each succeeding level (that is, divisional, departmental, individual) in the organization. Because lower unit managers jointly participate in setting their own goals, MBO works from the "bottom up" as well as the "top down." The result is a hierarchy that links objectives at one level to those at the next level. For the individual employee, MBO provides specific personal performance objectives. Each person therefore has an identified specific contribution to make to his or her unit's performance. If all the individuals achieve their goals, then their unit's goals will be attained, and the organization's overall objectives will become a reality.

There are four ingredients common to MBO programs. These are goal specificity, participative decision making, an explicit time period, and performance feedback.

The objectives in MBO should be concise statements of expected accomplishments. It's not adequate, for example, merely to state a desire to cut costs, improve service, or increase quality. Such desires have to be converted into tangible objectives that can be measured and evaluated. To cut departmental costs *by 7 percent,* to improve service by ensuring that all telephone orders are processed *within twenty-four hours of receipt,* or to increase quality by keeping returns to *less than 1 percent of sales* are examples of specific objectives.

In MBO the objectives are not unilaterally set by the boss and assigned to subordinates, as is characteristic of traditional objective setting. MBO replaces these imposed

FIGURE 7–5
Cascading of Objectives

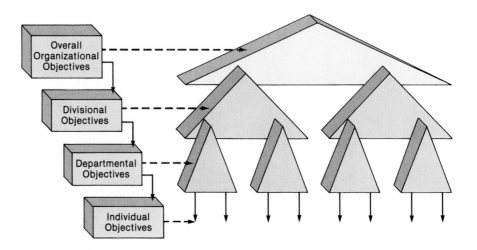

TABLE 7–3   Steps in a Typical MBO Program

1. The organization's overall objectives and strategies are formulated.
2. Major objectives are allocated among divisional and departmental units.
3. Unit managers collaboratively set specific objectives for their units with their superiors.
4. Specific objectives are collaboratively set for all department members.
5. Action plans, defining how objectives are to be achieved, are specified and agreed upon by managers and subordinates.
6. The action plans are implemented.
7. Progress toward objectives is periodically reviewed, and feedback is provided.
8. Successful achievement of objectives is reinforced by performance-based rewards.

goals with participatively determined goals. The superior and subordinate jointly choose the goals and agree on how they will be achieved.

Each objective has a concise time period in which it is to be completed. Typically, the time period is three months, six months, or a year. So not only do managers and subordinates have specific objectives but a stipulated time period in which to accomplish them.

The final ingredient in an MBO program is feedback on performance. MBO seeks to give continuous feedback on progress toward goals. Ideally, this is accomplished by ongoing feedback to individuals so they can monitor and correct their own actions. This is supplemented by periodic formal appraisal meetings in which superiors and subordinates can review progress toward goals and further feedback can be provided.

Table 7–3 summarizes the typical steps in an MBO program.

Does MBO Work?   Assessing the effectiveness of MBO is a complex task. Let's begin by briefly reviewing a growing body of literature on the relationship between goals and performance.

An overwhelming number of studies consistently confirm that hard or difficult goals result in a higher level of individual performance than do easy goals, that specific hard goals result in higher levels of performance than do no goals at all or the generalized goal of "do your best," and that feedback on one's performance leads to higher performance.[15]

In public sector organizations it is difficult to develop tangible, verifiable, and measurable objectives; reward structures are frequently fixed by legislative action; and many top-level government officials are elected and come up for reelection every two or four years, thus limiting their goal-setting horizon to little beyond twenty-four or thirty-six months.

If factors such as a person's ability and acceptance of goals are held constant, evidence demonstrates that more *difficult* goals lead to higher performance. Although individuals with very difficult goals achieve them far less often than those with very easy goals, they nevertheless perform at a consistently higher level. Of course, goals can be too hard. If individuals perceive a goal to be impossible instead of challenging, their desire to achieve it decreases, and the likelihood that they will abandon it increases.

Moreover, studies consistently support that *specific* hard goals produce a higher level of output than do no goals or generalized goals such as "do your best." *Feedback* also favorably affects performance. Feedback lets a person know whether his or her level of effort is sufficient or needs to be increased. It can induce a person to raise his or her goal level after attaining a previous goal and can inform a person of ways in which to improve his or her performance.

The results cited above are all consistent with MBO. MBO directly advocates specific goals and feedback. MBO implies, rather than explicitly states, that goals must be

ETHICAL DILEMMAS IN MANAGEMENT

Does MBO Require Manipulation?

A colleague once facetiously suggested that MBO stood for *manipulating by objectives*. He made his argument as follows:

1. Managers frequently have a specific set of goals in mind for an employee before the manager and employee ever sit down to begin the MBO process. These preconceived standards define the minimum goals that the manager is willing to accept.

2. Authentic employee participation therefore does not always take place. What takes place should more appropriately be called "pseudo-participation." That is, there is only the appearance of participation.

3. Nothing in the MBO process clarifies how to arrive at goals if the manager and subordinate are unable to reach agreement.

4. When conflicts exist, managers are prone to use the power of their position to impose their goals on the subordinate.

5. This scenario suggests that MBO can be a device that allows managers to appear to be setting goals participatively when, in fact, the goals are really being assigned.

Proponents of MBO would counter that, although the preceding scenario undoubtedly happens, it is not management by objectives. Moreover, managers must understand that anything less than complete participation by subordinates will undermine any MBO program's credibility and effectiveness. When differences occur, mature individuals can resolve them in a way that meets the needs of both the employee and the organization.

Is it unethical for a manager to enter a participative goal-setting session with a preestablished set of goals that the manager wants the employee to accept? Is it unethical for a manager to use his or her formal position to impose specific goals on an employee? What do *you* think?

perceived as feasible. Research on goal setting indicates that MBO is most effective if the goals are difficult enough to require the person to do some stretching.

But what about participation? MBO strongly advocates that goals be participatively set. Does the research demonstrate that participatively set goals lead to higher performance than those assigned by a superior? Interestingly, the research comparing participatively set and assigned goals on performance has not shown any strong or consistent relationships.[16] When goal difficulty has been held constant, assigned goals frequently do as well as participatively determined goals, contrary to MBO ideology. Therefore it is not possible to argue for the superiority of participation as MBO propo-

MANAGERS WHO MADE A DIFFERENCE

Robert Kiley of New York's Metropolitan Transportation Authority

In 1983, Robert Kiley took over as head of New York's Metropolitan Transportation Authority and, among other things, became responsible for the New York subway system.[17]

To say that the subway system was a mess at the time would be a gross understatement. Subway cars and stations were filthy, service was awful, and equipment was inadequate. As one transit system executive put it, "We thought the subways would collapse on themselves. We thought the track would fall apart, and people would just abandon it."

A quiet former CIA official and Boston deputy mayor, Kiley achieved one of recent history's great public management turnarounds in less than half a dozen years. While a ride on the New York subway can still provide adventures and surprises that passengers might rather avoid, Kiley has made remarkable improvements in service. In five years, he succeeded in cutting the breakdown rate in half, virtually eliminated spray-painted graffiti from cars, and increased ridership to its highest level since 1975.

How did Kiley do it? His methods involved a blend of conciliation and confrontation, a long-term focus, and concentration on limited goals. For instance, he repaired track and replaced more than 20 percent of the system's cars, but he also initiated drastic management reforms. He fought to get legislation to remove middle managers from union membership. The criteria for promotion in the management ranks were changed from seniority and civil service scores to measures of job performance. The pay system for field managers was redesigned and tied to job performance. Decision making was decentralized, and goal setting was introduced. Kiley found that field managers had been afraid to take steps such as disciplining workers because of fear that they would be challenged by unions or headquarters. When decisions were decentralized and a goal-setting program was implemented, major improvements in the system began to surface. At one major repair facility, managers introduced challenging daily output goals and dismissed employees for insubordination or inebriation—two actions that would have been unheard of in the pre-Kiley days. The work force at this repair facility dropped from over 1,000 people to 680, while productivity increased 35 percent.

nents advocate. One major benefit from participation, however, is that it appears to induce individuals to establish more difficult goals.[18] Thus participation may have a positive impact on performance by increasing one's goal aspiration level.

When we turn to studies of actual MBO programs to assess their effect on employee performance, we find a mixed bag of results.[19] A review of these studies suggests that three contingency variables may explain the instances when MBO has failed. These variables are an unsupportive culture, lack of top management commitment, and organizational constraints that undermine MBO ideology.

MBO is more likely to succeed if the organizational culture allows a high degree of individual initiative, provides a lot of direction, supports risk taking, and establishes performance as the primary determinant of rewards. Cultures that encourage individual initiative and provide high direction are directly compatible with MBO. Employees are treated as responsible, and there are clear organizational objectives and performance expectations. Because employees often see risk in the concept of holding individuals accountable for attaining specific goals, the culture needs to support risk. Risk-aversive cultures contain strong pressures to set goals at comfortable rather than difficult levels. Maybe the most important cultural factor needed for MBO to succeed is a commitment to rewarding performance. MBO is designed to pay off when objectives are achieved. With MBO, it's performance that counts! The best performers might not be management's favorites. Conversely, employees who are cheerful, loyal, and well liked might not do well on objective performance criteria. Since MBO is a results-oriented system, you can expect it to fail if rewards are not based on performance results.

A lack of top management commitment and involvement will quickly undermine any MBO program. It might be an unwillingness to back up the efforts of lower-level managers who attempt to apply MBO in their units. Or it might take the form of failing to do the sustained follow-up work necessary to make MBO effective. Either way, MBO is likely to be ineffective at best and could even fail totally.

It's more difficult to make MBO succeed in public-sector organizations than in business firms.[20] The added constraints in the public sector make identifying specific goals, rewarding performance, and using participation more of a challenge to successfully execute.

SUMMARY

This summary is organized by the chapter-opening learning objectives found on page 189.

1. Planning is the process of determining objectives and assessing the way these objectives can best be achieved.

2. Planning gives direction, reduces the impact of change, minimizes waste and redundancy, and sets the standards to facilitate controlling.

3. Strategic plans cover an extensive time period (usually three or more years), cover broad issues, and include the formulation of objectives. Operational plans cover shorter periods of time, focus on specifics, and assume that objectives are already known.

4. Directional plans are preferred over specific plans when uncertainty is high and when the organization is in the formative and decline stages of its life cycle.

5. Four contingency factors in planning include a manager's level in the organization, the life stage of the organization, the degree of environmental uncertainty, and the length of future commitments.

6. A manager should plan just far enough ahead to see through those commitments he or she makes today.

7. An organization's stated objectives might not be its real objectives because management might want to tell people what they want to hear and because it is simpler to state a set of consistent, understandable objectives than to explain a multiplicity of objectives.

8. A typical MBO program includes eight steps: (1) The organization's overall objectives and strategies are formulated; (2) major objectives are allocated among divisions and departmental units; (3) unit managers collaboratively set specific objectives for their units with their superiors; (4) specific objectives are collaboratively set for all department members; (5) action plans are specified and agreed upon by managers and subordinates; (6) the action plans are implemented; (7) progress toward objectives is periodically reviewed, and feedback is provided; and (8) successful achievement of objectives is reinforced by performance-based rewards.

9. MBO makes motivators out of goals because, with MBO, people know exactly what is expected of them, they get to participate in setting their goals, they receive continuous feedback on how well they're progressing toward their goals, and their rewards are contingent on achieving their goals. Such factors increase motivation.

10. MBO is most likely to succeed when an organization's culture allows a high degree of individual initiative, provides a lot of direction, supports risk, and establishes performance as the primary determinant of rewards; and when top management is strongly committed to it.

REVIEW QUESTIONS

1. Contrast *formal* with *informal* planning.
2. Do organizations that plan outperform those that don't?
3. Can planning eliminate change? Explain.
4. How can planning be inaccurate yet still be valuable to management?
5. How does the planning done by a top executive differ from that performed by a supervisor?
6. "Business has a single objective—to make a profit." Do you agree or disagree? Explain.
7. How would you identify an organization's stated objectives? Its real objectives?
8. Contrast traditional objective setting and MBO.
9. What qualities should MBO-type objectives have?
10. Does participation lead to higher levels of employee performance? Explain.

DISCUSSION QUESTIONS

1. "Planning and objective setting are the same thing." Do you agree or disagree? Discuss.

2. "Planning and controlling functions are intertwined." Do you agree or disagree? Discuss.

3. Why might planning not reduce flexibility?

4. A father tells his sixteen-year-old daughter, "All I ask is that you do your best in school. I can't ask any more of you." If this father wants his daughter to make high grades, what should he tell her instead?

5. What basic factors in MBO make it a logical technique for setting objectives? Would you expect it to work better in large or small organizations? Why?

SELF-ASSESSMENT EXERCISE

Are You a Good Planner?

Instructions: Answer either Yes or No to each of the following eight questions:

	Yes	No
1. My personal objectives are clearly spelled out in writing.	————	————
2. Most of my days are hectic and disorderly.	————	————
3. I seldom make any snap decisions and usually study a problem carefully before acting.	————	————
4. I keep a desk calendar or appointment book as an aid.	————	————
5. I make use of "action" and "deferred action" files.	————	————
6. I generally establish starting dates and deadlines for all my projects.	————	————
7. I often ask others for advice.	————	————
8. I believe that all problems have to be solved immediately.	————	————

Now turn to page 671 for scoring directions and key.

Sources: Ted Pollock, "Are You a Good Planner?," *Supervision,* January 1980, pp. 26–27; "How Good a Planner Are You?," *Supervision,* July 1983, p. 24; and "How to Be a Good Planner," *Supervision,* April 1984, pp. 25–26. Reprinted by permission of *Supervision.* Copyright © 1984 by The National Research Bureau, Inc., 424 North Third Street, Burlington, Iowa 52601.

CASE APPLICATION 7A

Grand Union

Mark Osco worked his way through Boston University while holding a part-time job bagging groceries at a Grand Union supermarket. When Mark graduated from BU in 1984 with a degree in business management, he decided to accept a job with Grand Union as a management trainee. Five years passed, and Mark gained wide experience in operating a large supermarket. Sixteen months ago, Mark became an assistant store manager in Newton, a Boston suburb. Last week, Mark Osco was made store manager at the Grand Union supermarket in Cambridge. He reports to Frank Sullivan, district manager for the Cambridge-Somerville-Medford area, who is responsible for fourteen stores.

One of the things Mark liked about the Grand Union chain was that it gave its managers a great deal of autonomy in running the stores. The company provided very general policies to guide its managers. The concern was with the bottom line; for the most part, how the managers got there was their business.

On the basis of what he had learned at BU, Mark wanted to install an MBO program when he had a store of his own. He liked the idea that everyone would have clear goals to work toward and that he could evaluate his personnel against those goals, thus eliminating excuses like "I didn't know what was expected of me" or "But I tried my best." Now that the time had come for him to run his own store, Mark felt it was also the time to implement an MBO program.

The Cambridge store employs ninety people, although, except for the managers, most work only twenty to thirty hours a week. Mark has five people reporting to him: an assistant manager and grocery, produce, meat, and bakery managers. The only highly skilled jobs belong to the butchers. Other, less-skilled jobs include cashiering, shelf stocking, cleanup, and grocery bagging.

Questions

1. What factors should Mark consider in order to determine whether MBO would be effective in his store?

2. Assuming that Mark decides to go forward with an MBO program, *specifically* describe how he should go about it.

3. Give two poor examples of objectives that a cashier might set. What, specifically, is wrong with each of these objectives?

4. Give two good examples of objectives that a cashier might establish.

CASE APPLICATION 7B

The Oak Bluffs Inn

Oak Bluffs is a resort town of 1,700 people on Martha's Vineyard off the coast of Massachusetts. Mike and Jan Christensen bought the Oak Bluffs Inn on the island about three years ago.

The Oak Bluffs is a quaint little inn. Its ten rooms can handle a maximum of forty guests, and the restaurant can seat seventy-five people. Since purchasing the inn for $325,000, Mike and Jan have spent another $80,000 and some 3,000 hours in renovating the place.

The Christensens have their own apartment in the inn and live there year-round. So far, they've kept the inn open only six months a year—April through September. Last year, after meeting all their expenses (including a $2,200 monthly mortgage payment), they showed a profit of $17,000.

Jan thinks that they could earn more money if they had a formal plan. Mike agrees but admits that he doesn't have the slightest idea of where to start.

Questions

1. How could formal plans for the inn help the Christensens?
2. What form might such plans take? Why?

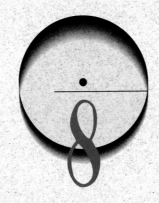

STRATEGIC PLANNING AND MANAGEMENT

1. Explain the importance of strategic planning.
2. Differentiate corporate-, business-, and functional-level strategies.
3. Contrast strategic management with strategic planning.
4. Outline the steps in the strategic management process.
5. Identify the four grand strategy options.
6. Describe how managers should allocate resources among the four business groups in the BCG matrix.
7. Contrast defenders, prospectors, and analyzers.
8. Describe how to assess an organization's competitive advantage.
9. Explain what entrepreneurship is.
10. Identify the personality characteristics of entrepreneurs.

alt Disney died in 1966, and with him died much of the creative energy at Walt Disney Co.[1] By the mid-1980s, the Disney empire was in trouble. Walt's successors had let the creative side of the company wither while they focused their attention on real estate development. The last major film hit had been *The Love Bug* in 1969. By 1984, Wall Street investors were beginning to think that the company was worth more in pieces than as a whole under the leadership it had then.

Things began to change, however, when Michael Eisner was brought in from Paramount Pictures to provide new leadership for Disney. He immediately began setting to work on a new strategy for the company that could capitalize on Disney's assets, talents, and reputation. He aggressively expanded Disney's Touchstone film group, added 50 percent more employees to the animation staff, introduced several new television cartoon shows, revived the famed Walt Disney Imagineering group to develop new rides and attractions at Disney theme parks, and ambitiously exploited opportunities for selling Disney-licensed products.

By 1988, Walt Disney Co. was reaping the rewards of Eisner's strategy. Film successes like *Down and Out in Beverly Hills, Ruthless People, Three Men and a Baby, Good Morning, Vietnam,* and *Who Framed Roger Rabbit?* made the Disney movie studio Number 1 in Hollywood. Its market share of U.S. box-office revenues had increased to an astounding 30 percent from merely 4 percent just four years earlier. The newly created *DuckTales* had become the Number 1 syndicated cartoon show on television. Attendance at the company's theme parks was up 22 percent, in spite of an increase in ticket fees of more than 50 percent.

From movies to theme parks to television to retail products, Eisner's strategy had made Disney the hottest all-around entertainment maker in the United States. Between 1984 and 1988, Disney's annual revenues more than doubled, profits increased nearly fourfold, and the value of the company's stock zoomed from $2 billion to $10 billion. Needless to say, the company was the darling of Wall Street.

Michael Eisner has directed the move of Mickey Mouse and Donald Duck out of the Disney theme parks and into shopping malls. He is rapidly expanding the company's concept of Disney Stores, where thousands of licensed products are sold.

THE INCREASING IMPORTANCE OF STRATEGIC PLANNING

The Disney case illustrates the value of strategic planning. An underlying theme in this chapter is that better strategies result in better organizational performance. Yet the fact that strategic planning plays a critical role in an organization's success has been widely recognized for only about twenty years.

Before the early 1970s, managers who made long-range plans generally assumed that better times lay ahead. Plans for the future were merely extensions of where the organization had been in the past. A number of environmental shocks in the 1970s and 1980s undermined this approach to long-range planning. The energy crisis, deregulation, accelerating technological change, the maturing or stagnation of certain markets, threats of takeover, and increased global competition are a few of the more obvious.[2] These changes in the rules of the game forced managers to develop a systematic means of analyzing the environment, assessing their organization's strengths and weaknesses, and identifying opportunities where the organization could have a competitive advantage. The value of strategic planning began to be recognized.

Today, strategic planning has moved beyond the confines of corporate America to include government agencies, hospitals, and educational institutions. For example, the skyrocketing costs of a college education, cutbacks in federal aid for students and research, and the decline in the absolute number of high school graduates have led many university administrators to assess their colleges' aspirations and identify a market niche in which they can survive and prosper.[3]

LEVELS OF STRATEGY

If all organizations produced only a single product or service, the management of any organization could develop a single strategic plan that encompassed everything it did. But many organizations are in diverse lines of businesses, many of which are only

MANAGERS WHO MADE A DIFFERENCE

Chuck Knight at Emerson Electric

When Chuck Knight became CEO of Emerson Electric in 1973, at the "ripe old age" of 37, the company had annual sales of $940 million, mostly derived from manufacturing motors.[4] Knight immediately instituted a fast-paced growth strategy propelled by detailed planning.

Knight seeks to achieve market leadership and be the "best-cost" supplier in every business in which Emerson competes. He tells his people that he will not accept anything less than best cost, which means the lowest cost at a differentiated-quality level. To get market leadership, he relies on buying other companies and developing new products. His goal is to get 20 percent of sales from products that are five years old or less. In mid-1989 the company had reached 18 percent.

Knight estimates that he devotes 60 percent of his time to reviewing plans submitted to him. Each of the heads of Emerson's fifty or so businesses spends about three days a year at headquarters in St. Louis presenting plans, in very specific detail, to Knight and his top assistants.

Knight is proud of the fact that the heads of his businesses actively develop their plans. "The people who develop the plans implement them," he says. When planning fails, according to Knight, the problem usually isn't in the plan, but in its implementation. To control for this, Emerson executives submit monthly operating reports indicating how well they are doing; the criteria are sales growth, profitability, and return on capital.

Knight's success at Emerson speaks for itself. He has successfully shifted the company's core from electromechanical technology to electronic technology, and sales at the end of the 1980s exceeded $7 billion a year.

Photo courtesy of Chuck Knight.

vaguely related. A firm like General Electric, for instance, is in a variety of businesses—everything from the manufacture of aircraft engines and light bulbs to ownership of the NBC television network. Additionally, GE also has diverse functional departments such as finance and marketing that support each of its businesses. Organizations that are in multiple businesses need to develop different strategies for different levels of activities. Therefore it's necessary to differentiate between corporate-level, business-level, and functional-level strategies (see Figure 8–1).

Corporate-Level Strategy

If an organization is in more than one line of business, it will need a **corporate-level strategy.** This strategy seeks to answer the question: In what set of businesses should we be? Corporate-level strategy determines the roles that each business in the organization will play. At a company like Eastman Kodak, top management's corporate-level strategy integrates the business-level strategies for its film, pharmaceutical, chemical, computer-disk, battery, and other divisions.

corporate-level strategy
Seeks to determine what businesses a corporation should be in.

Business-Level Strategy

Business-level strategy seeks to answer the question: How should we compete in each of our businesses? For the small organization in only one line of business, or the large organization that has avoided diversification, business-level strategy is typically the same as the organization's strategy. For organizations in multiple businesses, each division will have its own strategy that will define the products or services that it will offer, the customers it wants to reach, and the like. A company like Paramount Communications Corp. owns and operates entertainment businesses such as Paramount Pictures and Madison Square Garden as well as the publishing giant Simon & Schuster. Paramount's publishing division has its own unique business strategy that encompasses its trade, educational, and other publication products.

business-level strategy
Seeks to determine how a corporation should compete in each of its businesses.

When an organization is in a number of different businesses, planning can be facilitated by creating strategic business units. A **strategic business unit (SBU)** represents a single business or collection of related businesses. Each SBU will have its

FIGURE 8–1
Levels of Strategy

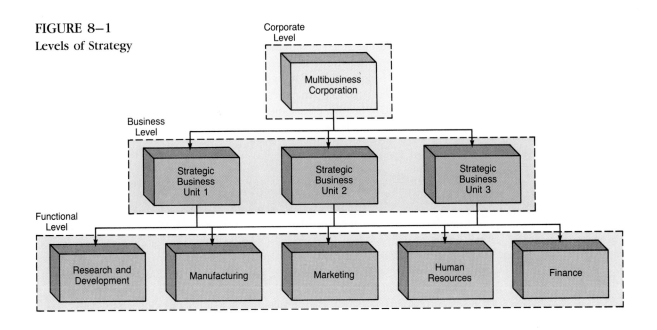

strategic business unit (SBU)
A single business or collection of businesses that is independent and formulates its own strategy.

own distinct mission and competitors. This allows an SBU to have a strategy independent from the other businesses of the larger organization. In a company like General Electric, because it is in so many diverse lines of business, management may create a dozen or more SBUs.

The SBU concept of planning breaks business units up based on the following principles:

The organization is managed as a "portfolio" of businesses, each business unit serving a clearly defined product-market segment with a clearly defined strategy.

Each business unit in the portfolio develops a strategy tailored to its capabilities and competitive needs but consistent with the overall organization's capabilities and needs.

The total portfolio is managed to serve the interests of the organization as a whole—to achieve balanced growth in sales, earnings, and asset mix at an acceptable and controlled level of risk.[5]

Functional-Level Strategy

functional-level strategy
Seeks to determine how to support the business-level strategy.

Functional-level strategy seeks to answer the question: How do we support the business-level strategy? Functional departments such as research and development, manufacturing, marketing, human resources, and finance need to conform to the business-level strategy. If the trade division at Paramount's Simon & Schuster commits millions of dollars to sign and develop former President Ronald Reagan's multibook autobiography, then the division's marketing department will need to develop a functional-level strategy to ensure that the Reagan books are properly promoted when they are published.

In the remainder of this chapter, we'll focus our attention on corporate-level and business-level strategies. This is not to demean the importance of functional-level managers developing strategies for their units. Rather, it reflects the emphasis that researchers and practitioners have placed on developing strategic frameworks.

THE STRATEGIC MANAGEMENT PROCESS

strategic management process
A nine-step process encompassing strategic planning, implementation, and evaluation.

Figure 8–2 illustrates the nine steps in the **strategic management process.** *Strategic planning* encompasses the first seven steps—through the formulation of corporate-, business-, and functional-level strategies. However, the best strategy can go awry if management fails to translate strategies into operational plans, structural designs, control systems, and other necessary means to carry them out; or fails to evaluate results. In this section, we'll look at the larger concept of the strategic *management* process.

Step 1: Identifying the Organization's Current Mission, Objectives, and Strategies

mission
The purpose of an organization.

Every organization has a **mission** that defines its purpose and answers the question: What business or businesses are we in? Defining the organization's mission forces management to identify carefully the scope of its products or services. It has been argued, for instance, that the demise of the railroads has been due to their misdefining the business they were in. During the 1930s and 1940s, had the railroads considered themselves to be in the transportation business instead of the railroad business, their fate might have been quite different.

FIGURE 8–2
The Strategic Management Process

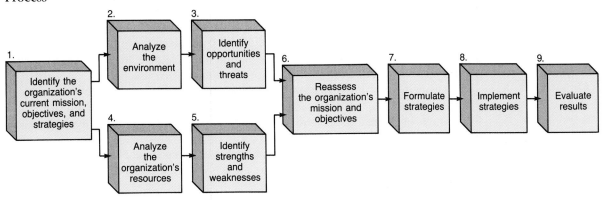

Determining the nature of their business is equally important for not-for-profit organizations. Hospitals, government agencies, and colleges must also identify their mission. For example, is a college training students for the professions, training students for particular jobs, or developing well-rounded students through a liberal education? Is it seeking students from the top 5 percent of high school graduates, students with low academic grades but high aptitude test scores, or students in the vast middle ground? Answers to questions such as these clarify the organization's current purpose.

Step 2: Analyzing the Environment

In Chapter 3, we presented the environment as a primary constraint on management action. Analyzing that environment is also a critical component of the strategy process. Why? Because an organization's environment, to a large degree, defines management's options. A successful strategy will be one that aligns well with the environment.

Objectives and strategies translate the mission into concrete terms. Black & Decker defines its mission as manufacturing and marketing tools and electrical equipment. One of the objectives of its power tools group is to increase sales by 20 percent a year for the next three years. A current strategy to achieve this objective is to modify the product line so that it can be sold worldwide.

As a case in point, IBM might be able to offer a customer a mainframe computer for $200,000 that can handle all of the customer's accounting and inventory control needs. However, microcomputers from competitors like Compaq and Apple now use state-of-the-art, high-power microprocessors, and the same customer's needs can be met by a microcomputer that costs less than $10,000. Because technological breakthroughs are changing IBM's markets for its mainframe computers, the success of IBM's mainframe strategy depends on understanding the technological changes that are taking place in its environment.

Management of every organization needs to analyze its environment. It needs to know, for instance, what its competition is up to, any pending legislation that might affect the organization, and the supply of labor in locations where the organization operates.

Step 2 of the strategy process is complete when management has an accurate grasp of what is taking place in its environment and is aware of important trends that might affect its operations.

Step 3: Identifying Opportunities and Threats

After analyzing the environment, management needs to evaluate what it has learned in terms of opportunities that the organization can exploit and threats that the organization faces.[6]

Keep in mind that the same environment can present opportunities to one organization and pose threats to another in the same industry because of their different resources. In 1989, high interest rates and a weak state economy were threats to many savings and loans in Texas. Dozens of S&Ls had become insolvent and were being taken over by the Federal Savings and Loan Insurance Corporation (FSLIC). For several of Texas's more prosperous and well-managed S&Ls, however, this situation was an opportunity. They were able to buy up potentially valuable assets from the FSLIC at bargain prices. Clearly, what an organization considers an opportunity or threat depends on the resources that it controls. This takes us to Step 4 in the strategic management process.

Step 4: Analyzing the Organization's Resources

Now we move from looking outside the organization to looking inside. What skills and abilities do the organization's employees have? What is the organization's cash position? Can it raise additional capital? Has it been successful at developing new and innovative products? How modern and efficient is the physical plant? How does the public perceive the organization and the quality of its products or services?

This step forces management to recognize that every organization, no matter how large and powerful, is constrained in some way by the resources and skills it has available. An undercapitalized manufacturer of office furniture can't move into the business of manufacturing minivans simply because management sees opportunities there. The office furniture manufacturer is unlikely to possess the expertise, capital, physical plant, or distribution system to compete successfully in the minivan market against the likes of General Motors, Chrysler, and Toyota.

Step 5: Identifying Strengths and Weaknesses

distinctive competence
The unique skills and resources that determine the organization's competitive weapons.

The analysis in Step 4 should lead to a clear assessment of the organization's strengths and weaknesses. Management can identify the organization's **distinctive competence.** That is, an internal analysis of strengths and weaknesses will identify the unique skills and resources that determine the organization's competitive weapons. Black & Decker, for instance, bought General Electric's small appliances division—

Chrysler has used its cost-cutting expertise to make Jeep and Eagle vehicles more profitable than when they were part of an independent American Motors.

which made coffeemakers, toasters, irons, and the like—renamed them, and capitalized on Black & Decker's reputation for quality and durability to make these appliances far more profitable than they had been under the GE name.

An understanding of the organization's culture and the strengths and liabilities it offers management is a crucial part of Step 5 that has only recently been getting the attention it deserves.[7] Specifically, you should be aware that strong and weak cultures have different effects on strategy and that the content of a culture has a major effect on the content of the strategy.

In a strong culture, for instance, almost all employees will have a clear understanding of what the organization is about. This should make it easier for management to convey to new employees the organization's distinctive competence. A department store chain like Nordstrom, which has a very strong culture that embraces service and customer satisfaction, should be able to instill its cultural values in new employees in a much shorter time than can a competitor with a weak culture. The negative side of a strong culture, of course, is that it is more difficult to change. A strong culture may act as a significant barrier to acceptance of a change in the organization's strategies. In fact, the strong culture at General Motors undoubtedly kept top management from perceiving the need to adopt a new corporate strategy in the 1970s and early 1980s in response to changes in the automobile industry. Successful organizations with strong cultures can become prisoners of their own past successes.

Cultures differ in the degree to which they encourage risk taking, exploit innovation, and reward performance. Since strategic choices encompass such factors, cultural values influence managerial preferences for certain strategies. In a risk-aversive culture, for instance, management is more likely to favor strategies that are defensive, that minimize financial exposure, and that react to changes in the environment rather than try to anticipate those changes. Where risk is shunned, you shouldn't be surprised to find management emphasizing cost cutting and improving established product lines. Conversely, where innovation is highly valued, management is likely to favor new technology and product development instead of more service locations or a superior sales force.

Step 6: Reassessing the Organization's Mission and Objectives

A merging of Steps 3 and 5 results in an assessment of the organization's opportunities (see Figure 8–3). In light of these opportunities, management now needs to reevaluate its mission and objectives. Are they realistic? Do they need modification? If changes are needed in the organization's overall direction, this is where they are likely to originate. On the other hand, if no changes are necessary, management is ready to begin the actual formulation of strategies.

Step 7: Formulating Strategies

Strategies need to be set at the corporate, business, and functional levels. The formulation of these strategies follows the decision-making process described in Chapter 6. Specifically, management needs to develop and evaluate alternative strategies and then select a set that is compatible at each level and will allow the organization to best capitalize on its resources and the opportunities available in the environment.

Step 7 is complete when management has developed a set of strategies that will give the organization a competitive advantage. That is, management will seek to position the organization so that it can gain a relative advantage over its rivals. As you'll see later in this chapter, this requires a careful evaluation of the competitive forces that dictate the rules of competition within the industry in which the organization operates. Successful managers will choose strategies that give their organization the most favorable competitive advantage; then they will try to sustain that advantage over time.

Step 8: Implementing Strategies

The next-to-last step in the strategic management process is implementation. No matter how effective strategic planning has been, it cannot succeed if it is not implemented properly. Later chapters in this book will address a number of issues related to strategy implementation. A preview of some "coming attractions" will highlight these.

In Chapter 10, we'll discuss the strategy-structure relationship. We'll show how successful strategies require an organization structure that is properly matched. If an organization significantly changes its corporate-level strategy, it will need to make appropriate changes in its overall structural design.

FIGURE 8–3
Identifying the Organization's
Opportunities

General Electric's new corporate-level strategy focuses solely on technology, service, and core manufacturing. Any of GE's 100 or more businesses that don't fit into one of these three categories are being sold off. This new strategy has resulted in the elimination of more than 100,000 jobs at GE. On the other hand, the acquisition of RCA has made GE's satellite business much bigger.

Top management leadership is a necessary ingredient in a successful strategy. So, too, is a motivated group of middle- and lower-level managers to carry out senior management's specific plans. Chapters 14 and 15 will discuss ways to motivate people and offer suggestions for improving leadership effectiveness.

Management might need to recruit, select, train, discipline, transfer, promote, and possibly even lay off employees to achieve the organization's strategic objectives. In Chapter 12, we'll show that if new strategies are to succeed, they often will require hiring new people with different skills, transferring some current employees to new positions, and laying off some employees.

Step 9: Evaluating Results

The final step in the strategic management process is evaluating results. How effective have our strategies been? What adjustments, if any, are necessary?

In Chapter 18, we'll review the control process. The concepts and techniques that we introduce in that chapter can be used to assess the results of strategies and to correct significant deviations.

CORPORATE-LEVEL STRATEGIC FRAMEWORKS

We defined corporate-level strategy as asking the question: In what set of businesses should we be? Two popular approaches for answering this question are the grand strategies framework and the corporate portfolio matrix.

Grand Strategies

The WD-40 Co., Wal-Mart, and AT&T are successful and highly profitable companies. However, in recent years, each seems to be going in a different direction. WD-40's management seems content to essentially maintain the status quo. Wal-Mart is rapidly expanding its operations and developing new businesses. Meanwhile, AT&T is cutting back and selling off some of its businesses. These different directions can be explained in terms of grand strategies.[8]

ETHICAL DILEMMAS IN MANAGEMENT

Are Certain Businesses Inherently Unethical?

The U.S. Surgeon General says that smoking causes lung cancer. Would you work for a tobacco company? Each year, 55,000 Americans lose their lives in alcohol-related traffic fatalities. Would you work for a beer or spirits manufacturer? Thousands of college graduates have to answer questions like these each spring as they begin their job searches. Large corporations must address similar concerns when they develop their corporate strategies.

When management asks: What set of businesses should we be in?, the answer should not only consider the organization's resources and opportunities in the environment. It also needs to address more basic questions: Is the business morally good? Are its products or services socially worthwhile?

Before management considers acquiring another firm, it typically spends a lot of time assessing the financial aspects of the purchase. More recently, managers have begun also to carefully assess the cultural fit between the parent firm and the acquisition candidate. The time might now have arrived when managers need to look at the ethical factors in acquisition decisions as well. Does the firm sell products that might harm consumers? Does it have business connections with South Africa, whose laws specifically discriminate against the black majority? Does it treat women and minority groups fairly in pay and promotions? Does the firm add to environmental pollution?

Are certain businesses inherently unethical? What do *you* think? How did you arrive at your answer?

---

stability strategy
A corporate-level strategy characterized by an absence of significant change.

Stability   A **stability strategy** is characterized by an absence of significant change. Examples of this strategy include continuing to serve the same clients by offering the same product or service, maintaining market share, and sustaining the organization's past return-on-investment record.

When should management pursue stability? When it views the organization's performance as satisfactory and the environment appears stable and unchanging.

It's not easy to identify organizations that are pursuing a stability strategy, if for no other reason than that few top executives are willing to admit it. In North America, growth tends to have universal appeal, and retrenchment is often accepted as a necessary evil. Moreover, the active pursuit of stability can result in management's being considered complacent or even smug.

We mentioned the WD-40 Co. as an example of a firm using this strategy. The company's single product, a petroleum-based lubricant, has been around since the 1950s, and management has little interest in changing the status quo.[9] Management seems happy to keep its good thing going.

WD-40 is found in 75 percent of U.S. homes and encounters little competition. The company only has seventy employees, but it recently earned an impressive $15.8 million on sales of $81.7 million.

growth strategy
A corporate-level strategy that seeks to increase the level of the organization's operations. This typically includes increasing revenues, employees, and/or market share.

Growth   The pursuit of growth has traditionally had a magic appeal for North Americans. Supposedly, bigger is better, and biggest is best. In our terms, a **growth strategy** means increasing the level of the organization's operations. This includes such popular measures as more revenues, more employees, and more of the market share. Growth can be achieved through direct expansion, a merger with similar firms, or diversification.

Firms like Wal-Mart and McDonald's have pursued a growth strategy by way of direct expansion. When Texaco absorbed Gulf Oil, it chose the merger route to growth. When Philip Morris bought General Foods, it was using diversification to achieve growth.

retrenchment strategy
A corporate-level strategy that seeks to reduce the size or diversity of an organization's operations.

Retrenchment   Until the 1980s, *retrenchment* was a dirty word in North American management circles. No one wanted to admit that they were pursuing a **retrenchment strategy**—reducing the size or diversity of their operations. However, in the last decade, managing decline has become one of the most actively investigated issues in the field of management.[10] The reasons for this are numerous. Aggressive foreign competition, deregulation, mergers and acquisitions, and major technological breakthroughs are some of the more obvious. For instance, within months after Grand Metropolitan International bought Pillsbury, they laid off several thousand employees in Pillsbury's Minneapolis headquarters. Most of these jobs could be absorbed by Grand Met's staff.

There is no shortage of firms that have recently pursued a retrenchment strategy. A partial list would include some of the biggest names in corporate America—AT&T, General Motors, Eastman Kodak, Polaroid, and Union Carbide. Recent changes in Eastern Europe and reductions in world tensions increase the likelihood that American military defense organizations, like the U.S. Army and Air Force, as well as major defense contractors such as Lockheed and Northrop, might also soon be pursuing retrenchment strategies.

combination strategy
A corporate-level strategy that pursues two or more of the following strategies—stability, growth, or retrenchment—simultaneously.

Combination   A **combination strategy** is the pursuit of two or more of the previous strategies simultaneously. For example, one business in the company may be pursuing growth while another in the same company is contracting. In the spring of 1989, for instance, Texas Air was rapidly expanding its Continental Airlines unit. But its Eastern Airlines operation was being consolidated. Eastern's management was selling off routes and planes, cutting back the number of cities served, and making plans for operating a much smaller airline.

Corporate Portfolio Matrix

One of the most popular approaches to corporate-level strategy has been the corporate portfolio matrix.[11] Developed by the Boston Consulting Group in the early 1970s, this approach introduced the idea that each of an organization's SBUs could be plotted on a two-by-two matrix to identify which SBUs offer high potential and which are a drain on the organization's resources.[12] Their **BCG matrix** is shown in Figure 8–4. The horizontal axis represents market share, and the vertical axis indicates anticipated market growth. For definitional purposes, high market share means that a business is the leader in its industry; the cutoff between high and low market growth is 10 percent annual growth in sales (after adjusting for inflation). The matrix identifies four business groups:

BCG matrix
Strategy tool to guide resource allocation decisions based on market share and growth of SBUs.

cash cows
Products that demonstrate low growth but have a high market share.

stars
Products that demonstrate high growth and high market share.

Cash cows (low growth, high market share). Products in this category generate large amounts of cash, but their prospects for future growth are limited.

Stars (high growth, high market share). These products are in a fast-growing market and hold a dominant share of that market but might or might not produce a positive cash flow, depending on the need for investment in new plant and equipment or product development.

FIGURE 8–4
The BCG Matrix

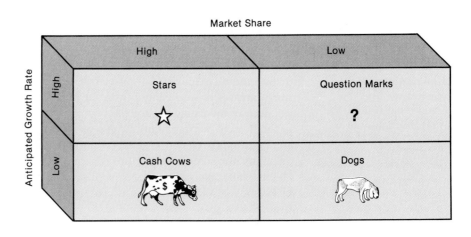

question marks
Products that demonstrate high growth but low market share.

dogs
Products that demonstrate low growth and low market share

cumulative learning curve
Assumes that when a business increases the amount of product manufactured, the per-unit cost of the product will decrease.

Question marks (high growth, low market share). These are speculative products that entail high risks. They may be profitable but hold a small percent of market share.

Dogs (low growth, low market share). The residual category doesn't produce much cash, nor does it require much. These products hold no promise for improved performance.

It is important to understand that the BCG matrix assumes the existence of a **cumulative learning curve.** This is the assumption that if a company is producing a product and managing its production process properly, every significant increase in the cumulative amount of product manufactured will bring a predictable decrease in the per-unit cost of the product. Specifically, the Boston Consulting Group argues that doubling volume typically leads to a 20 to 30 percent reduction in unit costs. The obvious conclusion is therefore that businesses that hold the largest market share will have the lowest costs.

Now let's turn specifically to the implications of the BCG matrix for strategy. What strategy should management pursue with each group?

BCG's research finds that organizations that sacrifice short-run profits to gain market share yield the highest long-run profits. So management should "milk" the cows for as much as they can, limit any new investment in cows to the minimal maintenance level, and use the large amounts of cash the cows generate to invest in more promising opportunities. The stars are those "more promising opportunities." Heavy investment in the stars pays high dividends. The stars, of course, will eventually develop into cash cows as their markets mature and growth declines. The hardest decisions relate to the question marks. Some should be sold off and others turned into stars. But question marks are risky, and management wants to have only a limited number of these speculative ventures. The dogs propose no strategic problems—they should be sold off or liquidated at the earliest opportunity. There is little to recommend their retention or further investment by the company. Money obtained from selling off dogs can be used to buy or finance question marks. For a company like McGraw-Hill, the BCG matrix might advise management to sell off its trade book business because it's a dog, "milk" a cash cow like its college textbook business, and invest in a star like *Business Week* or a question mark like database information products.

In recent years, the corporate portfolio concept (and the BCG matrix in particular) has lost much of its luster. Why? There are at least four reasons.[13] First, cost reduction due to greater cumulative experience has not been automatic. To successfully proceed down the curve, management must tightly control costs. Unfortunately, not all managements have been able to do this. Second, the portfolio concept assumes that an organization's businesses can be divided into a reasonable number of independent units. For large, complex organizations, this has been a lot easier in theory than in practice. Third, contrary to predictions, many so-called dogs have shown consistently higher levels of profitability than their growing competitors with dominant market shares. Finally, given the rate at which the economy has been growing in recent years and the fact that a market can have only one leader, well over half of all businesses fall by definition into the dog category. Following the corporate portfolio concept, most organizations' businesses are cash cows and dogs, and there are few stars and question marks in which to invest.

In spite of these problems, the corporate portfolio matrix is not a useless concept. It provides a framework for understanding disparate businesses and establishes priorities for making strategic resource allocation decisions. However, it has clear limitations as a device for guiding management in setting corporate-level strategy.

MANAGING FROM A GLOBAL PERSPECTIVE

global strategies
The search for competitive advantages outside an organization's domestic borders.

strategic alliances
Joint partnerships between two or more firms to gain a competitive advantage in a market.

The Pursuit of Global Strategies

The Ford automobile that a customer buys in the United Kingdom was probably designed in West Germany and built in Spain. In the United States, Inland Steel and Japan's Nippon Steel are jointly building the world's most advanced continuous cold steel mill at New Carlisle, Indiana. Inland's motivation is to get to use Nippon's technology, while Nippon will be able to bypass import quotas.

These are examples of **global strategies.** These firms are seeking competitive advantages outside their domestic borders.[14] Through global strategies, firms can exploit economies of scale through global volume and taking preemptive positions through large investments in other countries. Interdependent companies may achieve synergies by carefully combining different activities. Don't be surprised if your photocopying machine that was designed in Toronto, incorporates microprocessing chips made in Taiwan and a physical case manufactured in Japan, was assembled in South Korea, and was sold out of warehouses in Melbourne, London, and Los Angeles. Each of these locations was strategically chosen to gain a competitive advantage.

One of the most popular techniques for achieving a global strategy is to develop **strategic alliances** by finding partners in another country with whom strengths can be shared.[15] Inland Steel has done that with Nippon Steel in Indiana. Boeing and Europe's Airbus are currently doing research jointly in order to spread the risk in developing the next generation of commercial aircraft. As the cost of "going it alone" to reach global markets becomes prohibitively expensive, you can expect to see an increasing number of strategic alliances, some of which will even be among former rivals. For instance, Texas Instruments sued Hitachi of Japan in 1986 for patent infringement. The two have since teamed up to develop the next generation of memory chips.

BUSINESS-LEVEL STRATEGIC FRAMEWORKS

Now we move to the business level. The most popular frameworks to guide SBU managers are the adaptive strategy and competitive strategy approaches.

Adaptive Strategies

The adaptive strategy framework was developed from the study of business strategies by Raymond Miles and Charles Snow.[16] First, Miles and Snow identified four strategic types: defenders, prospectors, analyzers, and reactors. Then they demonstrated that success can be achieved with any of the first three strategies if there is a good fit between the strategy and the business unit's environment, internal structure, and managerial processes. However, Miles and Snow found that the reactor strategy often led to failure (see Table 8–1). Let's take a look at each of these four strategic types and explore how organizations have used them to their advantage.

Defenders   McDonald's has followed a defender strategy in the fast-food business. **Defenders** seek stability by producing only a limited set of products directed at a narrow segment of the total potential market. Within this limited niche, defenders strive aggressively to prevent competitors from entering their "turf." This strategy tends to be achieved through standard economic actions such as competitive pricing or creation of high-quality products or services. Defenders tend to ignore developments and trends outside their narrow niche, choosing instead to grow through market penetration and some limited product development. Over time, true defenders are able to carve out and maintain small niches within their industries that are difficult for competitors to penetrate.

Prospectors   Federal Express has followed a prospector strategy with its overnight parcel business. In direct contrast to defenders, **prospectors** seek innovation. Their strength is finding and exploiting new product and market opportunities. Prospectors depend on developing and maintaining the capacity to survey a wide range of environmental conditions, trends, and events. As a result, flexibility is critical to the success of prospectors.

Analyzers   Most of IBM's business units follow an analyzer strategy. They try to minimize risk and maximize the opportunity for profit. **Analyzers** live by imitation. They copy the successful ideas of prospectors. IBM essentially follows its smaller and more innovative competitors with superior products, but only after the competitors have demonstrated that the market is there.

Analyzers must have the ability to respond to the lead of key prospectors, yet at the same time maintain operating efficiency in their stable product and market areas. Analyzers tend to have smaller profit margins than do prospectors, but analyzers are more efficient. Prospectors must have high margins to justify the risks that they take and to compensate for their productive inefficiencies.

defenders
A business-level strategy that seeks stability by producing only a limited set of products directed at a narrow segment of the total potential market.

prospectors
A business-level strategy that seeks innovation by finding and exploiting new product and market opportunities.

analyzers
A business-level strategy that seeks to minimize risk by following competitors' innovations but only after they have proven successful.

TABLE 8–1   Miles and Snow's Adaptive Strategies

Strategy	Goal(s)	Appropriate Environment	Appropriate Structure and Processes
Defenders	Stability and efficiency	Stable	Tight control, efficient operations, low overhead
Prospectors	Flexibility	Dynamic	Loose structure, innovative
Analyzers	Stability and flexibility	Moderate change	Tight control and flexibility, efficient operations, innovative
Reactors	Not clear	Any condition	Not clear

reactors
A business-level strategy that characterizes inconsistent and unstable decision patterns.

Reactors   **Reactors** represent a residual strategy. The label is meant to describe the inconsistent and unstable patterns that arise when one of the other three strategies is pursued improperly. In general, reactors respond inappropriately, perform poorly, and are reluctant to commit themselves aggressively to a specific strategy for the future. In recent years, Avon Products' management reluctantly found itself pursuing a reactor strategy. After its original strategy—selling cosmetics door-to-door to women in their homes—faultered, Avon's management has struggled to find a new focus. In 1988 alone, Avon posted a loss of over $400 million.

Competitive Strategies

The most important recent ideas in strategic planning have come from the work of Michael Porter at Harvard's Graduate School of Business.[17] His competitive strategies framework demonstrates that managers can choose from among three generic strategies. Success depends on selecting the right strategy—one that fits the competitive posture of the organization and the industry of which it is a part. Porter's major contribution has been to detail carefully how management can create and sustain a competitive advantage that will achieve profitability above the industry average.

Industry Analysis   Porter begins by acknowledging that some industries are inherently more profitable than others. Pharmaceuticals, for instance, is an industry in which all competitors can achieve extremely high markups. However, this doesn't mean that a company can't make a lot of money in a "lean" industry. The key is gaining a competitive advantage. Consistent with this logic, we should expect that firms can lose money in so-called glamour industries like personal computers and cable television and make bundles in mundane industries like manufacturing fire trucks and selling junk auto parts. Porter would argue that success can be achieved in most industries; the trick is to find the right strategy.

For much of the 1980s, Sears retail department stores appeared to follow a reactor strategy. Management wasn't sure whether Sears was a general merchandiser, a discounter, or a group of specialty boutiques. Management seemed confused, and so were Sears' customers.

FIGURE 8–5

Forces in the Industry Analysis

Based on Michael E. Porter, *Competitive Strategy: Techniques for Analyzing Industries and Competitors* (New York: Free Press, 1980).

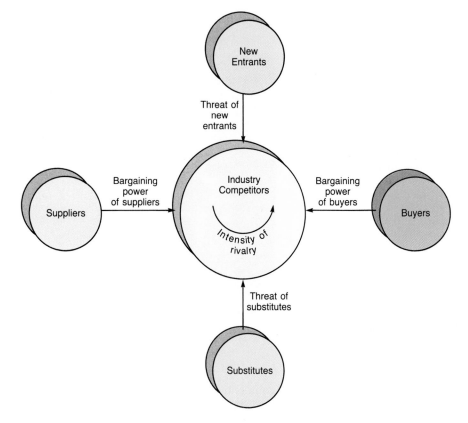

In any industry, five competitive forces dictate the rules of competition:

1. *Barriers to entry:* Factors like economies of scale, brand identity, and capital requirements determine how easy or hard it is for new competitors to enter an industry.

2. *Threats of substitutes:* Factors like switching costs and buyer loyalty determine the degree to which customers are likely to switch their business to a competitor.

3. *Bargaining power of buyers:* Factors like a buyer's volume, buyer information, and the availability of substitute products determine the amount of influence that buyers will have in an industry.

4. *Bargaining power of suppliers:* Factors like the degree of supplier concentration and the availability of substitute inputs determine the power that suppliers will have over firms in the industry.

5. *Rivalry among existing competitors:* Factors like industry growth and product differences determine how intense rivalry will be among firms in the industry.

These five forces, in aggregate (see Figure 8–5), determine industry profitability because they directly influence the prices that a firm can charge, its cost structure, and its investment requirements. Management should assess its industry's attractiveness by evaluating it in terms of these five factors. According to this framework, in 1990 the electronic toy business tended to be unattractive, while the data base publishing industry looked promising. Of course, industry dynamics are always changing. An industry that is favorable one day can become unfavorable the next. Managers need to regularly reevaluate the status of their industry.

Selecting a Competitive Advantage   According to Porter, no firm can successfully perform at an above-average level by trying to be all things to all people. He proposes that management must select a strategy that will give its organization a

There are substantial barriers to entry in the airline industry, in which seven carriers control 90 percent of U.S. air traffic. TWA, for instance, dominates flights into and out of St. Louis' Lambert International Airport. This allows TWA to charge prices that are higher than if there were numerous competitors in the St. Louis market.

competitive advantage. Management can choose from among three strategies: cost-leadership, differentiation, and focus. Which one management chooses depends on the organization's strengths and competitor's weaknesses. Management should avoid a position in which it has to slug it out with everybody in the industry. Rather, the organization should put its strength where the competition isn't.

When an organization sets out to be the low-cost producer in its industry, it is following a **cost-leadership strategy.** Success with this strategy requires that the organization be *the* cost leader and not merely one of the contenders for that position. Additionally, the product or service being offered must be perceived as comparable to that offered by rivals, or at least acceptable to buyers.

How does a firm gain such a cost advantage? Typical means include efficiency of operations, economies of scale, technological innovation, low-cost labor, or preferential access to raw materials. Examples of firms that have used this strategy include Wal-Mart, Gallo wines, and Hyundai automobiles.

The firm that seeks to be unique in its industry in ways that are widely valued by buyers is following a **differentiation strategy.** It might emphasize high quality, extraordinary service, innovative design, technological capability, or an unusually positive brand image. The key is that the attribute chosen must be different from those offered by rivals and significant enough to justify a price premium that exceeds the cost of differentiating.

There is no shortage of firms that have found at least one attribute that allows them to differentiate themselves from competitors. Cray supercomputers (technology), Honda (reliability), Mary Kay cosmetics (distribution), and L.L. Bean (service) are a few.

The first two strategies sought a competitive advantage in a broad range of industry segments. The **focus strategy** aims at a cost advantage (cost focus) or differentiation advantage (differentiation focus) in a narrow segment. That is, management will select a segment or group of segments in an industry (such as product variety, type of end buyer, distribution channel, or geographic location of buyers) and tailor the strategy

cost-leadership strategy
The strategy an organization follows when it wants to be the lowest-cost producer in its industry.

differentiation strategy
The strategy a firm follows when it wants to be unique in its industry along dimensions widely valued by buyers.

focus strategy
The strategy a company follows when it pursues a cost or differentiation advantage in a narrow segment.

to serve them to the exclusion of others. The goal is to exploit a narrow segment of a market. Of course, whether a focus strategy is feasible or not depends on the size of a segment and whether it can support the additional cost of focusing. Stouffer's used a cost-focus strategy in its Lean Cuisine line to reach calorie-conscious consumers seeking both high-quality products and convenience. Similarly, colleges that appeal to working students by offering only night classes hope to gain a competitive advantage over their rivals by following a differentiation-focus strategy. Recent research suggests that the focus strategy may be the most potent for small business firms.[18] This is because they typically don't have the economies of scale or internal resources to successfully pursue one of the other two strategies.

stuck in the middle
Descriptive of organizations that cannot compete through cost-leadership, differentiation, or focus strategies.

Porter uses the term **stuck in the middle** to describe organizations that are unable to gain a competitive advantage by one of these strategies. Such organizations find it very difficult to achieve long-term success. When they do, it is usually a result of competing in a highly favorable industry or having all their rivals similarly stuck in the middle.

Porter notes that successful organizations frequently get into trouble by reaching beyond their competitive advantage and ending up stuck in the middle. Laker Airways provides such a case. It began in 1977 by offering no-frills flights between London and New York at rock-bottom prices. This cost-leadership strategy resulted in a resounding success. In 1979, however, the firm began to add new routes and offer upscale services. This blurred the public's image of Laker, allowed the competition to make significant inroads, and led to Laker's declaration of bankruptcy in 1982.

Sustaining a Competitive Advantage   Long-term success with any one of the three strategies requires that the advantage be sustainable. That is, it must resist erosion by the actions of competitors or by evolutionary changes in the industry. This is no simple task. Technology changes, as do the tastes of customers. Most important, some advantages can be imitated by competitors. Management needs to create barriers that make imitation difficult or that reduce competitive opportunities. The use of patents and copyrights reduces opportunities for imitation. When there are strong economies of scale, reducing price to gain volume is a useful tactic. Tying up suppliers with exclusive contracts limits their ability to supply rivals. Encouraging government policies that impose import tariffs can limit foreign competition. Yet whatever actions it takes to sustain a competitive advantage, management cannot become complacent. Sustaining a competitive advantage requires constant action by management in order to keep one step ahead of the competition.

ENTREPRENEURSHIP: A SPECIAL CASE OF STRATEGIC PLANNING

Strategic planning carries a "big business" bias. It implies a formalization and structure that fits well with large, established organizations with abundant resources. But the primary interest of many students is not in managing large and established organizations. They're excited by the idea of starting up their own businesses from scratch. Some want to be the next Steve Jobs (of Apple Computer and NeXt fame), R. David Thomas (Wendy's), or Fred Smith (Federal Express), while others have no delusions of grandeur but merely want to control their own destinies. In this final section, we'll demonstrate that many strategic planning concepts can be applied directly by those who wish to pursue the entrepreneurial route in management, but with a different emphasis.

What Is Entrepreneurship?

entrepreneurship
Undertaking ventures, pursuing opportunities, innovating, and starting businesses.

Entrepreneurship refers to undertaking a venture, pursuing opportunities, fulfilling needs and wants through innovation, and starting businesses.[19] Entrepreneurs are individuals who fill this role. When we describe entrepreneurs, we use adjectives like bold, innovative, venturesome, and risk-taking. We also tend to associate entrepreneurs with small businesses.

It's important not to confuse small-business management with entrepreneurship. Why? Because not all small-business managers are entrepreneurs.[20] Many don't innovate or take risks. A great many small-business managers are merely scaled-down versions of the conservative, conforming bureaucrats who staff many large corporations and public agencies.

Can entrepreneurs exist in large, established organizations? The answer to that question depends on one's definition of entrepreneur. Peter Drucker, for instance, argues that they can.[21] He describes an entrepreneurial manager as someone who is confident of his or her ability, who seizes opportunities for innovation, and who not only expects surprises but capitalizes on them. He contrasts that with the trustee type of manager who feels threatened by change, is bothered by uncertainty, prefers predictability, and is inclined to maintain the status quo.

intrapreneurship
Creating the entrepreneurial spirit in a large organization.

Drucker's use of the term entrepreneurial, however, is misleading. By almost any definition of good management, his entrepreneurial type would be preferred over the trustee type. Moreover, the term **intrapreneurship** is now widely used to describe the effort to create the entrepreneurial spirit in a large organization.[22] Yet intrapreneurship can never capture the autonomy and riskiness inherent in true entrepreneurship. This is because intrapreneurship takes place within a larger organization; all financial risks are carried by the parent company; rules, policies, and other constraints are imposed by the parent; intrapreneurs have bosses or superiors to report to; and the payoff for success is not financial independence but career advancement.[23]

Characteristics of Entrepreneurs

One of the most-researched topics in entrepreneurship has been the search to determine what, if any, psychological characteristics entrepreneurs have in common. A number of characteristics have been found to be associated with entrepreneurship. These include hard work, self-confidence, optimism, determination, and a high energy level.[24] But three factors regularly sit on the top of most lists that profile the entrepreneurial personality. Entrepreneurs have a high need for achievement, strongly believe that they can control their own destinies, and take only moderate risks.[25]

The research allows us to draw a general description of entrepreneurs. They tend to be independent types who prefer to be personally responsible for solving problems, for setting goals, and for reaching these goals by their own efforts. They value independence and particularly don't like being controlled by others. While they're not afraid of taking chances, they're not wild risk takers. They prefer to take calculated risks where they feel they can control the outcome.

The evidence on entrepreneurial personalities leads us to two obvious conclusions. First, people with this personality makeup are not likely to be contented, productive employees in the typical large corporation or government agency. The rules, regulations, and controls that these bureaucracies impose on their members frustrate entrepreneurs. Second, the challenges and conditions inherent in starting one's own business mesh well with the entrepreneurial personality. Starting a new venture,

TABLE 8–2   The Order of Strategic Questions

Typical Bureaucratic Manager

What resources do I control?
What structure determines our organization's relationship to its market?
How can I minimize the impact of others on my ability to perform?
What opportunity is appropriate?

Typical Entrepreneur

Where is the opportunity?
How do I capitalize on it?
What resources do I need?
How do I gain control over them?
What structure is best?

Source: Reprinted by permission of *Harvard Business Review.* An excerpt from "The Heart of Entrepreneurship" by Howard H. Stevenson and David E. Gumpert, March–April 1985, pp. 86–87. Copyright © 1985 by the President and Fellows of Harvard College; all rights reserved.

which they control, appeals to their willingness to take risks and determine their own destinies. But because entrepreneurs believe that their future is fully in their own hands, the risk they perceive as moderate is often seen as high by nonentrepreneurs.

Strategy and the Entrepreneur

Entrepreneurs approach strategy differently from typical bureaucratic managers. This can be seen in the order in which they address key strategic questions (see Table 8–2).

The entrepreneur's strategic emphasis is driven by perception of opportunity rather than by availability of resources.[26] The entrepreneur's inclination is to monitor the environment closely in search of opportunities. The resources at his or her disposal take a back seat to identifying an idea that can be capitalized upon.

Once an opportunity is spotted, the entrepreneur begins to look for ways to take advantage of it. Because of his or her personality makeup, the entrepreneur is confident that the opportunity can be exploited. Moreover, the entrepreneur is not afraid to risk financial security, career opportunities, family relations, or psychic well-being to get the new venture off the ground. Entrepreneurs tend to ignore the hard statistics against success: New businesses with fewer than ten employees have little more than a 75 percent chance of surviving a year and only about one chance in three of lasting four years or more.[27] Nevertheless, the entrepreneur who sees an opportunity has the confidence and determination to believe that he or she will be on the winning side of those statistics.

Only after the entrepreneur has identified an opportunity and a way to exploit it does he or she begin to feel concerned about resources. But the entrepreneur's priorities are first to find out what resources are needed and then determine how they can be obtained. This is in contrast to typical bureaucratic managers, who focuses on the resources that are at their disposal. Entrepreneurs are often able to make imaginative and highly efficient use of very limited resources. Further, as entrepreneurship has grown in popularity, the availability of financial resources to support new ventures has increased. The rise of venture capital firms makes it more true than ever that if a new idea is promising enough, the capital to get it underway can be found.

Norman Pattiz created West-wood One in 1974 with his life savings—$10,000—and the perception of an opportunity. He would prepackage and sell syndicated radio programming. The idea hit, and his company grew. His firm recently purchased the Mutual Broadcasting System, NBC Radio, and stations in New York and Los Angeles. Today, Westwood One is the second largest radio network in the United States.

Finally, when the resource obstacles have been overcome, the entrepreneur will put together the organizational structure, people, marketing plan, and other components necessary to implement the overall strategy.

SUMMARY

This summary is organized by the chapter-opening learning objectives found on page 215.

1. A dynamic and uncertain environment has increased the importance of strategic planning for management. Changes in the environment have forced managers to develop a systematic means of analyzing the environment, assessing their organization's strengths and weaknesses, and identifying opportunities in which their organization could have a competitive advantage.

2. Corporate-level strategy seeks to determine what set of businesses the organization should be in. Business-level strategy is concerned with how the organization should compete in each of its businesses. Functional-level strategy is concerned with how functional departments can support the business-level strategy.

3. Strategic planning together with strategy implementation and evaluation forms strategic management.

4. The strategic management process is made up of nine steps: (1) identifying the organization's current mission, objectives, and strategies; (2) analyzing the environment; (3) identifying opportunities and threats in the environment; (4) analyzing the organization's resources; (5) identifying the organization's strengths and weaknesses; (6) reassessing the organization's mission and objectives based on its strengths, weaknesses, opportunities, and threats; (7) formulating strategies; (8) implementing its strategies; and (9) evaluating results.

5. The four grand strategies are stability, growth, retrenchment, and a combination of any two or more of the previous strategies pursued simultaneously.

6. The BCG matrix identifies four business groups: stars, cash cows, question marks, and dogs. Management should sell its dogs and use this money and that generated by the cash cows to invest in its stars and the potentially high-performing question marks.

7. At the business level, there are four adaptive strategies. Defenders operate in stable environments and produce a limited set of products for a narrow market segment. Prospectors operate in a dynamic environment, innovate, and seek flexibility. Analyzers minimize risk and maximize profit opportunities by seeking both flexibility and stability at the same time. Reactors are inconsistent and reluctant to commit themselves to any specific situation.

8. Management assesses its organization's competitive advantage by analyzing the forces that dictate the rules of competition within its industry (barriers to entry, substitutes, bargaining power of buyers and suppliers, and rivalry among competitors) and then selecting a strategy (cost-leadership, differentiation, or focus) that can best exploit its competitive posture.

9. Entrepreneurship refers to the innovative and risk-taking activities associated with starting up a new business.

10. Entrepreneurs have a high need for achievement, strongly believe that they can control their own destiny, and are willing to take moderate risks.

REVIEW QUESTIONS

1. What level of strategies would be relevant to a large firm that produced only a single product?

2. Define an SBU.

3. Compare an organization's *mission* with its *objectives*.

4. What relevance does an organization's culture have to its strategy?

5. What is an organization's *distinctive competence*?

6. Is growth always the best strategy for an organization to pursue? Explain.

7. What are the advantages of the BCG matrix? What are its limitations?

8. What are *global strategies*? Why do organizations use them?

9. What are the forces that dictate the rules of competition within an industry?

10. Compare how entrepreneurs and bureaucratic managers approach strategy.

DISCUSSION QUESTIONS

1. What is McDonald's competitive advantage in its industry?

2. What role, if any, do lower- and middle-level managers play in strategic planning?

3. Assume that you are a manager in a business that produces and markets baby food, such as Gerber Products. How might your strategies have changed between (a) 1961 and 1991? (b) 1981 and 1991?

4. A publisher of college textbooks decided to pursue the strategy of cost-leadership because no one in the industry had taken this route. Yet the strategy failed. Why? Can a lesson be learned from this example?

5. More than 200 colleges now offer courses in entrepreneurship. Do you think entrepreneurship can be taught? Explain your answer. How might a major in entrepreneurship differ from a traditional major in management or marketing?

SELF-ASSESSMENT EXERCISE

Are You an Entrepreneur?

Instructions: This quiz is designed to give you an idea of whether you have the entrepreneurial spirit. Circle your answer to each of the following twenty-six questions:

1. How were your parents employed?
   a. Both worked and were self-employed for most of their working lives.
   b. Both worked and were self-employed for some part of their working lives.
   c. One parent was self-employed for most of his or her working life.
   d. One parent was self-employed at some point in his or her working life.
   e. Neither parent was ever self-employed.

2. Have you ever been fired from a job?
   a. Yes, more than once.
   b. Yes, once.
   c. No.

3. Are you an immigrant, or were your parents or grandparents immigrants?
   a. I was born outside of the United States.
   b. One or both of my parents were born outside of the United States.
   c. At least one of my grandparents was born outside of the United States.
   d. Does not apply.

4. Your work career has been:
   a. Primarily in small business (under 100 employees).
   b. Primarily in medium-sized business (100 to 500 employees).
   c. Primarily in big business (over 500 employees).

5. Did you operate any businesses before you were 20?
   a. Many.
   b. A few.
   c. None.

6. What is your present age?
   a. Under 31.
   b. 31–40.
   c. 41–50.
   d. 51 or over.

7. You are the _____ child in the family.
   a. Oldest.
   b. Middle.
   c. Youngest.
   d. Other.

8. You are:
   a. Married.
   b. Divorced.
   c. Single.

9. Your highest level of formal education is:
   a. Some high school.
   b. High school diploma.
   c. Bachelor's degree.
   d. Master's degree.
   e. Doctor's degree.

10. What is your primary motivation in starting a business?
   a. To make money.
   b. I don't like working for someone else.
   c. To be famous.
   d. As an outlet for excess energy.

11. Your relationship to the parent who provided most of the family's income was:
   a. Strained.
   b. Comfortable.
   c. Competitive.
   d. Nonexistent.

12. If you could choose between working hard and working smart, you would:
   a. Work hard.
   b. Work smart.
   c. Both.

13. On whom do you rely for critical management advice?
    a. Internal management teams.
    b. External management professionals.
    c. External financial professionals.
    d. No one except myself.

14. If you were at the racetrack, which of these would you bet on?
    a. The daily double—a chance to make a killing.
    b. A 10-to-1-shot.
    c. A 3-to-1-shot.
    d. The 2-to-1 favorite.

15. The only ingredient that is both necessary and sufficient for starting a business is:
    a. Money.
    b. Customers.
    c. An idea or product.
    d. Motivation and hard work.

16. If you were an advanced tennis player and had a chance to play a top pro like Boris Becker, you would:
    a. Turn it down because he could easily beat you.
    b. Accept the challenge but not bet any money on it.
    c. Bet a week's pay that you would win.
    d. Get odds, bet a fortune, and try for an upset.

17. You tend to "fall in love" too quickly with:
    a. New product ideas.
    b. New employees.
    c. New manufacturing ideas.
    d. New financial plans.
    e. All of the above.

18. Which of the following personality types is best suited to be your right-hand person?
    a. Bright and energetic.
    b. Bright and lazy.
    c. Dumb and energetic.

19. You accomplish tasks better because:
    a. You are always on time.

b. You are superorganized.
c. You keep good records.

20. You hate to discuss:
    a. Problems involving employees.
    b. Signing expense accounts.
    c. New management practices.
    d. The future of the business.

21. Given a choice, you would prefer:
    a. Rolling dice with a 1-in-3 chance of winning.
    b. Working on a problem with a 1-in-3 chance of solving it in the allocated time.

22. If you could choose between the following competitive professions, it would be:
    a. Professional golf.
    b. Sales.
    c. Personnel counseling.
    d. Teaching.

23. If you had to choose between working with a partner who is a close friend and working with a stranger who is an expert in your field, you would choose:
    a. The close friend.
    b. The expert.

24. You enjoy being with people:
    a. When you have something meaningful to do.
    b. When you can do something new and different.
    c. Even when you have nothing planned.

25. In business situations that demand action, clarifying who is in charge will help produce results.
    a. Agree.
    b. Agree, with reservations.
    c. Disagree.

26. In playing a competitive game, you are concerned with:
    a. How well you play.
    b. Winning or losing.
    c. Both of the above.
    d. Neither of the above.

Turn to page 671 for scoring directions and key.

Source: Joseph R. Mancuso, "The Entrepreneur in You," *Across the Board,* July–August 1984, pp. 1–4, 43–47. With permission.

CASE APPLICATION 8A

Playboy Enterprises

In November 1988, after six years as president, Christie Hefner took over as CEO of the Playboy empire her father had founded nearly 35 years earlier.[28] Hugh Hefner's *Playboy* magazine grew and prospered by promoting a life-style of guiltless sex and fast living. It became a staple of U.S. pop culture in the 1960s. But times changed. Unfortunately for Playboy Enterprises, the company didn't respond very well to those changes.

The flagship of the firm's business, its *Playboy* magazine, suffered declining circulation throughout the late 1970s and 1980s. Circulation peaked at nearly 7 million in the 1970s, fell to 4.7 million in 1982, and was down to 3.4 million when Ms. Hefner took over as CEO in 1988. The magazine was suffering from attacks by feminists, increased competition from more sexually explicit magazines and X-rated home videos, and a shift toward more conservative sexual mores.

Other parts of Playboy Enterprises weren't fairing much better. The last of its bunny-hosted clubs in the United States closed in 1987. Its lucrative gambling casinos in London, Atlantic City, and the Bahamas were sold in the early 1980s. The company's pay-cable service, the Playboy Channel, was losing both subscribers and money. One of the few bright spots for the company was its licensing and merchandising business.

For fiscal 1988, Playboy's earnings plunged 76 percent to $2.6 million on flat sales of $159.8 million. Christie Hefner knew that she had a challenge ahead of her, but she was confident of her ability to respond. Convinced that Playboy had to move beyond her father's original vision of an empire built exclusively for men, Ms. Hefner planned on making Playboy into an international media and marketing company.

Questions

1. Describe Playboy Enterprises' environment. What opportunities and threats are present?
2. What are the company's strengths and weaknesses?
3. What corporate-level strategy do you think Christie Hefner should pursue? Why?

CASE APPLICATION 8B

The Falcone Piano Co.

According to the old adage, build a better mousetrap and the world will beat a path to your door. Santi Falcone doesn't buy it! He's built the "better mousetrap" and no one is knocking at *his* door.[29]

The mousetrap, in this case, is a piano. Not just any piano, mind you, but a product that many believe is the finest in the world—one capable of going up against the likes of Steinway and Yamaha and beating them. But Santi Falcone is caught in a bind. Although he might make the world's best piano, people won't buy it until the world's best pianists play it. However, the world's best pianists won't play it until more people buy it.

Falcone grew up loving pianos. By the time he decided to build the world's best, in 1983, he had spent 25 years repairing, rebuilding, and selling pianos. Using his life savings, he created the Falcone Piano Co. in a Boston suburb. Today, he and his staff of sixty craftspeople slowly and carefully build three sizes of grand pianos. Each piano is virtually custom made for a narrow market that includes professional musicians, music schools, and others willing to pay between $18,000 and $32,000 for his product.

Falcone believes that he has the physical capabilities to produce between 850 and 1000 pianos a year. Were he able to reach this objective, he would gross $20 million annually and earn a profit of around $6 million. But his sales objective might not be attainable. Falcone's firm is currently building and selling pianos at the rate of seven per month and losing money. The problem is that he competes in a declining industry, with two dominant U.S. players (Steinway and Baldwin) whose size allows them to offer service and availability that are beyond Falcone's current resources.

Like basketball sneakers and tennis rackets, real industry status comes from big-name endorsements. In the concert piano industry, Steinway and Baldwin have signed the major artists' to exclusive agreements. Artists agree to use only a specific brand of piano; in return, the piano manufacturer can use the artists' names and agrees to make a properly tuned piano available wherever and whenever the artists play. Such a relationship would be exceedingly difficult and expensive for Santi Falcone to duplicate.

To make matters worse, the number of pianos sold in the United States has declined by 40 percent since 1980. U.S. exports have dropped 80 percent. Imports, mostly Japanese and Korean, have more than doubled over this same period. A number of factors seem to be plaguing the U.S. industry: a decline in quality, high labor costs, high prices of raw materials, a strong market for used pianos, and a decline in the number of children at peak piano-lesson ages.

Santi Falcone is perplexed. He knows that he has a quality product. Several famous pianists have told him his is the best. But any determination of "best" in the piano business is a subjective judgment. He already prices his product competitively with Baldwin and well below comparable Steinways and major foreign brands. Yet he is able to maintain his price advantage only because he bypasses independent piano dealers and sells directly to customers. Being a little guy, Falcone can't match the kind of support system that Steinway offers its exclusive artists. Steinway has a $15 million inventory of concert pianos in the field and uses its 126 dealers in more than 195 markets to ensure that pianos are available to its artists when they're needed.

Questions

1. Describe Falcone's environment. What opportunities and threats are present?

2. What are the company's strengths and weaknesses?

3. What strategy do you think the company should pursue? Why?

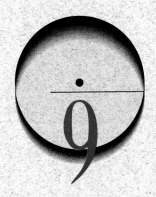

PLANNING TOOLS AND TECHNIQUES

1. Describe techniques for scanning the environment.
2. Contrast quantitative and qualitative forecasting.
3. Describe why budgets are popular.
4. List three approaches to budgeting.
5. Differentiate Gantt and load charts.
6. Identify the steps in a PERT network.
7. State the factors that determine a product's break-even point.
8. Describe the requirements for using linear programming.
9. Discuss how simulation can be a planning tool.
10. List five steps toward better time management.

If you were to walk by the factory manager's office in this Torrington Co. manufacturing plant, you might think that the plant manager and his top engineers were playing a video game on company time. Huddled in front of a computer screen, they're threading little cartoon-style symbols through mazes. On closer investigation, you would see that they're using a computer-based simulation planning tool. The screen display is a recreation of the factory floor, complete with work areas, machines, materials-handling equipment, and simulated workers. The manager and his staff are designing a complicated manufacturing line for making ball bearings. Their goal is to find the layout and processing flow that can turn out the highest-quality, lowest-cost product.[1]

The managers' computations indicated that they would need seventy-seven machine tools performing sixteen different processes. But when they fed the information into the computer and simulated the line in operation, they quickly realized that the plan could be improved. In a matter of a few hours and for an investment of several hundred dollars, these managers were able to eliminate four machines and save their firm $750,000.

This simulation tracks diesel engine castings through a production cycle. Such simulations help even small firms both to solve everyday problems and to make major strategic decisions.

Simulation is only one of many planning tools and techniques that are available to managers. In this chapter, we'll discuss two strategic planning techniques to assist managers in assessing their environment—environmental scanning and forecasting. We'll review the most popular planning tool used by managers: budgets. We'll then discuss scheduling, break-even analysis, and other operational planning tools. Finally, we'll conclude this chapter by offering some ideas to help you in your personal, day-to-day planning. We'll present the key things you need to know about time management.

TECHNIQUES FOR ASSESSING THE ENVIRONMENT

In Chapter 8, we detailed the strategic management process. In this section, we want to review several techniques that have been developed to help managers with one of the most challenging aspects of this process: assessing their organization's environment. Twenty years ago, environmental analysis was an informal endeavor based on intuitive judgments. Today, using structured techniques such as environmental scanning and forecasting, a manager's ability to accurately analyze an organization's environment has improved measurably.

Environmental Scanning

Maria Iriti, who runs a glass company in Massachusetts, put in a bid of $18,000 to repair stained glass windows in a church. She won the bid but lost her shirt. She later found out that the next lowest bid had come in at $76,000. Iriti learned a valuable lesson from her mistake. She now keeps a folder on each competitor, socializes with them at trade shows, and has friends write to competitors for price lists and brochures.[2]

environmental scanning
The screening of much information to detect emerging trends and create scenarios.

Managers in both small and large organizations are increasingly turning to **environmental scanning** to anticipate and interpret changes in their environment.[3] The term, as we'll use it, refers to screening large amounts of information to detect emerging trends and create a set of scenarios.

The importance of environmental scanning was first recognized (outside of the national security establishment) by firms in the life insurance industry in the late 1970s.[4] Life insurance companies found that the demand for their product was declining. Yet all the key environmental signals they were receiving strongly favored the sale of life insurance. The economy and population were growing. Baby boomers were finishing school, entering the labor force, and taking on family responsibilities. The market for life insurance should have been expanding, but it wasn't. What the insurance companies had failed to recognize was a fundamental change in family structure in the United States.

Young families, who represented the primary group of buyers of new insurance policies, tended to be dual-career couples who were increasingly choosing to remain childless. The life insurance needs of a family with one income, a dependent spouse, and a houseful of kids are much greater than those of a two-income family with few, if any, children. That a multibillion-dollar industry could overlook such a fundamental social trend underscored the need to develop techniques for monitoring important environmental developments.

competitor intelligence
Environmental scanning activity that seeks to identify who competitors are, what they're doing, and how their actions will affect the focus organization.

One of the fastest-growing areas of environmental scanning is **competitor intelligence**.[5] It seeks basic information about competitors: Who are they? What are they doing? How will what they're doing affect us? As Maria Iriti learned the hard way, accurate information on the competition can allow managers to *anticipate* competitor actions rather than merely *react* to them.

One expert on competitive intelligence emphasizes that 95 percent of the competitor-related information an organization needs to make crucial strategic decisions is available and accessible to the public.[6] In other words, competitive intelligence isn't organizational espionage. Advertisements, promotional materials, press releases, reports filed with government agencies, annual reports, want ads, newspaper reports, and industry studies are examples of readily accessible sources of information. Trade

How do managers go about scanning the environment? How do they ascertain trends? The most effective method is to follow a formal search process. This includes reading mainstream publications such as newspapers, magazines, popular books, and trade journals; fringe literature such as politically extreme publications; and periodicals directed at particular groups such as *Working Woman* and *Ebony*. The objective is to tap into social, technological, economic, and political trends when they're in their infancy.

Firms like Dialog sell inexpensive data bases that can provide management with extracts on competitor's SEC filings, patent information, income and balance sheet data, and in-depth profiles on key executives in competitors' firms.

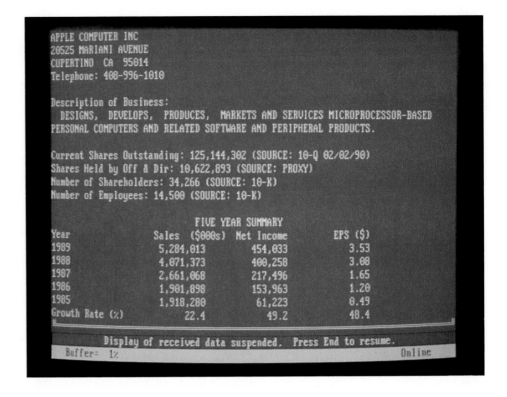

shows and debriefing of your own sales force can be other good sources of information on competitors. Many firms even regularly buy competitors' products and have their own engineers break them down to learn about new technical innovations.

Extensive environmental scanning is likely to reveal a number of issues and concerns that could affect your organization's current or planned operations. Not all of these are likely to be equally important, so it's usually necessary to focus in on a limited set—say, three or four—that are most important and to develop scenarios based on each of these.

scenario
An internally consistent view of what the future is likely to be.

A **scenario** is an internally consistent view of what the future is likely to be. If, for instance, scanning uncovers increasing interest in Congress for raising the national minimum wage, McDonald's could create a multiple set of scenarios to assess the possible consequences of such an action. What would be the implications for its labor supply if the minimum was raised to $4.75 an hour? How about $5.50 an hour? What effect would these changes have on labor costs? How might competitors respond? Different assumptions would lead to different outcomes. The intention of this exercise is not to try to predict the future, but to reduce uncertainty by playing out plausible future states under different specified conditions.[7] McDonald's could, for example, develop a set of scenarios ranging from optimistic to pessimistic in terms of the minimum-wage issue. It would then be better prepared to initiate changes in its strategy to gain and hold a competitive advantage.

Forecasting

forecasts
Predictions of future outcomes.

Environmental scanning creates the foundation for forecasts. Information obtained through scanning is used to form scenarios. These, in turn, establish premises for **forecasts,** which are predictions of future outcomes.

When Does Competitive Intelligence Become Espionage?

Texas Instruments hires a senior engineering executive from Motorola. While the new executive is certainly well qualified for his new position, so were a dozen or so other candidates. However, they didn't work for Motorola and have up-to-date knowledge of what new microchip products Motorola was developing. Is it unethical for Texas Instruments, one of Motorola's primary microchip competitors, to hire this executive? Is it acceptable to hire this executive but unacceptable to question him about Motorola's plans?

The vice president at a major book publishing company encourages one of her editors to interview for an editorial vacancy at a competing book publisher. The editor isn't interested in the position. The sole purpose of the interview will be to gain as much information as possible on the competitor's near-term publishing list and relay that information back to the vice president. Is going to such an interview unethical? Is asking a subordinate to engage in this intelligence mission unethical?

Neither of these situations involves obtaining publicly available information. Yet tactics like these are practiced by organizations in a number of highly competitive businesses. When does competitive intelligence become espionage? Does any effort to conceal one's real motives when attempting to gather information automatically brand that action as unethical? What do *you* think?

Types of Forecasts   Probably the two most popular outcomes of which management is likely to seek forecasts are future revenues and new technological breakthroughs. However, virtually any component in the organization's general and specific environment can receive forecasting attention.

Sara Lee's sales level drives purchasing requirements, production goals, employment needs, inventories, and numerous other decisions. Similarly, the University of Arizona's income from tuition and state appropriations will determine course offerings, staffing needs, salary increases for faculty, and the like. Both of these examples illustrate that predicting future revenues—**revenue forecasting**—is a critical element of planning for both profit and not-for-profit organizations.

revenue forecasting
Predicting future revenues.

Where does management get the data for developing revenue forecasts? Typically, it begins with historical revenue figures. For example, what were last year's revenues? This figure can then be adjusted for trends. What revenue patterns have evolved over recent years? What changes in social, economic, or other factors in the general environment might alter the pattern in the future? In the specific environment, what actions can we expect from our competitors? Answers to questions like these provide the basis for revenue forecasts.

Between 1986 and 1990, firms like Columbia and MCA saw one of their basic products—vinyl long-playing records—almost disappear. Consumers still wanted to listen to music, but they preferred a new technology: compact discs. The record companies that successfully forecasted this technology and foresaw its impact on their business were able to convert their production facilities, adopt the technology, and beat their competition to the record store racks.

Technological forecasting attempts to predict changes in technology and the time frame in which new technologies are likely to be economically feasible. The rapid pace of technological change has seen innovations in lasers, biotechnology, robotics, and data communications dramatically change surgery practices, the processes used for manufacturing almost every mass-produced product, pharmaceutical offerings, and the practicality of cellular telephones. Few organizations are exempt from the possibility that technological innovation might dramatically change the demand for their current products or services. The environmental scanning techniques discussed in the previous section can provide data on potential technological innovations.

Forecasting Techniques   Forecasting techniques fall into two categories: quantitative and qualitative. **Quantitative forecasting** applies a set of mathematical rules to a series of past data to predict future outcomes. These techniques are preferred when management has sufficient "hard" data from which to work. **Qualitative forecasting,** on the other hand, uses the judgment and opinions of knowledgeable individuals. Qualitative techniques are typically used when precise data is scarce or difficult to obtain.

Table 9–1 lists some of the better-known quantitative and qualitative forecasting techniques.

technological forecasting
Predicting changes in technology and when new technologies are likely to be economically feasible.

quantitative forecasting
Applies a set of mathematical rules to a series of past data to predict future outcomes.

qualitative forecasting
Uses the judgment and opinions of knowledgeable individuals to predict future outcomes.

TABLE 9–1   Forecasting Techniques

Quantitative Techniques	Description	Application
Time-series analysis	Fits a trend line to a mathematical equation and projects into the future by means of this equation	Predict next quarter's sales based on four years of previous sales data
Regression models	Predicts one variable on the basis of known or assumed other variables	Seek factors that will predict a certain level of sales (i.e., price, advertising expenditures)
Econometric models	Uses a set of regression equations to simulate segments of the economy	Predict change in car sales as a result of changes in tax laws
Economic indicators	Uses one or more economic indicators to predict a future state of the economy	Use change in GNP to predict discretionary income
Substitution effect	Uses a mathematical formulation to predict how, when, and under what circumstances a new product or technology will replace an existing one	Predict the effect of microwave ovens on the sale of conventional ovens

(Continued)

TABLE 9–1 (*Continued*)

Qualitative Techniques	Description	Application
Jury of opinion	Combining and averaging the opinions of experts	Polling all the company's personnel managers to predict next year's college recruitment needs
Sales-force composition	Combining estimates from field sales personnel of customers' expected purchases	Predict next year's sales of industrial lasers
Customer evaluation	Combining estimates from established customers of expected purchases	Survey of its major dealers' expected orders by a car manufacturer

BUDGETS

budget
A numerical plan.

Few of us are unfamiliar with budgets. Most of us learned about them at an early age, when we discovered that unless we allocated our "revenues" carefully, we would consume our weekly allowance before half the week was out.

A **budget** is a numerical plan. Managers typically prepare budgets for revenues, expenses, and capital expenditures like machinery and equipment. It's not unusual, though, for budgets to be used for improving time, space, and the use of material resources. These latter types of budgets substitute nondollar numbers for dollar terms. Items like person-hours, capacity utilization, or units of production can be budgeted for daily, weekly, or monthly activities. However, we'll emphasize dollar-based budgets in this section.

Why are budgets so popular? Probably because they are applicable to a wide variety of organizations and units within an organization. We live in a society that expresses

Budgets can be used for control as well as for planning. When a budget is established, it becomes a planning tool because it gives direction. It tells what activities are important and how many resources should be allocated to each activity. A budget becomes a control mechanism when it provides standards against which resource consumption can be measured and compared. Keep in mind that a budget is not only a numerical plan, but also a control device for assessing how well activities are going.

Department Expense Budget
Calender Year 1990

ITEM	QUARTER			
	1ST	2ND	3RD	4TH
Salaries/Fixed	$ 93,600	$ 93,600	$ 93,600	$ 93,600
Salaries/Variable	10,000	15,000	10,000	30,000
Performance Bonuses				35,000
Office Supplies	2,500	2,500	2,500	2,500
Photocopying	3,000	3,000	3,000	3,000
Telephone	8,000	8,000	8,000	8,000
Mail	2,500	2,500	2,500	2,500
Travel	8,000	3,000	3,000	3,000
Library Development	1,500	1,500	1,500	1,500
Outside Consultants	0	12,000	0	0
Recruitment/Entertainment	5,000	2,000	2,000	3,000
Corporate Overhead	23,500	23,500	23,500	23,500
Total Quarterly Expenses	$157,600	$166,600	$149,600	$205,600

IN PRACTICE

Management's Ability to Forecast Accurately

In spite of the importance of forecasting to strategic planning, managers have mixed success in forecasting events and outcomes accurately.[8] Inaccuracies, when they occur, have more to do with the nature of the environment than with management effort.

There is no shortage of dramatic examples to illustrate carefully designed forecasts that were widely off the mark. In the 1970s, school administrators closed elementary schools as enrollments dropped. Forecasting that women's liberation had permanently reduced the birth rate, administrators acted to close schools permanently and, in some cases, even sell them. What happened, however, was that women merely delayed their childbearing years. In the mid-1980s, many of these same administrators found enrollments back at near-record levels.

The three most important economic outcomes of the Reagan era (1981–1988) have been characterized as a high structural fiscal deficit, a chronic balance of payments deficit, and high real interest rates. Yet not one of these was predicted in 1979–1980. Most experts thought that the October 1987 stock market crash would bring on a recession in 1988. Managers who strategically positioned their organizations for the 1988 recession found that it didn't come.

Forecasting techniques are most accurate when the environment is static. The more dynamic the environment, the more likely management is to develop inaccurate forecasts. Forecasting has a relatively unimpressive record in predicting nonseasonal turning points such as recessions, unusual events, discontinuities, and the actions or reactions of competitors. The only major consolation for managers is that their competitors are unlikely to be any better than they are at forecasting accurately in a dynamic environment.

Although forecasting has a mixed record, managers continue to engage in the practice. They find that for many factors—such as revenues, demographic trends, new laws, and labor supplies—forecasting's record is quite solid. Moreover, by shortening the length of forecasts, managers improve their accuracy.

almost everything in the single common denominator of dollars. Even human life has a dollar value. Insurance actuaries regularly compute the value of a lost eye, arm, or leg. While theologians may argue that life is priceless, insurance companies and juries regularly convert the loss of human body parts or life itself into dollars and cents. It seems logical, then, that dollar budgets make a useful common denominator for directing activities in such diverse departments as production and marketing research or at various levels in an organization. Budgets are one planning device that most managers, regardless of level in the organization, help to formulate.

Types of Budgets

There is no shortage of items or areas for which budgets can be used. The following represent the ones managers are most likely to use.

revenue budget
A budget that projects future sales.

Revenue Budgets   The **revenue budget** is a specific type of revenue forecast. It is a budget that projects future sales. If the organization could be sure of selling everything it produced, revenue budgets would undoubtedly be quite accurate. Managers would need only to multiply the sales price of each product by the quantity it could produce. But such situations rarely exist. Managers must take into consideration their competitors, advertising budget, sales force effectiveness, and other relevant factors, and they must make an estimate of sales volume. Then, on the basis of estimates of demand at various prices, managers must select an appropriate sales price. The result is the revenue budget.

expense budget
A budget that lists the primary activities undertaken by a unit and allocates a dollar amount to each.

Expense Budgets   While revenue budgets are essentially a planning device for marketing and sales activities, expense budgets are found in all units within a firm and in not-for-profit and profit-making organizations alike. **Expense budgets** list the primary activities undertaken by a unit to achieve its goals and allocate a dollar amount to each. Lower expenses, when accompanied by stable quantity and quality of output, translate into greater efficiency. In times of severe competition, recession, or the like, managers typically look first at the expense budget as a place to make cuts and achieve economic efficiencies. Since all expenses do not vary in direct proportion to volume, they do not decline commensurately when the demand for products or services drops. Managers therefore give particular attention to so-called fixed expenses— that is, those that remain relatively unchanged regardless of volume. As production drops, the variable expenses tend to control themselves because they fall with volume.

profit budget
A budget that combines revenue and expense budgets into one.

Profit Budgets   The units in an organization that have clearly delineated revenues are often designated as profit centers and use profit budgets for planning and control. **Profit budgets** combine revenue and expense budgets into one. They are typically used in large organizations with multiple plants and divisions. Each manufacturing plant in a corporation, for instance, might charge its monthly expenses plus a charge for corporate overhead against its monthly billing revenues. Some organizations create artificial profit centers by developing transfer prices for interorganizational transactions. As a case in point, the exploration division of Texaco produces oil only for Texaco's refining division. The exploration unit has no real sales. However, Texaco has made the exploration unit a profit center by establishing prices for each barrel of oil the division drills and then "sells" to the refining division. The internal transfers create revenue for the exploration division and allows its managers to formulate and be evaluated against their profit budget.

cash budget
A budget that forecasts how much cash an organization will have on hand and how much it will need to meet expenses.

Cash Budgets   **Cash budgets** are forecasts of how much cash the organization will have on hand and how much it will need to meet expenses. This budget can reveal potential shortages or the availability of surplus cash for short-term investments.

Capital Expenditure Budgets   Investments in property, buildings, and major equipment are called *capital expenditures.* These are typically substantial expenditures both in terms of magnitude and duration. The decision by Chrysler, for example, to build a new production plant would represent a commitment of more than $100 million. It would require an outlay of funds over several years, and it would require many years for management to recoup its investment. The magnitude and duration of these investments can justify the development of separate budgets for these expendi-

capital expenditure budget
A budget that forecasts investments in property, buildings, and major equipment.

fixed budget
A budget that assumes a fixed level of sales or production.

variable budget
A budget that takes into account those costs that vary with volume.

tures. Such **capital expenditure budgets** allow management to forecast future capital requirements, to keep on top of important capital projects, and to ensure that adequate cash is available to meet these expenditures as they come due.

Variable Budgets   The budgets previously described are based on the assumption of a single specified volume—that is, they are **fixed budgets.** They assume a fixed level of sales or production volume. Most organizations, however, are not able to accurately predict volume. Moreover, a number of costs—such as labor, material, and some administrative expenses—vary with volume. **Variable budgets** are designed to deal with these facts. Since plans can change, standards need to be flexible to adjust to these changes. Variable budgets represent flexible standards. They can help managers to better plan costs by specifying cost schedules for varying levels of volume.

Approaches to Budgeting

There are essentially three approaches managers can take to budgeting. By far, the most popular approach is the traditional, or *incremental budget.* But in recent years, managers in some organizations have been experimenting to make budgets more effective. The *program budget* and the *zero-base budget* are results of these experiments. Let's look at each of these approaches.

incremental budget
A budget that allocates funds to departments according to allocations in the previous period.

Incremental Budgets   The **incremental** (or traditional) **budget** has two identifying characteristics. First, funds are allocated to departments or organizational units. The managers of these units then allocate funds to activities as they see fit. Second, an incremental budget develops out of the previous budget. Each period's budget begins by using the last period as a reference point. Only incremental changes in the budget request are reviewed. Each of these characteristics, however, creates a problem.

When funds are allocated to organizational units, it becomes difficult to differentiate activities within units. Why? Because organizational units typically have a multiple set of goals and hence engage in a number of activities. Incremental budgets don't take this diversity of activities into consideration. They focus on providing funds for units rather than for activities within the units. Given that units have multiple goals, it seems reasonable to conclude that (1) some goals are more important than others and (2) unit managers have varying degrees of success in achieving these multiple goals. Incremental budgets throw everything into the same pot. Thus as planning devices, they lack sufficient focus and specificity.

The incremental budget is particularly troublesome when top management seeks to identify inefficiencies and waste. In fact, inefficiencies tend to grow in the incremental budget because they tend to get hidden. In the typical incremental budget, nothing ever gets cut. Each budget begins with the funds allocated for the last period—to which unit managers add a percentage for inflation and requests for those new or expanded activities they seek to pursue. Top management looks only at the requests for incremental changes. The result is that money can be provided for activities long after their need is gone.

program budget
A budget that allocates funds to activities that are needed to achieve a specific objective.

Planning-Programming-Budgeting System (PPBS)
A program budget that combines budgeting with MBO and that allocates funds for the achievement of specific objectives.

Program Budgets   **Program budgets** allocate funds to groups of activities (programs) that are needed to achieve a specific objective. They are designed to deal with one of the major problems of incremental budgets; that is, funds are allocated to activities, not to departments.

The best-known elaboration of the program budget is called the **Planning-Programming-Budgeting System (PPBS).**[9] Originally developed for the Air Force by the Rand Corporation, PPBS has at one time or another been used by every department and agency of the federal government. Of course, it has been implemented in a number of business firms as well.

FIGURE 9–1   PPBS Process

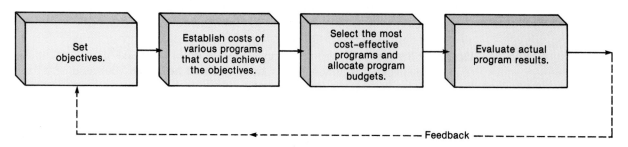

As shown in Figure 9–1, PPBS combines budgeting with management by objectives. Objectives are set to reflect the major activities of a department. Programs are determined, including possible alternatives, to achieve the stated objectives. Budgets are then allocated to programs, not to individual departments. Finally, the output of the program is compared with its objectives.

The idea behind PPBS is to attain objectives, not to merely allocate funds to a department. If a program takes a number of years to complete, PPBS can provide continuity that is often missing in incremental budgets. Moreover, in public organizations, in which there is no profit-and-loss statement and there are always far more objectives than resources to achieve them, PPBS provides a mechanism for choosing among objectives and ensuring that a dollar's worth of service is obtained for each dollar spent.

zero-base budgeting (ZBB)
A system in which budget requests start from scratch, regardless of previous appropriations.

Zero-Base Budgets **Zero-base budgeting (ZBB),** originally developed by Texas Instruments, requires managers to justify their budget requests in detail from scratch, regardless of previous appropriations.[10] It's designed to attack the second drawback we mentioned in incremental budgets: activities that have a way of becoming immortal. Once established, organizational activities can take on lives of their own. This is especially true in public organizations. For instance, one researcher noted that the State of New York's *Temporary* Commission of Investigation had issued its *sixteenth* annual report and that the Federal Metal and Nonmetallic Mine Safety Board of Review was abolished only after its executive secretary admitted in a front-page newspaper interview that he had no work to perform.[11]

ZBB shifts the burden of proof to the manager to justify why his or her unit should get any budget at all. The ZBB process reevaluates all organizational activities to see which should be eliminated, funded at a reduced level, funded at the current level, or increased. The process consists of three steps:

1. Each discrete departmental activity is broken down into a decision package.
2. The individual decision packages are ranked according to their benefit to the organization during the budget period.
3. Budget resources are allocated to the individual packages according to preferential rank in the organization.[12]

The *decision package* is a document that identifies and describes a specific activity. Usually prepared by operating managers, it includes a statement of the expected result or purpose of the activity, its costs, personnel requirements, measures of performance, alternative courses of action, and an evaluation of the benefits from performance and consequences of nonperformance from an organizationwide perspective. In more specific terms, each package lists a number of alternative methods of performing the activity, recommends one of these alternatives, and delineates effort levels. These *effort levels* identify spending targets—for instance, how the activity would be completed at 70, 90, and 110 percent of the current budget level. Any large organization that adopts ZBB will have literally thousands of these packages.

Once department managers have completed the decision packages, the packages are forwarded to the top executive group, which determines how much to spend and where to spend it. This is done by ascertaining the total amount to be spent by the organization and then by ranking all packages in order of decreasing benefits to the organization. Packages are accepted down to the spending level. When properly executed, the ZBB process carefully evaluates every organizational activity, assigns it a priority, and results in either the continuation, modification, or termination of the activity.

ZBB is no panacea. Like incremental budgeting, it has its own set of drawbacks.[13] It increases paperwork and requires time to prepare; the important activities that managers want funded tend to have their benefits inflated; and the eventual outcome rarely differs much from what would occur through an incremental budget.

The difficulty and expense of implementing ZBB suggest that it is not for every organization. The politics of large organizations often undermine any potential gain that ZBB might produce. It is possibly most effective in smaller public organizations, in supporting staff units in business firms, or in declining organizations. For example, because the resource requirements of staff units in business firms, which include areas like market research and personnel, are rarely related directly to the firm's output, it's difficult to determine whether their budgets are realistic or denote efficient operation. Thus for this type of unit, ZBB may be a valuable planning and control device. Also, ZBB is compatible with managing declining resources.[14] When organizations face cutbacks and financial restraints, their managers particularly look for devices that allocate limited resources effectively. ZBB can be just such a device.

OPERATIONAL PLANNING TOOLS

Flo's Take-Out Chicken is a large, highly successful fast-food restaurant in Miami, Florida. Florence Jackson, who owns and runs the restaurant, spends much of her time setting up work schedules for the forty-five people she employs, deciding how many registers to keep open during various times throughout the day, and solving similar day-to-day problems. In the following pages, we'll discuss some operational planning tools that can help managers like Florence to be more effective.

Scheduling

If you were to observe a group of supervisors or department managers for a few days, you would see them regularly detailing what activities have to be done, the order they are to be done in, who is to do each, and when they are to be completed. The managers are doing what we call **scheduling.** In this section, we will review some useful scheduling devices.

scheduling
A listing of necessary activities, their order of accomplishment, who is to do each, and time to completion.

The Gantt Chart   As we noted in Chapter 2, the Gantt chart was developed around the turn of the century by Henry Gantt, a protégé of Frederick Taylor. The idea is inherently simple. It is essentially a bar graph with time on the horizontal axis and the activities to be scheduled on the vertical axis. The bars show output, both planned and actual, over a period of time. The Gantt chart visually shows when tasks are supposed to be done and compares that to the actual progress on each. It is a simple but important device that allows managers to detail easily what has yet to be done to complete a job or project and to assess whether it is ahead, behind, or on schedule.

FIGURE 9–2
A Gantt Chart

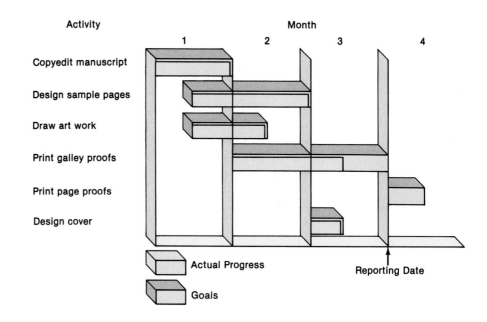

Figure 9–2 depicts a simplified Gantt chart that was developed for producing a book by a manager in a publishing firm. Time is expressed in months across the top of the chart. The major activities are listed down the left side. The planning comes in deciding what activities need to be done to get the book finished, the order in which they need to be done, and the time that should be allocated to each activity. Where a box sits within a time frame reflects its planned sequence. The shading represents actual progress. The chart becomes a control device when the manager looks for deviations from the plan. In this case, everything has been accomplished on schedule except the printing of galley proofs. This is two weeks behind schedule. Given this information, the manager of this project might want to take some corrective action either to pick up the two weeks lost or to ensure that no further delays occur. At this point, the manager can expect that the book will be published at least two weeks later than planned if no corrective action is taken.

load chart
A modified Gantt chart that schedules capacity by work stations.

The Load Chart   A **load chart** is a modified Gantt chart. Instead of listing activities on the vertical axis, load charts list either whole departments or specific resources. This allows managers to plan and control for capacity utilization. In other words, load charts schedule capacity by work stations.

For example, Figure 9–3 shows a load chart for six production editors at the same publishing firm. Each editor supervises the production and design of a number of books. By reviewing a load chart like the one shown in Figure 9–3, the executive editor, who supervises the six production editors, can see who is free to take on a new book. If everyone is fully scheduled, the executive editor might decide not to accept any new projects, to accept new projects and delay others, to make the editors work overtime, or to employ more production editors. In Figure 9–3, only Cindy and Maurice are completely booked for the next six months. Since the other editors have some unassigned time, they might be able to accept one or more new projects.

PERT Network Analysis   Gantt and load charts are helpful as long as the activities or projects being scheduled are few in number and independent of each other. But what if a manager had to plan a large project such as a reorganization, the launching of a cost-reduction campaign, or developing a new product that required coordinating

FIGURE 9–3
A Load Chart

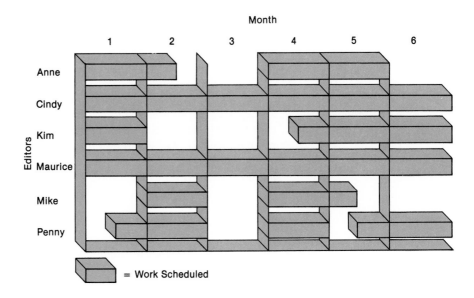

= Work Scheduled

inputs from marketing, production, and product design personnel? Such projects require coordinating hundreds or thousands of activities, some of which must be done simultaneously and some of which cannot begin until earlier activities have been completed. If you're constructing a building, you obviously can't start erecting walls until the foundation is laid. How, then, can you schedule such a complex project? You could use the Program Evaluation and Review Technique.

The **Program Evaluation and Review Technique**—usually just called PERT or PERT network analysis—was originally developed in the late 1950s for coordinating the more than 3,000 contractors and agencies working on the Polaris submarine weapon system.[15] This project was incredibly complicated, with hundreds of thousands of activities that had to be coordinated. PERT is reported to have cut two years off the completion date for the Polaris project.

A PERT network is a flowchartlike diagram that depicts the sequence of activities needed to complete a project and the time or costs associated with each activity. With a PERT network, a project manager must think through what has to be done, determine which events depend on one another, and identify potential trouble spots. PERT also makes it easy to compare what effect alternative actions will have on scheduling and costs. Thus PERT allows managers to monitor a project's progress, identify possible bottlenecks, and shift resources as necessary to keep the project on schedule.

To understand how to construct a PERT network, you need to know three terms: *events, activities,* and *critical path.* Let's define these terms, outline the steps in the PERT process, and then develop an example.

Events are end points that represent the completion of major activities. **Activities** represent the time or resources required to progress from one event to another. The **critical path** is the longest or most time-consuming sequence of events and activities in a PERT network.

Developing a PERT network requires the manager to identify all key activities needed to complete a project, rank them in order of dependence, and estimate each activity's completion time. This can be translated into five specific steps:

1. Identify every significant activity that must be achieved for a project to be completed. The accomplishment of each activity results in a set of events or outcomes.

2. Ascertain the order in which these events must be completed.

Program Evaluation and Review Technique (PERT)
A technique for scheduling complicated projects comprising many activities, some of which are interdependent.

events
End points that represent the completion of major activities in a PERT network.

activities
The time or resources needed to progress from one event to another in a PERT network.

critical path
The longest sequence of activities in a PERT network.

PERT network
A flowchartlike diagram showing the sequence of activities needed to complete a project and the time or cost associated with each.

3. Diagram the flow of activities from start to finish, identifying each activity and its relationship to all other activities. Use circles to indicate events and arrows to represent activities. This results in a flowchart diagram that we call the **PERT network.**

4. Compute a time estimate for completing each activity. This is done with a weighted average that employs an *optimistic* time estimate (t_o) of how long the activity would take under ideal conditions, a *most-likely* estimate (t_m) of the time the activity normally should take, and a *pessimistic* estimate (t_p) that represents the time that an activity should take under the worst possible conditions. The formula for calculating the expected time (t_e) is then

$$t_e = \frac{t_o + 4t_m + t_p}{6}$$

5. Finally, using a network diagram that contains time estimates for each activity, the manager can determine a schedule for the start and finish dates of each activity and for the entire project. Any delays that occur along the critical path require the most attention because they delay the entire project. That is, the critical path has no slack in it; therefore any delay along that path immediately translates into a delay in the final deadline for the completed project.

As was noted at the beginning of this section, most PERT projects are quite complicated and may be composed of hundreds or thousands of events. Such complicated computations are best done with a computer using specialized PERT software.[16] But for our purposes, let's work through a simplified example. Assume that you are the superintendent of a construction company. You have been assigned to oversee the construction of an office building. Since time really is money in your business, you must determine how long it will take to put up the building. You have carefully dissected the entire project into activities and events. Table 9–2 outlines the major events in the construction project and your estimate of the expected time required to complete each activity. Figure 9–4 depicts the PERT network based on the data in Table 9–2.

TABLE 9–2   A PERT Network for Erecting an Office Building

Event	Description	Expected Time (in weeks)	Preceding Event
A	Approve design and get permits	10	None
B	Dig subterranean garage	6	A
C	Erect frame and siding	14	B
D	Construct floors	6	C
E	Install windows	3	C
F	Put on roof	3	C
G	Install internal wiring	5	D,E,F
H	Install elevators	5	G
I	Put in floor covering and paneling	4	D
J	Put in doors and interior decorative trim	3	I,H
K	Turn over to building management group	1	J

FIGURE 9–4
PERT Network Diagram

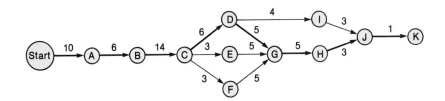

Your PERT network tells you that if everything goes as planned, it will take fifty weeks to complete the building. This is calculated by tracing the network's critical path: A-B-C-D-G-H-J-K. Any delay in completing the events along this path will delay the completion of the entire project. For example, if it took six weeks instead of four to put in the floor covering and paneling (event I), this would have no effect on the final completion date. Why? Because C-D + D-I + I-J equals only thirteen weeks, while C-E + E-G + G-H + H-J equals sixteen weeks. However, if you wanted to cut the fifty-week time frame, you would give attention to those activities along the critical path that could be speeded up.

Break-Even Analysis

How many units of a product must an organization sell in order to break even—that is, have neither profit nor loss? A manager might want to know the minimum number of units that must be sold to achieve her profit objective or whether a current product should continue to be sold or dropped from the organization's product line. **Break-even analysis** is a widely used technique for helping managers to make profit projections.[17]

Break-even analysis is a simplistic formulation, yet it is valuable to managers because it points out the relationship between revenues, costs, and profits. To compute the break-even point (*BE*), the manager needs to know the unit price of the product being sold (*P*), the variable cost per unit (*VC*), and total fixed costs (*TFC*).

break-even analysis
A technique for identifying the point at which total revenue is just sufficient to cover total costs.

•

Aerospace and construction firms like General Dynamics and Bechtel regularly use PERT schedules to manage complex projects.

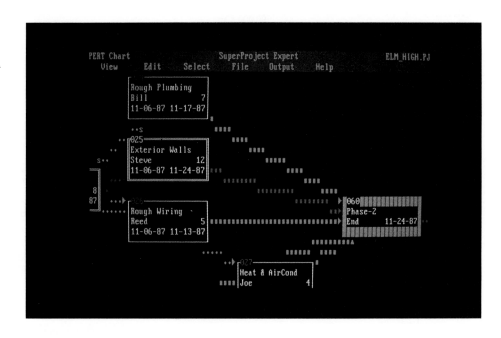

An organization breaks even when its total revenue is just enough to equal its total costs. But total cost has two parts: a fixed component and a variable component. *Fixed costs* are expenses that do not change, regardless of volume. Examples include insurance premiums and property taxes. Fixed costs, of course, are fixed only in the short term because, in the long run, commitments terminate and are thus subject to variation. *Variable costs* change in proportion to output and include raw materials, labor costs, and energy costs.

The break-even point can be computed graphically or by using the following formula:

$$BE = \frac{TFC}{P - VC}$$

This formula tells us that (1) total revenue will equal total cost when we sell enough units at a price that covers all variable unit costs and (2) the difference between price and variable costs, when multiplied by the number of units sold, equals the fixed costs.

For example, assume that Dave's Photocopying Service charges $0.10 per photocopy. If fixed costs are $27,000 a year and variable costs are $0.04 per copy, Dave can compute his break-even point as follows: $27,000/($0.10 − $0.04) = 450,000 copies, or when annual revenues are $45,000. This same relationship is shown graphically in Figure 9–5.

As a planning tool, break-even analysis could help Dave to set his sales objective. For example, he could establish the profit he wants and then work backward to determine what sales level is needed to reach that profit. Break-even analysis could also tell Dave how much volume has to increase to break even if he's currently running at a loss or how much volume he can afford to lose and still break even if he's currently operating profitably. In some cases, such as the management of professional sports franchises, break-even analysis has shown the projected volume of ticket sales

FIGURE 9–5
Break-Even Analysis

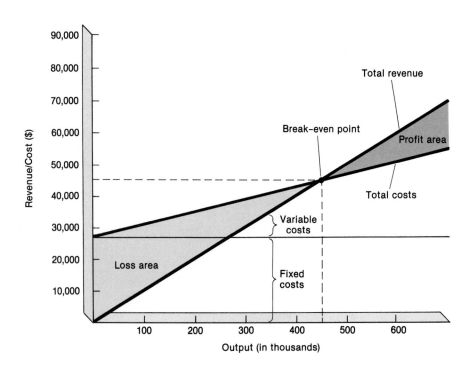

required to cover all costs to be so unrealistically high that the best action for management to take is to get out of the business.

Linear Programming

Dan Collier has a manufacturing plant that produces two kinds of sporting rifles, a basic 38-caliber rifle (the AT-38) and a deluxe model (the DL-38). Business is good. He can sell all of the rifles he can produce. His dilemma is: Given that both rifles go through the same production departments, how many of each model should he make to maximize his profits?

A closer look at Dan's operation tells us that he can use a mathematical technique, called **linear programming,** to solve his resource allocation dilemma. As we'll show, linear programming is applicable to Dan's problem, but it can't be applied to all resource allocation situations. Besides requiring limited resources and the objective of optimization, it requires that there be alternative ways of combining resources to produce a number of output mixes. There must also be a linear relationship between variables.[18] This means that a change in one variable will be accompanied by an exactly proportional change in the other. For Dan's business, this condition would be met if it took exactly twice the amount of raw materials and hours of labor to produce two of a given rifle model as it took to produce one.

What kinds of problems lend themselves to linear programming? Selecting transportation routes that minimize shipping costs, allocating a limited advertising budget among various product brands, making the optimum assignment of personnel among projects, and determining how much of each product to make with a limited number of resources are a few. Let's return to Dan's problem and see how linear programming could help him to solve it. Fortunately, Dan's problem is relatively simple, so we can solve it rather quickly. For complex linear programming problems, there is computer software that has been designed specifically to help develop solutions.

First, we need to establish some facts about Dan's business. Dan has computed the profit margins on the rifles as $25 for the AT model and $45 for the DL. He can therefore express his *objective function* as: maximum profit = $25A + $45D, where A is the number of AT's produced and D is the number of DL's produced. Additionally, Dan knows the time each rifle must spend in each department and the monthly production capacity (1,200 hours in manufacturing and 900 hours in assembly) for the two departments (see Table 9–3). The production capacity numbers act as *constraints* on his overall capacity. Now Dan can establish his constraint equations:

$$2A + 4D \leq 1,200$$
$$2A + 2D \leq 900$$

linear programming
A mathematical technique that solves resource allocation problems.

TABLE 9–3   Production Data for Rifles

Department	Number of Hours Required (per unit)		Monthly Production Capacity (in hours)
	Model AT	*Model DL*	
Manufacturing	2	4	1,200
Assembly	2	2	900
Profit per unit	$25	$45	

Of course, since neither rifle can be produced in a volume less than zero, Dan can also state that $A \geq 0$ and $D \geq 0$.

FIGURE 9–6
Graphical Solution to Dan
Collier's Linear Programming
Problem

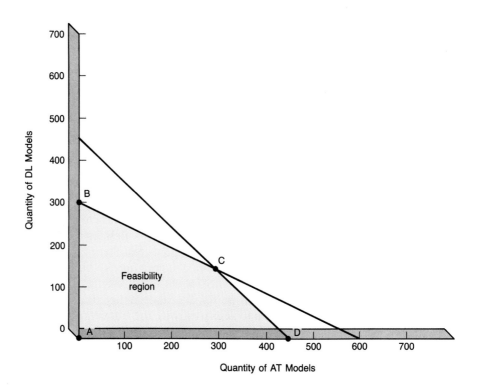

Dan has graphed his solution as shown in Figure 9–6. The shaded area represents the options that don't exceed the capacity of either department. This area represents his *feasibility region.* Dan's optimal resource allocation will be defined at one of the corners within this feasibility region. Point *C* is the farthest from the origin and provides the maximum profits within the constraints stated. At point *A*, profits would be 0. At points *B* and *D*, profits would be $13,500 and $11,250, respectively. At point *C*, however, profits would be $14,250.

Queuing Theory

You are a supervisor for the San Francisco Bay Bridge Toll Authority. One of the decisions you have to make is how many of the thirty-six toll booths you should keep open at any given time. Queuing theory, or what is frequently referred to as *waiting-line theory,* could assist you with this problem.

Whenever a decision involves balancing the cost of having a waiting line against the cost of service to maintain that line, it can be made easier with **queuing theory.** This includes such common situations as determining how many gas pumps are needed at gas stations, tellers at bank windows, or check-in lines at airline ticket counters. In each situation, management wants to minimize cost by having as few stations open as possible, yet not so few as to test the patience of customers. Referring back to our toll-booth example, during rush hours you could open all thirty-six and keep waiting time to a minimum, or you could open only one, minimize staffing costs, and risk a riot.

The mathematics underlying queuing theory is beyond the scope of this book. But you can see how the theory works in a simple example. Assume that you're a bank supervisor. One of your responsibilities is assigning tellers. You have five teller windows, but you want to know whether you can get by with only one window open during an average morning. You consider 12 minutes to be the longest you would

queuing theory
A technique that balances the cost of having a waiting line against the cost of service to maintain that line.

expect any customer to wait patiently in line. If it takes four minutes, on average, to serve each customer, the line should not be permitted to get longer than 3 deep (12 minutes ÷ 4 minutes per customer = 3 customers). If you know from past experience that, during the morning, people arrive at the average rate of 2 per minute, you can calculate the probability that the line will become longer than any number (n) customers as follows:

$$P_n = \left(1 - \frac{arrival\ rate}{service\ rate}\right) \times \left(\frac{arrival\ rate}{service\ rate}\right)^n$$

where n = 3 customers, *arrival rate* = 2 per minute, and *service rate* = 4 minutes per customer. Putting these numbers into the above formula generates the following:

$$P_3 = \left(1 - \frac{2}{4}\right) \times \left(\frac{2}{4}\right)^3 = \left(\frac{1}{2}\right)\left(\frac{8}{64}\right) = \frac{8}{128} = .0625$$

Probability Theory

probability theory
The use of statistics to analyze past predictable patterns and to reduce risk in future plans.

With the help of **probability theory,** managers can use statistics to reduce the amount of risk in plans. By analyzing past predictable patterns, a manager can improve current and future decisions. It makes for more effective planning when, for example, the marketing manager at Porsche/North America, who is responsible for the 944 line, knows that the mean age of his customers is 35.5 years, with a standard deviation of 3.5. If he assumes a normal distribution of ages, the manager can use probability theory to calculate that 95 of every 100 customers are between 28.6 and 42.4 years of age. If he were developing a new marketing program, he could use this information to target his marketing dollars more effectively.

Marginal Analysis

marginal analysis
A planning technique that assesses the incremental costs or revenues in a decision.

The concept of marginal, or incremental, analysis helps decision makers to optimize returns or minimize costs. **Marginal analysis** deals with the additional cost in a

---

What does a P_3 of .0625 mean? It tells you that the likelihood of having more than three customers in line during the morning is one chance in sixteen. Are you willing to live with four or more customers in line about 6 percent of the time? If so, keeping one teller window open will be enough. If not, you'll need to add windows and assign additional personnel to staff them.

particular decision, rather than the average cost. For example, the dry cleaner who wonders whether she should take on a new customer would consider not the total revenue and the total cost that would result after the order was taken, but rather what additional revenue would be generated by this particular order and what additional costs. If the incremental revenues exceeded the incremental costs, total profits would be increased by accepting the order.

Simulation

simulation

A model of a real-world phenomenon that contains one or more variables that can be manipulated in order to assess their impact.

At the beginning of this chapter, we showed how the Torrington Co. used a computer simulation to model its actual operating floor. Managers are increasingly turning to simulation as a means for trying out various planning options. They are using **simulation** to create a model of a real-world phenomenon and then manipulating one or more variables in the model to assess their impact. Simulation can deal with problems addressed by linear programming, but it can also deal with more complex situations.

How might a manager use simulation? Let's see how it was used by a library director at a large university. She was planning the interior design and layout for a new library building. The proper location of certain collections, study areas, offices, and information desks was crucial for the effective operation of the new facility. The director gathered information on the various collections, their usage rates, the demand pattern for periodicals, and the like. Then, with the assistance of a simulation expert, she developed a computer simulation model of the facility. The model expressed, in mathematical terms, the key variables in the library's design and layout. By altering these variables, the simulation model described the possible effects on library operations and cost. Most important, because the entire exercise was simulated on a computer, thousands of options could be plugged in and their probable results evaluated. This allowed for the identification of an optimum design, while minimizing any disruption in the ongoing operations of the library.

Probably the best-known use of simulation is the flight simulator used by the military and commercial airlines like this one at American Airlines to train pilots and update their skills. While these simulators cost millions of dollars, they are less expensive to use than real equipment, and, of course, a mistake on a simulator is a learning experience rather than a fatality.

TIME MANAGEMENT: A GUIDE FOR PERSONAL PLANNING

Do any of the following describe you?

You do interesting things before the uninteresting things?

You do things that are easy before things that are difficult?

You do things that are urgent before things that are important?

You work on things in the order of their arrival?

You wait until a deadline approaches before really moving on a project?[19]

time management

A personal form of scheduling time effectively.

If you answered Yes to one or more of these questions, you could benefit from time management. In this section, we'll present some suggestions to help you manage your time better. We'll show you that **time management** is actually a personal form of scheduling. Managers who use their time effectively know what activities they want to accomplish, the best order in which to take the activities, and when they want to complete those activities.

Time as a Scarce Resource

Time is a unique resource in that, if it's wasted, it can *never* be replaced. While people talk about *saving time,* the fact is that time can never actually be saved. It can't be stockpiled for use in some future period. If wasted, it can't be retrieved. When a minute is gone, it is gone forever.

The positive side of this resource is that all managers have it in equal abundance. While money, labor, and other resources are distributed unequally in this world, thus putting some managers at a disadvantage, every manager is allotted twenty-four hours every day and seven days every week. Some just use their allotments better than others.

Focusing on Discretionary Time

response time

Uncontrollable time spent responding to requests, demands, and problems initiated by others.

discretionary time

The part of a manager's time that is controllable.

Managers can't control all of their time. They are routinely interrupted and have to respond to unexpected crises. It's necessary, therefore, to differentiate between response time and discretionary time.[20]

The majority of a manager's time is spent responding to requests, demands, and problems initiated by others. We call this **response time** and treat it as uncontrollable. The portion that *is* under a manager's control is called **discretionary time.** Most of the suggestions offered to improve time management apply to its discretionary component. Why? Because only this part is manageable!

Unfortunately, for most managers, particularly those in the lower and middle ranks of the organization, discretionary time makes up only about 25 percent of their work hours.[21] Moreover, discretionary time tends to become available in small pieces—five minutes here, five minutes there. Thus it is very difficult to use effectively. The challenge, then, is to know what time is discretionary and then to organize activities so as to accumulate discretionary time in blocks large enough to be useful. Managers who are good at identifying and organizing their discretionary time accomplish significantly more, and the things they accomplish are more likely to be high-priority activities.

The best log is a daily diary or calendar broken into fifteen-minute intervals. To get enough information from which to generalize, you need about two weeks' worth of entries. During this two-week period, enter everything you do in the diary in fifteen-minute segments. To minimize memory loss, post the entries as you do them. Keep in mind that honesty is important. You want to record how you actually spent your time, not how you *wished* you had spent your time!

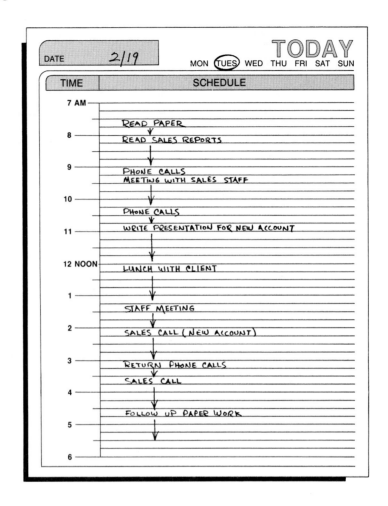

TABLE 9—4   Analyzing Activities for Importance and Urgency

Rate Each Activity for

Importance

A. Very important: must be done
B. Important: should be done
C. Not so important: may be useful, but is not necessary
D. Unimportant: doesn't accomplish anything

Urgency

A. Very urgent: must be done now
B. Urgent: should be done now
C. Not urgent: can be done sometime later
D. Time not a factor

How Do You Use Your Time?

How do managers, or anyone for that matter, determine how well they use their time? The answer is that they should keep a log or diary of daily activities for a short period of time, then evaluate the data they gather.

Try keeping such a diary. When it is complete, you will have a detailed time and activity log. Then you can analyze how effectively you use your time. Rate each activity in terms of its importance and urgency. (See Table 9–4.) If you find that many activities received C's or D's, you'll find the next sections valuable. They provide detailed guidelines for better time management.[22]

Five Steps to Better Time Management

The essence of time management is to use your time effectively. This requires that you know the objectives you want to accomplish, the activities that will lead to the accomplishment of those objectives, and the importance and urgency of each activity. We've translated this into a five-step process.

1. *Make a list of your objectives.* What specific objectives have you set for yourself and the unit you manage? If you're using MBO, these objectives are already in place.

2. *Rank the objectives according to their importance.* Not all objectives are of equal importance. Given the limitations on your time, you want to make sure you give highest priority to the most important objectives.

3. *List the activities necessary to achieve your objectives.* What specific actions do you need to take to achieve your objectives? Again, if you're using MBO, these action plans are already laid out.

4. *For each objective, assign priorities to the various activities required to reach the objective.* This step imposes a second set of priorities. Here, you need to emphasize both importance and urgency. If the activity is not important, you should consider delegating it to someone below you. If it's not urgent, it can usually wait. This step will identify activities that you *must* do, those you *should* do, those you'll get to *when you can,* and those that can be *delegated to others.*

5. *Schedule your activities according to the priorities you've set.* The final step is to prepare a daily plan. Every morning, or at the end of the previous work day, make a list of the five or so most important things you want to do for the day. If the list grows to ten or more activities, it becomes cumbersome and ineffective. Then set priorities for the activities listed on the basis of importance and urgency.

Some Additional Points to Ponder

Follow the 10–90 Principle   Ten percent of most managers' time produces 90 percent of their results. It's easy for managers to get caught up in the activity trap and confuse actions with accomplishments. Those who use their time well make sure that the critical 10 percent gets highest priority.

Know Your Productivity Cycle   Each of us has a daily cycle. Some of us are morning people, while others are late-afternoon or evening people. Managers who know their cycle and schedule their work accordingly, can significantly increase their effectiveness. They handle their most demanding problems during the high part of their cycle, when they are most alert and productive. They relegate their routine and undemanding tasks to their low periods.

Remember Parkinson's Law   Parkinson's Law says that work expands to fill the time available. The implication for time management is that you can schedule *too* much time for a task. If you give yourself an excess amount of time to perform an activity, you're likely to pace yourself so that you use up the entire time allocation.

Group Less Important Activities Together   Set aside a regular time period each day to make phone calls, do follow-ups, and perform other kinds of busywork. Ideally, this should be during your low cycle. This avoids duplication, waste, and redundancy; it also prevents trivia from intruding on high-priority tasks.

Minimize Disruptions   When possible, try to minimize disruptions by setting aside that part of the day when you are most productive as a block of discretionary time. Then, try to insulate yourself. During this time you should limit access to your work area and interruptions. Refuse phone calls or visits during these certain hours. You can set aside other blocks of time each day when your door is open for unexpected visits and when you can initiate or return all your calls. The ability to insulate yourself depends on your organization's culture, your boss, and how much faith you have in your subordinates. But most critical is your level in the organization. Generally, the higher up you are in an organization, the less crucial it is that you be available for every emergency. In contrast, most supervisors can be out of touch with the work areas they oversee for only short periods of time.

Beware of Wasting Time in Poorly Run Meetings   Meetings take a large proportion of a manager's time. They also tend to run on at length. If you're running a meeting, you should set a time limit at the outset. You should prepare a written agenda for the meeting and stick to it. Another suggestion, which is a bit bizarre but works wonders for keeping meetings brief, is to require all members to remain standing. As soon as people sit down and get comfortable, they lose any motivation to keep a discussion tightly focused on the issues. Some managers have no chairs in their office other than the one they occupy. Visitors are subtly encouraged to avoid wasting the manager's time. Managers usually move important meetings that demand a long and thoughtful discussion to an adjoining conference room that has an ample supply of chairs.

SUMMARY

This summary is organized by the chapter-opening learning objectives found on page 245.

1. Techniques for scanning the environment include reading newspapers, magazines, books, and trade journals; reading competitors' ads, promotional materials, and press releases; attending trade shows; debriefing sales personnel; purchasing data bases that describe competitors' actions; and reverse engineering of competitor's products.

2. Quantitative forecasting applies a set of mathematical rules to a set of past data to predict future outcomes. Qualitative forecasting uses judgments and the opinions of knowledgeable individuals to predict future outcomes.

3. Budgets are popular planning devices because dollars are a universal common denominator that can be used in all types of organizations and by managers at all levels.

4. The most popular approach to budgeting is the traditional, or incremental, budget. However, its drawbacks have led to increased interest in program budgets, which allocate funds based on specific objectives, and zero-base budgets, which make no reference to past allocations.

5. Gantt and load charts are scheduling devices. Both are bar graphs. The former monitor planned and actual activities over time; the latter focus on capacity utilization by monitoring whole departments or specific resources.

6. The five steps in developing a PERT network are: (1) identify every significant activity that must be achieved for a project to be completed; (2) ascertain the order in which these activities must be completed; (3) diagram the flow of activities in a project from start to finish; (4) estimate the time needed to complete each activity; and (5) use the network diagram to determine a schedule for the start and finish dates of each activity and for the entire project.

7. A product's break-even point is determined by the unit price of the product, its variable cost per unit, and its total fixed costs.

8. For linear programming to be applicable, a problem must have limited resources, constraints, an objective function to optimize, alternative ways of combining resources, and a linear relationship between variables.

9. Simulation is an effective planning tool because it allows managers to simulate, on a computer, thousands of potential options. By simulating a complex situation, managers can see how changes in variables will affect outcomes.

10. Five steps toward better time management include: (1) making a list of objectives, (2) ranking the objectives in order of importance, (3) listing the activities necessary to achieve the objectives, (4) assigning priorities to each activity, and (5) scheduling activities according to the priorities set.

REVIEW QUESTIONS

1. What industry precipitated the recognition that effective planning required environmental scanning? How did it come to this recognition?

2. Is competitor intelligence equivalent to organizational espionage? Explain.

3. How is scanning the environment related to forecasting?

4. What is a budget? Must it always be in dollars?

5. Compare incremental and zero-base budgets.

6. What is the significance of the critical path in a PERT network?

7. What is the value of break-even analysis as a planning tool?

8. Give three examples of planning problems for which simulation would be helpful.

9. How can managers assess how well they currently manage their time?

10. How might a manager use his or her discretionary time more effectively?

DISCUSSION QUESTIONS

1. Assume that you manage an upscale restaurant in downtown Portland, Oregon. What specific resources would you use to effectively scan your environment?

2. "Budgets are both a planning and control tool." Explain this statement.

3. Develop a Gantt chart for writing a college term paper.

4. "You can't teach time management. People who are good at it tend to be structured and compulsive individuals by nature." Do you agree or disagree? Discuss.

5. "Forecasting is a waste of a manager's time." Do you agree or disagree with this statement? Discuss.

SELF-ASSESSMENT EXERCISE

Are You an Effective Time Manager?

Instructions: Which of the following statements best describe you? Make a check (✔) next to those characteristics that are appropriate to your usual behavior.

1. I am a hard worker and, as such, try to do every job with total commitment. Even though I am frequently tired at the end of a day, I feel a great sense of accomplishment. ☐

2. If asked to take on an extra assignment, I will consent. Even if this new responsibility makes it nearly impossible for me to finish current projects on schedule, it is hard for me to refuse. ☐

3. Most people consider me a workaholic. I am usually involved in several projects at once. No one can make an appointment to see me without having to wait at least two weeks. I'd like to exercise more, but cannot seem to fit such a program into my heavy schedule. ☐

4. I pride myself on the ability to anticipate most problems before they occur. To me, the work schedule is sacred. Therefore I rarely deviate from it. Interruptions must be discouraged. As much as possible, I limit phone calls and prolonged conversations. ☐

5. The top and inside of my desk are covered with papers. A collector, I save telephone messages, reports, relevant newspaper articles, schedules, and letters. In fact, my filing system is so well organized that I can pull out a year-old memo at a moment's notice. Colleagues kid me about my tendency to store so many items, but I am sure that this is an asset. ☐

6. I tend to pay considerable attention to small details. I am an expert at catching even the tiniest mistake, whether in typing, grammar, or figures. Although most assignments take me hours to complete, I am known for my thoroughness and dedication. If necessary, I will take work home to ensure that a job is finished on schedule. ☐

7. Large projects are not my forte. I find them too overwhelming and confusing. I much prefer to be given more routine tasks. It is generally difficult for me to focus on too many details at once. I enjoy the involvement and sense of accomplishment that result from a small job brought to completion. ☐

Turn to page 671 for scoring directions and key.

Source: Dorri Jacobs, "Your Time Management Profile," *Manage,* May 1983, p. 4. With permission.

CASE APPLICATION 9A

Transport Systems

Transport Systems, a regional trucking company operating out of Denver, Colorado, is having profitability problems as a result of deregulation in the trucking industry.[23] Management wants to decrease driver turnover and reduce the use of its own trucks by hiring more independent owner-operators to haul products and materials. Top management has therefore instructed the director of operations to launch a program to recruit owner-operators. The director has identified the following activities that will be required for such a program.

Activities to decrease turnover of all drivers (company and owner-operator):

A. Establish terminal facilities for drivers (food, showers, parking, and so on).
B. Implement terminal facility standards.
C. Design a diesel fuel purchase program.
D. Implement the diesel fuel purchase program.

Activities to recruit the desired number of owner-operators:

E. Advertise for owner-operators.
F. Establish a bonus system for employees who recommend new owner-operators who are placed under contract.
G. Revise procedures, train staff to sign up new owner-operators, and begin sign-ups.

After careful thought, the director of operations has concluded that some activities must be completed before others can begin. The sequencing requirements among all activities are shown in Table CA9–1.

The director has also computed estimates of the activity times for the driver program. They are shown in Table CA9-2.

TABLE CA9–1   Sequencing of Activities

Activity	Preceding Activity
A. Establish terminal facility standards	None
C. Design fuel program	None
B. Implement terminal facility standards	A
D. Implement fuel program	C
F. Establish bonus system	B,D
E. Advertise	B,D
G. Sign up owner-operators	F,E

TABLE CA9–2   Activity Time Estimates for Driver Program (in weeks)

Activity	Optimistic Time t_o	Most Likely Time t_m	Pessimistic Time t_p
A	2½	6½	7½
B	15	20	37
C	2	4	6
D	5	6½	11
E	3	5	7
F	½	2	3½
G	5	6	7

Questions

1. Draw a PERT network of this program.

2. Calculate the expected time for each activity and include it in the PERT network.

3. How long should this program take?

4. What's the critical path in this program? What are the implications of delays in activities along this path?

CASE APPLICATION 9B

Meetings, Meetings, Meetings

You are 35 years old and manager of special projects in a large construction and land development firm that employs 1,500 people and specializes in the development of leisure parks and shopping centers.[24] You are a professional engineer and have been with the organization five years. You hope to stay at least another five and to rise to the level of vice president of engineering services. Your department employs a professional staff of sixty people and a support staff of thirty people. It plays a central part in overseeing and managing the firm's major construction projects. It is a highly visible department and is regarded as a linchpin in the organization's overall operations.

It is a Monday morning, and you are reviewing your calendar for the coming month. You have three sets of clashing priorities.

1. There is a routine project review meeting, held on the second Monday of every month, that clashes with a special hospital appointment for your son. Your spouse will be out of town on the day in question, and you have been waiting for the appointment for two months.

2. The CEO of your company has called a special briefing on a project that is in a critical stage of development. All departmental managers are expected to attend. Unfortunately, you have a high-profile visitor arriving from France as part of a special international delegation on shopping center development. This meeting has been arranged and carefully planned for six weeks.

3. A special day-long "retreat" of the corporate planning budget committee has been called to review financial plans that have a bearing on three of your projects. You are scheduled to give a luncheon address to the local chamber of commerce on the same day.

Questions

1. What are you going to do about each of the three clashes?

2. What facts and considerations will have a bearing on your decisions?

Goal Setting

PURPOSE

1. To practice goal setting.
2. To compare performance among groups.

REQUIRED KNOWLEDGE

1. The value of goals on performance.

TIME REQUIRED

Approximately 30 minutes.

INSTRUCTIONS

Your instructor will divide the class into approximately three equal groups. The first group is to remain in the class. Students in the other two groups are to wait outside the classroom.

Your instructor will now start the exercise. Follow his or her directions carefully.

Source: This exercise is based on Jiing-Lih Farh and Arthur G. Bedeian, "Understanding Goal Setting: An In-Class Experiment," *Organizational Behavior Teaching Review,* Vol. 12, Issue 3, 1987–88, pp. 75–79.

America West
Airlines

In an era when frequent flyers would rank U.S. carriers down there with lawyers for service, when most pilots and flight attendants seem to be either striking or threatening to, when industry executives seem more attuned to Wall Street than to the flying public, the likelihood of finding a passenger willing to stand up and fight for an airline seems, at best, remote. But passengers do at America West.

America West Airlines (AWA) has a winning formula: low fares, great service, an unbeatable on-time record, and a high-energy spirit that has managed to satisfy millions of passengers—so much so that it has developed almost a cult following in the West and Southwest. Ever since it started with three planes making nine flights a day to five southwestern cities in 1983, AWA's growth curve has been almost straight up. Its 74 planes now serve fifty cities, from Phoenix to Las Vegas to Honolulu, with 285 daily flights. It is nearly twice the size of Chicago's ten-year-old Midway Airlines, another upstart with which it is often compared.

Now the "Pearl of Deregulation" faces a dilemma common to every fast-growing company: With annual revenues now surpassing $1 billion, can AWA sustain the small-company culture that got it where it is? America West's image—and its unique entrepreneurial style—is largely the work of Edward Beauvais, the consultant who founded the airline in 1983 and who is still its chairman and chief executive. A passionate believer in customer service and team spirit, Beauvais has built an airline that seems almost a throwback to the days of the aviation pioneers who handled the controls, knew everybody's name, and brazenly plotted new routes as fast as they could get the planes and the pilots. That was the way entrepreneurs like Eddie Rickenbacker, the architect of Eastern, ran their shows, and it worked for decades, until the numbers crunchers of the 1960s and

the deregulators of the 1970s profoundly changed the airline industry's environment.

Alone among major airline CEO's, Beauvais insists that almost everyone—from gate agent to reservations agent—be able to perform all of the functions of reservations, sales, ticketing, baggage handling, and in-flight cabin attendance. The skills are acquired in a rigorous eighteen-week cross-training boot camp for new employees, who, upon graduation, earn the designation customer service representative—CSR.

To ensure total commitment to the airline's future, Beauvais also requires every new employee to invest an amount equivalent to 20 percent of his or her first year's salary in AWA stock. The shares currently generate no dividends; Beauvais believes that all profits should be channeled into new planes, ground facilities, and other capital projects—and that all eyes should be on the long-term success of the venture rather than short-term profits. As Linda Simmons, a manager of AWA's employee-training operation, puts it: "Because everyone who applies for a job here knows that he or she will be required to buy stock and go through rigorous training, we attract people who want to get into the airline industry, not just the freedom to fly around the world. People who don't want to accept the responsibilities of ownership go to work for our competitors. We recruit risk takers."

None of this was especially on Ed Beauvais's mind when he set out to invent America West. An airline economist specializing in rate structures, route systems, and evaluations of operational efficiencies, he had done consulting work for many of the carriers that later figured in the makeover of America's airline map: Continental, Frontier, New York Air, and USAir. Working with Texas International, he got to know Don Burr, who launched deregulation's most publicized showcase of cut-rate fares for the mass market, People Express.

By Beauvais's own definition, an entrepreneur is "a person who identifies a market, makes the decision to go after it, and takes the risk"; and in launching America West, he took those words seriously, point for point.

With American Airlines and TWA giving the potentially rich Phoenix market only a second glance as they pursued bigger fish in the wake of deregulation, Beauvais saw an opening, and away he went. The decision was part hunch and part analysis. "Ed has two characteristics as a strategic planner," says senior director Rod Cox. "First, he's a careful, numbers-oriented guy. Second, he's a man with phenomenal intuition. Personally, I think the latter is his strongest suit. Sure, he can handle more data than anyone I know. But the trick is he never gets lost in it. He never loses sight of the big picture."

To this day, students of America West's brand of airline management compare it to that of People Express, which was also employee owned. Beauvais acknowledges that it was, in fact, Don Burr who gave him some ideas on how to finance a fledgling airline. But any parallels stop there. For example, People Express grew by acquiring a traditionally managed, non-employee-owned airline, Frontier. When the progressive and traditional partners tried to set up house together, they found that their cultures were incompatible. By contrast, once America West was operating, Beauvais favored growing from within. "We started with a clean slate," says Beauvais. "We weren't influenced by People Express."

Incorporated in 1981, the carrier began business on August 1, 1983, with three aircraft and 280 employees. It wasn't long before Beauvais found the confines of Phoenix too tame for his restless nature. He developed a twin-superhub concept, basing AWA in Las Vegas as well as in Phoenix. If the airline did better than all others on taking off on time, it wasn't just because of the chairman's organizational skills. In the rough winter months, when Chicago's O'Hare and other northerly airports unexpectedly shut down, carriers like AWA, which fly more southerly routes, benefit from the good weather that goes with their territory. "America West found a niche through luck or insight," says Edmund S. Greenslet, an aviation expert who publishes *The Airline Monitor*. "The other airlines left a gap, and Beauvais moved in to fill it. America West didn't get roughed up by the big guys the way, say, Braniff did when it went head-to-head against American at Dallas/Fort Worth."

More than anything else, Beauvais constructed a system that would feed passengers to and from California, the magnet of the Far West. "Did you know that one out of three people flying west of the Mississippi is bound for California or coming back from there?" says an AWA executive. "That's what our market studies showed." So it's not surprising that, early on, America West began flying nonstops from Phoenix to absolutely every field in the Los Angeles area that can handle a modern commercial jet—not only LAX but Burbank, Ontario, John Wayne, and Long Beach. Within a few years, AWA accounted for one of every two departures out of Phoenix.

In the beginning, Beauvais was convinced that the best way for AWA to compete was to be the lowest-fare carrier on all of its routes. Unlike People Express, however, America West would provide the frills of full-fare travel—assigned seats, free booze, spacious legroom, and complimentary copies of *The Wall Street Journal* and *USA Today,* all designed to attract the business traveler and not just starving students. Again unlike People Express, AWA chose not to pick fights with the heavyweights of the industry. Mark Coleman, senior vice president of sales and product development, explains, "We wanted to avoid confrontation with the biggies by competing with each on only a couple of their routes." So far the strategy has worked: American Airlines quietly withdrew from the Phoenix–New York market, and Republic—before becoming part of Northwest—chose to reduce its service drastically into and out of Phoenix rather than do battle with AWA's numerous feeder routes in the Southwest and Midwest.

That extensive feeder network is the key, according to Beauvais. Customers from some fifty cities funnel into AWA's twin hubs, a concept that offers the convenience of two good-weather airports only an hour's flying time from each other. Having bases in both Phoenix and Las Vegas affords more connecting points, a nearby backup in case of technical glitches, and fewer delays due to missed connections. AWA has grouped its departures into "banks" of flights that repeat regularly throughout the day. Miss a flight in Phoenix, and one need only wait 45 minutes for the next bank to cycle through.

However, it hasn't always been fair weather during AWA's rapid expansion. In the free-for-all environment of deregulation, AWA's slogan—"Less fare, more care"—took a drubbing. The care was there, helping Beauvais build customer loyalty without trumpeting a frequent-flier program. But Dallas-based Southwest matched fares with AWA and even today gives the airline more trouble than any other. The two go up against each other on about 25 percent of their routes. Another smaller carrier, Alaska Airlines, scrambled to lure AWA passengers on some routes, using Beauvais's own tactic of providing service with frills. USAir, out to build a national network like that of megacarriers American, Delta, and

United, bought Pacific Southwest and tripled gate capacity at Phoenix's Sky Harbor.

In 1987, with AWA's debt above industry norms and load factors on some routes low, Wall Street began drafting death notices for the upstart. Not helping matters was the fact that Beauvais found the East Coast an irresistible market. He put six new Boeing 757's on routes linking Phoenix and Las Vegas with New York and Baltimore/Washington. But even with the elasticity of seat demand out of New York (there's always room for one more carrier or flight) Beauvais had to trim his ailerons by some 25 percent. Then, after restoring AWA to profitability, Beauvais raised some eyebrows by bidding against bumptious billionaire Donald Trump for Eastern Airline's Bos-Wash shuttle. What looked like a repeat of Donald Burr's ill-fated takeover of culturally incompatible Frontier Airlines was merely an attempt to gain Eastern's valuable terminal slots at LaGuardia, Logan, and National airports. In fact, Beauvais had put Eastern's feisty "Lorenzo-ized" unions on notice that they would be free to join AWA only as shareholding associates and not as unionized adversaries. Nonetheless, Beauvais was eventually trumped on the Eastern deal, and he has since turned his eyes westward—to Hawaii, where AWA began service to Phoenix and Las Vegas in November 1989. In its typical counterintuitive style, the airline is transporting surf-surfeited Hawaiians to their favorite vacation spot: the felt-green mesas of Vegas.

Wiser for its experiences, America West today can claim that it's the only major American airline started since deregulation that is still around to talk about it. The mortality rate of regional airlines has been high: Air Cal, Air Florida, Frontier, PSA, Western, and more have folded. But the doomsayers have changed their tune on AWA and now pat it on the back. "I don't think there's any question that it will survive," says consultant Greenslet. "They've stopped trying to be all things to all people at all times."

Beauvais depicts his army of nearly 11,000 employees as a family. "The idea is always to share information, to find ways collectively to help the other person," says senior director Cox, describing the chairman's managerial style at the regularly scheduled market-review and competitive-strategy meetings. "No matter what bad news you might bring, Ed is always the warm, personable father figure who's looking for ways to make you look good. He asks questions. He asks others if they have any suggestions. He creates an atmosphere in which you don't have to defend your own turf."

Colleagues like to call Beauvais a "visionary." That conjures up—well, visions of someone peering into the future and plotting grand strategies. It also suggests that someone else must be minding the store. Both interpretations are accurate. Beauvais, trained in the school of management consulting, where visions as well as practical advice sell, thinks big—about routes to Australia (encouraged by AWA's connection with Australia's Ansett Airlines, which owns 20 percent of AWA's stock) and to points along the booming Pacific Rim. At the same time, he's smart enough to know that you can dream only when you're not encumbered with day-to-day details. And so it was only logical that he decided to choose Michael J. Conway, a rough-hewn New Yorker out of Continental Airlines, as his number two. His decision has proved to be right on.

A no-nonsense executive, age 44, Conway peppers his language with undeleted expletives as he spurs the troops into action. Soon after becoming president, he called a meeting of his top managers and announced, "We'll have only one rule at America West—no rules." Says a disgruntled executive who has yet to adapt totally to Conway's flexible approach: "We'd all come from airlines where there had been rule books, union contracts, and job descriptions spelled out in minute detail. Then Conway says, 'Treat everyone as an individual. Treat every case as special.' We told him he was asking for anarchy. He snapped back, 'Don't put people in boxes. Give them responsibility. No goddamn rules!'"

Pushing entrepreneurship to its limits, AWA goes so far as to trash one standard piece of airline equipment, the employee policy-and-procedures manual. United's loose-leaf manual, for instance, contains the works, from how to write a fourteen-day, advance, nonrefundable ticket to how to assess whether a passenger has had too much to drink. It would seem natural for AWA to distribute a manual like that—after all, Conway himself spent several of his earlier years at one of the Big Six accounting firms. But he'll have none of it.

In any case, both Beauvais and Conway are adamant about letting their staff and AWA's employees at large make decisions without running to the corner office for approval. "We think delegating authority is a good management method," says Beauvais. "It's a way of complimenting people on their intelligence."

So deeply ingrained is the decentralization that, on a good day, you could almost believe that Beauvais has nothing to do except think. Down in the ranks, the beavers are doing everything—with barely a verbal okay from their superiors. "Sending memos around takes too long," says one executive. "We're in a business where time is a luxury."

Nowhere is this more obvious than in AWA's eighty-person planning department, run by forty-year-old Peter Otradovec. A hotshot specialist in yield management who worked at American and Piedmont, he's one of

Beauvais's sharpest acquisitions. It is his department that juggles fares at lightning speed to fill planes and maximize profits. Does Otradovec go running to the big boss for approval? Hardly at all. And that's undoubtedly one of the factors that has enabled AWA to execute tricky pricing maneuvers with the nimbleness of a fighter plane.

"I started here in April of 1988," Otradovec recalls. "In the first three months I spoke, I'd guess, ten sentences with Ed. He really believes in delegating authority. At American, we'd wait for a proposal to go up the line to the top, to Bob Crandall, and back down." He adds, "Ed pretty much told me, Here's your office; now go to work. It's a unique experience. My entire background was with large corporations. Let's face it. They have big support staffs and directors of planning for everything—fleet planning, operations planning, future planning. Here I'm running hard from 7 to 7 every day."

Since its decision makers are closer to line operations—employees deal with the daily headaches that demand quick problem solving—one can make the case that AWA is better than most of its competitors in knowing what customers need. That may sound like a homily, but it gets at the America West way of managing. Knowing what's right—in effect, what passengers want—requires a people-to-people network, and that is just what AWA has developed. There is an obvious camaraderie not only at one level but also up and down the pecking order. Call it a collective entrepreneurial spirit.

The crux of the employee system is the customer service representative—by now, an almost exalted fixture around AWA. "What we want is to cross-utilize people," Beauvais explains. "We consider that all our employees are in marketing, and all of them are in human resources. They're there to create economic opportunities for America West." As a result, CSRs, like most other AWA employees, act as though they own the airline.

And at truly critical times, the investment in cross-training pays a hefty dividend. A few months ago, for example, an America West jet had to make an emergency landing at a remote airport where there was no ground crew. It was only a matter of minutes before the cabin attendants were out of their uniforms and into jeans. They unloaded bags for the stranded passengers, booked hotel rooms, and the next morning reloaded the luggage, put their uniforms back on, and served coffee to a planeload of impressed customers. "That would never happen at another airline," says Linda Simmons. "Anywhere else, the employee would probably be punished for doing that. Here," she adds, "you're expected to act as though you own the place."

At AWA, cross-utilization—coupled with stock ownership and profit sharing—creates powerful peer pressure to perform productively. Lazy or careless employees are seen as taking money from the pockets of their fellow workers. If an employee damages a plane with a meal truck, says CSR Kerry Covey, "you're on everyone's dirt list." Adds Lisa Jones, also a CSR, "You really think twice before calling in sick."

Employees, from the upper echelons on down, seem to be brimming with ideas about how to improve the airline's productivity. To keep the innovative spirit going, pilots, maintenance people, and CSRs elect representatives to advisory boards that meet regularly with AWA's executives. As in any organization, few suggestions—luckily—get implemented, but America West vows that its worker bees are unlike the usual corporate drones and are all abuzz with bright ideas. It could be something as simple as, Why do we waste money putting the America West logo on trash bags? (The airline no longer does.)

Or a proposal could be as sophisticated as the one that came out of a ticketing problem at Sky Harbor airport: If there's no more room for ticket counters in the terminal, why not check people in outside? (That notion led to Fast Chek, an express service that allows business travelers making the rounds in Phoenix to drive up to a kiosk near the terminal, check their tickets and bags, drop off their rental cars, and go straight to the gate.)

In many companies, even the niblets of fresh ideas generally languish in dead storage because they're blocked from discussion by clearly defined lines of authority. People at different levels just don't talk to one another very much, if at all, and when they do, it's usually in rather formal, stiff meetings that resemble military briefings rather than democratic forums. Not so at America West. If an open-door policy had not already been a proud tradition at some enlightened companies—Nestlé, for one, believes in it—the airline would have invented it. Easy entrance even extends to the offices of Beauvais and Conway.

Why is it that AWA executives behave in such an open, nondirective style? The guiding principle, if there is one, is fairness, says Conway. "Companies don't get in trouble with employees in bad times," he says. "When the survival of a firm is threatened, everyone is willing to make sacrifices and tighten their belts." That's precisely what occurred during AWA's brief tailspin in 1987. The ownership attitude paid off. "People went nuts," CSR Jones recalls. "They were saving napkins!"

"You get morale problems mostly when you're making lots of money," Conway goes on to say. "That's when people ask, Am I getting my share?" And so AWA follows a policy of sharing 15 percent of pretax profits, paid quarterly, with all employees. Beyond that there are such tranquilizing benefits as child care either at the company's center or at home.

Still, America West isn't just a utopian community with a lot of happy people wearing Ipana smiles. Senior director Cox admits that the Beauvais-Conway style of flexibility and trust isn't for everybody. "If you have the 9-to-5 mentality of a banker and if you need rules, consistency, and guidance, you'd go crazy here," he says. "One frustrated manager said the place was run like a third-world democracy."

The bottom-line numbers say something different. By keeping unions out, AWA has kept labor costs down. It can crow about the fact that its payroll accounts for only 24 percent of total costs against an industry average of 35 percent. In revenue per passenger mile, as aviation consultant Greenslet points out, the airline was up 13 percent over 1988 in the first quarter of 1989, and up 11 percent in the second.

The improved yield stems partly from the savvy way manager Otradovec goes about filling the seats of AWA's 78 Boeing 737s, 757s, Dash-8s, and just delivered 747-200s (largely for the new Phoenix–Honolulu–Las Vegas routes). "We have the building blocks that snap in and out like the Tinker Toys I played with as a kid," he says, rattling on about the tricks of allocating discount inventory on particular flights and "getting the right balance in schedules."

Even with AWA's emphasis on the human factor, Otradovec is upgrading his planning department's fare-setting software and experimenting with "expert systems," computer programs modeled on the pricing patterns of real-life experts.

It would appear that AWA can expand a lot larger than its current size without having to jettison its entrepreneurial spirit. For one thing, at a time when many airline executives and those in numerous other industries job hop, both Beauvais and Conway are in for the long pull. "Our real goal is to be as enthusiastic about being here in the company's twentieth year as we were in year one," says Beauvais.

The most direct challenge to AWA's wing-and-a-prayer style of management would be a takeover by a more traditional company. But as the airline is now structured, that's unlikely. Beauvais and Conway have cleverly put half of AWA's stock in friendly hands—with 20 percent owned by Ansett, 12 percent by executives, and 18 percent by employees. In an attempted hostile takeover, the poison pill is a huge payoff to employees— 250 percent of their annual salaries—that should prove to be prohibitively costly.

Looking to a future with broader horizons for his company—with routes to the richest markets—Beauvais argues that "we're creating a management tradition that becomes clearer the more we employ it." He adds confidently, "It should be workable no matter how large the company is."

Source: Adapted from James O'Toole, "The Spirit of Phoenix," *Business Month*, October 1989, pp. 27–37. With permission. Copyright © 1989 by Goldhirsh Group, Inc., 38 Commercial Wharf, Boston, MA 02110.

QUESTIONS

1. Review AWA's strengths, weaknesses, opportunities, and threats.

2. How has effective planning played a role in AWA's success?

3. What types of plans are most appropriate for AWA today—specific or directional? Why?

4. How is the strategy process consistent with the belief that AWA can't "be all things to all people at all times?"

5. Does intuition have a role in planning? Explain.

6. How has AWA gotten its employees to focus on long-term goals rather than short-term ones? Is AWA's approach applicable to all organizations?

7. Compare Beauvais's style of running AWA with that of American Airlines' Bob Crandall described in Case Application 1A.

FOUNDATIONS OF ORGANIZING

1. Define organization structure.
2. Identify the advantages and disadvantages of division of labor.
3. Differentiate line and staff authority.
4. Contrast power with authority.
5. Identify five sources of power.
6. Contrast mechanistic and organic organizations.
7. Explain the strategy-determines-structure thesis.
8. Summarize the effect of size on structure.
9. Explain the effect of technology on structure.
10. Describe how environmental uncertainty affects structure.

o Siegel and John Hay were just a couple of "free spirits" trying to make ends meet in the 1960s.[1] More interested in religion, music, and health than in the security of an eight-to-five job, they would comb the canyons near their homes in Boulder, Colorado, pick herbs, mix them into an herbal tea concoction they called Mo's 24, then stuff it into bags and sell it to natural food stores in the Boulder area. It was fun, and it allowed Mo and John the freedom and fresh air they so valued.

But something began to happen that would change Mo and John's lives. People liked Mo's 24. Stores clamored for more. So Mo and John got their wives to help them. In the morning, the guys would pick herbs while their wives sewed herb tea bags. In the afternoon, the two couples would screen the hundreds of pounds of herbs that had been collected, mix them, and fill the bags. Every few days, one or more of the four would deliver the finished bags to the local stores.

Demand continued to increase. The big supermarket chains such as Safeway and A&P wanted to stock Mo's 24, and the health stores were asking for more variety. The Siegels and Hays could no longer do everything. They hired some additional people to help them out, and their little business grew to six people, ten people, fifteen people . . . .

Mo and John soon found that the informality that worked fine when there were just the two couples didn't work so well with ten or fifteen people. Of course, they had to rent space—a lot of space. Then various tasks had to be clarified so that everything got done. To avoid overlaps and omissions, each individual needed to be assigned specific duties. Some people picked herbs, some made bags, some blended, and some filled bags. Others handled the design of packages, sales, deliveries, accounts payable, and similar responsibilities needed to keep the business going. Communication, which had been easy when the two couples worked in the same small room and could interchange jobs as needed, became a great deal more difficult. So they created departments. To improve coordination and provide direction, they designated some people as formal leaders of these departments. As more people were hired, Mo and John realized they needed job descriptions to clarify people's assignments and responsibilities. There was also a need for policies and procedures to standardize accounting, purchasing, and personnel practices.

What started out as two guys trying to make a couple of bucks while working outdoors turned into Celestial Seasonings Inc., perhaps the best-known maker of herbal teas. Mo and John learned that, to efficiently handle the increased demand for their product, they had to develop a formal organization structure. In this chapter, we'll discuss the key components of organization structure, introduce organization design options, and provide some insights into when certain design options work better than others.

Today, Mo Siegel and John Hay's "little" enterprise—Celestial Seasonings Inc.— makes dozens of herbal teas, employs more than 200 people, and has annual sales in excess of $40 million.

DEFINING ORGANIZATION STRUCTURE AND DESIGN

organization structure
An organization's degree of complexity, formalization, and centralization.

Organization structure describes the organization's framework. Human beings have skeletons that define their parameters; organizations have structures that define theirs. An organization's structure can be dissected into three parts: complexity, formalization, and centralization.[2]

complexity
The amount of differentiation in an organization.

Complexity considers how much differentiation there is in an organization. The more division of labor, the more vertical levels in the hierarchy, and the more geographically dispersed the organization's units, the more difficult it is to coordinate people and their activities. Hence we use the term *complexity*.

formalization
The degree to which an organization relies on rules and procedures to direct the behavior of employees.

The degree to which an organization relies on rules and procedures to direct the behavior of employees is **formalization.** Some organizations operate with a minimum of such standardized guidelines, whereas others, some of them quite small, have all kinds of regulations instructing employees in what they can and cannot do. The more rules and regulations in an organization, the more formalized the organization's structure.

centralization
The concentration of decision-making authority in upper management.

Centralization considers where the decision-making authority lies. In some organizations, decision making is highly centralized. Problems flow up to senior executives, who choose the appropriate action. In other organizations, decision-making authority is passed down to lower levels. This is known as **decentralization.**

decentralization
The handing down of decision-making authority to lower levels in an organization.

When managers construct or change an organization's structure, they are engaged in **organization design.** When we discuss managers making structural decisions—for example, the level at which decisions should be made or the number of standardized rules for employees to follow—we are referring to organization design. In the next chapter, we'll show how the three parts of organization structure can be mixed and matched to create various organization designs.

organization design
The construction or changing of an organization's structure.

BASIC ORGANIZATION DESIGN CONCEPTS

The classical concepts of organization design were formulated by the general administrative theorists we discussed in Chapter 2. They offered a set of principles for managers to follow in organization design. More than sixty years have passed since most of these principles were originally proposed. Given the passing of that much time and all the changes that have taken place in our society, you might think that these principles would be pretty worthless today. Surprisingly, they're not! For the most part, they still provide valuable insights into how to design effective and efficient organizations. Of course, we have also gained a great deal of knowledge over the years as to the limitations of these principles.

In this section, we'll discuss the five basic classical principles that have guided organization design decisions over the years. We'll also present an updated analysis of how each has had to be modified to reflect the increasing sophistication and changing nature of organizational activities.

Division of Labor

The Classical View   We mentioned division of labor in our discussion of Adam Smith and the evolution of management thought. Division of labor means that, rather than an entire job being done by one individual, it is broken down into a number of steps, each step being completed by a separate individual. In essence, individuals specialize in doing part of an activity rather than the entire activity. Assembly-line production, in which each worker does the same standardized task over and over again, is an example of division of labor.

That organizations should be designed around a high degree of division of labor was a widely accepted classical principle. A brief review of the advantages of the

Division of labor produces efficiencies. Could Cessna produce one Citation jet a year if one person had to build the entire plane? One's skills at performing a task successfully increase through repetition. Less time is spent in changing tasks, in putting away one's tools and equipment from a prior step in the work process, and in getting ready for another. It is easier and less costly to find and train workers to do specific and repetitive tasks, especially for highly sophisticated and complex operations.

division of labor, as perceived by the classical writers, centers around economic efficiencies.

Division of labor makes efficient use of the diversity of skills that workers hold. In most organizations, some tasks require highly developed skills; others can be performed by the untrained. If all workers were engaged in each step of, say, an organization's manufacturing process, all would have to have the skills necessary to perform both the most demanding and the least demanding jobs. The result would be that, except when performing the most highly skilled or highly sophisticated tasks, employees would be working below their skill level. Since skilled workers are paid more than unskilled workers and their wages tend to reflect their highest level of skill, it represents an inefficient usage of resources to pay highly skilled workers to do easy tasks.

The Contemporary View   Classical writers viewed division of labor as an unending source of increased productivity. At the turn of the twentieth century and earlier, this generalization was undoubtedly accurate. Because specialization was not widely practiced, its introduction almost always generated higher productivity. But a good thing can be carried too far. There is a point at which the human diseconomies from division of labor—which surface as boredom, fatigue, stress, low productivity, poor quality, increased absenteeism, and high turnover—exceed the economic advantages (see Figure 10–1).

By the 1960s, that point had been reached in a number of jobs. In such cases, productivity could be increased by enlarging, rather than narrowing, the scope of job activities.[3] For instance, in the next chapter, we'll discuss successful efforts to increase productivity by giving employees a variety of activities to do, allowing them to do a whole and complete piece of work, and putting them together into teams. Each of these ideas, of course, runs counter to the division of labor concept. Yet, overall, the division of labor concept is alive and well in most organizations today. We recognize the economies it provides in certain types of jobs, but we also recognize its limitations.

FIGURE 10–1
Economies and Diseconomies
of Division of Labor

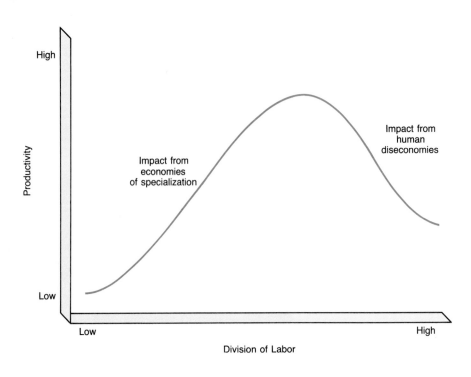

Impact from
economies
of specialization

Impact from
human
diseconomies

Division of Labor

Unity of Command

unity of command
The principle that a subordinate
should have one and only one
superior to whom he or she is
directly responsible.

The Classical View   Classical writers professing the **unity of command** principle
argued that a subordinate should have one and only one superior to whom he or she
is directly responsible. No person should report to two or more bosses. Otherwise, a
subordinate might have to cope with conflicting demands or priorities from several
superiors. In those rare instances when the unity of command principle had to be

Aid Association for Lutherans
(AAL) operates a huge insurance business. Its 500 clerks,
technicians, and managers no
longer perform narrow, individualized tasks. Rather, they have
been organized into all-purpose
teams that operate with minimal
supervision. The time required
to process complicated cases
has been cut from twenty days
to five.

violated, the classical viewpoint always explicitly designated that there be a clear separation of activities and a supervisor responsible for each.

The Contemporary View   The unity of command concept was logical when organizations were comparatively simple. Under most circumstances, it is still sound advice. Most organizations today closely adhere to this principle. Yet there are instances, which we'll introduce in the next chapter, when strict adherence to the unity of command creates a degree of inflexibility that hinders an organization's performance.[4]

Authority and Responsibility

authority
The rights inherent in a managerial position to give orders and expect them to be obeyed.

The Classical View   **Authority** refers to the rights inherent in a managerial position to give orders and expect the orders to be obeyed. Authority was a major tenet of the classical writers; it was viewed as the glue that held the organization together. It was to be delegated downward to subordinate managers, giving them certain rights while providing certain prescribed limits within which to operate.

Each management position has specific inherent rights that incumbents acquire from the position's rank or title. Authority therefore relates to one's position within an organization and ignores the personal characteristics of the individual manager. It has nothing directly to do with the individual. The expression "The king is dead; long live the king" illustrates the concept. Whoever is king acquires the rights inherent in the king's position. When a position of authority is vacated, the person who has left the position no longer has any authority. The authority remains with the position and its new incumbent.

responsibility
An obligation to perform.

When we delegate authority, we must allocate commensurate **responsibility.** That is, when one is given "rights," one also assumes a corresponding "obligation" to perform. Allocating authority without responsibility creates opportunities for abuse, and no one should be held responsible for something over which he or she has no authority.

Classical writers recognized the importance of equating authority and responsibility. Additionally, they stated that responsibility cannot be delegated. They supported this contention by noting that the delegator was held responsible for the actions of his delegates. But how is it possible to equate authority and responsibility, if responsibility cannot be delegated?

The classicists' answer was to recognize two forms of responsibility: *operating* responsibility and *ultimate* responsibility. Managers pass on operating responsibility, which may then be passed on further. But there is an aspect of responsibility—its ultimate component—that must be retained. A manager is ultimately responsible for the actions of his or her subordinates to whom the operating responsibility has been passed. Therefore managers should delegate operating responsibility equal to the delegated authority; however, ultimate responsibility can never be delegated.

line authority
The authority that entitles a manager to direct the work of a subordinate.

chain of command
The flow of authority from the top to the bottom of an organization.

The classical writers also distinguished between two forms of authority relations: line authority and staff authority. **Line authority** is the authority that entitles a manager to direct the work of a subordinate. It is the superior-subordinate authority relationship that extends from the top of the organization to the lowest echelon, following what is called the **chain of command.** This is shown in Figure 10–2. As a link in the chain of command, a manager with line authority has the right to direct the work of subordinates and make certain decisions without consulting others. Of course, in the chain of command, every manager is also subject to the direction of his or her superior.

Sometimes the term *line* is used to differentiate *line* managers from *staff* managers. In this context, line emphasizes managers whose organizational function contributes directly to the achievement of organizational objectives. In a manufacturing firm, line

FIGURE 10–2
The Chain of Command

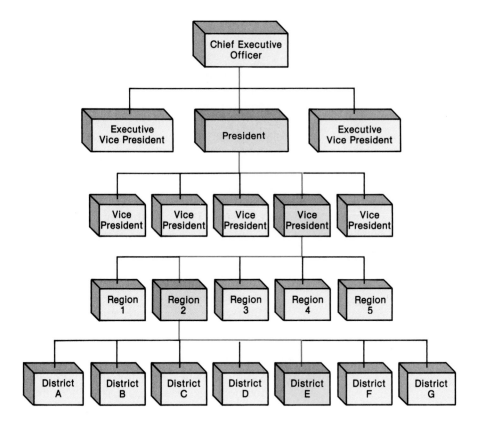

managers are typically in the production and sales functions, whereas executives in personnel and accounting are considered staff managers. But whether a manager's function is classified as line or staff depends on the organization's objectives. At a firm like Snelling and Snelling, which is a personnel placement organization, personnel interviewers have a line function. Similarly, at the accounting firm of Price Waterhouse, accounting is a line function.

The definitions given above are not contradictory but, rather, represent two ways of looking at the term *line*. Every manager has line authority over his or her subordinates, but not every line manager is in a line function or position. This latter determination depends on whether or not a function directly contributes to the organization's objectives.

As organizations get larger and more complex, line managers find that they do not have the time, expertise, or resources to effectively get their jobs done. In response, they create **staff authority** functions to support, assist, advise, and in general reduce some of the informational burdens they have. The hospital administrator can't effectively handle all the purchasing of supplies that the hospital needs, so she creates a purchasing department. The purchasing department is a staff department. Of course, the head of the purchasing department has line authority over her subordinate purchasing agents. The hospital administrator might also find that she is overburdened and needs an assistant. In creating the position of assistant to the hospital administrator, she has created a staff position.

Figure 10–3 illustrates line and staff authority.

The Contemporary View   The classical writers were enamored with authority. They naively assumed that the rights inherent in one's formal position in an organization were the sole source of influence. They believed that managers were all-powerful.

staff authority
Authority that supports, assists, and advises holders of line authority.

FIGURE 10–3
Line and Staff Authority

——— Line authority

– – – Staff authority

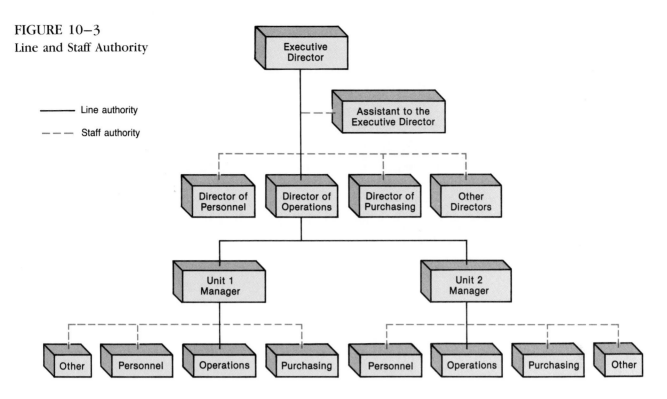

power
The capacity to influence decisions.

This might have been true sixty or more years ago. Organizations were simpler. Staff was less important. Managers were only minimally dependent on technical specialists. Under such conditions, influence is the same as authority; and the higher a manager's position in the organization, the more influence he or she had. However, those conditions no longer hold. Researchers and practitioners of management now recognize that you don't have to be a manager to have power, nor is power perfectly correlated to one's level in the organization. Authority is an important concept in organizations, but an exclusive focus on authority produces a narrow, unrealistic view of influence in organizations. Today, we recognize that authority is but one element in the larger concept of power.[5]

The terms *authority* and *power* are frequently confused. Authority is a right, the legitimacy of which is based on the authority figure's position in the organization. Authority goes with the job. **Power,** on the other hand, refers to an individual's capacity to influence decisions. Authority is part of the larger concept of power; that is, the formal rights that come with an individual's position in the organization are just one means by which an individual can affect the decision process.

Figure 10–4 visually depicts the difference between authority and power. The two-dimensional arrangement of boxes in part A portrays authority. The area in which the authority applies is defined by the horizontal dimension. Each horizontal grouping represents a functional area. The influence one holds in the organization is defined by the vertical dimension in the structure. The higher one is in the organization, the greater one's authority.

Power, on the other hand, is a three-dimensional concept (see the cone in part B of Figure 10–4). It includes not only the functional and hierarchical dimensions, but also a third dimension called *centrality*. While authority is defined by one's vertical position in the hierarchy, power is made up of both one's vertical position and one's distance from the organization's *power core,* or center.

FIGURE 10–4   Authority Versus Power

A. Authority

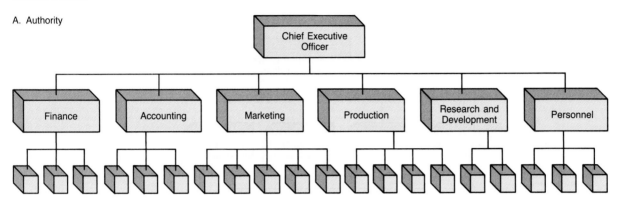

B. Power

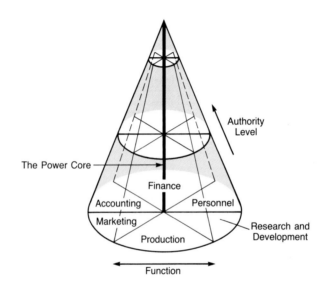

Think of the cone in Figure 10–4 as being an organization. The center of the cone is the power core. The closer you are to the power core, the more influence you have on decisions. The existence of a power core is, in fact, the only difference between A and B in Figure 10–4. The vertical hierarchy dimension in A is merely one's level on the outer edge of the cone. The top of the cone corresponds to the top of the hierarchy, the middle of the cone to the middle of the hierarchy, and so on. Similarly, the functional groups in A become wedges in the cone. Each wedge represents a functional area.

The cone analogy explicitly acknowledges two facts: (1) the higher one moves in an organization (an increase in authority), the closer one moves to the power core; and (2) it is not necessary to have authority in order to wield power because one can move horizontally inward toward the power core without moving up.

Have you ever noticed that secretaries of high-ranking executives usually have a great deal of power, even though they have little authority? As gatekeepers for their bosses, secretaries have considerable say over whom their bosses see and when. Furthermore, because they are regularly relied upon to pass information on to their bosses, they have some control over what their bosses hear. It's not unusual for $75,000-a-year middle managers to tread very carefully in order not to upset their boss's $25,000-a-year secretary. Why? Because the secretary has power! The secretary may be low in the authority hierarchy but close to the power core. Low-ranking employees who have relatives, friends, or associates in high places might also be close to the power core. So, too, are employees with scarce and important skills. The lowly production engineer with twenty years of experience in a company might be the only one in the firm who knows the inner workings of all the old production machinery. When pieces of this old equipment break down, no one but this engineer understands how to fix them. Suddenly, the engineer's influence is much greater than would appear from his level in the vertical hierarchy.

How does one acquire power? John French and Bertram Raven have identified five sources or bases of power: coercive, reward, legitimate, expert, and referent.[6]

coercive power
Power dependent on fear.

Coercive power base is defined by French and Raven as depending on fear. One reacts to this power out of fear of the negative results that might occur if one failed to comply. It rests on the application, or the threat of application, of physical sanctions such as the infliction of pain, deformity, or death; the generation of frustration through restriction of movement; or the controlling by force of basic physiological or safety needs.

In the 1930s, when John Dillinger went into a bank, held a gun to a teller's head, and asked for money, he was incredibly successful at getting compliance with his request. His power base was coercive. A loaded gun gives its holder power because others are fearful that they will lose something that they hold dear: their life.

If you are a manager, you typically have some coercive power. You may be able to suspend or demote employees. You may be able to assign them work activities they find unpleasant. You may even have the option of dismissing employees. These all represent coercive actions. But you don't have to be a manager to hold coercive power. For instance, a subordinate who is in a position to embarrass his or her boss in public and who successfully uses this power to gain advantage is using coercion.

**ETHICAL
DILEMMAS IN
MANAGEMENT**

Should You Follow Orders With Which You Don't Agree?

A few years back, a study of business executives revealed that most had obeyed orders that they had found personally objectionable or unethical.[7] Far more thought-provoking was a survey taken among the general public near the end of the Vietnam War. In spite of public dismay over the actions of some military personnel during that war, about half the respondents said that they would have shot civilian men, women, and children in cold blood if they had been ordered to do so by their commanding officer![8]

If you were asked to follow orders that you believed were unconscionable, would you comply? For example, what if your boss asked you to destroy evidence that he or she had been stealing a great deal of money from the organization?

What if you merely disagreed with the orders? For instance, what if your boss asked you to bring him or her coffee each morning even though no such task is included in your job description? What would *you* do?

reward power
Power based on the ability to distribute anything that others may value.

legitimate power
Power based on one's position in the formal hierarchy.

expert power
Power based on one's expertise, special skill, or knowledge.

referent power
Power based on identification with a person who has desirable resources or personal traits.

The opposite of coercive power is **reward power.** People comply with the wishes or directives of another because it produces positive benefits; therefore one who can distribute rewards that others view as valuable will have power over them. These rewards can be anything that another person values. In an organizational context, we think of money, favorable performance appraisals, promotions, interesting work assignments, friendly colleagues, and preferred work shifts or sales territories.

Coercive and reward power are actually counterparts of each other. If you can remove something of positive value from another or inflict something of negative value upon him or her, you have coercive power over that person. If you can give someone something of positive value or remove something of negative value, you have reward power over that person. Again, as with coercive power, you don't need to be a manager to be able to exert influence through rewards. Rewards such as friendliness, acceptance, and praise are available to everyone in the organization. To the degree that an individual seeks such rewards, your ability to give or withhold them gives you power over that individual.

Legitimate power and authority are one and the same. Legitimate power represents the power a person receives as a result of his or her position in the formal hierarchy.

Positions of authority include coercive and reward powers. Legitimate power, however, is broader than the power to coerce and reward. Specifically, it includes acceptance by members of an organization of the authority of a position. When school principals, bank presidents, or army captains speak (assuming that their directives are viewed to be within the authority of their positions), teachers, tellers, and first lieutenants listen and usually comply.

Expert power is influence wielded as a result of expertise, special skill, or knowledge. In recent years, as a result of the explosion in technical knowledge, expert power has become an increasingly potent power source in organizations. As jobs have become more specialized, management has increasingly become dependent on staff "experts" to achieve the organization's goals. As an employee increases his or her knowledge of information that is critical to the operation of a work group, and to the degree that that knowledge is not possessed by others, expert power is enhanced. To illustrate the point, if a computer system is critical to a unit's work, and if one employee, say Chris, knows how to repair it and no one else within 200 miles does, then the unit is dependent on Chris. If the system breaks down, Chris can use her expertise to obtain ends that she could never achieve by her position's authority alone. In such a situation, you should expect the unit's manager to try to have others trained in the workings of the computer system or to hire someone with this knowledge in order to reduce Chris's power. As others become capable of duplicating Chris's specialized activities, her expert power diminishes.

The last category of influence that French and Raven identified was **referent power.** Its base is identification with a person who has desirable resources or personal traits. If I admire and identify with you, you can exercise power over me because I want to please you.

Referent power develops out of admiration of another and a desire to be like that person. You might consider the person you identify with as having *charisma*. If you admire someone to the point of modeling your behavior and attitudes after him or her, this person possesses referent power over you. Referent power explains why celebrities are paid millions of dollars to endorse products in commercials. Marketing research shows that people like Bill Cosby, Cher, and Michael Jordan have the power to influence your choice of photo processors, perfume, and athletic shoes. With a little practice, you or I could probably deliver as smooth a sales pitch as these celebrities, but the buying public does not identify with you and me. In organizations, the charismatic individual—manager or otherwise—can influence superiors, peers, and subordinates.

MANAGERS WHO MADE A DIFFERENCE

Martina Bradford at AT&T

Martina Bradford is AT&T's vice president of external affairs for the New York/New England region. Her rapid ascent to this position appears to be the result of a lot of talent, a solid career plan, a string of visible accomplishments, and a shrewd understanding of power.[9]

Bradford's career plan was directed early on toward preparing her for a high-level position in the telecommunications industry. She knew that a key environmental force in this industry was government and regulatory issues, so she took a law degree at Duke University. She then spent thirteen years gaining experience working on legislative and regulatory law issues, first as chief of staff to the vice chairman of the Interstate Commerce Commission, then as minority counsel with Congress, and later as a lobbyist with her current employer AT&T.

Her decision to join AT&T was carefully thought out. She knew that AT&T was a company with an outstanding track record for promoting women and minorities into management positions. Furthermore, she figured that an understanding of regulatory issues would be a scarce and important resource in the company. At AT&T, she sought out high-profile assignments. For example, Bradford monitored the action of congressional committees on deregulation and prepared witnesses to testify in government hearings. She also successfully lobbied against the lifting of restraints that allowed the Baby Bells to manufacture telephone equipment and provide long-distance services, the company's two key revenue producers.

Her strategy obviously worked. After five years at AT&T, she was promoted to her current position as vice president. She and her staff of ninety people seek new and innovative ways of introducing telecommunications services and reducing access fees, the charge AT&T pays local telephone companies for acting as a conduit for its long-distance services. Because these expenses account for 50 cents out of every dollar earned, cutting costs is paramount if AT&T is to achieve its profit objectives. Clearly, Bradford has built a power base by gaining responsibility for a unit that makes vital contributions to AT&T's bottom-line.

Photo courtesy of Martina Bradford.

Span of Control

span of control
The number of subordinates a manager can direct efficiently and effectively.

The Classical View How many subordinates can a manager efficiently and effectively direct? This question of **span of control** received a great deal of attention from early writers. While there was no consensus on a specific number, the classical writers favored small spans—typically no more than six—in order to maintain close control.[10] However, several writers did acknowledge level in the organization as a contingency variable. They argued that as a manager rises in an organization, he or she has to deal with a greater number of ill-structured problems, so top executives need a smaller span than do middle managers, and middle managers require a smaller span than do supervisors.

FIGURE 10–5
Contrasting Spans of Control

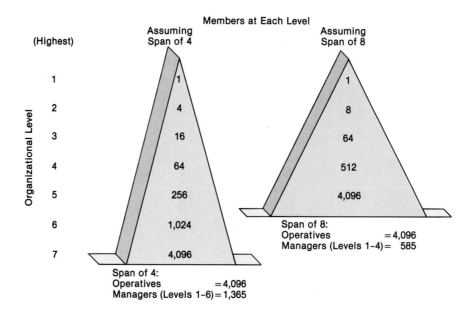

Why is the span of control concept important? To a large degree, it determines the number of levels and managers an organization has. All things being equal, the wider or larger the span, the more efficient the organization design. An example can illustrate the validity of this statement.

Assume that we have two organizations, each of which has approximately 4,100 operative employees. As Figure 10–5 illustrates, if one has a uniform span of four and the other a span of eight, the wider span would have two fewer levels and approximately 800 fewer managers. If the average manager made $35,000 a year, the wider span would save over $28 million a year in management salaries! Obviously, wider spans are more *efficient* in terms of cost. But at some point, wider spans reduce *effectiveness*.

The Contemporary View   Management guru Tom Peters recently predicted that Wal-Mart would pass Sears, Roebuck as the number one retailer in the United States: "Sears doesn't have a chance!" he said. "A twelve-layer company can't compete with a three-layer company."[11] Peters might have exaggerated the point a bit, but it clearly reflects the fact that the pendulum has swung in recent years toward designing flat structures with wide spans of control.

More and more organizations are increasing their spans of control. For example, the span for managers at companies like General Electric and Reynolds Metals has expanded to ten or twelve subordinates—twice the number of ten years ago.[12] The span of control is increasingly being determined by looking at contingency variables. For instance, it's obvious that the more training and experience subordinates have, the less direct supervision they need. Therefore managers who have well-trained and experienced employees can function with a wider span. Other contingency variables that will determine the appropriate span include similarity of subordinate tasks, the complexity of those tasks, the physical proximity of subordinates, the degree to which standardized procedures are in place, the sophistication of the organization's management information system, the strength of the organization's culture, and the preferred style of the manager.[13]

Departmentalization

The Classical View   The classical writers argued that activities in the organization should be specialized and grouped into departments. Division of labor creates specialists who need coordination. This coordination is facilitated by putting specialists together in departments under the direction of a manager. Creation of these departments is typically based on the work functions being performed, the product or service being offered, the target customer or client, the geographic territory being covered, or the process being used to turn inputs into outputs. No single method of departmentalization was advocated by the classical writers. The method or methods used should reflect the grouping that would best contribute to the attainment of the organization's objectives and the goals of individual units.

One of the most popular ways to group activities is by functions performed—**functional departmentalization.** A manufacturing manager might organize his or her plant by separating engineering, accounting, manufacturing, personnel, and purchasing specialists into common departments. (See Figure 10–6.) Departmentalization by function can be used in all types of organizations. Only the functions change to reflect the organization's objectives and activities. A hospital might have departments devoted to research, patient care, accounting, and so forth. A professional football franchise might have departments entitled Player Personnel, Ticket Sales, and Travel and Accommodations.

Figure 10–7 illustrates the **product departmentalization** method used at Sun Petroleum Products. Each major product area in the corporation is placed under the authority of a vice president who is a specialist in, and is responsible for, everything having to do with his or her product line. Notice, for example, in contrast to functional departmentalization, that manufacturing and other major activities have been divided up to give the product managers (vice presidents, in this case) considerable autonomy and control.

If an organization's activities are service-related rather than product-related, each service would be autonomously grouped. For instance, an accounting firm would have departments for tax, management consulting, auditing, and the like. Each offers a common array of services under the direction of a product or service manager.

The particular type of customer the organization seeks to reach can also be used to group employees. The sales activities in an office supply firm, for instance, can be broken down into three departments to serve retail, wholesale, and government customers. (See Figure 10–8.) A large law office can segment its staff on the basis of whether they serve corporate or individual clients. The assumption underlying **customer departmentalization** is that customers in each department have a common set of problems and needs that can best be met by having specialists for each.

Another way to departmentalize is on the basis of geography or territory—

functional departmentalization
Grouping activities by functions performed.

product departmentalization
Grouping activities by product line.

customer departmentalization
Grouping activities on the basis of common customers.

FIGURE 10–6
Departmentalization by Function

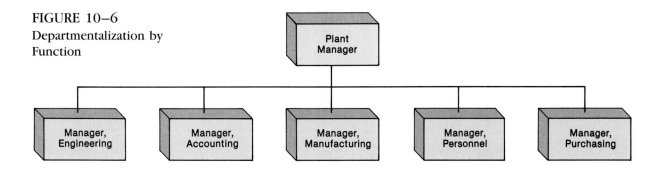

FIGURE 10–7
Departmentalization by
Product

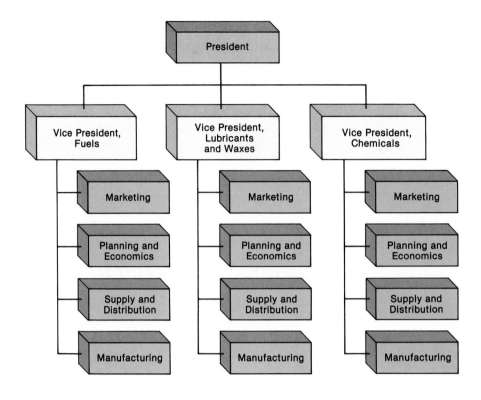

geographic departmentalization. The sales function might have western, south-ern, midwestern, and eastern regions. (See Figure 10–9.) A large school district might have six high schools to provide for each of the major geographical territories within the district. If an organization's customers are scattered over a large geographic area, this form of departmentalization can be valuable.

Figure 10–10 depicts the various production departments in an aluminum plant. Each department specializes in one specific phase in the production of aluminum tubing. The metal is cast in huge furnaces; sent to the press department, where it is extruded into aluminum pipe; transferred to the tube mill, where it is stretched into various sizes and shapes of tubing; moved to finishing, where it is cut and cleaned; and finally arrives in the inspect, pack, and ship department. Since each process requires different skills, this method offers a basis for the homogeneous categorizing of activi-ties.

FIGURE 10–8
Departmentalization by
Customer

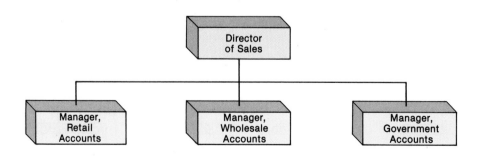

FIGURE 10–9
Departmentalization by
Geography

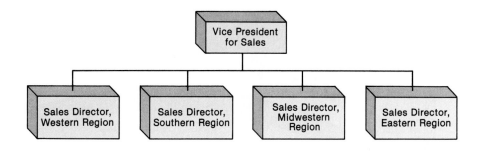

process departmentalization
Grouping activities on the basis
of product or customer flow.

Process departmentalization can be used for processing customers as well as products. If you have ever been to a state motor vehicle office to get a driver's license, you probably went through several departments before receiving your license. In one state, applicants must go through three steps, each handled by a separate department: (1) validation, by the motor vehicles division; (2) processing, by the licensing department; and (3) payment collection, by the treasury department.

The Contemporary View   Most large organizations continue to use most or all of the departmental groups suggested by the classical writers. A major electronics firm, for instance, organizes each of its divisions along functional lines, organizes its manufacturing units around processes, departmentalizes sales around four geographic regions, and divides each sales region into three customer groupings. But two recent trends need to be mentioned. First, the customer form of departmentalization has become increasingly emphasized. Second, rigid departmentalization is being complemented by the use of teams that cross over traditional departmental lines.

Today's competitive environment has refocused management's attention on its customers. To better monitor the needs of customers and to be able to respond to changes in those needs, many organizations have given greater emphasis to customer departmentalization. Xerox, for example, has eliminated its corporate marketing staff and placed marketing specialists out in the field.[14] This allows the company to better understand who their customers are and to respond faster to their requirements.

We are seeing a great deal more use of teams today as a device for accomplishing organizational objectives. As tasks have become more complex and diverse skills are needed to accomplish these tasks, management has increasingly introduced the use of teams and task forces.

FIGURE 10–10
Departmentalization by
Process

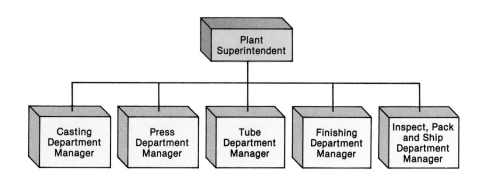

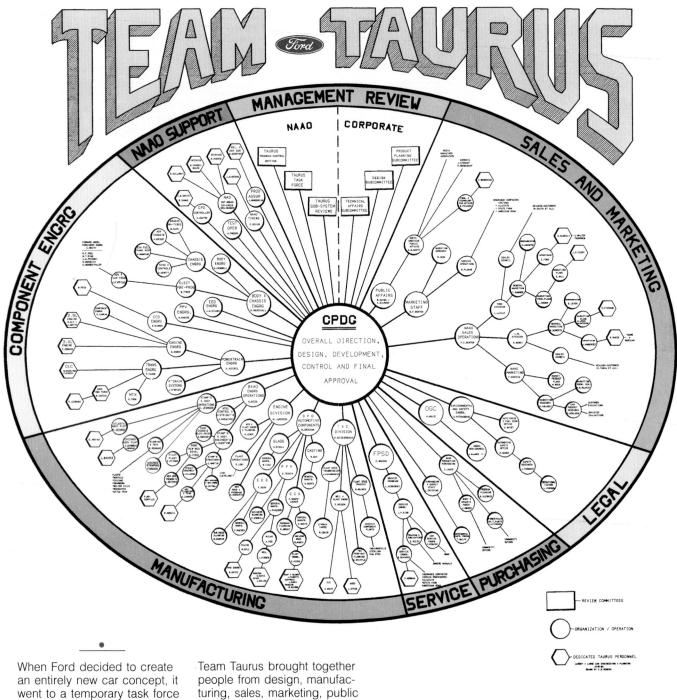

When Ford decided to create an entirely new car concept, it went to a temporary task force that crossed the company's traditional departmental lines.

Team Taurus brought together people from design, manufacturing, sales, marketing, public relations, legal, and other departments.

CONTEMPORARY ORGANIZATION DESIGN CONCEPTS

If we combine the classical principles, we arrive at what most of the early writers believed to be the ideal structural design: the mechanistic or bureaucratic organization. Today, we recognize that there is no single "ideal" organization design for all situations. In this section, we'll look at two generic models of organization design and then look at the situational factors that favor each.

Mechanistic and Organic Organizations

mechanistic organization (bureaucracy)
A structure that scores high on complexity, formalization, and centralization.

Figure 10–11 describes two diverse organizational forms.[15] The **mechanistic organization** (or **bureaucracy**) was the natural outcome from applying the classical principles. Adherence to the unity of command principle ensured the existence of a formal hierarchy of authority, with each person controlled and supervised by one superior. Keeping the span of control small at increasingly higher levels in the organization created tall, impersonal structures. As the distance between the top and the bottom of the organization expanded, top management would increasingly impose rules and regulations to ensure that standard practices were followed. Because top managers couldn't control lower-level activities through direct observation, they substituted rules and regulations. The classical writers' belief in a high degree of division of labor created jobs that were simple, routine, and standardized. Further specialization through the use of departmentalization increased impersonality and the need for multiple layers of management to coordinate the specialized departments.

In terms of our definition of organization structure, we find the classicists advocating that *all* organizations be high in complexity, high in formalization, and high in centralization. Structures would be efficiency machines, well oiled by rules, regulations, and routinization. The impact of personalities and human judgments, which impose inefficiencies and inconsistencies, would be minimized. Standardization would lead to stability and predictability. Confusion and ambiguity would be eliminated.

organic organization (adhocracy)
A structure that scores low on complexity, formalization, and centralization.

The **organic organization** (also referred to as an **adhocracy**) is a direct contrast to the mechanistic form. It is low in complexity, low in formalization, and decentralized.

The organic organization is a highly adaptive form that is as loose and flexible as the mechanistic organization is rigid and stable. Rather than having standardized jobs and regulations, the adhocracy's loose structure allows it to change rapidly as needs require. Adhocracies have division of labor, but the jobs people do are not standardized. Employees tend to be professionals who are technically proficient and trained to handle diverse problems. Their formal training has prepared them to handle an array of problems. They need very few formal rules and little direct supervision because their training has instilled in them standards of professional conduct. For instance, a computer engineer is given an assignment. He doesn't need to be given procedures on how to do it. Most problems he can solve himself or resolve after conferring with

FIGURE 10–11
Mechanistic Versus Organic Organizations

MECHANISTIC

ORGANIC

- High horizontal differentiation
- Rigid hierarchical relationships
- Fixed duties
- High formalization
- Formalized communication channels
- Centralized decision authority

- Low horizontal differentiation
- Collaboration (both vertical and horizontal)
- Adaptable duties
- Low formalization
- Informal communication
- Decentralized decision authority

colleagues. Professional standards guide his behavior. The organic organization is low in centralization in order for the professional to respond quickly to problems and because top management cannot be expected to possess the expertise to make necessary decisions.

Strategy and Structure

An organization's structure is a means to help management achieve its objectives. Since objectives are derived from the organization's overall strategy, it is only logical that strategy and structure should be closely linked. More specifically, structure should follow strategy. If management makes a significant change in its organization's strategy, structure will need to be modified to accommodate and support this change.

The first important research on the strategy-structure relationship was a study of close to 100 large U.S. companies conducted by Alfred Chandler.[16] After tracing the development of these organizations over a period of fifty years and compiling extensive case histories of companies such as DuPont, General Motors, Standard Oil of New Jersey, and Sears, Chandler concluded that changes in corporate strategy precede and lead to changes in an organization's structure. Specifically, he found that organizations usually begin with a single product or line. The simplicity of the strategy requires only a simple or loose form of structure to execute it. Decisions can be centralized in the hands of a single senior manager, while complexity and formalization will be low. As organizations grow, their strategies become more ambitious and elaborated.

From the single product line, companies often expand their activities within their industry by acquiring suppliers or selling their products directly to customers. For example, General Motors not only assembles automobiles but also owns companies that make air conditioners, electrical equipment, and other car components. This vertical integration strategy makes for increased interdependence between organizational units and creates the need for a more complex coordination device. This is achieved by redesigning the structure to form specialized units based on functions performed. Finally, if growth proceeds further into product diversification, structure needs to be adjusted again to gain efficiency. A product diversification strategy demands a structural form that allows for the efficient allocation of resources, accountability for performance, and coordination between units. This can be achieved best by creating many independent divisions, each responsible for a specified product line. In summary, Chandler proposed that as strategies move from single product to vertical integration to product diversification, management will move from an organic to a more mechanistic organization.

Recent research has generally confirmed the strategy-structure relationship but has used the strategy terminology presented in Chapter 8.[17] For instance, organizations pursuing a prospector strategy must innovate to survive. An organic organization matches best with this strategy. In contrast, a defender strategy seeks stability and efficiency. This can best be achieved with a mechanistic organization.

Size and Structure

There is considerable historical evidence that an organization's size significantly affects its structure.[18] For instance, large organizations—those typically employing 2,000 or more employees—tend to have more specialization, horizontal and vertical differentiation, and rules and regulations than do small organizations. However, the relationship isn't linear. Rather, size affects structure at a decreasing rate. The impact of size becomes less important as an organization expands. Why is this? Essentially, once an organization has around 2,000 employees, it is already fairly mechanistic. An additional 500 employees will not have much impact. On the other hand, adding 500 employees to an organization that has only 300 members is likely to result in a shift toward a more mechanistic structure.

IN PRACTICE

Lean, Mean, and Flexible

Historically, the size-structure relationship was clouded by two assumptions. First, managers assumed that large organizations were more efficient. Economies of scale were supposed to result in larger firms being able to produce at a lower cost than their smaller counterparts. Second, large organizations could achieve this efficiency only by adopting a mechanistic structure.

Recent evidence indicates that neither of these assumptions was correct.[19] For instance, minimills run by Nucorp and Chaparral can produce steel significantly more cheaply than can the huge plants run by USX and Bethlehem. Large, successful companies like Ford and 3M Co. have become highly decentralized and have taken on many of the characteristics of small, organic organizations. This new evidence that "small may be beautiful" hasn't been lost on practicing managers. We are seeing an increasing number of large organizations downsizing or reorganizing to cut excess layers of management and reorganizing around groups of smaller units.

The management of almost every *Fortune* 500 corporation has cut vertical layers from its organization in the past decade. Diverse companies like General Motors, Sears, and BankAmerica have made their organizations flatter by laying off employees, reducing hierarchy, and increasing their managers' spans of control. Companies like The Limited, GE, AT&T, Johnson & Johnson, and Hewlett-Packard have made their firms more flexible by organizing themselves into groups of smaller companies.

One lesson that managers seemed to have learned in the 1980s was that bigger doesn't necessarily mean more efficient. When Compaq Computer can develop a new computer three to five times faster than IBM, efficiency begins to take a back seat in the marketplace to flexibility.

Technology and Structure

Every organization uses some form of technology to convert its inputs into outputs. To attain its objectives, the organization uses equipment, materials, knowledge, and/or experienced individuals and puts them together into certain types and patterns of activities. All organizations use one or more technologies to obtain their objectives. For instance, college instructors teach students by a variety of methods: formal lectures, group discussions, case analyses, programmed learning, and so forth. Each of these methods is a type of technology.

In the early 1960s, Joan Woodward demonstrated that organization structures adapt to their technology. While few researchers in organization design would argue today that technology is the *sole* determinant of structure, clearly it is an important contributor. Let's look at Woodward's research and update the work on classifying different types of technology.

Joan Woodward   The initial interest in technology as a determinant of structure can be traced to the work of Joan Woodward.[20] She studied nearly 100 small manufactur-

3M makes a conscious effort to keep its work units as small as possible. The 52,000 U.S. employees of 3M are divided among thirty-seven divisions and nine subsidiaries. Among the company's ninety-one manufacturing plants, only five employ 1,000 people or more, and the average company installation has 270 employees.

unit production
The production of items in units or small batches.

mass production
Large-batch manufacturing.

process production
Continuous-process production.

ing firms in the south of England to determine the extent to which classical principles such as unity of command and span of control were related to firm success. She was unable to derive any consistent pattern from her data until she segmented her firms into three categories based on the size of their production runs. The three categories, representing three distinct technologies, had increasing levels of complexity and sophistication. The first category, **unit production,** was comprised of unit or small-batch producers that manufactured custom products such as tailor-made suits and turbines for hydroelectric dams. The second category, **mass production,** included large-batch or mass-production manufacturers that made items like refrigerators and automobiles. The third and most complex group, **process production,** included continuous-process producers like oil and chemical refiners.

Woodward found that (1) distinct relationships existed between these technology classifications and the subsequent structure of the firms and (2) the effectiveness of the organizations was related to the "fit" between technology and structure.

For example, the number of vertical levels increased with technical complexity. The median number of vertical levels for firms in the unit, mass, and process categories were three, four, and six, respectively. More important, from an effectiveness standpoint, the more successful firms in each category clustered around the median for their production group. But not all the relationships were linear. As a case in point, the mass-production firms scored high in terms of overall complexity and formalization, whereas the unit and process firms rated low on these structural dimensions. Imposing rules and regulations, for instance, was impossible with the nonroutine technology of unit production and unnecessary in the highly standardized process technology. A summary of her findings is shown in Table 10–1.

After carefully analyzing her findings, Woodward concluded that specific structures were associated with each of the three categories and that successful firms met the requirements of their technology by adopting the proper structural arrangements. Within each category, the firms that most nearly conformed to the median figure for each structural component were the most effective. She found that there was no one best way to organize a manufacturing firm. Unit and process production are most effective when matched with an organic structure; mass production is most effective when matched with a mechanistic structure.

TABLE 10–1   Woodward's Findings on Technology,
Structure, and Effectiveness

	Unit Production	Mass Production	Process Production
Structural characteristics	Low vertical differentiation Low horizontal differentiation Low formalization	Moderate vertical differentiation High horizontal differentiation High formalization	High vertical differentiation Low horizontal differentiation Low formalization
Most effective structure	Organic	Mechanistic	Organic

task variability
The number of exceptions individuals encounter in their work.

problem analyzability
The type of search procedures employees follow in responding to exceptions.

Charles Perrow   One of the major limitations of Woodward's technological classification scheme was that it applied only to manufacturing organizations. Since manufacturing firms represent fewer than half of all organizations, technology needed to be operationalized in a more generic way if the concept was to have meaning across all organizations. Charles Perrow suggested such an alternative.[21]

Perrow directed his attention to knowledge technology rather than production technology. He proposed that technology be viewed in terms of two dimensions: (1) the number of exceptions individuals encounter in their work and (2) the type of search procedures followed to find successful methods for responding adequately to these exceptions. The first dimension he termed **task variability**; the second he called **problem analyzability.**

The exceptions in task variability are few when the job is high in routineness. Examples of jobs that normally have few exceptions in their day-to-day practice include a worker on a manufacturing assembly line and a fry cook at McDonald's. At the other end of the spectrum, if a job has a great deal of variety, it will have a large number of exceptions. This would characterize top management positions, consulting jobs, and jobs such as putting out fires on off-shore oil platforms.

The second dimension, problem analyzability, assesses search procedures. The search can, at one extreme, be described as well defined. An individual can use logical and analytical reasoning in the search for a solution. If you're basically a high B student and you suddenly fail the first exam in a course, you logically analyze the problem and find a solution. Did you spend enough time studying for the exam? Did you study the right material? Was the exam fair? How did other good students do? Using this kind of logic, you can find the source of the problem and rectify it. At the other extreme are ill-defined problems. If you're an architect given an assignment to design a building to conform to standards and constraints that you've never encountered before or read about, you won't have any formal search technique to use. You will have to rely on your prior experience, judgment, and intuition to find a solution. Through guesswork and trial and error you might find an acceptable choice.

Perrow used these two dimensions, task variability and problem analyzability, to construct a two-by-two matrix, shown in Figure 10–12. The four cells in this matrix represent four types of technology: routine, engineering, craft, and nonroutine.

Routine technologies (cell 1) have few exceptions and have easy-to-analyze problems. The mass-production processes used to make steel and automobiles or to refine petroleum belong in this category. Engineering technologies (cell 2) have a large number of exceptions, but they can be handled in a rational and systemized manner. The construction of bridges falls in this category. Craft technologies (cell 3) deal with relatively difficult problems but with a limited set of exceptions. Shoemaking and

FIGURE 10–12
Perrow's Technology Classification

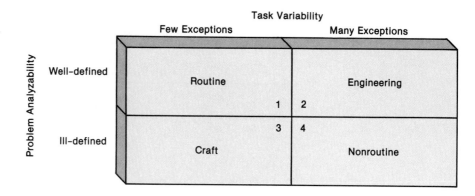

Task Variability

Few Exceptions | Many Exceptions

Problem Analyzability

Well-defined — Routine (1) | (2) Engineering

Ill-defined — (3) Craft | (4) Nonroutine

furniture restoring fit in this category. Finally, nonroutine technologies (cell 4) are characterized by many exceptions and by difficult-to-analyze problems. This technology describes many aerospace operations, such as Rockwell International's development of the Space Shuttle.

In summary, Perrow argued that if problems can be systematically analyzed, cells 1 and 2 are appropriate. Problems that can be handled only by intuition, guesswork, or unanalyzed experience require the technology of cell 3 or 4. Similarly, if new, unusual, or unfamiliar problems appear regularly, they would be in either cell 2 or 4. If problems are familiar, then cell 1 or 3 is appropriate.

What Does It Mean?   The common theme in studies of technology is that the processes or methods that transform inputs into outputs differ by their degree of routineness. In general, the more routine the technology, the more standardized the structure can be. We should expect management to meet routine technologies with a mechanistic organization. The more nonroutine the technology, the more organic the structure.[22]

Major Japanese automakers are not standing still while U.S. firms like GM become more flexible. Toyota has recently reorganized and cut out two vertical levels in its hierarchy.

Environment and Structure

In Chapter 3 we introduced the organization's environment as a constraint on managerial discretion. Research has demonstrated that environment is also a major influence on structure.[23] General Motors provides a good illustration.[24]

In the 1950s and 1960s, GM faced a relatively stable environment. Its competition was restricted to Ford, Chrysler, American Motors, and a few foreign imports like Volkswagen and Fiat. GM's share of the U.S. market during this period was almost 50 percent. Regardless of GM's styling, model offerings, or repair record, its cars sold well year in and year out. The only major uncertainty that GM faced in its environment was downturns in the economy, but even recessions hurt GM less than they hurt its competition.

We now fast-forward to the late 1980s and early 1990s. GM's market share has slipped to 34 percent. Ford is a much stronger domestic competitor, and the combined Chrysler-AMC management team is increasingly aggressive under Lee Iacocca. Japanese manufacturers like Nissan, Toyota, and Honda have built plants in the United States. GM faces formidable competition from car manufacturers in Germany, Sweden, France, and South Korea. Government regulations, which were minimal 25 years ago, now dictate mileage standards, safety equipment, and other requirements. To make matters worse, new government regulations pop up every few years. Clearly, GM's environment has gone from stable to dynamic.

GM's structure has had to change to reflect this change in environment. Its highly mechanistic organization, which worked well in stable times, was no longer effective.

MANAGING FROM A GLOBAL PERSPECTIVE

Expect Different Structures in India Than in Germany

An organization's structure must adapt to its environment. Included in that environment is the national culture of the country in which the organization is located. Research confirms that organizations mirror, to a considerable degree, the cultural values of their host country.[25]

In a country with a high power distance rating, people prefer that decisions be centralized. Similarly, uncertainty avoidance relates to formalization. High uncertainty avoidance relates to high formalization. Based on these relationships, we find certain patterns. French and Italian managers tend to create rigid bureaucracies that are high in both centralization and formalization. Managers in India prefer centralization and low formalization. Germans prefer formalization with decentralization.

The extensive use of work teams in a country like Japan can also be explained in terms of national culture. Japan scores high on collectivism. In such a culture, employees prefer more organic organizations built around work teams. In contrast, employees in India—where power distance values are high—are likely to perform poorly in teams. They feel more comfortable working in mechanistic, authority-dominated structures.

It was too burdensome and slow to respond to changing regulations, competitor's actions, and the like. While it might have been acceptable in the 1950s for GM to take six years from conception of a new car to its availability in showrooms, that time frame wouldn't work by the 1980s. Competitors had cut the process to barely two years. GM had to become more adaptive if it was to compete effectively. So GM reorganized. It cut out a number of layers, laid off thousands of administrative staffers, decentralized decision making, and began increasingly to rely on teams and task forces. In other words, GM became more organic.

The GM story is fully consistent with the research on the environment-structure relationship. Mechanistic organizations are most effective in stable environments. Organic organizations are best matched with dynamic and uncertain environments. This helps to explain why, for example, public utilities tend to be mechanistic while manufacturers of microchips and business software typically use organic organizations.

SUMMARY

This summary is organized by the chapter-opening learning objectives found on page 283.

1. An organization's structure is a measure of its degree of complexity, formalization, and centralization.

2. The advantages of division of labor relate to economic efficiencies. It makes efficient use of the diversity of skills that workers hold. Skills are developed through repetition. Less time is wasted. Training is also easier and less costly. The disadvantage of division of labor is that it can result in human diseconomies. Excessive division of labor can cause boredom, fatigue, stress, low productivity, poor quality, increased absence, and high turnover.

3. Line authority is the authority that entitles a manager to direct the work of a subordinate. Staff authority supports, assists, and advises. Line authority provides greater discretion and legitimate power.

4. Authority is a subset of power. Authority is synonymous with legitimate power. One can have influence in an organization without holding a managerial position.

5. Beyond the legitimate authority acquired through a position, a person can also exercise coercive, reward, expert, and referent power.

6. The mechanistic organization or bureaucracy rates high in complexity, formalization, and centralization. The organic organization or adhocracy scores low on these same three structural dimensions.

7. The "strategy-determines-structure" thesis argues that structure should follow strategy. As strategies move from single-product, to vertical integration, to product diversification, structure must move from organic to mechanistic.

8. Size affects structure at a decreasing rate. As size increases, so too do specialization, formalization, vertical differentiation, and decentralization. But it has less of an impact on large organizations than on small ones.

9. All other things equal, the more routine the technology, the more mechanistic the organization should be. The more nonroutine the technology, the more organic the structure should be.

10. All others things equal, stable environments are better matched with mechanistic organizations, while dynamic environments fit better with organic organizations.

REVIEW QUESTIONS

1. Why is the unity of command principle important?
2. All things being equal, which is more efficient: a wide or a narrow span of control? Why?
3. Why did the classical writers argue that authority should equal responsibility?
4. Can the manager of a staff department have line authority? Explain.
5. Why is an understanding of power important?
6. In what ways can management departmentalize?
7. Explain Perrow's technology framework and discuss its implications for organization design.
8. How do the classical principles of organization combine to favor the mechanistic organization?
9. Under what conditions is the mechanistic organization most effective?
10. Under what conditions is the organic organization most effective?

DISCUSSION QUESTIONS

1. Would there be any conflict in (a) having as few organizational levels as possible to foster coordination and (b) having a narrow span of control to facilitate control? Explain.
2. How are authority and organization structure interlocked?
3. "You need authority to make decisions." Build an argument to support this statement. Then build an argument against this statement.
4. As a new first-line supervisor in an organization, what specific tactics could you pursue to develop a power base?
5. Should your college be organized as a mechanistic or an organic organization? Explain.

SELF-ASSESSMENT EXERCISE

Is a Management Career in a Large Organization Right for You?

Instructions: For each statement, check the response that best represents your feelings.

	1 Strongly Disagree	2 Disagree	3 Unde- cided	4 Agree	5 Strongly Agree
1. I dislike following somebody else's orders.	_____	_____	_____	_____	_____
2. I dislike having to compete against others with whom I work.	_____	_____	_____	_____	_____
3. It is important for me to be liked by the people with whom I work.	_____	_____	_____	_____	_____
4. I prefer to act in customary ways; to blend in with the crowd.	_____	_____	_____	_____	_____
5. It is important for me to do things better or more efficiently than they've ever been done before.	_____	_____	_____	_____	_____
6. I like to assert myself and take charge.	_____	_____	_____	_____	_____
7. I enjoy giving directions to others.	_____	_____	_____	_____	_____
8. It doesn't bother me to do routine tasks.	_____	_____	_____	_____	_____

Turn to page 672 for scoring directions and key.

CASE APPLICATION 10A

Mrs. Fields

Debbi Fields opened her first cookie store in 1977. Within a decade, she had expanded her business into a 600-store chain with outlets from Los Angeles to New York, as well as such far-flung places as London and Hong Kong.[26]

Debbi Fields made an important decision early in her firm's growth. She would not franchise her stores. Rather, to maintain quality, she would own and run all the stores out of her Park City, Utah headquarters. With the assistance of her husband, Mrs. Fields added stores at a rapid rate and controlled operations through a comprehensive computerized information system that allowed the headquarters staff to closely monitor day-to-day activities. Token efforts were made at diversification, such as adding muffins and brownies, but Mrs. Fields was essentially a single-product company until 1987. In that year, Mrs. Fields bought La Petite Boulangerie, a chain of approximately 100 bakery stores.

With the purchase of La Petite Boulangerie, Debbi Fields began to redirect her firm. All future growth would be directed into combination stores that would merge Mrs. Fields cookie stores with La Petites. These stores would be three times the size of her cookie stores and, besides cookies, would sell items such as soups, bagels, and sandwiches.

Additionally, Mrs. Fields began to reorganize. She sold control of her European stores. She also closed some ninety-five of the cookie stores. The latter action was meant to reduce overlapping locations with the new combination stores.

These changes have put strains on the company's management ranks and its management systems. These changes have also found their way to the company's bottom line. While sales in 1988 were up 26 percent, the company went from profits of over $6 million in 1987 to a loss in 1988.

Questions

1. Describe the evolution of Mrs. Fields' strategy.
2. How should the company's structure change to reflect the changes in strategy?
3. How is control different in a 600-store chain in which all units are franchised from that in a similar chain that is completely owner-operated?
4. What recommendations would you make to improve Mrs. Fields' organization structure?

CASE APPLICATION 10B

Barnes Hospital

The following episode took place on a cool October day at Barnes Hospital in St. Louis.

Diane Polanski called Dr. Davis, the hospital's administrative director, and asked for an immediate appointment. Davis could sense by the anxiousness in

Diane's voice that something was up. He told her to come right up. About five minutes later, Polanksi walked into Davis's office and handed him her letter of resignation.

"I can't take it any longer here, Dr. Davis," she began. "I've been a nursing supervisor in the maternity wing for four months, but I can't get the job done. How can I do a job when I've got two or three bosses, each one with different demands and priorities? Listen, I'm only human. I've tried my darndest to adapt to this job but I don't think it's possible. Let me give you an example, but believe me, this is not an unusual case. Things like this are happening every day.

"When I came into my office yesterday morning at about 7:45, I found a message on my desk from Dana Jackson [the hospital's head nurse]. She told me that she needed the bed-utilization report by 10:00 A.M. that day, so that she could make her presentation to the Board in the afternoon. I knew the report would take at least an hour and a half to prepare. Thirty minutes later, Joyce [the nursing floor supervisor and Diane's immediate supervisor] came in and asked me why two of my nurses were not on duty. I told her that Dr. Reynolds [head of surgery] had taken them off my floor and was using them to handle an overload in the emergency surgical wing. I told her I had objected, but Reynolds said there were no other options. So what did Joyce say? She told me to get those nurses back in the maternity section immediately. What's more, she would be back in an hour to ensure that I got things straightened out! I'm telling you, Dr. Davis, things like this happen a couple of times a day. Is this any way to run a hospital?"

Questions

1. What is the formal chain of command?

2. Has anyone acted outside his or her authority?

3. What can Dr. Davis do to improve conditions?

4. "There's nothing wrong with the structure at Barnes Hospital. The problem is that Diane Polanski is an ineffective supervisor." Do you agree or disagree? Support your position.

5. Could Ms. Polanski have developed any power bases that might have allowed her to deal better with the competing demands on her?

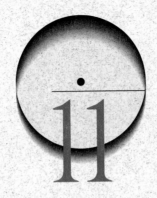

11

ORGANIZATION AND JOB DESIGN OPTIONS

During a ninety-day period in early 1986, NASA suffered an unprecedented series of setbacks. On January 28, the *Challenger* exploded less than two minutes after lift-off, killing its seven-member crew and destroying one of the three space shuttles. On April 18, NASA lost an unmanned Titan rocket in an explosion during a launch in California. The final blow came on May 3, when an engine on a Delta rocket failed, requiring the destruction of the spacecraft and its $60 million weather satellite. The fact that three dramatic failures happened in such a short period of time in an organization noted for its safety record was probably partly a result of bad luck. But NASA's problems were due to more than a streak of poor luck.[1]

Only hours before the launch of the *Challenger,* an intense debate occurred between senior engineers at Morton Thiokol, the manufacturer of the spacecraft's booster rocket, and managers at the Marshall Space Flight Center over the safety of the O-rings that sealed the joints between the rocket's sections. However, because of NASA's structure, the objections of Morton Thiokol's engineers to the launch and the fact that there was even any concern by the technical specialists with the rocket's O-rings never reached NASA's top managers who made the final launch decision.

Instead of facilitating the upward flow of all critical decision information, NASA's top management had chosen a structure that allowed the Johnson Space Center in Texas, the Marshall Center in Alabama, the Kennedy Space Center in Florida, and its other operations to behave as quasi-independent baronies that did not communicate with one another or with the top. Moreover, NASA's structure was poorly designed to identify safety problems. The safety oversight team, for instance, reported to the headquarters engineering office—whose decisions it was supposed to oversee—rather than directly to the head of the agency.

One specific example demonstrates the inherent flaws in NASA's organization design. At hearings of the presidential commission on the *Challenger* disaster, the manager of solid rocket booster operations at Marshall testified that there had been absolutely no evidence of erosion in the critical O-rings during the previous twelve months. On the same day, that manager was contradicted by NASA's own internal analysis of flight results, which showed that the incidence of erosion in the O-ring seals had *increased* during the prior year and had been the subject of growing alarm among Marshall's engineers.

The NASA example illustrates how important it is for management to select the right organization structure. It's a decision that should not be treated lightly. To arbitrarily implement a flexible, decentralized design because "that's what our major competitor is using" or to establish a highly formalized bureaucracy because "if it's good enough for General Motors, it should be good enough for us" is to openly court disaster.

But making the right structural decision requires more than merely knowing that the structural decision has an important bearing on the organization's overall effectiveness. You need to know your options. In the previous chapter, you learned that management can choose either a mechanistic or an organic organization. Which type management selects depends on the organization's strategy, size, technology, and environment. While the previous chapter provided the foundations of organization theory, it oversimplified structural designs. In the real world, there are few purely mechanistic or organic organizations. Rather, there are a variety of structural options that tend *toward* the mechanistic or *toward* the organic. This chapter presents a number of these options, loosely categorized as either mechanistic or organic.

However, this chapter is concerned with more than just organization design. It is also concerned with job design. Managerial decisions on how employees' day-to-day jobs should be designed and arranged—which includes considerations such as the amount of freedom and discretion an employee should have, whether individuals should work alone or as part of a group, the most effective arrangement of work hours, and the like—are an essential part of the organizing function. Moreover, making organizational design decisions is not a universal activity for all managers. Most supervisors and other low-level managers have little or no say about the number or kind of rules and regulations their unit will contain or how many levels of hierarchy will exist between the top and the bottom of the organization. For the most part, decisions concerning an organization's overall structure are made by senior-level executives, possibly with some consultation with subordinate managers. In performing the organizing function, lower-level managers are usually far more concerned with designing tasks or jobs than with making major decisions about the organization's structure. Therefore in this chapter, we'll also consider the job design options that managers need to consider as part of their organizing responsibilities.

MECHANISTIC DESIGN OPTIONS

When contingency factors favor a mechanistic design, one of two options is most likely to be considered. The *functional* structure's primary focus is on achieving the efficiencies of division of labor by grouping like specialists together. The *divisional* structure creates self-contained, autonomous units that are usually organized along mechanistic lines.

One point needs reiterating before we describe these structures: while both generally fall into the mechanistic category (they are clearly more mechanistic than organic), in practice few take on all the properties of a purely mechanistic structure.

The Functional Structure

"Listen, nothing happens in this place until we *produce* something," stated the production executive. "Wrong," interrupted the research and development manager. "Nothing happens until we *design* something!" "What are you talking about?" asked the marketing executive. "Nothing happens here until we *sell* something!" Finally, the exasperated accountant responded, "It doesn't matter what you produce, design, or sell. No one knows what's happening until we *tally up the results!*"

This dialogue is an undesirable result of the functional structure. We introduced departmentalization in the previous chapter, so the idea of organizing around functions is already familiar to you. The **functional structure** merely expands the functional orientation to make it the dominant form for the entire organization. As depicted in Figure 11–1, management can choose to organize its structure by grouping similar and related occupational specialties together. When it does this, management has chosen a functional structure.

The strength of the functional structure lies in the advantages that accrue from specialization. Putting like specialties together results in economies of scale, minimizes duplication of personnel and equipment, and makes employees comfortable

functional structure
A design that groups similar or related occupational specialties together.

FIGURE 11–1   Functional Structure in a Manufacturing Organization

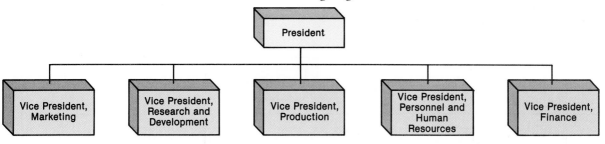

and satisfied because it gives them the opportunity to "talk the same language" with their peers.

The obvious weakness of the functional structure was illustrated at the opening of this section: The organization frequently loses sight of its best interests in the pursuit of functional goals. Members within individual functions become insulated and have little understanding of what people in other functions are doing. Each function focuses on what it does. No one function is totally responsible for end results, so top management must assume the coordination role, since only top management can see the whole picture. The diversity of interests and perspectives that exists between functions can result in continual conflict between functions as each tries to assert its importance. An additional weakness of the functional structure is that it provides little or no training for future chief executives. The functional executives only see one narrow segment of the organization: the one dealing with their function. Exposure to other functions is limited. As a result, the structure does not give managers a broad perspective on the organization's activities.

The Divisional Structure

General Motors, Hershey Foods, Burlington Industries, and Xerox are examples of organizations that have adopted the divisional structure. An illustration of what this structural form looks like at General Motors can be seen from the organization chart in Figure 11–2.

divisional structure

An organization structure made up of autonomous, self-contained units.

The **divisional structure,** which was pioneered in the 1920s by General Motors and DuPont, is designed to foster self-contained units. Each unit or division is generally autonomous, with a division manager responsible for performance and holding complete strategic and operating decision-making authority. At GM, each of the groups is a separate division headed by a vice president who is totally responsible for results. As in most divisional structures, a central headquarters provides support services to the divisions. This typically includes financial and legal services. Of course, the headquarters also acts as an external overseer to coordinate and control the various divisions. Divisions are, therefore, autonomous within given parameters. Division managers are usually free to direct their division as they see fit, as long as it is within the overall guidelines set down by headquarters.

A closer look at divisional structures reveals that their "innards" contain functional structures. The divisional framework creates a set of autonomous "little companies." Within each of these companies lies another organizational form, and it is almost always of the functional variety.

What advantages does the divisional structure offer? It focuses on results. Division managers have full responsibility for a product or service. The divisional structure also frees headquarters staff from being concerned with day-to-day operating details so

FIGURE 11–2   The Divisional Structure at General Motors Corporation

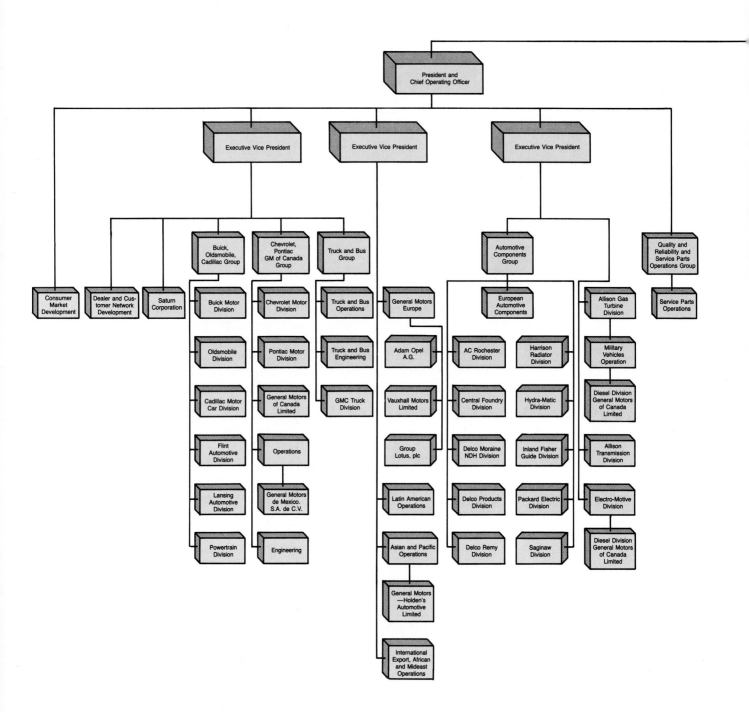

that they can pay attention to long-term and strategic planning. At GM, for instance, senior executives in Detroit can wrestle with the world's future transportation needs, while the division managers can go about the business of producing Chevrolets and GMC trucks as efficiently as possible.

In contrast to functional structures, the divisional form is also an excellent vehicle for developing senior executives. Division managers gain a broad range of experience in running their autonomous units. The individual responsibility and independence

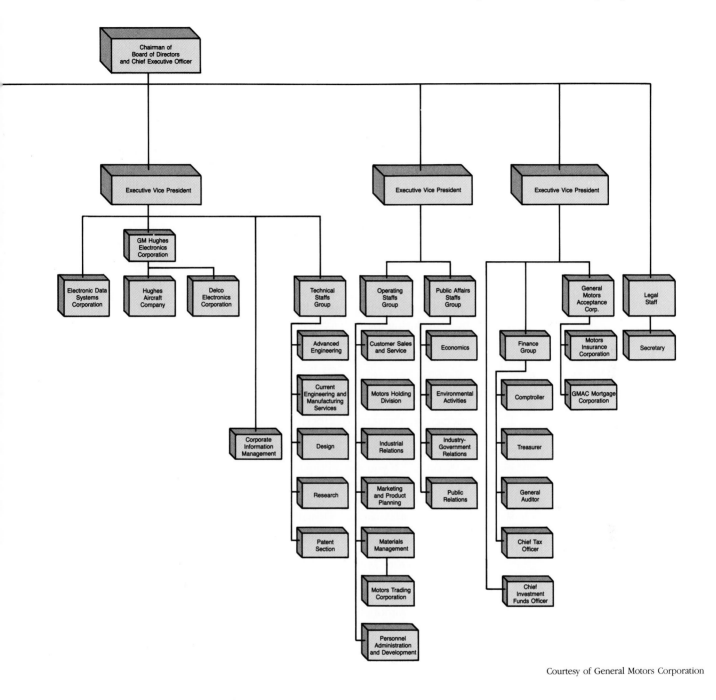

Courtesy of General Motors Corporation

give them an opportunity to run an entire company, with its frustrations and satisfactions. So a large organization with fifteen divisions has fifteen division managers who are developing the kind of generalist perspective that is needed in the organization's top spots.

The major disadvantage of the divisional structure is duplication of activities and resources. Each division, for instance, may have a marketing research department. In the absence of autonomous divisions, all of the organization's marketing research might be centralized and done for a fraction of the cost that divisionalization requires. Thus the divisional form's duplication of functions increases the organization's costs and reduces efficiency.

ORGANIC DESIGN OPTIONS

In this section, we present a selection of organic design options. These include the simple, matrix, network, task force, and committee structures.

Most organizations in North America are small. To be specific, 94 percent of all businesses in the United States have fewer than fifty employees.[2] Small organizations don't require a highly complex, formal structural design. What they need is a *simple* structure—that is, one that minimizes structural complexity. The *matrix* structure is an organic device that provides management with both high accountability for results and economies of specialization. It's popular in aerospace industries, high-tech companies, and professional organizations that operate in dynamic environments. The organic design of the future may be the *network* structure. The network design is a small central organization that contracts with other companies and suppliers to perform its manufacturing, distribution, marketing, or other crucial business functions. Its flexibility lies in the fact that management can move quickly to exploit new markets or new technologies because it "rents" the people, manufacturing facilities, and services it needs instead of "owning" them. We wrap up our discussion of organic design options by considering the *task force* and *committee* structures. Each can be used as an organic appendage to a mechanistic organization. Each adds flexibility to the typically inflexible mechanistic structure.

The Simple Structure

If "bureaucracy" is the term that best describes most large organizations, "simple structure" is the one that best characterizes most small ones.

simple structure
An organization that is low in complexity and formalization but high in centralization.

A **simple structure** is defined more by what it is not than by what it is. It is not an elaborate structure.[3] If you see an organization that appears to have almost no structure, it is probably of the simple variety. By that we mean that it is low in complexity, has little formalization, and has its authority centralized in a single person. The simple structure is a "flat" organization; it usually has only two or three vertical levels, a loose body of employees, and one individual in whom the decision-making authority is centralized.

The simple structure is most widely practiced in small businesses in which the manager and the owner are one and the same. This, for example, is illustrated in Figure 11–3—an organization chart for a retail men's store. Jack Gold owns and manages this store. Although Jack Gold employs five full-time salespeople, a cashier, and extra personnel for weekends and holidays, he "runs the show."

The strengths of the simple structure are obvious. It is fast, flexible, and inexpensive to maintain, and accountability is clear. One major weakness is that it is effective

FIGURE 11–3
Organization Chart for a Simple Structure (Jack Gold's Men's Store)

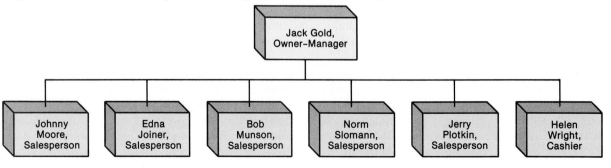

Decision making in the simple structure is basically informal. All important decisions are centralized in the senior executive, who, because of the organization's low complexity, can obtain key information readily and act rapidly when required. In addition, since complexity is low and decision making is centralized, the senior executive in the simple structure frequently has a wide span of control.

only in small organizations. It becomes inadequate as an organization grows because its low formalization and high centralization result in information overload at the top. As size increases, decision making becomes slower and can eventually come to a standstill as the single executive tries to continue making all the decisions. This often proves to be the undoing of many small businesses. When a company's sales begin to exceed about $5 million a year, it's very difficult for the owner-manager to make all the choices. If the structure isn't changed and made more elaborate, the firm is likely to lose momentum and eventually fail. The simple structure's other weakness is that it is risky: everything depends on one person. One heart attack can literally destroy the organization's information and decision-making center.

The Matrix Structure

The functional structure offers the advantages that accrue from specialization. The divisional structure has a greater focus on results but suffers from duplication of activities and resources. If the organization were to be completely organized around products—that is, if each product the company produced had its own supporting functional structure—the focus on results would again be high. Each product could have a product manager responsible for all activities related to that product. This, too, would result in redundancy, however, since each product would require its own set of functional specialists. Does any structure combine the advantages of functional specialization with the focus and accountability that product departmentalization provides? The answer is Yes, and it's called the **matrix structure.**

matrix structure

A structural design that assigns specialists from functional departments to work on one or more projects that are led by a project manager.

The matrix structure creates a *dual chain of command.* It explicitly breaks the classical principle of unity of command. Functional departmentalization is used to gain the economies from specialization. But overlaying the functional departments is a set of managers who are responsible for specific products, projects, or programs within the organization. (We will use these terms—products, projects, programs—interchangeably, since matrix structures can use any of the three.) Figure 11–4 illustrates the matrix structure of an aerospace firm. Notice that along the top of the figure are the familiar functions of engineering, accounting, personnel, and so forth. Along

FIGURE 11–4   A Matrix Organization in an Aerospace Firm

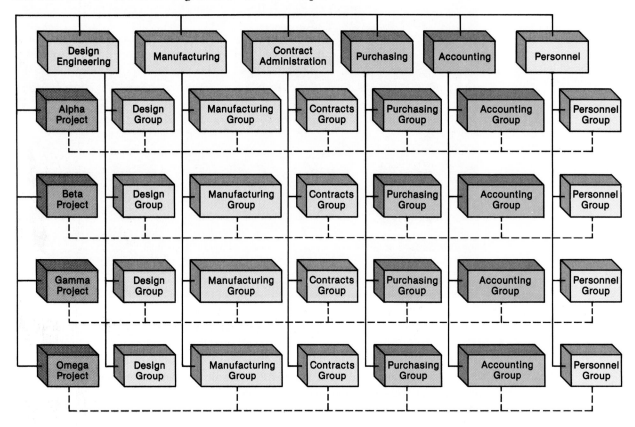

the vertical dimension, however, have been added the various projects that the aerospace firm is currently working on. Each project is directed by a manager who staffs his or her project with people from the functional departments. The addition of this vertical dimension to the traditional horizontal functional departments, in effect, weaves together elements of functional and product departmentalization—hence the term *matrix*.

How does the matrix work? Employees in the matrix have two bosses: their functional departmental manager and their product or project manager. The project managers have authority over the functional members who are part of that manager's project team. The purchasing specialists, for instance, who are responsible for procurement activities on the Gamma project are responsible to both the manager of Purchasing and the Gamma project manager. Authority is shared between the two managers. Typically, this is done by giving the project manager authority over project employees relative to the project's goals. However, decisions such as promotions, salary recommendations, and annual reviews remain the functional manager's responsibility. To work effectively, project and functional managers must communicate regularly and coordinate the demands upon their common employees.

The matrix creates an overall structure that possesses the strengths of both functional and product departmentalization, while avoiding the weaknesses of both.[4] That is, the functional form's strength lies in putting like specialists together, which minimizes the number necessary, and it allows for the pooling and sharing of specialized resources across products. Its primary drawback is the difficulty in coordinating the tasks of the specialists so that their activities are completed on time and within the budget. The product form, on the other hand, has exactly the opposite benefits and disadvantages. It facilitates the coordination among specialties to achieve on-time completion and meet budget targets. Furthermore, it provides clear responsibility for all activities related to a product or project. But no one is responsible for the long-run technical development of the specialties, and this results in duplication of costs.

If management chooses to implement a matrix structure, it can opt for either the temporary or the permanent variety. The aerospace structure shown in Figure 11–4 illustrates a temporary matrix. Because the projects the organization undertakes change over time, the structure at any given time is temporary. When new contracts are secured in the aerospace firm, project teams are created by drawing members from functional departments. A team exists only for the life of the project it is working on. This might be a few months or a half-dozen years. In an organization that has a number of projects, at any given time some are just starting up, others are well along on the way, and still others are winding down.

The product dimension of the permanent matrix stays relatively intact over time. Large business colleges use the permanent matrix when they superimpose product structures—undergraduate programs, graduate programs, executive programs, and so forth—over functional departments of management, marketing, and accounting. (See Figure 11–5.) Directors of product groups utilize faculty from the departments in order to achieve their goals. For example, the director of the master's program staffs his or her courses from members of the various departments. Notice that the matrix provides clear lines of responsibility for each product line. The responsibility for success or failure, for instance, of the executive development program lies directly with its director. Without the matrix, it would be difficult to coordinate faculty among the development program's various course offerings. Furthermore, if there are any problems with the program, the matrix avoids the buck-passing of responsibility among the functional department chairpersons.

Our examples should make the matrix's strengths evident: it can facilitate coordination of a multiple set of complex and interdependent projects while still retaining the economies from keeping functional specialists grouped together.

The major disadvantages of the matrix lie in the confusion it creates and its propensity to foster power struggles. When you dispense with the unity of command princi-

FIGURE 11–5   Matrix Structure in a College of Business

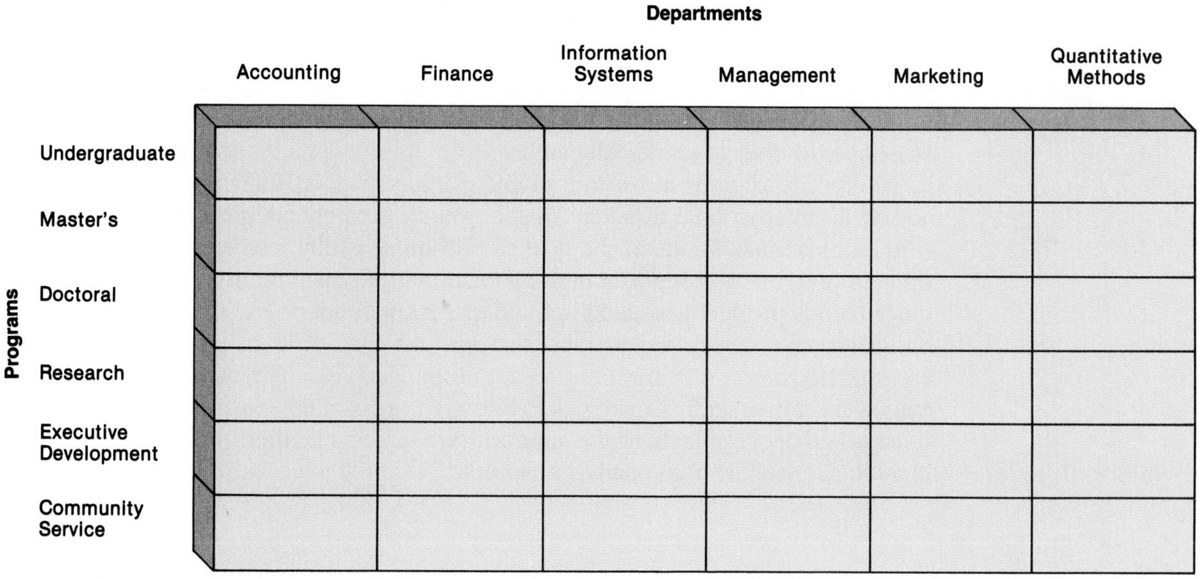

ple, you significantly increase ambiguity. Confusion can exist over who reports to whom. This confusion and ambiguity, in turn, plant the seeds for power struggles. Because the relationships between functional and project managers are not specified by rules and procedures, they must be negotiated, and this gives rise to power struggles. Deciding whether to implement the matrix requires managers to weigh these disadvantages against the advantages.

The Network Structure

network structure

A small centralized organization that relies on other organizations to perform its basic business functions on a contract basis.

A new form of organization design is currently gaining popularity. It allows management great flexibility in responding to new technology, fashion, or low-cost foreign competition. It is the **network structure**—a small central organization that relies on other organizations to perform manufacturing, distribution, marketing, or other crucial business functions on a contract basis.[5]

The network structure is a viable option for the small organization. Magicorp, for example, runs a small shop that makes graphics transparencies. It relies on other companies for the rest of its operations. People who use graphics software on their personal computers send data by phone lines to Magicorp's office in Wilmington, Ohio. Why is Magicorp in Wilmington? Because the Airborne Express hub is there, making fast turnarounds possible. Rather than do its own marketing, Magicorp relies on graphics software vendors to promote its services, paying these vendors on a royalty basis.

MANAGING FROM A GLOBAL PERSPECTIVE

The Structure of Multinationals

The challenge in managing a multinational corporation (MNC) is greater than in the traditional domestic firm.[6] For instance, in addition to the normal risks in a business enterprise, the MNC is more vulnerable to political instability, changes in laws, and exchange-rate fluctuations. Therefore MNC's must have a structure that provides greater environmental scanning capability to allow managers to monitor, and quickly respond to, changes in their environment. Moreover, the high complexity created by geographically dispersed units requires superior structural mechanisms to allow for communicating over distances, often in different languages, and to facilitate rapid responses to diverse market demands.

When organizations move into global markets, they typically begin by adding an international division. This, however, is rarely adequate for the true multinational. To attain the goal of becoming a fully integrated global organization, many move to a multinational matrix structure. This simultaneously blends product and geographic departmentalization. For instance, a multinational might have a product manager for each of its major marketing areas in North America, Latin America, Europe, and Asia. The major advantage of the multinational matrix is to allow an organization to respond more quickly and appropriately to the unique requirements of these various geographic markets for a company's products.

The network structure is also applicable to large organizations. Nike, Esprit apparel, Emerson Radio, and Schwinn Bicycle are large companies that have found that they can sell hundreds of millions of dollars of products every year and earn a very competitive return with few or no manufacturing facilities of their own and only a few hundred employees.[7] What these firms have done is to create an organization of relationships. They connect with independent designers, manufacturers, commissioned sales representatives, or the like to perform, on a contract basis, the functions they need.

The network stands in sharp contrast to divisional structures that have many vertical levels of management and in which organizations seek to control their destiny through ownership. In such organizations, research and development is done in-house, production occurs in company-owned manufacturing plants, and sales and marketing are performed by their own employees. To support all this, management has to employ extra personnel such as accountants, human resource specialists, and lawyers. In the network structure, most of these functions are bought outside the organization. This gives management a high degree of flexibility and allows the organization to concentrate on what it does best. For most U.S. firms, that means focusing on design or marketing and buying manufacturing capability outside. Emerson Radio Corporation, for example, designs and engineers its TVs, stereos, and other consumer electronic products, but it contracts out their manufacture to Asian suppliers.

Figure 11–6 shows a network structure in which management contracts out all of the primary functions of the business. The core of the network organization is a small group of executives. Their job is to oversee directly any activities that are done in-house and to coordinate relationships with the other organizations that manufacture, distribute, and perform other crucial functions for the network organization. The dotted lines in Figure 11–6 represent those contractual relationships. In essence, managers in network structures spend most of their time coordinating and controlling external relations.

The network organization is not appropriate for all endeavors. It fits industrial companies like toy and apparel firms, which require very high flexibility in order to respond quickly to fashion changes. It also fits firms whose manufacturing operations require low-cost labor that is available only outside the United States and can best be

FIGURE 11–6
A Network Structure

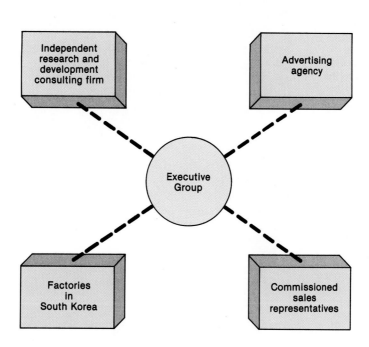

utilized by contracting with foreign suppliers. On the negative side, management in network structures lacks the close control of manufacturing operations that exists in more traditional organizations. Reliability of supply is also less predictable. Finally, any innovation in design that a network organization acquires is susceptible to being "ripped off." It is very difficult, if not impossible, to closely guard innovations that are under the direction of management in another organization. Yet with computers in one organization now interfacing and communicating with computers in other organizations, the network structure is becoming an increasingly viable alternative.

Organic Appendages

The design options previously described are intended for organizationwide application. Sometimes, however, management might want to maintain an overall mechanistic structure but gain the flexibility of an organic structure. An alternative is to append an organic structural unit to a mechanistic organization. Two examples of such appendages are the task force and the committee structure.

task force structure

A temporary structure created to accomplish a specific, well-defined, complex task that requires the involvement of personnel from other organizational subunits.

The Task Force   The **task force structure** is a temporary structure created to accomplish a specific, well-defined, and complex task that requires the involvement of personnel from a number of organizational subunits. It can be thought of as a scaled-down version of the temporary matrix. Members serve on the task force until its goal is achieved, at which time the task force is disbanded. Then the members move on to a new task force, return to their permanent functional department, or leave the organization.[8]

The task force is a common tool of consumer product firms. For instance, when Kellogg decides to create a new breakfast cereal, it brings together people with exper-

Because the task force is temporary, it can be used to attack problems that cut across functional lines with only minimal disturbance to the organization's main mechanistic structure. Johnson & Johnson's response to the Tylenol poisoning incidents in 1982 and 1986 was to create immediately an internal task force to assess the exact nature of the problem and to develop a rapid, effective response. Members included representatives from public relations, legal affairs, advertising, marketing, product design, manufacturing, and finance. Since any action J&J took would affect all these areas, the task force ensured that their concerns would be taken into consideration and that the best possible response would result. This task force allowed J&J to be adaptive while maintaining its efficient bureaucracy.

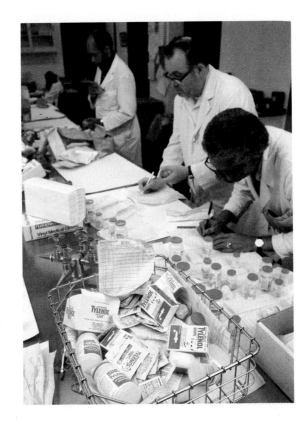

tise in product design, food research, marketing, manufacturing, finance, and other relevant functions to formulate the product, design its package, determine its market, compute its manufacturing costs, and project its profits. Once the problems have been worked out and the product is ready to be mass produced, the task force disbands, and the cereal is integrated into the permanent structure. At Kellogg, the new cereal is then assigned its own product manager and becomes a part of Kellogg's matrix structure.

committee structure

A structure that brings together a range of individuals from across functional lines to deal with problems.

The Committee Structure   Another option that combines a range of individual experiences and backgrounds for dealing with problems that cut across functional lines is the **committee structure.**

Committees may be of a temporary or permanent nature. A temporary committee is typically the same as the task force. Permanent committees, however, facilitate the bringing together of diverse inputs like the task force, but they offer the stability and consistency of the matrix. However, committees are appendages. Members of the committee are permanently attached to a functional department. They can meet at regular or irregular intervals to analyze problems, make recommendations or final decisions, coordinate activities, or oversee projects. As a result, they are mechanisms for bringing together the input of diverse departments. Colleges frequently use permanent committees for everything from student admissions to faculty promotions and alumni relations. Large business firms use committees as coordinating and control mechanisms. For instance, many firms have a compensation committee to review salary and bonuses provided to management personnel and an audit committee to objectively evaluate the organization's operations. A few firms even use the committee as the central coordinating device in their structure. J.C. Penney has a management committee that consists of the firm's top fourteen executives. They debate and pass on such disparate areas as strategic planning, public affairs, personnel, and merchandising. Permanent subcommittees are used to focus on key parts of the business, while temporary committees are formed for specific issues, such as what to do with the company's troubled Treasury discount store operation.

A BUYER'S GUIDE TO ORGANIZATION DESIGN OPTIONS

What conditions make one organization design preferable to another? Table 11–1 summarizes the options we have discussed and notes the conditions that favor each.

Certain structures are designed to work well in large organizations that are specialized. These include the functional and divisional structures. Both are essentially bureaucracies or mechanistic structures.

The simple structure is effective when the number of employees is few, when the organization is new, and when the environment is simple and dynamic.[9] Small size usually means less repetitive work, so standardization is less attractive. Small size also makes informal communication both convenient and effective. All new organizations tend to adopt the simple structure because management has not had the time to elaborate the structure. A simple environment is easily comprehended by a single individual, yet the structure's flexibility allows it to respond rapidly to unpredictable contingencies.

The matrix attempts to obtain the advantages of specialization without its disadvantages. When the organization has multiple programs or products and functional departmentalization, it can create program or product managers who direct activities across functional lines.

TABLE 11-1   Organization Design Options

Design	Strengths	When and Where to Use
Functional	Economies through specialization	Single-product or -service organizations
Divisional	High accountability for results	Large organizations; multiple-product or multiple-market organizations
Simple	Speed, flexibility, economy	Small organizations; formative years of development; simple and dynamic environments
Matrix	Economies through specialization and accountability for product results	Multiple products or programs that rely on functional expertise
Network	Speed, flexibility, economy	Industrial firms; formative years of development; many reliable suppliers available; low-cost foreign labor available
Task force	Flexibility	Important tasks that have specific time and performance standards, that are unique and unfamiliar, that require expertise that crosses functional lines
Committee	Flexibility	Tasks that require expertise that crosses functional lines

The network structure is a product of the computer revolution. By being linked to other organizations, an industrial firm can be in the manufacturing business without having to build and operate its own plants. The network is an excellent vehicle for the manufacturing firm that is just getting started because it minimizes risks and commitments. It also lessens financial demands on the organization, since it requires few fixed assets. To succeed, however, management must be skilled in developing and maintaining relationships with suppliers. If any one of the firms that the network organization has contracted with fails to meet its commitments, the network organization ends up the loser.

The task force and committee structures were offered as appendages to mechanistic structures. Both are meant to be used when it is necessary to bring together personnel from across functional lines. Because the task force is a temporary design, it is also an ideal vehicle for tackling important tasks that have specific time and performance standards and that are unique and unfamiliar. Once a task is familiar and needs to be repeated, a mechanistic design can handle it in a more standardized and efficient manner.

JOB DESIGN OPTIONS

If you put an organization under a microscope, you would find that it is composed of thousands, maybe even millions, of tasks. These tasks, in turn, are aggregated into jobs.[10] The jobs that people do in any organization should not evolve by chance.

Instead of an assembly line, Buick Reatta's 700 workers are grouped into teams that install entire systems on cars.

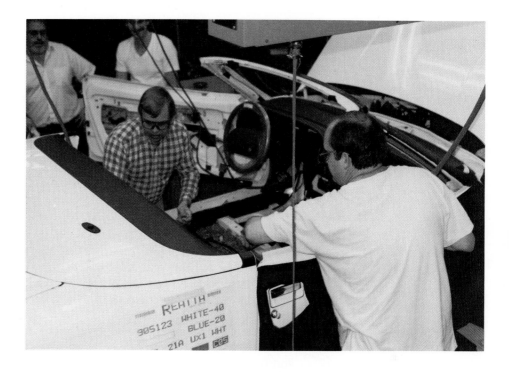

Management should thoughtfully design jobs to reflect the organization's technology, as well as the skills, abilities, and preferences of its employees. When this is done, employees can reach their full productive capabilities.

job design
The way in which tasks are combined to form complete jobs.

We use the term **job design** to refer to the way in which tasks are combined to form complete jobs. Some jobs are routine because the tasks are standardized and repetitive; others are nonroutine. Some require a large number of varied and diverse skills; others are narrow in scope. Some jobs constrain employees by requiring them to follow very precise procedures; others allow employees substantial freedom in how they do their work. Some jobs are most effectively accomplished by groups of employees working as a team, whereas other jobs are best done by individuals acting independently. Our point is that jobs differ in the way their tasks are combined, and these different combinations create a variety of job designs.

Job Specialization

For the first half of this century, job design was synonymous with division of labor or job specialization. Using guidelines laid down by the likes of Adam Smith and Frederick Taylor, managers sought to make jobs in organizations as simple as possible. This meant dividing them into minute, specialized tasks (see Figure 11-7). However, as we noted earlier, jobs can become too specialized. When this happens, employees often begin to rebel. They express their frustrations and boredom by taking "mental health days" off, socializing around the workplace instead of being productive, ignoring the quality of their work, or abusing alcohol and drugs. Efficiency declines.

The principles of job specialization continue to guide the design of many jobs. Manufacturing workers still perform simple, repetitive jobs on assembly lines. Office clerks sit at computer terminals and perform standardized tasks. Even nurses, accountants, and other professionals find that many of their tasks require performing narrow, specialized activities.

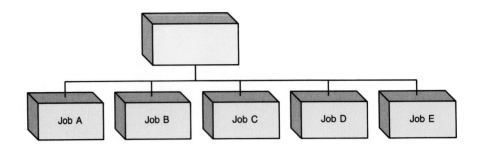

Job Rotation

One of the earliest efforts at moving away from job specialization and its drawbacks was the introduction of **job rotation.** This approach to job design allows workers to diversify their activities and avoid boredom.

job rotation
Lateral job transfers.

There are actually two types of rotation: vertical and horizontal. *Vertical rotation* refers to promotions and demotions. When we talk about job rotation, however, we mean the horizontal variety.

Horizontal job transfers can be instituted on a planned basis—that is, by means of a training program whereby the employee spends two or three months in an activity and is then moved on. (See Figure 11–8.) This approach, for example, is common among large Wall Street law firms, in which new associates work for many different partners before choosing an area of specialization. Horizontal transfers can also be made on a situational basis by moving the person to another activity when the first is no longer challenging or when the needs of work scheduling require it. In other words, people may be put in a continual transfer mode. Rotation, as employed by many large organizations in their programs to develop managerial talent, may include moving people between line and staff positions, often allowing an employee to understudy a more experienced employee.

The advantages of job rotation are clear. It broadens employees and gives them a range of experiences. Boredom and monotony, which develop after a person has acquired the skills to perform his or her task effectively, are reduced when transfers are frequently made. Finally, since a broader experience permits a greater understanding of other activities within the organization, people are prepared more rapidly to assume greater responsibility, especially at the upper echelons. In other words, as one moves up in the organization, it becomes increasingly necessary to understand the intricacies and interrelationships of activities; and these skills can be more quickly acquired by moving about within the organization.

On the other hand, job rotation is not without its drawbacks. Training costs are increased, and productivity is reduced by moving a worker into a new position just when his or her efficiency at the prior job was creating organizational economies. An extensive rotation program can result in a vast number of employees being situated in positions for which their experience is very limited. Even though there might be

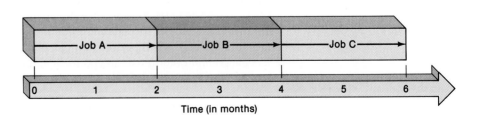

FIGURE 11–9
Job Enlargement Increases
Job Scope

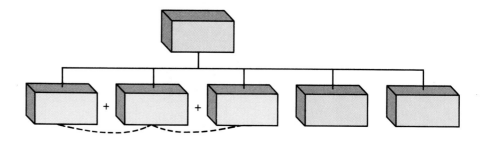

significant long-term benefits from the program, the organization must be equipped to deal with the day-to-day problems that arise when inexperienced personnel perform new tasks and when rotated managers make decisions based on little experience with the activity at hand. Job rotation can also demotivate intelligent and aggressive trainees who seek specific responsibility in their chosen specialty. Finally, there is some evidence that rotation that is involuntarily imposed on employees increases absenteeism and accidents.[11]

Job Enlargement

job enlargement
The horizontal expansion of a job; an increase in job scope.

job scope
The number of different operations required in a job and the frequency with which the job cycle is repeated.

Another early effort at increasing the horizontal diversity in a worker's tasks was **job enlargement.** This option increases **job scope;** that is, it increases the number of different operations required in a job and decreases the frequency with which the job cycle is repeated. (See Figure 11–9.) By increasing the number of tasks an individual performs, job enlargement increases job diversity. Instead of only sorting the incoming mail by department, for instance, a mail sorter's job could be enlarged to include physically delivering the mail to the various departments or running outgoing letters through the postage meter.

Efforts at job enlargement have met with less-than-enthusiastic results. As one employee who experienced such a redesign on his job remarked, "Before I had one lousy job. Now, through enlargement, I have three lousy jobs!" Job enlargement attacked the lack of diversity in overspecialized jobs, but it provided few challenges and little meaning to a worker's activities.

Job Enrichment

job enrichment
Vertical expansion of a job by adding planning and evaluating responsibilities.

job depth
The degree of control employees have over their work.

The production workers at GM's Delco-Remy Plant in Fitzgerald, Georgia have jobs that are unlike those in most manufacturing facilities. They do budget preparations, help determine staffing levels, keep track of their own time, take complete responsibility for plant safety, generate requirements for new equipment, do all maintenance and make minor repairs on machines, and perform quality control inspections on their own work.[12] These GM employees have had their jobs enriched. Job enrichment has proven effective in dealing with some of the shortcomings of job enlargement.

Job enrichment increases **job depth** (see Figure 11–10). What this means is that job enrichment allows employees greater control over their work. They're allowed to assume some of the tasks typically done by their supervisor—particularly planning and evaluating their own work. The tasks in an enriched job should allow workers to do a complete activity with increased freedom, independence, and responsibility; they should also provide feedback so that individuals can assess and correct their own performance.

FIGURE 11–10
Job Enrichment Increases Job Depth

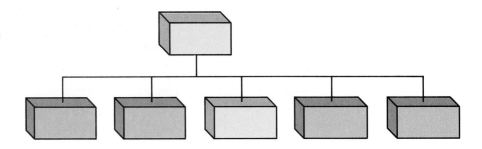

How does management enrich jobs? This question can be answered by an example. Travelers Insurance was displeased with the performance of its keypunch operators.[13] Output seemed inadequate, the error rate excessive, and absenteeism too high. Travelers' management therefore introduced the following changes to enrich the keypunch operators' jobs:

1. The random assignment of work was replaced by assigning to each operator continuing responsibility for certain accounts.

2. Some planning and control functions were combined with the central task of keypunching.

3. Each operator was given several channels of direct contact with clients. When problems arose, the operator, not the supervisor, took up the problems with the client.

4. Operators were given the authority to set their own schedules, plan their daily work, and correct obvious coding errors on their own.

5. Incorrect cards were returned by the computer department to the operators who punched them, and the operators corrected their own errors. Weekly computer printouts of errors and productivity were sent directly to the operator rather than the supervisor.

These workers are performing enriched jobs in an auto assembly plant.

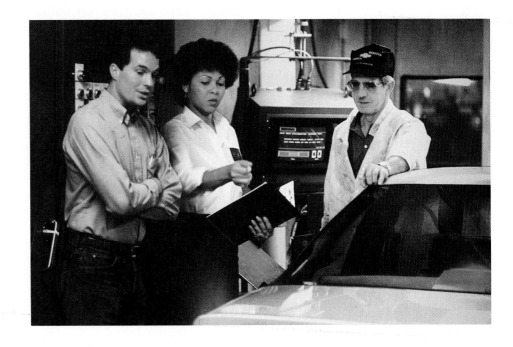

This Volvo plant in Sweden is designed to mass-produce the midline 740 without using assembly lines. The plant employs teams of seven to ten hourly workers. Each team works in one area and assembles four cars per shift.

The enrichment efforts cited above led to some impressive results. Fewer keypunch operators were needed, the quantity of output increased, error rates and absenteeism declined, and job attitudes improved. The changes reportedly saved Travelers over $90,000 a year.

The above examples shouldn't be taken as a blanket endorsement of job enrichment. The evidence generally shows that job enrichment reduces absenteeism and turnover costs; but on the critical issue of productivity, the evidence is inconclusive.[14] In some situations, job enrichment has increased productivity; in others, it has decreased it. However, when productivity decreases, there does appear to be consistently more conscientious use of resources and a higher quality of product or service.

Work Teams

work teams
Groups of individuals that cooperate in completing a set of tasks.

integrated work team
A group that accomplishes many tasks by making specific assignments to members and rotating jobs among members as the tasks require.

autonomous work team
A vertically integrated team that is given almost complete autonomy in determining how a task will be done.

When jobs are designed around groups rather than individuals, the result is **work teams.** When cooperation is important for completing a set of tasks, it can be desirable to build jobs around the team concept.

There are basically two types of work teams: integrated and autonomous. In **integrated work teams,** a large number of tasks are assigned to a group. The group then decides the specific assignments of members and is responsible for rotating jobs among the members as the tasks require. The team still has a supervisor who oversees the group's activities. (See Figure 11–11.) Integrated work teams are used frequently in activities like building maintenance and construction. In the cleaning of a large office building, for example, the foreman will identify the tasks to be completed and then let the maintenance workers, as a group, choose how the tasks are to be allocated. Similarly, a road construction crew frequently decides, as a group, how its various tasks are to be completed.

Autonomous work teams are more vertically integrated and have a wider range of discretion than their integrated counterparts. The autonomous work team is given a

FIGURE 11–11
Integrated Work Teams

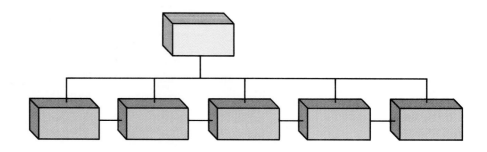

goal to achieve and then is free to determine work assignments, rest breaks, inspection procedures, and so forth.[15] Fully autonomous work teams even select their own members and have the members evaluate one another's performance. As a result, supervisory positions become less important and may sometimes even be eliminated. (See Figure 11–12.) Goodyear Tire and Rubber has had remarkable success with autonomous work teams at its radial-tire plant in Lawton, Oklahoma.[16] The 164 teams are made up of five to twenty-seven people. The team members set their own production schedule and their own goals and screen applicants to decide on new members. Goodyear's management has found that the plant can produce double the daily volume of comparable-sized, traditionally designed plants and can beat the cost of comparable tires made by its lowest-cost foreign competitors.

job characteristics model
A framework for analyzing and designing jobs; identifies five primary job characteristics, their interrelationships, and impact on outcome variables.

The Job Characteristics Model

None of the prior approaches provided a conceptual framework for analyzing jobs or for guiding managers in designing jobs. The **job characteristics model** (JCM) offers such a framework.[17] It identifies five primary job characteristics, their interrelationships, and their impact on employee productivity, motivation, and satisfaction.

FIGURE 11–12
Autonomous Work Teams

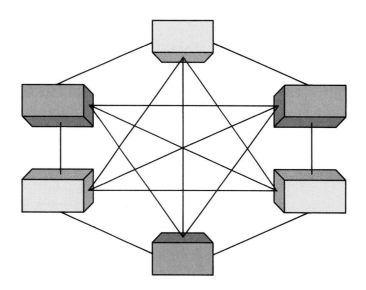

The network structure is also applicable to large organizations. Nike, Esprit apparel, Emerson Radio, and Schwinn Bicycle are large companies that have found that they can sell hundreds of millions of dollars of products every year and earn a very competitive return with few or no manufacturing facilities of their own and only a few hundred employees.[7] What these firms have done is to create an organization of relationships. They connect with independent designers, manufacturers, commissioned sales representatives, or the like to perform, on a contract basis, the functions they need.

The network stands in sharp contrast to divisional structures that have many vertical levels of management and in which organizations seek to control their destiny through ownership. In such organizations, research and development is done in-house, production occurs in company-owned manufacturing plants, and sales and marketing are performed by their own employees. To support all this, management has to employ extra personnel such as accountants, human resource specialists, and lawyers. In the network structure, most of these functions are bought outside the organization. This gives management a high degree of flexibility and allows the organization to concentrate on what it does best. For most U.S. firms, that means focusing on design or marketing and buying manufacturing capability outside. Emerson Radio Corporation, for example, designs and engineers its TVs, stereos, and other consumer electronic products, but it contracts out their manufacture to Asian suppliers.

Figure 11–6 shows a network structure in which management contracts out all of the primary functions of the business. The core of the network organization is a small group of executives. Their job is to oversee directly any activities that are done in-house and to coordinate relationships with the other organizations that manufacture, distribute, and perform other crucial functions for the network organization. The dotted lines in Figure 11–6 represent those contractual relationships. In essence, managers in network structures spend most of their time coordinating and controlling external relations.

The network organization is not appropriate for all endeavors. It fits industrial companies like toy and apparel firms, which require very high flexibility in order to respond quickly to fashion changes. It also fits firms whose manufacturing operations require low-cost labor that is available only outside the United States and can best be

FIGURE 11–6
A Network Structure

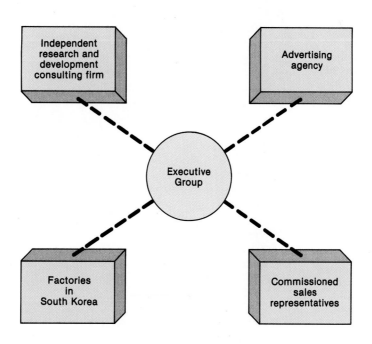

utilized by contracting with foreign suppliers. On the negative side, management in network structures lacks the close control of manufacturing operations that exists in more traditional organizations. Reliability of supply is also less predictable. Finally, any innovation in design that a network organization acquires is susceptible to being "ripped off." It is very difficult, if not impossible, to closely guard innovations that are under the direction of management in another organization. Yet with computers in one organization now interfacing and communicating with computers in other organizations, the network structure is becoming an increasingly viable alternative.

Organic Appendages

The design options previously described are intended for organizationwide application. Sometimes, however, management might want to maintain an overall mechanistic structure but gain the flexibility of an organic structure. An alternative is to append an organic structural unit to a mechanistic organization. Two examples of such appendages are the task force and the committee structure.

task force structure

A temporary structure created to accomplish a specific, well-defined, complex task that requires the involvement of personnel from other organizational subunits.

The Task Force   The **task force structure** is a temporary structure created to accomplish a specific, well-defined, and complex task that requires the involvement of personnel from a number of organizational subunits. It can be thought of as a scaled-down version of the temporary matrix. Members serve on the task force until its goal is achieved, at which time the task force is disbanded. Then the members move on to a new task force, return to their permanent functional department, or leave the organization.[8]

The task force is a common tool of consumer product firms. For instance, when Kellogg decides to create a new breakfast cereal, it brings together people with exper-

Because the task force is temporary, it can be used to attack problems that cut across functional lines with only minimal disturbance to the organization's main mechanistic structure. Johnson & Johnson's response to the Tylenol poisoning incidents in 1982 and 1986 was to create immediately an internal task force to assess the exact nature of the problem and to develop a rapid, effective response. Members included representatives from public relations, legal affairs, advertising, marketing, product design, manufacturing, and finance. Since any action J&J took would affect all these areas, the task force ensured that their concerns would be taken into consideration and that the best possible response would result. This task force allowed J&J to be adaptive while maintaining its efficient bureaucracy.

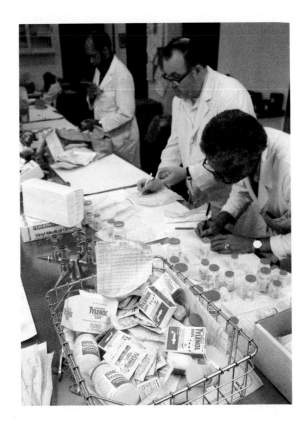

Core Dimensions   According to the JCM, any job can be described in terms of five core dimensions, defined as follows:

skill variety
The degree to which a job includes a variety of activities that call for a number of different skills and talents.

task identity
The degree to which a job requires completion of a whole and identifiable piece of work.

task significance
The degree to which a job has a substantial impact on the lives or work of other people.

autonomy
The degree to which a job provides substantial freedom, independence, and discretion to an individual in scheduling and carrying out his or her work.

feedback
The degree to which carrying out the work activities required by a job results in an individual's obtaining direct and clear information about the effectiveness of his or her performance.

Skill variety, the degree to which a job requires a variety of activities so that one can use a number of different skills and talents.

Task identity, the degree to which a job requires completion of a whole and identifiable piece of work.

Task significance, the degree to which a job has a substantial impact on the lives or work of other people.

Autonomy, the degree to which a job provides substantial freedom, independence, and discretion to the individual in scheduling the work and determining the procedures to be used in carrying it out.

Feedback, the degree to which carrying out the work activities required by a job results in the individual's obtaining direct and clear information about the effectiveness of his or her performance.

Figure 11–13 presents the model. Notice how the first three dimensions—skill variety, task identity, and task significance—combine to create meaningful work. That is, if these three characteristics exist in a job, we can predict that the person will view his or her job as being important, valuable, and worthwhile. Notice, too, that jobs that possess autonomy give the job incumbent a feeling of personal responsibility for the results and that, if a job provides feedback, the employee will know how effectively he or she is performing.

From a motivational standpoint, the model says that internal rewards are obtained when one *learns* (knowledge of results) that one *personally* (experienced responsibility) has performed well on a task that one *cares about* (experienced meaningfulness).[18] The more these three conditions are present, the greater will be the employee's motivation, performance, and satisfaction and the lower his or her absenteeism and likelihood of resigning. As the model shows, the links between the job dimen-

FIGURE 11–13
Job Characteristics Model

Source: J. Richard Hackman and J. Lloyd Shuttle, eds., *Improving Life at Work* (Glenview, IL: Scott, Foresman and Co., 1977). With permission of author.

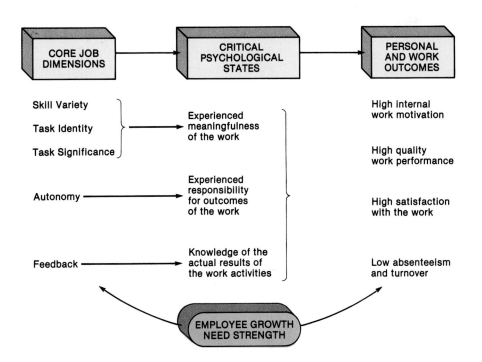

FIGURE 11–14

Computing a Motivating Potential Score

Source: J. Richard Hackman and J. Lloyd Shuttle, eds., *Improving Life at Work* (Glenview, IL: Scott, Foresman and Co., 1977). With permission of author.

$$\text{Motivating Potential Score (MPS)} = \left[\frac{\text{Skill Variety} + \text{Task Identity} + \text{Task Significance}}{3} \right] \times \text{Autonomy} \times \text{Feedback}$$

sions and the outcomes are moderated or adjusted for by the strength of the individual's growth need—that is, the employee's desire for self-esteem and self-actualization. This means that individuals with a high growth need are more likely to experience the psychological states when their jobs score high on the core dimensions than are their low-growth-need counterparts. High-growth-need individuals will respond more positively to the psychological states, when they are present, than will low-growth-need individuals.

Predictions from the Model   The core dimensions can be combined into a single index as shown in Figure 11–14. Jobs that are high on motivating potential must be high on at least one of the three factors that lead to experiencing meaningfulness; they must also be high on both autonomy and feedback. If jobs score high on motivating potential, the model predicts that motivation, performance, and satisfaction will be positively affected, while the likelihood of absence and turnover will be lessened.[19]

Guides for Managers   The JCM provides specific guidance to managers in the designing of jobs. (See Figure 11–15.) The following suggestions, which derive from the JCM, specify the types of changes in jobs that are most likely to lead to improvements in each of the five core dimensions:

1. *Combine tasks.* Managers should put existing fractionalized tasks back together to form a new, larger module of work. This increases skill variety and task identity.

2. *Create natural work units.* Managers should design tasks that form an identifiable and meaningful whole. This increases employee "ownership" of the work and encourages employees to view their work as meaningful and important rather than as irrelevant and boring.

3. *Establish client relationships.* The client is the user of the product or service that the employee works on. Wherever possible, managers should establish direct relationships between workers and their clients. This increases skill variety, autonomy, task identity, and feedback for the employee.

4. *Expand jobs vertically.* Vertical expansion gives employees responsibilities and controls that were formerly reserved for management. It partially closes the gap

FIGURE 11–15

Guidelines for Job Redesign

Source: J. Richard Hackman and J. Lloyd Shuttle, eds., *Improving Life at Work* (Glenview, IL: Scott, Foresman and Co., 1977). With permission of author.

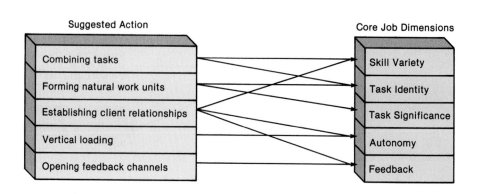

between the "doing" and "controlling" aspects of the job, and it increases employee autonomy.

5. *Open feedback channels.* By increasing feedback, employees not only learn how well they are performing their jobs but also whether their performance is improving, deteriorating, or remaining at a constant level. Ideally, employees should receive performance feedback directly as they do their jobs rather than from management on an occasional basis.[20]

Scheduling Options

A final set of job design options deals with the scheduling of work. For instance, a job for most people in North America means leaving home and going to a place of work, arriving at 8:00 or 9:00 in the morning, putting in a fixed set of approximately eight hours, and doing this routine five days a week. However, it doesn't have to be this way. Depending on labor-market conditions, the type of work that has to be done, and employee preferences, management might consider implementing a compressed workweek of four days, flexible work hours, or job sharing; using contingent or temporary workers; or allowing employees to work at home through telecommuting.

compressed workweek
A workweek comprised of four ten-hour days.

The Compressed Workweek   We define the **compressed workweek** as comprised of four ten-hour days. While there have been experiments with three-day weeks and other compressed workweek variants, we limit our attention to four-day, forty-hour (4–40) programs.

Proponents of 4–40 programs claim that they have a favorable effect on employee absenteeism, job satisfaction, and productivity.[21] It is argued that a four-day workweek provides employees with more leisure time, decreases commuting time, decreases requests for time off for personal matters, makes it easier for an organization to recruit employees, and decreases time spent on tasks such as setting up equipment. However, some potential disadvantages have been noted. Among these are a decrease in worker's productivity near the end of the longer workday, a decrease in service to customers and clients, unwillingness to work longer days when needed to meet deadlines, and underutilization of equipment.[22]

Maybe the most telling characteristic of the four-day workweek, from management's perspective, is that it appears to have different short-term and long-term effects.[23] When first implemented, the compressed workweek achieves many of the results claimed by its advocates: improved morale, less dissatisfaction, and less absenteeism and turnover. However, after approximately one year, many of these advantages disappear. Employees then begin to complain about increased fatigue and the difficulty of coordinating their jobs with their personal lives (the latter is a particular problem for working mothers). Managers also find drawbacks. More scheduling of work is involved, overtime rates must frequently be paid for hours worked in excess of eight during the workday, and general difficulties arise in coordinating work. Moreover, since managers still tell employees when to arrive and when to leave, the compressed workweek does little to increase the worker's freedom, specifically in the selecting of work hours that suit him or her best.

As a result, the compressed workweek is no panacea for dealing with the problems of standardized jobs. It has been suggested, however, that the desire for increased worker freedom can be achieved through flexible work hours.

flexible work hours (flextime)
A scheduling system in which employees are required to work a number of hours a week, but are free, within limits, to vary the hours of work.

Flexible Work Hours   **Flexible work hours** (also popularly known as **flextime**) is a scheduling system in which employees are required to work a specific number of hours a week, but are free to vary the hours of work within certain limits. As shown in Figure 11–16, each day consists of a common core, usually five or six hours, with a flexibility band surrounding the core. For example, not counting a one-hour lunch

FIGURE 11—16
A Flexible Work Schedule

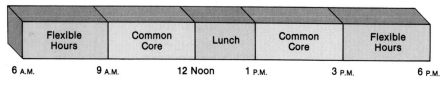

Time During the Day

break, the core may be 9:00 A.M. to 3:00 P.M., with the office actually opening at 6:00 A.M. and closing at 6:00 P.M. All employees are required to be at their jobs during the common-core periods, but they are allowed to accumulate their remaining hours from before and/or after the core time. Some flextime programs allow extra hours to be accumulated and turned into a free day off each month.

What is flextime's record? Most of the evidence stacks up favorably. Flextime tends to reduce absenteeism, improve morale, and improve worker productivity.[24] Why? Employees can better schedule their work hours to align with personal demands, and they are able to exercise discretion over their work hours. The result is that employees are more likely to adjust their work activities to the hours in which they are individually more productive and which better align with their off-work commitments.

Of course, flextime does have drawbacks, especially in its effect on the manager's job.[25] It produces problems for managers in directing subordinates outside the common-core period, causes confusion in shift work, increases difficulties when someone with a particular skill or knowledge is not available, and makes planning and controlling more cumbersome and costly for managers. Also, keep in mind that many jobs can't be converted to flextime: salesperson in a department store, office receptionist, and assembly-line operator are examples of jobs in which the jobholder must depend on others inside or outside the organization—and vice versa. Where such interdependence exists, flextime is usually not a viable alternative.

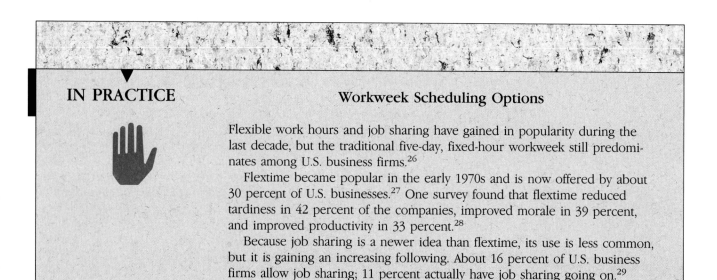

IN PRACTICE   **Workweek Scheduling Options**

Flexible work hours and job sharing have gained in popularity during the last decade, but the traditional five-day, fixed-hour workweek still predominates among U.S. business firms.[26]

Flextime became popular in the early 1970s and is now offered by about 30 percent of U.S. businesses.[27] One survey found that flextime reduced tardiness in 42 percent of the companies, improved morale in 39 percent, and improved productivity in 33 percent.[28]

Because job sharing is a newer idea than flextime, its use is less common, but it is gaining an increasing following. About 16 percent of U.S. business firms allow job sharing; 11 percent actually have job sharing going on.[29]

job sharing
The practice of having two or more people split a forty-hour-a-week job.

Job Sharing **Job sharing** is a recent work-scheduling innovation. It allows two or more individuals to split a traditional forty-hour-a-week job. So, for example, one person might perform the job from 8 A.M. to noon, while another performs the same job from 1 P.M. to 5 P.M. Why would management opt for such an arrangement? It allows the organization to draw upon the talents of more than one individual in a given job. It also opens up the opportunity to acquire skills that might not be available on a full-time basis. For instance, women with school-age children and retirees often won't accept the responsibilities that go with a full-time position but would work in a job in which the demands could be shared with others.

contingent workers
Temporary and part-time workers who supplement an organization's permanent work force.

Contingent Workers Organizations that face dynamic environments need job flexibility as well as overall structural flexibility. That explains why more and more organizations are using **contingent workers**—temporaries and part-timers who supplement an organization's permanent work force.[30] For instance, almost 17 percent of Apple Computer's work force is temporary.[31] Contingent workers allow Apple and other organizations to boost productivity in busy times and avoid painful layoffs and bad publicity in slack periods by keeping the stable core of permanent employees small. The use of contingent workers allows management a great deal of increased flexibility. Contingent jobs, in turn, satisfy workers' needs for autonomy and job diversity. On the negative side, for people who want the stability of permanent jobs, contingent-worker status can be demoralizing and even perceived as a second-class status in the labor force.[32]

Contingent workers now represent 25 percent of the work force, and their number is growing at a rate of 20 percent annually.[33] Contingent workers include low-skilled

ETHICAL DILEMMAS IN MANAGEMENT

Are Organizations Exploiting Contingent Workers?

Contingent workers provide management with increased flexibility—but at what price to the workers themselves?

For some workers, the rapid growth in demand for contingent workers is a blessing. For example, it is an opportunity for people who want to work only on a part-time basis. Being a disposable employee, however, is not necessarily a status everyone seeks willingly. Data from the Bureau of Labor Statistics indicate that 3.8 million part-timers would prefer full-time work but can't find it.[34]

Contingent workers often suffer in terms of pay and benefits. On average, they earn 40 percent less than permanent employees. Some 70 percent of part-timers have no employee-provided retirement plan, and 42 percent receive no health insurance coverage.[35]

Are organizations that use contingent workers cutting costs by exploiting these people? Are these organizations shirking their responsibilities to these workers and to society as a whole? Should federal legislation be passed that would mandate minimum fringe benefits for part-time workers? What do *you* think? How did you arrive at your conclusions?

This person is at work, but doing it from home. There are no dress codes and no commuting. Computer networks allow an increasing number of people to do their work from home.

part-time employees and office temporaries, but the contingent work force also includes a growing pool of professionals like computer designers, accountants, and lawyers. As management seeks devices to increase organizational flexibility, we can expect to see more organizations creating two-tier labor systems—a small core of permanent employees supplemented by a continually expanding and shrinking pool of contingent workers.

telecommuting
The linking by computer and modem of workers at home with co-workers and management at an office.

Telecommuting   Computer technology is opening still another alternative for managers in the way they arrange jobs. That alternative is to allow employees to perform their work at home by **telecommuting**.[36] Many white-collar occupations can now, at least technically, be carried out at home. A computer in an employee's home can be linked to those of co-workers and managers by modems. Approximately two million people now telecommute, doing things like taking orders over the phone, filling out reports and other forms, and processing or analyzing information. Some experts believe that the number will grow to 20 million by the year 2000. Whether that forecast proves accurate depends on some questions for which we do not yet have answers. For example, will people balk at losing the regular social contact that a formal office provides? Would employees who do their work at home be at a political disadvantage? Might they be less likely to be considered for salary increases and promotions? Is being out of sight equivalent to being out of mind? As we get answers to questions such as these, the future of telecommuting will become far more clear.

SUMMARY

This summary is organized by the chapter-opening learning objectives found on page 313.

1. The functional structure groups similar and related occupational specialties together. It takes advantage of specialization and is probably the most popular form of bureaucracy.

2. The divisional structure is made up of multiple, self-contained units. It provides high accountability for results.

3. The simple structure is low in complexity, has little formalization, and has authority centralized in a single person. It is fast, flexible, and inexpensive to maintain.

4. The matrix structure combines functional and product departmentalization in order to get the advantages of both specialization and high accountability.

5. The network structure is a small, centralized organization that relies on other organizations to perform manufacturing, distribution, marketing, or other crucial business functions on a contract basis. It is fast, flexible, and economical.

6. The task force structure is a temporary structure created to accomplish a specific, well-defined, complex task that requires the involvement of personnel from a number of organizational subunits. Its strength lies in its flexibility.

7. The committee structure is a temporary or permanent form that is an appendage to a larger structure. Committee members are chosen across functional lines. Like the task force, the committee structure's basic strength is its flexibility.

8. The functional structure works well with single-product or -service organizations. The divisional structure is appropriate for large organizations with multiple products or multiple markets. The simple structure is suited to small organizations, the early years of an organization's development, and a simple and dynamic environment. The matrix should be used for multiple and changing products or programs that rely on functional expertise. The network structure works well for industrial firms that use a large number of suppliers and whose products require a lot of low-cost labor. The task force is appropriate for specific tasks that have unique and unfamiliar characteristics and that require expertise that crosses functional lines. The committee structure is appropriate for tasks that require expertise that crosses functional lines.

9. Job specialization is concerned with breaking jobs down into ever smaller tasks. Job enlargement is the reverse. It expands jobs horizontally by increasing their scope. Like enlargement, job enrichment expands jobs, but vertically rather than horizontally. Enriched jobs increase depth by allowing employees greater control over their work.

10. The core job dimensions in the job characteristics model are skill variety, task identity, task significance, autonomy, and feedback.

11. The main advantage of flexible work hours is greater freedom for employees. It allows them to complete nonwork commitments without incurring absences. Additionally, it allows employees to better align their work schedule with their personal productivity cycle. The major drawback of flexible work hours is that it creates coordination problems for managers.

12. Contingent workers increase management's ability to respond rapidly to a changing environment. They can be hired or released as needed with minimal disruptions. For organizations whose business tends to be cyclical, contingent workers can be added to meet the peak periods.

REVIEW QUESTIONS

1. Which is most prevalent in practice—the functional or the matrix structure? What do you think explains its popularity?

2. Why is the simple structure inadequate in large organizations?

3. When should management use
   a. the simple structure?
   b. the matrix structure?
   c. the network structure?
   d. the task force?

4. Contrast *job enlargement* with *job enrichment* in terms of the job characteristics model.

5. What kind of jobs are likely to be better done by teams than by individuals?

6. Describe how a job can be enriched.

7. What kind of jobs do not adapt easily to flexible work hours? Explain.

8. If you were a manager, why might you resist offering flexible work hours to your employees?

9. Why might professionals who could find permanent jobs seek employment as contingent workers?

10. Why might telecommuting prove to be better in theory than in practice?

DISCUSSION QUESTIONS

1. Can an organization have *no* structure?

2. Which structural design—divisional, simple, or matrix—do you think most people would prefer to work in? Least prefer? Why?

3. Do you think that in twenty years most jobs will score high on motivating potential? Explain.

4. Identify two jobs that you're familiar with: one that you think you would like to do continuously and one that you would never want to do. Compare them in terms of the JCM. Compare them also in terms of compensation and prestige in the community. Do you think compensation and prestige are positively correlated with a high MPS?

5. "What a manager does in terms of the *organizing function* depends on what level he or she occupies in the organizational hierarchy." Discuss.

SELF-ASSESSMENT EXERCISE

Is an Enriched Job for You?

Instructions: People differ in what they like and dislike in their jobs. Listed below are twelve pairs of jobs. For each pair, indicate which job you would prefer. Assume that everything else about the jobs is the same—pay attention only to the characteristics actually listed for each pair of jobs. If you would prefer the job in the left-hand column (Column A), indicate how much you prefer it by putting a check mark in a blank to the left of the Neutral point. If you prefer the job in the right-hand column (Column B), check one of the blanks to the right of Neutral. Check the Neutral blank only if you find the two jobs equally attractive or unattractive. Try to use the Neutral blank rarely.

Column A		Column B
1. A job that offers little or no challenge.	Strongly prefer A — Neutral — Strongly prefer B	A job that requires you to be completely isolated from co-workers.
2. A job that pays very well.	Strongly prefer A — Neutral — Strongly prefer B	A job that allows considerable opportunity to be creative and innovative.
3. A job that often requires you to make important decisions.	Strongly prefer A — Neutral — Strongly prefer B	A job in which there are many pleasant people to work with.
4. A job with little security in a somewhat unstable organization.	Strongly prefer A — Neutral — Strongly prefer B	A job in which you have little or no opportunity to participate in decisions that affect your work.
5. A job in which greater responsibility is given to those who do the best work.	Strongly prefer A — Neutral — Strongly prefer B	A job in which greater responsibility is given to loyal employees who have the most *seniority*.
6. A job with a supervisor who sometimes is highly critical.	Strongly prefer A — Neutral — Strongly prefer B	A job that does not require you to use much of your talent.
7. A very routine job.	Strongly prefer A — Neutral — Strongly prefer B	A job in which your co-workers are not very friendly.

Column A		Column B
8. A job with a supervisor who respects you and treats you fairly	Strongly Neutral Strongly prefer A prefer B	A job that provides constant opportunities for you to learn new and interesting things.
9. A job that gives you a real chance to develop yourself personally.	Strongly Neutral Strongly prefer A prefer B	A job with excellent vacations and fringe benefits.
10. A job in which there is a real chance you could be laid off.	Strongly Neutral Strongly prefer A prefer B	A job with very little chance to do challenging work.
11. A job with little freedom and independence to do your work in the way you think best.	Strongly Neutral Strongly prefer A prefer B	A job with poor working conditions.
12. A job with very satisfying teamwork.	Strongly Neutral Strongly prefer A prefer B	A job that allows you to use your skills and abilities to the fullest extent.

Turn to page 672 for scoring directions and key.

Source: J. R. Hackman and G. R. Oldham (1974). *The Job Diagnostic Survey: An Instrument for the Diagnosis of Jobs and the Evaluation of Job Redesign Projects.* Technical Report No. 4. New Haven, Conn.: Yale University, Department of Administrative Sciences. With permission.

CASE APPLICATION 11A

The Valdosta City Library

The Valdosta Library serves the city of Valdosta, Georgia. The director, Betty Hunt, has a staff of seventeen people working for her. Five of these are professional librarians with master's degrees. The remaining twelve people are nonprofessional.

Betty has designed a structure with carefully written job descriptions, a number of rules that all employees are expected to follow, and centralized decision making.

Three people report directly to Betty: an administrative assistant, an associate director for cataloging and technical services, and an associate director for reference and operations. The two associate directors regularly express to Betty their concern that they are not consulted about important decisions that affect their work groups. Betty's response is, "We're a small organization. I know everything that's going on, and coordination will work best when I make the decisions."

Questions

1. How is the Valdosta Library organized?
2. What are the advantages and disadvantages of this structure?
3. What changes, if any, would you make? Why?

CASE APPLICATION 11B

Retail Credit Reports

Retail Credit Reports (RCR) operates out of Minneapolis, Minnesota. Employing approximately 125 people, the company supplies credit reports on individuals to department stores, oil companies, banks, and other organizations in Minnesota and western Wisconsin that use the information to make credit decisions. Firms pay a flat membership fee per year to use RCR's services plus a fee for each credit report, the cost varying with the amount of information desired.

In 1989, RCR employed seven managers, one assistant to the manager, fifteen supervisors, seventy-three service clerks, twenty secretaries, and nine investigators. Figure CA11–1 shows the organization chart. The service clerks were organized by the last names of individuals. For instance, if a bank wanted a credit report on Nan Greenberg, the F to I account manager was responsible for developing the report. If the account manager needed more information than had been obtained in mail and phone reports from credit sources, she called upon the investigations group to gather additional data. The investigations group also verified secondary data, did reference checks, and performed similar activities.

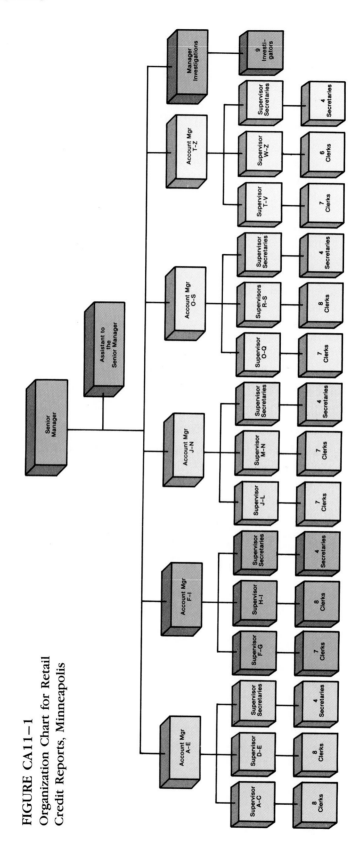

FIGURE CA11–1
Organization Chart for Retail
Credit Reports, Minneapolis

The structure of jobs at RCR differed within areas. For instance, the investigators typically dropped by the office every day or every other day, picked up their assignments, dropped off finished reports, and departed. As long as they completed their assignments competently and on time, they experienced very little in terms of control. The service clerks and secretaries, on the other hand, performed routine and standardized activities. Supervisors and managers monitored their on-the-job behavior closely.

The investigators' freedom was a sore point in the office, particularly among service clerks. In terms of education and experience, the investigators were little different from the service clerks. Even their salaries were quite similar. The continuous griping about the "soft hours that the investigators have" led Jill Friedman, the senior manager in charge of the Minneapolis office, to decide to introduce a four-day workweek in February 1990. It applied to all RCR employees except the investigators. The investigators could work a four-day week if they chose.

Jill was unsure of just what was involved and the effect that it would have on the company's performance, so she hired a consultant from a local university to help implement the program. The consultant's strategy included tracking absence and satisfaction data before and after the shorter workweek was implemented. In this way, the consultant believed, it would be possible to assess the actual impact of the change.

The consultant had employees complete a questionnaire that assessed job satisfaction. He also reviewed employee personnel records to calculate absence figures. These became the base rates against which later figures could be compared.

Shortly after this information was obtained, employees were advised that RCR was moving to a four-day, forty-hour week. The announcement was made in a management staff meeting. It was further announced that Mondays would be the extra day off. No mention was made of the criteria for deciding whether or not the program would be continued.

One month after the 4–40 workweek went into effect, the consultant made a follow-up survey of employee job satisfaction. Absence data was also obtained. However, unbeknownst to the consultant, Jill Friedman was not pleased with how the change was working out. She was finding it increasingly difficult to schedule RCR's work activities. One month and three days after the 4–40 schedule was introduced, Jill announced that RCR would be returning to the standard five-day week. The consultant, somewhat surprised, decided to make the best of the situation. He asked for and received approval from Jill to do a third employee satisfaction survey. It was administered a month after the program was terminated. Absence data was also computed. This gave the consultant three sets of data. He had job satisfaction and absence data covering the period before the change was announced, a month after it had been implemented, and a month after it was terminated.

In June, the consultant provided a report to Jill giving the results he obtained. Job satisfaction improved significantly after the 4–40 was implemented. After the program was discontinued, satisfaction dropped severely, to a level well below what it had been before the shorter workweek was introduced. Absence data followed a similar pattern. Using the first set of data as a base (equal to 100), absenteeism dropped to 27 a month after 4–40 was introduced but was up to 112 a month after 4–40 was terminated.

Questions

1. Redesign Figure CA11–1 to centralize all secretarial activities directly under the senior manager. What advantages might centralization offer? What disadvantages?

2. What suggestions can you make to improve the overall structure of RCR?

3. What factors should Jill have considered before implementing the 4–40 schedule?

4. Do you think that the final job satisfaction and absentee data would have been different if the employees had been consulted before the 4–40 program was initiated? If they had been consulted after it was initiated but before it was discontinued?

5. What implications does this case have for instituting a structural change and then withdrawing it?

12

HUMAN
RESOURCE
MANAGEMENT

LEARNING
OBJECTIVES

After Reading
This Chapter,
You Should
Be Able To:

1. Describe the human resource management process.
2. Identify the key laws and regulations that influence human resource decisions.
3. Differentiate between job descriptions and job specifications.
4. List some recruitment and decruitment options.
5. Explain the importance of validity and reliability in selection.
6. Describe the selection devices that work best with various kinds of jobs.
7. Identify and describe the various training methods.
8. Describe five performance appraisal methods.
9. Outline the five stages in a career.
10. Explain the collective bargaining process.
11. Describe the organizational implications from dual-career couples.
12. Explain why sexual harassment is a growing concern of management.

ob candidates applying for work at Mazda Motor Corp.'s assembly plant in Flat Rock, Michigan should prepare themselves for a grueling selection process and, if chosen for a job, an extensive follow-up training program. Mazda spends a great deal of time and expense in hiring and training to make sure it selects new employees who have high levels of skill and motivation and an aptitude for learning new work methods.[1]

Mazda has a five-step screening process that all applicants must go through that is specifically designed to assess interpersonal skills, aptitude for teamwork, planning skills, and flexibility. This screening process encompasses a lot more than taking a paper-and-pencil test, enduring a few interviews, and providing some references. At Mazda, applicants must also perform tasks that simulate jobs that they might do on the actual factory floor. For example, applicants might have to bolt fenders onto a car or attach hoses in a simulated engine compartment. This helps Mazda's management to match workers' abilities with specific job requirements, and it also provides applicants with a realistic preview of what they're getting into.

For the initial work force, 10,000 applicants passed the five-step screening process. Of these, only 1,300 were hired. The cost of screening each one of these new employees was about $13,000 per employee.

But new hires at Mazda don't just report to the factory floor and join a work team. First, they have to undergo detailed training. It starts with a three-week hodgepodge of sessions in which they learn about interpersonal relations, charting quality, stimulating creativity, and the like. This is followed by three days devoted to learning Mazda's philosophy of increasing efficiency through continual improvement. After this basic training comes job-specific training. Line workers, for example, spend five to seven more weeks picking up specific technical skills, then spend another three or four weeks being supervised on the assembly line.

The internal screening process at Mazda's Flat Rock, Michigan plant to find and prepare auto workers to do fairly standardized jobs in a manufacturing plant might seem like overkill. But Mazda is convinced that its effort pays dividends. Mazda wants literate, versatile employees who accept the company's emphasis on teamwork, loyalty, efficiency, and quality. On the basis of performance figures from this plant, Mazda's hiring and training seem to be working.

This example illustrates what many organizations are rapidly learning: People are an organization's most valuable asset. What is IBM without its employees? A lot of factories, expensive equipment, and some impressive bank balances. It certainly would have no resemblance to the IBM that you and I know. Similarly, if you removed the employees from such varied organizations as the Boston Celtics, the U.S. Army, Exxon, and McDonald's, what would be left? Not much! The quality of an organization is, to a large degree, merely the summation of the quality of people it hires and holds. Getting and keeping competent personnel is critical to the success of every organization, whether the organization is just starting or well established. Therefore, part of every manager's job in the organizing function is filling positions; that is, putting the right person into the right job.

MANAGERS AND PERSONNEL DEPARTMENTS

Some readers may be thinking, "Sure, personnel decisions are important but aren't they made by people in personnel departments? These aren't decisions that *all* managers are involved in!"

It's true that, in large organizations, a number of the activities grouped under the label *human resource management* (HRM) are often done by specialists in personnel or human resource development. However, not all managers work in organizations that have formal personnel departments; and even those who do still have to be engaged in some human resource activities.

Small-business managers are an obvious example of individuals who must frequently do their hiring without the assistance of a personnel department. But even managers in billion-dollar corporations are involved in recruiting, reviewing application forms, interviewing applicants, inducting new employees, appraising employee performance, making decisions about employee training, and providing career advice to subordinates. Whether or not an organization has a personnel department, *every* manager is involved with human resource decisions in his or her unit.

THE HUMAN RESOURCE MANAGEMENT PROCESS

human resource management process
Activities necessary for staffing the organization and sustaining high employee performance.

Figure 12–1 introduces the key components of an organization's **human resource management process.** It represents nine activities, or steps (the blue-colored boxes), that, if properly executed, will staff an organization with competent, high-performing employees who are capable of sustaining their performance level over the long term.

The first four steps represent *human resource planning,* the adding of staff through *recruitment,* the reduction in staff through *decruitment,* and *selection,* resulting in the *identification and selection* of competent employees. Once you've got competent people, you need to help them adapt to the organization and ensure that their job skills and knowledge are kept current. You do this through *orientation* and *training.* The last steps in the HRM process are designed to identify performance problems, correct them, and help employees to sustain a high level of performance over their entire career. The activities included here include *performance appraisal, career development,* and, where employees are unionized, *labor-management relations.*

Notice in Figure 12–1 that the entire HRM process is influenced by the external environment. In Chapter 3 we elaborated on the constraints that the environment places on management. Those constraints are probably most severe in the management of human resources. Before we review the nine steps in the process, therefore, we will briefly examine how environmental forces influence the process.

IMPORTANT ENVIRONMENTAL CONSIDERATIONS

Numerous environmental forces impinge on human resource management activities. For instance, approximately 16 percent of the U.S. work force is unionized. In unionized organizations, many key personnel decisions are regulated by the terms of collec-

FIGURE 12–1   The Human Resource Management Process

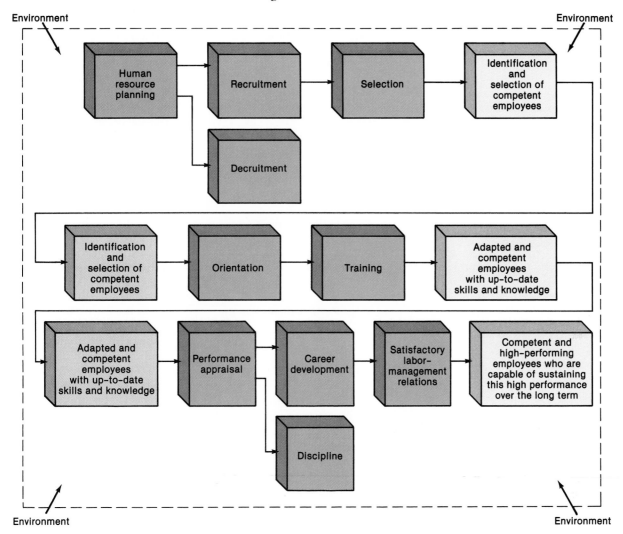

tive bargaining agreements. These agreements usually define such things as recruitment sources; criteria for hiring, promotions, and layoffs; training eligibility; and disciplinary practices. But no environmental constraint can match the influence of government laws and regulations.

During the 1960s and 1970s, the federal government greatly expanded its influence over HRM decisions by enacting new laws and regulations. (See Table 12–1.) As a result of this legislation, employers today must ensure that equal employment opportunities exist for job applicants and current employees. Decisions regarding who will be hired, for example, or which employees will be chosen for a management training program must be made without regard to race, sex, religion, age, color, or national origin. Exceptions can occur only for requirements that are **bona fide occupational qualifications (BFOQ).** This explains why, for instance, airlines today have flight attendants of both sexes and of varying ages. In the early 1960s, airlines hired almost exclusively flight attendants who were young, attractive females. But youth and being female are not BFOQs for this job; hence such criteria had to be dropped.

**bona fide occupational quali-
fications (BFOQ)**
A criterion such as sex, age, or national origin may be used as a basis for hiring if it can be clearly demonstrated to be job related.

TABLE 12–1 Major Federal Laws and Regulations Related to Human Resource Management Passed During the 1960s and 1970s

Year	Law or Regulation	Description
1963	Equal Pay Act	Prohibits pay differences based on sex for equal work
1964 (amended in 1972)	Civil Rights Act, Title VII	Prohibits discrimination based on race, color, religion, national origin, or sex
1967 (amended in 1975)	Age Discrimination in Employment Act	Prohibits age discrimination against employees between 40 and 65 years of age
1973	Vocational Rehabilitation Act	Prohibits discrimination on the basis of physical or mental handicaps
1974	Veterans' Readjustment Act	Prohibits discrimination against disabled veterans and Vietnam War veterans
1974	Privacy Act	Gives employees the legal right to examine letters of reference concerning them
1978	Pregnancy Discrimination Act, Title VII	Prohibits dismissal of women because of pregnancy alone and protects job security during maternity leaves
1978	Mandatory Retirement Act	Prohibits the forced retirement of most employees before the age of 70

affirmative action programs
Programs that enhance the organizational status of members of protected groups.

Many organizations have **affirmative action programs** to ensure that decisions and practices enhance the employment, upgrading, and retention of members from minority, female, and other protected groups. That is, not only will the organization refrain from discrimination, but it will actively seek to enhance the status of members from protected groups. Why are organizations taking this affirmative stance? On the ethical side, they have a social responsibility to improve the status of protected group members. On the economic side, the cost of defending the organization against charges of discrimination can be enormous. Sears, Roebuck, as an example, spent over twelve years and $20 million in legal fees, and employed 250 full-time people to defend itself successfully against accusations by the Equal Employment Opportunity Commission that its past hiring practices had discriminated against females.[2]

While there were fewer new federal regulations in the 1980s on equal employment opportunity, the environment facing managers continues to be highly dynamic. At the federal level, Supreme Court decisions have failed to clarify precisely which of an employer's actions are legal and which are not.[3] At the state level, new legislation changing the rules of the game is being passed continually.

Thus managers are not completely free to choose who they hire, promote, or fire. Federal and state regulations, enacted to ensure that all applicants and employees are assessed on the basis of job performance criteria alone, have reduced management's discretion over human resource decisions.

The laws increasingly favor the employee in wrongful firing suits. There are currently more than 25,000 wrongful discharge cases pending in U.S. state and federal courts. The average jury award in these cases is $602,000, and 64 percent of all trial verdicts in wrongful discharge suits favor the plaintiff employees.

HUMAN RESOURCE PLANNING

human resource planning
The process by which management ensures that it has the right personnel, who are capable of completing those tasks that help the organization reach its objectives.

Human resource planning is the process by which management ensures that it has the right number and kinds of people at the right places, and at the right times, who are capable of effectively and efficiently completing those tasks that will help the organization achieve its overall objectives. Human resource planning, then, translates the organization's objectives into terms of the workers needed to meet those objectives.[4]

Human resource planning can be condensed into three steps: (1) assessing current human resources, (2) assessing future human resource needs, and (3) developing a program to meet future human resource needs.

Current Assessment

Management begins by reviewing its current human resource status. This is typically done by generating a *human resource inventory*. In an era of sophisticated computer systems, it is not too difficult a task for most organizations to generate a human resource inventory report. The input for this report is derived from forms completed by employees. Such reports might include a list of names, education, training, prior employment, languages spoken, capabilities, and specialized skills for all employees in the organization. This inventory allows management to assess what talents and skills are available.

job analysis
An assessment that defines jobs and the behaviors necessary to perform them.

Another part of the current assessment is the **job analysis.** While the human resource inventory is concerned with telling management what individual employees can do, job analysis is more fundamental. It defines the jobs within the organization and the behaviors that are necessary to perform these jobs. For instance, what are the duties of a purchasing specialist, grade 3, who works for Boise Cascade? What minimal knowledge, skills, and abilities are necessary for the adequate performance of a grade

3 purchasing specialist's job? How do the requirements for a purchasing specialist, grade 3, compare with those for a purchasing specialist, grade 2, or for a purchasing analyst? These are questions that job analysis can answer. It seeks to determine the kind of people needed to fill each job and culminates in job descriptions and job specifications.

There are several methods for analyzing jobs. There is the observation method, in which employees are either watched directly or filmed on the job. Employees can also be interviewed individually or in a group. A third method is the use of structured questionnaires on which employees check or rate the items they perform in their jobs from a long list of possible task items. A fourth method is the use of a technical conference at which "experts"—usually supervisors with extensive knowledge of a job—identify its specific characteristics. A fifth method is to have employees record their daily activities in a diary or notebook, which can then be reviewed and structured into job activities.

Information gathered by using one or more of these methods allows management to draw up a **job description** and **job specification.** The former is a written statement of what a jobholder does, how it is done, and why it is done. It typically portrays job content, environment, and conditions of employment. An example of a job description for a billing adjustments supervisor is provided in Table 12–2. The job

job description

A written statement of what a jobholder does, how it is done, and why it is done.

job specification

A statement of the minimum acceptable qualifications that an incumbent must possess to perform a given job successfully.

TABLE 12–2   Job Description at a Large Public Utility

Title: Billing Adjustments Supervisor

General Function: To supervise, direct and control the formulation, testing, implementation and revision of customer billing programs and operating procedures; assist in the rate design process involving commercial and residential accounts; and pre-billing file maintenance and post-billing adjustment activities.

Supervisory Responsibility: Supervises approximately twenty-five clerical employees.

Operating Responsibilities:

1. Supervise the formulation and maintenance of billing system documentation; formulate and analyze the design of special programs needed to respond to other departmental needs.

2. Coordinate information, as well as assist in the rate design process and rate implementation for commercial and residential accounts.

3. Act as liaison with Information Systems in initiating major changes or enhancements to the Customer Master File and Billing Systems to ensure compatibility with the existing billing system.

4. Analyze, prepare and maintain billing-related programs and operating procedures for pre-billing and post-billing; provide guidance in the use of these procedures.

5. Oversee the formulation and revision of billing policies and programs including the development of related manual and automated systems and procedures.

6. Resolve billing discrepancies by the correcting of computer file listings and the investigation of customer accounts rejected owing to unequal reads or extreme high/low consumption.

7. Coordinate testimony for, as well as testify in court hearings, involving the Company's billing records and record systems.

8. Analyze and assist in the formulation and revision of meter deposit policies and programs including the development of related manual and automated systems and procedures.

Contacts: Has contact with all levels of personnel throughout the Company. Has frequent contact with meter reading and customer service supervisors.

Working conditions: Works in an office area; occasionally makes field trips.

TABLE 12–3   Job Specification at a Large Public Utility

Title: Billing Adjustments Supervisor

Education: Requires a bachelor's degree or equivalent, preferably in business administration or accounting. Knowledge of the use and application of computer systems is desirable.

Experience: Requires a minimum of four years of experience, two of which should have been in a lead or supervisory capacity and have involved the application and interpretation of billing policies.

Mental Complexities: Requires a thorough knowledge of Company billing procedures, techniques and rules as well as applicable State and Federal codes and regulations governing billing practices. Excellent oral and written communication skills are required.

specification states the minimum acceptable qualifications that an incumbent must possess to perform a given job successfully. It identifies the knowledge, skills, and abilities needed to do the job effectively. An example of a job specification for a billing adjustments supervisor is shown in Table 12–3.

The job description and specification are important documents when managers begin recruiting and selecting. The job description can be used to describe the job to potential candidates. The job specification keeps the manager's attention on the list of qualifications necessary for an incumbent to perform a job and assists in determining whether candidates are qualified.

Future Assessment

Future human resource needs are determined by the organization's objectives and strategies.

Demand for human resources is a result of demand for the organization's products or services. On the basis of its estimate of total revenue, management can attempt to establish the number and mix of human resources needed to reach these revenues. In some cases, the situation may be reversed. Where particular skills are necessary and in scarce supply, the availability of satisfactory human resources determines revenues. This might be the case, for example, in a tax consulting firm that finds it has more business opportunities than it can handle. Its only limiting factor in building revenues might be its ability to locate and hire staff with the qualifications necessary to satisfy the consulting firm's clients. In most cases, however, the overall organizational goals and the resulting revenue forecast provide the major input determining the organization's human resource demand requirements.

Developing a Future Program

After it has assessed both current capabilities and future needs, management is able to estimate shortages—both in number and in kind—and to highlight areas in which the organization will be overstaffed. A program can then be developed that can match these estimates with forecasts of future labor supply. So human resource planning not only provides information to guide current staffing needs, but also provides projections of future personnel needs and availability.

RECRUITMENT AND DECRUITMENT

recruitment
The process of locating, identifying, and attracting capable applicants.

decruitment
Techniques for reducing the labor supply within an organization.

Once managers know their current personnel status (whether they are understaffed or overstaffed), they can begin to do something about it. If one or more vacancies exist, they can use the information gathered through job analysis to guide them in **recruitment**—that is, the process of locating, identifying, and attracting capable applicants.[5] On the other hand, if human resource planning indicates a surplus, management will want to reduce the labor supply within the organization. This activity is called **decruitment.**[6]

Where does a manager look to recruit potential candidates? Table 12–4 offers some guidance. The source that is used should reflect the local labor market, type or level of position, and size of the organization.

Regardless of the type of position or its attractiveness, it is generally easier to recruit in large labor markets than in small ones. If for no other reasons, large labor markets like New York or Chicago have a greater supply of workers. Of course, this generalization has to be moderated by unemployment levels, wage rates, and other factors. But in large markets, recruitment efforts can be directed locally—to newspapers, employment agencies, colleges, or referrals by current employees.

The type or level of a position influences recruitment methods. The greater the skill required or the higher the position in the organization's hierarchy, the more the recruitment process will expand to become a regional or national search.

TABLE 12–4
Major Sources of Potential Job Candidates

Source	Advantages	Disadvantages
Internal search	Low cost; builds employee morale; familiarity with organization	Limited supply; may not increase proportion of employees from protected groups
Advertisements	Wide distribution; can be targeted to specific groups	Generates many unqualified candidates
Employee referrals	Knowledge about the organization; can generate strong candidates because a good referral reflects on the recommender	Does not increase the diversity and mix of employees
Public employment agencies	Free or nominal cost	Candidates tend to be unskilled or minimally trained
Private employment agencies	Wide contacts; careful screening; short-term guarantees often given	High cost
School placement	Large, centralized body of candidates	Limited to entry-level positions
Temporary help services	Fills temporary needs	Expensive; generally limited to routine or narrowly defined skills

To fill senior executive positions, for which compensation is above $150,000 a year, management is likely to rely on executive search firms with national contacts or regional publications like the *Wall Street Journal.* A wider set of candidates is justified because of the potential impact the decisions of such managers will have on an organization's future.

The scope of recruitment and the amount of effort devoted to it will also be influenced by the size of the organization. Generally, the larger the organization, the easier it is to recruit job applicants. Larger organizations have a larger pool of internal candidates from which to choose to fill positions above the lowest level. Larger organizations have more visibility and, typically, more prestige. Larger organizations are also often perceived as offering greater opportunities for promotions and increased responsibility.

In the 1980s, most of the largest U.S. corporations, as well as many government agencies and smaller businesses, were forced to engage in some decruitment activities. The decline in many manufacturing industries, market changes, foreign competition, and mergers have been the primary causes of personnel cutbacks.

Decruitment is not a pleasant task for any manager to perform. But as many organizations are forced to shrink the size of their work force or restructure their skill composition, decruitment is becoming an increasingly important part of human resource management.

What are a manager's decruitment options? Obviously, people can be fired. But other choices may be more beneficial to the organization and/or the employee.[7] Table 12–5 summarizes a manager's major options.

TABLE 12–5
Decruitment Options

Option	Description
Firing	Permanent involuntary termination.
Layoffs	Temporary involuntary termination; may last only a few days or extend to years.
Attrition	Not filling openings created by voluntary resignations or normal retirements.
Transfers	Move employees either laterally or downward; usually does not reduce costs but can reduce intra-organizational supply-demand imbalances.
Reduced workweeks	Employees work fewer hours per week, share jobs, or perform their jobs on a part-time basis.
Early retirements	Incentives are provided to older and more senior employees for retiring before their normal retirement date.

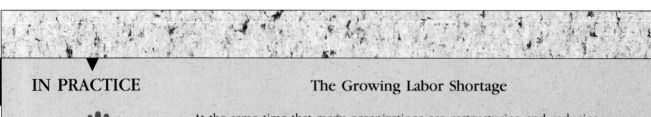

IN PRACTICE   The Growing Labor Shortage

At the same time that many organizations are restructuring and reducing their work forces, another phenomenon is developing that could prove to be a far more pervasive challenge for managers: a spreading labor *shortage*.[8]

The demographics and statistics are unchallengable. An average of only 1.3 million people will enter the labor force every year throughout the 1990s, down considerably from 3 million a year during the 1970s. A slower-growing population, compounded by a widening mismatch between the skills that workers have and the skills employers need, is creating a labor shortage that is likely to last throughout the 1990s.

Organizations are already taking steps to deal with this problem. In many communities, "minimum-wage" jobs are paying $6 and $7 an hour because employers can't fill them at $4.25. Have you noticed that many fast-food chains have installed self-service drink-dispensing machines? This is an example of another option managers are taking—namely, substituting capital for labor. Many employers are also expanding child care and maternity leave benefits in order to attract and keep female employees.

One of the most valuable groups of potentially skilled and committed employees that organizations are beginning to tap aggressively is the pool of retired workers. In many cases, organizations are bringing back their own retirees. Older workers now compose 25 percent of Days Inns' 650-person reservation sales staff. According to Days Inns' management, annual turnover among this group is less than 2 percent compared to 70 percent for younger employees. This reduction in turnover has brought down recruitment and training costs at the hotel's reservation center by 40 percent.

Incidentally, this labor shortage should be welcome news to upcoming college graduates. They will find increased demand for their services, more job choices, and better opportunities to fully utilize their educations.

SELECTION

A new college graduate with a degree in accounting walked into the personnel office of a medium-sized corporation not long ago in search of a job. Immediately, she was confronted by two doors, one of which displayed the sign "Applicants With College Degree" and the other, "Applicants Without College Degree." She opened the first door. As soon as she did so, she confronted two more doors. The first said: "Applicants with Grade Point Average of 3.0 or Greater," and the other: "Applicants with Grade Point Average of Less Than 3.0." Having achieved a 3.6 average, she again chose the first door—and was once again faced by two doors, one reading: "Applicants with Management Majors," and the other: "Applicants with Nonmanagement Majors." Having an accounting degree, she opened the second of these doors—and found herself out in the street.[9]

Although this story is fictitious, it does convey the essence of the selection process. When human resource planning identifies a personnel shortage and develops a pool of applicants, it needs some method for screening the applicants to ensure that the most appropriate candidate is awarded the job. That screening method is the **selection process.**

selection process
The process of screening job applicants to ensure that the most appropriate candidates are hired.

Foundations of Selection

Selection is a prediction exercise. It seeks to predict which applicants will be successful if hired. "Successful" in this case means performing well on the criteria the organization uses to evaluate personnel. In filling a sales position, for example, the selection process should be able to predict which applicants will generate a high volume of sales; for a position as a high school teacher, it should predict which applicants will get high student evaluations.

Prediction   Consider, for a moment, that any selection decision can result in four possible outcomes. As shown in Figure 12–2, two of these outcomes would indicate correct decisions, but two would indicate errors.

A decision is correct when the applicant was predicted to be successful and later proved to be successful on the job or when the applicant was predicted to be unsuccessful and would perform accordingly if hired. In the former case, we have successfully accepted; in the latter case, we have successfully rejected. Thus the purpose of selection activities is to develop outcomes shown as "correct decisions" in Figure 12–2.

Problems occur when we make errors by rejecting candidates who would later perform successfully on the job (reject errors) or accepting those who subsequently perform poorly (accept errors). These problems are, unfortunately, far from insignificant. Reject errors historically meant only that the costs of selection would be increased because more candidates would have to be screened. Today, selection techniques that result in reject errors can open the organization to charges of discrimination, especially if applicants from protected groups are disproportionately rejected. Accept errors, on the other hand, have very obvious costs to the organization, including the cost of training the employee, the costs generated or profits forgone because of the employee's incompetence, and the cost of severance and the subsequent costs of further recruiting and selection screening. The major thrust of any selection activity is therefore to reduce the probability of making reject errors or accept errors, while increasing the probability of making correct decisions.

FIGURE 12–2   Selection Decision Outcomes

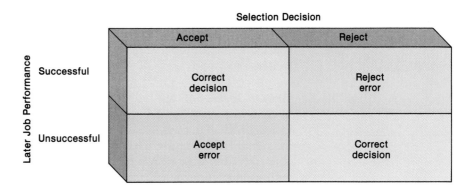

validity
The proven relationship that exists between a selection device and some relevant criterion.

Validity   Any selection device that a manager uses—such as application forms, tests, interviews, or background investigations—must demonstrate **validity.** That is, there must be a proven relationship between the selection device and some relevant criterion. For example, the law prohibits management from using a test score as a selection device unless there is clear evidence that individuals with high scores on this test outperform, on the job, individuals with low test scores.

The burden is on management to support that any selection device it uses to differentiate applicants is related to job performance. While management can give applicants an intelligence test and use the results to help make selection decisions, it must be prepared to demonstrate, if challenged, that this intelligence test is a valid measure, that is, that scores on the test are positively related to later job performance.

reliability
The ability of a selection device to measure the same thing consistently.

Reliability   In addition to being valid, a selection device must also demonstrate reliability. **Reliability** indicates whether the device measures the same thing consistently. For example, if a test is reliable, any single individual's score should remain fairly stable over time, assuming that the characteristics it is measuring are also stable.

The importance of reliability should be evident. No selection device can be effective if it is low in reliability. That is equivalent to weighing yourself everyday on an erratic scale. If the scale is unreliable—randomly fluctuating, say, ten to fifteen pounds every time you step on it—the results will not mean much. The same applies to selection devices. To be effective predictors, they must possess an acceptable level of consistency.

Selection Devices

Managers can use a number of selection devices to reduce accept and reject errors. The best-known devices include an analysis of the prospects' completed application form, written and performance-simulation tests, interviews, background investigations, and in some cases a physical examination. Let us briefly review each of these devices, giving particular attention to how valid each is in predicting job performance. After we review the devices, we will discuss when each should be used.

The Application Form   Almost all organizations require candidates to fill out an application. It may be only a form on which a prospect gives his or her name, address, and telephone number. At the other extreme, it might be a comprehensive personal history profile, detailing the applicant's activities, skills, and accomplishments.

Hard and relevant biographical data that can be verified—for example, rank in high school graduating class—have shown to be valid measures of performance for some jobs.[10] Additionally, when application form items have been appropriately weighted to reflect job relatedness, the device has proven a valid predictor for such diverse groups as salesclerks, engineers, factory workers, district managers, clerical employees, and technicians.[11] But typically, only a couple of items on the application prove to be valid predictors, and then only for a specific job. Use of weighted applications for selection purposes is difficult and expensive because the weights have to be validated for each specific job and must be continually reviewed and updated to reflect changes in weights over time.

Written Tests   Typical written tests include tests of intelligence, aptitude, ability, and interest. Tests have long been popular as selection devices, but there has been a marked decline in their use since the late 1960s.[12] The reason is that such tests have frequently been characterized as discriminating, and many organizations cannot validate such tests as being job related.[13]

Tests in intellectual ability, spatial and mechanical ability, perceptual accuracy, and motor ability have shown to be moderately valid predictors for many semiskilled and

The trend in recent years has been toward shorter application forms. This is to avoid requesting information that is not relevant to the job.

APPLICATION FOR EMPLOYMENT

NAME _____ SOCIAL SECURITY NO. _____

    LAST   FIRST   MIDDLE

ADDRESS _____

    STREET   CITY   STATE   ZIP

PHONE NO. _____ DATE _____

WHAT KIND OF WORK ARE YOU LOOKING FOR? _____

WHAT SPECIAL QUALIFICATIONS DO YOU HAVE? _____

WHAT MACHINES CAN YOU OPERATE? _____

EDUCATION

SCHOOL	NAME OF SCHOOL	NO. OF YEARS ATTENDED	MAJOR	DID YOU GRADUATE?
HIGH				
COLLEGE				
OTHER				

EXPERIENCE

JOB TITLE	NAME AND ADDRESS OF EMPLOYER	DATE FROM	TO

MILITARY SERVICE RECORD

BRANCH OF SERVICE _____ DISCHARGE DATE _____

PRESENT MEMBER IN NATIONAL GUARD OR RESERVES _____

BUSINESS REFERENCES

NAME	ADDRESS	OCCUPATION

unskilled operative jobs in industrial organizations.[14] Intelligence tests are reasonably good predictors for supervisory positions.[15] Again, the burden is on management to demonstrate that any test used is job related. Since the characteristics that many of these tests tap are considerably removed from the actual performance of the job itself, getting high validity coefficients has often been difficult. The result has been a decreased use of traditional written tests and increased interest in performance simulation tests.

Performance Simulation Tests   What better way to find out whether an applicant can do a job successfully than by having him or her do it? The logic of this question has resulted in increased usage of performance simulation tests. Undoubtedly, the enthusiasm for these tests lies in the fact that they are based on job analysis data and therefore should more easily meet the requirement of job relatedness than do written tests. Performance simulation tests are made up of actual job behaviors rather than surrogates.

The best-known performance simulation tests are work sampling and assessment centers. The former is suited to routine jobs, the latter to selecting managerial personnel.

Work sampling involves presenting applicants with a miniature replica of a job and letting them perform a task or set of tasks that are central to the job. Applicants demonstrate that they possess the necessary talents by actually doing the tasks. By carefully devising work samples based on job analysis data, management can determine the knowledge, skills, and abilities needed for each job. Each work sample element is then matched with a corresponding job performance element. For instance, a work sample for a job that involves computations on a calculator would require applicants to make similar computations.

The results from work sample experiments have generally been impressive. They have almost always yielded validity scores that are superior to that of written aptitude, personality, or intelligence tests.[16]

A more elaborate set of performance simulation tests, specifically designed to evaluate a candidate's managerial potential, is administered in **assessment centers.** In assessment centers, line executives, supervisors, or trained psychologists evaluate

work sampling

A personnel selection device in which job applicants are presented with a miniature replica of a job and allowed to perform tasks central to that job.

assessment centers

Places in which job candidates undergo performance simulation tests that evaluate managerial potential.

candidates as they go through two to four days of exercises that simulate real problems they would confront on the job. Based on a list of descriptive dimensions that the actual job incumbent has to meet, activities might include interviews, in-basket problem-solving exercises, group discussions, and business decision games.

The evidence for the effectiveness of assessment centers is extremely impressive. They have consistently demonstrated results that predict later job performance in managerial positions.[17] Although they are not cheap, the selection of an ineffective manager is undoubtedly far more costly.

Interviews   The interview, along with the application form, is an almost universal selection device. Not many of us have ever gotten a job without one or more interviews. The irony of this is that the value of the interview for selection has been the subject of considerable debate, with most of the evidence stacking up *against* the interview as a valid predictive tool.

Studies of the interview as a predictor have found it to generally achieve low reliability and validity scores.[18] It has been called "a costly, inefficient, and usually invalid procedure."[19] A review of the research leads us to the following conclusions:

1. Prior knowledge about the applicant will bias the interviewer's evaluation.
2. The interviewer holds a stereotype of what represents a "good" applicant.
3. The interviewer tends to favor applicants who share his or her own attitudes.
4. The order in which applicants are interviewed will influence evaluations.
5. The order in which information is elicited during the interview will influence evaluations.
6. Negative information is given unduly high weight.
7. The interviewer makes a decision concerning the applicant's suitability early in the interview.
8. The interviewer forgets much of the interview's content within minutes after its conclusion.
9. Structured and well-organized interviews are more reliable.
10. The interview is most valid in determining an applicant's intelligence, level of motivation, and interpersonal skills.[20]

The conclusions listed above are, in aggregate, rather devastating evidence against the interview. Nevertheless, interviews are widely used and, unfortunately, tend to be given considerable weight in the final selection decision.[21]

Given the fact that interviews are widely used and are influential in the selection decision, is there anything managers can do to make interviews more effective? While there is no sure-fire formula for making the interview a highly reliable and valid device, its value can be increased by: (1) structuring a fixed set of questions; (2) possessing detailed information about the job for which an applicant is interviewing; (3) minimizing any foreknowledge of the applicant's background, experience, interests, test scores, or other characteristics; (4) using a standardized evaluation form; (5) taking notes during the interview; and (6) avoiding short interviews that encourage premature decision making.[22]

Background Investigation   Background investigations are of two types: verifications of application data and reference checks. The first type has proven to be a valuable source of selection information, whereas the latter is essentially worthless. Let's briefly review each.

Several studies indicate that verifying "facts" given on the application form pays dividends. A significant percentage of job applicants—upwards of 15 percent—exaggerate or misrepresent dates of employment, job titles, past salaries, or reasons for leaving a prior position.[23] Confirmation of hard data on the application with prior employers is therefore a worthwhile endeavor.

The reference check is used by many organizations but is extremely difficult to justify. Whether they are work related or personal, references provide little valid information for the selection decision.[24] Employers are frequently reluctant to give candid evaluations of a former employee's job performance for fear of legal repercussions. In fact, a recent survey found that only 55 percent of human resource executives would "always" provide accurate references to a prospective employer. Seven percent said they would never give an accurate reference.[25] Personal likes and dislikes also heavily influence the type of recommendation given. Personal references are likely to provide biased information. Who among us doesn't have three or four friends who will speak in glowing terms about our integrity, work habits, positive attitudes, knowledge, and skills?

Physical Examination For jobs that require certain physical requirements, the physical examination has some validity. However, this includes a very small number of jobs today. In almost all cases, the physical examination is done for insurance purposes. Management wants to eliminate insurance claims for injuries or illnesses contracted prior to being hired.

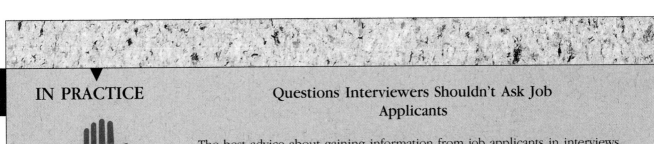

IN PRACTICE

Questions Interviewers Shouldn't Ask Job Applicants

The best advice about gaining information from job applicants in interviews is to ask only for information that is directly related to the applicant's ability to perform the job in question. As a rule, the following questions either are illegal or at least may suggest an intention to discriminate. To be on the safe side, these are questions interviewers should avoid:

Where were you born?

How old are you?

What church do you attend?

What religious holidays do you observe?

Are you married?

Do you have children?

If you're not married, are you currently involved with someone?

What social clubs do you belong to?

What are your hobbies?

If you're a veteran, what type of discharge do you have?

Great care must be taken to ensure that physical requirements are job related and do not discriminate. Some physical requirements may exclude certain handicapped persons, when, in fact, such requirements do not affect job performance. Similarly, height and weight requirements may discriminate against female applicants.

What Works Best and When

Many selection devices are of limited value to managers in making selection decisions. An understanding of strengths and weaknesses of each will help you to determine when each should be used. We offer the following advice to guide your choices.

Since the validity of selection devices varies for different types of jobs, you should use only those devices that predict for a given job. (See Table 12–6.) The application form offers limited information. Traditional written tests are reasonably effective devices for routine jobs. Work samples, however, are clearly preferable to written tests. For managerial selection, the assessment center is strongly recommended. If the interview has a place in the selection decision, it is most likely among less-routine jobs, particularly middle- and upper-level managerial positions. The interview is a reasonably good device for discerning intelligence and interpersonal skills.[26] These are more likely to be related to job performance in nonroutine activities, especially senior managerial positions. Verification of application data is valuable for all jobs. Conversely, reference checks are generally worthless for all jobs. Finally, physical examinations rarely provide any valid selection information.

ORIENTATION

orientation

The introduction of a new employee into his or her job and the organization.

Once a job candidate has been selected, he or she needs to be introduced to the job and organization. This introduction is called **orientation.**

The major objectives of orientation are to reduce the initial anxiety all new employees feel as they begin a new job; to familiarize new employees with the job, the work unit, and the organization as a whole; and to facilitate the outsider-insider transition. Job orientation expands on the information the employee obtained during the recruit-

TABLE 12–6   Quality of Selection Devices as Predictors

Selection Device	Position[a]			
	Senior Management	Middle and Lower Management	Complex Nonmanagerial	Routine Operative
Application form	2	2	2	2
Written tests	1	1	2	3
Work samples	—	—	4	4
Assessment center	5	5	—	—
Interviews	3	2	1	1
Verification of application data	3	3	3	3
Reference checks	1	1	1	1
Physical exam	1	1	1	2

[a]Validity is measured on a scale from 5 (highest) to 1 (lowest).

ETHICAL DILEMMAS IN MANAGEMENT

Is It Wrong to Write a "Creative" Résumé?

Almost all of us have written, or will write, a résumé to give to prospective employers. It summarizes our background, experiences, and accomplishments. Should it be 100 percent truthful? Let's take a few examples:

Person A leaves a job where his title was "Credit Clerk." When looking for a new job, he describes his previous title as "Credit Analyst." He thinks it sounds more impressive. Is this retitling of a former job wrong?

Person B made $1700 a month when she left her previous job. On her résumé, she says that she was making $1900. Is that wrong?

Person C, about eight years ago, took nine months off between jobs to travel around Europe. Afraid that people might consider her unstable or lacking in career motivation, she puts down on her résumé that she was engaged in "independent consulting activities" during the period. Was she wrong?

Person D is fifty years old with an impressive career record. He spent five years in college, thirty years ago, but never got a degree. He is being considered for a $150,000 a year vice presidency at another firm. He knows he has the ability and track record to do the job but won't get the interview if he admits to not having a college degree. He knows that the probability is very low that anyone would check his college records. Should he put on his résumé that he attained his degree?

Person E is writing brief descriptions of her accomplishments next to each job on her résumé. In truth, she has accomplished very little on her own. Should she say that, say nothing, or "shape" the descriptions to give the appearance that she has accomplished more than she has?

Falsehoods on résumés are widespread. A recent survey of 200 applicants found that 30 percent reported incorrect dates of employment.[27] Eleven percent misrepresented reasons for leaving a previous job to cover up the fact that they were fired. Some falsely claimed college degrees or totally fabricated work histories. In a larger study of 11,000 applicants, 488 failed to disclose criminal records; most of these were drug or alcohol offenses, but some were as serious as rape or attempted murder.

Is it wrong to write a "creative" résumé? What deviations from the truth, if any, would *you* make?

---

ment and selection stages. The new employee's specific duties and responsibilities are clarified, as well as how his or her performance will be evaluated. This is also the time to rectify any unrealistic expectations new employees might hold about the job. Work unit orientation familiarizes the employee with the goals of the work unit, makes clear how his or her job contributes to the unit's goals, and includes introduction to his or her co-workers. Organization orientation informs the new employee about the organization's objectives, history, philosophy, procedures, and rules. This should include relevant personnel policies and benefits such as work hours, pay procedures, over-

Every one of the employees at Walt Disney World in Florida—from vice presidents to janitors—attends a two-day training and orientation course. Its purpose is to initiate new employees into the Disney philosophy of teamwork and cooperation and convey the company's corporate culture. Sessions include a range of lectures and discussions and a three-hour tour of Disney's 28,000-acre grounds. Topics cover everything from appropriate grooming to techniques for greeting customers—called "guests"—to the history of the Disney organization.

time requirements, and fringe benefits. A tour of the organization's physical facilities is often part of the organization orientation.

Many organizations, particularly large ones, have formal orientation programs. Such a program might include a tour of the offices or plant, a film describing the history of the organization, and a short discussion with a representative of the personnel department, who describes the organization's benefit programs. Other organizations utilize an informal orientation program in which, for instance, the manager assigns the new employee to a senior member of the unit, who introduces the new employee to immediate co-workers and shows him or her the locations of the rest rooms, cafeteria, coffee machine, and the like.

Management has an obligation to make the integration of the new employee into the organization as smooth and as free of anxiety as possible. Successful orientation, whether formal or informal, results in an outsider-insider transition that makes the new member feel comfortable and fairly well adjusted, lowers the likelihood of poor work performance, and reduces the probability of a surprise resignation by the new employee only a week or two into the job.

EMPLOYEE TRAINING

On the whole, planes don't cause airline accidents, people do. Most collisions, crashes, and other mishaps—about 74 percent to be exact—result from errors by the pilot or air traffic controller or inadequate maintenance. Weather and structural failures cause only 15 percent of accidents.[28] We cite these statistics to illustrate the importance of training in the airline industry. These maintenance and human errors could be prevented or significantly reduced by better employee training.

As job demands change, employee skills have to be altered and updated. It has been estimated, for instance, that U.S. business firms alone spend an astounding $30

MANAGERS WHO MADE A DIFFERENCE

Photo courtesy of Susan DeNuccio.

Susan DeNuccio at Target Stores

Target employs more than 42,000 people in its 246 discount department stores. Most of these employees are part-timers, so some turnover is expected. But in 1986, turnover reached an intolerable 100 percent a year! Although Target administered pretests, screened applicants heavily, and checked references, it was unable to find people willing to make a commitment to the company. In addition, the pool of 18- to 24-year-old recruits, which made up the bulk of the applicant supply, was quickly evaporating. An innovative solution was needed. Susan DeNuccio, Target's vice president of stores and distribution personnel, came up with it. Her answer was a flexible staffing program.[29]

DeNuccio noticed that employees regularly complained that their work shifts were too short. Since they were trained to do only one task and such tasks required only a few hours a day to do, it would be difficult to lengthen their shifts. DeNuccio concluded that her people were being underutilized. After many months of planning and field testing, she unveiled her flex-team staffing concept.

No longer would employees be pigeonholed into one narrow job category. Now they would be trained to be part of a team. A member of the merchandise-flow team, for instance, might rebag merchandise, mark new items, unload trailers, stock shelves, or any one of eight other jobs in his or her team category. To gain even more flexibility, employees could also cross-train between teams. For example, employees in the merchandise-flow team could learn to do the jobs of the sales floor team and earn additional pay.

After being in place for three years, DeNuccio's flex-team staffing program has proven to be a winner. At some stores, the turnover rate has dropped by 40 percent.

billion a year on formal courses and training programs to build workers' skills.[30] Management, of course, is responsible for deciding when subordinates are in need of training and what form that training should take.

Skill Categories

We can dissect employee skills into three categories: technical, interpersonal, and problem solving. Most employee training activities seek to modify one or more of these skills.

Technical   Most training is directed at upgrading and improving an employee's technical skills. This applies as much to white-collar jobs as to blue-collar jobs. Jobs change as a result of new technologies and improved methods. Postal sorters have had to undergo technical training to learn to operate automatic sorting machines. Many auto repair personnel have had to undergo extensive training to fix and maintain recent models with front-wheel-drive trains, electronic ignitions, diesel engines, and other innovations. Not many clerical personnel during the past decade have been unaffected by the computer. Literally millions of such employees have had to be trained to operate and interface with a computer terminal.

Interpersonal Almost every employee belongs to a work unit. To some degree, work performance depends on the employee's ability to effectively interact with co-workers and the boss. Some employees have excellent interpersonal skills. Others require training to improve theirs. This includes learning how to be a better listener, how to communicate ideas more clearly, and how to reduce conflict.

One employee who had had a history of being difficult to work with found that a three-hour group session in which she and co-workers openly discussed how each perceived the others significantly changed the way she interacted with her peers. Her co-workers were unanimous in describing her as arrogant. They all interpreted her requests as sounding like orders. Unaware of this tendency, she began to make conscious efforts to change the tone and content of her requests and this had very positive results in her relationships with her colleagues.

Problem Solving Many employees find that they have to solve problems on their job. This is particularly true in jobs that are of the nonroutine variety. When employees' problem-solving skills are deficient, management might want to improve these skills through training. This would include activities to sharpen logic, reasoning, and skills at defining problems, assessing causation, developing alternatives, analyzing alternatives, and selecting solutions.

One of management's greatest challenges in the 1990s will be to upgrade the basic reading, writing, and arithmetic skills of workers to handle the more complicated jobs of the future. The degree of the problem can be seen in New York Telephone Company's recent experience. In one year, 57,000 applicants took its entry-level exam, a simple test that measures basic skills in math, reading, and reasoning. Only 2,100 of the applicants passed!

Training Methods

Most training takes place on the job. This can be attributed to the simplicity of such methods and their usually lower cost. However, on-the-job training can disrupt the workplace and result in an increase in errors while learning takes place. Also, some skill training is too complex to learn on the job. In such cases, it should take place outside the work setting.

On-the-Job Training Popular on-the-job training methods include job rotation and understudy assignments. Job rotation involves lateral transfers that enable employees to work at different jobs. Employees get to learn a wide variety of jobs and gain increased insight into the interdependency between jobs and a wider perspective on organizational activities. New employees frequently learn their jobs by understudying a seasoned veteran. In the trades, this is usually called an *apprenticeship.* In white-collar jobs, it is called a *coaching,* or *mentor,* relationship. In each, the understudy works under the observation of an experienced worker, who acts as a model whom the understudy attempts to emulate.

Both job rotation and understudy assignments apply to the learning of technical skills. Interpersonal and problem-solving skills are acquired more effectively by training that takes place off the job.

vestibule training
Training conducted away from the work floor in which employees learn on the same equipment they will be using.

Off-the-Job Training There are a number of off-the-job training methods that managers may want to make available to employees. The more popular are classroom lectures, films, and simulation exercises. *Classroom lectures* are well suited for conveying specific information. They can be used effectively for developing technical and problem-solving skills. *Films* can also be used to explicitly demonstrate technical skills that are not easily presented by other methods. Interpersonal and problem-solving skills may be best learned through *simulation exercises* such as case analyses, experiential exercises, role playing, and group interaction sessions. However, complex computer models, such as those used by airlines in the training of pilots, are another kind of simulation exercise, which in this case is used to teach technical skills. So, too, is **vestibule training,** in which employees learn their jobs on the same equipment they will be using, only the training is conducted away from the actual work floor. Many large department stores train cashiers how to operate their new computer cash registers in specially created vestibule labs that simulate the actual checkout environment. This way, mistakes result in learning experiences rather than irate customers.

PERFORMANCE APPRAISAL

performance appraisal
The evaluation of an individual's work performance in order to arrive at objective personnel decisions.

Performance appraisal is a process of evaluating individuals in order to arrive at objective personnel decisions. As illustrated in Table 12–7, organizations use performance appraisals to make a number of human resource decisions. Performance appraisals are used to decide who gets merit pay increases and other rewards. They provide feedback to employees on how the organization views their performance. Appraisals also identify training and development needs; they pinpoint employee skills and competencies that are currently inadequate but for which remedial programs can be developed. They provide input into human resource planning and guide promotion, transfer, and termination decisions. Finally, performance appraisals are occasionally used for personnel research—specifically, as a criterion against which to validate selection and development programs.

TABLE 12–7   Primary Uses for Performance Appraisals

Use	Percent[a]
Compensation	85.6
Performance feedback	65.1
Training	64.3
Promotion	45.3
Personnel planning	43.1
Retention/discharge	30.3
Research	17.2

[a]Based on responses from 600 organizations.

Source: "Performance Appraisal: Current Practices and Techniques," *Personnel,* May–June 1984, p. 57. © 1984 American Management Association, New York. By permission of the publisher. All rights reserved.

Performance Appraisal Methods

Obviously, performance appraisals are important. But how do you evaluate an employee's performance? That is, what are the specific techniques for appraisal? The following discussion reviews the major performance appraisal methods.[31]

written essay
A performance appraisal technique in which an evaluator writes out a description of an employee's strengths, weaknesses, past performance, and potential and then makes suggestions for improvement.

Written Essays   Probably the simplest method of appraisal is to write a narrative describing an employee's strengths, weaknesses, past performance, and potential and then to provide suggestions for improvement. The **written essay** requires no complex forms or extensive training to complete. However, a "good" or "bad" appraisal may be determined as much by the evaluator's writing skill as by the employee's actual level of performance.

critical incidents
A performance appraisal technique in which an evaluator lists key behaviors that separate effective from ineffective job performance.

Critical Incidents   The use of **critical incidents** focuses the evaluator's attention on those critical or key behaviors that separate effective from ineffective job performance. The appraiser writes down little anecdotes that describe what the employee did that was especially effective or ineffective. The key here is that only specific behaviors are cited, not vaguely defined personality traits. A list of critical incidents on a given employee provides a rich set of examples from which to point out to the employee his or her desirable and undesirable behaviors.

graphic rating scales
A performance appraisal technique in which an evaluator rates a set of performance factors on an incremental scale.

Graphic Rating Scales   One of the oldest and most popular methods of appraisal is **graphic rating scales.** This method lists a set of performance factors such as quantity and quality of work, job knowledge, cooperation, loyalty, attendance, honesty, and initiative. The evaluator then goes down the list and rates each on an incremental scale. The scales typically specify five points; a factor like job knowledge might be rated from 1 ("poorly informed about work duties") to 5 ("has complete mastery of all phases of the job").

    Why are graphic ratings scales so popular? Though they don't provide the depth of information that essays or critical incidents do, they are less time consuming to develop and administer. They also allow for quantitative analysis and comparison.

behaviorally anchored rating scales (BARS)
A performance appraisal technique in which an evaluator rates employees on specific job behaviors derived from performance dimensions.

Behaviorally Anchored Rating Scales   An approach that has received a great deal of attention in recent years involves **behaviorally anchored rating scales (BARS).**[32] These scales combine major elements from the critical incident and graphic rating scale approaches: The appraiser rates an employee according to items along a continuum, but the points are examples of actual behavior on a given job rather than general descriptions or traits.

TABLE 12–8   Examples of Behavioral Dimensions for Appraising Supervisors

1. Explains job requirements to new employees in a clear manner (e.g., talks slowly, shows them how to do it).
   Almost never   0   1   2   3   4   Almost always
2. Tells workers that if they have questions or problems to feel free to come and talk to him or her.
   Almost never   0   1   2   3   4   Almost always
3. Distributes overtime equally taking seniority into account.
   Almost never   0   1   2   3   4   Almost always

Source: Gary P. Latham and Kenneth N. Wexley, *Increasing Productivity Through Performance Appraisal* (Reading, Mass.: Addison-Wesley, 1981), p. 45. With permission.

Behaviorally anchored rating scales specify definite, observable, and measurable job behavior. Examples of job-related behavior and performance dimensions are generated by asking participants to give specific illustrations of effective and ineffective behavior on each performance dimension. These behavioral examples are then retranslated into appropriate performance dimensions. Key behaviors are retained. The final group of behavior incidents is then numerically scaled to a level of performance that each behavior is perceived to represent. The incidents that are retranslated and that have high rater agreement on performance effectiveness are retained for use as anchors on the performance dimension. This process produces behavioral descriptions such as "anticipates," "plans," "executes," "solves immediate problems," "carries out orders," and "handles emergency situations." Table 12–8 provides examples of behavioral dimensions for appraising a first-level supervisor.

multiperson comparison
A performance appraisal technique in which individuals are compared to one another.

group order ranking
A performance appraisal approach that groups employees into ordered classifications.

individual ranking
A performance appraisal approach that ranks employees in order from highest to lowest.

paired comparison
A performance appraisal approach in which each employee is compared to every other employee and rated as either the superior or weaker member of the pair.

Multiperson Comparisons   **Multiperson comparisons** compare one individual's performance to those of one or more others. It is a relative, not an absolute, measuring device. The three most popular uses of this method are group order ranking, individual ranking, and paired comparisons.

The **group order ranking** requires the evaluator to place employees into a particular classification such as "top one-fifth" or "second one-fifth." This method is often used in recommending a student for graduate school. Evaluators are asked to rank the student in the top 5 percent, the next 5 percent, the next 15 percent, and so forth. When this method is used to appraise employees, managers deal with all their subordinates. If a rater has twenty subordinates, only four can be in the top fifth, and, of course, four must be relegated to the bottom fifth.

The **individual ranking** approach requires the evaluator merely to list the employees in order from highest to lowest. Only one can be "best." In an appraisal of thirty subordinates, the difference between the first and second employee is assumed to be the same as that between the twenty-first and twenty-second. Even though some employees may be closely grouped, there can be no ties.

In the **paired comparison** approach, each employee is compared to every other employee in the comparison group and rated as either the superior or weaker member of the pair. After all paired comparisons are made, each employee is assigned a summary ranking based on the number of superior scores he or she achieved. While this approach ensures that each employee is compared against every other, it can become unwieldly when large numbers of employees are being assessed.

Multiperson comparisons can be combined with other methods to yield a blend of the best from both absolute and relative standards. For example, a college could use the graphic rating scale and the individual ranking methods to provide more accurate information about its students' performance. An absolute grade (A, B, C, D, or F) could be assigned and a student's relative rank in a class ascertained. A prospective employer or graduate school admissions committee could then look at two students who each got a "B" in financial accounting and draw considerably different conclusions about each when next to one grade it says "ranked fourth out of twenty-six," while the other says "ranked seventeenth out of thirty." Obviously, the latter instructor gives out many more high grades!

Providing Feedback in the Appraisal Review

Many managers are reluctant to give a formal performance appraisal review for each employee. Why? Probably the two main reasons are that (1) they lack complete confidence in the appraisal method used and (2) they fear a confrontation with the employee and dealing with his or her reaction if the results are not overwhelmingly positive. Nevertheless, managers should conduct such reviews because they are the primary means by which employees gain feedback on their performance.

An effective review—in which the employee perceives the appraisal as fair, the manager as sincere, and the climate as constructive—is likely to result in the employee leaving the interview in an upbeat mood, informed about the performance areas in which he or she needs to improve and determined to correct the deficiencies. Unfortunately, this is not the usual outcome of appraisal reviews.

The problem is that performance appraisal reviews have a built-in barrier. Statistically speaking, half of all employees must be below-average performers. But evidence tells us that the average employee's estimate of his or her own performance level generally falls around the seventy-fifth percentile.[33] In other words, employees tend to form inflated assessments of their own performances. The good news the manager does convey may be perceived as not good enough. In chapter 16, in our discussion of feedback skills, we'll provide suggestions for making the best of a tough situation.

CAREER DEVELOPMENT

The term *career* has a number of meanings. In popular usage, it can mean advancement ("his career is progressing nicely"), a profession ("she has chosen a career in medicine"), or a lifelong sequence of jobs ("his career has included fifteen jobs in six different organizations"). For our purposes, we define a **career** as the "sequence of positions occupied by a person during the course of a lifetime."[34] By this definition, it is apparent that we all have, or will have, careers. Moreover, the concept is as relevant to transient, unskilled laborers as to engineers or physicians.

Why should an organization be concerned with careers? More specifically, why should management spend time on career development? Focusing on careers forces management to adopt a long-term perspective on its human resources. Table 12–9 summarizes the primary positive outcomes that can accrue from effective career development efforts.

Career Stages

The most popular way of analyzing and discussing careers is to view them as a series of stages.[35] In this section, we'll develop a five-stage model that is generalizable to most people during their adult years, regardless of the type of work they do.

**TABLE 12–9   The Value of Effective Career
Development**

Ensures that needed talent will be available

Improves the organization's ability to attract and retain highly
   talented personnel

Ensures that minorities and women get opportunities for
   growth and development

Reduces employee frustration

Most individuals begin to form ideas about their careers during their elementary and secondary school years. Their careers begin to wind down as they reach retirement age. We can identify five career stages that most people will go through during these years: exploration, establishment, midcareer, late career, and decline. These stages are depicted in Figure 12–3.

Exploration   Individuals make critical choices about their careers even before they enter the work force on a paid basis. The influence of relatives, teachers, and friends, as well as television programs and films, begins to narrow alternatives very early in people's lives and lead them in certain directions.

The exploration period ends for most people when they are in their mid-20s as they make the transition from school to work. From an organizational standpoint, this stage has the least relevance, since it occurs prior to employment. It is relevant, however. The exploration period is a time when a person develops a number of expectations about his or her career, many of which are unrealistic. Such expectations may, of course, lie dormant for years and then pop up later to frustrate both employee and employer.

Establishment   The establishment period begins with the search for work and includes getting the first job, being accepted by one's peers, learning the job, and

FIGURE 12–3

Stages in Career Development

Source: D. T. Hall, *Careers in Organizations.* (Glenview, IL: Scott, Foresman and Company, 1976), p. 57. With permission of author.

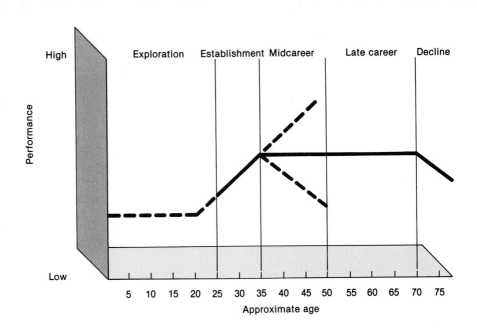

gaining the first tangible evidence of success or failure in the real world. This stage is characterized by the making of mistakes and learning from those mistakes.

Midcareer   Most people don't face their first severe career dilemmas until they reach the midcareer stage. This is a time when a person may continue to make improvements in performance, level off, or begin to deteriorate. An important fact about this stage is that the individual is no longer seen as a "learner." Mistakes carry greater penalties. Individuals who successfully make the transition to this stage receive greater responsibilities and rewards. For others, it may be a time of reassessment, job changes, adjustment of priorities, or pursuit of alternative life-styles (for example, divorce, going back to school, making a major geographical move).

Late Career   For people who continue to grow through the midcareer stage, the late career usually is a pleasant time when they can relax a bit and play the part of elder statesperson. Their value to the organization lies in their judgment, built up over many years and through varied experiences, and their ability to share their knowledge with others.

For those who have stagnated or deteriorated during the previous stage, the late career brings the reality that they will not have an everlasting impact or change the world as they had once thought. It is a time when individuals recognize that they have decreased work mobility and might be locked into their current job.

Decline   The final stage in a career is difficult for everyone but, ironically, is probably hardest on those who have had continued success in the earlier stages. After several decades of achievement and high levels of performance, the time has come for retirement. One is forced to step out of the limelight and give up a major component of one's identity. For modest performers or those who have seen their performance deteriorate over the years, it may be a pleasant time. The frustrations that have been associated with work will be left behind.

Applying the Career Stage Model   The concept of career stages can be of great benefit to managers. The following are some possible insights.

New employees often hold unrealistic expectations about their work. A **realistic job preview**—in which job candidates are exposed to negative as well as positive information about the job and organization—can reduce the number of surprise resignations.[36] Employees in the establishment stage need training and mentoring to ensure that they have the abilities to perform their jobs well and to provide them with guidance and encouragement.

Managers should keep an eye out for employees who, in midcareer, fail to understand that they are no longer apprentices and that mistakes now carry penalties. Disciplinary action is more likely to be necessary at this stage, when employees first start to show signs of insecurity. Younger employees may be threats. Midcareer failures will occur, but so too will frustration, boredom, and burnout. Managers should be prepared to help employees with their insecurities and consider ways of making jobs more interesting or varied.

Individuals in their late careers make excellent mentors. Managers should exploit this resource. Managers also need to recognize that people in the late career stage frequently undergo significant changes in personal priorities. They may become less interested in work or prefer more free time or a less stressful position instead of more money.

Finally, managers should recognize that the decline stage is difficult for every employee to confront. Periods of depression are not uncommon. Employees may also become more hostile and aggressive.

realistic job preview
Exposing job candidates to both negative and positive information about a job and an organization.

Keys to a Successful Management Career

If you choose a career in management, there are certain keys to success you should consider. The following discussion makes some suggestions based on proven tactics that managers have used to advance their careers.[37]

Do Good Work Good work performance is a necessary (but not sufficient) condition for managerial success. The marginal performer may be rewarded in the short term, but his or her weaknesses are bound to surface eventually and cut off career advancement. Good work performance is no guarantee of success, but without it the probability of a successful management career is low.

Present the Right Image Assuming that a set of managers are all performing well, the ability to align one's image with that sought by the organization is certain to be interpreted positively.

The manager should evaluate the organization's culture so that he or she understands what the organization wants and values from its managers. Then the manager is equipped to project the appropriate image—in terms of style of dress; associates one should and should not cultivate; whether one should project a risk-taking or risk-aversive stance; the organization's preferred leadership style; whether conflict should be avoided, tolerated, or encouraged; the importance attributed to getting along well with others; and so forth.

Learn the Power Structure The authority relationships defined by the organization's formal structure explain only part of the influence patterns within an organization. It's of equal or greater importance to know and understand the organization's power structure. The effective manager needs to learn "who is really in charge, who has the goods on whom, what are the major debts and dependencies—all things that are not reflected by the neat boxes in the table of organization. Once he has this knowledge he can navigate with more skill and ease."[38]

Gain Control of Organizational Resources The control of organizational resources that are scarce and important is a source of power. Knowledge and expertise are particularly effective resources to control. They make you more valuable to the organization and therefore more likely to gain security and advancement.

Stay Visible Since the evaluation of managerial effectiveness has a substantial subjective component, it is important that your boss and those in power in the organization be made aware of your contribution. If you are fortunate enough to have a job that brings your accomplishments to the attention of others, taking direct measures to increase your visibility might not be needed. But your job may require you to handle activities that are low in visibility, or your specific contribution may be indistinguishable because you are part of a group endeavor. In such cases—without creating the image of being a braggart—you will want to call attention to yourself by giving progress reports to your boss and others, being seen at social functions, being active in your professional associations, developing powerful allies who speak positively about you, and engaging in other similar tactics.

Stay Mobile Managers are likely to move upward more rapidly if they indicate a willingness to move to different geographical locations and across functional lines within the organization. Career advancement may also be facilitated by a willingness to change organizations. In slow-growth, stagnant, or declining organizations, mobility should be of even greater importance to the ambitious manager.

The appearance of maintaining interorganizational mobility, when coupled with control of organizational resources, can be particularly effective. If senior management needs what you have and is fearful that you might leave, it is not likely to ignore your needs. One fast-rising manager was very competent, possessed some unique skills, but also took great strides to keep himself visible in his industry. He made a habit of regularly mentioning to those in the powerful inner circle of his firm that he received a steady stream of job offers from competitors (which was true) but that as long as he continued to receive increasingly responsible positions and large salary increases, he had no intention of leaving his firm. This strategy has continued to pay dividends for this manager. He has received three promotions in five years and increased his salary fourfold.

mentor
A person who sponsors or supports another employee who is lower in the organization.

Find a Mentor   A **mentor** is an individual, typically someone higher up in the organization, who takes on a protégé as an ally. A mentor is someone from whom you can learn and who can encourage and help you. The evidence indicates that acquiring a sponsor who is part of the organization's power core is essential for managers who aspire to make it to the top.[39]

Where do employees get a mentor? Some organizations have formal mentoring programs. Young managers for whom the organization has high expectations are assigned to a senior manager who plays a mentoring role. More typically, you are informally selected to become a protégé by your boss or someone in the organization with whom you share similar interests. If your mentor is someone other than your boss, be sure that you do nothing through your mentor-protégé relationship that threatens your boss or suggests disloyalty on your part.

Support Your Boss   Your immediate future is in the hands of your current boss. He or she evaluates your performance, and few young managers are powerful enough to challenge their boss and survive. You should make the effort to help your boss succeed, be supportive if your boss is under siege, and find out what criteria he or she will be using to assess your effectiveness. Don't undermine your boss. Don't speak negatively of your boss to others. If your boss is competent, visible, and in possession of a power base, he or she is likely to be on the way up in the organization. By being perceived as supportive, you might find yourself pulled along too. At worst, you will have established an ally higher up in the organization. If your boss's performance is poor and his or her power is low, you should use your mentor (if you have one) to arrange a transfer. It's hard to have your competence recognized or your positive performance evaluations taken seriously if your boss is perceived as incompetent.

LABOR-MANAGEMENT RELATIONS

labor union
An organization that represents workers and seeks to protect their interests through collective bargaining.

labor-management relations
The formal interactions between unions and an organization's management.

As was mentioned at the beginning of this chapter, approximately 16 percent of the labor force belongs to a **labor union.** These unions represent workers and seek to protect and promote their members' interests through collective bargaining. (See Table 12–10.) In this section, we want to briefly discuss **labor-management relations**—that is, the formal interactions between these unions and the organization's management.

Why Good Labor-Management Relations Are Important

For many managers in unionized organizations, the management of human resources is largely composed of following procedures and policies laid out in the labor con-

MANAGING FROM A GLOBAL PERSPECTIVE

Selecting Managers for Global Assignments

Most global organizations have made significant strides since the 1970s, when it was widely believed that "working abroad is working abroad."[40] Transferring managers into new and different national cultures, without careful thought and proper selection, is setting those managers up to fail.

Most research on the transfer of managers between diverse countries—particularly the moving of U.S. executives overseas—indicates a fairly high failure rate. Of particular interest is the finding that U.S. executives seem to fail at a rate that is considerably higher than those of European and Japanese managers transferred to new countries.

Why don't more managers succeed when they are placed in foreign countries? One possible reason is that most organizations still select transfer candidates on the basis of technical competence alone, ignoring other predictors of success such as language skills, flexibility, and family adaptability.[41]

A contingency approach to selecting managers for foreign assignments in subsidiaries has been proposed, based on the type of information and control required.[42] When jobs are largely technical, information is objective, and control is bureaucratic, organizations will probably do best by selecting technically competent outsiders for relatively short tours to foreign subsidiaries. However, for longer-term assignments in posts where social information and an understanding of organizational norms are more important, long-time insiders steeped in the organization's culture should be more effective both working in the subsidiary and communicating what they learn back to headquarters.

TABLE 12–10   Why Do Employees Join Unions?

1. *Unions influence the wage and effort outcome.* Unions bargain for their members over wages, hours, and working conditions. The result of this bargaining determines the amount of pay, the hours of employment, the amount of work required during a given period, and the conditions of employment.

2. *Unions establish a security system with employers.* Unions have a security agreement with employers that, in effect, defines the union's power. It can control, for example, whom the employer may hire and whether employees must join the union. It may also restrict the employer from contracting out work to other organizations.

3. *Unions influence the administration of rules.* Unions provide workers with an opportunity to participate in determining the conditions under which they work; unions also have specific grievance procedures by which they can protest conditions they believe to be unfair.

4. *Unions have political power in the state and over the economy.* Unions have not been reluctant to exert political muscle to gain through legislation what they have been unable to win at the bargaining table. Unions use their lobbying efforts to support legislation that is in labor's interests.

A good rapport with a union is likely to foster a climate of cooperation before and during negotiations. Negotiations are more likely to result in favorable outcomes for management. Changes can be agreed upon that will improve the organization's productivity, and work rules can be negotiated that don't place unreasonable constraints on management's decision-making options. Perhaps the most obvious benefit of good labor-management relations is a reduced threat of costly strikes and work stoppages.

tract. Decisions about where recruitment is done, how employees are selected, who is trained, how compensation is determined, and disciplinary procedures are no longer unilateral prerogatives of management for jobs within the union's province. Such decisions are substantially made at the time the labor contract is negotiated. The development of good labor-management relations produces a number of positive outcomes for management as described with the accompanying photo.[43]

The Collective Bargaining Process

collective bargaining
A process for negotiating a union contract and for administrating the contract after it has been negotiated.

The negotiation, administration, and interpretation of a labor contract are achieved through **collective bargaining.** The following discussion summarizes how the process typically flows in the private sector.

Organizing and Certification   Efforts to organize a group of employees may begin when employee representatives ask union officials to visit the employee's organization and solicit members or when the union itself initiates a membership drive. Either way, the law requires that a union must secure signed authorization cards from at least 30 percent of the employees that it desires to represent. If the 30 percent goal is achieved, either the union or management will file a petition with a federal agency—the National Labor Relations Board (NLRB)—requesting a representation election.

When the NLRB receives the required number of authorization cards, it evaluates them, verifies that legal requirements have been satisfied, and then clarifies the appropriate bargaining unit—that is, identifies which employees the union will represent if it wins the election.

A secret ballot election is usually called within twenty-five days of receiving the authorization cards. If the union gets a majority in this election, the NLRB certifies the union and recognizes it as the exclusive bargaining representative for all employees within the specified bargaining unit. Should the union fail, another election cannot be held for one year.

Occasionally, employees become dissatisfied with a certified union. In such instances, employees may request a decertification election by the NLRB. If a majority of the members vote for decertification, the union is out.

Preparation for Negotiation   Once a union has been certified, management will begin preparing for negotiations. It will gather information on the economy, copies of recently negotiated contracts between other unions and employers, cost-of-living data, labor market statistics, and similar environmental concerns. It will also gather internal information on grievance and accident records, employee performance reports, and overtime figures.

This information will tell management where it is, what similar organizations are doing, and what it can anticipate from the economy in the near term. Management then uses these data to determine what it can expect to achieve in the negotiation. What can it expect the union to ask for? What is management prepared to acquiesce on?

Negotiation   Negotiation customarily begins when the union delivers a list of demands to management. These are typically ambitious in order to create room for trading in the later stages of negotiation. Not surprisingly, management's initial response is typically to counter by offering little more than the terms of the previous contract. It has not even been unusual, in recent years, for management to begin by proposing a reduction in wages and benefits and demanding that the union take a lesser role in the organization's decision-making process.

These introductory proposals usually initiate a period of long and intense bargaining. Compromises are made, and after an oral agreement is achieved, it is converted into a written contract. Finally, negotiation concludes with the union's representatives submitting the contract to its members for ratification.

Contract Administration   Once a contract is agreed upon and ratified, it must be administered. The way in which it will be administered is included in the contract itself.

Probably the most important element of contract administration has to do with the spelling out of a procedure for handling contractual disputes. Almost all collective bargaining agreements contain formal procedures for resolving grievances over the interpretation and application of the contract.

CURRENT ISSUES IN HUMAN RESOURCE MANAGEMENT

We conclude by discussing several contemporary issues facing today's managers. These include developing female and minority managers, dual-career couples, sexual harassment, and compensation based on comparable worth.

Developing Female and Minority Managers

While the majority of today's managers are white males, the changing characteristics of the work force suggest that tomorrow's new managers are increasingly likely to be women and members of minorities.

Between the years 1986 and 2000, the work force growth rate for white men is projected to be 8.5 percent. When you compare that to the rates for Asian-Americans (11.4 percent), African-Americans (17.4 percent), Hispanic-Americans (28.7 percent), and white women (34.8 percent), you quickly recognize that women and minorities are rapidly expanding their presence in organizations.[44] Naturally, many of these women and members of minorities aspire to management positions.

Unfortunately, women and members of minorities face a number of obstacles in their efforts to advance into upper management.[45] White male bosses, for instance, tend to promote people with whom they are comfortable—people like themselves. This works against women and minorities, as does the lack of mentors. Older white male executives, who occupy most of the seats in the executive suite and the ones most likely to do mentoring, often find it hard to relate to members of minorities and are afraid of the sexual innuendoes that might accompany mentoring females.[46] To these problems we can add exclusion from clubs and other social settings, stereotyping, harassment, and erroneous assumptions about assignments. In aggregate, these create real obstacles for women and minorities aspiring to senior management jobs.

However, not everything is bleak for aspiring managers who are not white males. For instance, while fewer than 16 percent of all management and administrative positions were filled by women in the early 1970s, today that number is over 35 percent.[47] Although women are still largely concentrated in supervisory and lower-level management positions, many are rapidly filling the ranks of middle management. The real challenge today is to increase women's access to upper executive positions.

Organizations need to ensure that capable women and members of minorities are given opportunities to move into increasingly responsible management positions. Organizations can expedite this by changing organizational policies and practices, and modifying the organization's education, training, and career development programs.

Organizational policies and practices should reflect the needs of a diversified management cadre. For instance, women are more likely to be attracted to, and stay with, an organization that provides paid maternity leaves, flexible work hours, and on-site child care facilities.

The organization's education, training, and career development programs need to be modified to reflect problems that are unique to female and minority managers. All employees, for instance, can benefit from consciousness-raising workshops on sexism and racism in the workplace. Special mentoring programs should be created to deal with the reality that lower-level female and minority managers have few role models with whom to identify.

Dual-Career Couples

dual-career couples
Couples in which both partners have a professional, managerial, or administrative occupation.

The number of **dual-career couples**—couples in which both partners have a professional, managerial, or administrative occupation[48]—has expanded dramatically in the United States in recent years as married women have gained professional credentials and sought jobs outside the home. An organization's human resource management policies need to reflect this trend and the special problems it creates for couples. Special attention needs to be specifically given to the organization's policies regarding nepotism, transfers, and conflicts of interest.[49]

The issue of nepotism concerns both spouses working for the same employer. Recent evidence indicates that only about 10 percent of organizations have a strict no-relatives-allowed policy. However, most organizations prohibit spouses from working in the same department or one directly supervising the other.[50]

Dual-career couples have become a major factor affecting organizations' relocation policies. Promotions represent a good illustration. When managers were predominantly male and their wives either were not employed or held low-skilled jobs, organizations could design development programs entailing extensive transfers and correctly assume that their managers would readily accept such moves. However, dual-career couples have shown far greater reluctance to pull up roots for one member's promotion opportunity. For dual-career couples, promotion of one member that requires a geographical move becomes a joint decision that must consider the financial implications for both members and job opportunities for the other member in the new location. As a result, organizations will have to expand formal spouse relocation policies to include assuming a portion of the spouse's job search costs, giving the spouse priority on jobs at the new location, and career counseling that includes assessment, planning, and placement assistance.[51]

Another challenge that dual-career couples create for organizations is conflict of interest created by a partner who holds a key position in a competing organization. Such situations can allow confidential information to easily find its way into the competitor's hands. Most organizations will probably continue to trust their employees to use good judgment in handling potential conflicts of interest. However, we can expect to see an increasing number of organizations requiring employees to sign loyalty statements or even developing policies that prohibit spouses from working for or holding key positions with major competitors.[52]

Sexual Harassment

sexual harassment
Behavior marked by sexually suggestive remarks, unwanted touching and sexual advances, requests for sexual favors, or other verbal or physical conduct of a sexual nature.

The large increase in the number of women entering the work force has created a new problem for managers: dealing with sexual harassment.[53] While the definition of the term continues to be modified in the courts, **sexual harassment** generally encompasses sexually suggestive remarks, unwanted touching and sexual advances, requests for sexual favors, and other verbal and physical conduct of a sexual nature. It is now considered illegal, a violation of the federal civil rights law.

From management's standpoint, sexual harassment is a growing concern because it intimidates employees, interferes with job performance, and exposes the organization to liability. On this last point, the courts have ruled that if the employee who is guilty of sexual harassment is a supervisor or agent for an organization, then the organization is liable for sexual harassment, regardless of whether the act was authorized or forbidden by the organization or whether the organization knew of the act.

To avoid liability, management must establish a clear and strong policy against sexual harassment. That policy should then be reinforced by regular discussion sessions in which managers are reminded of the rule and carefully instructed that even the slightest sexual overture to another employee will not be tolerated.

Comparable Worth

comparable worth
The doctrine that jobs equal in value to an organization should be equally compensated.

We have made considerable progress in the United States during the past two decades in tearing down the barriers that have prevented women from entering certain occupations. However, women still earn only 70 cents for each dollar that men earn. One method of reducing this gap, strongly advocated by women's groups and now receiving increased support from the courts and many large corporations, is to base employee pay on comparable jobs.[54]

Comparable worth is a doctrine that holds that jobs equal in value to the organization should be equally compensated, whether or not the work content of those jobs is similar.[55] That is, if the jobs of secretary and draftsman (historically viewed as female and male jobs, respectively) require similar skills and make comparable demands on employees, they should be paid the same, regardless of external market factors.

The idea of comparable worth is controversial. It assumes that totally dissimilar jobs can be accurately compared and that pay rates based on supply and demand factors in the job market are frequently inequitable and discriminatory. But managers cannot ignore its implications. They must establish fair and equitable job evaluation systems.[56]

job evaluation
A procedure that ranks jobs according to criteria such as knowledge and skills, mental demands, responsibility, and working conditions.

Job evaluation is a procedure that ranks all the jobs in an organization according to criteria such as knowledge and skills, mental demands, responsibility, and working conditions. The factors are given points, and jobs are ranked by total points. Points then determine the range of a job's base pay. Well-designed job evaluation systems should lead to fair pay for all employees and protect the organization from charges of pay inequity.

SUMMARY

This summary is organized by the chapter-opening learning objectives found on page 349.

1. The human resource management process encompasses human resource planning, recruitment or decruitment, selection, orientation, training, performance appraisal, career development, and labor-management relations.

2. Key laws and regulations that influence human resource decisions include the Civil Rights Act, the Equal Pay Act, the Age Discrimination in Employment Act, the Privacy Act, and the Mandatory Retirement Act.

3. A job description is a written statement of what a jobholder does, how it is done, and why it's done. A job specification states the minimum acceptable qualifications that an incumbent must possess to perform a given job successfully.

4. Recruitment seeks to develop a pool of potential job candidates. Typical sources include an internal search, advertisements, employee referrals, employment agencies, school placement centers, and temporary help services. Decruitment reduces the labor supply within an organization through options such as firing, layoffs, attrition, transfers, reduced workweeks, and early retirements.

5. The quality of a selection device is determined by its validity and reliability. If a device is not valid, then no proven relationship exists between it and relevant job criteria. If a selection device isn't reliable, then it cannot be assumed to be a consistent measure.

6. Selection devices must match the job in question. Work samples work best with low-level jobs. Assessment centers work best for managerial positions. The validity of the interview as a selection device increases at progressively higher levels of management.

7. Employee training can be on-the-job or off-the-job. Popular on-the-job methods include job rotation, understudying, and apprenticeships. The more popular off-the-job methods are classroom lectures, films, and simulation exercises.

8. Performance appraisal methods include written essays, critical incidents, graphic rating scales, behaviorally anchored rating scales, and multiperson comparisons.

9. The five career stages are exploration, establishment, midcareer, late career, and decline.

10. The collective bargaining process consists of organizing and certification, preparation for negotiation, and contract administration.

11. Human resource management policies need to be modified to attract and keep members of dual-career couples. Nepotism policies need to be reviewed because partners may both be working for the same organization. Transfers and promotions become more complex as two decision makers are involved. Potential conflicts of interest are created, and special policies are sometimes necessary, when a spouse holds a key position in a competing organization.

12. Sexual harassment is a growing concern for management because it intimidates employees, interferes with job performance, and exposes the organization to liability.

REVIEW QUESTIONS

1. Define *human resource planning*.
2. What is the relationship between selection, recruitment, and job analysis?

3. Contrast reject errors and accept errors. Which one is most likely to open an employer to charges of discrimination? Why?

4. What selection devices are most effective in filling top management positions? Low-level and routine positions?

5. What are the major problems of the interview as a selection device?

6. How are selection and training related?

7. What is *validity?* Why is it important in selection?

8. What is the goal of orientation?

9. Review the five career stages and identify problems that managers should be aware of in each.

10. What can management do to facilitate the upward movement of females and members of minorities into senior-level management positions?

DISCUSSION QUESTIONS

1. "The right of an employee to keep a job is as protected by society as one's right to hold property." Do you agree or disagree with this statement? Discuss.

2. "Female managers today still face barriers that male managers do not." Do you agree or disagree with this statement? Discuss.

3. When employees want to slow down their work effort, they often "work to rule," which is a euphemism for doing only what one's job description says. What does this imply about job descriptions?

4. "Career development is a waste of money for a company. Employees have their expectations raised and then, frustrated, they quit." Do you agree or disagree? Discuss.

5. Do you think there are moral limits on how far a prospective employer should delve into an applicant's life by means of interviews and tests?

SELF-ASSESSMENT EXERCISE

What's the Right Career for You?

Complete the following questionnaire by circling the answer that best describes your feelings about each statement. For each item, circle your response according to the following:

SA = Strongly agree
 A = Agree
 D = Disagree
SD = Strongly disagree

1. I would leave my company rather than be promoted out of my area of expertise.   SA A D SD

2. Becoming highly specialized and highly competent in some specific functional or technical area is important to me.   SA A D SD

3. A career that is free from organization restriction is important to me.   SA A D SD

4. I have always sought a career in which I could be of service to others.   SA A D SD

5. A career that provides a maximum variety of types of assignments and work projects is important to me.   SA A D SD

6. To rise to a position in general management is important to me.   SA A D SD

7. I like to be identified with a particular organization and the prestige that accompanies that organization.   SA A D SD

8. Remaining in my present geographical location rather than moving because of a promotion is important to me.   SA A D SD

9. The use of my skills in building a new business enterprise is important to me.   SA A D SD

10. I would like to reach a level of responsibility in an organization where my decisions really make a difference.   SA A D SD

11. I see myself more as a generalist as opposed to being committed to one specific area of expertise.   SA A D SD

12. An endless variety of challenges in my career is important to me.   SA A D SD

13. Being identified with a powerful or prestigious employer is important to me.   SA A D SD

14. The excitement of participating in many areas of work has been the underlying motivation behind my career.   SA A D SD

15. The process of supervising, influencing, leading, and controlling people at all levels is important to me.   SA A D SD

16. I am willing to sacrifice some of my autonomy to stabilize my total life situation.   SA A D SD

17. An organization that will provide security through guaranteed work, benefits, a good retirement, and so forth, is important to me.   SA   A   D   SD

18. During my career I will be mainly concerned with my own sense of freedom and autonomy.   SA   A   D   SD

19. I will be motivated throughout my career by the number of products that I have been directly involved in creating.   SA   A   D   SD

20. I want others to identify me by my organization and job.   SA   A   D   SD

21. Being able to use my skills and talents in the service of an important cause is important to me.   SA   A   D   SD

22. To be recognized by my title and status is important to me.   SA   A   D   SD

23. A career that permits a maximum of freedom and autonomy to choose my own work, hours, and so forth, is important to me.   SA   A   D   SD

24. A career that gives me a great deal of flexibility is important to me.   SA   A   D   SD

25. To be in a position in general management is important to me.   SA   A   D   SD

26. It is important for me to be identified by my occupation.   SA   A   D   SD

27. I will accept a management position only if it is in my area of expertise.   SA   A   D   SD

28. It is important for me to remain in my present geographical location rather than move because of a promotion or new job assignment.   SA   A   D   SD

29. I would like to accumulate a personal fortune to prove to myself and others that I am competent.   SA   A   D   SD

30. I want to achieve a position that gives me the opportunity to combine analytical competence with supervision of people.   SA   A   D   SD

31. I have been motivated throughout my career by using my talents in a variety of different areas of work.   SA   A   D   SD

32. An endless variety of challenges is what I really want from my career.   SA   A   D   SD

33. An organization that will give me long-run stability is important to me.   SA   A   D   SD

34. To be able to create or build something that is entirely my own product or idea is important to me.   SA   A   D   SD

35. Remaining in my specialized area, as opposed to being promoted out of my area of expertise, is important to me.   SA   A   D   SD

36. I do not want to be constrained by either an organization or the business world.   SA   A   D   SD

37. Seeing others change because of my efforts is important to me.   SA   A   D   SD

38. My main concern in life is to be competent in my area of expertise.   SA   A   D   SD

39. The chance to pursue my own life-style and not be constrained by the rules of an organization is important to me.   SA   A   D   SD

40. I find most organizations to be restrictive and intrusive.   SA   A   D   SD
41. Remaining in my area of expertise, rather than being promoted into general management, is important to me.   SA   A   D   SD
42. I want a career that allows me to meet my basic needs through helping others.   SA   A   D   SD
43. The use of my interpersonal and helping skills in the service of others is important to me.   SA   A   D   SD
44. I like to see others change because of my efforts.   SA   A   D   SD

Turn to page 672 for scoring direction and key.

Source: Adapted from Thomas J. Delong, "Reexamining the Career Anchor Model," *Personnel,* May–June 1982, pp. 56–57. © 1982 AMACOM, a division of American Management Associations, New York. All rights reserved.

CASE APPLICATION 12A

Von's Supermarkets

Susan Chapman is southern regional manager for Von's Supermarkets, a chain in the western United States. Five district supervisors report to her. Each of the district supervisors, in turn, oversees the activities of eight to twelve stores.

One spring morning, as Susan was going over her morning reports, her secretary buzzed her on the intercom. "Ms. Chapman, did you see the business section in this morning's paper?" "No, why?" Susan responded. "Well, it says here that Chuck Bailey has accepted the position of Arizona regional manager for Safeway." Leaping to her feet, Susan went to see the article for herself.

Susan's concern was not unwarranted. Chuck Bailey was one of her district supervisors. He had been in his current job with Von's for four years. Von's had hired him away from Alpha Beta Markets, where he had been a store manager. Susan felt hurt that she had to learn of Chuck's departure through the newspaper, but she knew she'd get over that fast. What was more relevant was that Chuck was a very effective supervisor—his district consistently outperformed her other four. Where was she going to find a competent replacement?

Several days passed. She talked with Chuck and sincerely wished him well in his new job. She also discussed with him the problem of finding a replacement. Her final decision was to transfer one of the supervisors from a smaller district in her region into Chuck's district and to begin an immediate search for someone to fill the smaller district's supervisory vacancy.

Susan went to her files and pulled out the job description for a district supervisor's position (no job specification was available). The job's duties included ensuring the maintenance of corporate standards of cleanliness, service, and product quality; supervising store managers and evaluating their performance; preparing monthly, quarterly, and annual revenue and expense forecasts for the district; making cost-savings suggestions to head office and/or store managers; coordinating buying; negotiating cooperative advertising programs with suppliers; and participating in union negotiations.

Questions

1. What recruitment sources would you recommend that Susan use? Why?
2. Define the factors that should predict success in this job.
3. Which selection devices would you recommend that Susan use to screen applicants? Why?
4. In terms of career development, what might Susan have done to ensure Chuck's continued employment with Von's?

CASE APPLICATION 12B

Danville Bank & Trust

Jane Broderick joined Danville Bank & Trust in 1986 as an assistant operations manager at the Springfield, Missouri branch office. During her first three and a half years, her operations manager and boss was Debbie Clark. Jane and Debbie had a good working relationship, and Debbie gave Jane excellent performance evaluations at each six-month review period.

About four months ago, Debbie was promoted to a larger branch of the bank. Gregg McCracken was transferred to the Springfield office to replace Debbie. Things haven't been the same for Jane since Gregg's arrival.

Although Jane is single, she has had a steady boyfriend for five years. Gregg, by contrast, was recently divorced and—at least in Jane's mind—behaves toward her in ways that she considers inappropriate and unprofessional. Four specific concerns particularly upset Jane.

During his second week as Jane's new boss, Gregg asked Jane out for dinner. She politely declined. Since that time, he has asked her out on at least four other occasions. She has declined each invitation as politely as possible, but his persistence makes her uncomfortable. She is concerned that Gregg might retaliate against her by giving her lower performance evaluations, though he has said nothing that might suggest such a response.

Gregg is fond of telling off-color jokes in her presence. He seems to find Jane's embarrassment amusing.

Last week, Gregg threw his arm around Jane while discussing a problem about one of the bank's clients. She quickly removed his hand from her shoulder. Obviously put off, Gregg exclaimed, "What's your problem, woman? I put my arm around all my associates—male as well as female. You take every friendly gesture I make as a come-on." After thinking about it, Jane had to admit that Gregg did put his arm around a number of people in the office when he talked with them—male and female alike.

Yesterday, when Jane came into the office, Gregg's first comment was, "I love that leather mini-skirt you're wearing. You have great legs. You should wear mini-skirts more often."

Questions

1. Which, if any, of Jane's concerns do you think represent sexual harassment? Why?

2. If you were Jane, how would you handle these incidents?

Organization Charts

PURPOSE

To analyze different organization charts.

REQUIRED KNOWLEDGE

1. Components in an organization structure.
2. Organization design options.

TIME REQUIRED

Approximately 30 minutes.

INSTRUCTIONS

1. Study the three organization charts in Figures IV-A, IV-B, and IV-C.
2. Determine what type of organization might use each and why.
3. Analyze the method of organizing for each.
4. Predict the management problems you think might surface from each.

Based on Judith R. Gordon, *A Diagnostic Approach to Organizational Behavior,* 2nd ed. (Boston: Allyn & Bacon, Inc., 1987), pp. 571–72.

FIGURE IV-A

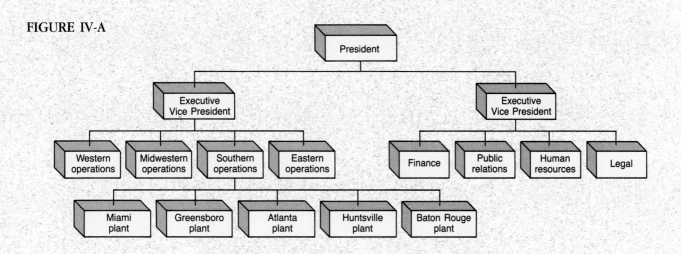

FIGURE IV-B

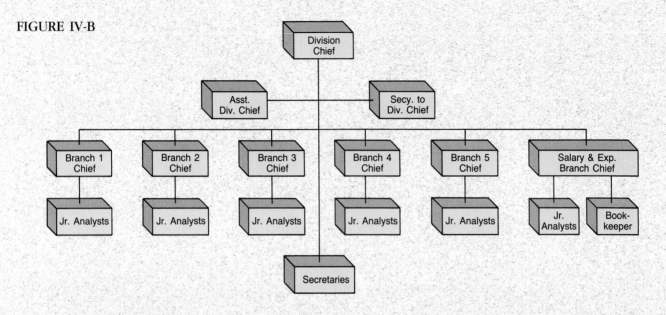

FIGURE IV-C

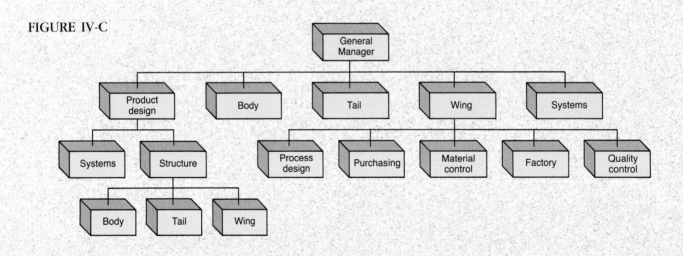

The Larger Company (A)

The phone rang and highly indignant words blared, "Masters, what do you mean by submitting a report to all the executives without first talking it over with the division manager!"

Masters replied, "My men made every effort to see him. They never got past his secretary. He instructed her to have them talk to the works manager."

"I don't believe a word of it. Vining is up in arms. He says the report is vindictive. What are you trying to do—embarrass the division manager? I don't believe your men ever tried to see Vining and I question the veracity of their statements!" The phone on the other end was hung up with a bang.

Masters said to himself, "Gunn must be hot under the collar or he wouldn't have called me when I was away from my own office visiting another plant."

The next day Masters' office received Gunn's letter confirming this telephone conversation and demanding an explanation. A week later Masters received a letter from Gunn's superior, a Mr. Jordan, stating: "I have read the aforementioned report and discussed it with Mr. Gunn. He has advised me that the report is essentially untrue, inaccurate, and overstated. I am not satisfied to have such wide differences of opinion and have scheduled a meeting to be held in my office on————. I would appreciate it if you would be present."

In light of the phone call and the two letters, Mr. Masters decided to reassess all events leading to this climax.

The cast of characters is shown in Figure IV-1. The Larger Company had an elaborate organizational structure as a result of its scale of operations. At the headquarters office of the corporation, the president had a group of staff vice presidents in charge of functions. Mr. Masters was a staff department head reporting to the vice president of manufacturing. The headquarters staff departments assisted in policy formulation and made

staff studies for the operating organization when requested. Members of such departments were encouraged to offer ideas for the good of the company. Their proposals were considered by a management committee consisting of the vice presidents at the headquarters level and the operating vice presidents in charge of product groups. Mr. Jordan of this case was the operating vice president, Product Group B.

Under the product groups there were general managers of product classes. They supervised the division managers, who were in charge of the sales and manufacturing operations of one or more plants. Mr. Gunn was general manager of Product Class Y. One of the four division managers under him was Mr. Vining of Division II.

Two years before this incident occurred, Mr. Masters' staff department proposed to the management committee, with the approval of the vice president of manufacturing, that representatives of Mr. Masters' office join with representatives of the vice president of accounting, to make studies in each plant of the procedures for and actual practices regarding expense control. The suggestion was approved and endorsed enthusiastically by the general managers. They sent a letter through channels to each division manager advising that periodically a team of two people would visit each plant to make a comprehensive analysis of expense-control practices and systems.

After a visit these field representatives of headquarters were to prepare a report giving findings and recommendations. They were to discuss it with the appropriate division manager and his or her staff. Thus they would be able to incorporate any specific plans of action set in motion by division managers. Next, a report was to be submitted to Mr. Masters. Both his department and the accounting office were to make comments. The final document was then to be submit-

FIGURE IV–1
The Larger Company Organization Chart

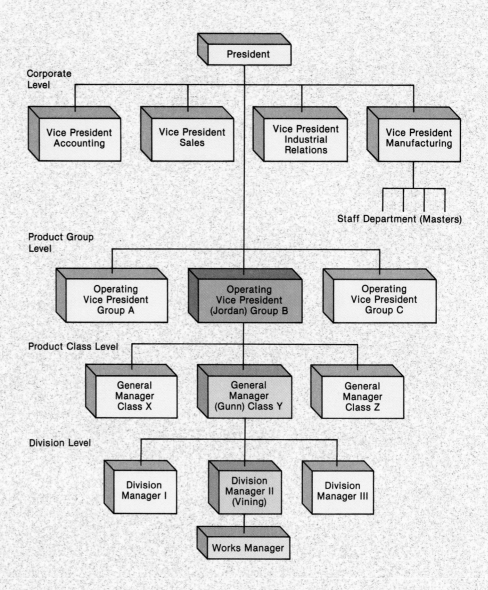

ted to the vice president of accounting, the vice president of manufacturing, the operating vice president of the product group, the general manager of the product class, and the division manager concerned.

This general procedure had worked smoothly within the company until General Manager Gunn of Product Class Y exploded. In the first plant studied, the two team members spent approximately four weeks examining documents, interviewing line management, interrogating industrial engineers, observing operations, and so on. The employees of this plant were very cooperative. Some of the facts revealed by them could have been embarrassing to the division manager. The team was able to make specific recommendations for improvement to the division manager. His reception of the report was good. According to him, the study had given an opportunity to review his situation and get his house in order. He intended to implement the recommenda-

tions unless they were changed in the review process at the higher level. Sixteen other plants were visited with reasonably good acceptance of the work of the team.

In his review of the Division II situation, Mr. Masters found that the team had observed all the required organization routines. Mr. Sawyer, representing Mr. Masters, had a master's degree in industrial engineering and had twelve years with the company. Mr. Peters, from the accounting office, had served that department for thirty years. Both had shown ability to gain confidences and to use them discreetly. They were considered straightforward, conscientious, and unobtrusive in their work. In Division II the team obtained from plant personnel considerable information that pointed up a number of practices and procedures requiring improvement. In the opinion of the team members, the operating organization at the lower levels sincerely wanted to make these changes. The team thought that there was some resistance at some level within the division to these suggestions and, in fact, to any from headquarters.

While the study was in process, Mr. Sawyer advised Mr. Masters about the possible impact of the information that was being collected. Mr. Masters emphasized the necessity to report to the division manager, and Mr. Sawyer promised that he and Mr. Peters would do so.

The team made several efforts to see the division manager, but his secretary informed them that he was busy. They questioned the secretary closely to learn if the manager had knowledge of the procedural requirement that he and his staff go over the report with the team. She replied that he knew the requirements but was too busy to discuss a headquarters program. He would ask his assistant, the works manager, and several staff members to go over it, and what they approved would be all right with him. Eventually this meeting was held.

The members of the local management staff took a very reasonable attitude; they admitted the bad situation portrayed in the analysis and offered their assurances that immediate steps would be taken toward improvement. The team members thought that the local management staff was glad to have their problems brought out in the open and were delighted to have the suggestions of the headquarters representatives.

When Mr. Masters reviewed the report, both team members expressed their complete dissatisfaction with the brushoff they got from the division manager. Masters took this as a cue to question them extensively concerning their findings and recommendations. In view of the sensitive character of the situation and the possible controversy that it might create, he was reluctant to distribute the report. It was the consensus of the remainder of the staff and the representatives of the accounting office that the usual transmittal letter should be prepared, and distribution made. Mr. Masters signed this letter and took no other action until the telephone call came from Mr. Gunn.

QUESTIONS

1. What kind of organization structure does the Larger Company have? Why do you think it is organized as it is?

2. Who, if anyone, in this case acted outside his or her authority?

3. Does the organization's structure need changing? Support your position.

4. What does this case tell you about delegating authority?

5. If you were Mr. Jordan, what would you do now?

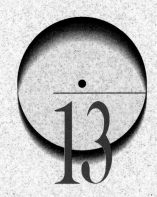

13

FOUNDATIONS OF INDIVIDUAL AND GROUP BEHAVIOR

●
──────────

LEARNING OBJECTIVES
──────────

After Reading
This Chapter,
You Should
Be Able To:

1. Define the focus and goals of organizational behavior.
2. Clarify the relationship between attitudes and behavior.
3. Identify several personality attributes that may explain behavior in organizations.
4. Identify the major sources of perceptual distortion.
5. Describe the two primary ways in which people learn.
6. Explain why people join groups.
7. Describe the stages of group development.
8. State how roles and norms influence an employee's behavior.
9. Explain what determines a group's performance and member satisfaction.

Nancy Lincoln is a nursing supervisor at a large hospital in Portland, Oregon. She has just received a letter of resignation from one of her nurses. That makes three resignations in the last thirty days. What's the problem? That's precisely what Nancy asked each of the three. Their answers were all the same: "The salaries here are not competitive with other hospitals in town." This really bothered Nancy. The hospital's personnel department had completed a thorough area survey sixty days earlier, and the results clearly showed that her nurses' salaries were in the top 20 percent. Nancy explained this to the resignees, but they disagreed. As Nancy said in an interview, "They're quitting for a reason that has no basis." Nancy was confusing reality with perceptions. The nurses' behavior was based on their perceptions, not on facts. From Nancy's perspective, of course, she lost three good employees. The irony in this case is that the hospital has one of the highest pay schedules for nurses in Portland, but the nurses are just as gone as if the hospital's salaries actually were low.

Jeff Davis is considering promoting Andy Settle to a supervisory position in United Parcel Service's Dayton office. Andy has been a UPS driver for four years and is one of the office's most able and conscientious employees. However, one thing is bothering Jeff: Andy's views on married working women. Andy regularly comments that he thinks married women should stay home, take care of the house, and raise children. If Andy is made supervisor, half of his subordinates will be female, and many of these women are married. Jeff knows that Andy is capable of being a top-grade supervisor, but Andy's attitude toward women could be a problem. Jeff wants to know how attitudes affect behavior. Will Andy's attitude toward married women cause him to discriminate against them when he allocates daily routes or completes their annual performance review?

Larry Gelber manages the bookstore at a state college in Pennsylvania. He has a problem, but he doesn't know what to do about it: The students he hires to stock shelves and control inventory seem to limit their work efforts. The students all know one another and seem pretty close, both on the job and off. They also seem to be in collusion not to work too fast or to get too much done. Larry has talked to them individually, offered them incentives to work harder, but nothing has worked. Larry thinks that each of the students is a hard worker. But there seems to be some group chemistry that is restricting their output.

Each of these problems involves employee behavior, but Nancy Lincoln, Jeff Davis, and Larry Gelber don't seem to have a very good understanding of employee behavior. If they did, they could probably explain and act on what they have encountered. The purpose of this chapter is to help you understand the kinds of behavior problems these managers are facing and what you could do about them if you were in their shoes.

TOWARD EXPLAINING AND PREDICTING BEHAVIOR

behavior
The observable actions of people.

This chapter draws heavily on the field of study that has come to be known as *organizational behavior* (OB). It is concerned with the subject of **behavior**—that is, the

organizational behavior
The study of the actions of people at work.

observable actions of people—but not all behavior. **Organizational behavior** is concerned specifically with the actions of people at work.

Focus of Organizational Behavior

Organizational behavior focuses primarily on two major areas. First, OB looks at *individual behavior*. Based predominantly on contributions from psychologists, this area includes such topics as attitudes, personality, perception, learning, and motivation. Second, OB is concerned with *group behavior,* which includes norms, conformity, roles, and group dynamics. Our knowledge about groups comes basically from the work of sociologists and social psychologists. Unfortunately, the behavior of a group of employees cannot be understood by merely summing up the actions of each individual, since individuals in groups behave differently from individuals acting alone. You see this characteristic when a street gang in a large city harasses innocent citizens. The gang members, acting individually, might never engage in such behavior. Put them together, and they act differently. The same is true at work. Therefore since employees in an organization are both individuals and members of groups, we need to study them at two levels.

Goals of Organizational Behavior

The goals of OB are to *explain* and *predict behavior*. Why do managers need this skill? Simply, in order to manage their employees' behavior. We know that a manager's success depends on getting things done through other people. Toward this goal, the manager needs to be able to explain why employees engage in some behaviors rather than others and to predict how employees will respond to various actions the manager might take.

Organizational behavior is also a *descriptive* field of study. It provides managers with accurate descriptions of how employees and groups of employees behave on the job. Managers can then use this information to *prescribe* action. That is, when managers can accurately explain and predict employee behavior, they can take the appropriate action to direct and control that behavior. For example, if I know what motivates a certain employee, then I can use that information to design an effective motivation program for that employee.

Intuition Versus Systematic Study

A final point needs to be made before we survey the field of organizational behavior and demonstrate its implications for managers: OB seeks to replace intuition with systematic study.

intuition
Gut feelings and interpretations based on personal experience.

systematic study
Study conducted in an objective and rigorous manner.

Most of us like to think we have pretty good **intuition**—that is, insight into human behavior. After all, haven't we been explaining and predicting the behavior of parents, brothers, sisters, teachers, friends, and enemies all our lives? We have. But much of that has been based on "gut" feelings and interpretations from our own personal experience. In some cases our intuitions are right, but often they are not. The conclusions that we reach in this chapter have come from the **systematic study** of people in organizations. OB researchers have gathered their data under controlled conditions, measured it in a reasonably objective and rigorous manner, attempted to attribute causes and effects, and based their conclusions as much as possible on scientific evidence. Organizational behavior is highly complex, but the material presented here should make you a more accurate observer.

INDIVIDUAL BEHAVIOR

The foundation of organizational behavior is the individual employee. Let's look at how an employee's attitudes, personality, perceptions, and learning processes influence his or her behavior. Employee needs and motives—a critical determinant of individual behavior—are discussed in detail in Chapter 14.

Attitudes

attitudes
Evaluative statements concerning objects, people, or events.

Attitudes are evaluative statements—either favorable or unfavorable—concerning objects, people, or events. An employee who says, "I really like my job" is expressing his or her attitude about work. Popular job-related attitudes include:

job satisfaction
An employee's general attitude toward his or her job.

job involvement
The degree to which an employee identifies with his or her job, actively participates in it, and considers his or her performance important to his or her sense of self-worth.

Job satisfaction: An employee's general attitude toward his or her job. When people speak of employee attitudes, more often than not they mean job satisfaction.

Job involvement: The degree to which an employee identifies with his or her job, actively participates in it, and considers his or her performance important to his or her self-worth.

organizational commitment
An employee's orientation toward an organization in terms of his or her loyalty to, identification with, and involvement in the organization.

Organizational commitment: An employee's orientation toward the organization in terms of his or her loyalty to, identification with, and involvement in the organization.

dissonance
Inconsistencies among attitudes or between attitudes and behavior.

The Search to Reduce Dissonance   Did you ever notice how people change what they say so that it doesn't contradict what they do? Research evidence shows that people seek to reduce **dissonance,** or inconsistencies among their attitudes and between their attitudes and behavior.[1] Individuals seek to reconcile divergent attitudes and align their attitudes and behavior in order to appear rational and consistent.

It's hard for employees to strongly dislike their job and the company they work for and yet come to work regularly and on time and exert a high level of effort. Similarly, a person who strongly believes that cigarettes are a major cause of lung cancer would probably have difficulty being a successful sales representative for a tobacco company. Of course, this doesn't mean that all people who dislike their jobs will resign or that you can't be a successful tobacco salesperson and think cigarettes and cancer are linked. The evidence suggests that when there is an inconsistency, forces are initiated to return the individual to a state of *equilibrium,* in which attitudes and behavior are again consistent. This can be done by altering either the attitudes ("This job isn't so bad after all") or the behavior (increasing absenteeism, looking for another job, quitting), or by developing a rationalization for the discrepancy ("Cigarettes may cause cancer, but jobs are tight, and I have a family to support").

No person can totally avoid dissonance. If the elements creating the dissonance are relatively unimportant, the pressure to correct the imbalance will be low. But if they are important, then employees will seek a balance. This, too, can be affected by the degree of influence the employee believes he or she has over the elements and the rewards that may be involved in dissonance. If the dissonance is seen as something over which the employee has little control ("The boss told me to do it"), pressure to reduce dissonance is less than it would be if the behavior were performed voluntarily. The inconsistency is still there, but it can be rationalized and justified. Rewards also influence an employee's motivation to reduce dissonance. High rewards can act to make dissonance less important. Since people in organizations are given some form of reward or remuneration for their services, employees can often deal with greater dissonance on their jobs than off their jobs.

Are Satisfied Workers Productive?   From the 1930s to the mid-1960s it was taken as a truism that happy workers were productive workers. As a result of the Hawthorne studies, managers generalized that if their employees were satisfied on their jobs, they would then transfer their satisfaction into high productivity. It sounded good, but studies that tested this relationship rarely achieved significant results.[2] Most findings showed a consistent, but not very large, positive relationship.[3]

A more careful analysis of these studies suggests another interpretation. The causal relationship is the reverse of that originally thought. That is, productive workers tend to be happy workers.[4] This position appears to hold the greatest credibility today. We can state that satisfaction and productivity do have a low but consistent relationship, but it is more likely that high productivity leads to high satisfaction than the other way around.

Personality

Some people could be described as quiet and passive, whereas others are loud and aggressive. When we describe people in terms of traits such as quiet, passive, loud, aggressive, ambitious, extroverted, loyal, tense, or sociable, we are categorizing them in terms of *personality traits*. An individual's **personality** is the combination of the psychological traits we use to classify that person.

There are literally dozens of personality traits. However, several have received the bulk of attention in the search to link personality attributes to behavior in organizations. They include *locus of control, authoritarianism, Machiavellianism,* and *risk propensity.*

Some people believe that they are masters of their own fate. Others see themselves as pawns of fate, believing that what happens to them in their lives is due to luck or chance. The locus of control in the first case is *internal:* these people believe that they control their destiny. In the second case it is *external:* these people believe that their lives are controlled by outside forces.[5] The evidence indicates that employees who rate high in externality are less satisfied with their jobs, more alienated from the work setting, and less involved in their jobs than those who rate high in internality.[6] A manager might also expect to find that externals blame a poor performance evaluation on their boss's prejudice, their co-workers, or other events outside their control, whereas internals explain the same evaluation in terms of their own actions.

Authoritarianism refers to a belief that there should be status and power differences among people in organizations.[7] The extremely high authoritarian personality is intellectually rigid, judgmental of others, deferential to those above, exploitative of those below, distrustful, and resistant to change. Since few people are extreme authoritarians, our conclusions must be guarded. It seems reasonable to postulate, however, that possessing a high authoritarian personality would be negatively related to the performance of a job that demands sensitivity to the feelings of others, tact, and the ability to adapt to complex and changing situations.[8] On the other hand, in a job that is highly structured and in which success depends on close conformance to rules and regulations, the highly authoritarian employee should perform quite well.

Closely related to authoritarianism is the characteristic of **Machiavellianism** ("Mach"), named after Niccolo Machiavelli, who wrote in the sixteenth century on how to gain and manipulate power. An individual who is high in Machiavellianism—in contrast to someone who is low—is pragmatic, maintains emotional distance, and believes that ends can justify means.[9] "If it works, use it" is consistent with a high Mach

personality
A combination of traits that classifies a person.

authoritarianism
A measure of a person's belief that there should be status and power differences among people in organizations.

Machiavellianism
A measure of the degree to which people are pragmatic, maintain emotional distance, and believe that ends justify means.

A person with a high risk-taking propensity might perform effectively as a stock trader in a brokerage firm. This type of job demands rapid decision making. On the other hand, this personality characteristic might be a major obstacle in an accountant who has to perform auditing activities. Such a position is better filled by someone with a low risk-taking propensity.

perspective. Do high Machs make good employees? That answer depends on the type of job and whether you consider ethical implications in evaluating performance. In jobs that require bargaining skills (such as labor negotiator) or that have substantial rewards for winning (such as a commissioned salesperson), high Machs are productive. In jobs in which ends do not justify the means or that lack absolute standards of performance, it is difficult to predict the performance of high Machs.

risk propensity
A measure of a person's willingness to take chances.

People differ in their willingness to take chances. Individuals with a high **risk propensity** make decisions more rapidly and use less information in making their choices than do low-risk-propensity individuals.[10] Managers might use this information to align employee risk-taking propensity with specific job demands.

Perception

perception
The process of organizing and interpreting sensory impressions in order to give meaning to the environment.

Perception is a process by which individuals organize and interpret their sensory impressions in order to give meaning to their environment. Research on perception consistently demonstrates that individuals may look at the same thing, yet perceive it differently. One manager, for instance, can interpret the fact that her assistant regularly takes several days to make important decisions as evidence that the assistant is slow, disorganized, and afraid to make decisions. Another manager, with the same assistant, might interpret the same action as evidence that the assistant is thoughtful, thorough, and deliberate. The first manager would probably evaluate her assistant negatively, while the second manager would evaluate the person positively. The point is that none of us actually sees reality. We interpret what we see and call it *reality*. And, of course, as the above example illustrates, we act according to our perceptions.

Factors Influencing Perception   How do we explain the fact that people can perceive the same thing differently? A number of factors operate to shape and sometimes distort perception. These factors can reside in the *perceiver,* in the object, or *target,* being perceived, or in the context of the *situation* in which the perception is made.

When an individual looks at a target and attempts to interpret what he or she sees, the individual's personal characteristics are going to heavily influence the interpretation. These personal characteristics include attitudes, personality, motives, interests, past experiences, and expectations.

The characteristics of the target being observed can also affect what is perceived. Loud people are more likely than quiet people to be noticed in a group. So, too, are extremely attractive or unattractive individuals. Because targets are not looked at in isolation, the relationship of a target to its background also influences perception, as does our tendency to group close things and similar things together.

The context in which we see objects or events is also important. The time at which an object or event is seen can influence attention, as can location, light, heat, and any number of other situational factors.

Shortcuts in Judging Others   People in organizations judge and evaluate others. As examples, managers conduct interviews and do performance appraisals, and operatives assess whether or not their co-workers are putting forth their full effort. Making judgments about others is difficult. To make the task easier, individuals take shortcuts. Some of these shortcuts are valuable because they allow us to make quick, accurate judgments and provide valid data for making predictions. However, they can also result in significant distortions.

selectivity
The process by which people assimilate certain bits and pieces of what they observe, depending on their interests, background, and attitudes.

Individuals cannot assimilate all they observe, so they engage in **selectivity.** They take in bits and pieces. These bits and pieces are not chosen randomly; rather, they are selectively chosen depending on the interests, background, experience, and attitudes of the observer. Selective perception allows us to "speed read" others, but not without the risk of drawing an inaccurate picture.

assumed similarity
The belief that others are like oneself.

It is easy to judge others if we assume that they are similar to us. In **assumed similarity,** or the "like me" effect, the observer's perception of others is influenced more by the observer's own characteristics than by those of the person observed. For example, if you want challenge and responsibility in your job, you will assume that others want the same. People who assume that others are like them are right some of the time, but only in cases when they judge someone who actually is like them. The rest of the time, they're wrong.

stereotyping
Judging a person on the basis of one's perception of the group to which he or she belongs.

When we judge someone on the basis of our perception of the group to which he or she belongs, we are using the shortcut called **stereotyping.** "Married people are more stable employees than singles" and "union people expect something for nothing" are examples of stereotyping. To the degree that a stereotype is based on fact, it may produce accurate judgments. However, many stereotypes have no foundation in fact. In such cases, stereotypes distort judgments.

halo effect
A general impression of an individual based on a single characteristic.

When we form a general impression about an individual based on a single characteristic such as intelligence, sociability, or appearance, we are being influenced by the **halo effect.** This effect frequently occurs when students evaluate their classroom instructor. Students may isolate a single trait such as enthusiasm and allow their entire evaluation to be tainted by their perception of this one trait. An instructor might be quiet, assured, knowledgeable, and highly qualified, but if his style lacks zeal, he will be rated lower on a number of other characteristics.

Learning

The psychologist's definition of learning is considerably broader than the lay person's, which usually defines it as "what I did when I went to school." In actuality, each of us is continuously "going to school." Learning is going on all the time. A more sophisticated definition of **learning** is therefore any relatively permanent change in behavior that occurs as a result of experience.

learning
Any relatively permanent change in behavior that occurs as a result of experience.

How do we learn? Figure 13–1 summarizes the learning process. First, learning helps us to adapt to and master our environment. By altering our behavior to changing

MANAGERS WHO MADE A DIFFERENCE

King Ming Young at Hewlett-Packard

King Ming Young is head of the managing-diversity project at Hewlett-Packard Co. Born in Hong Kong, raised in Honduras, and educated in the United States, Ms. Young is responsible for developing more than 200 in-house trainers who, in turn, have helped thousands of H-P employees change their beliefs that a woman or a member of a minority is deficient in some ways.[11] Young wants H-P employees to look at how, because of cultural conditioning, some people have difficulties working together and how to make the most of that situation. In other words, it's all right to accept that not everyone is the same. Young wants H-P employees to recognize individual differences, avoid stereotyping, and help the company to create a climate that encourages diversity.

At H-P, 45 percent of employees are women, and nearly 20 percent are members of minorities, but minority members fill only about 2 percent of upper-management positions. Young's trainers run internal programs at H-P to make managers aware of the biases and assumptions that control their comfort zones and boundaries and then show them how these harm individuals and the company. Young points, for instance, to the unconscious tendency for managers to promote others who are similar to themselves and with whom they feel comfortable. This practice excludes others who may be equally or more qualified.

Young describes her project as focusing on a wide range of management interactions among diverse employees—women managing men, African-Americans managing white males, Asians managing Hispanics, and so forth. The importance of her project is dramatized by the changing makeup of the American work force. Over the next decade, women will account for 51 percent of employment growth, Hispanics 15 percent, African-Americans 13 percent, and Asians and other minorities 6 percent. By the year 2000, white, non-Hispanic males will have become the true minority, comprising only 39 percent of the total work force.

Photo courtesy of Ms. King Ming Young.

law of effect
The principle that behavior is a function of its consequences.

conditions, we become responsible citizens and productive employees. But learning is built on the **law of effect,** which says that behavior is a function of its consequences.[12] Behavior that is followed by a favorable consequence tends to be repeated, whereas behavior that is followed by an unfavorable consequence tends not to be repeated. *Consequences,* in this terminology, are anything a person considers rewarding—for instance, money, praise, promotions, or a smile. If your boss compliments you on your sales approach, you are likely to repeat that behavior. Conversely,

FIGURE 13–1
The Learning Process

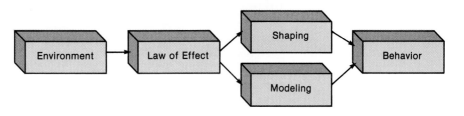

shaping
Learning that occurs in graduated steps.

modeling
Learning that occurs by observing others and copying their behavior.

•

Management training programs are increasingly using modeling as a learning device. Individuals watch others exhibit "good" managerial behaviors, then they practice doing the same.

if you are reprimanded for your sales approach, you're less likely to repeat it. The keys to the learning process are the two theories or explanations of how we learn. One is *shaping,* and the other is *modeling.*

When learning takes place in graduated steps, it is called **shaping.** Managers shape employee behavior by systematically reinforcing, through rewards, each successive step that moves the employee closer to the desired behavior. Much of our learning occurs by shaping. When we speak of "learning by mistakes," we are referring to shaping. We try, we fail, and we try again. Through such trials and errors, most of us have mastered many skills such as riding a bicycle, performing basic mathematical computations, taking classroom notes, and answering multiple-choice tests.

In addition to shaping, much of what we learn is obtained through observing others and **modeling** our behavior after them. While the trial-and-error process is usually a slow one, modeling can produce complex behavioral changes quite rapidly. For instance, at one time or another, most of us, when having trouble in school or in a particular class, have looked around to find someone who seems to have the system down pat. Then we observe that person to see what he or she is doing differently from us. If we find some differences, we then incorporate them into our behavior repertoire. If our performance improves (a favorable consequence), we're likely to change our behavior permanently to reflect what we have seen work for others. The process is the same at work as it is in school. A new employee who wants to be successful on his or her job is likely to look for someone in the organization who is well respected and successful and then try to imitate that person's behavior.

MANAGING FROM A GLOBAL PERSPECTIVE

culture shock
Confusion, disorientation, and emotional upheaval caused by being immersed in a new culture.

Culture Shock

When people move to a foreign country, they experience a certain amount of confusion, disorientation, and emotional upheaval. We call this **culture shock.** A transfer from the United States to Canada, for example, would require relatively little adjustment, but one would still experience some culture shock. The differences would include the form of representative government (Canadians have a parliamentary system), language (Canada is a bilingual—English- and French-speaking—country), and even holidays (Canadian Thanksgiving is in early October). However, culture shock will obviously be more severe when individuals move to cultures that are quite unlike their old environment.

The adjustment to a foreign country has been found to follow a U-shaped curve that contains four distinct stages.[13] This is shown in Figure 13–2.

The initial stage (I) is one of novelty. The newcomer is excited and optimistic. His or her mood is high. For the temporary visitor to a foreign country this stage is all one typically goes through. A person who spends a week or two on vacation in a strange land considers cultural differences to be interesting, even educational. However, the employee who makes a permanent or relatively permanent move experiences euphoria and then disillusionment. In this stage (II) the "quaint" quickly becomes "obsolete," and the "traditional" becomes "inefficient." The "opportunity" to learn a new language turns into the reality of struggling to communicate. After a few months the newcomer hits bottom. At this point (stage III), any and all of the culture's differences have become blatantly clear. The newcomer's basic interpretation system, which worked fine at home, now no longer functions. He or she is bombarded by millions of sights, sounds, and other cues that are uninterpretable. Frustration and confusion are highest and mood lowest in stage III. Finally, the newcomer begins to adapt, and the negative responses related to culture shock dissipate. In this stage (IV) the newcomer has learned what is important and what can be ignored.

What are the implications of this model? There are at least two. First, if you're a newcomer in a foreign country or you are managing a newcomer, expect culture shock. It's not abnormal. Everyone goes through it to some degree. Second, culture shock follows a relatively predictable pattern. Expect early euphoria, followed by depression and frustration. However, after about four to six months, most people have adjusted to their new culture. What was previously different and strange becomes understandable.

The Individual Behavior Model

Figure 13–3 summarizes our discussion of individual behavior. In very simplified terms we can say that people enter an organization with a set of attitudes and a substantially established personality. How they see the world (perception) influences their level of motivation (the topic of our next chapter), what they learn on the job, and, eventually, their individual work behavior. Their behavior is also influenced by

FIGURE 13–2
Culture Shock Cycle

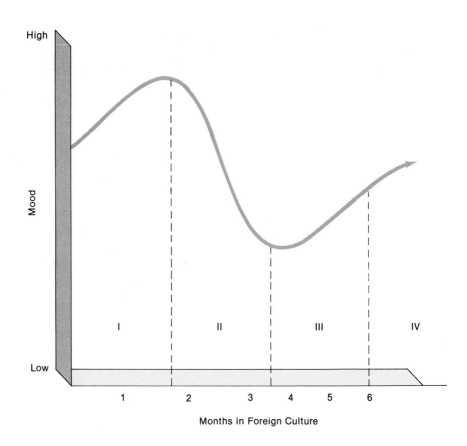

their ability—the talents and skills they have when they join an organization. Learning, of course, will alter this variable over time.

Some Suggestions for Managers

As a manager, how could you use the insights we have discussed about individual behavior to be more effective? The following are some suggestions.

Attitudes   We know that employees can be expected to try to reduce dissonance. Therefore, not surprisingly, there is relatively strong evidence that committed and

FIGURE 13–3
Key Variables Affecting Individual Behavior

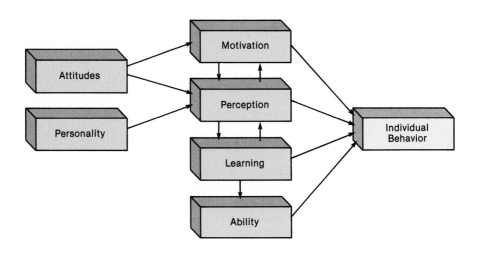

satisfied employees have lower rates of turnover and absenteeism.[14] Since most managers want to minimize the number of resignations and absences—especially among their more productive employees—they should do those things that will generate positive job attitudes. Dissonance, however, can be managed. If employees are required to engage in activities that appear inconsistent to them or that are at odds with their attitudes, managers should remember that pressure to reduce the dissonance is lessened when the employee perceives that the dissonance is externally imposed and uncontrollable. The pressure is also lessened if rewards are significant enough to offset the dissonance.

The findings about the satisfaction-productivity relationship have important implications for managers. They suggest that the goal of making employees happy on the assumption that this will lead to high productivity is probably misdirected. Managers who follow this strategy could end up with a very happy but poorly performing group of employees. Managers would get better results by directing their attention primarily at what will help employees to become more productive. Successful job performance should then lead to feelings of accomplishment, increased pay, promotions, and other rewards—all desirable outcomes—which then lead to satisfaction with the job.

Personality   An understanding of personality differences helps managers to select employees. Managers who try to match personality types with jobs are likely to have more productive and more satisfied employees. Managers can also anticipate how specific employees are likely to perform in their jobs. For instance, individuals with an external locus of control will probably be less satisfied with their jobs and also less willing to accept responsibility for their actions than individuals with an internal locus of control.

Perception   Managers need to recognize that they and their employees react to perceptions, not reality. Whether a job is actually interesting or challenging is irrelevant. Whether a manager actually helps his or her subordinates to structure their work more efficiently and effectively is also irrelevant. The key is what is perceived. Similarly, issues such as fair pay for work performed, the validity of performance appraisals, and the adequacy of work conditions affect an employee's performance and satisfaction. But reality must first be organized and interpreted, and that allows the potential for perceptual distortion.

Learning   The issue isn't whether or not employees continually learn on the job. They do! The issue is whether managers are going to let employee learning occur randomly or manage learning through the rewards they allocate and the examples they set. If marginal employees are rewarded with pay raises and promotions, they will have little reason to change their behavior. If managers want behavior A but reward behavior B, they shouldn't be surprised when employees engage in behavior B.[15] Similarly, managers should expect employees to look to them as models. Managers who are constantly late for work, take two hours for lunch, or help themselves to company office supplies for personal use should expect employees to read the message they're sending and model their behavior accordingly.

GROUP BEHAVIOR

The behavior of individuals in groups is something more than the sum total of each acting in his or her own way. More specifically, individuals act differently in groups than when they are alone. Therefore if we want to more fully understand organizational behavior, we need to study groups.

ETHICAL DILEMMAS IN MANAGEMENT

Is Shaping Behavior a Form of Manipulative Control?

Animal trainers use rewards—typically food—to get dogs, porpoises, and whales to perform extraordinary stunts. Behavioral psychologists have put rats through thousands of experiments by manipulating their food supply. These trainers and researchers have shaped the behavior of these animals by controlling consequences. Such learning techniques may be appropriate for animals performing in zoos, circuses, or laboratories, but are they appropriate for managing the behavior of people at work?

Critics argue that human beings are not rats in an experiment. Human beings should be treated with respect and dignity. To explicitly use rewards as a learning device—to encourage the repetition of desired behaviors—is manipulative. Human beings in organizations should act of free will and not be subjected to manipulative control techniques by their bosses.

No well-schooled behavioral scientist would argue that shaping isn't a powerful tool for controlling behavior. But when used by managers, is it a form of manipulation? If an employee engages in behaviors that the organization later judges "wrong" but that were motivated by a manager's control of rewards, is that employee any less responsible for his or her actions than if such rewards were not involved? What do *you* think?

Defining and Classifying Groups

group
Two or more interacting and interdependent individuals who come together to achieve particular objectives.

A **group** is defined as two or more interacting and interdependent individuals who come together to achieve particular objectives. Groups can be either formal or informal. By *formal*, we mean a group that is defined by the organization's structure, with designated work assignments establishing tasks. In formal groups, the behaviors in which one should engage are stipulated by and directed toward organizational goals. In contrast, *informal groups* are alliances that are neither structured nor organizationally determined. These groups are natural formations that appear in the work environment in response to the need for social contact.

It is possible to further subclassify groups as *command, task, interest,* or *friendship* groups.[16] Command and task groups are dictated by the formal organization, whereas interest and friendship groups are informal alliances.

command group
A group composed of subordinates who report directly to a given manager.

The **command group** is determined by the organization chart. It is composed of the subordinates who report directly to a given manager. An elementary school principal and his twelve teachers form a command group, as do a director of postal audits and her five inspectors.

task group
A group of people who work together to complete a job task.

The **task group,** also organizationally determined, represents people working together to complete a job task. However, a task group's boundaries are not limited to its immediate hierarchical superior. It can cross command relationships. For instance, when a college student is accused of a campus crime, communication and coordination between the dean of academic affairs, the dean of students, the registrar, the director of security, and the student's advisor may be required. Such a formation would constitute a task group. It should be noted that all command groups are also task groups; but because task groups can cut across the organization, the reverse is not necessarily true.

People who may or may not be aligned into common command or task groups might affiliate to attain a specific objective with which each is concerned. This is an **interest group.** Employees who band together to have their vacation schedules altered, to support a peer who has been fired, or to seek increased fringe benefits represent the formation of a united body to further their common interest.

Groups often develop because the individual members have one or more characteristics in common. We call this type of formation a **friendship group.** Social alliances, which frequently extend outside the work situation, can be based on similar age, support for "Big Red" Nebraska football, attendance at the same college, or similar political views, to name just a few.

Why People Join Groups

There is no single reason why individuals join groups. Since most people belong to a number of groups, it's obvious that different groups provide different benefits to their members. Most people join a group out of needs for security, status, self-esteem, affiliation, power, and goal achievement.

Security   "There's strength in numbers." By joining a group we can reduce the insecurity of "standing alone"—we feel stronger, have fewer self-doubts, and are more resistant to threats. New employees are particularly vulnerable to a sense of isolation; they turn to the group for guidance and support. However, whether we are talking about new employees or those with years on the job, we can state that few individuals like to stand alone. Human beings get reassurances from interacting with others and being part of a group. This often explains the appeal of unions; if management creates a climate in which employees feel insecure, they are likely to turn to unionization to reduce their feelings of insecurity.

interest group
A group of people who affiliate to attain a specific objective with which each is concerned.

friendship group
A group that develops because members have one or more characteristics in common.

Informal groups provide a very important service by satisfying their members' social needs. Because of interactions that result from the close proximity of work stations or task interactions, we find workers playing golf together, riding to and from work together, lunching together, and spending their breaks around the water cooler together. We must recognize that although these types of interactions among individuals are informal, they deeply affect individuals' behavior.

Status   "I'm a member of our company's running team. Last month, at the National Corporate Relays, we won the national championship. Didn't you see our picture in the company newsletter?" Comments like this demonstrate the power of a group to give prestige. Inclusion in a group that others view as important provides recognition and status for its members.

Self-Esteem   "Before I was asked to pledge Phi Omega Chi, I felt like a nobody. Being in a fraternity makes me feel a lot more important." This quote demonstrates that groups can increase people's feelings of self-worth. That is, in addition to conveying status to those outside the group, membership can also raise feelings of self-esteem. Our self-esteem is bolstered, for example, when we are accepted into a highly valued group. Being assigned to a task force to review and make recommendations for the location of the company's new corporate headquarters can fulfill one's needs for competence and growth as well as for status.

Affiliation   "I'm independently wealthy, but I wouldn't give up my job. Why? Because I really like the people I work with!" This quote, from a $25,000-a-year purchasing agent who inherited several million dollars' worth of real estate, verifies that groups can fulfill our social needs. People enjoy the regular interaction that comes with group membership. For many people, these on-the-job interactions are their primary means of fulfilling their need for affiliation. For almost all people, work groups significantly contribute to fulfilling their need for friendships and social relations.

Power   "I tried for two years to get the plant management to increase the number of female restrooms on the production floor to the same number as the men have. It was like talking to a wall. But I got about fifteen other women who were production employees together and we jointly presented our demands to management. The construction crews were in here adding female restrooms within ten days!"

This episode demonstrates that one of the appealing aspects of groups is that they represent power. What often cannot be achieved individually becomes possible through group action. Of course, this power might not be sought only to make demands on others. It might be desired merely as a countermeasure. To protect themselves from unreasonable demands by management, individuals may align with others.

Informal groups additionally provide opportunities for individuals to exercise power over others. For individuals who desire to influence others, groups can offer power without a formal position of authority in the organization. As a group leader, you might be able to make requests of group members and obtain compliance without any of the responsibilities that traditionally go with formal managerial positions. For people with a high power need, groups can be a vehicle for fulfillment.

Goal Achievement   "I'm part of a three-person team studying how we can cut our company's transportation costs. Since they've been going up at over 30 percent a year for several years now, the corporate controller assigned representatives from cost accounting, shipping, and marketing to study the problem and make recommendations."

This task group was created to achieve a goal that would be considerably more difficult if pursued by a single person. There are times when it takes more than one person to accomplish a particular task; there is a need to pool talents, knowledge, or power in order to get a job completed. In such instances, management will rely on the use of a formal group.

FIGURE 13–4   Stages of Group Development

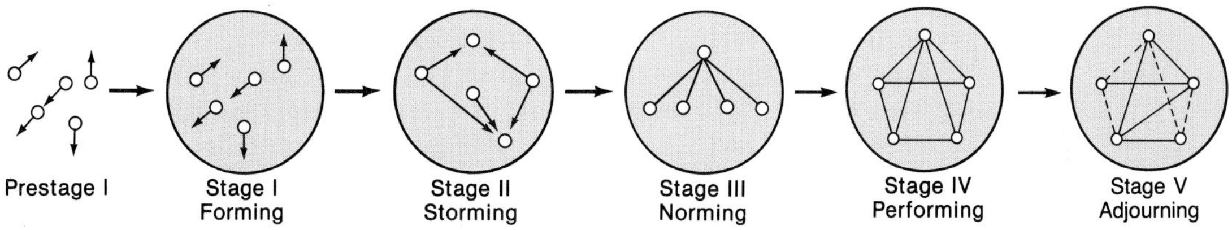

Prestage I → Stage I Forming → Stage II Storming → Stage III Norming → Stage IV Performing → Stage V Adjourning

Stages of Group Development

Group development is a dynamic process. Most groups are in a continual state of change. But even though groups probably never reach complete stability, there is a general pattern that describes how most groups evolve. There is strong evidence that groups pass through a standard sequence of five stages.[17] As shown in Figure 13–4, these five stages have been labeled *forming, storming, norming, performing,* and *adjourning.*

The first stage, **forming,** is characterized by a great deal of uncertainty about the group's purpose, structure, and leadership. Members are "testing the waters" to determine what types of behavior are acceptable. This stage is complete when members have begun to think of themselves as part of a group.

The **storming** stage is one of intragroup conflict. Members accept the existence of the group, but there is resistance to the control that the group imposes on individuality. Further, there is conflict over who will control the group. When stage II is complete, there will be a relatively clear hierarchy of leadership within the group.

The third stage is one in which close relationships develop and the group demonstrates cohesiveness. There is now a strong sense of group identity and comaraderie. This **norming** stage is complete when the group structure solidifies and the group has assimilated a common set of expectations of what defines correct member behavior.

The fourth stage is **performing.** The structure at this point is fully functional and accepted. Group energy has moved from getting to know and understand each other to performing the task at hand.

For permanent work groups, performing is the last stage in their development. However, for temporary committees, task forces, teams, and similar groups that have a limited task to perform, there is an **adjourning** stage. In this stage the group prepares for its disbandment. High levels of task performance are no longer the group's top priority. Instead, attention is directed toward wrapping-up activities. Responses of group members vary in this stage. Some are upbeat, basking in the group's accomplishments. Others may be depressed over the loss of comaraderie and friendships gained during the work group's life.

Most of you have probably encountered each of these stages in a group project for a class. Group members are selected and then meet for the first time. There is a "feeling out" period to assess what the group is going to do and how it is going to do it. This is usually rapidly followed by the battle for control: Who is going to lead us? Once this is resolved and a hierarchy is agreed upon, the group identifies specific aspects of the task, who is going to do them, and dates by which the parts need to be completed. General expectations become set and agreed upon for each member. This forms the foundation for what you hope will be a coordinated group effort culminating in a job well done. Once the group project is complete and turned in, the group

---

forming
The first stage in group development, characterized by much uncertainty.

storming
The second stage of group development, characterized by intragroup conflict.

norming
The third stage of group development, characterized by close relationships and cohesiveness.

performing
The fourth stage in group development, when the group is fully functional.

adjourning
The final stage in group development for temporary groups, characterized by concern with wrapping-up activities rather than task performance.

breaks up. Of course, groups occasionally don't get much beyond the first or second stage, which typically results in disappointing projects and grades.

Should one assume from the foregoing that a group becomes more effective as it progresses through the first four stages? Some argue that effectiveness of work units increases at advanced stages, but it is not that simple.[18] While this assumption may be generally true, what makes a group effective is a complex issue. Under some conditions, high levels of conflict are conducive to high levels of group performance. We might expect to find situations in which groups in stage II outperform those in stages III or IV. Similarly, groups do not always proceed clearly from one stage to the next. Sometimes, in fact, several stages are going on simultaneously, as when groups are storming and performing at the same time. Groups even occasionally regress to previous stages. Therefore one should not always assume that all groups precisely follow this developmental process or that stage IV is always the most preferable. It is better to think of this model as a general framework. It reminds you that groups are dynamic entities and can help you better understand the problems and issues that are most likely to surface during a group's life.

Basic Group Concepts

In this section we introduce the foundation concepts upon which an understanding of group behavior can be built. These are *roles, norms* and *conformity, status systems,* and *group cohesiveness.*

role
A set of behavior patterns expected of someone occupying a given position in a social unit.

Roles   We introduced the concept of roles in Chapter 1 when we discussed what managers do. Of course, managers are not the only individuals in an organization who have roles. The concept of roles applies to all employees in organizations and to their life outside the organization as well.

A **role** refers to a set of expected behavior patterns attributed to someone who occupies a given position in a social unit. Individuals play multiple roles, adjusting their roles to the group to which they belong at the time. In an organization, employees attempt to determine what behaviors are expected of them. They'll read their job descriptions, get suggestions from their boss, and watch what their co-workers do. An individual who is confronted by divergent role expectations experiences *role conflict.* Employees in organizations often face such role conflicts. The credit manager expects her credit analysts to process a minimum of thirty applications a week, but the work group pressures members to restrict output to twenty applications a week so that everyone has work to do and no one gets laid off. A young college instructor's colleagues want him to give out very few high grades in order to maintain the department's "tough standards" reputation, whereas students want him to give out lots of high grades to enhance their grade point averages. To the degree that the instructor sincerely seeks to satisfy the expectations of both his colleagues and his students, he faces role conflict.

norms
Acceptable standards shared by a group's members.

Norms and Conformity   All groups have established **norms,** or acceptable standards that are shared by the group's members. Norms dictate things like output levels, absenteeism rates, promptness or tardiness, the amount of "horseplay" allowed, and whom one should socialize with.

Norms dictate the behavior a student is expected to project in the classroom. Depending upon the climate created by the instructor, the norms may support unequivocal acceptance of the material suggested by the instructor; or, at the other extreme, students may be expected to challenge and question the instructor on any point that is unclear. In most classroom situations the norms dictate that one not humiliate the instructor or engage in loud, boisterous discussion that makes it impos-

You behave differently in class on Monday morning than you did at the dance you attended on Saturday night. You understand that role expectations differ considerably in college classrooms from those expected in a night club.

sible to understand the lecture. Should some in the classroom group violate these norms, pressure is brought to bear on them to make their behavior conform with established group standards.

status

A prestige grading, position, or rank within a group.

Status Systems   **Status** is a prestige grading, position, or rank within a group. As far back as scientists have been able to trace human groupings, they have found status hierarchies: tribal chiefs and their followers, noblemen and peasants, the haves and have-nots. Status systems are an important factor in understanding behavior. Status is a significant motivator and has behavioral consequences when individuals see a disparity between what they perceive their status to be and what others perceive it to be.

Status may be informally conferred by characteristics such as education, age, sex, skill, or experience. Anything can have status value if others in the group evaluate it as such. Of course, just because status is informal does not mean that it is less important or that there is less agreement on who has it or who does not. Members of groups have no problem placing people into status categories, and they usually agree closely about who is high, low, and in the middle.

It is important for employees to believe that the organization's formal status system is congruent. That is, there should be equity between the perceived ranking of an individual and the status accoutrements he or she is given by the organization. For instance, incongruence occurs when a supervisor is earning less than his or her subordinates, a desirable office is occupied by a lower-ranking individual, or paid country club membership is provided by the company for division managers but not for vice presidents. Employees expect the things an individual has and receives to be congruent with his or her status. When they are not congruent, employees are likely to reject the authority of their superiors, the motivation potential of promotions decreases, and the general pattern of order and consistency in the organization is disturbed.

Group Cohesiveness   Intuitively, it would appear that groups in which there is a lot of internal disagreement and lack of cooperation are less effective in completing their tasks than groups in which individuals generally agree, cooperate, and like each other.

We are all familiar with the formal trappings that are associated with organizational status: large offices with thick carpeting on the floor, impressive titles, high pay and fringe benefits, preferred work schedules, and so on. Whether or not management acknowledges the existence of status symbols or a status hierarchy, organizations are filled with amenities that are not uniformly available to everyone and hence carry status value.

group cohesiveness

The degree to which members are attracted to one another and share the group's goals.

Research on this position had focused on **group cohesiveness,** or the degree to which members are attracted to one another and share the group's goals. The more the members are attracted to one another and the more the group's goals align with their individual goals, the greater the group's cohesiveness.

Research has generally shown that highly cohesive groups are more effective than those with less cohesiveness,[19] but the relationship is more complex. A key moderating variable is the degree to which the group's attitude aligns with its formal goals or those of the larger organization of which it is a part.[20] The more cohesive a group, the more its members will follow its goals. If these goals are favorable (for instance, high output, quality work, cooperation with individuals outside the group), a cohesive group is more productive than a less cohesive group. But if cohesiveness is high and attitudes are unfavorable, productivity decreases. If cohesiveness is low and goals are supported, productivity increases but not as much as when both cohesiveness and support are high. When cohesiveness is low and goals are not supported, cohesiveness has no significant effect upon productivity. These conclusions are summarized in Figure 13–5.

FIGURE 13–5

The Relationship Between Cohesiveness and Productivity

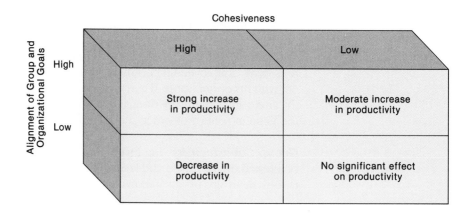

From Basic Concepts to Practice: Making Groups Effective

Based on our discussion of basic group concepts, there are a number of things managers might want to consider in order to make groups—both formal and informal—work for them.

Managers should clarify an employee's role in his or her work group. Expectations should be made clear. Role conflicts can be minimized by clarifying authority relations (but in certain structures, such as the matrix, managers should expect heightened role conflicts among employees). Finally, managers should use their understanding of roles to predict behaviors. Knowledge of a person's role can make it easier for a manager to deal with that person. Why? Because roles give us insight into expected behavior patterns. A drill press operator is likely to be more aggressive and argumentative during labor negotiations, when he or she is on the union bargaining team and playing the role of "abused worker," than during work, when he or she is playing the role of "mentor" to a new operator in the drill press department.

Managers should carefully monitor group norms because these norms can enhance or retard the group's performance. Knowing the norms of a group can help the manager explain and predict the behavior of its members. For example, when norms support high output, a manager can expect individual performance to be markedly higher than when norms restrict output.

Status incongruence creates frustration for employees and can negatively affect their performance and satisfaction. To minimize incongruence, managers should consider formal hierarchical rank and informal group rank in the allocation of status items.

Managers should strive to promote cohesiveness among their work groups and to align the groups' goals with those of the organization. A manager should keep in mind, however, that group cohesiveness is desirable only when accompanied by group and organization goal agreement.

Toward Understanding Work Group Behavior

Why are some groups more successful than others? The answer to that question is complex, but it includes variables such as the abilities of the group's members, the size of the group, the level of conflict, and internal pressures on members to conform to the group's norms. Figure 13–6 presents the major components that determine group performance and satisfaction.[21] It can help you to sort out the key variables and their interrelationships.

FIGURE 13–6
Group Behavior Model

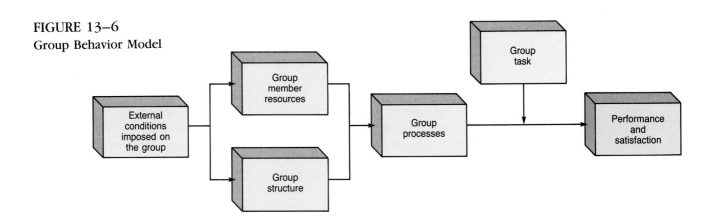

External Conditions Imposed on the Group   To begin understanding the behavior of a work group, you need to view it as a subsystem embedded in a larger system.[22] When we realize that groups are subsets of a larger organization system, we can extract part of the explanation of the group's behavior from an explanation of the organization to which it belongs.

Work groups don't exist in isolation. They are part of a larger organization. A design team in General Dynamics' Convair Division in San Diego, for instance, must live within the rules and policies dictated from the division's headquarters and GD's corporate offices in St. Louis. Every work group is influenced by external conditions imposed from outside it.

What are some of these external conditions? They include the organization's overall strategy, authority structures, formal regulations, the abundance or absence of organizationwide resources, personnel selection criteria, the organization's performance evaluation and reward system, the organization's culture, and the general physical layout of the group's work space set by the organization's industrial engineers and office designers.

Group Member Resources   A group's potential level of performance depends to a large extent on the resources that its members individually bring to the group. This would include member abilities and personality characteristics.

Part of a group's performance can be predicted by assessing the task-relevant and intellectual abilities of its individual members. We do occasionally read about an athletic team composed of mediocre players who, because of excellent coaching, determination, and precision teamwork, beat a far more talented group of players. Such cases make the news precisely because they are aberrations. As the old saying goes, "The race doesn't always go to the swiftest nor the battle to the strongest, but that's the way to bet." Group performance is not merely the summation of its individual members' abilities. However, these abilities set parameters for what members can do and how effectively they will perform in a group.

There has been a great deal of research on the relationship between personality traits and group attitudes and behavior. The general conclusion is that attributes that tend to have a positive connotation in our culture tend to be positively related to group productivity and morale. These include traits such as sociability, self-reliance, and independence. In contrast, negatively evaluated characteristics such as authoritarianism, dominance, and unconventionality tend to be negatively related to productivity and morale.[23] These personality traits affect group performance by strongly influencing how the individual will interact with other group members.

Group Structure   Work groups are not unorganized mobs. They have a structure that shapes members' behavior and makes it possible to explain and predict a larger portion of individual behavior within the group as well as the performance of the group itself. These structural variables include roles, norms, and formal leadership. Since we have already discussed roles and norms in this chapter and leadership will be covered in Chapter 15, we don't need to elaborate on these variables here. Just keep in mind that every work group has an internal structure that defines member roles, norms, and formal leadership positions.

Group Processes   The next component in our group behavior model considers the processes that go on within a work group—the communication patterns used by members to exchange information, group decision processes, leader behavior, power dynamics, conflict interactions, and the like.

Why are processes important to understanding work group behavior? Because in groups, one and one do not necessarily add up to two. Every group begins with a potential defined by the group's constraints, resources, and structure. Then you need to add in process gains and losses created within the group itself. Four people on a research team, for instance, may be able to generate far more ideas as a group than the members could produce individually. This positive synergy results in a process gain. You also have to subtract out process losses. High levels of conflict, for example, may hinder group effectiveness.

To determine a group's *actual* effectiveness, you need to *add* in process gains and *subtract* out process losses from the group's *potential* effectiveness.

Group Tasks   The final box in our model points out that the impact of group processes on the group's performance and member satisfaction depends on the task that the group is doing. More specifically, the *complexity* and *interdependence* of tasks influence the group's effectiveness.[24]

Tasks can be generalized as being either simple or complex. Complex tasks are ones that tend to be novel or nonroutine. Simple tasks are routine and standardized. We would hypothesize that the more complex the task, the more the group will benefit from discussion among members about alternative work methods. If the task is simple, group members don't need to discuss such alternatives. They can rely on standardized operating procedures. Similarly, if there is a high degree of interdependence among the tasks that group members must perform, they'll need to interact more. Effective communication and minimal levels of conflict should therefore be more relevant to group performance when tasks are interdependent.

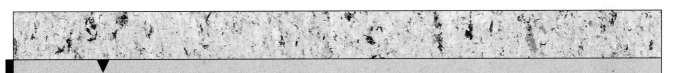

IN PRACTICE   The Growing Popularity of Work Teams

British, American, and Scandinavian firms have been experimenting with work teams for forty years.[25] Volvo, for instance, has been building its cars for decades using teams rather than individuals on assembly lines.

In recent years, however, work teams have been replacing individuals as the central focus of job design in many North American organizations. Some organizations have hundreds of work teams, composed of 20 to 30 employees each, that do the work that previously was done by individuals performing narrowly specialized and repetitive tasks.

Why have work teams become so popular? They generate a number of benefits: expanded use of employee skills, more stimulating and rewarding work for employees, more sustained effort at team goals, improved quality of output, and greater member satisfaction.

The work team concept is now being practiced in a number of U.S. manufacturing industries—autos, food processing, electronics, paper, oil refining, steel, and electrical products. It is also gaining popularity in service industries such as financial services and insurance.

These conclusions are consistent with what we know about information-processing capacity and uncertainty.[26] Tasks that have higher uncertainty (which are those that are complex and interdependent) require more information processing. This, in turn, puts more importance on group processes. So, just because a group is characterized by poor communication, weak leadership, high levels of conflict, and the like, does not necessarily mean that it will be low-performing. If the group's tasks are simple and require little interdependence among members, the group still may be effective.

SUMMARY

This summary is organized by the chapter-opening learning objectives found on page 397.

1. The field of organizational behavior is concerned with the actions of people—managers and operatives alike—in organizations. By focusing on individual- and group-level concepts it seeks to explain and predict behavior. Since managers get things done through other people, they will be more effective leaders if they have an understanding of behavior.

2. Individuals try to make their behavior consistent with their attitudes, and vice versa, to reduce dissonance and to appear rational.

3. Popular personality attributes that have been shown to explain behavior in organizations include locus of control, authoritarianism, Machiavellianism, and risk propensity.

4. The major sources of perceptual distortion reside in the perceiver, the target being perceived, or the context of the situation in which the perception occurs.

5. The two primary ways by which people learn are shaping and modeling.

6. People join groups because of their needs for security, status, self-esteem, affiliation, power, and goal achievement.

7. Groups develop by passing through a standard sequence of stages: forming, storming, norming, performing, and adjourning.

8. A role refers to a set of behavior patterns expected of someone occupying a given position in a social unit. Employees adjust their role behaviors at any given time to the group of which they are a part. Norms are standards shared by group members. They informally convey to employees which behaviors are acceptable and which are unacceptable.

9. A group's performance and satisfaction is determined by five variables. First, a group is influenced by the larger organization of which it is a part. Second, a group's potential level of performance depends to a large extent on the resources that its members individually bring to the group. Third, there is a group structure that shapes the behavior of members. Fourth, there are internal processes within the group that aid and hinder interaction and the ability of the group to perform. Finally, the impact of group processes on the group's performance and member satisfaction depends on the task that the group is doing.

REVIEW QUESTIONS

1. What is *organizational behavior?*
2. What is *dissonance?* How is it related to *attitudes?*

3. Are happy workers productive workers?

4. What behavioral predictions would you make about an employee who has an external locus of control?

5. Explain how perceptual distortions can affect the outcome of a performance appraisal.

6. Explain how employees might learn bad work habits.

7. How might organizations create role conflicts for an employee?

8. What's the relationship between *group cohesiveness* and *effectiveness?*

9. Why are some groups more successful than others?

10. What benefits might accrue from using work teams to accomplish tasks?

DISCUSSION QUESTIONS

1. How could you use personality traits to improve employee selection?

2. What relationship, if any, can you find between the law of effect and MBO?

3. Given that perception affects behavior, is there anything management can do to reduce employee perceptual distortion?

4. Why is group behavior something more than the sum total of each person acting in his or her own way?

5. In North America, we have historically built organizations around individuals. What would happen if we took groups seriously and used them as the basic building block for an organization? What if we *selected* groups rather than individuals, *trained* groups rather than individuals, *paid* groups rather than individuals, *promoted* groups rather than individuals, *fired* groups rather than individuals, and so forth?

SELF-ASSESSMENT EXERCISE

Who Controls Your Life?

Instructions: Read the following statements and indicate whether you agree more with choice A or choice B.

A	B	
1. Making a lot of money is largely a matter of getting the right breaks.	1. Promotions are earned through hard work and persistence.	_____
2. I have noticed that there is usually a direct connection between how hard I study and the grades I get.	2. Many times the reactions of teachers seem haphazard to me.	_____
3. The number of divorces indicates that more and more people are not trying to make their marriages work.	3. Marriage is largely a gamble.	_____
4. It is silly to think that one can really change another person's basic attitudes.	4. When I am right I can convince others.	_____
5. Getting promoted is really a matter of being a little luckier than the next person.	5. In our society a person's future earning power depends upon his or her ability.	_____
6. If one knows how to deal with people, they are really quite easily led.	6. I have little influence over the way other people behave.	_____
7. The grades I make are the result of my own efforts; luck has little or nothing to do with it.	7. Sometimes I feel that I have little to do with the grades I get.	_____
8. People like me can change the course of world affairs if we make ourselves heard.	8. It is only wishful thinking to believe that one can really influence what happens in our society at large.	_____
9. A great deal that happens to me is probably a matter of chance.	9. I am the master of my fate.	_____
10. Getting along with people is a skill that must be practiced.	10. It is almost impossible to figure out how to please some people.	_____

Turn to page 674 for scoring directions and key.

Source: Adapted from Julian B. Rotter, "External Control and Internal Control," *Psychology Today,* June 1971, p. 42. Copyright 1971 by the American Psychological Association. Adapted with permission.

CASE APPLICATION 13A

Big Time Foods

It has been a year since Bob Doreen and Nina Hollins were hired out of college and joined Big Time Foods, a large consumer products company with sales of over a billion dollars a year. Both Bob and Nina graduated with B.S. degrees in business from the University of Alabama. They were hired by Big Time as sales management trainees.

Bob and Nina decided to have lunch together to celebrate their first full year out of school. As it happened, the conversation centered on their individual perceptions and experiences at Big Time.

Nina described herself as "alienated." She was one of only three female sales management trainees in a group of forty-two. Among the thirty-five product managers in the company, all were male. Only one assistant product manager was a female. Nina said that she wished she had a female role model whom she could look up to and emulate. Nina also commented on a number of recent events that bothered her. First, there was much infighting between product managers to get company resources for their product lines. She couldn't figure out why top management didn't do something to eliminate this infighting. Second, Big Time's college recruiters had emphasized the company's long-standing reputation for promoting from within. Yet during the past twelve months, three senior marketing positions had opened up, and all had been filled from outside the company. Third, Nina felt she had done an excellent job during her first year with the company, but no one seemed to notice. She received a rating of 92 out of 100 from her boss and a $200-a-month raise. Other than a two-minute interview in which her boss complimented her on her cooperative attitude, she felt her efforts were not being appropriately recognized.

Listening to Bob talk, Nina couldn't believe they worked for the same company, never mind that they were both part of the same training program. Bob thought the company was great. A regional marketing manager, J.B. Neeley, had remembered Bob's heroics as a running back on Alabama's football team. In very short order, they had become friends. Bob had even become a regular part of a Saturday golfing foursome made up of Neeley, Neeley's boss, and two Big Time vice presidents. Bob was somewhat confused by the reaction to Nina's performance evaluation. He received an 85 rating and a similar $200-a-month raise. But his boss had spent more than a hour with Bob reviewing his evaluation, commending him on his performance, and talking about the numerous opportunities he could look forward to in the company.

As they finished lunch, Bob sensed Nina's frustrations. She was extremely conscientious. She seemed disheartened by what she considered inefficient management practices and the belief that her contributions were not being recognized. Bob's positive impressions of Big Time only seemed to upset her more. It didn't surprise Bob when Nina concluded their conversation by saying, "I don't think there's any future for me here. I'm going to start looking for another job."

Questions

1. How have Bob's and Nina's perceptions influenced their attitudes and behaviors?

2. Should Nina have been surprised by the management practices she observed? Can you explain why they differ from management theory?

3. If Nina asked you for advice, what would you tell her?

4. Are there any reasonable actions that top management could have taken to make Nina's first year a more positive experience?

CASE APPLICATION 13B

AT&T Credit Corporation

AT&T Credit Corporation (ATTCC) is a newly created subsidiary of American Telephone & Telegraph Co. It provides financing for customers who lease equipment from AT&T and other companies.[27]

ATTCC's problems began when a bank it initially retained to process lease applications couldn't keep up with the volume of new business. ATTCC President Thomas C. Wajnert saw that the fault lay in the bank's method of dividing labor into narrow tasks and organizing work by function. One department handled applications and checked customers' credit standings, a second drew up contracts, and a third collected payments. No one person or group had responsibility for providing full service to a customer.

Wajnert decided to hire his own employees and give them "ownership and accountability." His first concern was to increase efficiency, not to provide more rewarding jobs. In the end, however, he did both.

ATTCC created eleven teams of ten to fifteen members each. The three major lease-processing functions were combined into each team so calls from customers no longer had to be transferred from department to department.

ATTCC also divided its national staff of field agents into seven regions and assigned two or three teams to handle business from each region. Team members were responsible for solving customers' problems. ATTCC's new slogan was "Whoever gets the calls owns the problem."

Teams are essentially on their own on how to deal with customers, scheduling, reassigning work when people are absent, and interviewing prospective new employees. The only supervisors are seven regional managers who advise the team members.

This new organizational set-up has resulted in a one-hundred percent increase in the number of lease applications processed each day. The teams also have cut decision making time by more than thirty percent. ATTCC is now growing at a forty to fifty percent compounded annual rate and the new team-based organization design has facilitated this increase in volume.

Questions

1. Why do you think teams have doubled productivity at ATTCC?

2. Are groups more productive than individuals? Discuss.

3. What negatives do you see teams creating for management? For team members?

4. Would you want to work in a team-based organization? Explain your answer.

14

MOTIVATING EMPLOYEES

•

LEARNING
OBJECTIVES

**After Reading
This Chapter,
You Should
Be Able To:**

1. Define the motivation process.
2. Explain the hierarchy of needs theory.
3. Differentiate Theory X from Theory Y.
4. Explain the motivational implications of the motivation-hygiene theory.
5. Identify the characteristics that high achievers seek in a job.
6. Explain how goals motivate people.
7. Differentiate reinforcement theory from goal-setting theory.
8. Describe the motivational implications of equity theory.
9. Explain the key relationships in expectancy theory.
10. Identify the conditions under which money can motivate.

n 1984, when Tina Irwin started Friendship Cards, she wanted to use her degree in commercial design to make and sell greeting cards. Of course, she hoped to make a decent living, too. Today, Tina's firm employs twelve people and provides her with an annual income that exceeds $100,000.

In March 1990, Tina decided to share her firm's success with her employees. She announced that, during the upcoming months of June, July, and August, Friendship Cards would close on Fridays. All employees could therefore enjoy a three-day weekend. Of course, they would continue to be paid as if they had worked a full five-day week.

The three-day weekend had been in place about a month when one of Tina's most trusted employees confided to her that he would have preferred a pay increase instead of the extra days off. He was sure that several others felt the same way.

Tina was surprised. Most of her employees were under 30 years of age, yet were paid an average of $35,000 a year. This was a good 20 percent more than other employers in town were paying for comparable jobs. Tina knew that if *she* were making $35,000 a year and were given the choice of more money or more free time, she would have no trouble deciding. She'd take the free time. She thought her employees would too. But Tina had an open mind. At the next staff meeting she polled all twelve employees. She asked, "What's your preference? Do you want the four-day workweek for the summer months, or would you rather have a $4,000 cash bonus? How many want to continue the four-day week?" Six hands rose. "How many would prefer the money instead?" The other six hands went up.

This incident taught Tina something about rewarding and motivating her employees. Moreover, Tina's lesson can be generalized to all students of management. Successful managers understand that not everyone is like them. What motivates them may have little or no effect on others. Effective managers know that if they want their employees to make a maximum effort, they should tailor their motivational practices to reflect this fact.[1]

WHAT IS MOTIVATION?

To understand what motivation *is*, let us begin by pointing out what motivation *isn't*. Why? Because many people incorrectly view motivation as a personal trait—that is, some have it and others don't. In practice, this would characterize the manager who labels a certain employee as lazy. Such a label assumes that an individual is always lazy or is lacking in motivation. Our knowledge of motivation tells us that this just isn't true. What we know is that motivation is the result of the interaction between the individual and the situation. Certainly, individuals differ in motivational drive. You may read a complete novel at one sitting yet find it difficult to stay with a textbook for more than twenty minutes. It's not necessarily you—it's the situation. As we analyze

Tina learned something about people when she assumed that everyone desires more free time. People's needs differ. Just because Tina values free time over money doesn't mean that everyone who works for her feels the same.

The same employee who is quickly bored when pulling the lever on his drill press might pull the lever on a slot machine in Las Vegas for hours on end without the slightest hint of boredom. Why do you think that is?

motivation
The willingness to exert high levels of effort to reach organizational goals, conditioned by the effort's ability to satisfy some individual need.

need
An internal state that makes certain outcomes appear attractive.

the concept of motivation, keep in mind that level of motivation varies both between individuals and within individuals at different times.

We'll define **motivation** as the willingness to exert high levels of effort to reach organizational goals, conditioned by the effort's ability to satisfy some individual need. While general motivation refers to effort toward *any* goal, here it will refer to *organizational goals* because our focus is on work-related behavior. The three key elements in our definition are effort, organizational goals, and needs.

The *effort* element is a measure of intensity. When someone is motivated, he or she tries hard. But high levels of effort are unlikely to lead to favorable job performance outcomes unless the effort is channeled in a direction that benefits the organization.[2] Therefore we must consider the quality of the effort as well as its intensity. Effort that is directed toward, and consistent with, the organization's goals is the kind of effort that we should be seeking. Finally, we will treat motivation as a need-satisfying process. This is depicted in Figure 14-1.

A **need,** in our terminology, means some internal state that makes certain outcomes appear attractive. An unsatisfied need creates tension that stimulates drives within an individual. These drives generate a search behavior to find particular goals that, if attained, will satisfy the need and reduce the tension.

We can say that motivated employees are in a state of tension. To relieve this tension, they exert effort. The greater the tension, the higher the effort level. If this

FIGURE 14-1   The Motivation Process

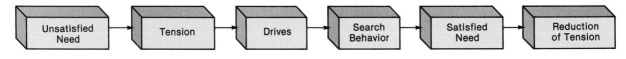

Unsatisfied Need → Tension → Drives → Search Behavior → Satisfied Need → Reduction of Tension

effort successfully leads to the satisfaction of the need, it reduces tension. Since we are interested in work behavior, this tension-reduction effort must also be directed toward organizational goals. Therefore, inherent in our definition of motivation is the requirement that the individual's needs be compatible and consistent with the organization's goals. When this does not occur, individuals may exert high levels of effort that run counter to the interests of the organization. Incidentally, this is not so unusual. Some employees regularly spend a lot of time talking with friends at work in order to satisfy their social needs. There is a high level of effort, but it's being unproductively directed.

ETHICAL DILEMMAS IN MANAGEMENT

Are "Loyalty Expectations" Making Managers Unethical?

Is it unethical to say that one is committed to his or her employer but not actually believe it? Is it unethical for a manager to *use* an organization for his or her own interests? These questions force us to assess the role of loyalty in today's organizations.[3]

Before the 1980s—before the merger and acquisition wave, when foreign competition was essentially irrelevant, and no one had heard terms like "downsizing" and "lean and mean"—employees tended to join organizations for the long haul. Employees were willing to sacrifice for their organization and, in return, were provided with a sense of belonging and job security. Companies made a commitment to employees and vice versa. Loyalty was valued and expected.

In the 1980s, when organization after organization laid off thousands or tens of thousands of employees in order to become more competitive, these organizations, in effect, unilaterally broke that bond. Some observers even believe that today's organizations don't want to build the expectation in their employees that it is the organization's responsibility to take care of them. They contend that commitment, from the organization's standpoint, is increasingly being defined in days rather than decades.

Even if the bond of loyalty between employee and employer is disintegrating, role expectations regarding *managers'* loyalty aren't changing accordingly. Very few organizational cultures tolerate managers openly admitting that loyalty to their organization is passé. Managers are expected to speak and behave as if they are totally committed to their organization.

Are managers being placed in an ethical dilemma that requires them to say one thing though they believe something very different? Is it unethical for managers to espouse loyalty to their organizations but, in actuality, use their organizations to further their personal career ambitions? What do *you* think?

EARLY THEORIES OF MOTIVATION

hierarchy of needs theory
Five human needs identified by Maslow: physiological, safety, social, esteem, and self-actualization. As each need is substantially satisfied, the next need becomes dominant.

physiological needs
Basic hunger, thirst, shelter, and sexual needs

safety needs
A person's needs for security and protection from physical and emotional harm.

social needs
A person's needs for affection, belongingness, acceptance, and friendship.

esteem needs
Internal factors such as self-respect, autonomy, and achievement; and external factors such as status, recognition, and attention.

self-actualization needs
A person's drive to become what he or she is capable of becoming.

lower-order needs
Physiological and safety needs.

higher-order needs
Social, esteem, and self-actualization needs.

The 1950s were a fruitful time for the development of motivation concepts. Three specific theories were formulated during this period, which, though heavily attacked and now considered of questionable validity, are probably still the best-known explanations for employee motivation. These are the *hierarchy of needs theory, Theories X and Y,* and the *motivation-hygiene theory.* While we have developed more valid explanations of motivation, you should know these theories for at least two reasons: (1) They represent a foundation from which contemporary theories grew, and (2) practicing managers regularly use these theories and their terminology in explaining employee motivation.

Hierarchy of Needs Theory

The best-known theory of motivation is probably Abraham Maslow's **hierarchy of needs theory.**[4] He hypothesized that within every human being there exists a hierarchy of five needs. These are:

1. **Physiological needs:** food, drink, shelter, sexual satisfaction, and other bodily requirements
2. **Safety needs:** security and protection from physical and emotional harm
3. **Social needs:** affection, belongingness, acceptance, and friendship
4. **Esteem needs:** internal esteem factors such as self-respect, autonomy, and achievement; and external esteem factors such as status, recognition, and attention
5. **Self-actualization needs:** growth, achieving one's potential, and self-fulfillment; the drive to become what one is capable of becoming

As each need is substantially satisfied, the next need becomes dominant. In terms of Figure 14–2, the individual moves up the hierarchy. From the standpoint of motivation, the theory says that although no need is ever fully gratified, a substantially satisfied need no longer motivates. If you want to motivate someone, according to Maslow, you need to understand where that person is in the hierarchy and focus on satisfying needs at or above that level.

Maslow separated the five needs into higher and lower levels. Physiological and safety needs were described as **lower-order needs** and social, esteem, and self-actualization as **higher-order needs.** The differentiation between the two orders was made on the premise that higher-order needs are satisfied internally, whereas

FIGURE 14–2
Maslow's Hierarchy of Needs

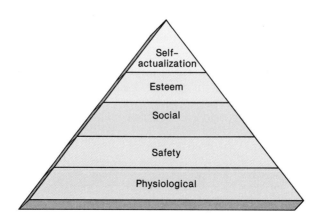

lower-order needs are predominantly satisfied externally (by such things as wages, union contracts, and tenure). In fact, the natural conclusion to be drawn from Maslow's classification is that, in times of economic plenty, almost all permanently employed workers have their lower-order needs substantially met.

Maslow's need theory has received wide recognition, particularly among practicing managers. This can be attributed to the theory's intuitive logic and ease of understanding. Unfortunately, however, research does not generally validate the theory. Maslow provided no empirical substantiation for his theory, and several studies that sought to validate it found no support.[5]

Old theories, especially ones that are intuitively logical, apparently die hard. One researcher reviewed the evidence and concluded that "although of great societal popularity, need hierarchy as a theory continues to receive little empirical support."[6] Further, the researcher stated that the "available research should certainly generate a reluctance to accept unconditionally the implication of Maslow's hierarchy."[7] Another review came to the same conclusion.[8] Little support was found for the prediction that need structures are organized along the dimensions proposed by Maslow, for the prediction of a negative relationship between the level of need gratification and the activation of that need, or for the prediction of a positive relationship between the level of need gratification and the activation level of the next higher need.

Theory X and Theory Y

Douglas McGregor proposed two distinct views of the nature of human beings: a basically negative view, labeled *Theory X,* and a basically positive view, labeled *Theory Y.*[9] After viewing the way managers dealt with employees, McGregor concluded that a manager's view of human nature is based on a group of assumptions and that the manager molds his or her behavior toward subordinates according to these assumptions.

Under **Theory X,** the four assumptions held by a manager are the following:

Theory X
The assumption that employees dislike work, are lazy, seek to avoid responsibility, and must be coerced to perform.

1. Employees inherently dislike work and, whenever possible, will attempt to avoid it.
2. Since employees dislike work, they must be coerced, controlled, or threatened with punishment to achieve desired goals.
3. Employees will shirk responsibilities and seek formal direction whenever possible.
4. Most workers place security above all other factors associated with work and will display little ambition.

In contrast to these negative views of human nature, McGregor listed four other assumptions, which he called **Theory Y:**

Theory Y
The assumption that employees are creative, seek responsibility, and can exercise self-direction.

1. Employees can view work as being as natural as rest or play.
2. Men and women will exercise self-direction and self-control if they are committed to the objectives.
3. The average person can learn to accept, even seek, responsibility.
4. The ability to make good decisions is widely dispersed throughout the population and is not necessarily the sole province of managers.

What does McGregor's analysis imply about motivation? The answer is best expressed in the framework presented by Maslow. Theory X assumes that lower-order needs dominate individuals. Theory Y assumes that higher-order needs dominate individuals. McGregor himself held to the belief that the assumptions of Theory Y were more valid than those of Theory X. Therefore he proposed that participation in decision making, responsible and challenging jobs, and good group relations would maximize job motivation.

Unfortunately, there is no evidence to confirm that either set of assumptions is valid or that accepting Theory Y assumptions and altering one's actions accordingly will make one's employees more motivated. As we shall see, the assumptions of either theory may be appropriate in a particular situation.

Motivation-Hygiene Theory

motivation-hygiene theory
The theory that intrinsic factors are related to job satisfaction, while extrinsic factors are associated with dissatisfaction.

The **motivation-hygiene theory** was proposed by psychologist Frederick Herzberg.[10] In the belief that an individual's relation to his or her work is a basic one and that his or her attitude to work can very well determine success or failure, Herzberg investigated the question: What do people want from their jobs? He asked people to describe in detail situations in which they felt exceptionally good or bad about their jobs. These responses were tabulated and placed into one of sixteen categories. A summary of what Herzberg found is shown in Figure 14–3.

From analyzing the responses, Herzberg concluded that the replies people gave when they felt good about their jobs were significantly different from the replies given when they felt bad. As seen in Figure 14–3, certain characteristics were consistently related to job satisfaction (factors on the left side of the figure), and others to job dissatisfaction (the right side of the figure). Intrinsic factors such as achievement, recognition, the work itself, responsibility, advancement, and growth were related to job satisfaction. When those questioned felt good about their work, they tended to attribute these characteristics to themselves. On the other hand, when they were dissatisfied, they tended to cite extrinsic factors such as company policy and administration, supervision, interpersonal relationships, and working conditions.

The data suggest, said Herzberg, that the opposite of satisfaction is not dissatisfaction, as was traditionally believed. Removing dissatisfying characteristics from a job does not necessarily make the job satisfying. As illustrated in Figure 14–4, Herzberg proposed that his findings indicate the existence of a dual continuum: The opposite of "satisfaction" is "no satisfaction," and the opposite of "dissatisfaction" is "no dissatisfaction."

According to Herzberg, the factors leading to job satisfaction are separate and distinct from those that lead to job dissatisfaction. Therefore managers who seek to eliminate factors that create job dissatisfaction can bring about peace, but not necessarily motivation. They are placating their work force rather than motivating it. As a result, company policy and administration, supervision, interpersonal relations, work-

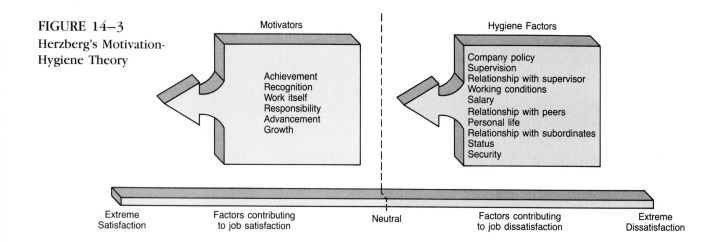

FIGURE 14–3
Herzberg's Motivation-Hygiene Theory

FIGURE 14–4
Contrasting Views of Satisfaction-Dissatisfaction

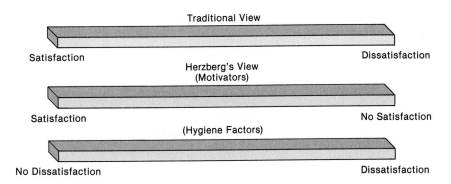

hygiene factors
Factors that eliminate dissatisfaction.

motivators
Factors that increase job satisfaction.

ing conditions, and salary were characterized by Herzberg as **hygiene factors.** When these factors are adequate, people will not be dissatisfied; however, neither will they be satisfied. To motivate people on their jobs, Herzberg suggested emphasizing **motivators** such as achievement, recognition, the work itself, responsibility, and growth. Herzberg argued that these are the characteristics that people find intrinsically rewarding.

The motivation-hygiene theory is not without its detractors. The criticisms of the theory include the following:

1. The procedure that Herzberg used was limited by its methodology. When things are going well, people tend to take the credit themselves. They blame failure on extrinsic factors.

2. The reliability of Herzberg's methodology was questionable. Since raters had to make interpretations, they might have contaminated the findings by interpreting one response in one manner while treating another similar response differently.

3. No overall measure of satisfaction was utilized. A person may dislike part of his or her job yet still think the job is acceptable.

4. The theory is inconsistent with previous research. The motivation-hygiene theory ignores situational variables.

5. Herzberg assumed that there is a relationship between satisfaction and productivity, but the research methodology he used looked only at satisfaction, not at productivity. To make such research relevant, one must assume a close relationship between satisfaction and productivity.[11]

Regardless of these criticisms, Herzberg's theory has been widely popularized, and few managers are unfamiliar with his recommendations. Much of the enthusiasm for job enrichment, discussed in Chapter 11, can be attributed to Herzberg's findings and recommendations.

CONTEMPORARY THEORIES OF MOTIVATION

While the previous theories are well known, they unfortunately have not held up well under close examination. However, all is not lost. A number of contemporary theories have one thing in common: each has a reasonable degree of valid supporting documentation. The following theories represent the current "state-of-the-art" explanations of employee motivation.

Three-Needs Theory

three-needs theory
The needs for achievement, power, and affiliation are major motives in work.

need for achievement
The drive to excel, to achieve in relation to a set of standards, to strive to succeed.

need for power
The need to make others behave in a way that they would not have behaved otherwise.

need for affiliation
The desire for friendly and close interpersonal relationships.

David McClelland and others have proposed the **three-needs theory**—that there are three major relevant motives or needs in work situations:

1. **Need for achievement *(nAch)*:** the drive to excel, to achieve in relation to a set of standards, to strive to succeed
2. **Need for power *(nPow)*:** the need to make others behave in a way that they would not have behaved otherwise
3. **Need for affiliation *(nAff)*:** the desire for friendly and close interpersonal relationships[12]

Some people have a compelling drive to succeed, but they are striving for personal achievement rather than for the rewards of success per se. They have a desire to do something better or more efficiently than it has been done before. This drive is the need for achievement. From research concerning the achievement need, McClelland found that high achievers differentiate themselves from others by their desire to do things better.[13] They seek situations in which they can attain personal responsibility for finding solutions to problems, in which they can receive rapid and unambiguous feedback on their performance in order to tell whether they are improving or not, and in which they can set moderately challenging goals. High achievers are not gamblers; they dislike succeeding by chance. They prefer the challenge of working at a problem and accepting the personal responsibility for success or failure, rather than leaving the outcome to chance or the actions of others. An important point is that they avoid what they perceive to be very easy or very difficult tasks. (See Figure 14–5.)

High achievers perform best when they perceive their probability of success as being 0.5—that is, when they estimate that they have a fifty-fifty chance of success. They dislike gambling when the odds are high because they get no achievement satisfaction from happenstance success. Similarly, they dislike low odds (high probability of success) because then there is no challenge to their skills. They like to set goals that require stretching themselves a little. When there is an approximately equal chance of success or failure, there is the optimum opportunity to experience feelings of successful accomplishment and satisfaction from their efforts.

The need for power is the desire to have impact and to be influential. Individuals high in *nPow* enjoy being "in charge," strive for influence over others, prefer to be in competitive and status-oriented situations, and are more concerned with gaining influence over others and prestige than with effective performance.

The third need isolated by McClelland is affiliation. This need has received the least attention by researchers. Affiliation can be viewed as a Dale Carnegie type of need: the desire to be liked and accepted by others. Individuals with high *nAff* strive for friendships, prefer cooperative situations rather than competitive ones, and desire relationships involving a high degree of mutual understanding.

How do you find out if someone is, for instance, a high achiever? All three motives are typically measured by a projective test in which subjects respond to a set of pictures. Each picture is briefly shown to a subject who then writes a story based on the picture.

Based on an extensive amount of research, some reasonably well-supported predictions can be made between the relationship of the achievement need and job

FIGURE 14–5
Matching Achievers and Jobs

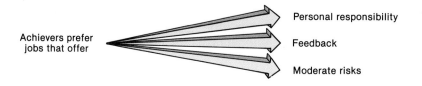

performance. Though less research has been done on power and affiliation needs, there are consistent findings here too. First, individuals with a high need to achieve prefer job situations with personal responsibility, feedback, and an intermediate degree of risk. When these characteristics are prevalent, high achievers are strongly motivated. The evidence consistently demonstrates, for instance, that high achievers are successful in entrepreneurial activities like running their own business, managing a self-contained unit within a large organization, and many sales positions.[14] Second, a high need to achieve does not necessarily lead to being a good manager, especially in large organizations. High *nAch* salespeople do not necessarily make good sales managers, and good managers in a large organization do not necessarily have a high need to achieve.[15] Third, the needs for affiliation and power are closely related to managerial success.[16] The best managers are high in the need for power and low in the need for affiliation. Last, employees can be trained successfully to stimulate their achievement need.[17] If a job calls for a high achiever, management can select a person with a high *nAch* or develop its own candidate through achievement training.

Goal-Setting Theory

goal-setting theory
Specific goals increase performance and difficult goals, when accepted, result in higher performance than easy goals.

In Chapter 7, in our discussion of MBO, we found substantial support for the thesis that specific goals increase performance and that difficult goals, when accepted, result in higher performance than do easy goals. This thesis has been labeled **goal-setting theory.** It's not necessary to review the evidence again, but the results are important, so let's summarize what we know about goals as motivators.

Intention to work toward a goal is a major source of job motivation. Studies on goal setting have demonstrated the superiority of specific and challenging goals as motivating forces.[18] While we can't state that having employees participate in the goal-setting process is always desirable, participation is probably preferable to assigning goals when you expect resistance to accepting more difficult challenges.

The highly astute reader may have noted what appears to be a contradiction between the research findings on achievement motivation and goal setting. Is it a contradiction that achievement motivation is stimulated by moderately challenging goals, whereas goal-setting theory says that motivation is maximized by difficult goals? The answer is No. The explanation is twofold.[19] First, goal-setting theory deals with people in general. The conclusions on achievement motivation are based only on people who have a high *nAch*. Given the probability that not more than 10 to 20 percent of North Americans are naturally high achievers, difficult goals are still recommended for the majority of workers. Second, the conclusions of goal-setting theory apply to those who accept and are committed to the goals. Difficult goals will lead to higher performance only if they are accepted.

Reinforcement Theory

reinforcement theory
Behavior is a function of its consequences.

A counterpoint to goal-setting theory is **reinforcement theory.** Goal-setting theory is a cognitive approach; it proposes that an individual's purposes direct his or her actions. Reinforcement theory is a behavioristic approach; it argues that reinforcement conditions behavior. The two are clearly at odds philosophically. Reinforcement theorists see behavior as environmentally caused. You need not be concerned, they would argue, with internal cognitive events; what controls behavior are **reinforcers:** consequences that, when immediately following a response, increase the probability that the behavior will be repeated.

reinforcer
Any consequence immediately following a response that increases the probability that the behavior will be repeated.

Reinforcement theory ignores the inner state of the individual and concentrates solely on what happens to a person when he or she takes some action. Because it does not concern itself with what initiates behavior, it is not, strictly speaking, a theory of

Emery Air Freight's management wanted packers to use freight containers for shipments whenever possible because of cost savings. When packers were queried as to the percentage of shipments that were containerized, the standard reply was 90 percent. But Emery found the true figure to be 45 percent. Using positive reinforcement, Emery asked each packer to keep a checklist of his or her daily packings, both containerized and noncontainerized. At the end of each day the packer computed his or her container utilization rate. Container utilization jumped to more than 90 percent on the first day of the program and held to that level.

motivation. But it does provide a powerful means of analyzing what controls behavior, and for this reason it is considered in discussions of motivation.

In the last chapter we introduced the law of effect as it relates to learning. We showed that reinforcers condition behavior and help to explain how people learn. But the law of effect and the concept of reinforcement are also widely believed to explain motivation. The strongest proponent has undoubtedly been the psychologist B.F. Skinner.[20] The basic logic of reinforcement theory can be explained as follows: People will most likely engage in desired behavior if they are rewarded for doing so; these rewards are most effective if they immediately follow a desired response; and behavior that is not rewarded, or is punished, is less likely to be repeated. We can expand somewhat upon the research base of this argument.

Skinner assumes that behavior is determined from without, not from within. Therefore he believes it can be exactly predicted. Since people repeat behaviors that are positively rewarded and avoid behaviors that are punished, managers can influence others' behavior by reinforcing acts they deem favorable. However, since the emphasis is on positive reinforcement, not punishment, they should ignore, not punish, unfavorable behavior. Even though punishment eliminates undesired behavior more quickly than nonreinforcement does, its effect is often only temporary and may later have unpleasant side effects such as dysfunctional conflictual behavior, absenteeism, or turnover.

continuous reinforcement schedule

A schedule that reinforces a desired behavior each and every time it is demonstrated.

intermittent reinforcement schedule

A schedule in which reinforcement is given only often enough to make the behavior worth repeating.

The two major schedules of reinforcement are called *continuous* and *intermittent.* A **continuous reinforcement schedule** reinforces the desired behavior each and every time it is demonstrated. For example, in the case of a woman who is chronically late for work, every time she is *not* tardy, her manager might compliment her on her desirable behavior. In an **intermittent reinforcement schedule,** on the other hand, not every instance of the desirable behavior is reinforced. Reinforcement is given only often enough to make the behavior worth repeating. The intermittent schedule can be compared to the workings of a Las Vegas slot machine, which people will continue to play even when they know that it is adjusted to give a considerable return to the gambling house. The intermittent payoffs occur just often enough to reinforce the behavior of slipping in coins and pulling the handle. Evidence indicates that the intermittent, or varied, form of reinforcement promotes steadier and stronger behavior than does the continuous form.[21]

The evidence indicates that reinforcement is undoubtedly an important influence on work behavior. But reinforcement is not the *only* explanation for differences in employee motivation.[22] Goals, for instance, affect motivation, as do levels of achievement motivation, inequities in rewards, and expectations.

Equity Theory

Employees don't work in a vacuum. They make comparisons. If someone offered you $40,000 a year on your first job upon graduation from college, you'd probably grab the offer and report to work enthusiastic and certainly satisfied with your pay. How would you react if you found out a month or so into the job that a co-worker—another recent graduate, your age, with comparable grades from a comparable college—was getting $45,000 a year? You would probably be upset! Even though, in absolute terms, $40,000 is a lot of money for a new graduate to make (and you know it!), that suddenly would not be the issue. The issue would now center around relative rewards and what you believe is fair. There is considerable evidence that employees make comparisons of their job inputs and outcomes relative to others and that inequities influence the degree of effort that employees exert.[23]

Developed by J. Stacey Adams, **equity theory** says that employees perceive what they get from a job situation (outcomes) in relation to what they put into it (inputs) and then compare their inputs-outcomes ratio with the inputs-outcomes ratio of relevant others. This is shown in Table 14–1. If they perceive their ratio to be equal to those of the relevant others with whom they compare themselves, a state of equity exists. They perceive that their situation is fair—that justice prevails. If the ratios are unequal, inequity exists; that is, they view themselves as underrewarded or overrewarded. When inequities occur, employees attempt to correct them.

The **referent** with whom employees choose to compare themselves is an important variable in equity theory.[24] The three referent categories have been classified as "other," "system," and "self." The "other" category includes other individuals with similar jobs in the same organization and also includes friends, neighbors, or professional associates. On the basis of information they receive through word of mouth, newspapers, and magazine articles on issues such as executive salaries or a recent union contract, employees compare their pay with that of others.

The "system" category considers organizational pay policies and procedures and the administration of this system. It considers organizationwide pay policies, both implied and explicit. Precedents by the organization in terms of allocation of pay are major determinants in this category.

The "self" category refers to inputs-outcomes ratios that are unique to the individual. This category is influenced by criteria such as past jobs or family commitments.

equity theory
The theory that an employee compares his or her job's inputs-outcomes ratio to that of relevant others and then corrects any inequity.

referents
The persons, systems, or selves against which individuals compare themselves to assess equity.

TABLE 14–1   Equity Theory

Perceived Ratio Comparison*	Employee's Assessment
$\dfrac{\text{Outcomes A}}{\text{Inputs A}} < \dfrac{\text{Outcomes B}}{\text{Inputs B}}$	Inequity (underrewarded)
$\dfrac{\text{Outcomes A}}{\text{Inputs A}} = \dfrac{\text{Outcomes B}}{\text{Inputs B}}$	Equity
$\dfrac{\text{Outcomes A}}{\text{Inputs A}} > \dfrac{\text{Outcomes B}}{\text{Inputs B}}$	Inequity (overrewarded)

*Person A is the employee, and Person B is a relevant other or referent.

The choice of a particular set of referents is related to the information available about referents as well as to their perceived relevance. On the basis of equity theory, when employees perceive an inequity, they may:

1. distort either their own or others' inputs or outcomes;
2. behave in some way to induce others to change their inputs or outcomes;
3. behave in some way to change their own inputs or outcomes;
4. choose a different comparison referent; and/or
5. quit their job.

Equity theory recognizes that individuals are concerned not only with the absolute rewards they receive for their efforts, but also with the relationship of these rewards to what others receive. They make judgments concerning the relationship between their inputs and outcomes and the inputs and outcomes of others. On the basis of one's inputs, such as effort, experience, education, and competence, one compares outcomes such as salary levels, raises, recognition, and other factors. When people perceive an imbalance in their inputs-outcomes ratio relative to those of others, they experience tension. This tension provides the basis for motivation as people strive for what they perceive as equity and fairness.

Specifically, the theory establishes the following four propositions relating to inequitable pay:

1. *Given payment by time, overrewarded employees will produce more than equitably paid employees.* Hourly and salaried employees will generate a high quantity or quality of production in order to increase the input side of the ratio and bring about equity.

2. *Given payment by quantity of production, overrewarded employees will produce fewer but higher-quality units than equitably paid employees.* Individuals paid on a piece-rate basis will increase their effort to achieve equity, which can result in greater quality or quantity. However, increases in quantity will only increase inequity, since every unit produced results in further overpayment. Therefore effort is directed toward increasing quality rather than quantity.

3. *Given payment by time, underrewarded employees will produce less or poorer-quality output.* Effort will be decreased, which will bring about lower productivity or poorer-quality output than equitably paid subjects.

4. *Given payment by quantity of production, underrewarded employees will produce a large number of low-quality units in comparison with equitably paid employees.* Employees on piece-rate pay plans can bring about equity because trading off quality of output for quantity will result in an increase in rewards with little or no increase in contributions.

The propositions listed above have generally proven to be correct.[25] A review of the research consistently confirms the equity thesis: Employee motivation is influenced significantly by relative rewards as well as absolute rewards. Whenever employees perceive inequity, they will act to correct the situation.[26] The result might be lower or higher productivity, improved or reduced quality of output, increased absenteeism, or voluntary resignation.

From the discussion above, however, we should not conclude that equity theory is without problems. The theory leaves some key issues still unclear.[27] For instance, how do employees select who is included in the "other" referent category? How do they define inputs and outcomes? How do they combine and weigh their inputs and outcomes to arrive at totals? When and how do the factors change over time? Regardless of these problems, equity theory has an impressive amount of research support and offers us some important insights into employee motivation.

IN PRACTICE

Two-tier pay system
A system in which new employees are hired at a significantly lower wage than that paid to those already employed in the same job.

Two-Tier Pay Systems

In the early 1980s, a number of companies introduced something called a **two-tier pay system** as a way to hold down labor costs. In this system, new employees are hired at significantly lower wage rates than those already employed in the same job.[28] For instance, new machinists at Boeing were starting at $6.70 an hour, while co-workers who had been hired before implementation of the two-tier contract made a minimum of $11.38 an hour.[29]

Two-tier pay systems reached their peak in popularity around 1985, when 11 percent of collective bargaining agreements made with unions included them. Since then, however, the frequency of two-tier wage plans have been declining.[30] These systems built resentment among new hires, undermined employee loyalty, and worked against new employees contributing their best efforts to the organization.

Anyone with a knowledge of equity theory could have predicted this result. The two-tier pay system is inconsistent with equity theory. Equity theory tells us that employees compare their inputs-outcomes ratio against those of others. One of the most obvious "others" is co-workers. If you're doing the same job as someone else for significantly less money, yet feel that your background and experience are relatively similar, you're not likely to ignore this perceived discrepancy. Remember, too, that new employees soon become old ones. After a few years, the lower-paid workers can't see any reason why they should be paid less than other people doing the same job.

Expectancy Theory

expectancy theory
The theory that the tendency to act in a certain way depends on the strength of the expectation that the act will be followed by a given outcome and on the attractiveness of that outcome to the individual.

The most comprehensive explanation of motivation is Victor Vroom's **expectancy theory**.[31] Though it has its critics,[32] most of the research evidence is supportive of the theory.[33]

The expectancy theory argues that the strength of a tendency to act in a certain way depends on the strength of the expectation that the act will be followed by a given outcome and on the attractiveness of that outcome to the individual. It includes three variables or relationships:

1. *Attractiveness:* the importance that the individual places on the potential outcome or reward that can be achieved on the job. This considers the unsatisfied needs of the individual.

2. *Performance-reward linkage:* the degree to which the individual believes that performing at a particular level will lead to the attainment of a desired outcome.

3. *Effort-performance linkage:* the probability perceived by the individual that exerting a given amount of effort will lead to performance.[34]

While this might sound pretty complex, it really is not that difficult to visualize. Whether one has the desire to produce at any given time depends on one's particular goals and one's perception of the relative worth of performance as a path to the attainment of these goals.

Figure 14–6 shows a very simple version of the expectancy theory that expresses its major contentions. The strength of a person's motivation to perform (effort) depends on how strongly that individual believes that he or she can achieve what is being attempted. If this goal is achieved (performance), will he or she be adequately rewarded by the organization? If so, will the reward satisfy his or her individual goals? Let us consider the four steps inherent in the theory and then attempt to apply it.

First, what perceived outcomes does the job offer the employee? Outcomes may be positive: pay, security, companionship, trust, fringe benefits, a chance to use talent or skills, or congenial relationships. On the other hand, employees may view the outcomes as negative: fatigue, boredom, frustration, anxiety, harsh supervision, or threat of dismissal. Reality is not relevant here; the critical issue is what the individual employee *perceives* the outcome to be, regardless of whether his or her perceptions are accurate.

Second, how attractive do employees consider these outcomes to be? Are they valued positively, negatively, or neutrally? This obviously is an internal issue and considers the individual's personal attitudes, personality, and needs. The individual who finds a particular outcome attractive—that is, values it positively—would rather attain it than not attain it. Others may find it negative and therefore prefer not attaining it to attaining it. Still others may be neutral.

Third, what kind of behavior must the employee exhibit to achieve these outcomes? The outcomes are not likely to have any effect on an individual employee's performance unless the employee knows, clearly and unambiguously, what he or she must do to achieve them. For example, what is "doing well" in terms of performance appraisal? What criteria will be used to judge the employee's performance?

Fourth and last, how does the employee view his or her chances of doing what is asked? After the employee has considered his or her own competencies and ability to control those variables that will determine success, what probability does he or she place on successful attainment?[35]

Let's use the classroom organization as an illustration of how one can use the expectancy theory to explain motivation.

Most students prefer an instructor who tells them what is expected of them in the course. They want to know what the assignments and examinations will be like, when they are due or to be taken, and how much weight each carries in the final term grade. They also like to think that the amount of effort they exert in attending classes, taking notes, and studying will be reasonably related to the grade they will make in the course. Let us assume that you, as a student, feel this way. Consider that five weeks into a class you are really enjoying (we'll call it MGT 301), an examination is given back to you. You studied hard for this examination, and you have consistently made A's and B's on examinations in other courses in which you have expended similar effort. The reason you work so hard is to make top grades, which you believe are important for getting a good job upon graduation. Also, you are not sure, but you might want to go on to graduate school. Again, you think grades are important for getting into a good graduate school.

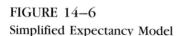
FIGURE 14–6
Simplified Expectancy Model

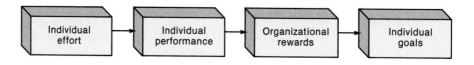

Individual effort → Individual performance → Organizational rewards → Individual goals

Why are many people not motivated at work? Expectancy theory suggests some possible answers: They don't believe that high levels of effort will lead to high performance evaluations. High evaluations may not necessarily result in a significant increase in rewards. Even if high performance is rewarded by the organization, the reward might not be tailored to the needs of the employee.

Well, the results of that five-week examination are in. The class median was 72. Ten percent of the class scored an 85 or higher and got an A. Your grade was 46; the minimum passing mark was 50. You're mad. You're frustrated. Even more, you're perplexed. How could you possibly have done so poorly on the examination when you usually score in the top range in other classes by preparing as you did for this one?

Several interesting things are immediately evident in your behavior. Suddenly, you are no longer driven to attend MGT 301 classes regularly. You find that you do not study for the course either. When you do attend classes, you daydream a lot—the result is an empty notebook instead of several pages of notes. One would probably be correct in describing you as "lacking in motivation" in MGT 301. Why did your motivation level change? You know and I know, but let's explain it in expectancy terms.

If we use Figure 14–6 to understand this situation, we might say the following: Studying and preparing for MGT 301 (effort) are conditioned by their resulting in correctly answering the questions on the examination (performance), which will produce a high grade (reward), which will lead, in turn, to the security, prestige, and other benefits that accrue from obtaining a good job (individual goal).

The attractiveness of the outcome, which in this case is a good grade, is high. But what about the performance-reward linkage? Do you feel that the grade you received truly reflects your knowledge of the material? In other words, did the test fairly measure what you know? If the answer is Yes, then this linkage is strong. If the answer is No, then at least part of the reason for your reduced motivational level is your belief that the test was not a fair measure of your performance. If the test was of an essay type, maybe you believe that the instructor's grading method was poor. Was too much weight placed on a question that you thought was trivial? Maybe the instructor does not like you and was biased in grading your paper. These are examples of perceptions that influence the performance-reward linkage and your level of motivation.

Another possible demotivating force may be the effort-performance relationship. If, after you took the examination, you believed that you could not have passed it regardless of the amount of preparation you had done, then your desire to study will drop. Possibly the instructor wrote the examination under the assumption that you had a considerably broader background in the subject matter. Maybe the course had several prerequisites that you did not know about, or possibly you had the prerequisites but took them several years ago. The result is the same: You place a low value on your effort leading to answering the examination questions correctly; hence your motivational level decreases, and you lessen your effort.

The key to the expectancy theory is therefore understanding an individual's goal—and the linkage between effort and performance, between performance and rewards, and, finally, between rewards and individual goal satisfaction. As a contingency model, the expectancy theory recognizes that there is no universal principle for explaining everyone's motivations. In addition, knowing what needs a person seeks to satisfy does not ensure that the individual will perceive that high performance will necessarily lead to the satisfaction of these needs. If you desire to take MGT 301 in order to meet new people and make social contacts, but the instructor organizes the class on the assumption that you want to make a good grade in the course, the instructor may be personally disappointed should you perform poorly on the examinations. Unfortunately, most instructors assume that their ability to allocate grades is a potent force in motivating students. It will be so only if students place a high importance on grades, if students know what they must do to achieve the grade desired, and if the students consider that there is a high probability of their performing well should they exert a high level of effort.

Let us summarize some of the issues surrounding the expectancy theory. First, it emphasizes payoffs, or rewards. As a result, we have to believe that the rewards the organization is offering align with what the employee wants. It is a theory based on self-interest, wherein each individual seeks to maximize his or her expected satisfaction: "Expectancy theory is a form of calculative, psychological *hedonism* in which the ultimate motive of every human act is asserted to be the maximization of pleasure and/or the minimization of pain."[36] Second, we have to be concerned with the attractiveness of rewards, which requires an understanding and knowledge of what value the individual puts on organizational payoffs. We shall want to reward individuals with those things they value positively. Third, the expectancy theory emphasizes expected behaviors. Do individuals know what is expected of them and how they will be appraised? Finally, the theory is concerned with expectations. What is realistic is irrelevant. An individual's own expectations of performance, reward, and goal satisfaction outcomes will determine his or her level of effort, not the objective outcomes themselves.

Integrating Contemporary Theories of Motivation

We have presented a number of theories in this chapter. There is a tendency, at this point, to view them independently. This is a mistake. The fact is that many of the ideas underlying the theories are complementary, and your understanding of how to motivate people is maximized when you see how the theories fit together.

Figure 14–7, on page 447, presents a model that integrates much of what we know about motivation. Its basic foundation is the simplified expectancy model shown in Figure 14–6. Let's work through Figure 14–7, beginning at the left.

The individual effort box has an arrow leading into it. This arrow flows out of the individual's goals. Consistent with goal-setting theory, this goals-effort loop is meant to remind us that goals direct behavior.

Expectancy theory predicts that an employee will exert a high level of effort if he or she perceives that there is a strong relationship between effort and performance, performance and rewards, and rewards and satisfaction of personal goals. Each of these relationships, in turn, is influenced by certain factors. For effort to lead to good performance, the individual must have the requisite ability to perform, and the performance evaluation system that measures the individual's performance must be perceived as being fair and objective. The performance-reward relationship will be strong

MANAGING FROM A GLOBAL PERSPECTIVE

Modifying Motivation Theories for Different Cultures

Theories of motivation have been developed largely by U.S. psychologists and validated by studying American workers. These theories need to be modified for different cultures.[37]

The self-interest concept is consistent with capitalism and the extremely high value placed on individualism in the United States. Since almost all the motivation theories presented in this chapter are based on the self-interest motive, they should be applicable to organizations in countries like Great Britain and Australia, where capitalism and individualism are highly valued. In more collectivist nations—Venezuela, Yugoslavia, Singapore, Japan, and Mexico—the link to the organization is the individual's *loyalty* to the organization or society, rather than his or her self-interest. Employees in collectivist cultures should be more receptive to team-based job design, group goals, and group performance evaluations. Reliance on the fear of being fired in such cultures is likely to be less effective, even if the laws in these countries allow managers to fire employees.

The need-achievement concept provides another example of a motivation theory with a U.S. bias. The view that a high need for achievement acts as an internal motivator presupposes the existence of two cultural characteristics: a willingness to accept a moderate degree of risk and a concern with performance. These characteristics would exclude countries with high uncertainty avoidance scores and high femininity ratings. The remaining countries are exclusively Anglo-American countries like New Zealand, South Africa, Ireland, the United States, and Canada.

Keep in mind that the road goes two ways. Motivation techniques that work well in China, for instance, may be inappropriate in North America. A large department store in Xian, China, selects its forty *worst* sales clerks each year.[38] They have to write self-criticisms and analyze their shortcomings. Management then hangs a plaque over their work stations, complete with picture, proclaiming them as members of the "Forty Worst." This approach was a response to the generally poor service that management felt its clerks were giving customers and the fact that lifetime employment is guaranteed for Chinese employees. The store's management has found that those employees selected for the "Forty Worst" are strongly motivated to improve their performance and to get the plaques removed from their work area. Motivation through humiliation might be acceptable and effective in China, but it isn't likely to work in North America.

if the individual perceives that it is performance (rather than seniority, personal favorites, or other criteria) that is rewarded. The final link in expectancy theory is the rewards-goals relationship. Need theories would come into play at this point. Motivation would be high to the degree that the rewards an individual received for his or her high performance satisfied the dominant needs consistent with his or her individual goals.

FIGURE 14-7
Integrating Contemporary
Theories of Motivation

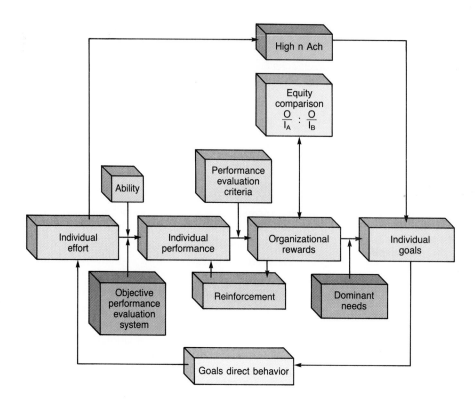

A closer look at Figure 14–7 will also reveal that the model considers the achieve-ment-need and reinforcement and equity theories. The high achiever is not motivated by the organization's assessment of his or her performance or organizational rewards; hence the jump from effort to individual goals for those with a high *nAch*. Remember that high achievers are internally driven as long as the jobs they are doing provide them with personal responsibility, feedback, and moderate risks. They are not con-cerned with the effort-performance, performance-rewards, or rewards-goal linkages.

Reinforcement theory enters our model by recognizing that the organization's rewards reinforce the individual's performance. If management has designed a reward system that is seen by employees as "paying off" for good performance, the rewards will reinforce and encourage continued good performance.

Finally, rewards also play the key part in equity theory. Individuals will compare the rewards (outcomes) they receive from the inputs they make with the inputs-outcomes ratio of relevant others (O/I_A:O/I_B), and inequities may influence the effort expended.

CONTEMPORARY ISSUES IN MOTIVATION

Several topics within the subject of motivation have particular relevance to today's managers. For instance, does money motivate? How do you motivate low-paid service workers? In the following pages we'll look at three such issues.

Does Money Motivate?

According to the contents of this chapter, the answer to the question "Does money motivate?" depends on which theory you accept. According to the motivation-hygiene theory, for instance, money doesn't motivate. It is a hygiene factor, so its presence can only placate workers, not motivate them. On the other hand, expectancy theory would argue that money motivates people if it is contingent on performance and satisfies their personal goals.

Money is a medium of exchange. Therefore it should motivate to the degree that people see it as a means to acquire the things they want. Of course, money also conveys symbolic meaning. Employees use money as a scorecard to assess the value that the organization places on their services. Maybe the strongest case for money as a motivator lies in a comprehensive study that looked at the effect of four different motivational techniques on employee performance. Goal setting, the use of participation, and job redesign were found to produce erratic results on performance—with increases ranging, on average, from less than 1 percent up to 17 percent. Money, however, was consistently shown to improve employee performance, with an average increase of 30 percent.[39]

If we look at the motivational power of money in a contingency framework, it is clear that money motivates *some* people under *some* conditions. To motivate, money must be important to the employee, it must be perceived as a direct reward for performance, the *marginal* increase that is being offered for higher performance must be seen as significant to the employee, and management must have the discretion to provide these significant monetary rewards for higher performance. When these conditions *aren't* met, don't expect money to stimulate much increased effort.

Do Organizations Pay for Performance?

If you asked the question "Do organizations pay for performance?" ten years ago, the answer would have been, with a few exceptions, No. Wage earners got paid by the hour and salary earners by the year. Raises were largely a result of automatic cost-of-living adjustments. The only group that was paid for its performance was senior executives, who received bonuses based on their organizations' overall profitability.

Times have changed. As shown in Table 14–2, incentive plans such as profit sharing, lump-sum bonuses, individual incentives, small-group incentives, and gainsharing have increased dramatically in recent years. In aggregate, about 75 percent of employers now have some form of pay-for-performance incentive plan, roughly 80 percent of these having been adopted since the early 1980s.[40] In other words, the widespread adoption of these plans is a relatively recent phenomenon.

In one recent year, Paul Fireman, CEO at Reebok International, received salary and bonuses equal to more than $11.4 million. Multimillion-dollar compensation packages for top executives act as rewards for superior performance and also motivate other managers to work hard so that someday they, too, might be able to reach the top and earn millions.

TABLE 14–2   Popular Pay-for-Performance Incentive Plans

Plan	Description	Percentage of Organizations Adopting the Plan
Profit sharing	Employees receive a varying annual bonus based on corporate profits	32
Lump-sum bonus	One-time cash payments in place of wage or salary increase	30
Individual incentives	Any pay-for-performance plan that is tied to an employee's individual performance	28
Small-group incentives	Performance rewards based on work-group performance	14
Gainsharing	All members of a unit share in bonuses when they exceed productivity, quality, service, or other performance targets	13

Source: Based on Carla O'Dell and Jerry McAdams, "The Revolution in Employee Rewards," *Management Review,* March 1987, pp. 29–33; and Nancy J. Perry, "Here Come Richer, Riskier Pay Plans," *Fortune,* December 19, 1988, pp. 50–58.

The increasing popularity of pay-for-performance plans is the good news. The bad news is that employees don't seem to be perceiving the changes that are taking place. According to expectancy theory, for pay to be an effective motivator, not only must it be linked to performance, but employees need to see the linkage. A recent national survey found that only 28 percent of workers see any clear tie between their work performance and the pay increases they receive.[41]

The previous data suggests that organizations have come a long way in the last decade toward redesigning pay systems and making them more effective motivating devices. However, there is still plenty of room for improvement, especially in changing employees' perceptions.

Motivating Low-Pay Service Workers

The rapid demise of low-skilled, blue-collar manufacturing jobs that paid $12 to $20 an hour has moved the United States toward a bimodal, service-oriented work force. A significant number of jobs are filled by skilled and well-educated workers who earn high pay. Many other jobs pay at, or slightly above, the minimum wage, such as those offered by fast-food chains. Theories of motivation provide reliable guidelines for dealing with people in the skilled category. They don't, however, provide much help to managers who must motivate low-skilled, low-paid service workers.

The basic problem is this: The low-skilled worker of previous generations could get a unionized job in an automobile or steel plant and earn enough to become a member, in good standing, of the middle class. This worker might have had little opportunity for advancement, but that wasn't a major problem. The worker was committed to job and employer because they provided the means to satisfy most of

MANAGERS WHO MADE A DIFFERENCE

Bill Gates at Microsoft

Most of the media attention that Bill Gates has received tends to focus on the fact that he was a self-made billionaire by the age of thirty. What has often been overlooked is how he made that much money.[42]

Bill Gates is co-founder and chief executive officer of Microsoft, one of the fastest growing computer software firms around. Between 1980 and 1988, his firm grew from annual sales of $8 million to in excess of $600 million. During that same period, Microsoft's payroll increased from eighty people to 1800. The secret to success when your business is developing software products is getting, keeping, and motivating creative people. Bill Gates has demonstrated that he has that ability.

How does Gates motivate and harness innovation at Microsoft? For one thing, the jobs of software designers are enriched. Every couple of months, innovation retreats are held at which marketing and software development people exchange ideas about particular products. Regular product reviews, in which programs are discussed from all angles, include design people as well as program managers. Software designers also are the heart of the company's recruiting. Ninety percent of new hires come right out of college, and software developers visit college campuses, do the interviewing, and essentially determine who will be hired.

In addition to job enrichment, Microsoft stimulates employee motivation and creativity by creating a special promotion track for product designers. In this track, employees get promoted without having to become managers or become involved in management issues. They get increased salary and stock options with each promotion. But most important, they get increased recognition and the autonomy to work on the projects that stimulate them. The top tier for developers is called *architect*. By 1988, only six developers had achieved this level, and they report informally to Gates.

The rapid growth and success of Microsoft have created an unusual motivation problem for Gates. The company's generous stock option program has made many of his employees very wealthy. They have the freedom to go off and do other things besides work at Microsoft. Gates is proud of having created a work climate that is challenging and fun for Microsoft employees—one in which even the rich want to continue to participate.

Photo courtesy of Mr. William Gates.

the family's material needs. Today's low-skilled worker makes $4.00 to $6.00 an hour. That doesn't come close to allowing the worker to move into the middle class. Moreover, promotion opportunities are limited. This leads to the inevitable question: How do you motivate individuals who are making very low wages and have little opportunity to significantly increase their pay either in their current jobs or through promotions?

McDonald's has increasingly turned to retirees to work in their restaurants. Older people have proven to be very effective and loyal employees. Their absentee rates are typically much lower than those of their teenage co-workers.

The problem is real. Unfortunately, there is no ready solution.[43] Pay will need to be increased, but it's unlikely that significantly higher basic wage rates can be passed on to consumers. The public doesn't seem ready yet for the $10 Big Mac. Another option may be merit bonuses based on shift performance. But unless accompanied by higher productivity, such bonuses increase operating costs and have to be passed on to consumers in terms of higher prices. Still a third alternative is to offer benefits such as tuition reimbursement, which used to be reserved for full-time, skilled employees. By linking the amount of benefits to length of employment, employees may be induced to stay longer with a firm. A fourth option is to fill these jobs with teenagers, young adults who are still in school, and retirees whose financial needs are less. Another alternative is to make these jobs more interesting and challenging, though just how this can be done is not clear. The eventual solution will probably involve widening the recruiting net, making jobs more appealing, raising pay levels, instituting performance bonuses, and expanding benefits.

SUMMARY

This summary is organized by the chapter-opening learning objectives found on page 425.

1. Motivation is the willingness to exert high levels of effort toward organizational goals, conditioned by the effort's ability to satisfy some individual need. The motivation process begins with an unsatisfied need, which creates tension and drives an individual to search for goals that, if attained, will satisfy the need and reduce the tension.

2. The hierarchy of needs theory states that there are five needs—physiological, safety, social, esteem, and self-actualization—that individuals attempt to satisfy in a steplike progression. A substantially satisfied need no longer motivates.

3. Theory X is basically a negative view of human nature: assuming that employees dislike work, are lazy, seek to avoid responsibility, and must be coerced to

perform. Theory Y is basically positive: assuming that employees are creative, seek responsibility, and can exercise self-direction.

4. The motivation-hygiene theory proposes that hygiene factors merely placate employees. If you want to motivate them, you need to emphasize factors such as achievement, recognition, the work itself, responsibility, and growth. These are factors people find intrinsically rewarding.

5. High achievers prefer jobs that offer personal responsibility, feedback, and moderate risks.

6. Goals motivate employees by providing specific and challenging bench marks to guide and stimulate performance.

7. Reinforcement theory emphasizes the pattern in which rewards are administered. It assumes that behavior is environmentally caused. Goal-setting theory views motivation as coming from an individual's internal statements of purpose.

8. Equity theory argues that an individual's motivation declines when the individual perceives an inequity between his or her inputs and outcomes relative to relevant others.

9. The expectancy theory argues that the strength of a tendency to act in a certain way depends on the strength of the expectation that the act will be followed by a given outcome and on the attractiveness of that outcome to the individual. Its prime components are the relationships between effort and performance, performance and rewards, and rewards and individual goals.

10. For money to motivate, it must be important to the employee, it must be perceived as a direct reward for performance, the marginal increase that is offered for higher performance must be seen as significant to the employee, and management must have the discretion to provide significant monetary rewards for higher performance.

REVIEW QUESTIONS

1. What are the three key elements in the text's definition of *motivation*?
2. Contrast the hierarchy of needs theory with the motivation-hygiene theory.
3. Which set of assumptions—Theory X or Theory Y—should effective managers hold?
4. Would an individual with a high *nAch* be a good candidate for a management position? Explain.
5. High achievers seek only moderately difficult goals, whereas goal-setting theory argues for difficult goals. Are these two recommendations contradictory?
6. What may employees do if they perceive inequity between their inputs and rewards?
7. What are *two-tier pay systems*? Why have they been declining in popularity?
8. What role does perception play in (a) expectancy theory, (b) equity theory, and (c) reinforcement theory?
9. Do organizations pay for performance?
10. How can management motivate low-paid service workers?

DISCUSSION QUESTIONS

1. Can an employee be *so* motivated that his or her performance declines as a result of excessive effort? Discuss.

2. "Goal setting is part of both reinforcement and expectancy theories." Do you agree or disagree? Explain.

3. What role would money play in (a) the hierarchy of needs theory, (b) motivation-hygiene theory, (c) equity theory, (d) expectancy theory, and (e) employees with a high *nAch* rating?

4. "Job design has specific motivational implications." Discuss.

5. On a scale of 1 to 10 (10 being highest), how would you rate the importance of the following in a job: (a) pay closely tied to performance, (b) recognition, (c) challenging work, (d) promotion opportunities? How do you think your ratings compare with those of most college graduates? How do you think your ratings compare with most jobs filled by college graduates?

SELF-ASSESSMENT EXERCISE

What Needs Are Most Important to You?

Instructions: Rank your responses for each of the following questions. The response that is most important or most true for you should receive a 5; the next should receive a 4; the next a 3; the next a 2; and the least important or least true should receive a 1.

Example

The work I like best involves:

A   _4_   Working alone.

B   _3_   A mixture of time spent with people and time spent alone.

C   _1_   Giving speeches.

D   _2_   Discussion with others.

E   _5_   Working outdoors.

1. Overall, the most important thing to me about a job is whether or not:

   A _____ The pay is sufficient to meet my needs.

   B _____ It provides the opportunity for fellowship and good human relations.

   C _____ It is a secure job with good employee benefits.

   D _____ It allows me freedom and the chance to express myself.

   E _____ There is opportunity for advancement based on my achievements.

2. If I were to quit a job, it would probably be because:

   A _____ It was a dangerous job, such as working with inadequate equipment or poor safety procedures.

   B _____ Continued employment was questionable because of uncertainties in business conditions or funding sources.

   C _____ It was a job people looked down on.

   D _____ It was a one-person job, allowing little opportunity for discussion and interaction with others.

   E _____ The work lacked personal meaning to me.

3. For me, the most important rewards in working are those that:

   A _____ Come from the work itself—important and challenging assignments.

B _____ Satisfy the basic reasons why people work—good pay, a good home, and other economic needs.

C _____ Are provided by fringe benefits—such as hospitalization insurance, time off for vacations, security for retirement, etc.

D _____ Reflect my ability—such as being recognized for the work I do and knowing I am one of the best in my company or profession.

E _____ Come from the human aspects of working—that is, the opportunity to make friends and to be a valued member of a team.

4. My morale would suffer most in a job in which:

A _____ The future was unpredictable.

B _____ Other employees received recognition, when I didn't, for doing the same quality of work.

C _____ My co-workers were unfriendly or held grudges.

D _____ I felt stifled and unable to grow.

E _____ The job environment was poor—no air conditioning, inconvenient parking, insufficient space and lighting, primitive toilet facilities.

5. In deciding whether or not to accept a promotion, I would be most concerned with whether:

A _____ The job was a source of pride and would be viewed with respect by others.

B _____ Taking the job would constitute a gamble on my part, and I could lose more than I gained.

C _____ The economic rewards would be favorable.

D _____ I would like the new people I would be working with, and whether or not we would get along.

E _____ I would be able to explore new areas and do more creative work.

6. The kind of job that brings out my best is one in which:

A _____ There is a family spirit among employees and we all share good times.

B _____ The working conditions—equipment, materials, and basic surroundings—are physically safe.

C _____ Management is understanding and there is little chance of losing my job.

D _____ I can see the returns on my work from the standpoint of personal values.

E _____ There is recognition for achievement.

7. I would consider changing jobs if my present position:

A _____ Did not offer security and fringe benefits.

B _____ Did not provide a chance to learn and grow.

C _____ Did not provide recognition for my performance.

D _____ Did not allow close personal contacts.

E _____ Did not provide economic rewards.

8. The job situation that would cause the most stress for me is:

A _____ Having a serious disagreement with my co-workers.

B _____ Working in an unsafe environment.

C _____ Having an unpredictable supervisor.

D _____ Not being able to express myself.

E _____ Not being appreciated for the quality of my work.

9. I would accept a new position if:

A _____ The position would be a test of my potential.

B _____ The new job would offer better pay and physical surroundings.

C _____ The new job would be secure and offer long-term fringe benefits.

D _____ The position would be respected by others in my organization.

E _____ Good relationships with co-workers and business associates were probable.

10. I would work overtime if:

A _____ The work is challenging.

B _____ I need the extra income.

C _____ My co-workers are also working overtime.

D _____ I must do it to keep my job.

E _____ The company recognizes my contribution.

Turn to page 674 for scoring directions and key.

Source: George Manning and Kent Curtis, *Human Behavior: Why People Do What They Do* (Cincinnati, Ohio: Vista Systems/Southwestern Publishing, 1988), pp. 17–20. With permission.

CASE APPLICATION 14A

Systems One

"I thought I was pretty good at managing people, but I've had to rethink a lot of my premises," began Todd Colberg. "I moved up fast through the ranks at Black & Decker. After twelve years, I was vice president for manufacturing. But I knew I'd never get the top spot—the CEO was only two years older than I was—so when the opportunity came to head up Systems One, I grabbed it."

Systems One is a leading manufacturer of electronic-warfare equipment. The company is young and growing. Founded in 1980, it now has annual sales exceeding $70 million. It employs 350 people, mostly engineers and technical specialists. When interviewed, Todd Colberg had been with Systems One for eight months.

"The design and manufacturing of power tools and small appliances are very different from the kind of work we do here. Most of our contracts are part of the 'Star Wars' program. At Black & Decker we had a number of engineers, but they handled routine types of problems. Here, we're on the cutting edge. We're inventing the future. Our people are incredible. We have some of the smartest people I've ever met. Did I tell you that over 30 percent of our people have Ph.D.'s? You just can't treat the people here the way we did at Black & Decker.

"The typical Systems One employee is a thirty-year-old electrical engineer with a graduate degree. Probably graduated at or near the top of his or her class. This person seeks personal fulfillment and growth from his work. He wants to be challenged! Money and job titles don't mean much. Of course, we pay well. Our starting salary for an electrical engineer is $50,000 a year. A few—those who joined us in the first year or two—make $90,000 plus profit sharing and stock options."

Questions

1. Compare the typical electrical engineer's job at Black & Decker and Systems One. How might the differences influence the needs of the engineers at each firm?
2. What can Todd Colberg do to keep and motivate his technical innovators?
3. Do you think the needs of technical innovators are different from those of other professionals like managers, lawyers, or accountants? Discuss.

CASE APPLICATION 14B

Lincoln Electric

Lincoln Electric is a Cleveland-based firm with sales of $440 million a year, 2,400 employees, and a very unusual way of motivating its employees.[44] What is its business? About 90 percent of its sales come from manufacturing arc-welding equipment and supplies.

Factory workers at Lincoln receive piece-rate wages with no guaranteed minimum hourly pay. After working for the firm for two years, employees begin to participate in the year-end bonus plan. Determined by a formula that considers the company's gross profits, the employees' base piece rate, and merit rating, it might be the most lucrative bonus system for factory workers in U.S. manufacturing. The *average* size of the bonus over the past 56 years has been 95.5 percent of base wages. A handful of Lincoln factory workers make more than $100,000 a year! In recent good years, average employees have earned about $44,000 a year, well above the $17,000 average for U.S. manufacturing workers as a whole. But in a bad year, as during the 1982 recession, Lincoln employees' average fell to $27,000—still not bad, but a significant drop from the better years.

The company has a guaranteed-employment policy, which it put in place in 1958. Since that time, it has not laid off a single worker. In return for job security, however, employees agree to several things. During slow times they will accept reduced work periods. They also agree to accept work transfers, even to lower-paid jobs, if that is necessary to maintain a minimum of 30 hours of work per week.

Lincoln Electric is extremely cost and productivity conscious. If a worker produces a part that does not meet quality standards, he is not paid for that part until it is fixed. The piecework wage system and a highly competitive merit rating system create a pressure-cooker atmosphere that some workers might find excessive. But "the proof of the pudding is in the eating." One company executive estimates that Lincoln's overall productivity is about double that of its domestic competitors. The company has earned a profit every year since the depths of the 1930s depression and has never missed a quarterly dividend. Lincoln has one of the lowest employee turnover rates in U.S. industry. Recently, *Fortune* magazine cited its two U.S. plants as among the ten best-managed in the country.

Questions

1. How does Lincoln's approach to motivating employees differ from most manufacturing firms?

2. Why does it work?

3. Why don't other companies use it?

4. What problems, if any, do you think this system might create for management?

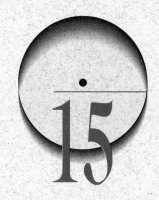

15

LEADERSHIP

●

LEARNING OBJECTIVES

After Reading
This Chapter,
You Should
Be Able To:

1. Explain the difference between managers and leaders.
2. Summarize the conclusions of trait theories.
3. Identify the two underlying behaviors in the Managerial Grid.
4. Describe the Fiedler Contingency Model.
5. Explain the Hersey-Blanchard Situational Theory.
6. Summarize the Path-Goal Model.
7. Explain when leaders may not be that important.
8. Identify the key characteristics of charismatic leaders.

He's a real-life Indiana Jones. Like the swashbuckling movie hero, he fancies himself an expert at wriggling out of the most harrowing predicaments. He lives life to its fullest and takes on risks few of us would even consider. The man we're referring to is Ted Turner.[1]

He has dared to do what others said couldn't be done. He was the first to exploit the possibilities of cable television by beaming a signal via satellite across the country from his Atlanta station (now called WTBS). He bought the Atlanta Braves baseball team in order to have something to broadcast besides old reruns of "Leave It to Beaver" and "Father Knows Best." Turner created CNN, the unique, twenty-four-hour news channel for cable TV. He bought the Metro-Goldwyn-Mayer film studio to get its valuable library of old films. He created the Goodwill Games, an Olympic-style contest featuring U.S. and Soviet athletes. If that weren't enough, along the way Turner proved his yachtman's talents by leading his boat to a win in the America's Cup race.

By almost any definition, Ted Turner is a leader. Among his many accomplishments, he took a small, debt-ridden outdoor billboard business in Atlanta, Georgia and built it into what eventually became the Turner Broadcasting System.

Ted Turner reminds us of the importance of leadership. It's the leaders in organizations who make things happen. But if leadership is so important, it's only natural to ask: Are leaders born or made? What differentiates leaders from nonleaders? What can *you* do if you want to be seen as a leader? In this chapter we'll try to answer such questions.

MANAGERS VERSUS LEADERS

Let's begin by clarifying the distinction between managers and leaders. Writers frequently confuse the two, although they are not necessarily the same.

Managers are appointed. They have legitimate power that allows them to reward and punish. Their ability to influence is founded upon the formal authority inherent in their positions. In contrast, leaders may either be appointed or emerge from within a group. Leaders can influence others to perform beyond the actions dictated by formal authority.

Should all managers be leaders? Conversely, should all leaders be managers? Since no one yet has been able to demonstrate through research or logical argument that leadership ability is a handicap to a manager, we can state that all managers should *ideally* be leaders (see Table 15–1). However, not all leaders necessarily have the capabilities in other managerial functions, and hence not all should hold managerial positions. The fact that an individual can influence others does not tell whether he or she can also plan, organize, and control. Given (if only ideally) that all managers should be leaders, we will pursue the subject from a managerial perspective. Therefore **leaders** in this chapter mean those who are able to influence others and who possess managerial authority.

leaders
Those who are able to influence others and who possess managerial authority.

TABLE 15–1   The Most Effective Leaders in U.S. Business

Whom do *Fortune* 500 CEO's consider the most effective business leaders in the United States?[2] A 1988 poll provided the following top ten:

1. Don Petersen, Ford
2. Lee Iacocca, Chrysler
3. Jack Welch, GE
4. John Reed, Citicorp
5. John Akers, IBM
6. Roy Vagelos, Merck
7. Charles Knight, Emerson
8. Ken Olsen, DEC
9. John Young, Hewlett-Packard
10. James Burke, Johnson & Johnson

What do these men (notice that all are males!) have in common other than gender? *Fortune* magazine claims that consultants, academics, and executives largely agree on seven guidelines that, in aggregate, produce effective leadership.[3] The obvious conclusion is that the CEO's in the previous list have these qualities:

1. Trust your subordinates
2. Develop a vision
3. Keep your cool
4. Encourage risk
5. Be an expert
6. Invite dissent
7. Simplify

By the time you finish reading this chapter, you should be able to assess the validity of these seven leadership qualities.

TRAIT THEORIES

trait theories
Theories isolating characteristics that differentiate leaders from nonleaders.

Ask the average person on the street what comes to mind when he or she thinks of leadership. You're likely to get a list of qualities such as intelligence, charisma, decisiveness, enthusiasm, strength, bravery, integrity, and self-confidence. These responses represent, in essence, **trait theories** of leadership. The search for traits or characteristics that differentiate leaders from nonleaders, though done in a more sophisticated manner than our on-the-street survey, dominated the early research efforts in the study of leadership.

Is it possible to isolate one or more traits in individuals who are generally acknowledged to be leaders—for instance, Martin Luther King, Jr., Lee Iacocca, Joan of Arc, Ted Turner, Adolph Hitler, Mahatma Gandhi—that nonleaders do not possess? We may agree that these individuals meet our definition of a leader, but they represent individuals with utterly different characteristics. If the concept of traits was to prove valid, there had to be found specific characteristics that all leaders possess.

Research efforts at isolating these traits resulted in a number of dead ends. Attempts failed to identify a set of traits that would always differentiate leaders from followers and effective leaders from ineffective leaders. Perhaps it was a bit optimistic to believe that a set of consistent and unique personality traits could apply across the board to all effective leaders, whether they were in charge of the Hell's Angels, the New York Yankees, Federal Express, Shell Oil, Massachusetts General Hospital, the Church of Jesus Christ of Latter-Day Saints, or Playboy Enterprises.

However, attempts to identify traits consistently associated with leadership were more successful. For example, intelligence, dominance, self-confidence, high energy level, and task-relevant knowledge are five traits that show consistently positive correlations with leadership.[4] But "positive correlations" should not be interpreted to mean "definitive predictors." The correlations between these traits and leadership have generally ranged from +0.25 to +0.35—which means that between 6 and 12 percent of the variance in leadership can be explained by traits.[5] An interesting result, but not earth-shattering!

The above results represent conclusions based on seventy years of trait research. Such modest correlations, coupled with the inherent limitations of the trait approach—which ignores the needs of followers, generally fails to clarify the relative importance of various traits, and ignores situational factors—naturally led researchers in other

MANAGERS WHO MADE A DIFFERENCE

Scott McNealy at Sun Microsystems

Scott McNealy is a man on a mission.[6] As a co-founder and currently CEO of Sun Microsystems, he heads up one of the fastest growing companies in America. Sun was founded in 1982, yet reached a billion dollars in sales six years later. The primary source of this growth was the company's high-powered workstations used by engineers and programmers.

Much of Sun's success is undoubtedly attributable to the leadership of McNealy. Only 33 years old when the company hit the billion-dollar mark, McNealy goes to great lengths to build unity and commitment among his executives. Major decisions reflect a consensus of senior executives who meet in noisy, table-pounding meetings. He sees conflict as functional as long as executives are committed. As McNealy puts it, "Agree and commit, disagree and commit—or just get the hell out of the way." Additionally, McNealy has created a decentralized organization made up of small business units. The key to his organization is to get individuals to take responsibility with little direction from managers. Says McNealy, "to ask permission is to seek denial."

But the past is history. Sun's future will depend on McNealy's ability to respond to increasingly aggressive competitors. He's betting Sun's future on achieving increased market share by adding a wealth of new computer products. This will put him up against a number of new competitors, many of them—like IBM, Digital Equipment, and Hewlett-Packard—that are far larger than Sun. But Sun should continue to reflect McNealy's aggressiveness and action-oriented philosophy, aptly captured in this remark on responding to the market, "The right answer is the best answer. The wrong answer is second-best. No answer is the worst."

Photo courtesy of Scott G. McNealy.

directions. Although there has been some resurgent interest in traits during the past decade, a major movement away from trait theories began as early as the 1940s. Leadership research from the late 1940s through the mid-1960s emphasized the preferred behavioral styles that leaders demonstrated.

BEHAVIORAL THEORIES

behavioral theories
Theories identifying behaviors that differentiate effective from ineffective leaders.

The inability to strike gold in the trait mines led researchers to look at the behavior that specific leaders exhibited. Researchers wondered whether there was something unique in the behavior of effective leaders. For example, do leaders tend to be more democratic than autocratic?

Not only, it was hoped, would the **behavioral theories** approach provide more definitive answers about the nature of leadership, but, if successful, it would have practical implications quite different from those of the trait approach. If trait research had been successful, it would have provided a basis for *selecting* the "right" people to assume formal positions in organizations requiring leadership. In contrast, if behavioral studies were to turn up critical behavioral determinants of leadership, we could *train* people to be leaders. The difference between trait and behavioral theories, in terms of application, lies in their underlying assumptions. Trait theories maintained that leaders are born: Either you have it or you don't! On the other hand, if specific behaviors identified leaders, then we could teach leadership—we could design programs to implant these behavioral patterns in individuals who desired to be effective leaders. This was surely a more exciting avenue, since it meant that the supply of leaders could be expanded. If training worked, we could have an infinite supply of effective leaders.

A number of studies looked at behavioral styles. We shall briefly review the two most popular studies: the Ohio State group and the University of Michigan group. Then we shall see how the concepts that these studies developed could be used to create a grid for looking at and appraising leadership styles.

The Ohio State Studies

The most comprehensive and replicated of the behavioral theories resulted from research that began at Ohio State University in the late 1940s.[7] These studies sought to identify independent dimensions of leader behavior. Beginning with over 1,000 dimensions, they eventually narrowed the list down to two categories that accounted for most of the leadership behavior described by subordinates. They called these two dimensions *initiating structure* and *consideration.*

initiating structure
The extent to which a leader defines and structures his or her role and those of subordinates to attain goals.

Initiating structure refers to the extent to which a leader is likely to define and structure his or her role and those of subordinates in the search for goal attainment. It includes behavior that attempts to organize work, work relationships, and goals. For example, the leader who is characterized as high in initiating structure assigns group members to particular tasks, expects workers to maintain definite standards of performance, and emphasizes the meeting of deadlines.

consideration
The extent to which a person has job relationships characterized by mutual trust, respect for subordinates' ideas, and regard for their feelings.

Consideration is defined as the extent to which a person has job relationships characterized by mutual trust, respect for subordinates' ideas, and regard for their feelings. He or she shows concern for his or her followers' comfort, well-being, status, and satisfaction. A leader who is high in consideration helps subordinates with personal problems, is friendly and approachable, and treats all subordinates as equals.

high-high leader
A leader high in both initiating structure and consideration.

Extensive research based on these definitions found that a leader who is high in initiating structure *and* consideration (a **"high-high" leader**) achieved high subordinate performance and satisfaction more frequently than one who rated low on either consideration, initiating structure, or both. However, the high-high style did not *always* yield positive results. For example, leader behavior characterized as high on initiating structure led to greater rates of grievances, absenteeism, and turnover and lower levels of job satisfaction for workers performing routine tasks. Other studies found that high consideration was negatively related to performance ratings of the leader by his or her superior. In conclusion, the Ohio State studies suggested that the high-high style generally produced positive outcomes, but enough exceptions were found to indicate that situational factors needed to be integrated into the theory.

The University of Michigan Studies

Leadership studies undertaken at the University of Michigan's Survey Research Center, at about the same time as those being done at Ohio State, had similar research objectives: to locate behavioral characteristics of leaders that were related to performance effectiveness.

The Michigan group also came up with two dimensions of leadership behavior that they labeled *employee* oriented and *production* oriented.[8] Leaders who were *employee oriented* were described as emphasizing interpersonal relations; they took a personal interest in the needs of their subordinates and accepted individual differences among members. The *production-oriented* leaders, in contrast, tended to emphasize the technical or task aspects of the job, were concerned mainly with accomplishing their group's tasks, and regarded group members as a means to that end.

The conclusions of the Michigan researchers strongly favored leaders who were employee oriented. Employee-oriented leaders were associated with higher group productivity and higher job satisfaction. Production-oriented leaders were associated with low group productivity and lower worker satisfaction.

The Managerial Grid

managerial grid
A two-dimensional portrayal of leadership based on concerns for people and for production.

A two-dimensional view of leadership style was developed by Blake and Mouton.[9] They proposed a **managerial grid** based on the styles of "concern for people" and "concern for production," which essentially represent the Ohio State dimensions of consideration and initiating structure or the Michigan dimensions of employee orientation and production orientation.

The grid, depicted in Figure 15–1, has nine possible positions along each axis, creating eighty-one different positions into which a leader's style may fall. The grid does not show results produced, but rather the dominating factors in a leader's thinking in regard to getting results.

Although there are eighty-one positions on the grid, the five key positions identified by Blake and Mouton are as follows:

1,1: *Impoverished:* The leader exerts a minimum effort to accomplish the work.

9,1: *Task:* The leader concentrates on task efficiency but shows little concern for the development and morale of subordinates.

1,9: *Country-club:* The leader focuses on being supportive and considerate of subordinates to the exclusion of concern for task efficiency.

5,5: *Middle-of-the-road:* Adequate task efficiency and satisfactory morale are the goals of this style.

9,9: *Team:* The leader facilitates task efficiency and high morale by coordinating and integrating work-related activities.

FIGURE 15–1

The Managerial Grid

Source: Reprinted by permission of *Harvard Business Review*. An exhibit from "Breakthrough in Organization Development" by Robert R. Blake, Jane S. Mouton, Louis B. Barnes, and Larry E. Greiner, November–December 1964, p. 136. Copyright © 1964 by the President and Fellows of Harvard College; all rights reserved.

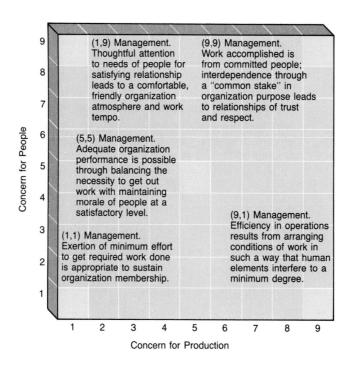

From these findings, Blake and Mouton concluded that managers perform best using a 9,9 style. Unfortunately, the grid offers a better framework for conceptualizing leadership style than for presenting any tangible new information to clarify the leadership quandry. In fact, there is little substantive evidence to support the conclusion that a 9,9 style is most effective in all situations.[10]

Summary of Behavioral Theories

We have described the most popular and important attempts to explain leadership in terms of behavior. There were other efforts,[11] but they faced the same problem that confronted the Ohio State and Michigan researchers: They had very little success in identifying consistent relationships between patterns of leadership behavior and successful performance. General statements could not be made because results would vary over different ranges of circumstances. What was missing was consideration of the situational factors that influence success or failure. For example, would Cesar Chavez have been a great leader of agricultural workers at the turn of the century? Would Ralph Nader have risen to lead a consumer activist group had he been born in 1834 rather than in 1934 or in Costa Rica rather than Connecticut? It seems quite unlikely, yet the behavioral approaches we have described could not clarify such situational factors.

CONTINGENCY THEORIES

It became increasingly clear to those studying the leadership phenomenon that predicting leadership success involved something more complex than isolating a few traits or preferable behaviors. The failure to obtain consistent results led to a new focus on situational influences. The relationship between leadership style and effectiveness suggested that under condition *a*, style *x* would be appropriate, whereas style *y* would be more suitable for condition *b*, and style *z* for condition *c*. But what were the conditions *a*, *b*, *c*, and so forth? It was one thing to say that leadership effectiveness depended on the situation and another to be able to isolate those situational conditions.

There has been no shortage of studies attempting to isolate critical situational factors that affect leadership effectiveness. One author, in reviewing the literature, found that the task being performed (that is, the complexity, type, technology, and size of the project) was a significant moderating variable; but he also uncovered studies that isolated situational factors such as style of the leader's immediate supervisor, group norms, span of control, external threats and stress, and organizational culture.[12]

Several approaches to isolating key situational variables have proven more successful than others and, as a result, have gained wider recognition. We shall consider four of these: the Fiedler model, Hersey and Blanchard's situational theory, the Vroom-Yetton participation model, and path-goal theory.

The Fiedler Model

The first comprehensive contingency model for leadership was developed by Fred Fiedler.[13] The **Fiedler contingency model** proposes that effective group performance depends upon the proper match between the leader's style of interacting with his or her subordinates and the degree to which the situation gives control and influence to the leader. Fiedler developed an instrument, which he called the **least-preferred co-worker (LPC) questionnaire**, that purports to measure whether a person is task or relationship oriented. Further, he isolated three situational criteria—leader-member relations, task structure, and position power—that he believes can be manipulated to create the proper match with the behavioral orientation of the leader. In a sense the Fiedler model is an outgrowth of trait theory, since the LPC questionnaire is a simple psychological test. However, Fiedler goes significantly beyond trait and behavioral approaches by isolating situations, relating an individual's personality to the situation, and then predicting leadership effectiveness as a function of the two.

The above description of the Fiedler model can appear somewhat abstract. Let us now look at the model in more pragmatic detail.

Fiedler believes a key factor in leadership success to be an individual's basic leadership style. Thus he first tries to find out what that basic style is. Fiedler created the LPC questionnaire for this purpose. As shown in Figure 15–2, it contains sixteen pairs of contrasting adjectives. Respondents are asked to think of all the co-workers they have ever had and to describe the one person they *least enjoyed* working with by rating him or her on a scale of 1 to 8 for each of the sixteen sets of adjectives. Fiedler believes that, on the basis of the respondents' answers to this LPC questionnaire, he can determine most people's basic leadership style.

If the least preferred co-worker is described in relatively positive terms (a high LPC score), then the respondent is primarily interested in good personal relations with this co-worker. That is, if you describe the person you are least able to work with in favorable terms, Fiedler would label you *relationship oriented*. In contrast, if you see the least preferred co-worker in relatively unfavorable terms (a low LPC score), you are primarily interested in productivity and thus would be labeled *task oriented*. Using the LPC instrument, Fiedler is able to place most respondents into either of two leadership styles: relationship oriented or task oriented. A small group of people has been found to fall in between. Fiedler acknowledges that it is difficult to draw a personality sketch for those in this group.

It's important to note that Fiedler assumes that an individual's leadership style is fixed. As we'll show in a moment, this means that if a situation requires a task-oriented leader and the person in that leadership position is relationship oriented, either the

---

Fiedler contingency model The theory that effective groups depend on a proper match between a leader's style of interacting with subordinates and the degree to which the situation gives control and influence to the leader.

least-preferred co-worker (LPC) questionnaire A questionnaire that measures whether a person is task or relationship oriented.

FIGURE 15–2
Fiedler's LPC Scale

Source: From Fred E. Fiedler and Martin M. Chemers, *Leadership and Effective Management* (Scott, Foresman & Co., 1974). Reprinted by permission of author.

	8	7	6	5	4	3	2	1	
Pleasant	8	7	6	5	4	3	2	1	Unpleasant
Friendly	8	7	6	5	4	3	2	1	Unfriendly
Rejecting	1	2	3	4	5	6	7	8	Accepting
Helpful	8	7	6	5	4	3	2	1	Frustrating
Unenthusiastic	1	2	3	4	5	6	7	8	Enthusiastic
Tense	1	2	3	4	5	6	7	8	Relaxed
Distant	1	2	3	4	5	6	7	8	Close
Cold	1	2	3	4	5	6	7	8	Warm
Cooperative	8	7	6	5	4	3	2	1	Uncooperative
Supportive	8	7	6	5	4	3	2	1	Hostile
Boring	1	2	3	4	5	6	7	8	Interesting
Quarrelsome	1	2	3	4	5	6	7	8	Harmonious
Self-assured	8	7	6	5	4	3	2	1	Hesitant
Efficient	8	7	6	5	4	3	2	1	Inefficient
Gloomy	1	2	3	4	5	6	7	8	Cheerful
Open	8	7	6	5	4	3	2	1	Guarded

leader-member relations
The degree of confidence, trust, and respect subordinates have in their leader.

task structure
The degree to which the job assignments are procedurized.

position power
The degree of influence a leader has over power variables such as hiring, firing, discipline, promotions, and salary increases.

situation has to be modified or the leader has to be removed and replaced if optimum effectiveness is to be achieved. Fiedler argues that leadership style is innate—you *can't* change your style to fit changing situations!

After an individual's basic leadership style has been assessed through the LPC, it is necessary to match the leader with the situation. Fiedler has identified three contingency dimensions that, he argues, define the key situational factors that determine leadership effectiveness. These are *leader-member relations, task structure,* and *position power.* They are defined as follows:

1. **Leader-member relations:** The degree of confidence, trust, and respect subordinates have in their leader

2. **Task structure:** The degree to which the job assignments are procedurized (i.e., structured or unstructured)

3. **Position power:** the degree of influence a leader has over power variables such as hiring, firing, discipline, promotions, and salary increases

The next step in the Fiedler model is to evaluate the situation in terms of these three contingency variables. Leader-member relations are either good or poor, task structure either high or low, and position power either strong or weak.

Fiedler states that the better the leader-member relations, the more highly structured the job, and the stronger the position power, the more control or influence the

According to Fiedler, an unfavorable leadership situation might be that of a disliked chairman of a voluntary United Way fund-raising team. In this job, the leader has very little control.

leader has. For example, a very favorable situation (in which the leader would have a great deal of control) might involve a payroll manager who is well respected and whose subordinates have confidence in her (good leader-member relations). The activities to be done—such as wage computation, check writing, report filing—would be specific and clear (high task structure), and the job would give her considerable freedom to reward and punish subordinates (strong position power). Altogether, by mixing the three contingency variables, there are potentially eight different situations or categories in which a leader could find himself or herself.

The Fiedler model proposes matching an individual's LPC and an assessment of the three contingency variables to achieve maximum leadership effectiveness. In his studies of over 1,200 groups, in which he compared relationship- versus task-oriented leadership styles in each of the eight situational categories, Fiedler concluded that task-oriented leaders tend to perform better in situations that were *very favorable* to them and in situations that were *very unfavorable* (see Figure 15–3). Fiedler would predict that, when faced with a category I, II, III, VII, or VIII situation, task-oriented leaders perform better. Relationship-oriented leaders, however, perform better in moderately favorable situations—categories IV through VI.

How would you apply Fiedler's findings? You would seek to match leaders and situations. Individuals' LPC scores would determine the type of situation for which they were best suited. That "situation" would be defined by evaluating the three contingency factors of leader-member relations, task structure, and position power.

Remember that according to Fiedler, an individual's leadership style is fixed. Therefore there are really only two ways in which to improve leader effectiveness. First, you can change the leader to fit the situation. Analogous to a baseball game, management can reach into its bullpen and put in a right-handed pitcher or a left-handed pitcher, depending on the situational characteristics of the hitter. For example, if a group situation rates as highly unfavorable but is currently led by a relationship-oriented manager, the group's performance could be improved by replacing that manager with one who is task oriented. The second alternative would be to change the situation to fit the leader. That could be done by restructuring tasks or increasing or decreasing the power that the leader has to control factors such as salary increases,

FIGURE 15–3
The Findings of the Fiedler Model

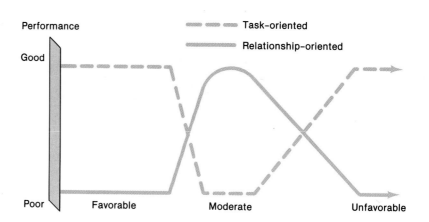

Category	I	II	III	IV	V	VI	VII	VIII
Leader–member relations	Good	Good	Good	Good	Poor	Poor	Poor	Poor
Task structure	High	High	Low	Low	High	High	Low	Low
Position power	Strong	Weak	Strong	Weak	Strong	Weak	Strong	Weak

promotions, and disciplinary actions. To illustrate, assume that a task-oriented leader is in a category IV situation. If this leader could significantly increase his or her position power, then the leader would be operating in category III, and the leader-situation match would be compatible for high group performance.

One should not surmise that Fiedler has closed all the gaps and put to rest all the questions underlying leadership effectiveness. Research finds that the Fiedler model predicts all except category II when laboratory studies are reviewed; however, when field studies are analyzed, the model produces supportive evidence only for categories II, V, VII, and VIII.[14] Therefore, we have conflicting results depending on the type of studies used.

As a whole, reviews of the major studies undertaken to test the overall validity of the Fiedler model lead to a generally positive conclusion. That is, there is considerable evidence to support the model.[15] But additional variables are probably needed if an improved model is to fill in some of the remaining gaps. Moreover, there are problems with the LPC and the practical use of the model that need to be addressed. For instance, the logic underlying the LPC is not well understood, and studies have shown that respondents' LPC scores are not stable.[16] Also, the contingency variables are complex and difficult for practitioners to assess. It's often difficult in practice to determine how good the leader-member relations are, how structured the task is, and how much position power the leader has.[17]

Our conclusion is that Fiedler has clearly made an important contribution toward understanding leadership effectiveness. His model has been the object of much controversy and probably will continue to be. Field studies fall short of providing full support, and the model could benefit by including additional contingency variables. Nevertheless, Fiedler's work continues to be a dominant input in the development of a contingency explanation of leadership effectiveness.

The Hersey-Blanchard Situational Theory

situational leadership theory
A contingency theory that focuses on followers' maturity.

One of the most widely followed leadership models is Paul Hersey and Kenneth Blanchard's **situational leadership theory.**[18] It has been used as a major training device at such *Fortune* 500 companies as BankAmerica, Caterpillar, IBM, Mobil Oil, and Xerox; it has also been widely accepted in all the military services.[19] Although the theory has not undergone extensive evaluation to test its validity, we include it here because of its wide acceptance and its strong intuitive appeal. Furthermore, in defense of the theory, at this point in its development it's too early to dismiss it out of hand merely because researchers have not chosen to evaluate it more thoroughly.

Situational leadership is a contingency theory that focuses on followers. Successful leadership is achieved by selecting the right leadership style, which Hersey and Blanchard argue is contingent on the level of the followers' maturity. Before we proceed, we should clarify two points: Why focus on followers? and What is meant by the term *maturity?*

The emphasis on followers in leadership effectiveness reflects the reality that it is they who accept or reject the leader. Regardless of what the leader does, effectiveness depends on the actions of his or her followers. This is an important dimension that has been overlooked or underemphasized in most leadership theories.

maturity
The ability and willingness of people to take responsibility for directing their own behavior.

The term **maturity,** as defined by Hersey and Blanchard, is the ability and willingness of people to take responsibility for directing their own behavior. It has two components: job maturity and psychological maturity. The first encompasses one's knowledge and skills. Individuals who are high in job maturity have the knowledge, ability, and experience to perform their job tasks without direction from others. Psychological maturity relates to the willingness or motivation to do something. Individuals who are high in psychological maturity don't need much external encouragement; they are already intrinsically motivated.

Situational leadership uses the same two leadership dimensions that Fiedler identified: task and relationship behaviors. However, Hersey and Blanchard go a step further by considering each as either high or low and then combining them into four specific leadership styles: telling, selling, participating, and delegating. They are described as follows:

Telling (high task–low relationship): The leader defines roles and tells people what, how, when, and where to do various tasks. It emphasizes directive behavior.

Selling (high task–high relationship): The leader provides both directive behavior and supportive behavior.

Participating (low task–high relationship): The leader and follower share in decision making, the main role of the leader being facilitating and communicating.

Delegating (low task–low relationship): The leader provides little direction or support.

The final component in Hersey and Blanchard's theory is defining four stages of maturity:

M1: People are both unable and unwilling to take responsibility for doing something. They are neither competent nor confident.

M2: People are unable but willing to do the necessary job tasks. They are motivated but currently lack the appropriate skills.

M3: People are able but unwilling to do what the leader wants.

M4: People are both able and willing to do what is asked of them.

This employee has the ability but lacks the willingness to do his job. This is an example of an M3 level of maturity, which, according to Hersey and Blanchard, is best matched with a participating style.

Figure 15–4 integrates the various components into the situational leadership model. As followers reach high levels of maturity, the leader responds not only by continuing to decrease control over activities, but also by continuing to decrease relationship behavior. At stage M1, followers need clear and specific directions. At stage M2, both high-task and high-relationship behavior is needed. The high-task behavior compensates for the followers' lack of ability, and the high-relationship behavior tries to get the followers psychologically to "buy into" the leader's desires. M3 creates motivational problems that are best solved by a supportive, nondirective, participative style. Finally, at stage M4 the leader doesn't have to do much because followers are both willing and able to take responsibility.

The astute reader might have noticed the high similarity between Hersey and Blanchard's four leadership styles and the four extreme "corners" in the managerial grid. The telling style equates to the 9,1 leader; selling equals 9,9; participating is equivalent to 1,9; and delegating is the same as the 1,1 leader. Is situational leadership, then, merely the managerial grid with one major difference: the replacement of the 9,9 ("one style for all occasions") contention with the recommendation that the "right" style should align with the maturity of the followers? Hersey and Blanchard say No.[20] They argue that the grid emphasizes *concern* for production and people, which are attitudinal dimensions. Situational leadership, in contrast, emphasizes task and relationship *behavior*. In spite of Hersey and Blanchard's claim, this is a pretty minute differentiation. The situational leadership theory is probably better understood by being considered as a fairly direct adaptation of the grid framework to reflect four stages of follower maturity.

Finally, we come to the critical question: Is there evidence to support situational leadership theory? As was noted earlier, the theory has received little attention from

FIGURE 15–4

The Situational Leadership Model

Source: Adapted from P. Hersey and K. Blanchard, *Management of Organizational Behavior: Utilizing Human Resources,* 4th ed. © 1982, p. 152. Adapted by permission of Prentice-Hall, Inc., Englewood Cliffs, NJ.

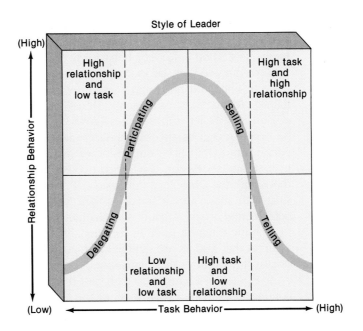

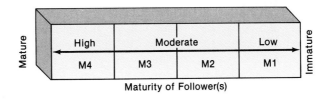

researchers. Fewer than half a dozen studies have been undertaken to empirically test its validity, and most of these were not comprehensive.[21] Hence any conclusions about situational leadership must be guarded. Probably the best summary statement we can currently make is that the present evidence provides partial support for the theory, especially for followers with low maturity (M1), but more research is clearly necessary.[22] Until additional, empirical research can more fully support the theory, any enthusiastic endorsement should be cautioned against.

Path-Goal Theory

Currently, one of the most respected approaches to leadership is path-goal theory. Developed by Robert House, path-goal theory is a contingency model of leadership that extracts key elements from the Ohio State leadership research on initiating structure and consideration and the expectancy theory of motivation.[23]

The essence of the theory is that it's the leader's job to assist his or her followers in attaining their goals and to provide the necessary direction and/or support to ensure that their goals are compatible with the overall objectives of the group or organization. The term "path-goal" is derived from the belief that effective leaders clarify the path to help their followers get from where they are to the achievement of their work goals and make the journey along the path easier by reducing roadblocks and pitfalls.

path-goal theory
The theory that a leader's behavior is acceptable to subordinates insofar as they view it as a source of either immediate or future satisfaction.

According to **path-goal theory,** a leader's behavior is *acceptable* to subordinates to the degree that they view it as an immediate source of satisfaction or as a means of future satisfaction. A leader's behavior is *motivational* to the degree that it (1) makes subordinate need satisfaction contingent on effective performance and (2) provides the coaching, guidance, support, and rewards that are necessary for effective performance. To test these statements, House identified four leadership behaviors. The *directive leader* lets subordinates know what is expected of them, schedules work to be done, and gives specific guidance as to how to accomplish tasks. This closely parallels the Ohio State dimension of initiating structure. The *supportive leader* is friendly and shows concern for the needs of subordinates. This is essentially synonymous with the Ohio State dimension of consideration. The *participative leader* consults with subordinates and uses their suggestions before making a decision. The *achievement-oriented leader* sets challenging goals and expects subordinates to perform at their highest level. In contrast to Fiedler's view of a leader's behavior, House assumes that leaders are flexible. Path-goal theory implies that the same leader can display any or all of these behaviors, depending on the situation.

As Figure 15–5 illustrates, path-goal theory proposes two classes of situational or contingency variables that moderate the leadership behavior-outcome relationship—those in the *environment* that are outside the control of the subordinate (task structure, the formal authority system, and the work group) and those that are part of the personal characteristics of the *subordinate* (locus of control, experience, and perceived ability). Environmental factors determine the type of leader behavior required as a complement if subordinate outcomes are to be maximized, while personal characteristics of the subordinate determine how the environment and leader behavior are interpreted. The theory proposes that leader behavior will be ineffective when it is redundant with sources of environmental structure or incongruent with subordinate characteristics.

The following are some examples of hypotheses that have evolved out of path-goal theory:

- Directive leadership leads to greater satisfaction when tasks are ambiguous or stressful than when they are highly structured and well laid out.
- Supportive leadership results in high employee performance and satisfaction when subordinates are performing structured tasks.
- Directive leadership is likely to be perceived as redundant among subordinates with high perceived ability or with considerable experience.
- The more clear and bureaucratic the formal authority relationships, the more leaders should exhibit supportive behavior and deemphasize directive behavior.
- Directive leadership will lead to higher employee satisfaction when there is substantive conflict within a work group.
- Subordinates with an internal locus of control (those who believe they control their own destiny) will be more satisfied with a participative style.
- Subordinates with an external locus of control will be more satisfied with a directive style.
- Achievement-oriented leadership will increase subordinates' expectancies that effort will lead to high performance when tasks are ambiguously structured.

Research to validate hypotheses such as these are generally encouraging.[24] The evidence supports the logic underlying the theory. That is, employee performance and satisfaction are likely to be positively influenced when the leader compensates for things lacking in either the employee or the work setting. However, if the leader spends time explaining tasks when those tasks are already clear or the employee has the ability and experience to handle them without interference, the employee is likely to see such directive behavior as redundant or even insulting.

FIGURE 15–5
Path-Goal Theory

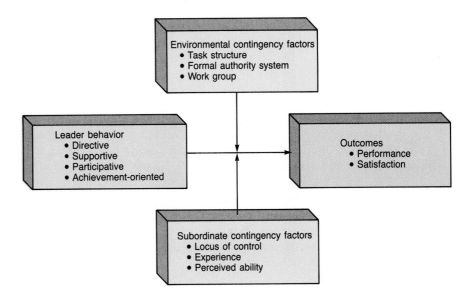

What does the future hold for path-goal theory? Its framework has been tested and appears to have moderate to high empirical support. We can, however, expect to see more research focused on refining and extending the theory by incorporating additional moderating variables.

Vroom-Yetton Leader-Participation Model

leader-participation model
A leadership theory that provides a set of rules to determine the form and amount of participative decision making in different situations.

One of the more recent additions to the contingency approach is the **leader-participation model** proposed by Victor Vroom and Phillip Yetton.[25] It relates leadership behavior and participation to decision making. Recognizing that task structures have varying demands for routine and nonroutine activities, these researchers suggest that leader behavior must adjust to reflect the task structure. Vroom and Yetton's model is normative—it provides a sequential set of rules that should be followed in determining the form and amount of participation in decision making, as determined by different types of situations. As shown in Figure 15–6, the model is a decision tree incorporating seven contingencies and five alternative leadership styles.

The model assumes that any of five behaviors may be feasible in a given situation: Autocratic I (AI), Autocratic II (AII), Consultative I (CI), Consultative II (CII), and Group II (GII):

AI: You solve the problem or make a decision yourself, using information available to you at that time.

AII: You obtain the necessary information from subordinates and then decide on the solution to the problem yourself. You may or may not tell subordinates what the problem is. The role played by your subordinates in making the decision is clearly one of providing the necessary information to you rather than generating or evaluating alternative solutions.

CI: You share the problem with relevant subordinates individually, getting their ideas and suggestions without bringing them together as a group. Then *you* make the decision that may or may not reflect your subordinates' influence.

CII: You share the problem with your subordinates as a group, collectively obtaining their ideas and suggestions. Then you make the decision that may or may not reflect your subordinates' influence.

FIGURE 15–6
The Leader-Participation Model

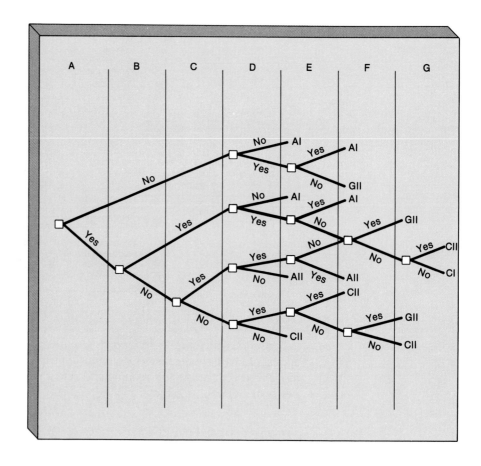

GII: You share the problem with your subordinates as a group. Together you generate and evaluate alternatives and attempt to reach an agreement (consensus) on a solution.

This model offers the leader a specific way of analyzing problems by means of seven contingency questions. By answering Yes or No to these questions, the leader can arrive at the preferred decision-making behavior—that is, the leader can determine how much participation should be used.

The seven questions must be answered in order from A to G:

A. Is there a quality requirement?

B. Do I have sufficient information to make a high-quality decision?

C. Is the problem structured?

D. Is acceptance of the decision by subordinates critical to its implementation?

E. If I were to make the decision by myself, is it reasonably certain that my subordinates would accept it?

F. Do subordinates share the organizational goals to be obtained in solving this problem?

G. Is obtaining the preferred solution likely to create conflict among subordinates?

Again, referring to Figure 15–6, on the basis of the answers to questions A through G, the leader follows the decision tree until reaching its end. The designation at the end of the branch (either AI, AII, CI, CII, or GII) tells the leader what to do.

You have four preferential parking spaces that can be allocated among yourself and your five department heads, all of whom are expecting the privilege. Using the leadership-participation model, you have concluded that the problem doesn't possess a quality requirement; acceptance of the decision by subordinates is important; and if you make the decision yourself, it is not reasonably certain that they will accept it. Following Figure 15–6, the best solution is GII.

To illustrate how the model would work, assume that you are a manufacturing manager in a large electronics plant.[26] The company's management has always been searching for ways of increasing efficiency. They have recently installed new machines and set up a new simplified work system, but to the surprise of everyone—including yourself—the expected increase in productivity was not realized. In fact, production has begun to drop, quality has fallen off, and the number of employee resignations has risen.

You do not believe that there is anything wrong with the machines. You have had reports from other companies that are using them, and they confirm this opinion. You have also had representatives from the firm that built the machines go over them, and they report that they are operating at peak efficiency.

You suspect that some parts of the new work system might be responsible for the change, but this view is not widely shared among your immediate subordinates, who are four first-line supervisors, each in charge of a section, and your supply manager. The drop in production has been variously attributed to poor training of the operators, lack of an adequate system of financial incentives, and poor morale. Clearly, this is an issue about which there is considerable depth of feeling within individuals and potential disagreement between your subordinates.

This morning you received a phone call from your division manager. He had just received your production figures for the last six months and was calling to express his concern. He indicated that the problem was yours to solve in any way that you think best but that he would like to know within a week what steps you plan to take.

You share your division manager's concern with the falling productivity and know that your employees are also concerned. The problem is to decide what steps to take to rectify the situation.

Referring back to Figure 15–6, what should you do? Answers to the seven questions would be: (A) Yes, (B) No, (C) No, (D) Yes, (E) No, (F) Yes, (G) Yes. Working along the model's flow chart, you arrive at the solution: GII. That is, you should share the problem with your subordinates and reach a consensus on a solution.

Research testing of the leader-participation model has been encouraging.[27] It has also undergone changes since its introduction. The latest and most sophisticated revi-

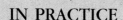

IN PRACTICE

Employee Participation Appears to be More Talk Than Action

Despite widespread recognition that participation in the workplace can help boost productivity, only one-quarter of the largest firms in the United States have actively promoted greater worker involvement in company operations, according to a study by the U.S. General Accounting Office and a team of researchers from the University of Southern California.[28]

The survey of senior managers at 479 of 1,000 large U.S. companies showed that while 70 percent of the companies had taken some action in the area of employee participation, most of the efforts were tentative at best. "The level of participation was a mile wide and a foot deep," says Gerald Ledford, Jr., a USC researcher and co-author of the study. "Companies could do much more."

Jerome Rosow, president of the Work in America Institute in New York, confirms that the participation rate is misleading. "Companies tend to claim more than they do," says Rosow. "I don't know of any single company that has more than 50 percent of their workers involved in participation programs."

Ledford says that the shallow nature of the participation programs is particularly striking given that more than two-thirds of the respondents said that worker involvement had a positive effect on productivity, while virtually none reported negative effects.

sion identifies twelve contingency questions (rather than seven) and expands responses from two (yes or no) to five for most questions.[29] However, the complexity of this new version requires a computer program to replace the decision tree for calculating the correct leadership style. While this new version improves the validity of the original model, we have excluded specific discussion of it here because of its complexity.

Where does this leave us? The leader-participation model provides an excellent guide for determining the form and degree of employee participation in organizational decision making. Moreover, it confirms existing empirical evidence that leaders use participation (1) when the quality of the decision is important, (2) when it is important that subordinates accept the decision and it is unlikely that they will do so unless they are allowed to take part in it, and (3) when subordinates can be trusted to pay attention to the goals of the group rather than simply to their own preferences.

Sometimes Leadership Is Irrelevant!

In keeping with the contingency spirit, we want to conclude this section by offering this notion: The belief that *some* leadership style *will always* be effective *regardless* of the situation may not be true. Leadership may not always be important. Data from numerous studies demonstrate that, in many situations, any behaviors a leader exhibits are irrelevant. Certain individual, job, and organizational variables can act as "substitutes for leadership," negating the influence of the leader.[30]

For instance, characteristics of subordinates such as experience, training, "professional" orientation, or need for independence can neutralize the effect of leadership. These characteristics can replace the need for a leader's support or ability to create structure and reduce task ambiguity. Similarly, jobs that are inherently unambiguous and routine or that are intrinsically satisfying may place fewer demands on the leadership variable. Finally, organizational characteristics like explicit formalized goals, rigid rules and procedures, or cohesive work groups can act in the place of formal leadership.

TRAIT THEORIES UPDATED: CHARISMATIC LEADERSHIP

transactional leaders
Leaders who guide or motivate their followers in the direction of established goals by clarifying role and task requirements.

transformational/charismatic leaders
Leaders who inspire followers to transcend their own self-interests for the good of the organization and who are capable of having a profound and extraordinary effect on their followers.

Most of the leadership theories discussed in this chapter have involved **transactional leaders.** These people guide or motivate their followers in the direction of established goals by clarifying role and task requirements. There is another type of leader who inspires followers to transcend their own self-interests for the good of the organization and who is capable of having a profound and extraordinary effect on his or her followers. These are **transformational** or **charismatic leaders.**[31] Ted Turner, Lee Iacocca, Mother Teresa, General Douglas MacArthur, and Franklin D. Roosevelt are of this latter type. By the force of their personal abilities they transform their followers by raising their sense of the importance and value of their tasks. "I'd walk through fire if my boss asked me" is the kind of support that charismatic leaders inspire.

MANAGING FROM A GLOBAL PERSPECTIVE

The Case Against the Universal Leader

One general conclusion that surfaces from the leadership literature is that effective leaders don't use any single style. They adjust their style to the situation. While not mentioned explicitly, national culture is certainly an important situational variable determining which leadership style will be most effective.

National culture affects leadership style by way of the subordinate. A leader cannot choose his or her style at will. "What is feasible depends to a large extent on the cultural conditioning of a leader's subordinates."[32] For example, a manipulative or autocratic style is compatible with high power distance, and we find high power distance scores in Arab, Far Eastern, and Latin countries. Power distance rankings should also be good indicators of employee willingness to accept participative leadership. Participation is likely to be most effective in low-power-distance cultures such as those in Norway, Finland, Denmark, and Sweden.

What characteristics differentiate charismatic leaders from noncharismatic ones? Five attributes seem most important:[33]

Self-confidence. They have complete confidence in their judgment and ability.

A vision. This is an idealized goal that proposes a future better than the status quo. The greater the disparity between this idealized goal and the status quo, the more likely that followers will attribute extraordinary vision to the leader.

Strong convictions in that vision. Charismatic leaders are perceived as being strongly committed. They are perceived as willing to take on high personal risk, incur high costs, and engage in self-sacrifice to achieve their vision.

Behave out of the ordinary. Leaders with charisma engage in behavior that is perceived as novel, unconventional, and counter to norms. When successful, these behaviors evoke surprise and admiration in followers.

Perceived as a change agent. Charismatic leaders are perceived as agents of radical change rather than as caretakers of the status quo.

What can we say about the charismatic leader's impact on his or her followers' attitudes and behavior? One study found that followers of charismatic leaders were more self-assured, experienced more meaningfulness in their work, reported more support from their leaders, worked longer hours, saw their leaders as more dynamic, and had higher performance ratings than the followers of the noncharismatic but effective leaders.[34] Another study found that people working under charismatic leaders were more productive and satisfied than those working under leaders who relied on the more traditional transactional behaviors of initiating structure and consideration.[35] Two studies, of course, provide only a limited set of information from which to generalize. We need more research on this subject. However, the early evidence is encouraging.

A final thought: Is charismatic leadership *always* desirable? Based on the media's connotation of leadership, which tends to treat *leadership* and *charismatic leadership* as synonymous, you would think so. But it's not true. First, charismatic leaders might

Mary Kay Ash, founder of Mary Kay Cosmetics, is a charismatic leader. Her vision was of using cosmetics as a path to help women become financially successful. She built a large, successful company and became rich herself along the way by conveying that vision. Her decision to award top salespeople with furs, jewelry, and pink automobiles—presented at annual sales meetings that took on a circuslike atmosphere—was widely seen as novel and unconventional.

not always be needed to achieve high levels of employee performance. Charismatic leadership might be most appropriate when the follower's task has an ideological component.[36] This could explain why charismatic leaders are more likely to surface in politics or religion, in wartime, or when a business firm is introducing a radically new product or facing a life-threatening crisis. Such conditions tend to involve ideological concerns. Second, charismatic leaders may be ideal for pulling an organization through a crisis but perform poorly after the crisis subsides and ordinary conditions return.[37] The forceful, confident behavior that was needed during the crisis now becomes a liability. Charismatic managers are often self-possessed, autocratic, and given to thinking that their opinions have a greater degree of certainty than they merit. These behaviors then tend to drive good people away and can lead their organizations down dangerous paths.

ETHICAL DILEMMAS IN MANAGEMENT

Is it Unethical to Create Charisma?

In 1990, no list of charismatic business leaders would have been complete without the names of Lee Iacocca, Donald Trump, and Ted Turner. They personified the contemporary idea of charisma in the corporate world. But are these men authentically charismatic figures or self-created images?

Each of these men employs public relations firms or has public relations specialists on his staff who spend a great deal of time shaping and honing their boss's image. Iacocca has done little to lessen the impressions that he fathered the highly successful Ford Mustang (although he was merely part of a large team that developed the car) and that he single-handedly turned Chrysler around. In fact, he used his autobiography to help reinforce those beliefs. Trump relishes his reputation for bold decision making and his excessive life-style. Ted Turner has worked hard to project his "to hell with tradition" and bad-boy images in the popular press.

One view of these men is that they are authentically charismatic leaders whose actions and achievements have caught the fancy of the media. This view assumes that these leaders couldn't hide their charismatic qualities. It was just a matter of time before they were found out and gained the public's eye. Another view—certainly a more cynical one—proposes that these men consciously created an image that they wanted to project and then purposely went about doing things that would draw attention to, and confirm, that image. They are not inherently charismatic individuals but rather highly astute manipulators of symbols, circumstances, and the media. In support of this latter position, one can identify leaders such as Jack Welch at GE, John Reed at Citicorp, and Chuck Knight at Emerson Electric, who are widely viewed as charismatic in their firms and industries but relatively unknown in the popular press.

Is charismatic leadership an inherent quality within a person, a label thrust upon an individual, or a purposely and carefully molded image? If charisma can be derived from the media, is it unethical for a person to engage in practices whose primary purposes are to create or enhance this perception? Is it unethical to *create* charisma? What do *you* think?

SUMMARY

This summary is organized by the chapter-opening learning objectives found on page 457.

1. Managers influence through formal authority. Leaders can influence others to perform beyond the actions dictated by formal authority. Leaders, therefore, may be appointed or emerge from within a group. In this chapter, leaders are described as individuals who are able to influence others but also hold managerial authority.

2. The early work on leadership sought traits that would differentiate leaders from nonleaders. While some traits (intelligence, dominance, self-confidence, high energy level, job knowledge) achieved positive correlations, the results were far from encouraging.

3. The Managerial Grid focused on two leader styles: concern for people and concern for production.

4. Fiedler's contingency model identifies three situational variables: leader-member relations, task structure, and position power. In situations that are highly favorable or highly unfavorable, task-oriented leaders tend to perform best. In moderately favorable or unfavorable situations, relations-oriented leaders are preferred.

5. Hersey-Blanchard's situational theory argues that leadership style (telling, selling, participating, or delegating) depends on the followers' maturity level.

6. The path-goal model essentially proposes that leader behavior depends on the degree of task structure in the job, the subordinate's perception of his or her own ability, and the subordinate's locus of control.

7. Leaders might not be important when individual variables replace the need for a leader's support or ability to create structure and reduce task ambiguity; when jobs are unambiguous, routine, or intrinsically satisfying; or when organizational characteristics like explicit goals, rigid rules and procedures, or cohesive work groups act in place of formal leadership.

8. Charismatic leaders are self-confident, possess a vision of a better future, have a strong belief in that vision, engage in unconventional behaviors, and are perceived as agents of radical change.

REVIEW QUESTIONS

1. "All managers should be leaders, but not all leaders should be managers." Do you agree or disagree with this statement? Support your position.

2. Discuss the strengths and weaknesses of the trait approach to leadership.

3. What is the managerial grid? Contrast its approach to leadership with that of the Ohio State and Michigan groups.

4. Is "high-high" the most effective leadership style? Explain.

5. What's the drawback of behavioral leadership theories?

6. What are the contingencies in Fiedler's contingency model? Develop an example in which you apply the Fiedler model.

7. Contrast the Hersey-Blanchard situational leadership theory with the managerial grid.

8. What are the contingencies in the path-goal model? What conclusions are obtained from this model?

9. According to the Vroom-Yetton leader-participation model, what contingencies dictate the degree of participation a leader should exercise?

10. Contrast transactional and transformational leaders.

DISCUSSION QUESTIONS

1. What similarities, if any, can you find between the Fiedler and path-goal models?

2. Which leadership theories, or parts of theories, appear to demonstrate reasonable predictive capability?

3. What role should personality tests and experience play in the selection of leaders for organizations?

4. Do most organizations use a contingency approach to increase leader effectiveness in practice? Discuss.

5. When average people on the street are asked to explain why a given individual is a leader, they tend to describe the person in terms such as competent, consistent, self-assured, inspiring a shared vision, invoking enthusiasm for goal-attainment, and supportive of his or her followers. Can you reconcile this description with leadership concepts presented in this chapter?

SELF-ASSESSMENT EXERCISE

What Kind of Leader Are You?

Instructions: The following items describe aspects of leadership behavior. Respond to each item according to the way you would be most likely to act if you were the leader of a work group. Circle whether you would be likely to behave in the described way Always (A), Frequently (F), Occasionally (O), Seldom (S), or Never (N).

If I Were the Leader of a Work Group . . .

A F O S N _____ 1. I would most likely act as the spokesperson of the group.

A F O S N _____ 2. I would encourage overtime work.

A F O S N _____ 3. I would allow members complete freedom in their work.

A F O S N _____ 4. I would encourage the use of uniform procedures.

A F O S N _____ 5. I would permit the members to use their own judgment in solving problems.

A F O S N _____ 6. I would stress being ahead of competing groups.

A F O S N _____ 7. I would speak as a representative of the group.

A F O S N _____ 8. I would needle members for greater effort.

A F O S N _____ 9. I would try out my ideas in the group.

A F O S N _____ 10. I would let the members do their work the way they think best.

A F O S N _____ 11. I would be working hard for a promotion.

A F O S N _____ 12. I would be able to tolerate postponement and uncertainty.

A F O S N _____ 13. I would speak for the group when visitors were present.

A F O S N _____ 14. I would keep the work moving at a rapid pace.

A F O S N _____ 15. I would turn the members loose on a job and let them go to it.

A F O S N _____ 16. I would settle conflicts when they occur in the group.

A F O S N _____ 17. I would get swamped by details.

A F O S N _____ 18. I would represent the group at outside meetings.

A F O S N _____ 19. I would be reluctant to allow the members any freedom of action.

A F O S N _____ 20. I would decide what shall be done and how it shall be done.

A F O S N _____ 21. I would push for increased production.

A F O S N _____ 22. I would let some members have authority which I could keep.

A F O S N   _____ 23. Things would usually turn out as I predict.

A F O S N   _____ 24. I would allow the group a high degree of initiative.

A F O S N   _____ 25. I would assign group members to particular tasks.

A F O S N   _____ 26. I would be willing to make changes.

A F O S N   _____ 27. I would ask the members to work harder.

A F O S N   _____ 28. I would trust the group members to exercise good judgment.

A F O S N   _____ 29. I would schedule the work to be done.

A F O S N   _____ 30. I would refuse to explain my actions.

A F O S N   _____ 31. I would persuade others that my ideas are to their advantage.

A F O S N   _____ 32. I would permit the group to set its own pace.

A F O S N   _____ 33. I would urge the group to beat its previous record.

A F O S N   _____ 34. I would act without consulting the group.

A F O S N   _____ 35. I would ask that group members follow standard rules and regulations.

Turn to page 675 for scoring directions and key.

Source: From J. William Pfeiffer and John E. Jones, eds, *A Handbook of Structural Experiences for Human Relations Training,* Vol. 1 (San Diego, CA: University Associates, Inc., 1974). With permission.

CASE APPLICATION 15A

Ronald Reagan Versus George Bush

When Ronald Reagan left the Presidency of the United States in January 1989, *Time* magazine claimed that he was "going home a winner."[38] Polls gave him a 64 percent approval rating. When adult Americans were asked whether the United States was better off as a result of Reagan's eight years in office, 60 percent said things were better, while only 27 percent said things were worse.

History, of course, will be the final judge of Reagan's record but the following list summarizes a few of the highlights and "lowlights" of his two terms in office:

- He pushed a massive tax reduction program through Congress
- He cut the inflation rate from 12 percent to less than 4.5 percent
- He broke the strike by the Professional Air Traffic Controllers' Association and obliterated the union
- He created the largest federal budget deficits in U.S. history
- He brought unemployment down to a fourteen-year low
- He oversaw the longest economic expansion in forty years
- He improved relations with the Soviet Union
- He expanded the Pentagon budget to gargantuan proportions
- He endured the Iran-Contra scandal
- He presided over the largest stock market crash in sixty years

Was Ronald Reagan a leader? Most experts think so. He sincerely believed in the United States and its future, and he could use his superb communication skills to project this optimism. He was particularly adept at selling nostalgia. He brought to life a sort of Norman Rockwell vision of America's bright and triumphant past. *Time* concluded that Reagan was able to give Americans a pride in themselves and their country that had been absent since John Kennedy's death. He restored self-assurance to the U.S. people and to the office of the Presidency.[39]

Reagan's themes were also singled out for their consistency and focus. He had a clear set of goals. He kept his agenda short and easy to understand: decrease taxes, reduce domestic spending, increase defense expenditures, and develop a tougher foreign policy. He used his previous acting experience and his stage presence to sell his ideas. Reagan defined the issues he wanted considered and then set out to control the agenda to ensure their implementation.

What about Reagan's successor, George Bush? Is he a leader? Some say that he was elected without an agenda. Bush was Reagan's vice president, and some say that his goals are merely to carry on the policies that Reagan began. Bush certainly had no shortage of problems to deal with when he took office. The more obvious ones included a huge budget deficit, rampant drug problems, ethical lapses by government officials, an increasingly polluted environment, and a staggering trade imbalance. In his first year in office, Bush was criticized by some in the media as "a nonideological caretaker destined to follow public opinion."[40] However, the White House preferred to call his style "simply cautious." In early 1990, the United States was at peace and the economy was relatively strong. A former Reagan pollster noted that there were "no big currents crying out for change." A political science professor concurred: "There is no great clamor for sweeping new programs."

Questions

1. Reagan was personally triumphant as President, but it is not clear whether this translated into durable accomplishments. Does this case suggest that leadership is more a *perceptual* phenomenon than an *actual* quality? Discuss.

2. Contrast Bush's and Reagan's leadership styles. Base your answer on theories and terminology introduced in this chapter.

3. As a consultant to George Bush, what specific suggestions would you make in order for him to become a more charismatic leader?

CASE APPLICATION 15B

Sue Reynolds at Connecticut Mutual

Sue Reynolds is twenty-two years old and will be receiving her B.S. degree in human resource management from the University of Hartford at the end of this semester. She has spent the past two summers working for Connecticut Mutual (CM), filling in on a number of different jobs while employees took their vacations. She has received and accepted an offer to join CM on a permanent basis upon graduation, as a supervisor in the policy renewal department.

Connecticut Mutual is a large insurance company. In the headquarters office alone, where Sue will work, 5,000 employees are employed. The company believes strongly in the personal development of its employees. This translates into a philosophy, emanating from the top executive offices, of trust and respect for all CM employees.

The job Sue will be assuming requires her to direct the activities of twenty-two clerks. Their jobs require little training and are highly routine. A clerk's responsibility is to ensure that renewal notices are sent on current policies, to tabulate any changes in premium from a standardized table, and to advise the sales division if a policy is to be canceled as a result of nonresponse to renewal notices.

Sue's group is composed of all females, ranging from nineteen to sixty-two years of age, with a median age of twenty-five. For the most part they are high school graduates with little prior working experience. The salary range for policy renewal clerks is $1,220 to $1,970 per month. Sue will be replacing a long-time CM employee, Mabel Fincher. Mabel is retiring after thirty-seven years with CM, the last fourteen spent as a policy renewal supervisor. Since Sue spent a few weeks in Mabel's group last summer, she is familiar with Mabel's style and knows most of the group members. She anticipates no problems from any of her soon-to-be employees, except possibly for Lillian Lantz. Lillian is well into her fifties, has been a policy renewal clerk for over a dozen years, and—as the "grand old lady"—carries a lot of weight with group members. Sue has concluded that her job could prove very difficult without Lantz's support.

Sue is determined to get her career off on the right foot. As a result, she has been doing a lot of thinking about the qualities of an effective leader.

Questions

1. What critical factors will influence Sue's success as a leader? Would these factors be the same if success were defined as group satisfaction rather than group productivity?

2. Do you think that Sue can choose a leadership style? If so, describe the style you think would be most effective for her. If not, why?

3. What suggestions might you make to Sue to help her win over or control Lillian Lantz?

COMMUNICATION AND INTERPERSONAL SKILLS

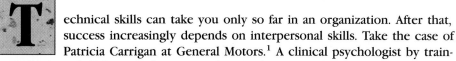

Technical skills can take you only so far in an organization. After that, success increasingly depends on interpersonal skills. Take the case of Patricia Carrigan at General Motors.[1] A clinical psychologist by training, she joined GM in 1976 in an employee-relations capacity. Six years later, at the age of fifty-three, she was named manager of the Lakewood assembly plant in Atlanta. This plant was famous throughout GM for its history of labor strife. Using her finely honed interpersonal skills, Carrigan broke down the traditionally antagonistic relationship between plant management and the unions. She got union members involved in operating decisions and achieved new standards of productivity and quality. Carrigan is now manager of the Bay City, Michigan, engine and transmission parts plant, where she is using her talents to achieve similar success.

Technical skills are necessary but not sufficient requirements for success in management. Patricia Carrigan has used her outstanding interpersonal skills to become one of General Motors' most highly rated managers.

Would it surprise you to know that more managers are probably fired because of poor interpersonal skills than for lack of technical ability on the job? Though the evidence is mostly anecdotal, this seems to be the case.[2] When managers with MBA's have been asked what skills, knowledge, and abilities they would consider most important in selecting someone to fill their current job, interpersonal skills and communication skills finished first and second out of a list of seventeen items.[3] If you need any further evidence of the importance of interpersonal skills, we would add that a recent comprehensive study found that the people who hire undergraduate business graduates and depend on them to fill future management vacancies claimed that the area in which these graduates were most deficient was in leadership and interpersonal skills.[4] These overall findings, of course, are consistent with our view of the manager's job. Since managers ultimately get things done through others, competencies in leadership, communication, and other interpersonal skills must be a prerequisite to managerial effectiveness.

UNDERSTANDING COMMUNICATION

The following episodes occurred in one eight-hour day in the head office of a major hotel chain.

Episode 1: The director of convention sales, Jan Decker, was on the phone with Kim Wong. Kim was the new head of convention sales at the chain's San Francisco hotel.

"Kim, I just saw your last quarter's sales report," Jan was saying. "I thought we had agreed on a goal of fourteen conventions for the quarter. Now I get this report and it says you booked only eleven. What happened?"

"I don't understand the problem," Kim responded. "Fourteen was a goal, a target. It was something we were trying to reach."

Clearly upset, Jan was now shouting into the receiver. "Kim, Fourteen was our goal, all right. But it wasn't some 'pie-in-the-sky' number. It was the minimum number of bookings we were counting on coming out of San Francisco. I told Dave [the general manager and Jan's immediate boss] we'd get at least fourteen from your hotel. Now I've got to explain why we missed our goal in San Francisco!"

Episode 2: A memo had gone out a number of months previously from the office of the vice president for human resources to the personnel managers at all the hotels in the chain. The topic of the memo was a change in the corporation's maternity leave policy. Now the head office had just received a complaint from a female employee at one of the chain's Chicago hotels. The employee's complaint was that her request for a two-week extension of maternity leave without pay had been denied. She felt her request was reasonable and should have been approved. The memo in question had specifically stated that such maternity leave extensions were to be uniformly approved. When a member of the headquarters staff relayed this fact to the Chicago personnel department, she was told, "We never knew there was a change of policy on maternity leaves."

Episode 3: The following conversation took place between two keypunch operators in the accounting department.
"Did you hear the latest? The president's daughter is marrying some guy from Pittsburgh who's serving a five-year sentence for stealing."
"You're kidding?"
"No, I'm not kidding! I heard it this morning from Chuck in purchasing. Can you imagine the heartache the family must feel?"
This rumor had some basis in fact but was far from accurate. The truth was that, the previous week, the hotel's president had announced the engagement of his daughter to a football star with the Pittsburgh Steelers who had just signed a new five-year contract.

These episodes demonstrate three facts about communicating in organizations. First, words mean different things to different people. In this instance, to Jan Decker a *goal* meant a minimum level of attainment, while to Kim Wong it meant a maximum target that one tried to reach. Second, the initiation of a message is no assurance that it is received or understood as intended. Third, communications often become distorted as they are transmitted from person to person. As the marriage rumor illustrates, "facts" in messages can lose much of their accuracy as they are transmitted and translated.

These episodes underscore how communication problems can surface in organizations. The importance of effective communication for managers can't be overemphasized for one specific reason: Everything a manager does involves communicating. Not *some* things, but everything! A manager can't make a decision without information. That information has to be communicated. Once a decision is made, communication must again take place. Otherwise, no one will know that a decision has been made. The best idea, the most creative suggestion, or the finest plan cannot take form without communication. Managers therefore need effective communication skills. We are not suggesting, of course, that good communication skills alone make a successful manager. We can say, however, that ineffective communication skills can lead to a continuous stream of problems for the manager.

What Is Communication?

Communication involves the transfer of meaning. If no information or ideas have been conveyed, communication has not taken place. The speaker who is not heard or the writer who is not read does not communicate. The philosophical question, "If a tree falls in a forest and no one hears it, does it make any noise?" must, in a communicative context, be answered negatively.

communication

The transference and understanding of meaning.

However, for communication to be successful, the meaning must be not only imparted, but also understood. A letter addressed to me but written in Portuguese (a language of which I am totally ignorant) cannot be considered a communication until I have it translated. **Communication** is the *transference* and *understanding* of meaning. Perfect communication, if such a thing were possible, would exist when a transmitted thought or idea was perceived by the receiver exactly the same as it was envisioned by the sender.

Another point to keep in mind is that *good* communication is often erroneously defined by the communicator as *agreement* instead of clarity of understanding.[5] If someone disagrees with us, many of us assume that the person just didn't fully understand our position. In other words, many of us define good communication as having someone accept our views. But I can understand very clearly what you mean and *not* agree with what you say. In fact, when observers conclude that a lack of communication must exist because a conflict has continued for a prolonged time, a close examination often reveals that there is plenty of effective communication going on. Each fully understands the other's position. The problem is one of equating effective communication with agreement.

interpersonal communication

Communication between two or more people in which the parties are treated as individuals rather than objects.

A final point before we move on: Our attention in this chapter will be on **interpersonal communication.** This is communication between two or more people in which the parties are treated as individuals rather than objects. Organizationwide communication—which encompasses topics such as the flow of organizational communication, communication networks, and the development of management information systems—will be covered in our discussion of information control systems in Chapter 19.

The Communication Process

message

A purpose to be conveyed.

encoding

Converting a message into symbols.

channel

The medium by which a message travels.

decoding

Retranslating a sender's message.

communication process

The seven steps by which meaning is transmitted and understood.

noise

Disturbances that interfere with the transmission of a message.

Before communication can take place, a purpose, expressed as a **message** to be conveyed, must exist. It passes between a source (the sender) and a receiver. The message is converted to symbolic form (called **encoding**) and passed by way of some medium **(channel)** to the receiver, who retranslates the sender's message (called **decoding**). The result is the transfer of meaning from one person to another.[6]

Figure 16–1 depicts the **communication process.** This model is made up of seven parts: (1) the communication source, (2) the message, (3) encoding, (4) the channel, (5) decoding, (6) the receiver, and (7) feedback. In addition, the entire process is susceptible to **noise**—that is, disturbances that interfere with the transmission of the message (depicted in Figure 16–1 as lightning bolts). Typical examples of noise include illegible print, telephone static, inattention by the receiver, or the background sounds of machinery on the production floor. Remember that anything that interferes with understanding—whether internal (such as the low speaking voice of the speaker/sender) or external (like the loud voices of co-workers talking at an adjoining desk)—represents noise. Noise can create distortion at any point in the communication process. Since the impact of external noise on communication effectiveness is self-evident, let's look at some potential internal sources of distortion in the communication process.

A source initiates a message by encoding a thought. Four conditions affect the encoded message: skill, attitudes, knowledge, and the social-cultural system.

If textbook authors are without the requisite skills, their message will not reach students in the form desired. My success in communicating to you depends upon my writing skills. One's total communicative success also includes speaking, reading, listening, and reasoning skills. As we discussed in Chapter 13, our attitudes influence our behavior. We hold preformed ideas on numerous topics, and these ideas affect our communications. Furthermore, we are restricted in our communicative activity by the

FIGURE 16–1   The Communication Process

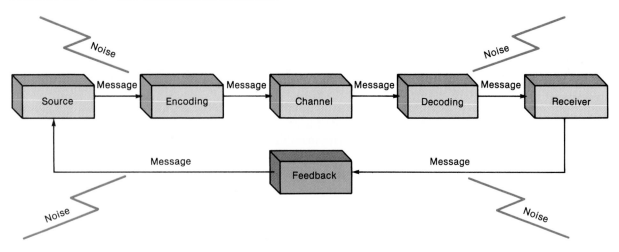

extent of our knowledge of a particular topic. We cannot communicate what we do not know; and should our knowledge be too extensive, it is possible that our receiver will not understand our message. Clearly, the amount of knowledge we have about a subject affects the message we seek to transfer. Finally, just as our attitudes influence our behavior, so does our position in the social-cultural system in which we exist. Our beliefs and values (all part of our culture) act to influence us as communication sources.

The message itself can cause distortion in the communication process, regardless of the supporting apparatus used to convey it. Our message is the actual physical product encoded by the source. "When we speak, the speech is the message. When we write, the writing is the message. When we paint, the picture is the message. When we gesture, the movements of our arms, the expressions on our face are the message."[7] Our message is affected by the code or group of symbols we use to transfer meaning, the content of the message itself, and the decisions that the source makes in selecting and arranging both codes and content. Each of these three segments can act to distort the message.

The *channel* is the medium through which the message travels. It is selected by the sender. Common channels are air for the spoken word and paper for the written word. If you decide to convey to a friend something that happened to you during the day in a face-to-face conversation, the channel becomes spoken words and gestures. But you have choices. A specific message—an invitation to a party, for example—can be communicated orally or in writing. In an organization, certain channels are more appropriate for certain messages. Obviously, if the building is on fire, a memo to convey the fact is inappropriate! If something is important, such as an employee's performance appraisal, a manager might want to use multiple channels—for instance, an oral review followed by a summary letter. This decreases the potential for distortion.

The *receiver* is the individual to whom the message is directed. But before the message can be received, the symbols in it must be translated into a form that can be understood by the receiver. This is the *decoding* of the message. Just as the encoder was limited by his or her skills, attitudes, knowledge, and social-cultural system, so is the receiver equally restricted. Just as the source must be skillful in writing or speaking, the receiver must be skillful in reading or listening, and both must be able to reason. A person's level of knowledge influences his or her ability to receive, just as it

Communication in organizations takes many forms. It ranges from computers talking to other computers to informal, one-on-one conversations.

does his or her ability to send. Moreover, the receiver's preformed attitudes and cultural background can distort the message being transferred.

The final link in the communicative process is a feedback loop. "If a communication source decodes the message that he encodes, if the message is put back into the system, we have feedback."[8] That is, *feedback* returns the message to the sender and provides a check on whether understanding has been achieved.

Methods of Communicating

The most popular communication methods used by people in organizations are verbal or oral interaction, written communications, nonverbal communication, and electronic media. In this section we'll briefly describe each method.

Oral   People communicate with each other most often by talking, or oral communication. Popular forms of oral communication include speeches, formal one-on-one and group discussions, and the informal rumor mill, or grapevine.

The advantages of oral communications are quick transmission and quick feedback. A verbal message can be conveyed and a response received in a minimum amount of time. If the receiver is unsure of the message, rapid feedback allows the sender to detect the uncertainty and to correct it.

The major disadvantage of oral communication surfaces whenever a message has to be passed through a number of people. The more people who are involved, the greater the potential for distortion. If you have ever played the game "telephone" at a party, you know the problem. Each person interprets the message in his or her own way. The message's content, when it reaches its destination, is often very different from the original. In an organization where decisions and other communiques are verbally passed up and down the authority hierarchy, considerable opportunity exists for messages to become distorted.

Written   Written communications include memos, letters, organizational periodicals, bulletin boards, or any other device that transmits written words or symbols.

Why would a sender choose to use written communications? Because they're permanent, tangible, and verifiable. Typically, both sender and receiver have a record of the communication. The message can be stored for an indefinite period of time. If there are questions about the content of the message, it is physically available for later reference. This is particularly important for complex or lengthy communications. The marketing plan for a new product is likely to contain a number of tasks spread out over several months. By putting it in writing, those who have to initiate the plan can readily refer to it over the life of the plan. A final benefit of written communication comes from the process itself. Except in rare instances, such as when presenting a formal speech, more care is taken with the written word than with the oral word. Having to put something in writing forces a person to think through more carefully what he or she wants to convey. Therefore written communications are more likely to be well thought out, logical, and clear.

Of course, written messages have their drawbacks. While writing may be more precise, it also consumes a great deal more time. You could convey far more information to your college instructor in a one-hour oral exam than in a one-hour written exam. In fact, you could probably say the same thing in ten to fifteen minutes that takes you an hour to write. The other major disadvantage is feedback or lack of it. Oral communications allow the receivers to respond rapidly to what they think they hear. However, written communications do not have a built-in feedback mechanism. The result is that sending a memo is no assurance that it will be received; if it is received, there is no guarantee that the recipient will interpret it as the sender meant. The latter point is also relevant in oral communiqués, except that it's easier in such cases merely to ask the receiver to summarize what you've said. An accurate summary presents feedback evidence that the message has been received and understood.

nonverbal communication
Communication transmitted without words.

Nonverbal   Some of the most meaningful communications are neither spoken nor written. These are **nonverbal communications.** A loud siren or a red light at an intersection tells you something without words. When a college instructor is teaching a large lecture class, she doesn't need words to tell her that her students are bored when eyes get glassy or students begin to read the school newspaper. Similarly, when papers start to rustle and notebooks begin to close, the message is clear: Class time is about over. The size of a person's office and desk or the clothes a person wears also convey messages to others. However, the best-known areas of nonverbal communication are body language and verbal intonation.

body language
Gestures, facial configurations, and other movements of the body that convey meaning.

Body language refers to gestures, facial configurations, and other movements of the body. A snarled face, for example, says something different from a smile. Hand motions, facial expressions, and other gestures can communicate emotions or temperaments such as aggression, fear, shyness, arrogance, joy, and anger.

verbal intonation
An emphasis given to words or phrases that conveys meaning.

Verbal intonations refers to the emphasis someone gives to words or phrases. To illustrate how intonations can change the meaning of a message, consider the student who asks the instructor a question. The instructor replies, "What do you mean by that?" The student's reaction will vary, depending on the tone of the instructor's response. A soft, smooth tone creates a different meaning from one that is abrasive and puts a strong emphasis on the last word. Most of us would view the first intonation as coming from someone who sincerely sought clarification, whereas the second suggests that the person is aggressive or defensive.

The fact that every oral communication also has a nonverbal message cannot be overemphasized. Why? Because the nonverbal component is likely to carry the greatest impact. One researcher found that 55 percent of an oral message is derived from facial expression and physical posture, 38 percent from verbal intonation, and only 7 percent from the actual words used.[9] Most of us know that animals respond to how we say something rather than what we say. Apparently, people aren't much different.

TABLE 16-1   How Communications Break Down

What the Manager Said	What the Manager Meant	What the Subordinate Heard
I'll look into hiring another person for your department as soon as I complete my budget review.	We'll start interviewing for that job in about three weeks.	I'm tied up with more important things. Let's forget about hiring for the indefinite future.
Your performance was below par last quarter. I really expected more out of you.	You're going to have to try harder, but I know you can do it.	If you screw up one more time, you're out.
I'd like that report as soon as you can get to it.	I need that report within the week.	Drop that rush order you're working on and fill out that report today.
I talked to the boss, but at the present time, due to budget problems, we'll be unable to fully match your competitive salary offer.	We can give you 95 percent of that offer, and I know we'll be able to do even more for you next year.	If I were you, I'd take that competitive offer. We're certainly not going to pay that kind of salary to a person with your credentials.
We have a job opening in Los Angeles that we think would be just your cup of tea. We'd like you to go out there and look it over.	If you'd like that job, it's yours. If not, of course, you can stay here in Denver. You be the judge.	You don't have to go out to L.A. if you don't want to. However, if you don't, you can kiss good-bye to your career with this firm.
Your people seem to be having some problems getting their work out on time. I want you to look into this situation and straighten it out.	Talk to your people and find out what the problem is. Then get with them and jointly solve it.	I don't care how many heads you bust, just get me that output. I've got enough problems around here without you screwing things up too.

Source: From Steven Altman, Enzo Valenzi, and Richard M. Hodgetts, *Organizational Behavior: Theory and Practice* (Orlando, FL: Harcourt Brace Jovanovich, 1985), p. 532. With permission.

Electronic Media   Today we rely on a number of sophisticated electronic media to carry our communications. In addition to the more common media—the telephone and public address system—we have closed-circuit television, voice-activated computers, xerographic reproduction, fax machines, and a host of other electronic devices that we can use in conjunction with speech or paper to create more effective communication. Maybe the fastest growing is **electronic mail.** Computers that are linked together, with the appropriate software, allow individuals to instantaneously transmit written messages among each other. Messages sit at the receiver's terminal to be read at the receiver's convenience. Electronic mail is fast and cheap and can be used to send the same message to dozens of people at the same time. Its other strengths and weaknesses generally parallel those of written communications.

Barriers to Effective Communication

In our discussion of the communication process, we noted the consistent potential for distortion. As illustrated in Table 16–1, what managers say can differ from what they

electronic mail
Instantaneous transmission of written messages on computers that are linked together.

mean, as well as from what a subordinate hears. What causes such communication breakdown? In addition to the general distortions identified in the communication process, there are a number of other barriers to effective communication.

filtering
The deliberate manipulation of information to make it appear more favorable to the receiver.

Filtering   **Filtering** is the deliberate manipulation of information to make it appear more favorable to the receiver. For example, when a manager tells his or her boss what the boss wants to hear, the manager is filtering information.

The extent of filtering tends to be a function of the height of the structure and the organizational culture. The more vertical levels there are in an organization's hierarchy, the more opportunities there are for filtering. The organizational culture encourages or discourages filtering by the emphasis it places on rewards. The more rewards emphasize style and appearance, the more managers are motivated to alter communications in their favor.

Selective Perception   We've mentioned selective perception in several places. The receiver in the communication process selectively sees and hears communications depending on his or her needs, motivations, experience, background, and other personal characteristics. The receiver also projects his or her interests and expectations into communications in decoding them. The employment interviewer who expects a female job candidate to put family before career is likely to *see* that in female candidates, regardless of whether the candidates feel that way. As we said in Chapter 13, we don't see reality; instead, we interpret what we see and call it reality.

Emotions   How the receiver feels at the time of receipt of a message influences how he or she interprets it. You will often interpret the same message differently, depending on whether you are happy or distressed. Extreme emotions such as jubilation or depression are most likely to hinder effective communication. In such instances, we often disregard our rational and objective thinking processes and substitute emotional judgments. It's best to avoid making decisions when you're upset because you're not likely to be thinking clearly.

Language   Words mean different things to different people. Age, education, and cultural background are three of the more obvious variables that influence the language a person uses and the definitions they give to words. The language of William F. Buckley, Jr. is clearly different from that of the typical high-school-educated factory worker. The latter, in fact, would undoubtedly have trouble understanding much of Buckley's vocabulary. In an organization, employees usually come from diverse backgrounds. Furthermore, horizontal differentiation creates specialists who develop their own jargon or technical language. In large organizations, members are often widely dispersed geographically (some even work in different countries), and employees in each locale will use terms and phrases that are unique to their area. Vertical differentiation can also cause language problems. For instance, differences in the meaning of words such as *incentives* and *quotas* occur at different levels of management.[10] Top managers often speak about the need for incentives and quotas, yet these terms imply manipulation and create resentment among lower managers.

The point is that while you and I might both speak the same language (English), our use of that language is far from uniform. A knowledge of how each of us modifies the language would minimize communication difficulties. The problem is that members in an organization usually don't know how others with whom they interact have modified the language. Senders tend to assume that the words and terms they use mean the same to the receiver as they do to them. This, of course, is often incorrect and creates communication difficulties.

MANAGING FROM A GLOBAL PERSPECTIVE

Cross-Cultural Insights Into Communication Processes

Interpersonal communication is not conducted in the same way around the world. For example, compare countries that place a high value on individualism (such as the United States) with countries where the emphasis is on collectivism (such as Japan).[11]

Owing to the emphasis on the individual in countries like the United States, communication patterns are individual-oriented and rather clearly spelled out. For instance, U.S. managers rely heavily on memoranda, announcements, position papers, and other formal forms of communication to stake out their positions in intra-organizational negotiations. Supervisors in the United States often hoard secret information in an attempt to promote their own advancement and as a way of inducing their subordinates to accept decisions and plans. For their own protection, lower-level employees also engage in this practice.

In collectivist countries like Japan, there is more interaction for its own sake and a more informal way of interpersonal contact. The Japanese manager, in contrast to U.S. managers, will engage in extensive verbal consultation over an issue first and only draw up a formal document later to outline the agreement that was made. Face-to-face communication is encouraged. Additionally, open communication is an inherent part of the Japanese work setting. Work spaces are open and crowded with individuals at different levels in the work hierarchy. U.S. organizations emphasize authority, hierarchy, and formal lines of communication.

These cultural differences between the United States and Japan can make negotiations difficult between executives from these countries.[12] Research on negotiations has found, for example, that executives from these countries come to the negotiating table with two different objectives. Americans come to make a deal, while their Japanese counterparts come to start a relationship. Americans want to begin talking immediately about numbers and details. Japanese executives start the process by talking in generalities. Americans tend to be blunt and forthright in their refusals. Many Japanese find this aggressiveness and frankness offensive.

Nonverbal Cues   Earlier, we noted that nonverbal communication is an important way in which people convey messages to others. But nonverbal communication is almost always accompanied by oral communication. As long as the two are in agreement, they act to reinforce each other. My boss's words tell me that he is angry; his tone of voice and body movements indicate anger. I can conclude—probably correctly—that he is angry. When nonverbal cues are inconsistent with the oral message, the receiver becomes confused, and the clarity of the message suffers. The boss who tells you that she sincerely wants to hear about your problem and then proceeds to read her mail while you talk is sending conflicting signals.

Overcoming the Barriers

Given these barriers to communication, what can managers do to overcome them? The following suggestions should help to make communication more effective.

Use Feedback   Many communication problems can be directly attributed to misunderstandings and inaccuracies. These are less likely to occur if the manager uses the feedback loop in the communication process. This feedback can be verbal or nonverbal.

If a manager asks a receiver, "Did you understand what I said?," the response represents feedback. Also, feedback should include more than Yes and No answers. The manager can ask a set of questions about a message in order to determine whether or not the message was received as intended. Better yet, the manager can ask the receiver to restate the message in his or her own words. If the manager then hears what was intended, understanding and accuracy should be enhanced. Feedback includes subtler things than the direct asking of questions or the summarizing of messages. General comments can give a manager a sense of the receiver's reaction to a message. In addition, performance appraisals, salary reviews, and promotions represent important, but more subtle, forms of feedback.

Of course, feedback does not have to be conveyed in words. Actions *can* speak louder than words. The sales manager who sends out a directive to his or her staff describing a new monthly sales report that all sales personnel will need to complete receives feedback if some of the salespeople fail to turn in the new report. This feedback suggests that the sales manager needs to clarify further the initial directive. Similarly, when you give a speech to a group of people, you watch their eyes and look for other nonverbal clues to tell you whether they are getting your message or not. This may explain why television performers on situation comedy shows prefer to tape their programs in front of a live audience. Immediate laughter and applause or their absence conveys to the performers whether their message is getting across as intended.

Simplify Language   Since language can be a barrier, managers should choose words and structure their messages in ways that will make them clear and understandable to the receiver. The manager needs to simplify his or her language and consider the audience to whom the message is directed so that the language will be tailored to the receivers. Remember, effective communication is achieved when a message is both received and *understood*. Understanding is improved by simplifying the language used in relation to the audience intended. This means, for example, that a hospital administrator should always try to communicate in clear, easily understood terms and that the language used in messages to the surgical staff should be purposely different from that used with office employees. Jargon can facilitate understanding when it is used with those who know what it means, but it can cause innumerable problems when used outside that group.

Consistent with the previous discussion on feedback, language problems in an important message can be minimized by trying out the message on someone who is unfamiliar with the issue. For example, having a friend read a speech or letter before it is officially communicated can be an effective device for identifying confusing terminology, unclear assumptions, or discontinuous logic flows. One author of a prominent introductory psychology textbook had her husband read the entire book before publication in spite of the fact that he knew nothing about the field of psychology. Her thinking, which made a great deal of sense, was that if her husband (who was a chemical engineer by training) could understand the material, then it should also be clear to freshman college students.

Listen Actively   When someone talks, we hear. But too often we don't listen. Listening is an active search for meaning, whereas hearing is passive. In listening, two people are thinking: the receiver and the sender.

Many of us are poor listeners. Why? Because it's difficult, and it's usually more satisfying to be on the offensive. Listening, in fact, is often more tiring than talking. It demands intellectual effort. Unlike hearing, **active listening** demands total concentration. The average person speaks at a rate of about 150 words per minute, whereas we have the capacity to listen at the rate of over 1,000 words per minute. The difference obviously leaves idle time for the brain and opportunities for the mind to wander.

Active listening is enhanced by developing empathy with the sender—that is, by placing yourself in the sender's position. Since senders differ in attitudes, interests, needs, and expectations, empathy makes it easier to understand the actual content of a message. An empathetic listener reserves judgment on the message's content and carefully listens to what is being said. The goal is to improve one's ability to receive the full meaning of a communication without having it distorted by premature judgments or interpretations. Active listening skills are discussed in considerable detail later in this chapter.

active listening
Listening for full meaning without making premature judgments or interpretations.

Constrain Emotions   It would be naive to assume that managers always communicate in a fully rational manner. We know that emotions can severely cloud and distort the transference of meaning. A manager who is emotionally upset over an issue is more likely to misconstrue incoming messages and fail to clearly and accurately express his or her outgoing messages. What can the manager do? The simplest answer is to desist from further communication until he or she has regained composure.

Watch Nonverbal Cues   If actions speak louder than words, then it's important to watch your actions to make sure they align with and reinforce the words that go along with them. We noted that nonverbal messages carry a great deal of weight. Given this fact, the effective communicator watches his or her nonverbal cues to ensure that they too convey the desired message.

DEVELOPING INTERPERSONAL SKILLS

Effective communication skills are only part of the larger set of interpersonal skills. In recent years, attention has been focused on a short list of interpersonal skills.[13] We'll call them the *basic* interpersonal skills in which every manager needs to become proficient. The rest of this chapter discusses these key skills: active listening, providing feedback, delegating, disciplining, and managing conflict.

ETHICAL DILEMMAS IN MANAGEMENT

Is it Unethical to Purposely Distort Information?

The issue of "ethics in lying" was introduced in Chapter 1. Since then, you've had ample time to think about this issue. Since lying is such a broad concern and so closely intertwined with interpersonal communication, this might be a good time to think again about dilemmas that managers face relating to the intentional distortion of information.

You have just seen your division's sales report for last month. Sales are down considerably. Your boss, who works 2,000 miles away in another city, is unlikely to see last month's sales figures. You're optimistic that sales will pick up this month and next so that your overall quarterly numbers will be acceptable. You also know that your boss is the type of person who hates to hear bad news. You're having a phone conversation today with your boss. He happens to ask, in passing, how last month's sales went. Do you tell him the truth?

A subordinate asks you about a rumor she's heard that your department and all its employees will be transferred from New York to Dallas. You know the rumor to be true, but you would rather not let the information out just yet. You're fearful that it could hurt departmental morale and lead to premature resignations. What do you say to your employee?

These two incidents illustrate dilemmas that managers face relating to evading, distorting, or lying to others.

It might not always be in a manager's best interest or those of his or her unit to provide full and complete information. In fact, a strong argument can be made for managers to purposely keep their communications vague and unclear.[14] Keeping communications fuzzy can cut down on questions, permit faster decision making, minimize objections, reduce opposition, make it easier to deny one's earlier statements, preserve the freedom to change one's mind, permit one to say No diplomatically, help to avoid confrontation and anxiety, and provide other benefits that work to the advantage of the manager.

Is it unethical to purposely distort communications to get a favorable outcome? Is distortion acceptable but lying not? What about "little white lies" that really don't hurt anybody? What do *you* think?

ACTIVE LISTENING SKILLS

The ability to be an effective listener is too often taken for granted. We confuse hearing with listening. Hearing is merely picking up sound vibrations. Listening is making sense of what we hear. Listening requires paying attention, interpreting, and remembering sound stimuli.

Active listening is hard work. It includes good eye contact, avoiding distractions, asking questions, paraphrasing, and not interrupting the speaker.

Active Versus Passive Listening

Effective listening is active rather than passive. In passive listening, you're much like a tape recorder. You absorb the information given. If the speaker provides you with a clear message and makes his or her delivery interesting enough to keep your attention, you'll probably get most of what the speaker is trying to communicate. But active listening requires you to get inside the speaker so that you can understand the communication from his or her point of view. As you'll see, active listening is hard work. You have to concentrate, and you have to want to fully understand what a speaker is saying. Students who use active listening techniques for an entire fifty-minute lecture are as tired as their instructor when that lecture is over because they have put as much energy into listening as the instructor put into speaking.

There are four essential requirements for active listening. You need to listen with (1) intensity, (2) empathy, (3) acceptance, and (4) a willingness to take responsibility for completeness.[15]

As noted previously, the human brain is capable of handling a speaking rate that is about six times the speed of the average speaker. That leaves a lot of time for idle mind wandering while listening. The active listener concentrates intensely on what the speaker is saying and tunes out the thousands of miscellaneous thoughts (about money, sex, vacations, parties, friends, getting the car fixed, and the like) that create distractions. What do active listeners do with their idle brain time? Summarize and integrate what has been said! They put each new bit of information into the context of what has preceded it.

Empathy requires you to put yourself in the speaker's shoes. You try to understand what the *speaker* wants to communicate rather than what *you* want to understand. Notice that empathy demands both knowledge of the speaker and flexibility on your part. You need to suspend your own thoughts and feelings and adjust what you see and feel to your speaker's world. In that way you increase the likelihood that you will interpret the message being spoken in the way the speaker intended.

An active listener demonstrates acceptance. He or she listens objectively without judging content. This is no easy task. It is natural to be distracted by the content of what a speaker says, especially when we disagree with it. When we hear something we disagree with, we begin formulating our mental arguments to counter what is being

TABLE 16–2   Behaviors Related to Effective Active Listening

- Make eye contact
- Exhibit affirmative nods and appropriate facial expressions
- Avoid distracting actions or gestures
- Ask questions
- Paraphrase
- Avoid interrupting the speaker
- Don't overtalk
- Make smooth transitions between the roles of speaker and listener

said. Of course, in doing this we miss the rest of the message. The challenge for the active listener is to absorb what is being said and to withhold judgment on content until the speaker is finished.

The final ingredient of active listening is taking responsibility for completeness. That is, the listener does whatever is necessary to get the full intended meaning from the speaker's communication. Two widely used active listening techniques to achieve this end are listening for feelings as well as for content and asking questions to ensure understanding.

Developing Effective Active Listening Skills

From a review of the active listening literature, we can identify eight specific behaviors that effective listeners demonstrate[16] (see Table 16–2). As you review these behaviors, ask yourself the degree to which they describe your listening practices. If you're not currently using these techniques, there is no better time than today to begin developing them.

Make Eye Contact   How do you feel when somebody doesn't look at you when you're speaking? If you're like most people, you're likely to interpret this as aloofness or disinterest. It's ironic that while "you listen with your ears, people judge whether you are listening by looking at your eyes."[17] Making eye contact with the speaker focuses your attention, reduces the likelihood that you will become distracted, and encourages the speaker.

Exhibit Affirmative Nods and Appropriate Facial Expressions   The effective listener shows interest in what is being said. How? Through nonverbal signals. Affirmative nods and appropriate facial expressions, when added to good eye contact, convey to the speaker that you're listening.

Avoid Distracting Actions or Gestures   The other side of showing interest is avoiding actions that suggest that your mind is somewhere else. When listening, *don't* look at your watch, shuffle papers, play with your pencil, or engage in similar distractions. They make the speaker feel that you're bored or uninterested. Furthermore, they indicate that you *aren't* fully attentive and might be missing part of the message that the speaker wants to convey.

Ask Questions   The critical listener analyzes what he or she hears and asks questions. This behavior provides clarification, ensures understanding, and assures the speaker that you're listening.

paraphrasing
Restating what a speaker has said but in your own words.

Paraphrase   **Paraphrasing** means restating *in your own words* what the speaker has said. The effective listener uses phrases like: "What I hear you saying is . . ." or "Do you mean . . . ?" Why rephrase what's already been said? There are two reasons. First, it's an excellent control device to check on whether you're listening carefully. You can't paraphrase accurately if your mind is wandering or if you're thinking about what you're going to say next. Second, it's a control for accuracy. By rephrasing in your own words what the speaker has said and feeding it back to the speaker, you verify the accuracy of your understanding.

Avoid Interrupting the Speaker   Let the speaker complete his or her thought before you try to respond. Don't try to second-guess where the speaker's thoughts are going. When the speaker is finished, you'll know it.

Don't Overtalk   Most of us would rather speak our own ideas than listen to what someone else says. Too many of us listen only because it's the price we have to pay to get people to let us talk. While talking might be more fun and silence might be uncomfortable, you can't talk and listen at the same time. The good listener recognizes this fact and doesn't overtalk.

Make Smooth Transitions Between the Roles of Speaker and Listener   As a student sitting in a lecture hall, you probably find it relatively easy to get into an effective listening frame of mind. Why? Because communication is essentially one-way; the instructor talks and you listen. But the instructor-student dyad is atypical. In most work situations you're continually shifting back and forth between the roles of speaker and listener. The effective listener makes transitions smoothly from speaker to listener and back to speaker. From a listening perspective this means concentrating on what a speaker has to say and practicing not thinking about what you're going to say as soon as you get your chance.

FEEDBACK SKILLS

Ask a manager about the feedback he or she gives subordinates, and you're likely to get a qualified answer. If the feedback is positive, it's likely to be given promptly and enthusiastically. Negative feedback is often treated very differently. Like most of us, managers don't particularly enjoy being the bearers of bad news. They fear offending or having to deal with the recipient's defensiveness. The result is that negative feedback is often avoided, delayed, or substantially distorted.[18] The purposes of this section are to show you the importance of providing both positive and negative feedback and to identify specific techniques to make your feedback more effective.

Positive Versus Negative Feedback

We said that managers treat positive and negative feedback differently. So, too, do recipients. You need to understand this fact and adjust your style accordingly.

Positive feedback is more readily and accurately perceived than negative feedback. Furthermore, while positive feedback is almost always accepted, negative feedback often meets resistance.[19] Why? The logical answer seems to be that people want to hear good news and block out the bad. Positive feedback fits what most people wish to hear and already believe about themselves.

TABLE 16–3   Behaviors Related to Providing Effective Feedback

- Focus on specific behaviors
- Keep feedback impersonal
- Keep feedback goal-oriented
- Make feedback well-timed
- Ensure understanding
- Direct negative feedback toward behavior that the recipient can control

Does this mean that you should avoid giving negative feedback? No! What it means is that you need to be aware of potential resistance and learn to use negative feedback in situations in which it is most likely to be accepted.[20] What are those situations? Research indicates that negative feedback is most likely to be accepted when it comes from a credible source or if it is objective in form. Subjective impressions carry weight only when they come from a person with high status and credibility.[21] This suggests that negative feedback that is supported by hard data—numbers, specific examples, and the like—has a good chance of being accepted. Negative feedback that is subjective can be a meaningful tool for experienced managers, particularly those high in the organization who have earned the respect of their employees. From less experienced managers, those in the lower ranks of the organization, and those whose reputations have not yet been established, negative feedback is not likely to be well received.

Developing Effective Feedback Skills

There are six specific suggestions that we can make to help you be more effective in providing feedback (see Table 16–3).

Focus on Specific Behaviors   Feedback should be specific rather than general.[22] Avoid statements like "You have a bad attitude" or "I'm really impressed with the good job you did." They're vague, and while they provide information, they don't tell the recipient enough to correct the "bad attitude" or *on what basis* you concluded that a "good job" had been done.

Suppose you said something like "Bob, I'm concerned with your attitude toward your work. You were a half hour late to yesterday's staff meeting and then told me you hadn't read the preliminary report we were discussing. Today you tell me you're taking off three hours early for a dental appointment"; or "Jan, I was really pleased with the job you did on the Phillips account. They increased their purchases from us by 22 percent last month, and I got a call a few days ago from Dan Phillips complimenting me on how quickly you responded to those specification changes for the MJ-7 microchip." Both of these statements focus on specific behaviors. They tell the recipient *why* you are being critical or complimentary.

Keep Feedback Impersonal   Feedback, particularly the negative kind, should be descriptive rather than judgmental or evaluative.[23] No matter how upset you are, keep the feedback job-related and never criticize someone personally because of an inappropriate action. Telling people they're "stupid," "incompetent," or the like is almost always counterproductive. It provokes such an emotional reaction that the performance deviation itself is apt to be overlooked. When you're criticizing, remember that you're censuring a job-related behavior, not the person. You might be tempted to tell someone he or she is "rude and insensitive" (which might well be true); however, that's hardly impersonal. It's better to say something like "You interrupted me three times, with questions that were not urgent, when you knew I was talking long-distance to a customer in Scotland."

Keep Feedback Goal-Oriented   Feedback should not be given primarily to "dump" or "unload" on another.[24] If you have to say something negative, make sure it's directed toward the recipient's goals. Ask yourself whom the feedback is supposed to help. If the answer is essentially *you*—"I've got something I just want to get off my chest"—bite your tongue. Such feedback undermines your credibility and lessens the meaning and influence of future feedback.

Make Feedback Well-Timed   Feedback is most meaningful to a recipient when there is a very short interval between his or her behavior and the receipt of feedback about that behavior.[25] To illustrate, a new employee who makes a mistake is more likely to respond to his manager's suggestions for improvement right after the mistake or at the end of that working day, rather than during a performance-review session several months later. If you have to spend time recreating a situation and refreshing someone's memory of it, the feedback you're providing is likely to be ineffective.[26] Moreover, if you are particularly concerned with *changing* behavior, delays in providing feedback on the undesirable actions lessen the likelihood that the feedback will be effective in bringing about the desired change.[27] Of course, making feedback prompt merely for promptness' sake can backfire if you have insufficient information, if you're angry, or if you're otherwise emotionally upset. In such instances, "well-timed" could mean "somewhat delayed."

Ensure Understanding   Is your feedback concise and complete enough that the recipient clearly and fully understands your communication? Remember that every successful communication requires both transference and understanding of meaning. If feedback is to be effective, you need to ensure that the recipient understands it.[28] Consistent with our discussion of listening techniques, you should have the recipient rephrase the content of your feedback to find out whether it fully captures the meaning you intended.

Direct Negative Feedback Toward Behavior That the Recipient can Control   There's little value in reminding a person of some shortcoming over which he or she has no control. Negative feedback should be directed toward behavior the recipient can do something about.[29] For example, to criticize an employee who is late because she forgot to set her wake-up alarm is valid. To criticize her for being late when the subway she takes to work every day had a power failure, trapping her underground for half an hour, is pointless. There is nothing she could have done to correct what happened.

Additionally, when negative feedback is given concerning something that the recipient can control, it might be a good idea to indicate specifically what can be done to improve the situation. This takes some of the sting out of the criticism and offers guidance to recipients who understand the problem but don't know how to resolve it.

DELEGATION SKILLS

Managers get things done through other people. This description recognizes that there are limits to any manager's time and knowledge. Effective managers, therefore, need to understand the value of delegating and how to do it.

delegation
The assignment of authority and responsibility to another person to carry out specific activities.

What Is Delegation?

Delegation is the assignment of authority to another person to carry out specific activities. It allows a subordinate to make decisions—that is, it's a shift of decision-making authority from one organizational level to another, lower one.[30]

Delegation should not be confused with participation. In participative decision making, there is a sharing of authority. With delegation, subordinates make decisions on their own.

Is Delegation Abdication?

When done properly, delegation is *not* abdication. The key word here is "properly." If you dump tasks on a subordinate without clarifying exactly what is to be done, the range of the subordinate's discretion, the expected level of performance, when the tasks are to be completed, and similar concerns, you are abdicating responsibility and inviting trouble.[31]

Don't fall into the trap of assuming that, to avoid the appearance of abdicating, you should minimize delegation. Unfortunately, this is the approach taken by many new and inexperienced managers. Lacking confidence in their subordinates or fearful that they will be criticized for their subordinates' mistakes, they try to do everything themselves.

It might very well be true that you're capable of doing the tasks better, faster, or with fewer mistakes. The catch is that your time and energy are scarce resources. It's not possible for you to do everything yourself. You need to learn to delegate if you're going to be effective in your job.[32] This suggests two important points. First, you should expect and accept some mistakes by your subordinates. They are part of delegation. Mistakes are often good learning experiences for your subordinates, as long as their costs are not excessive. Second, to ensure that the costs of mistakes don't exceed the value of the learning, you need to put adequate controls in place. As we'll discuss later in this section, delegation without feedback controls that let you know when there are serious problems *is* abdication.

Contingency Factors in Delegation

How much authority should a manager delegate? Should he or she keep authority centralized, delegating only the least number of duties? If not, what contingency factors should be considered in determining the degree to which authority is delegated? The following contingency factors provide some guidance.

The Size of the Organization   The larger the organization, the greater the number of decisions that have to be made. Since the top managers in an organization have only so much time and can obtain only so much information, they become increasingly dependent in larger organizations on the decision making of lower-level managers. Hence they resort to increased delegation.

The Importance of the Duty or Decision   The more important a duty or decision is (as expressed in terms of cost and impact on the future of the organization), the less likely it is to be delegated. For instance, a department head may be delegated authority to make expenditures up to $5,000, and division heads and vice presidents up to $25,000 and $100,000, respectively.

Task Complexity   The more complex the task, the more difficult it is for top management to possess current and sufficient technical information to make effective

TABLE 16–4   Behaviors Related to Effective Delegating

- Clarify the assignment
- Specify the subordinate's range of discretion
- Allow the subordinate to participate
- Inform others that delegation has occurred
- Establish feedback controls

decisions. Complex tasks require greater expertise, and decisions about them should be delegated to the individuals who possess the necessary technical knowledge.

Organizational Culture   If management has confidence and trust in subordinates, the culture will support a greater degree of delegation. However, if top management does not have confidence in the abilities of lower-level managers, it will delegate authority begrudgingly. In such instances, as little authority as possible will be delegated.

Qualities of Subordinates   A final contingency consideration is the qualities of subordinates. Delegation requires subordinates with the skills, abilities, and motivation to accept authority and act on it. If this is lacking, top management will be reluctant to relinquish authority.

Developing Effective Delegating Skills

A number of actions differentiate the effective from the ineffective delegator[33] (see Table 16–4).

Clarify the Assignment   The place to begin is to determine *what* is to be delegated and to *whom*. You need to identify the person who is best capable of doing the task and then determine whether he or she has the time and motivation to do the job.

Assuming that you have a willing and able subordinate, it is your responsibility to provide clear information on what is being delegated, the results you expect, and any time or performance expectations you hold.

Unless there is an overriding need to adhere to specific methods, you should delegate only the results. That is, get agreement on what is to be done and the results expected, but let the subordinate decide on the means. By focusing on goals and allowing the employee the freedom to use his or her own judgment as to how those goals are to be achieved, you increase trust between you and the employee, improve the employee's motivation, and enhance accountability for the results.

Specify the Subordinate's Range of Discretion   Every act of delegation comes with constraints. You are delegating authority to act, but not *unlimited* authority. What you are delegating is authority to act on certain issues and, on those issues, within certain parameters. You need to specify what those parameters are so that subordinates know, in no uncertain terms, the range of their discretion. When this has been successfully communicated, both you and the subordinate will have the same idea of the limits to the latter's authority and how far he or she can go without checking further with you.

How much authority do you give a subordinate? In other words, how tightly do you draw the parameters? The best answer is that you should allocate enough authority to allow the subordinate to complete the task successfully.

Allow the Subordinate to Participate   One of the best sources for determining how much authority will be necessary to accomplish a task is the subordinate who will be held accountable for that task. Be alert, however, that participation can present its own set of potential problems as a result of subordinates' self-interest and biases in evaluating their own abilities. Some subordinates might be personally motivated to expand their authority beyond what they need and beyond what they are capable of handling. Allowing such people too much participation in deciding what tasks they should take on and how much authority they must have to complete those tasks can undermine the effectiveness of the delegation process.

Inform Others That Delegation Has Occurred   Delegation should not take place in a vacuum. Not only do the manager and subordinate need to know specifically what has been delegated and how much authority has been granted, but anyone else who is likely to be affected by the delegation act also needs to be informed. This includes people outside the organization as well as inside it. Essentially, you need to convey what has been delegated (the task and amount of authority) and to whom. If you fail to follow through on this step, the legitimacy of your subordinate's authority will probably be called into question. Failure to inform others makes conflict likely and decreases the chances that your subordinate will be able to accomplish the delegated task efficiently.

Establish Feedback Controls   To delegate without instituting feedback controls is to invite problems. There is always the possibility that a subordinate will misuse the discretion that he or she has been delegated. The establishment of controls to monitor the subordinate's progress increases the likelihood that important problems will be identified early and that the task will be completed on time and to the desired specifications.

Ideally, controls should be determined at the time of the initial assignment. Agree on a specific time for completion of the task, and then set progress dates when the subordinate will report back on how well he or she is doing and any major problems that have surfaced. This can be supplemented with periodic spot checks to ensure that authority guidelines are not being abused, organization policies are being followed, proper procedures are being met, and the like.

Too much of a good thing can be dysfunctional. If the controls are too constraining, the subordinate will be deprived of the opportunity to build self-confidence and much of the motivational aspects of delegation will be lost. A well-designed control system, which we'll elaborate on in detail in Chapter 18, permits your subordinates to make small mistakes but quickly alerts you when big mistakes are imminent.

DISCIPLINE SKILLS

It has been fashionable in management circles for a number of years to talk about rewards and downplay punishment or discipline. This has essentially derived from the research on the law of effect, which was discussed in Chapter 13. According to this view, punishment can decrease or eliminate an undesirable behavior, but it will not necessarily lead to desirable behaviors. The negative connotation of punishment and discipline is not a sufficient reason to dismiss it as a management skill for modifying employee behavior.[34] As most practicing managers have learned, the use of discipline is sometimes necessary in dealing with problem employees.

discipline
Actions taken by a manager to enforce the organization's standards and regulations.

What specifically do we mean when we use the term **discipline?** It refers to actions taken by a manager to enforce the organization's standards and regulations.

MANAGERS WHO MADE A DIFFERENCE

Steve McCracken at DuPont

At age thirty-five, Steve McCracken was on the fast track at DuPont.[35] Between 1986 and 1988 he had been managing DuPont's apparel-marketing office in New York, overseeing sixty people. Before that, McCracken had held jobs in manufacturing, marketing, and finance, almost always the youngest person ever to have those assignments. In 1989, McCracken got another promotion—this time in Switzerland, where he was put in charge of European marketing for Lycra, one of DuPont's fastest-growing fibers businesses.

A large part of McCracken's success had to do with his management style. He knew the value of delegating authority and the increased importance delegation was playing in DuPont's culture. He gave his people freedom to try new ideas while he concentrated on creating a relaxed environment in which everyone felt a part of the effort. "In the old days," he said, "my head would roll if I didn't know where my people were and what they were doing. Now, it's more important that I'm motivating them. I'm not expected to know all the things my people know."

McCracken's style didn't always go over well with his bosses. For instance, he took all the secretaries from New York to Florida and included them in a three-day meeting with his marketing people. He purposely didn't clear this with headquarters ahead of time. "It's a whole lot easier to ask for forgiveness than it is for permission," he said.

Photo courtesy of DuPont de Nemours Int.

Types of Discipline Problems

With very little difficulty, we could list several dozen or more infractions that managers might believe require disciplinary action. For simplicity's sake, we have classified the most frequent violations into four categories: attendance, on-the-job behaviors, dishonesty, and outside activities.[36]

Attendance   The most serious disciplinary problems facing managers undoubtedly involve attendance. For instance, in a study of 200 organizations, 60 percent of which employed over 1,000 workers, absenteeism, tardiness, abuse of sick leave, and other aspects of attendance were rated as the foremost problems by 79 percent of the respondents.[37]

On-the-Job Behaviors   Our second category of discipline problems covers on-the-job behaviors. This blanket label includes insubordination, horseplay, fighting, gambling, failure to use safety devices, carelessness, and two of the most widely discussed problems in organizations today—alcohol abuse and drug abuse.

Dishonesty   Although it is not one of the more widespread employee problems confronting a manager, dishonesty has traditionally resulted in the most severe disciplinary actions. One study found that 90 percent of surveyed organizations would

Attendance problems are more widespread than those related to productivity, such as carelessness in doing work, neglect of duty, and not following established procedures.

discharge an employee for theft, even if it was only a first offense. Similarly, 88 percent would discharge employees who were found to have falsified information on their employment applications.[38] These findings reflect the strong cultural norm against dishonesty in North America.

Outside Activities   Our final problem category covers activities in which employees engage outside of their work that either affect their on-the-job performance or generally reflect negatively on the organization's image. Included here are unauthorized strike activity, having part of one's wages attached to satisfy a debt, outside criminal activities, and working for a competing organization. Among managerial personnel, this category would also include bad-mouthing the organization and questioning the organization's key values in public.

The "Hot Stove" Rule

"hot stove" rule
Discipline should immediately follow an infraction, provide ample warning, be consistent, and impersonal.

The **"hot stove" rule** is a frequently cited set of principles that can guide you in effectively disciplining an employee.[39] The name comes from the similarities between touching a hot stove and administering discipline. Both are painful, but the analogy goes further. When you touch a hot stove, you get an *immediate* response. The burn you receive is instantaneous, leaving no doubt in your mind about the relation between cause and effect. You have ample *warning.* You know what happens if you touch a hot stove. Furthermore, the result is *consistent.* Every time you touch a hot stove, you get the same result—you get burned. Finally, the result is *impersonal.* Regardless of who you are, if you touch a hot stove, you will be burned.

The analogy with discipline should be apparent, but let's briefly expand on each of these four points, since they are central tenets in developing your disciplining skills.

Immediacy   The effect of a disciplinary action will be reduced as the time between the infraction and the penalty lengthens. The more quickly the discipline follows the offense, the more likely it is that the employee will associate the discipline with the offense rather than with you as the imposer of the discipline. Therefore it is best to begin the disciplinary process as soon as possible after you notice a violation. Of course, the immediacy requirement should not result in undue haste. Fair and objective treatment should not be compromised for expediency.

Advance Warning   As a manager, you have an obligation to give advance warning before initiating formal disciplinary action. This means that the employee must be aware of the organization's rules and accept its standards of behavior. Disciplinary action is more likely to be interpreted as fair by employees when they have received clear warning that a given violation will lead to discipline and when they know what that discipline will be.

Consistency   Fair treatment of employees demands that disciplinary action be consistent. If you enforce rule violations in an inconsistent manner, the rules will lose their impact, morale will decline, and employees will question your competence. Productivity will suffer as a result of employee insecurity and anxiety. Your employees will want to know the limits of permissible behavior, and they will look to your actions for guidance. Consistency, by the way, need not result in treating everyone exactly alike because that ignores mitigating circumstances. It does put the responsibility on you to clearly justify disciplinary actions that might appear inconsistent to employees.

Impersonal Nature   The last guideline that flows from the "hot stove" rule is to keep the discipline impersonal. Penalties should be connected with a given violation, not with the personality of the violator. That is, discipline should be directed at what the employee has done, not at the employee. You are penalizing the rule violation, not the individual. Once the penalty has been imposed, you must make every effort to forget the incident. You should attempt to treat the employee just as you did before the infraction.

Developing Effective Discipline Skills

The essence of effective disciplining can be summarized in the seven behaviors listed in Table 16–5.[40]

Confront the Employee in a Calm, Objective, and Serious Manner   Managers can facilitate many interpersonal situations by a loose, informal, and relaxed manner. The idea in such situations is to put the employee at ease. Administering discipline is not one of those situations. Avoid anger or other emotional responses, and convey your comments in a calm, serious tone. But do *not* try to lessen the tension by cracking jokes or making small talk. Such actions are likely to confuse the employee because they send conflicting signals.

TABLE 16–5   Behaviors Related to Effective Disciplining

- Confront the employee in a calm, objective, and serious manner
- State the problem specifically
- Keep the discussion impersonal
- Allow the employee to explain his or her position
- Maintain control of the discussion
- Obtain agreement on how mistakes can be prevented in the future
- Select disciplinary action progressively, considering mitigating circumstances

512		PART FIVE	Leading

State the Problem Specifically   When you sit down with the employee, indicate that you have documentation and be specific about the problem. Give the date, time, place, individuals involved, and any mitigating circumstances surrounding the violation. Be sure to define the violation in exact terms instead of just citing company regulations or the union contract. It's not the breaking of the rules per se about which you want to convey concern. It's the effect that the rule violation has on the work unit's performance. Explain why the behavior can't be continued by showing how it specifically affects the employee's job performance, the unit's effectiveness, and the employee's colleagues.

Keep the Discussion Impersonal   As we stated in our discussion of feedback skills, criticism should focus on the employee's behavior rather than on the individual personally. For instance, if an employee has been late for work several times, point out how this behavior has increased the workload of others or has lowered departmental morale. Don't criticize the person for being thoughtless or irresponsible.

Allow the Employee to Explain His or Her Position   Regardless of what facts you have uncovered, even if you have the proverbial "smoking gun" to support your accusations, due process demands that you give the employee the opportunity to explain his or her position. From the employee's perspective, what happened? Why did it happen? What was his or her perception of the rules, regulations, and circumstances? If there are significant discrepancies between your version of the violation and the employee's, you might need to do more investigating.

Maintain Control of the Discussion   In most interpersonal exchanges, you want to encourage open dialogue. You want to give up control and create a climate of open communication between equals. This won't work in administering discipline. Why? Because violators are prone to use any opportunity to put you on the defensive. In other words, if you don't take control, they will. Disciplining an employee is, by definition, an authority-based act. You are *enforcing* the organization's standards and regulations, so take control. Ask the employee for his or her side of the story. Get the facts. But don't let the employee interrupt you or divert you from your objective.

Obtain Agreement on How Mistakes Can Be Prevented in the Future   Disciplining should include guidance and direction for correcting the problem. Let the employee state what he or she plans to do in the future to ensure that the violation isn't repeated. For serious violations, have the employee draft a step-by-step plan to change the problem behavior. Then set a timetable with follow-up meetings in which progress can be evaluated.

Select Disciplinary Action Progressively, Considering Mitigating Circumstances   Choose a punishment that is appropriate to the crime.[41] Penalties should get progressively stronger if, or when, an offense is repeated. Typically, progressive disciplinary action begins with a verbal warning and then proceeds through a written reprimand, suspension, a demotion or pay cut, and finally, in the most serious cases, dismissal. The punishment you select should be viewed as fair and consistent. This means acknowledging mitigating circumstances. For example, how severe is the problem? Have there been other disciplinary problems with this employee? If so, for how long? Is the problem part of a continuing pattern of discipline infractions? What is the employee's past track record? To what extent has the employee been previously warned about the offense? How have similar infractions been dealt with in the past? Answers to questions such as these can help to ensure that mitigating circumstances are considered.

CONFLICT MANAGEMENT SKILLS

The ability to manage conflict is undoubtedly one of the most important skills a manager needs to possess. A study of middle- and top-level executives by the American Management Association revealed that the average manager spends approximately 20 percent of his or her time dealing with conflict.[42] Its importance is reinforced by a survey of what topics practicing managers consider most important in management development programs; conflict management was rated as being more important than decision making, leadership, or communication skills.[43] In further support of our claim, one researcher studied a group of managers and looked at twenty-five skill and personality factors to determine which, if any, were related to managerial success (defined in terms of ratings by one's boss, salary increases, and promotions).[44] Of the twenty-five measures, only one—the ability to handle conflict—was positively related to managerial success.

What Is Conflict?

conflict
Perceived incompatible differences that result in interference or opposition.

When we use the term **conflict,** we are referring to perceived incompatible differences resulting in some form of interference or opposition. Whether the differences are real or not is irrelevant. If people perceive that differences exist, then a conflict state exists. In addition, our definition includes the extremes, from subtle, indirect, and highly controlled forms of interference to overt acts such as strikes, riots, and wars.

Over the years, three differing views have evolved toward conflict in organizations.[45] One argues that conflict must be avoided, that it indicates a malfunctioning within the organization. We call this the **traditional view of conflict.** A second, the **human relations view of conflict,** argues that conflict is a natural and inevitable outcome in any organization and that it need not be evil but, rather, has the potential to be a positive force in contributing to an organization's performance. The third and most recent perspective proposes not only that conflict can be a positive force in an organization, but also that some conflict is *absolutely necessary* for an organization or units within the organization to perform effectively. We label this third approach the **interactionist view of conflict.**

traditional view of conflict
The view that all conflict is bad and must be avoided.

human relations view of conflict
The view that conflict is a natural and inevitable outcome in any organization.

interactionist view of conflict
The view that some conflict is necessary for an organization to perform effectively.

The Traditional View   The early approach assumed that conflict was bad and would *always* have a negative impact on an organization. Conflict became synonymous with violence, destruction, and irrationality. Since conflict was harmful, it was to be avoided. Management had a responsibility to rid the organization of conflict. This traditional view dominated management literature during the late nineteenth century and continued until the mid-1940s.

The Human Relations View   The human relations position argued that conflict was a natural and inevitable occurrence in all organizations. Since conflict was inevitable, the human relations approach advocated acceptance of conflict. This approach rationalized the existence of conflict; it cannot be eliminated, and there are times when it may even benefit the organization. The human relations view dominated conflict thinking from the late 1940s through the mid-1970s.

The Interactionist View   The current theoretical perspective on conflict is the interactionist approach. While the human relations approach accepts conflict, the interactionist approach *encourages* conflict on the grounds that a harmonious, peaceful, tranquil, and cooperative organization is prone to becoming static, apathetic, and nonresponsive to needs for change and innovation. The major contribution of the interactionist approach, therefore, is that it encourages managers to maintain an ongoing minimum level of conflict—enough to keep units viable, self-critical, and creative.

Functional Versus Dysfunctional Conflict

The interactionist view does not propose that *all* conflicts are good. Rather, some conflicts support the goals of the organization; these are **functional conflicts** of a constructive form. However, some conflicts prevent an organization from achieving its goals; these are **dysfunctional conflicts** and are destructive forms.

Of course, it is one thing to argue that conflict can be valuable, but how does a manager tell whether a conflict is functional or dysfunctional? Unfortunately, the demarcation is neither clear nor precise. No one level of conflict can be adopted as acceptable or unacceptable under all conditions. The type and level of conflict that promote a healthy and positive involvement toward one department's goals may, in another department or in the same department at another time, be highly dysfunctional. Functionality or dysfunctionality, therefore, is a matter of judgment. Figure 16–2 illustrates the challenge facing managers. They want to create an environment within their organization or organizational unit in which conflict is healthy but not allowed to run to pathological extremes. Neither too little nor too much conflict is desirable. Managers should stimulate conflict to gain the full benefits of its functional properties, yet reduce its level when it becomes a disruptive force. Since we have yet to devise a sophisticated measuring instrument for assessing whether a given conflict level is functional or dysfunctional, it remains for managers to make intelligent judgments concerning whether conflict levels in their units are optimal, too high, or too low.

Developing Effective Conflict Resolution Skills

If conflict is dysfunctional, what can a manager do? In this section, we'll review conflict resolution skills. Essentially, you need to know your basic conflict-handling style as well as those of the conflicting parties, to understand the situation that has created the conflict, and to be aware of your options.

To ensure that issues are thoroughly discussed, top executives at Compaq Computer regularly take different sides in discussions. The objective is to keep the discussion honest so that the best idea is chosen. Compaq's culture encourages managers to put any question on the table without fear of being wrong.

FIGURE 16–2
Conflict and Organizational
Performance

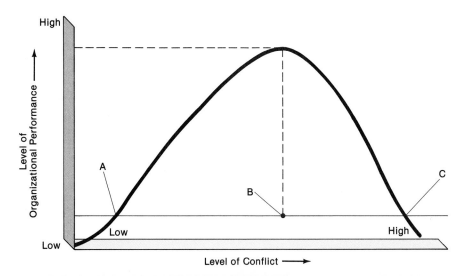

Situation	Level of Conflict	Type of Conflict	Organization's Internal Characteristics	Level Of Organizational Performance
A	Low or none	Dys-functional	Apathetic Stagnant Unresponsive to change Lack of new ideas	Low
B	Optimal	Functional	Viable Self-critical Innovative	High
C	High	Dys-functional	Disruptive Chaotic Uncooperative	Low

What Is Your Underlying Conflict-Handling Style?   While most of us have the ability to vary our conflict response according to the situation, each of us has a preferred style for handling conflicts.[46] The questionnaire in Table 16–6 can help you to identify your basic conflict-handling style. You might be able to change your preferred style to suit the context in which a certain conflict exists; however, your basic style tells you how you're *most likely* to behave and the conflict-handling approaches on which you *most often* rely.

Be Judicious in Selecting the Conflicts That You Want to Handle   Not every conflict justifies your attention. Some might not be worth the effort; others might be unmanageable.

Not every conflict is worth your time and effort to resolve. While avoidance might appear to be a "cop-out," it can sometimes be the most appropriate response. You can improve your overall management effectiveness, and your conflict-management skills in particular, by avoiding trivial conflicts. Choose your battles judiciously, saving your efforts for the ones that count.

Regardless of our desires, reality tells us that some conflicts are unmanageable.[47] When antagonisms are deeply rooted, when one or both parties wish to prolong a conflict, or when emotions run so high that constructive interaction is impossible, your efforts to manage the conflict are unlikely to meet with much success.

TABLE 16-6   Conflict-Handling Style Questionnaire

Indicate how often you do the following when you differ with someone.

When I Differ With Someone:	Usually	Sometimes	Seldom
1. I explore our differences, not backing down, but not imposing my view either.	☐	☐	☐
2. I disagree openly, then invite more discussion about our differences.	☐	☐	☐
3. I look for a mutually satisfactory solution.	☐	☐	☐
4. Rather than let the other person make a decision without my input, I make sure I am heard and also that I hear the other out.	☐	☐	☐
5. I agree to a middle ground rather than look for a completely satisfying solution.	☐	☐	☐
6. I admit I am half wrong rather than explore our differences.	☐	☐	☐
7. I have a reputation for meeting a person halfway.	☐	☐	☐
8. I expect to get out about half of what I really want to say.	☐	☐	☐
9. I give in totally rather than try to change another's opinion.	☐	☐	☐
10. I put aside any controversial aspects of an issue.	☐	☐	☐
11. I agree early on, rather than argue about a point.	☐	☐	☐
12. I give in as soon as the other party gets emotional about an issue.	☐	☐	☐
13. I try to win the other person over.	☐	☐	☐
14. I work to come out victorious, no matter what.	☐	☐	☐
15. I never back away from a good argument.	☐	☐	☐
16. I would rather win than end up compromising.	☐	☐	☐

Scoring Key and Interpretation

Total your choices as follows: Give yourself five points for "Usually," three points for "Sometimes," and one point for "Seldom." Then total them for each set of statements, grouped as follows:

Set A: Items 13–16
Set B: Items 9–12
Set C: Items 5–8
Set D: Items 1–4

Treat each set separately. A score of 17 or above on any set is considered high; scores of 12 to 16 are moderately high; scores of 8 to 11 are moderately low; and scores of 7 or less are considered low.

Sets A, B, C, and D represent different conflict-resolution strategies:

A = *Forcing/domination:* I win, you lose.

B = *Accommodation:* I lose, you win.

C = *Compromise:* Both win some, lose some.

D = *Collaboration:* I win, you win.

Source: From Thomas J. Von Der Embse, *Supervision: Managerial Skills for a New Era.* Copyright © 1987 by Macmillan Publishing Co. With permission.

Don't be naively lured into believing that a good manager can effectively resolve every conflict. Some aren't worth the effort. Some are outside your realm of influence. Still others may be functional and, as such, are best left alone.

Evaluate the Conflict Players   If you choose to manage a conflict situation, it's important that you take the time to get to know the players. Who is involved in the conflict? What interests does each party represent? What are each player's values, personality, feelings, and resources? Your chances of success in managing a conflict will be greatly enhanced if you can view the conflict situation through the eyes of the conflicting parties.

Assess the Source of the Conflict   Conflicts don't pop out of thin air. They have causes. Since your approach to resolving a conflict is likely to be determined largely by its causes, you need to determine the source of the conflict. Research indicates that while conflicts have varying causes, they can generally be separated into three categories: communication differences, structural differences, and personal differences.[48]

Communication differences are disagreements arising from semantic difficulties, misunderstandings, and noise in the communication channels. People are often quick to assume that most conflicts are caused by lack of communication but, as one author has noted, there is usually plenty of communication going on in most conflicts.[49] As we pointed out at the beginning of this chapter, the mistake many people make is equating good communication with having others agree with their views. What might at first look like an interpersonal conflict based on poor communication is usually found, upon closer analysis, to be a disagreement caused by different role requirements, unit goals, personalities, value systems, or similar factors. As a source of conflict for managers, poor communication probably gets more attention than it deserves.

As we discussed in Chapter 10, organizations are horizontally and vertically differentiated. This *structural differentiation* creates problems of integration. The frequent result is conflicts. Individuals disagree over goals, decision alternatives, performance criteria, and resource allocations. These conflicts are not due to poor communication or personal animosities. Rather, they are rooted in the structure of the organization itself.

The third conflict source is *personal differences.* Conflicts can evolve out of individual idiosyncrasies and personal value systems. The chemistry between some people makes it hard for them to work together. Factors like background, education, experience, and training mold each individual into a unique personality with a particular set of values. The result is people who may be perceived by others as abrasive, untrustworthy, or strange. These personal differences can create conflict.

•

Organizational resources that people want—budgets, promotions, pay increases, additions to staff, office space, influence over decisions, and the like—are scarce and must be divided up. The creation of horizontal units (departments) and vertical levels (the management hierarchy) brings about efficiencies through specialization and coordination but at the same time produces the potential for structural conflicts.

Know Your Options   What resolution tools or techniques can a manager call upon to reduce conflict when it is too high? Managers essentially can draw upon five conflict-resolution options: avoidance, accommodation, forcing, compromise, and collaboration.[50] Each has particular strengths and weaknesses, and no one option is ideal for every situation. You should consider each a "tool" in your conflict-management "tool chest." While you might be better at using some tools than others, the skilled manager knows what each tool can do and when it is likely to be most effective.

As we noted earlier, not every conflict requires an assertive action. Sometimes **avoidance** is the best solution—just withdrawing from or suppressing the conflict. When is avoidance a desirable strategy? When the conflict is trivial, when emotions are running high and time is needed to cool them down, or when the potential disruption from a more assertive action outweighs the benefits of resolution.

The goal of **accommodation** is to maintain harmonious relationships by placing another's needs and concerns above your own. You might, for example, yield to another person's position on an issue. This option is most viable when the issue under dispute isn't that important to you or when you want to build up credits for later issues.

In **forcing,** you attempt to satisfy your own needs at the expense of the other party. In organizations this is most often illustrated by a manager using his or her formal authority to resolve a dispute. Forcing works well when you need a quick resolution on important issues where unpopular actions must be taken, and when commitment by others to your solution is not critical.

A **compromise** requires each party to give up something of value. This is typically the approach taken by management and labor in negotiating a new labor contract. Compromise can be an optimum strategy when conflicting parties are about equal in power, when it is desirable to achieve a temporary solution to a complex issue, or when time pressures demand an expedient solution.

Collaboration is the ultimate win-win solution. All parties to the conflict seek to satisfy their interests. It is typically characterized by open and honest discussion among the parties, active listening to understand differences, and careful deliberation over a full range of alternatives to find a solution that is advantageous to all. When is

avoidance
Withdrawal from or suppression of conflict.

accommodation
Resolving conflicts by placing another's need and concerns above one's own.

forcing
Resolving conflict through the use of formal authority

compromise
A solution to conflict in which each party gives up something of value.

collaboration
Resolving conflict by seeking a solution advantageous to all parties.

collaboration the best conflict option? When time pressures are minimal, when all parties seriously want a win-win solution, and when the issue is too important to be compromised.

What About Conflict Stimulation?

What about the other side of conflict management—situations that require managers to *stimulate* conflict? The notion of stimulating conflict is often difficult to accept. For almost all of us the term "conflict" has a negative connotation, and the idea of purposely creating conflict seems to be the antithesis of good management. Few of us personally enjoy being in conflict situations. Yet the evidence demonstrates that there are situations in which an increase in conflict is constructive.[51] Given this reality and the fact that there is no clear demarcation between functional and dysfunctional conflict, we have listed in Table 16–7 a set of questions that might help you. While there is no definitive method for assessing the need for more conflict, an affirmative answer to one or more of the questions in Table 16–7 suggests a need for conflict stimulation.

We know a lot more about resolving conflict than stimulating it. That's only natural, since human beings have been concerned with the subject of conflict reduction for hundreds, maybe thousands, of years. The dearth of ideas on conflict stimulation techniques reflects the very recent interest in the subject. The following are some preliminary suggestions that managers might want to utilize.[52]

Change the Organization's Culture   The initial step in stimulating functional conflict is for managers to convey to subordinates the message, supported by actions, that conflict has its legitimate place. Individuals who challenge the status quo, suggest innovative ideas, offer divergent opinions, and demonstrate original thinking need to be visibly rewarded with promotions, salary increases, and other positive reinforcers.

Use Communication   As far back as Franklin Roosevelt's administration, and probably before, the White House has consistently used communication to stimulate con-

---

TABLE 16–7   Is Conflict Stimulation Needed?*

---

1. Are you surrounded by "yes people"?

2. Are subordinates afraid to admit ignorance and uncertainties to you?

3. Is there so much concentration by decision makers on reaching a compromise that they lose sight of values, long-term objectives, or the organization's welfare?

4. Do managers believe that it is in their best interest to maintain the impression of peace and cooperation in their unit, regardless of the price?

5. Is there an excessive concern by decision makers for not hurting the feelings of others?

6. Do managers believe that popularity is more important for obtaining organizational rewards than competence and high performance?

7. Are managers unduly enamored of obtaining consensus for their decisions?

8. Do employees show unusually high resistance to change?

9. Is there a lack of new ideas?

10. Is there an unusually low level of employee turnover?

An affirmative answer to any or all of these questions suggests the need for conflict stimulation.

Source: From Stephen P. Robbins, "'Conflict Management' and 'Conflict Resolution' Are Not Synonymous Terms," *California Management Review,* Winter 1978, Vol 2, No 2, p. 71. With permission of the Regents.

flict. Senior officials "plant" possible decisions with the media through the infamous "reliable source" route. For example, the name of a prominent judge is "leaked" as a possible Supreme Court appointment. If the candidate survives the public scrutiny, his or her appointment will be announced by the president. However, if the candidate is found lacking by the press, media, and public, the president's press secretary or other high-level official will make a formal statement such as, "At no time was this candidate under consideration." Regardless of party affiliation, occupants of the White House have regularly used the reliable source as a conflict stimulation technique. It is all the more popular because of its handy escape mechanism. If the conflict level gets too high, the source can be denied and eliminated.

Ambiguous or threatening messages also encourage conflict. Information that a plant might close, that a department is likely to be eliminated, or that a layoff is imminent can reduce apathy, stimulate new ideas, and force reevaluation—all positive outcomes as a result of increased conflict.

Bring in Outsiders   A widely used method for shaking up a stagnant unit or organization is to bring in—either by hiring from outside or by internal transfer—individuals whose backgrounds, values, attitudes, or managerial styles differ from those of present members. Many large corporations have used this technique during the last decade in filling vacancies on their boards of directors. Women, African-Americans, consumer activists, and others whose backgrounds and interests differ significantly from those of the board have been purposely selected to add a fresh perspective.

Restructure the Organization   We know that structural variables are a source of conflict. It is therefore only logical that managers look to structure as a conflict stimulation device. Centralizing decisions, realigning work groups, increasing formalization, and increasing interdependencies between units are all structural devices that disrupt the status quo and act to increase conflict levels.

devil's advocate
A person who purposely presents arguments that run counter to those proposed by the majority.

Appoint a Devil's Advocate   A **devil's advocate** is a person who purposely presents arguments that run counter to those proposed by the majority or against current practices. He or she plays the role of the critic, even to the point of arguing against positions with which he or she actually agrees.

A devil's advocate acts as a check against groupthink and practices that have no better justification than "that's the way we've always done it around here." When thoughtfully listened to, the advocate can improve the quality of group decision making. On the other hand, others in the group often view advocates as time wasters, and their appointment is almost certain to delay any decision process.

SUMMARY

This summary is organized by the chapter-opening learning objectives found on page 487.

1. Communication is the transference and understanding of meaning.
2. The communication process has seven parts: (1) the communication source, (2) the message, (3) encoding, (4) the channel, (5) decoding, (6) the receiver, and (7) feedback.
3. Barriers to effective communication include filtering, selective perception, emotions, language, and inconsistency between what is said and verbal cues.

4. Some techniques for overcoming these barriers include using feedback, simplifying language, listening actively, constraining emotions, and watching nonverbal cues.

5. Active listening requires concentration and requires understanding the communication from the sender's point of view. Passive listening requires only absorbing the information given.

6. Behaviors related to effective active listening are making eye contact, exhibiting affirmative nods and appropriate facial expressions, avoiding distracting actions or gestures, asking questions, paraphrasing, avoiding interruption of the speaker, not overtalking, and making smooth transitions between the roles of speaker and listener.

7. Behaviors related to providing effective feedback are focusing on specific behaviors; keeping feedback impersonal, goal-oriented, and well-timed; ensuring understanding; and directing negative feedback toward behavior that the recipient can control.

8. Contingency factors guide managers in determining the degree to which authority should be delegated. These factors include the size of the organization (larger organizations are associated with increased delegation), the importance of the duty or decision (the more important a duty or decision is, the less likely it is to be delegated), task complexity (the more complex the task is, the more likely it is that decisions about the task will be delegated), organizational culture (confidence and trust in subordinates is associated with delegation), and qualities of subordinates (delegation requires subordinates with the skills, abilities, and motivation to accept authority and act on it).

9. Behaviors related to effective delegating are clarifying the assignment, specifying the subordinate's range of discretion, allowing the subordinate to participate, informing others that delegation has occurred, and establishing feedback controls.

10. The "hot stove" rule proposes that effective disciplining should be equivalent to touching a hot stove. The response should be immediate, there should be ample warning, and enforcement of rules should be consistent and impersonal.

11. Behaviors related to effective disciplining are confronting the employee in a calm, objective, and serious manner; stating the problem specifically; keeping the discussion impersonal; allowing the employee to explain his or her position; maintaining control of the discussion; obtaining agreement on how mistakes can be prevented in the future; and selecting disciplinary action progressively, considering mitigating circumstances.

12. The steps to be followed in analyzing and resolving conflict situations begin by finding out your underlying conflict-handling style. Then select only conflicts that are worth the effort and that can be managed. Third, evaluate the conflict players. Fourth, assess the source of the conflict. Finally, choose the conflict-resolution option that best reflects your style and the situation.

REVIEW QUESTIONS

1. Why isn't *effective communication* synonymous with *agreement?*

2. Where in the communication process is distortion likely to occur?

3. What are the most popular communication methods used by people in organizations?

4. Is nonverbal communication as important as verbal communication? Explain.
5. What are the four essential requirements for active listening?
6. When should a manager avoid giving negative feedback?
7. Why isn't delegation synonymous with abdication?
8. What qualities would characterize an effective disciplinary program?
9. Contrast the traditional, human relations, and interactionist views of conflict.
10. What are the five primary conflict-resolution techniques?

DISCUSSION QUESTIONS

1. "Ineffective communication is the fault of the sender." Do you agree or disagree with this statement? Support your position.
2. Why do nonverbal communications carry such great weight?
3. Why are effective interpersonal skills so important to a manager's success?
4. "Most people are poor listeners." Do you agree or disagree with this statement? Support your answer.
5. "Most managers accept the interactionist view of conflict." Do you agree or disagree with this statement? Support your answer.

SELF-ASSESSMENT EXERCISE

What's Your Communication Style?

The following scale is used for each item:

YES—strong agreement with the statement
yes—agreement with the statement
?—neither agreement nor disagreement with the statement
no—disagreement with the statement
NO—strong disagreement with the statement

Next to each of the following statements, respond with a Y, y, ?, n, or N:

1. I am comfortable with all varieties of people.
2. I laugh easily.
3. I readily express admiration for others.
4. What I say usually leaves an impression on people.
5. I leave people with an impression of me which they definitely tend to remember.
6. To be friendly, I habitually acknowledge verbally other's contributions.
7. I am a very good communicator.
8. I have some nervous mannerisms in my speech.
9. I am a very relaxed communicator.
10. When I disagree with somebody, I am very quick to challenge them.
11. I can always repeat back to a person exactly what was meant.
12. The sound of my voice is very easy to recognize.
13. I am a very precise communicator.
14. I leave a definite impression on people.
15. The rhythm or flow of my speech is sometimes affected by nervousness.
16. Under pressure I come across as a relaxed speaker.
17. My eyes reflect exactly what I am feeling when I communicate.
18. I dramatize a lot.
19. I always find it very easy to communicate on a one-to-one basis with strangers.
20. Usually, I deliberately react in such a way that people know that I am listening to them.
21. Usually, I do not tell people much about myself until I get to know them well.
22. Regularly, I tell jokes, anecdotes, and stories when I communicate.
23. I tend to constantly gesture when I communicate.
24. I am an extremely open communicator.
25. I am vocally a loud communicator.
26. In a small group of strangers I am a very good communicator.
27. In arguments I insist upon very precise definitions.
28. In most social situations I generally speak very frequently.

29. I find it extremely easy to maintain a conversation with a member of the opposite sex whom I have just met.

30. I like to be strictly accurate when I communicate.

31. Because I have a loud voice, I can easily break into a conversation.

32. Often I physically and vocally act out when I want to communicate.

33. I have an assertive voice.

34. I readily reveal personal things about myself.

35. I am dominant in social situations.

36. I am very argumentative.

37. Once I get wound up in a heated discussion I have a hard time stopping myself.

38. I am always an extremely friendly communicator.

39. I really like to listen very carefully to people.

40. Very often I insist that other people document or present some kind of proof for what they are arguing.

41. I try to take charge of things when I am with people.

42. It bothers me to drop an argument that is not resolved.

43. In most social situations I tend to come on strong.

44. I am very expressive nonverbally in social situations.

45. The way I say something usually leaves an impression on people.

46. Whenever I communicate, I tend to be very encouraging to people.

47. I actively use a lot of facial expressions when I communicate.

48. I very frequently verbally exaggerate to emphasize a point.

49. I am an extremely attentive communicator.

50. As a rule, I openly express my feelings and emotions.

Turn to page 676 for scoring directions and key.

Source: Robert W. Norton, "Foundation of a Communicator Style Construct," *Human Communication Research,* Vol 4, No 2, 1978, pp. 99–111. Copyright © 1978 International Communication Assoc., Inc. With permission of Sage Publications, Inc.

CASE APPLICATION 16A

Danson Pharmaceuticals

Christine Hall is Director of Research and Development for Danson Pharmaceuticals.[53] Six people report directly to her: Sue Traynor (her secretary), Dale Morgan (the laboratory manager), Todd Connor (quality standards manager), Linda Peters (patent coordination manager), Ruben Gomez (market coordination manager), and Marjorie England (senior project manager). Dale is the most senior of the five managers and is generally acknowledged as the chief candidate to replace Christine when she is promoted.

Christine has recently received her annual instructions from the CEO to develop next year's budget for her department. The task is relatively routine but takes quite a bit of time. In the past, Christine has always done the annual budget herself. This year, because of an exceptionally heavy workload, she has decided to try something different. She is going to assign budget preparation to one of her subordinate managers. The obvious choice is Dale Morgan. He has been with the company longest, is highly dependable, and, as her probable successor, is most likely to gain from the experience. The budget is due on Christine's boss's desk in eight weeks. Last year it took her about thirty to thirty-five hours to complete. However, she had the experience of having done a budget many times before. For a novice it might take double that amount of time.

The budget process is generally straightforward. One starts with last year's budget and modifies it to reflect inflation and changes in departmental objectives. All the data that Dale will need are in Christine's files or can be obtained from her other managers.

Christine realizes that Dale has his hands full running the lab. He regularly comes in around 7:00 A.M., and it's unusual for him to leave before 7:00 P.M. She knows that four of the last five weekends he has even come in on Saturday mornings in order to keep his work current. So she knows that doing the annual budget will require Dale to reprioritize his projects. On the other hand, she also knows that he wants to expand his responsibilities to include some of Christine's tasks.

Christine has decided to walk over to Dale's office and inform him of her decision.

Question

1. Detail specifically what you would say to Dale, if you were Christine, when you arrived at his office.

CASE APPLICATION 16B

Albuquerque Metals

Marc Lattoni is supervisor of an eight-member cost-accounting department in a large metals-fabricating plant in Albuquerque, New Mexico. He was promoted about six months ago to his supervisory position after only a year as an accountant, mostly because of his education; he has an MBA degree, whereas no one else in the department has a college degree. The transition to supervisor went smoothly, and there were hardly any problems until this morning.

The need for another cost accountant in the office had been obvious to Marc for over a month. Overtime had become commonplace and was putting a strain on department members, as well as the department's budget (overtime was computed at time and a half). Marc had his eye on one particular individual in production control who he thought would fit his needs quite well. He had talked with the production control supervisor and the personnel manager, and the three had agreed that a young African-American clerk in production named Ralph might be a good candidate to move into cost accounting and help with the increased departmental work load. Ralph had been with the company for eight months, shown above-average potential, and was only six units shy of a bachelor's degree (with a major in accounting) that he was earning at night at the University of New Mexico.

Marc had discussed the cost-accounting position with Ralph earlier in the week, and Ralph had been enthusiastic. Marc had said that, while he could make no promises, he thought that he would recommend Ralph for the job. However, Marc emphasized that it would be a week or so before a final decision was made and the announcement made official.

When Marc came into his office this morning, he was confronted by Tip O'Malley, a 58-year-old cost accountant who had been at the plant since its opening over twenty-four years ago. Tip, who is white and was born and raised in a small town in the Deep South, had heard a rumor that Ralph would be coming up and working in the cost department. Tip minced no words: "I've never worked with a black and I never will." Tip's face was red, and it was obvious that this was an emotionally charged issue for him. His short, one-way confrontation closed with the statement: "I have no intention of working in the same department as that fellow."

Questions

1. What is the source of this conflict?

2. What conflict resolution techniques would be relevant in handling this situation?

3. Which do you recommend for Marc and why?

MANAGING
CHANGE

AT&T is struggling with its old culture just as competition is getting more aggressive. AT&T is facing price wars in many of its markets and anemic performance in its computer business. It is also facing aggressive competition in the international phone equipment market from foreign rivals.

In April 1988, Robert Allen took on the job of chairman and CEO of AT&T, the largest diversified service company in the United States. He also took on a lot of headaches.[1]

In January 1984, the U.S. government completed the final step in its breakup of the Bell System. AT&T would no longer monopolize the U.S. telephone system. Its operating telephone companies would become independent firms; in return, AT&T would be allowed to compete in the telecommunication and computer markets. The new AT&T would no longer have the luxuries associated with being a regulated monopoly: predictable price increases, complacency over competition, and the ability to ignore costs. It had to learn to get aggressive, to take chances, and, above all, to move quickly. Unfortunately, AT&T proved to be a slow learner. Employees found it hard to become market-oriented. The company was losing market share in the all-important long-distance market to upstarts like MCI and Sprint. A joint venture with Olivetti of Italy, which was intended to beef up AT&T's ability to compete globally in the computer market, was going nowhere.

Allen concluded that AT&T's culture had to change and change for good if the company was to move forward. In the four years since the breakup, management had talked a lot about the need for cultural change, but little had happened. "Every one of us can fall into the trap of thinking, 'I don't need to change,'" Allen said. "It's like drug or alcohol addiction. You first have to face up to the fact that you've got a problem."

Allen was not taking on an easy task. AT&T had the most entrenched organizational culture in the United States. The company was dominated by engineers, who had always put operational and technical concerns ahead of marketing, and most of its employees had joined AT&T because of the security and predictability that "Ma Bell" provided. What could Allen do, if anything, to change AT&T's culture?

change
An alteration in people, structure, or technology.

If it weren't for **change,** the manager's job would be relatively easy. Planning would be without problems because tomorrow would be no different from today. The issue of organizational design would be solved: Since the environment would be free from uncertainty and there would be no need to adapt, all organizations would be tightly structured. Similarly, decision making would be dramatically simplified because the outcome of each alternative could be predicted with almost certain accuracy. It would, indeed, simplify the manager's job if, for example, competitors didn't introduce new products or services, if customers didn't make new demands, if government regulations were never modified, or if employees' needs didn't change.

However, change is an organizational reality. Handling that change is an integral part of every manager's job. In this chapter of the book we address the key issues related to managing change, including actions that executives like Robert Allen can take to remake their organization's culture permanently.

FORCES FOR CHANGE

In Chapter 3, we pointed out that there are both external and internal forces that constrain managers. These same forces also bring about the need for change. Let's briefly look at the factors that can create the need for change.

External Forces

The external forces that create the need for change come from various directions. The *marketplace,* in recent years, has affected firms like UPS, BMW, and Domino's by introducing competition in the form of international overnight delivery services created by Federal Express's purchase of Flying Tiger, upscale Japanese cars produced by Lexus and Infiniti, and Pizza Hut's move into the home-delivery market. *Government laws and regulations* are a frequent impetus for change. The passing of equal rights legislation, as a case in point, required most employers to develop affirmative action plans to identify and hire more female and minority employees. The passage of a major tax revision in 1986, which included the phasing out of interest deductibility except for home mortgages, almost overnight created huge opportunities for firms like Citicorp and Home Savings of America to sell home equity loans.

Technology also creates the need for change. Firms that manufactured carbon paper saw the demand for their product nose-dive as xerographic technology revolutionized paper copying. Recent developments in complex, sophisticated, and extremely expensive diagnostic equipment have created significant economies of scale for hospitals and medical centers. The assembly line in many industries is undergoing dramatic changes as employers replace human labor with technologically advanced mechanical robots. The fluctuation of *labor markets* forces managers to initiate change. For instance, the current shortage of registered nurses has forced hospitals to redesign jobs and alter their reward and benefit packages.

Economic changes, of course, affect almost all organizations, but in different ways. The October 1987 stock market crash, for instance, forced many brokerage firms to cut costs and lay off thousands of employees. Meanwhile, escalating housing prices in Los Angeles and San Francisco have prompted a number of firms to relocate or expand to lower-cost West Coast cities like Sacramento, Portland, and Seattle.

Internal Forces

In addition to the external forces noted above, internal forces can also stimulate the need for change. These internal forces can originate primarily from the internal operations of the organization or from the impact of external changes.

When management redefines or modifies its *strategy,* it often introduces a host of changes. Sears, Roebuck recently switched its emphasis from selling moderately priced, private-label brand merchandise to "everyday low prices." It then had to redesign its structure. An organization's *work force* is rarely static. Its composition changes in terms of age, education, sex, and so forth. In a stable organization with an increasing number of older executives, there might be a need to restructure jobs in order to retain the younger and more ambitious managers who occupy the lower ranks. The compensation and benefits systems might also need to be reworked to reflect the needs of an older work force. The introduction of new *equipment* represents another internal force for change. Employees may have their jobs redesigned, need to undergo training to operate the new equipment, or be required to establish new interaction patterns within their formal group. *Employee attitudes,* such as increased job dissatisfaction, may lead to increased absenteeism, more voluntary resignations, and even strikes. Such events will, in turn, often lead to changes in management policies and practices.

The Manager as Change Agent

change agents
People who act as catalysts and manage the change process.

Changes within an organization need a catalyst. People who act as catalysts and assume the responsibility for managing the change process are called **change agents.**

MANAGING FROM A GLOBAL PERSPECTIVE

The Global Economy Intensifies the Need for Change

Probably no single external stimulus for change has been more influential in the past decade than the emergence of the global economy.

As we have discussed throughout this book, few organizations are so insulated that they can ignore foreign competition. In many cases, economies of scale dictate that firms either expand or merge with other organizations in order to compete effectively in world markets. A number of the major U.S. public accounting firms, for instance, have merged in recent years in order to better handle the rise of multinationals and consolidation going on in western Europe.

Additionally, as trade barriers are lessened, organizations find that their rivals are just as likely to come from 15,000 miles away as from across town. Remember that less than twenty years ago, Xerox owned almost 100 percent of the copier market; no one, including Kodak, had ever heard of Fuji Photofilm; and General Motors sold one of every two automobiles bought in the United States.

Any manager can be a change agent. As we review the topic of change, we assume that it is initiated and carried out by a manager within the organization. However, the change agent can be a nonmanager—for example, an internal staff specialist or outside consultant whose expertise is in change implementation. For major systemwide changes, internal management will often hire outside consultants to provide advice and assistance. Because they are from the outside, they can offer an objective perspective usually lacking in insiders. However, outside consultants are usually at a disadvantage because they have an inadequate understanding of the organization's history, culture, operating procedures, and personnel. Outside consultants are also often prone to initiate more drastic changes than insiders—which can be either a benefit or a disadvantage—because they do not have to live with the repercussions after the change is implemented. In contrast, internal managers who act as change agents may be more thoughtful (and possibly cautious) because they must live with the consequences of their actions.

TWO DIFFERENT VIEWS ON THE CHANGE PROCESS

"The organization is like a large ship traveling across the calm Mediterrean Sea to a specific port.[2] The ship's captain has made this exact trip hundreds of times before with the same crew. Every once in a while, however, a storm will appear, and the crew has to respond. The captain will make the appropriate adjustment—that is, implement changes—and, having maneuvered through the storm, will return to calm waters. Implementing change in organizations should therefore be seen as a response to a break in the status quo and needed only in occasional situations."

"The organization is more akin to a forty-foot raft than to a large ship. Rather than sailing a calm sea, this raft must traverse a raging river made up of an uninterrupted flow of permanent white-water rapids. To make things worse, the raft is manned by ten people who have never worked together, none have traveled the river before, much of the trip is in the dark, the river is dotted by unexpected turns and obstacles, the exact destination of the raft is not clear, and at irregular frequencies the raft needs to pull to shore, where new crew members are added and others leave. Change is a natural state and managing change is a continual process."

These two metaphors present very different approaches to understanding and responding to change. Let's take a closer look at each one.

The "Calm Waters" Metaphor

Until very recently, the "calm waters" metaphor dominated the thinking of practicing managers and academics. It is best illustrated in Kurt Lewin's three-step description of the change process[3] (see Figure 17–1).

According to Lewin, successful change requires *unfreezing* the status quo, *changing* to a new state, and *refreezing* the new change to make it permanent. The status quo can be considered an equilibrium state. To move from this equilibrium, unfreezing is necessary. It can be achieved in one of three ways:

1. The *driving forces,* which direct behavior away from the status quo, can be increased.

2. The *restraining forces,* which hinder movement from the existing equilibrium, can be decreased.

3. The two approaches can be *combined.*

Once unfreezing has been accomplished, the change itself can be implemented. However, the mere introduction of change does not ensure that it will take hold. The new situation therefore needs to be *refrozen* so that it can be sustained over time. Unless this last step is attended to, there is a very strong chance that the change will be short lived and employees will revert to the previous equilibrium state. The objective of refreezing, then, is to stabilize the new situation by balancing the driving and restraining forces.

Note how Lewin's three-step process treats change as a break in the organization's equilibrium state. The status quo has been disturbed, and change is necessary to establish a new equilibrium state. This view might have been appropriate to the relatively calm environment that most organizations faced in the 1950s, 1960s, and early 1970s. But one can argue that the "calm waters" metaphor no longer describes the kind of seas that current managers have to negotiate.

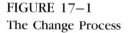

FIGURE 17–1
The Change Process

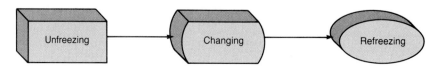

Unfreezing   Changing   Refreezing

The "White-Water Rapids" Metaphor

The "white-water rapids" metaphor is consistent with our discussion of uncertain and dynamic environments in Chapter 3. It is consistent with Mintzberg's observation, discussed in Chapter 1, that the manager's job is one of constant interruptions. It is also consistent with the dynamics associated with going from an industrial society to a world dominated by information and ideas.

To get a feeling for what managing change might be like when you have to continually maneuver in uninterrupted rapids, how would you like to attend a college that had the following curriculum? Courses vary in length. Unfortunately, when you sign up, you don't know how long a course will last. It might go for two weeks or thirty weeks. Furthermore, the instructor can end a course any time he or she wants, with no prior warning. If that wasn't bad enough, the length of the class changes each time it meets—sometimes it lasts twenty minutes, while other times it runs for three hours—and determination of when the next class meeting will take place is set by the instructor during the previous class. Oh yes, there's one more thing. The exams are all unannounced, so you have to be ready for a test at any time.

To succeed in this college, you would have to be incredibly flexible and able to respond quickly to every changing condition. Students who were overstructured or slow on their feet wouldn't survive.

A growing number of managers are coming to accept that their job is much like what a student would face in such a college. The stability and predictability of the "calm water" metaphor don't exist. Nor are disruptions in the status quo only occasional and temporary, followed by a return to calm waters. Many of today's managers never get out of the rapids. They face constant change, bordering on chaos. These managers are being forced to play a game they've never played before governed by rules that are created as the game progresses.[4]

Is the "white-water rapids" metaphor merely hyperbole? No! Take the case of Harry Quadracci, founder and president of Quad/Graphics Inc.[5] His firm is a commercial printer based in Wisconsin. Begun in 1971, the company is one of the largest and fastest-growing printers in the United States. It prints such magazines as *Time, People,* and *Architectural Digest.* The company now employs more than 3,500 people and has sales in excess of $400 million a year.

Quadracci attributes his company's success to its ability to act fast when opportunities arise. Change and growth are among the few constants at Quad/Graphics. He encourages his people to "act now, think later." The company has no budgets because it is moving too fast—its annual growth rate during the past decade has been an astounding 40 percent! As Quadracci points out, when every department looks 30 percent different every six months, budgets aren't much use. Instead of budgets, each of the company's ten divisions is measured against its own previous performance.

We have used the "white-water rapids" metaphor to describe an organization that confronts continual change; Quadracci makes the same point by comparing his company to a circus. "Rather than a single show on center stage, Quad is a continuous performance, in many rings, of highly creative and individualistic troupes. Clowns are a perfect symbol of Quad/Graphics philosophy of management, because, unlike so many others, they are not wedded to conventional wisdom. They retain their childlike ability to be surprised, and the flexibility to adapt to, or even thrive on, change."[6]

Putting the Two Views in Perspective

Does *every* manager face a world of constant and chaotic change? No, but the set of managers who don't is dwindling rapidly.

Managers in businesses like women's high-fashion clothing and computer software have long confronted a world that looks like white-water rapids. They used to look with envy at their counterparts in industries such as auto manufacturing, oil exploration, banking, fast-food restaurants, office equipment, publishing, telecommunications, and air transportation because these managers historically faced a stable and predictable environment. That might have been true in the 1960s, but it's not true in the 1990s!

Few organizations today can treat change as the occasional disturbance in an otherwise peaceful world. Even these few do so at great risk. Too much is changing too fast for any organization or its managers to be complacent.[7] Most competitive advantages last less than eighteen months. A firm like People Express was described in business periodicals as the model "new look" firm, then went bankrupt a short time later. As Tom Peters has aptly noted, the old saw "If it ain't broke, don't fix it" no longer applies. In its place, he suggests "If it ain't broke, you just haven't looked hard enough. Fix it anyway."[8]

ORGANIZATIONAL INERTIA AND RESISTANCE TO CHANGE

As change agents, managers should be motivated to initiate change because they're concerned with improving their organization's effectiveness. However, change can be a threat to managers. Of course, change can be a threat to nonmanagerial personnel as well.

In spite of all the reasons for organizations to accept change and learn to thrive on impermanence, there are strong internal forces within organizations that build inertia. In this section, we want to review why people in organizations resist change and what can be done to lessen this resistance.

Resistance to Change

It has been said that most people hate any change that doesn't jingle in their pockets. This awareness of resistance to change is well documented.[9] But why do people resist change? An individual is likely to resist change for three reasons: uncertainty, concern over personal loss, and the belief that the change is not in the organization's best interest.[10]

Changes substitute ambiguity and uncertainty for the known. Regardless of how much you may dislike attending college, at least you know the ropes. You understand what is expected of you. When you leave college and venture out into the world of full-time employment, regardless of how anxious you are to get out of college, you will have to trade the known for the unknown. Employees in organizations hold the same dislike for uncertainty. For example, the introduction in manufacturing plants of quality-control methods based on sophisticated statistical models means that many quality-control inspectors will have to learn these new methods. Some inspectors may fear that they will be unable to do so. They may, therefore, develop a negative attitude toward statistical control techniques or behave dysfunctionally if required to use them.

Another cause of resistance is the fear of losing something already possessed. Change threatens the investment one has already made in the status quo. The more people have invested in the current system, the more they resist change. Why? They fear the loss of status, money, authority, friendships, personal convenience, or other benefits that they value. This explains why older employees resist change more than

Individuals who spent twenty years as mail sorters for the post office were likely to resist automatic letter sorters more actively than recent hirees. The latter had less personal investment in the old system and were less threatened by automation.

do younger ones. Older employees have generally invested more in the current system and therefore have more to lose by adapting to a change.

A final cause of resistance is a person's belief that the change is incompatible with the goals and best interests of the organization. If an employee believes that a new job procedure proposed by a change agent will reduce productivity or product quality, that employee can be expected to resist the change. If the employee expresses his or her resistance positively (clearly expressing it to the change agent, along with substantiation), this form of resistance can be beneficial to the organization.

Techniques for Reducing Resistance

When management sees resistance to change as dysfunctional, what actions can it take? Six tactics have been suggested for use by managers or other change agents in dealing with resistance to change.[11]

Education and Communication   Resistance can be reduced through communicating with employees to help them see the logic of a change. This tactic assumes that the source of resistance lies in misinformation or poor communication: If employees receive the full facts and have their misunderstandings cleared up, their resistance will subside. This can be achieved through one-on-one discussions, memos, group presentations, or reports. Does it work? It does, provided that the source of resistance is inadequate communication and that management-employee relations are characterized by mutual trust and credibility. If these conditions do not exist, it is unlikely to succeed. Moreover, the time and effort that this tactic involves must be weighed against its advantages, particularly when the change affects a large number of people.

Participation   It's difficult for individuals to resist a change decision in which they participated. Before a change is made, those who are opposed can be brought into the decision process. Assuming that the participants have the expertise to make a meaningful contribution, their involvement can reduce resistance, obtain commitment, and increase the quality of the change decision. However, against these advantages are the negatives: the possibility of a poor solution and the consumption of a lot of time.

Facilitation and Support   Change agents can offer a range of supportive efforts to reduce resistance. When employee fear and anxiety are high, employee counseling and therapy, new skills training, or a short paid leave of absence might facilitate adjustment. The drawback of this tactic, as of the others, is that it is time consuming. Furthermore, it is expensive, and its implementation offers no assurance of success.

Negotiation   Another way for the change agent to deal with potential resistance to change is to exchange something of value for a lessening of the resistance. For instance, if the resistance is centered in a few powerful individuals, a specific reward package can be negotiated that will meet their individual needs. Negotiation as a tactic may be necessary when resistance comes from a powerful source. Yet one cannot ignore its potentially high costs. There is also the risk that, once a change agent negotiates to avoid resistance, he or she is open to the possibility of being blackmailed by others with power.

Manipulation and Cooptation   *Manipulation* refers to covert attempts to influence. Twisting and distorting facts to make them appear more attractive, withholding damaging information, and creating false rumors to get employees to accept a change are all examples of manipulation. A corporate management that threatens to close a particular manufacturing plant if the employees fail to accept an across-the-board pay cut, and that actually has no intention of doing so, is using manipulation. *Cooptation,* on the other hand, is a form of both manipulation and participation. It seeks to "buy off" the leaders of a resistance group by giving them a key role in the change decision. The leaders' advice is sought, not to arrive at a better decision but to get their endorsement. Both manipulation and cooptation are relatively inexpensive and easy ways to gain the support of adversaries, but the tactics can backfire if the targets become aware that they are being tricked or used. Once the deception has been discovered, the change agent's credibility may drop to zero.

Coercion   Last on the list of tactics is *coercion*—that is, the use of direct threats or force upon the resisters. A corporate management that is really determined to close a manufacturing plant if employees do not agree to a pay cut is using coercion. Other examples of coercion include threats of transfer, loss of promotions, negative performance evaluations, or a poor letter of recommendation. The advantages and drawbacks of coercion are approximately the same as those of manipulation and cooptation.

TECHNIQUES FOR MANAGING CHANGE

What *can* a manager change? The manager's options essentially fall into one of three categories: people, structure, or technology. (See Figure 17–2.) Changing *people* refers to changes in employee attitudes, skills, expectations, perceptions, or behavior. Changing *structure* includes any alteration in authority relations, coordination mechanisms, degree of centralization, job redesign, or similar structural variables. Changing *technology* encompasses modifications in the way work is processed or the methods and equipment used.

FIGURE 17–2
Change Options

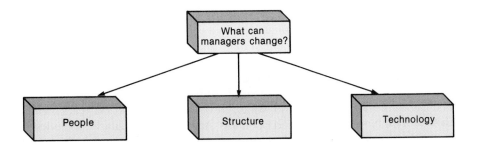

Changing People

The last twenty-five years have seen a dramatic increase in interest by academic researchers and practicing managers in helping individuals and groups within organizations to work more effectively together. The term **organizational development (OD),** though occasionally referring to all types of change, essentially focuses on techniques or programs to change people and the nature and quality of interpersonal work relationships.[12] The more popular OD techniques include sensitivity training, survey feedback, process consultation, team building, and intergroup development. The common thread running through these techniques is that each seeks to bring about changes in or among the organization's personnel.

organization development (OD)
Techniques to change people and the quality of interpersonal work relationships.

Sensitivity training is a method of changing behavior through unstructured group interaction. The group is made up of a professional behavioral scientist and a set of participants. There is no specified agenda. The professional—who accepts no leadership role—merely creates the opportunity for participants to express their ideas and feelings. The forum is free and open. Participants can discuss anything they like. What evolves is discussion that focuses on the individual participants and their interactive processes.

sensitivity training
A method of changing behavior through unstructured group interaction.

The research evidence on the effectiveness of sensitivity training as a change technique indicates mixed results. On the positive side, it appears to stimulate short-term improvement in communication skills, improve perceptual accuracy, and increase one's willingness to use participation.[13] However, the impact of these changes on job performance is inconclusive,[14] and the technique is not devoid of psychological risks.[15]

Survey feedback is a technique for assessing the attitudes of organizational members, identifying discrepancies in these attitudes and perceptions, and resolving the differences by using survey information in feedback groups. A questionnaire is typically completed by all members in the organization or unit. It asks members for their perceptions and attitudes on a broad range of topics such as decision-making practices, communication effectiveness, coordination between units, and satisfaction with the organization, job, peers, and immediate manager. The data from the questionnaire are tabulated and distributed to the relevant employees, and the information obtained becomes the springboard for identifying problems and clarifying issues that may be creating difficulties for people.

survey feedback
A technique for assessing attitudes, identifying discrepancies in them, and resolving the differences by using survey information in feedback groups.

In **process consultation,** an outside consultant helps the manager to "perceive, understand, and act upon process events" with which he or she must deal.[16] These might include, for example, work flow, informal relationships among unit members, and formal communication channels. The consultant gives the manager insight into what is going on around and within him or her and between the manager and other

process consultation
Help given by an outside consultant to a manager in perceiving, understanding, and acting upon process events.

people. The consultant is not there to solve the manager's problem. Rather, the consultant acts as a coach to help the manager diagnose what processes need improvement. If the manager, with the help of the consultant, cannot solve the problem, the consultant will help the manager to locate an expert who has the appropriate technical knowledge.

team building
Interaction among members of work teams to learn how each member thinks and works.

In **team building,** work-team members interact to learn how each member thinks and works. Through high interaction, team members learn to develop increased trust and openness. Activities that might be included in a team-building program include group goal setting, development of interpersonal relations among team members, role analysis to clarify each member's role and responsibilities, and team process analysis.

intergroup development
Changing the attitudes, stereotypes, and perceptions that work groups have of each other.

The attempt to change the attitudes, stereotypes, and perceptions that members of work groups have about each other is called **intergroup development.** For example, if two groups have a history of difficult work relationships, they can meet independently to develop lists of their perceptions of themselves, of the other group, and of how they believe the other group perceives them. The groups then share their lists, after which similarities and differences are discussed. Differences are clearly articulated, the groups look for the causes of the disparities, and efforts are made to develop solutions that will improve relations between the groups.

ETHICAL DILEMMAS IN MANAGEMENT

Do OD Techniques Compromise Employees' Privacy and Freedom?

OD techniques such as sensitivity training and team building rely heavily on processes such as participation, collaboration, and confrontation. They seek to increase openness and trust among organizational members. But not everyone feels comfortable participating in a process that requires being open about feelings and attitudes. When management asks employees to participate in change techniques that demand openness, doesn't that compromise the employee's privacy and freedom?

Management might respond by arguing that these change programs are voluntary. That sounds good, but it ignores the possibility that the decision not to participate might carry negative connotations, result in lower performance evaluations, and have adverse career effects.

Finally, what if an employee does participate in one of these change programs, is authentically open, and reveals to the group some very personal fears and concerns, and then someone in the group uses this information vindictively against that employee at some later date?

Don't OD techniques that seek to increase openness and trust compromise an employee's privacy and freedom? What do *you* think?

Changing Structure

In Chapters 10 and 11, we discussed structural issues. Managers were described as having responsibility for such activities as choosing the organization's formal design, allocating authority, determining the degree of decentralization that would prevail, and designing jobs. Once those structural decisions have been made, however, they are not set in concrete. Changing conditions demand changes in the structure. As a result, the manager, in his or her role as a change agent, might need to modify the structure.

What options does the manager have for changing structure? Essentially the same ones we introduced in our discussion of the organizing function. A few examples should make these options clearer.

An organization's structure is defined in terms of its degree of complexity, formalization, and centralization. Managers can alter one or more of these *structural components*. For instance, departmental responsibilities can be combined, vertical layers removed, and spans of control widened to make the organization flatter and less bureaucratic. More rules and procedures can be implemented to increase standardization. An increase in decentralization can be made to speed up the decision-making process.

Another option would be to introduce major changes in the actual *structural design*. This might include a shift from a functional to a product structure or the creation of a matrix design. Managers might consider redesigning jobs or work schedules. Job descriptions can be redefined, jobs enriched, or flexible work hours introduced. Still another option is to modify the organization's compensation system. Motivation could be increased by, for example, introducing performance bonuses or profit sharing.

Changing Technology

The final category over which managers exert control is the technology used to convert inputs into outputs. Most of the early studies in management—the work of Frederick Taylor and Frank Gilbreth certainly comes to mind—dealt with efforts aimed at technological change. Scientific management sought to implement changes that would increase production efficiency based on time-and-motion studies. Today, major technological changes usually involve the introduction of new equipment, tools, or methods; automation; or computerization.

Competitive factors or new innovations within an industry often require management to introduce *new equipment, tools, or operating methods*. As an example, many U.S. aluminum companies have significantly modernized their plants in recent years in order to compete more effectively against foreign manufacturers. More efficient handling equipment, furnaces, and presses have been installed to reduce the cost of manufacturing a ton of aluminum.

Automation is a technological change that replaces people with machines. It began in the Industrial Revolution and continues as a management option today. As we have seen, automation has been introduced (and sometimes resisted) in the U.S. Postal Service in the form of automatic mail sorters and in automobile assembly lines in the form of robots.

Probably the most visible technological change in recent years has come through management's efforts at expanding *computerization*. Many organizations now have sophisticated management information systems. Large supermarkets have converted their cash registers into input terminals and linked them to computers to provide instant inventory data. The office of 1991 is dramatically different from its counterpart of 1971, predominantly because of computerization. This is typified by desktop micro-computers that can run hundreds of business software packages and network systems that allow these computers to communicate with each other.

CONTEMPORARY ISSUES IN MANAGING CHANGE

- What can management do to change an organizational culture when it no longer supports the organization's mission?
- What, if anything, can management do to change its environment and lessen its dependence on it?
- Why is it that some organizations, like 3M Co., have a long history of innovation, while other firms don't? And what can managers do if they want to make their organizations more innovative?
- With all the recent pressure on managers to be more competitive, they have responded by cutting costs and streamlining their organizations. What unique problems and challenges confront managers as they shrink their organizations?
- Finally, today's competitive environment has made the workplace more stressful. What can managers do to help employees better handle this stress?

These change issues—altering organizational cultures, managing the environment, stimulating innovation, managing retrenchment, and handling employee stress—will be critical concerns to managers as they lead their organizations into the twenty-first century. In this section, we'll look at each of these issues and discuss what actions managers should consider for dealing with them.

Changing Organizational Cultures

This chapter opened by describing Robert Allen's determination to change AT&T's culture. If you were Robert Allen, how would you go about the task?

The fact that an organization's culture is made up of relatively stable and permanent characteristics (see Chapter 3) tends to make culture very resistant to change.[17] A culture takes a long time to form; and once established, it tends to become entrenched. Strong cultures, like that at AT&T, are particularly resistant to change because employees have become so committed to them. If a given culture, over time, becomes inappropriate to an organization and a handicap to management, there might be little management can do to change it. This is especially true in the short run. Under the most favorable conditions, cultural changes have to be measured in years, not weeks or months.

Understanding the Situational Factors   What "favorable conditions" *might* facilitate cultural change? The evidence suggests that cultural change is most likely to take place where most or all of the following conditions exist:

A dramatic crisis occurs. This can be the shock that undermines the status quo and calls into question the relevance of the current culture, for example, a surprising financial setback, the loss of a major customer, or a dramatic technological break-through by a competitor.

Leadership changes hands. New top leadership, which can provide an alternative set of key values, may be perceived as more capable of responding to the crisis. This would encompass the organization's chief executive but might need to include all senior management positions.

The organization is young and small. The younger the organization, the less entrenched its culture. Similarly, it's easier for management to communicate its new values when the organization is small.

The new CEO of Knight-Ridder, a newspaper chain that owns thirty papers, including the Philadelphia Inquirer, is determined to make his people rededicate themselves to serving their customers—both readers and advertisers. This is a particular challenge in an industry in which marketing questions pale besides such concerns as protection of First Amendment rights.

The culture is weak. The more widely held a culture is and the higher the agreement among members on its values, the more difficult it will be to change. Conversely, weak cultures are more amenable to change than strong ones.[18]

Do the above conditions describe AT&T? Yes and no. Deregulation might be considered a dramatic crisis, but only if employees sincerely believe that AT&T's survival is threatened. It seems, to date, that most AT&T employees haven't seen deregulation as life threatening. Even though Allen has spent his entire career in the Bell System, he offers a true change in leadership and an alternative set of cultural values. The other conditions, however, clearly work against Allen. AT&T is a large, mature organization, and its culture is very strong.

How Can Cultural Change Be Accomplished?   Now we ask the question: If conditions are right, how does management go about enacting the cultural change?

The challenge is to unfreeze the current culture. No single action is likely to have the impact necessary to unfreeze something that is so entrenched and highly valued. Therefore there needs to be a comprehensive and coordinated strategy for managing culture.

The best place to begin is with a cultural analysis.[19] This would include a cultural audit to assess the current culture, a comparison of the present culture with the culture that is desired, and a gap evaluation to identify what cultural elements specifically need changing.

We have discussed the importance of a dramatic crisis as a means to unfreeze an entrenched culture. Unfortunately, crises are not always evident to all members of the organization. It might be necessary for management to make the crisis more visible. It is important that it be clear to everyone that the organization's survival is legitimately threatened. If employees don't see the urgency for change, it's unlikely that a strong culture will respond to change efforts.

The appointment of a new top executive is likely to dramatize that "major changes are going to take place." He or she can offer a new role model and new standards of behavior. However, this executive needs to introduce quickly his or her new vision of the organization and to staff key management positions with individuals who are loyal to this vision. A large part of Lee Iacocca's success in changing Chrysler's culture is undoubtedly due to his rapid and wholesale shakeup of Chrysler's senior management, in which he brought in loyal associates with whom he had worked before at Ford.

Along with a shakeup among key management personnel, it also makes sense to initiate a reorganization. The creation of new units, the combining of some, and the elimination of others convey, in very visible terms, that management is determined to move the organization in new directions.

The new leadership will want to move quickly also to create new stories, symbols, and rituals to replace those currently in place. This needs to be done rapidly. Delays will allow the current culture to become associated with the new leadership, thus closing the window of opportunity for change.

Finally, management will want to change the selection and socialization processes and the evaluation and reward systems to support employees who espouse the new values that are sought.

The above suggestions, of course, provide no guarantee that change efforts will succeed. Organizational members don't quickly let go of values that they understand and that have worked well for them in the past. Managers must therefore show patience. Change, if it comes, will be slow. And management must keep on a constant alert to protect against reversion to old, familiar practices and traditions.

Managing the Environment

We know from our discussion in Chapter 3 that the environment constrains managerial choices. Is there anything management can do to reduce the constraints imposed by the environment?

Most organizations are relatively powerless to change their environment. Their environment acts upon them rather than they upon it. However, some organizations—especially the large and powerful ones—can manage their environment and thereby reduce the constraints that the environment seeks to impose.

For instance, commercial airlines reduce their dependence on fuel suppliers by writing contracts with Texaco, Shell, and similar suppliers. These contracts guarantee quantities and price for a certain period of time. Hertz, Avis, and other car rental firms reduce their prices on weekends. Since most of their revenues come from businesspeople who travel (and rent cars) during the week, lower weekend prices help to level out the demand fluctuations in the environment. Table 17–1 lists some of the actions management might be able to take to lessen environmental constraints.

Stimulating Creativity and Innovation

Some organizations—3M Co., Johnson & Johnson, and Merck & Co. are obvious examples—are consistently more innovative than others. 3M Co., for instance, has long set itself the goal of getting at least a quarter of its annual sales from products less than five years old.[20] In 1988, 32 percent of 3M's sales came from products like antistatic videotape, translucent dental braces, synthetic ligaments for damaged knees, and heavy-duty reflective sheeting for construction-site signs—all products that didn't exist in 1983.[21]

What differentiates organizations like 3M from less creative organizations? Do creative organizations do a better job of identifying and hiring creative people? Do they provide a supportive culture that brings out the creative potential in people? Or do innovative organizations utilize certain techniques to foster a creative way of thinking? Let's first define *creativity* and *innovation* and then assess what management can do if it wants to stimulate these forces within an organization.

creativity
The ability to combine ideas in a unique way or to make unusual associations between ideas.

Definitions   In general usage, **creativity** means the ability to combine ideas in a unique way or to make unusual associations between ideas.[22] An organization that

MANAGERS WHO MADE A DIFFERENCE

Jan Carlzon at Scandinavian Airlines

Jan Carlzon became president and CEO at Scandinavian Airlines in 1981.[23] It was a time of despair at SAS. The airline was losing $20 million a year, service was being severely cut back, employees were being laid off, and morale was low. In two years, Carlzon made the company profitable and won it *Air Transport World's* Airline of the Year award. By 1989, SAS was being widely acclaimed as one of the most successful airlines in the world. The essence of Carlzon's success was changing SAS's culture from being production oriented into a competitive service enterprise.

Upon taking charge at SAS, Carlzon identified his vision for the company. It would be "the best airline in the world for the frequent business traveler." SAS would not invest one penny or spend one resource in any activity not related to the business market. "We went through the entire company asking ourselves, 'Is this service, is this production, is this person related to the business traveler's needs or not?' If the answer is yes, we have to ask ourselves if we have enough or too much of that resource, and should we increase or decrease it. If the answer is no, we have to get rid of it immediately."

Since the quality that most differentiates airlines is its employees, Carlzon focused on what he called "moments of truth." Carlzon calculated that each of the ten million people who fly SAS came in contact with approximately five SAS employees and that each contact lasted only an average of fifteen seconds. In these fifty million moments of truth lay the success or failure of SAS, since these short contacts would be the basis upon which the customers would decide whether or not to fly SAS again.

Carlzon succeeded in changing SAS's culture by emphasizing communication, reorganization, and positive reinforcement. He took it upon himself to spread his new vision. Recognizing that people rarely read memos, but they do read articles about their company in the newspaper, he used the media to help spread the new gospel. Carlzon reorganized SAS by pushing operating decisions down so that employees would have the authority to solve a customer's problems on the spot. All front-line SAS employees know that they don't have to wait for a supervisor's permission to do what is right for the customer. Finally, Carlzon reinforced employees who accepted his new cultural values. When someone made a decision that he thought promoted the new culture, he made an example of that person and visibly rewarded him or her so other employees would learn from it.

Photo by Ted Fahn.

innovation
The process of taking a creative idea and turning it into a useful product, service, or method of operation.

stimulates creativity is one that develops novel approaches to things or unique solutions to problems. **Innovation** is the process of taking a creative idea and turning it into a useful product, service, or method of operation. Thus the innovative organization is characterized by the ability to channel its creative juices into useful outcomes. When managers talk about changing an organization to make it more creative, they

TABLE 17-1   Some Techniques for Managing the Environment

Change market niche: Some organizations can change their niche with respect to the products or services offered and markets served. They can move to a new niche with fewer or less powerful competitors, fewer regulations, more suppliers, no unions, less powerful public pressure groups, or the like.

Environmental scanning: To the extent that scanning can lead to accurate forecasts of environmental fluctuations, it can reduce uncertainty.

Buffering: Practices such as stockpiling materials and supplies or building up finished-goods inventory protect the organization from environmental surprises at the input or output side.

Smoothing: Offering lower prices at nonpeak times is a means to level out the impact of fluctuations in the environment.

Geographic dispersion: Having multiple locations, especially in different countries, reduces environmental uncertainties that might occur because of political unrest, changes in government or economic policies, labor strikes, weather, or the like.

Advertising: Advertising reduces competitive pressures, stabilizes demand, and allows the organization the opportunity to set prices with less concern for the response of its competitors.

Contracting: Contracting protects the organization from changes in quantity or price on either the input or the output side.

Joint action: Organizations can combine with one or more other organizations for the purpose of joint action. Joint ventures and mergers, for example, reduce environmental uncertainty by lessening interorganizational competition and dependency.

Lobbying: Large and powerful organizations regularly lobby government to achieve favorable outcomes. Smaller organizations often use trade, professional, and similar associations to do their lobbying for them.

Source: Adapted from Stephen P. Robbins, *Organization Theory: Structure, Design, and Applications,* 3rd ed. (Englewood Cliffs, NJ: Prentice Hall, 1990), pp. 358–78.

usually mean that they want to stimulate innovation. The 3M company is aptly described as innovative because it has taken novel ideas and turned them into profitable products like cellophane tape, Scotch-Guard protective coatings, Post-it note pads, and diapers with elastic waistbands.

Fostering Innovation   If you're a manager who wants to increase innovation in your organization, what can you do? One approach is to employ highly creative individuals.

Research tells us that creative people tend to be dissatisfied with the status quo, don't necessarily think in a logical and orderly fashion, are independent and achievement oriented, are willing to work very hard on activities that intrinsically interest them, and tend to be more flexible than their noncreative counterparts.[24] Moreover, contrary to many media stereotypes of creative people, they are rarely considered to be highly intelligent.[25] This may be due in part to the way we measure intelligence. Because they see things that others don't and tend to think in a zigzag fashion rather than sequentially, creative individuals often don't score well on standardized I.Q. tests. Such tests are designed to identify and reward traditional vertical thinking—that is, taking logical steps, one at a time, each step following the previous one in an unbroken sequence. The creative person frequently thinks laterally, skipping logical steps and going off in odd directions. For example, the lateral thinker may tackle a problem from the solution end rather than the starting end and back into various beginning states.

Hewlett-Packard stimulates creativity by fostering an atmosphere of freedom. The company's labs are open to engineers around the clock, and H-P encourages its 965 corporate researchers to devote 10 percent of company time to exploring their own ideas.

To build up innovation by hiring and holding onto creative people is to ignore two facts: (1) highly creative people are extremely scarce resources, and (2) everyone possesses some creative potential. Another alternative, therefore, is to develop a culture that supports and encourages every employee's creative potential.

What would this culture look like? The following characteristics will help to create a climate that stimulates creativity and innovation:[26]

1. *Tolerance of risk:* Employees are encouraged to experiment without fear of the consequences should they fail. Mistakes are treated as learning opportunities.

2. *Low external control:* Rules, regulations, policies, and similar controls are kept to a minimum.

3. *Low division of labor:* Narrowly defined jobs create myopia. Diverse job activities give employees a broader perspective.

4. *Acceptance of ambiguity:* Too much emphasis on objectivity and specificity constrains creativity.

5. *Tolerance of conflict:* Diversity of opinions should be encouraged. Harmony and agreement between individuals and/or units are *not* assumed to be evidence of high performance.

6. *Tolerance of the impractical:* Individuals who offer impractical, even foolish, answers to "what if" questions are not stifled. What seems impractical at first might lead to innovative solutions.

7. *Focus on ends rather than means:* Goals should be made clear, and individuals should be encouraged to consider alternative routes toward their attainment. Focusing on ends suggests that there might be several right answers to any given problem.

8. *All-channel communication:* Communication should flow laterally as well as vertically. The free flow of communication facilitates cross-fertilization of ideas.

Stimulating Creativity and Innovation   Given that everyone has some potential for creativity if the organization's culture is supportive, what specifically can be done to increase employee creativity?

Brainstorming, the nominal group technique, and the Delphi technique (discussed in Chapter 6 as methods for improving group decision making) are the three most popular ways of stimulating the development of unique solutions to problems. In addition, evidence indicates that *synectics* is a valuable tool for stimulating creative abilities.[27]

synectics
A method for fitting together different and irrelevant elements to arrive at new solutions to ·problems.

Synectics is a method for fitting together different and irrelevant elements to arrive at new solutions to problems. It recognizes that "most problems are not new. The challenge is to view the problem in a new way. This viewpoint in turn embodies the potential for a new basic solution."[28] Its goal, therefore, is to make the strange familiar and the familiar strange.

To find new approaches to old problems, it is necessary to abandon familiar ways of viewing things. For instance, most of us think of hens laying eggs. But how many of us have considered that a hen is only an egg's way of making another egg? Obviously, this represents another way of looking at the situation.

Synectics makes extensive use of *analogies* to look for similarities between relationships or functions. As a case in point, the direct analogy can reveal new alternatives by comparing parallel facts, knowledge, or technology. Alexander Graham Bell saw the possibility of taking concepts that operate in the human ear and applying them in his "talking box." After noticing that the massive bones in the ear are operated by a delicate membrane, he wondered why a thicker and stronger piece of membrane should not move a piece of steel. Out of that analogy the telephone was conceived.

Managing Organizational Retrenchment

"Managing change is never easy. But having to lay off 15 percent of our work force and significantly cut back the size of our organization has been the toughest task I've ever faced." These words from a senior executive describe a task that is becoming part of an increasing number of managers' jobs. In recent years, for instance, Ford cut its work force by more than 10,000, AT&T Information Systems eliminated 24,000 jobs, Eastman Kodak trimmed 4,500 jobs, CBS cut more than 2,000 people, Unisys Corp. reduced its work force by nearly 8,000 employees, and DuPont sweetened its retirement program to encourage 13,000 employees to make an early exit. Since the mid-1980s, few *Fortune* 500 companies have escaped this need to reduce the size of their work force. In some U.S. industries—such as steel and textiles—almost every firm has recently closed manufacturing plants and laid off large numbers of employees.

Managing organizational retrenchment may be a difficult and unpleasant task, but it does have a positive side. Declining conditions create a favorable climate for introducing change. Why? Because they provide the ultimate crisis for unfreezing the status quo. Therefore, while retrenchment is certainly hard on all the people it affects, it can be viewed as a window of opportunity for bringing about large-scale organizational change. The successful changes that have taken place at organizations such as Ford, USX, ITT, and Navistar International have undoubtedly been facilitated by the fact that each has gone through serious retrenchment.

What problems should managers expect during retrenchment? What actions might they consider to deal with these problems? Let's take a look.[29]

Potential Problems Associated with Retrenchment Six problems can typically be expected to surface during retrenchment: (1) increased conflict, (2) increased politicking, (3) loss of top-management credibility, (4) change in work force composition, (5) increased voluntary turnover, and (6) decaying employee motivation.

A manager has the opportunity to really test his or her conflict-management skills during organizational retrenchment. Growth creates slack that acts as a kind of grease to smooth over conflict-creating forces. Management uses this slack as a currency for buying off potentially conflicting interest groups within the organization. Conflicts can be resolved readily by expanding everyone's resources. However, in retrenchment, conflict over resources increases because there are fewer resources to divide up.

Of course, consistent with our approach to conflict in Chapter 16, we are not suggesting that the increased conflict that is evident during retrenchment is necessarily dysfunctional. If managed properly, it can be directed toward slowing the decline. Out of the conflict can come changes that may revitalize the organization: selection of a new domain, the creation of new products or services, and cost-cutting measures that can make the shrunken organization more efficient and viable.

Less slack also translates into more politicking. Many organized and vocal groups will emerge to actively pursue their self-interest. Politically naive managers will find their jobs difficult, if not impossible, as they are unable to adjust to changing decision-making criteria. Remember that under retrenchment conditions, the resource pie is shrinking. If one department can successfully resist a cut, the result will typically be that other departments have to cut more. Weak units not only will take a disproportional part of the cut but may be most vulnerable to elimination. In a "fight-for-life" situation, the standard rules are disregarded. Critical data for decisions are twisted and interpreted by various coalitions so as to further their groups' interests. Such an environment encourages "no-holds-barred" politicking.

Members of the organization in decline will look to some individual or group on which to place the blame for the retrenchment. Whether or not top management is directly responsible for the decline, it tends to become the scapegoat. This, in turn, leads to a loss of top-management credibility. Members compare their organizations with others that are growing or compare their plight with the situation of friends and relatives who are employed by healthy organizations, and then they look for some place to vent their frustrations.

Retrenchment requires personnel cuts. The most popular criterion for determining who gets laid off is seniority; that is, the most recent hirees are the first to go. However, laying off personnel on the basis of seniority tends to reshape the composition of the work force. Since newer employees tend to be younger, seniority-based layoffs typically create an older work force. When organizations operating in mature industries are required to make substantial cuts, the average age of employees may increase by ten years or more. Seniority-based layoffs can also undermine progress made under affirmative-action programs, resulting in a work force made up predominantly of white males.

The other side of employee departures is voluntary quits. This can become a major problem in organizational decline because the organization will want to retain its most valuable employees. Yet some of the first people to voluntarily leave an organization when it begins to decline are the most mobile individuals, such as skilled technicians, professionals, and talented managerial personnel. These, of course, are typically the individuals that the organization can least afford to lose.

Finally, employee motivation is different when an organization is contracting than when it is enjoying growth. During growth, motivation can be provided by promotional opportunities and the excitement of being associated with a dynamic organization. During decline, there are layoffs, reassignments of duties that frequently require employees to absorb the tasks that were previously done by others, and similar stress-inducing changes. It's usually hard for employees to stay motivated when there is high uncertainty as to whether they will still have a job next month or next year. When their organization is experiencing prolonged decline, managers are challenged to function effectively in an organizational climate typified by stagnation, fear, and stress.

Some Possible Solutions   There are no magic techniques available to management that can overcome the many negative outcomes associated with organizational retrenchment. But some things seem to work better than others.[30] These include clarifying the organization's strategy, increasing communication, redesigning jobs, and developing innovative approaches to cutbacks.

Management needs to attack directly the ambiguity that organizational retrenchment creates among employees. This is best done by clarifying the organization's strategy and goals. Where is the organization going? What are the organization's future and potential? By addressing these questions, management demonstrates that it understands the problem and has a vision of what the new, smaller organization will look like. Employees want to believe that management is not content to sit back and run a "going-out-of-business" sale.

Organizational retrenchment demands that management do a lot of communicating with employees. The primary focus of this communication should be downward—specifically, explaining the rationale for changes that will have to be made. But there should also be upward communication to give employees an opportunity to vent their fears and frustrations and have important questions answered. Remember that management's credibility is not likely to be high. Additionally, rumors will be rampant. This puts a premium on management's making every effort to explain clearly the reasons for, and implications of, all significant changes. That is not going to eliminate employee fears, but it will increase the likelihood that management will be perceived as honest and trustworthy. Under the circumstances, that may be about the best one can hope for.

When cuts are made in personnel, management has the opportunity to consolidate and redesign jobs. If the decline appears to be arrested and fears of further layoffs subside, the redesign of jobs to make them more challenging and motivating can turn a problem—eliminating functions and reassigning workloads—into an opportunity. For example, increasing the variety of work activities and allowing people to do complete jobs can give employees new assignments that offer a greater diversity of activities and more whole and identifiable work.

Our final suggestion is for management to look for innovative ways to deal with the problems inherent in cutbacks. A good place to begin is with the list of decruitment options that were identified in Chapter 12. Some organizations, for example, have offered attractive incentives to encourage employees to take early retirement; have provided outplacement services to laid-off employees; or have imposed work-hour reduction programs, whereby all employees share in the cutback by working only twenty-five or thirty hours a week, as an alternative to layoffs.

Handling Employee Stress

For many employees, change creates stress. In this final section, we want to review what is specifically meant by the term *stress,* what causes it, how to identify it, and what managers can do to reduce it.

stress

A dynamic condition in which an individual is confronted with an opportunity, constraint, or demand related to what he or she desires and for which the outcome is perceived to be both uncertain and important.

What Is Stress?   **Stress** is a dynamic condition in which an individual is confronted with an opportunity, constraint, or demand related to what he or she desires and for which the outcome is perceived to be both uncertain and important.[31] This is a complicated definition. Let's look at its components more closely.

Stress is not necessarily bad in and of itself. While stress is often discussed in a negative context, it also has a positive value, particularly when it offers a potential gain. Consider, for example, the superior performance that an athlete or stage performer gives in critical situations. Such individuals often use stress as an opportunity to rise to the occasion and perform at or near their maximum.

However, stress is more often associated with constraints and demands. A constraint prevents you from doing what you desire; demands refer to the loss of something desired. When you take a test at school or you undergo your annual performance review at work, you feel stress because you confront opportunity, constraints, and demands. A good performance review may lead to a promotion, greater responsibilities, and a higher salary. But a poor review may prevent you from getting the promotion. An extremely poor review might cause you to be fired.

Two conditions are necessary for potential stress to become actual stress.[32] There must be uncertainty over the outcome, and the outcome must be important. Regardless of the conditions, a stressful condition exists only when there is doubt or uncertainty regarding whether the opportunity will be seized, whether the constraint will be removed, or whether the loss will be avoided. That is, stress is highest for individuals who are uncertain whether they will win or lose and lowest for individuals who think that winning or losing is a certainty. The importance of the outcome is also a critical factor. If winning or losing is unimportant, there is no stress. If a subordinate feels that keeping a job or earning a promotion are unimportant, he or she will experience no stress before a performance review.

Causes of Stress   The causes of stress can be found in issues related to the organization or in personal factors that evolve out of the employee's private life.

Clearly, change of any kind has the potential to cause stress. It can present opportunities, constraints, or demands. Moreover, changes are frequently created in a climate of uncertainty and around issues that are important to employees. It's not surprising, then, for change to be a major stressor.

An employee's job and the organization's structure are also pervasive causes of stress. Excessive work loads create stress, as do pressures to maintain a machine-regulated pace. At the other extreme, job boredom can also create stress. Individuals with more challenging jobs have less anxiety, depression, and physical illness than those with less challenging jobs.[33] Role conflict and ambiguity create stress.[34] The former imposes contradictory demands on the employee, whereas unclear expectations and uncertain job requirements characterize the latter. A classic structural source of stress is when the unity of command is broken and employees must deal with more than one boss. Additional organizational factors that cause employee stress include excessive rules and regulations, an unresponsive and unsupportive boss, ambiguous communications, and unpleasant physical working conditions such as extreme temperatures, poor lighting, or distracting noises.

The death of a family member, a divorce, and personal financial difficulties are examples of private matters that can create personal stress.[35] Because employees bring their personal problems with them to work, a full understanding of employee stress requires consideration of these personal factors.

There is evidence that an employee's personality acts as a moderator to accentuate or diminish the impact of both organizational and personal stressors.[36] The most attention has been given to what has been called the Type A–Type B dichotomy.[37] Individuals exhibiting **Type A behavior** are characterized by a chronic sense of time urgency and an excessive competitive drive. They are impatient, do everything fast, and have great difficulty coping with leisure time. **Type B behavior** is just the opposite—relaxed, easygoing, and noncompetitive. Type As live with moderate to high levels of stress; they are more susceptible to heart disease than Type Bs. From a manager's standpoint, Type As are more likely to show symptoms of stress, even if organizational and personal stressors are low.

Symptoms of Stress   What signs indicate that an employee's stress level might be too high? Stress shows itself in a number of ways. For instance, an employee who is experiencing a high level of stress may develop high blood pressure, ulcers, irritability, difficulty in making routine decisions, loss of appetite, accident proneness, and the

Type A behavior

Behavior marked by a chronic sense of time urgency and an excessive competitive drive.

Type B behavior

Behavior that is relaxed, easygoing, and noncompetitive.

Research consistently finds the job of air traffic controller to be one of high stress. The work load in this job is high, total concentration is required, and a mistake can mean the loss of hundreds of lives.

like. These symptoms can be subsumed under three general categories: physiological, psychological, and behavioral.[38]

Most of the early concern with stress was directed at physiological symptoms. This was predominantly because the topic was researched by specialists in the health and medical sciences. This research led to the conclusion that stress could create changes in metabolism, increase heart and breathing rates, increase blood pressure, bring on headaches, and induce heart attacks.

The link between stress and particular physiological symptoms is not clear. There are few, if any, consistent relationships.[39] This is attributed to the complexity of the symptoms and the difficulty in measuring them objectively. But physiological symptoms have the least direct relevance to managers.

Of greater importance are the psychological symptoms. Stress can cause dissatisfaction. Job-related stress can cause job-related dissatisfaction. Job dissatisfaction, in fact, is "the simplest and most obvious psychological effect" of stress.[40] But stress shows itself in other psychological states—for instance, tension, anxiety, irritability, boredom, and procrastination. Behaviorally related stress symptoms include changes in productivity, absence, and turnover, as well as changes in eating habits, increased smoking or consumption of alcohol, rapid speech, fidgeting, and sleep disorders.

Reducing Stress   Not all stress is dysfunctional. Moreover, realistically, stress can never be totally eliminated from a person's life, either off the job or on. As we review stress reduction techniques, keep in mind that our concern is with reducing the part of stress that is dysfunctional.

In terms of organizational factors, any attempt to lower stress levels has to begin with employee *selection*. Management needs to make sure that an employee's abilities match the requirements of the job. When employees are in "over their heads," their stress levels will typically be high. A realistic job preview during the selection process will also lessen stress by reducing ambiguity. Improved organizational communications will keep ambiguity-induced stress to a minimum. Similarly, a performance-planning program such as MBO will clarify job responsibilities, provide clear performance objectives, and reduce ambiguity through feedback. Job redesign is also a way to reduce stress. If stress can be traced directly to boredom or work overload, jobs should be redesigned to increase challenge or reduce the work load. Redesigns that increase opportunities for employees to participate in decisions and to gain social support have also been found to lessen stress.[41]

Stress that arises from an employee's personal life creates two problems. First, it is more difficult for the manager to directly control. Second, there are ethical considerations. Specifically, does the manager have any right to intrude—even in the most subtle ways—in the employee's personal life? If a manager believes it is ethical and the employee is receptive, there are a few approaches the manager can consider. Employee *counseling* can provide stress relief. Employees often want to talk to someone about their problems; and the organization—through its managers, in-house personnel counselors, or free or low-cost outside professional help—can meet that need. For employees whose personal lives suffer from a lack of planning and organization that, in turn, creates stress, the offering of a *time management program* may prove beneficial in helping them to sort out their priorities.[42] Still another approach is organizationally sponsored *physical activity programs*.[43] Some large corporations employ physical fitness specialists who provide employees with exercise advice, teach relaxation techniques, and show individual employees physical activities they can use to keep their stress levels down.

SUMMARY

This summary is organized by the chapter-opening learning objectives found on page 527.

1. The "calm-waters" metaphor views change as a break in the organization's equilibrium state. Organizations are seen as stable and predictable, disturbed by an occasional crisis. The "white-water rapids" metaphor views change as a constant. Managers must deal with ongoing and unpredictable change.

2. Change is often resisted because of the uncertainty it creates, concern for personal loss, and a belief that it might not be in the organization's best interest.

3. Resistance to change can be reduced by increasing driving forces, decreasing restraining forces, or combining the two approaches.

4. The situational factors that facilitate cultural change in an organization are a dramatic crisis, a change in top leadership, having a young and small organization, and the existence of a weak culture.

5. Management should enact cultural change by beginning with a cultural analysis. This can be followed by actions to make a crisis more visible; appointing new personnel in top positions; reorganizing key functions; creating new stories, symbols, and rituals to replace ones that reflect the old culture; and altering the organization's selection and socialization processes and evaluation and reward systems to reflect the new cultural values.

6. Techniques for managing the environment include changing the organization's market niche, environmental scanning, buffering, smoothing, geographic dispersion, advertising, contracting, joint action, and lobbying.

7. Creativity refers to the ability to combine ideas in a unique way or to make unusual associations between ideas. Innovation is the process of taking a creative idea and turning it into a useful product, service, or method of operation.

8. Potential problems that are likely to surface during organizational retrenchment include increased conflict, increased politicking, loss of top-management credibility, change in work force composition, increased voluntary turnover, and decaying employee motivation.

9. Stress is a dynamic condition in which an individual is confronted with an opportunity, constraint, or demand related to what he or she desires and for which the outcome is perceived to be both uncertain and important.

10. Techniques for reducing employee stress include careful matching of applicants with jobs in the selection process, clear performance objectives, redesign of jobs to increase challenge and reduce the work load, employee counseling, provision of time management programs, and organizationally sponsored physical activity programs.

REVIEW QUESTIONS

1. Why is handling change an integral part of every manager's job?
2. Give half a dozen examples of internal and external forces that create the need for organizations to change.
3. Who are change agents?
4. Describe Lewin's three-step change process. Why is it inconsistent with the "white-water rapids" view of organizational change?
5. Contrast driving and restraining forces in unfreezing.
6. Give an example of a change in (a) people, (b) structure, and (c) technology.
7. Is it easier to change the culture of a small high-tech firm or the culture at General Electric? Explain.
8. How can managers stimulate innovation in their organization?
9. Is managing retrenchment more challenging than managing growth? Explain.
10. What signs indicate that an employee's stress level might be too high?

DISCUSSION QUESTIONS

1. As an outside change agent, what problems would you anticipate if you worked as a consultant for a company? What actions would you take to reduce these problems?
2. Compare techniques for changing people with your knowledge of the learning process. How are they related?
3. How can an innovative culture make an organization more effective? Could such an innovative culture make an organization less effective? Explain.
4. Explain how cultural change and managing the environment could significantly expand a manager's decision discretion.
5. Why is employee stress considered a problem for managers? Isn't this essentially a medical issue?

SELF-ASSESSMENT EXERCISE

How Ready Are You For Managing in a Turbulent World?

Instructions: Listed below are some statements a thirty-seven-year-old manager made about his job at a large, successful corporation. If your job had these characteristics, how would you react to them? After each statement are five letters, A to E. Circle the letter that best describes how you think you would react according to the following scale:

A *I would enjoy this very much; it's completely acceptable.*
B *This would be enjoyable and acceptable most of the time.*
C *I'd have no reaction to this feature one way or another, or it would be about equally enjoyable and unpleasant.*
D *This feature would be somewhat unpleasant for me.*
E *This feature would be very unpleasant for me.*

1. I regularly spend 30 to 40 percent of my time in meetings.
   A B C D E

2. A year and a half ago, my job did not exist, and I have been essentially inventing it as I go along.   A B C D E

3. The responsibilities I either assume or am assigned consistently exceed the authority I have for discharging them.   A B C D E

4. At any given moment in my job, I have on the average about a dozen phone calls to be returned.   A B C D E

5. There seems to be very little relation in my job between the quality of my performance and my actual pay and fringe benefits.   A B C D E

6. About two weeks a year of formal management training is needed in my job just to stay current.   A B C D E

7. Because we have very effective equal employment opportunity (EEO) in my company and because it is thoroughly multinational, my job consistently brings me into close working contact at a professional level with people of many races, ethnic groups, and nationalities and of both sexes.
   A B C D E

8. There is no objective way to measure my effectiveness.   A B C D E

9. I report to three different bosses for different aspects of my job, and each has an equal say in my performance appraisal.   A B C D E

10. On average, about a third of my time is spent dealing with unexpected emergencies that force all scheduled work to be postponed.   A B C D E

11. When I have to have a meeting of the people who report to me, it takes my secretary most of a day to find a time when we are all available, and even then, I have yet to have a meeting where everyone is present for the entire meeting.   A B C D E

12. The college degree I earned in preparation for this type of work is now obsolete, and I probably should go back for another degree.   A B C D E

13. My job requires that I absorb 100–200 pages per week of technical materials.
    A B C D E

14. I am out of town overnight at least one night per week.   A B C D E

15. My department is so interdependent with several other departments in the company that all distinctions about which departments are responsible for which tasks are quite arbitrary.   A   B   C   D   E

16. I will probably get a promotion in about a year to a job in another division that has most of these same characteristics.   A   B   C   D   E

17. During the period of my employment here, either the entire company or the division I worked in has been reorganized every year or so.
A   B   C   D   E

18. While there are several possible promotions I can see ahead of me, I have no real career path in an objective sense.   A   B   C   D   E

19. While there are several possible promotions I can see ahead of me, I think I have no realistic chance of getting to the top levels of the company.
A   B   C   D   E

20. While I have many ideas about how to make things work better, I have no direct influence on either the business policies or the personnel policies that govern my division.   A   B   C   D   E

21. My company has recently put in an "assessment center" where I and all other managers will be required to go through an extensive battery of psychological tests to assess our potential.   A   B   C   D   E

22. My company is a defendant in an antitrust suit, and if the case comes to trial, I will probably have to testify about some decisions that were made a few years ago.   A   B   C   D   E

23. Advanced computer and other electronic office technology is continually being introduced into my division, necessitating constant learning on my part.
A   B   C   D   E

24. The computer terminal and screen I have in my office can be monitored in my bosses' offices without my knowledge.   A   B   C   D   E

Turn to page 676 for scoring directions and key.

Source: From Peter B. Vaill, *Managing as a Performing Art: New Ideas for a World of Chaotic Change* (San Francisco: Jossey-Bass, 1989), pp. 8–9. With permission.

CASE APPLICATION 17A

Apple Computer

Apple Computer was only eight years old when John Sculley came over from PepsiCo in 1983 to head up the California computer maker. By the summer of 1989, he had succeeded in quadrupling Apple's annual revenues to over $4 billion and had quintupled profits to $420 million. Not willing to rest on his laurels, he introduced the third major organizational shakeup since his arrival.[44]

The realization that big changes were needed at Apple dawned on Sculley after he returned from a nine-week sabbatical during the summer of 1988. "The technical people didn't respect the marketing department," he said. "The marketing department was disorganized, and there was little possibility that we could afford all the projects it was working on." Moreover, the company was aggressively moving into the professional market—attempting to sell its Macintosh products to large corporations and government institutions—which required that Apple become a more serious and better organized firm.

Apple had grown by promoting a California life-style in the workplace. Every computer box contained not only a computer, but also a large potion of the California mystique: creativity flourishing in an informal work setting. Sculley says that those days are now over. California cool is on the way out. He is leading the company through a significant transition that will change how Apple sees the world and how the world sees Apple. New products will be less revolutionary and more evolutionary. Apple products and people will move from counterculture to mainstream.

Sculley sees change as necessary to better compete against the likes of IBM, Next, and Sun Microsystems. However, it won't be easy. He must pull off a delicate balancing act. He has to persuade corporations that Apple machines can fit into networks dominated by other vendors and that Apple won't suddenly bring out a new product that renders the company's old line obsolete. At the same time, he must convince customers that the Mac and its successor products can significantly outperform anything IBM has to offer. Sculley plans to concentrate on making the Mac easy to use, insisting on consistent, intuitively obvious commands throughout all models and in thousands of different software packages that are a pleasure for even a neophyte to run.

The most obvious sign of Apple's new work climate was the appointment of two people with very different personality types to key management slots. Sculley promoted Jean-Louis Gassée, a colorful Frenchman who had run Apple's operations in France, to manage all of Apple's R&D, new-product development, and manufacturing. Slender and irreverent, wearing a diamond in his left ear, Gassée symbolized Apple's countercultural past. In contrast, Sculley hired Allan Z. Loren, a former insurance executive, to develop a new in-house computer and communications network. New York born and bred, Loren is beefy, abrasive, and task-oriented. Sculley admits that "Allan scared the hell out of people, and I'm thrilled. I knew a tough guy from the East Coast demanding implementation would be unpopular. I told him that before he took the job." Sculley is quick to point out that Gassée and Loren agreed on the company they wanted Apple to be. There were no debates between them over what products or technologies to introduce or how an Apple computer should function.

Not all of Sculley's changes were received with open arms by Apple employees. There was enormous upheaval in the executive suite as people tried to adjust to

Gassée's and Loren's varied styles. Gassée and Loren have now both left Apple. Uncertainty is still high throughout the company. As one employee put it, "This place has none of the buoyancy of a few years ago. I dread coming to work."

Questions

1. What precipitated Sculley's actions?

2. What were the pros and cons of his new strategy?

3. Do you think Sculley tampered too much with the Apple mystique?

4. Do you think Sculley's efforts to change Apple's culture are succeeding? Explain your position.

CASE APPLICATION 17B

Wang Laboratories

The decline of Wang Laboratories Inc. illustrates what happens to a company that moves too slowly in a fast-moving industry.[45]

The company was started by An Wang, a Chinese immigrant, in 1951. In 1984, his company had become a member of the *Fortune* 500, and he held Wang stock worth more than $1.6 billion. But his company is now in serious trouble, and the value of his stock is down to about $250 million.

Through the 1970s and much of the 1980s, Wang Laboratories moved adroitly from one successful product to another. In the decade ending in 1983, Wang's growth averaged 40 percent a year. When the personal-computer revolution hit, Wang, with its huge base in office desktops, was in a position to own the industry.

But instead of meeting the competition head-on with aggressively priced computers that were compatible with IBM equipment, Wang sold high-priced, incompatible PCs that appealed only to its existing customers. Meanwhile, its lucrative word-processor business slumped, and its minicomputer business slowed sharply. To make matters worse, Wang's management chose to keep employment high and used heavy debt financing to pay for new product development.

By the summer of 1989, Wang was in deep trouble. It reported a third quarter loss of $63.7 million and was expecting further losses in the fourth quarter. Lenders were forcing renegotiation of its debt. And Frederick Wang, An Wang's 38-year-old son, who had become president and chief operating officer in early 1987, was asked by his father to resign. The senior Wang, aging and dying of cancer, brought in an outsider to replace his son.

Wang's expenses were far too high to support its current level of sales. Between May and December of 1989, 4,500 workers were laid off, but the company was still overstaffed. Furthermore, short-term debt, due within a year, had grown to $425 million from only $75 million in 1986.

Questions

1. How did Wang respond to change during the last half of the 1980s? What was wrong with this response?

2. What forces brought about the need for change?

3. What problems do you think Wang's retrenchment has created for management?

4. What, if anything, can new management do that Frederick Wang couldn't?

Active Listening

PURPOSE

1. To contrast passive and active listening
2. To apply paraphrasing skills

REQUIRED KNOWLEDGE

The skills of paraphrasing what others have said.

TIME REQUIRED

Approximately 15 minutes

INSTRUCTIONS

Most of us are pretty poor listeners. This is probably because active listening is very demanding. This exercise is specifically designed to dramatize how difficult it is to listen actively and to accurately interpret what is being said. It also points out how emotions can distort communication.

Break the class into pairs. In each pair, Person A is to choose a contemporary issue. Some examples include business ethics, stiffer college grading practices, gun control, legalization of abortion, on-site employee drug-testing, money as a motivator, and company-paid maternity benefits. Person B is then to select a position on that issue. Person A must automatically take the opposing position. The two individuals are now to debate the issue.

But not so fast! There's a catch. Before each speaks, he or she must first summarize, in his or her *own* words and without notes, what the other has said. If the summary doesn't satisfy the speaker, it must be corrected until it does.

Concrete Products

Concrete Products is a subsidiary of the Premix Company and is located in Bellevue, Washington. The main product of Concrete Products is building blocks. The firm is made up of about 150 unskilled production employees, twenty skilled metal workers, fifteen first-line supervisors, and a staff of twenty office and management personnel.

The president of Concrete Products was concerned about the company's profitability and hired a management consultant, Pete Thompson, to prepare a study. As a preliminary investigation, it was agreed that Pete Thompson would carefully evaluate three diverse positions in the firm. The individuals and jobs selected for evaluation were Mike Phillips (a production worker), Carol Hunt (a sales dispatcher), and Gary Riley (the company's sales manager). Their place in Concrete Products' organization can be seen in Figure V–1.

MIKE PHILLIPS

Mike Phillips had been employed by Tacoma Block and Concrete until 1986. In that year, Tacoma Block and Concrete was bought by Concrete Products, and Mike was transferred to the Bellevue location. He operates the off-bearer, a fork attachment that removes masonry blocks from a conveyor and places them in racks to be forwarded to the autoclave for curing. The job might be described as undesirable for two reasons. First, the surroundings are very noisy because the job is done in close proximity to the compaction equipment. Second, the job is monotonous because the production line has been designed to produce at a constant rate.

The Job

Mike's day begins at 7:00 A.M. He begins work on the production line almost immediately, since plant setup, repairs, and preventive maintenance are completed overnight by fitters. The job itself is quite straightforward. As the concrete blocks are pressed, Mike removes them from the conveyor and places them into special steel racks. He does this by swivelling the fork into position parallel to the racks. The procedure, while sounding simple, actually requires considerable skill. Mike has to adjust his methods according to the size and weight of each type of block.

Mike also acts as a control point on the production line, and this enables him to take corrective action in case of delays. These delays are usually caused by the failure of the forklift drivers to replace the steel shelving quickly. This, in turn, is caused by breakdowns, slowness of the strippers to empty the racks, general "orneriness" of the lift drivers, and absenteeism on any of these jobs. Other factors causing delays in Mike's job are poor quality control in batching, deflection of the block molds, and poor compaction of the blocks due to machine failure. Another increasing problem Mike faces is sabotage—specifically, employees who throw foreign materials into the batching system. This results in the fracturing or bending of molds and almost always requires a number of employees (including Mike) to work overtime. Mike estimates that, on average, at least one hour per day is lost due to delays. When a big job is on, Mike has noted that sabotage tends to increase and, with it, the length of delays.

Job Satisfaction

Mike describes himself as "reasonably satisfied" with his pay. This is probably due to the way in which his pay is calculated. He gets a basic wage rate plus a group bonus. The group bonus requires that each supervisor decide on performance rankings, and thus the bonus differentials, of the employees in his group of ten to twelve workers. Mike is consistently one of the highest bonus earners, and while money is probably not as

FIGURE V–1
Concrete Products

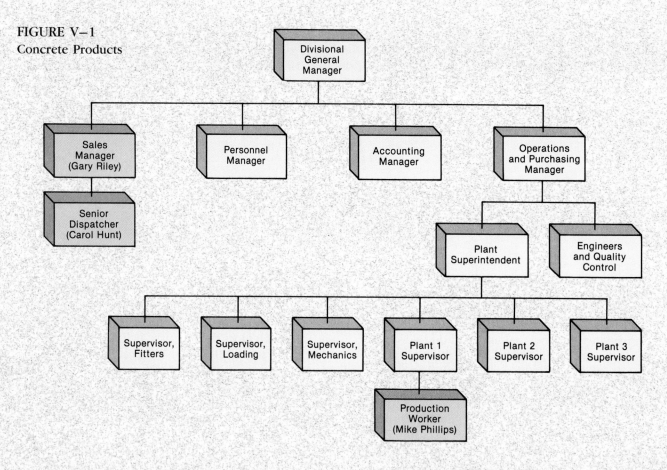

much of an incentive to Mike as it once was, it still remains an important measure of success for him. Mike told Pete Thompson that "the worth of a job is determined by how much money you're paid for doing that job."

The work group of which Mike is a part also gives him satisfaction. Mike's experience and skill level provide him with relatively high status in his work group. This status compensates for some of the job's disadvantages like limited opportunities for promotion or personal growth, poor working conditions, and the frustration from performing highly repetitive tasks.

When Mike was asked to talk about things that "turn him off" about his job, he mentioned three. There are the occasional verbal confrontations with the forklift drivers. Mike thinks this may be due to the fact that these drivers are not included in the bonus system. Another frustration is that "new workers are here one day and disappear the next." This lack of continuity makes it hard to develop smooth coordination. But Mike's biggest beef concerns the company's philosophy. "This place, like every other place I've ever worked, doesn't care about helping people to do a better job.

Nothing gets done to make our jobs more meaningful unless it increases profits or benefits someone in management."

Contact with Superiors

Mike's contacts with the "higher-ups" are limited to those with his supervisor. That relationship, however, is fairly positive. Mike considers his supervisor "reasonably objective" and "receptive to change." Mike's supervisor often gives him the opportunity to participate in efforts to improve block-handling methods. For instance, the redesign of the racking system and twin off-bearer are two of Mike's suggestions now in operation.

Mike has almost no contact with upper management except for passing "hello's." The president often walks through the factory but seldom talks with production people. Mike noted that this distancing works both ways. Few workers take any interest in the president. This, he surmised, is a result of frequent changes of company presidents. It has become generally accepted by production personnel that because Concrete Products is one of the smaller subsidiaries of Premix, it suffers from turnover in chief executives. The presidents take "little interest in the detailed operations here so we take little interest in presidents."

Contact with Peers

High turnover has resulted in the creation of two production groups: "newcomers" and "old pros." Each group tends to go its own way at break time, during lunch, and after work. Within his peer group, Mike's ability and competence is generally recognized, though occasionally new members within the group will question his skills, which "burns me to no end." Members of the "old pros" often rely on Mike for both personal and work-related advice. Pete Thompson noted, with interest, that there was little social interaction between the production workers and people such as fitters, mechanics, and forklift drivers.

CAROL HUNT

Carol Hunt has been with Concrete Products since 1984. Initially, she was employed as a salesclerk, but in the last two years she has been responsible for dispatching orders throughout the Seattle metropolitan area. As senior sales dispatcher, she also supervises three clerks involved in order taking.

The Job

Carol's day begins at 8:00 A.M., when she ensures that all orders allocated the previous day have been dispatched and checks on breakdowns and the number of trucks and cranes available for the day. She receives and prices orders, checks on pallet returns, and follows up on claims for waiting time, additional cartage, and credit. Claims for credit are forwarded to the accounts department and, occasionally, to the sales manager for consideration. By midmorning, the first set of drivers is returning for second loads. New orders are distributed to the drivers as they pass the dispatch office on their way to the loading areas.

This pattern continues throughout the day until approximately 3:00 P.M., when the transactions for the day are totalled for the sales manager's review. It is at this time that the allocation of orders for the next day begins and delivery lists are forwarded to the loading docks for use early the following day. Carol also handles all minor customer complaints and forwards details on these to the sales manager. On a typical day, Carol will make one or two trips to the loading docks to check on delays and driver complaints. Occasionally she

has found as many as eight or ten trucks sitting idle. Such incidents occur, according to Carol, because forklifts break down or are reallocated to production areas.

Job Satisfaction

Carol says she likes her job "when everything runs smoothly." Unfortunately, this isn't too often. She tends to be confronted continually with problems related to loading and delivery. This does, of course, add challenge to her daily activities; and when she successfully solves a problem, she feels "a sense of satisfaction."

Carol's job allows her a considerable degree of freedom and responsibility. Seldom are her decisions questioned by more senior staff. When discussing the satisfying aspects of her job, she talks about autonomy, responsibility, and achievement.

On the negative side, Carol becomes frustrated and dissatisfied when she is accused of favoring some drivers over others. The drivers are subcontractors and she is regularly accused of allocating "easy runs" to certain of these. Carol also spoke negatively about job pressures and the lack of rewards. Carol says sometimes the pressure of the job becomes so great that she feels that she is "running around in circles." She is disappointed by the lack of verbal recognition of her performance by her superiors. She also thinks the company is "exploiting" her by paying her less than a male would receive for doing the same job.

Contact with Superiors

Communication with her immediate boss, the sales manager, is inhibited because of "personality differences." In Carol's opinion, the sales manager "likes to talk rather than listen." This has eroded her belief that any suggestions regarding improvements in her area of responsibility would be heeded. Contact with other members of management is limited. She commented that this is probably due to her occupying "what was once regarded as a man's job."

Contact with Peers

All Carol's social contacts with her work peers occur on the job. Carol does not believe in socializing with colleagues outside working hours. "I have little in common with the people around here." Carol was described by the order clerks as "abrasive," "arrogant," and "self-centered."

GARY RILEY

Gary Riley has been with Concrete Products since 1982. He was initially an industrial salesman but has been sales manager since 1986.

The Job

Gary's work involves a diverse pattern of activity. Most of his time is occupied by reading and sending mail, by telephone calls, and by meetings with customers, subordinates, and superiors. Gary does not work to a plan in the accepted sense of the word, and the pressures of the job leave little room for reflection. Other activities during the day include delegating "calls" to sales representatives and informing sales reps of trade gossip, customer problems, promotional programs, as well as production and delivery problems. Gary is also responsible for supervising and coordinating all the activities in the sales department.

Gary devotes a major part of his day to immediate issues such as daily production analysis and calling personally on major customers. He also disseminates information returned by representatives—information on the quality of the blocks, credits, color range, competitive activity, and new process technology. In this way he attempts to piece together some tangible details of what products are being sold.

Job Satisfaction

The prior sales managers had been perceived as resistant to change and highly autocratic. "Middle management just didn't participate in the running of the company; the skills were there but in most cases were underutilized." Since becoming sales manager, Gary has greatly enjoyed the challenge of reorganizing and rejuvenating the sales department.

Gary believes he has developed a climate in the sales department that affords his staff the opportunity to develop their knowledge and skills and to contribute to the department's success. This development is a continual source of satisfaction to Gary.

Gary's goal has been to remove any social barriers within his department. Yet he is worried about how much control he should maintain and how much he should delegate.

Gary is also dissatisfied because he is often criticized by senior managers for his lack of decision-making ability and his "easygoing" manner. Gary admits his style is very different from that of most other managers. "Historically, this has been an extremely autocratic company," he says. Gary's estimate of his own abilities doesn't generally coincide with that of senior manage-

ment, with the notable exception of the current president. Other senior executives are regularly questioning "my competence as a manager."

Contact with Superiors

Gary communicates well with his immediate superior, the president, which is a direct result of the president's participative management style. This is a major departure from the highly autocratic style of the previous presidents appointed from the Premix group. Gary has been able to discuss many of his problems and ideas with the president, and the president regularly seeks Gary out for his opinions. The two-way interaction has given Gary access to information not available to previous sales managers, and he feels that this information has been extremely beneficial to his decision making.

Contact with Peers

Gary is generally liked by his peers, but some are suspicious of his motives. Gary's close contact with the current president has caused some resentment, especially in the operational and engineering departments. Organizational changes are being made in both areas, and Gary acknowledges that some of them are a result of his suggestions. He is concerned that he might be earning a reputation as a hatchetman. Because of the organizational changes that are taking place, Gary has noticed that his position within his peer group is also changing.

QUESTIONS

1. What motivates Mike Phillips? Carol Hunt? Gary Riley?
2. How is each person's job performance influenced by interactions with others in and around his or her work group? Discuss.
3. How are culture and leadership style interrelated in this case?
4. Analyze the conflicts that exist at Concrete Products. Are these functional or dysfunctional?
5. If you were Pete Thompson, what changes would you suggest the president make to improve the company's profitability? Be specific.

This case was prepared by Dr. Graham Kenny. Reprinted, with modifications, by permission of the author.

18

FOUNDATIONS OF CONTROL

After extensive time delays and cost overruns, the B-2 stealth bomber made its initial flight test on July 17, 1989.[1] It was a significant day for the U.S. Air Force, which ordered the plane, and for Northrop, which built it. It was not a very good day for the U.S. taxpayer, who was picking up the tab.

Following eighteen months of delays—the plane was originally scheduled to be flight-tested in January 1988—the plane did pass its preliminary tests. The cost overruns, however, had many Congressmen wondering out loud whether the whole B-2 program should be scuttled. The original plan was to build approximately 132 of the planes at a cost of about $170 million each. By the time of the actual flight tests, it had become the most expensive airplane in military history.

Of course, the Air Force has never been considered a paragon of management efficiency. Inadequate controls have permitted practices that are almost too outlandish to believe.[2] For instance, the Air Force paid $3,033.82 to Pratt & Whitney for a turbine air seal used in the F-111 fighter bomber. It had paid only $16 for the same kind of seal the year before. Similarly, it paid Boeing $1,118.26 apiece for one-inch-square plastic caps that fit on the legs of stools used by navigators in B-52 bombers, even though these caps were available from other suppliers for $4 each.

There are cost overruns, and then there are cost overruns! The B-2 bomber, which was originally supposed to cost $170 million apiece, will actually end up costing an astounding $815 million per plane! That represents more than a 320 percent escalation.

Such examples illustrate what can happen when an organization has a defective control system. While most business firms, hospitals, schools, and other government agencies do not have control problems as blatant as those of the U.S. Air Force, every organization can benefit from a well-designed control system.

WHAT IS CONTROL?

control
The process of monitoring activities to ensure they are being accomplished as planned and of correcting any significant deviations.

Control can be defined as the process of monitoring activities to ensure that they are being accomplished as planned and of correcting any significant deviations. All managers should be involved in the control function even if their units are performing as planned. They cannot really know whether their units are performing properly until they have evaluated what activities have been done and have compared the actual performance with the desired standard.[3] An effective control system ensures that activities are completed in ways that lead to the attainment of the organization's goals. "The criterion of an effective control system is the extent to which it creates goal congruence. If a control system sometimes leads to goal congruence and sometimes to goal conflict, it is ineffective or less effective than might be desired."[4]

THE IMPORTANCE OF CONTROL

Planning can be done, an organization structure can be created to efficiently facilitate the achievement of objectives, and employees can be directed and motivated. Still,

In 1986 and 1987, Mattel lost a total of $121.5 million, in spite of the continued success of Barbie and Ken. By introducing new cost and inventory controls, Mattel's management has turned the company around. By 1989 it had again become solidly profitable. Its 1989 profits of $79.6 million was the best in Mattel's 45-year history.

there is no assurance that activities are going as planned and that the goals managers are seeking are, in fact, being attained. Control is important, therefore, because it is the final link in the functional chain of management: checking up on activities to ensure that they are going as planned and, when there are significant deviations, taking the necessary action to correct the deviation. However, the value of the control function predominantly lies in its relation to planning and delegating activities.

In Chapter 7, we described objectives as the foundation of planning. Objectives give specific direction to managers. However, just stating objectives or having subordinates accept your objectives is no guarantee that the necessary actions have been accomplished. "The best-laid plans of mice and men oft go awry." The effective manager needs to follow up to ensure that the actions that others are supposed to take and the objectives they are supposed to accomplish are, in fact, being taken and achieved.

In our discussion of interpersonal skills we noted that many managers find it difficult to delegate. A major reason given was the fear that subordinates would do something wrong for which the manager would be held responsible. Thus many managers are tempted to do things themselves and avoid delegating. This reluctance to delegate, however, can be reduced if managers develop an effective control system. Such a control system can provide information and feedback on the performance of subordinates to whom they have delegated authority. An effective control system is therefore important because managers need to delegate authority; but since they are held ultimately responsible for the decisions that their subordinates make, managers also need a feedback mechanism.

THE CONTROL PROCESS

The **control process** consists of three separate and distinct steps:

control process
The process of measuring actual performance, comparing it against a standard, and taking managerial action to correct deviations or inadequate standards.

1. *Measuring* actual performance.

2. *Comparing* actual performance against a standard.

3. Taking *managerial action* to correct deviations or inadequate standards.

Before we consider each step in detail, you should be aware that the control process assumes that standards of performance *already exist*. These standards are the specific objectives against which progress can be measured. They are created in the planning function. If managers use MBO, then objectives are, by definition, tangible, verifiable, and measurable. In such instances, these objectives are the standards against which progress is measured and compared. If MBO is not practiced, then standards are the specific performance indicators that management uses. Our point is that these standards are developed in the planning function; planning must *precede* control.

Measuring

To determine what actual performance is, it is necessary to acquire information about it. The first step in control, then, is measuring. Let us consider *how* we measure and *what* we measure.

How We Measure   Four common sources of information, frequently used by managers to measure actual performance, are personal observation, statistical reports, oral reports, and written reports. Each has particular strengths and weaknesses; however, a combination of them increases both the number of input sources and the probability of receiving reliable information.

Personal observation provides firsthand, intimate knowledge of the actual activity—information that is not filtered through others. It permits intensive coverage, since minor as well as major performance activities can be observed, as well as opportunities for the manager to "read between the lines." Personal observation can pick up omissions, facial expressions, and tones of voice that may be missed by other sources. Unfortunately, in a time when quantitative information suggests objectivity, personal observation is often considered an inferior information source. It is subject to perceptual biases—what one manager sees, another might not. Personal observation also consumes a good deal of time. Finally, this method suffers from obtrusiveness. Employees might interpret a manager's overt observation as a sign of a lack of confidence in them or of mistrust.

The current wide use of computers in organizations has made managers rely increasingly on *statistical reports* for measuring actual performance. This measuring device, however, is not limited to computer outputs. It also includes graphs, bar charts, and numerical displays of any form that managers may use for assessing performance. Although statistical data is easy to visualize and effective for showing relationships, it provides limited information about an activity. Statistics report on only a few key areas and often ignore other important factors.

Information can also be acquired through *oral reports*—that is, through conferences, meetings, one-to-one conversations, or telephone calls. The advantages and disadvantages of this method of measuring performance are similar to those of personal observation. Although the information is filtered, it is fast, allows for feedback, and permits language expression and tone of voice, as well as words themselves, to convey meaning. Historically, one of the major drawbacks of oral reports was the problem of documenting information for later references. However, our technological capabilities have progressed in the last couple of decades to the point at which oral reports can be efficiently taped and become as permanent as if they were written.

Actual performance may also be measured by *written reports*. As with statistical reports, they are slower yet more formal than first- or secondhand oral measures. This formality also often means greater comprehensiveness and conciseness than is found in oral reports. In addition, written reports are usually easy to catalogue and reference.

Given the varied advantages and disadvantages of each of these four measurement techniques, comprehensive control efforts by managers should use all four.

What We Measure *What* we measure is probably more critical to the control process than *how* we measure. The selection of the wrong criteria can result in serious dysfunctional consequences. Besides, what we measure determines, to a great extent, what people in the organization will attempt to excel at.[5]

Some control criteria are applicable to any management situation. For instance, since all managers, by definition, direct the activities of others, criteria such as employee satisfaction or turnover and absenteeism rates can be measured. Most managers have budgets for their area of responsibility set in dollar costs. Keeping costs within budget is therefore a fairly common control measure. However, any comprehensive control system needs to recognize the diversity of activities among managers. A production manager in a manufacturing plant might use measures of the quantity of units produced per day, units produced per labor hour, scrap per unit of output, or percent of rejects returned by customers. The manager of an administrative unit in a government agency might use number of document pages typed per day, number of orders processed per hour, or average time required to process service calls. Marketing managers often use measures such as percent of market captured, average dollar value per sale, or number of customer visits per salesperson.

The performance of some activities is difficult to measure in quantifiable terms. It is more difficult, for instance, for an administrator to measure the performance of a research chemist or elementary school teacher than of a person who sells life insurance. But most activities can be broken down into objective segments that allow for

While a teacher's performance may be difficult to measure, it is not impossible. If the objectives of the teacher's job are stimulating students to continue learning, creating good work habits, and developing basic reading, writing, mathematical, and logical skills, a school administrator might include criteria such as percentage increase in reading speed during the school year, percentage of work assignments turned in on time, comparison of absenteeism rates with school norms, average number of outside books read by students during the school year, and comparison of scores on standardized mathematical computation tests between the beginning and end of the school year.

TABLE 18–1
Eastern States Distributors' Sales Performance for July (hundreds of cases)

Brand	Standard	Actual	Over (Under)
Heineken	1,075	913	(162)
Molson	630	634	4
Beck's	800	912	112
Moosehead	620	622	2
Labatt's	540	672	132
Corona	160	140	(20)
Amstel Light	80	65	(15)
Dos Equis	125	120	(5)
Tecate	170	286	116
Total Cases	4,200	4,364	164

measurement. The manager needs to determine what value a person, department, or unit contributes to the organization and convert the contribution into standards.

Most jobs and activities can be expressed in tangible and measurable terms. When a performance indicator cannot be stated in quantifiable terms, managers should look for and use subjective measures. Certainly, subjective measures have significant limitations. Still, they are better than having no standards at all and ignoring the control function. If an activity is important, the excuse that it is difficult to measure is inadequate. In such cases, managers should use subjective performance criteria. Of course, any analysis or decisions made based on subjective criteria should recognize the limitations of the data.

Comparing

The comparing step determines the degree of variation between actual performance and the standard. Some variation in performance can be expected in all activities; it is therefore critical to determine the acceptable **range of variation.** Deviations in excess of this range become significant and receive the manager's attention. In the comparison stage, managers are particularly concerned with the size and direction of the variation. An example should make this clearer.

Rich Tanner is sales manager for Eastern States Distributors. The firm distributes imported beers in a three-state area on the East Coast. Rich prepares a report during the first week of each month that describes sales for the previous month, classified by brand name. Table 18–1 displays both the standard and actual sales figures (in hundreds of cases) for the month of July.

Should Rich be concerned with the July performance? Sales were a bit higher than he had originally targeted, but does that mean that there were no significant deviations? Even though overall performance was generally quite favorable, several brands might deserve the sales manager's attention. However, the number of brands that deserve attention depends on what Rich believes to be *significant.* How much variation should Rich allow before he takes corrective action?

The deviation on several brands is very small and undoubtedly not worthy of special attention. These include Molson, Moosehead, and Dos Equis. Are the shortages for Corona and Amstel Light brands significant? That's a judgment Rich must make. Heineken sales were 15 percent below Rich's goal. This needs attention. Rich should

range of variation

The acceptable parameters of variance between actual performance and the standard.

look for a cause. In this case, Rich attributed the loss to aggressive advertising and promotion programs by the big domestic producers—Anheuser-Busch and Miller. Since Heineken is the number one selling import, it is most vulnerable to the promotion clout of the big domestic producers. If the decline in Heineken is more than a temporary slump, Rich will need to reduce his orders with the brewery and lower his inventory stock.

An error in understating sales can be as troublesome as an overstatement. For instance, is the surprising popularity of Tecate a one-month aberration, or is this brand increasing its market share? Our Eastern States' example illustrates that both over-variance and undervariance require managerial attention.

Taking Managerial Action

The third and final step in the control process is managerial action. Managers can choose among three courses of action: They can do nothing; they can correct the actual performance; or they can revise the standard. Since "doing nothing" is fairly self-explanatory, let's look more closely at the latter two.

Correct Actual Performance   If the source of the variation has been deficient performance, the manager will want to take corrective action. Examples of such corrective action might include changes in strategy, structure, compensation practices, or training programs; the redesign of jobs; or the replacement of personnel.

A manager who decides to correct actual performance has to make another decision: Should he or she take immediate or basic corrective action? **Immediate corrective action** corrects something right now and gets things back on track. **Basic corrective action** asks how and why performance deviated and then proceeds to correct the source of deviation. It is not unusual for managers to rationalize that they do not have the time to take basic corrective action and therefore must be content to perpetually "put out fires." Effective managers, however, analyze deviations and, when the benefits justify it, take the time to permanently correct significant variances between standard and actual performance.

To return to our example of the beer distributor, Rich Tanner might take basic corrective action on the negative variance for Heineken. He might increase promotion efforts, increase the advertisement budget for this brand, or reduce future orders with the manufacturer. The action he takes will depend on his assessment of each brand's potential effectiveness.

Revise the Standard   It is possible that the variance was a result of an unrealistic standard—that is, the goal may be too high or too low. In such cases it's the standard that needs corrective attention, not the performance. In our example, the sales manager might need to raise the standard for Tecate to reflect its increasing popularity. This frequently happens in sports when athletes adjust their performance goals upward during a season if they achieve their season goal early.

The more troublesome problem is the revising downward of a performance standard. If an employee or unit falls significantly short of reaching its target, the natural response is to shift the blame for the variance to the standard. For instance, students who make a low grade on a test often attack the grade cutoff points as too high. Rather than accept the fact that their performance was inadequate, students argue that the standards are unreasonable. Similarly, salespeople who fail to meet their monthly quota may attribute the failure to an unrealistic quota. It may be true that standards are too high, resulting in a significant variance and acting to demotivate those employees being assessed against it. But keep in mind that if employees or managers don't meet the standard, the first thing they are likely to attack is the standard itself. If you believe the standard is realistic, hold your ground. Explain your position, reaffirm to the

immediate corrective action
Correcting an activity right now in order to get things back on the track.

basic corrective action
Determining how and why performance has deviated and correcting the source of deviation.

employee or manager that you expect future performance to improve, and then take the necessary corrective action to turn that expectation into reality.

Summary

Figure 18–1 summarizes the control process. Standards evolve out of objectives, but since these are developed in the planning function, they are tangential to the control process. The process is essentially a continuous flow between measuring, comparing, and managerial action. Depending on the results of the comparing stage, management's courses of action are to do nothing, revise the standard, or correct the performance.

TYPES OF CONTROL

Management can implement controls before an activity commences, while the activity is going on, or after the fact. The first type is called *feedforward control,* the second is *concurrent control,* and the last is *feedback control.*

Feedforward Control

feedforward control
Control that prevents anticipated problems.

The most desirable type of control—**feedforward control**—prevents anticipated problems. It is called feedforward control because it takes place in advance of the actual activity. It is future-directed.[6] For instance, managers in an aerospace firm may

FIGURE 18–1
The Control Process

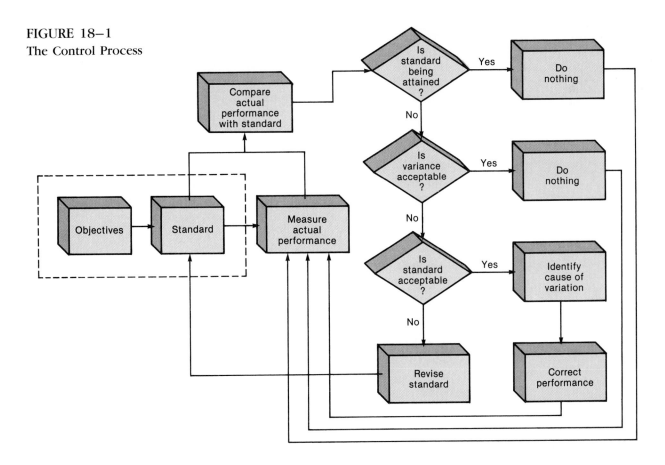

ETHICAL DILEMMAS IN MANAGEMENT

Are "Phantom Snoops" Unethical?

They come into retail stores and look like any other shopper, except that they're surly and impossible to please. They do everything and anything they can do to hassle employees. However, these are not real customers; they are management spies. Their objective is to give employees a hard time and report to management on what happens.

These "phantom spies" are widely used by retail chains like department stores and fast-food restaurants, as well as other service organizations such as airlines. Their primary purpose is to check on how employees treat customers. They rarely conduct themselves like typical customers. They're neither courteous nor understanding. They try to display the worst traits of the most demanding customers.

Are phantom snoops unethical? Almost all organizations employ auditors to check on the organization's financial well-being. Auditors snoop around looking for problems or potential problems. Their role in organizations is typically unquestioned because of the need to verify financial statements and the fact that auditors don't misrepresent who they are. Their arrival may be unannounced, but they almost always quickly identify themselves as part of the auditing staff.

To do their job successfully, phantom snoops must conceal their true identities. Moreover, they are not passive evaluators. They purposely attempt to create problems to see how employees respond. Is it unethical for the top management of an organization to hire such people to secretly hassle, observe, and evaluate employees? What do *you* think?

hire additional personnel as soon as the government announces that the firm has won a major military contract. The hiring of personnel ahead of time prevents potential delays. The key to feedforward controls, therefore, is taking managerial action before a problem occurs.

Feedforward controls are desirable because they allow management to prevent problems rather than cure them later. Unfortunately, these controls require timely and accurate information that is often difficult to develop. As a result, managers frequently have to use one of the other two types of control.

Concurrent Control

Concurrent control, as its name implies, takes place while an activity is in progress. When control is enacted while the work is being performed, management can correct problems before they become too costly.

The best-known form of concurrent control is direct supervision. When a manager directly oversees the actions of a subordinate, the manager can concurrently monitor the employee's actions and correct problems as they occur. While there is obviously some delay between the activity and the manager's corrective response, the delay is

concurrent control

Control that occurs while an activity is in progress.

minimal. Technical equipment can be designed to include concurrent controls. Most computers, for instance, are programmed to provide operators with immediate response if an error is made. If you input the wrong command, the program's concurrent controls reject your command and may even tell you why it was wrong.

Feedback Control

feedback control
Control imposed after an action has occurred.

The most popular type of control relies on feedback. The control takes place after the action. The control report that Rich Tanner used for assessing beer sales is an example of a **feedback control.**

The major drawback of this type of control is that, by the time the manager has the information and if there is a significant problem, the damage is already done. It's analogous to the proverbial closing the barn door after the horse has been stolen. But for many activities, feedback is the only viable type of control available.

We should note that feedback has two advantages over feedforward and concurrent control.[7] First, feedback provides managers with meaningful information on how effective its planning effort was. If feedback indicates little variance between standard and actual performance, this is evidence that planning was generally on target. If the deviation is great, a manager can use this information when formulating new plans to make them more effective. Second, feedback control can enhance employee motivation. People want information on how well they have performed. Feedback control provides that information.

THE FOCUS OF CONTROL

What do managers control? Most control efforts are directed at one of five areas: people, finances, operations, information, or the performance of the total organization.

People

Managers accomplish things by working through other people. They need and depend on subordinates to achieve their unit goals. It is therefore important for managers to get their employees to behave in ways that management considers desirable. But how do managers ensure that employees are performing as they are supposed to?

On a day-to-day basis, managers oversee employees' work and correct problems as they occur. The supervisor who spots an employee taking an unnecessary risk when operating his or her machine may point out the correct way to perform the task and tell the employee to do it the correct way in the future.

Managers assess the work of their employees in a more formal way by means of systematic performance appraisals. An employee's recent performance is evaluated. If performance is positive, the employee's behavior can be reinforced with a reward such as a pay increase. If performance is below standard, managers will seek to correct it or, depending on the nature of the deviation, discipline the employee.

Finances

The primary purpose of every business firm is to earn a profit. In pursuit of this objective, managers seek financial controls. Managers might, for instance, carefully

IN PRACTICE

Don't Ignore the Negative Side of Controls

Three managers at a big GM Chevrolet truck plant in Flint, Michigan, installed a secret control box in a supervisor's office to override the control panel that governed the speed of the assembly line.[8] The device allowed the managers to speed up the assembly line—a serious violation of GM's contract with the United Auto Workers. The managers explained that, while they knew what they were doing was wrong, the pressure from higher-ups to meet unrealistic production goals was so great that they felt the secret control panel was the only way they could meet their targets. As described by one manager, senior GM executives would say, "I don't care *how* you do it—just *do* it."

MiniScribe Corp., a computer disk-drive manufacturer, had posted thirteen consecutive record-breaking quarters.[9] These were impressive results—until it was found that the company's spectacular sales gains had been fabricated. Q. T. Wiles, MiniScribe's chairman, had created unrealistic sales targets and put terrific pressure on managers to achieve them. Achieve them they did, even if they had to book shipments as sales, manipulate reserves, and simply falsify figures.

These examples illustrate what can happen when control standards are unreasonable or when the controls are inflexible. People lose sight of the organization's overall goals and become motivated to literally lie and cheat to meet performance standards. Like the tail wagging the dog, controls can wag the organization.

Because any control system has imperfections, problems occur when individuals or organizational units attempt to look good exclusively in terms of the control devices. In actuality, the result is dysfunctional in terms of the organization's goals. More often than not, this is caused by incomplete measures of performance. If the control system evaluates only the quantity of output, people will ignore quality. Similarly, if the system measures activities rather than results, people will spend their time attempting to look good on the activity measures.

To avoid being reprimanded by managers because of the control system, people can engage in behaviors that are designed solely to influence the information system's data output during a given control period. Rather than actually performing well, employees can manipulate measures to give the appearance that they are performing well. Evidence indicates that the manipulation of control data is not a random phenomenon. It depends on the importance of an activity. Organizationally important activities are more likely to make a difference in a person's rewards; therefore, there is a greater incentive to look good on these particular measures.[10] When rewards are at stake, individuals will manipulate data to appear in a favorable light by, for instance, distorting actual figures, emphasizing successes, and suppressing evidence of failures. On the other hand, only random errors occur when the distribution of rewards is unaffected.[11]

search quarterly income statements for excessive expenses. They might also perform several financial ratio tests to ensure that sufficient cash is available to pay ongoing expenses, that debt does not become too large and burdensome, and that assets are being productively used. These are examples of how financial controls can be used to reduce costs and make the best use of financial resources.

Financial controls, of course, are used not only by managers in the private sector. Managers of not-for-profit organizations have objectives, one of the most important being efficiency. Financial controls like budgets are an important tool for controlling costs in hospitals, schools, and government agencies.

In Chapter 9, we discussed budgets as a planning tool. As we noted, they are used for both planning and control. They provide managers with quantitative standards against which to measure and compare resource consumption. And by pointing out deviations between standard and actual consumption, they become control devices.

Table 18–2 summarizes some of the most popular financial ratios used in organizations. Taken from the organization's financial statements (the balance sheet and income statement), they compare two significant figures and express them as a percentage, or ratio. Since you undoubtedly have encountered these ratios, or will in the near future, in introductory accounting and finance courses, we needn't elaborate on them. We mention them, however, to remind you that managers use such ratios as internal control devices for monitoring how efficiently the organization uses its assets, debt, inventories, and the like.

TABLE 18–2 Popular Financial Ratios

Objective	Ratio	Calculation	Meaning
Liquidity test	Current ratio	$\dfrac{\text{Current assets}}{\text{Current liabilities}}$	Tests the organization's ability to meet short-term obligations
	Acid test	$\dfrac{\text{Current assets less inventories}}{\text{Current liabilities}}$	Tests liquidity more accurately when inventories turn over slowly or are difficult to sell
Leverage test	Debt-to-assets	$\dfrac{\text{Total debt}}{\text{Total assets}}$	The higher the ratio, the more leveraged the organization
	Times-interest-earned	$\dfrac{\text{Profits before interest and taxes}}{\text{Total interest charges}}$	Measures how far profits can decline before the organization is unable to meet its interest expenses
Operations test	Inventory turnover	$\dfrac{\text{Sales}}{\text{Inventory}}$	The higher the ratio, the more efficiently inventory assets are being used
	Total asset turnover	$\dfrac{\text{Sales}}{\text{Total assets}}$	The fewer assets used to achieve a given level of sales, the more efficiently management is using the organization's total assets
Profitability	Profit-margin-on-sales	$\dfrac{\text{Net profit after taxes}}{\text{Total sales}}$	Identifies the profits that various products are generating
	Return-on-investment	$\dfrac{\text{Net profit after taxes}}{\text{Total assets}}$	Measures the efficiency of assets to generate profits

Operations

The success of an organization depends to a large extent on its ability to produce goods and services effectively and efficiently. Operations control techniques are designed to assess how effectively and efficiently an organization's transformation processes are working.

Operations control typically encompasses production activities to ensure that they are on schedule; assessing purchasing's ability to provide the proper quantity and quality of supplies needed at the lowest cost possible; monitoring the quality of the organization's products or services to ensure that they meet preestablished standards; and making sure that equipment is well maintained. These concerns will be elaborated upon in Chapter 20 in our discussion of operations management.

Information

Managers need information to do their job. Inaccurate, incomplete, excessive, or delayed information will seriously impede their performance. It's therefore necessary to develop a management information system that provides the right data in the right amount to the right person when he or she needs it.

The technology for managing information has changed dramatically in recent years. Fifteen years ago, for instance, managers in large organizations relied on a centralized data-processing department to service their information needs. If they wanted a breakdown of weekly sales by regional sales territory, they requested the report from the data-processing manager. A lucky manager might get a computer printout of the sales figures by late Monday or early Tuesday of the following week. Today's managers usually have terminals on their desks. They can type in their request at any time and call up the latest sales figures by territory. What used to take days to get can now be accessed in seconds.

Few areas of the manager's job have changed, and will continue to change, as rapidly as has management information systems. Technology is creating new options for managers at an unprecedented pace. Today's state-of-the-art system will almost certainly be antiquated in two or three years. The importance of management information systems and their rapid development require expanded discussion. Chapter 19 treats the issue of controlling information.

Organization Performance

Evaluations of an organization's overall performance or effectiveness are made regularly by a number of constituencies. Managers, of course, are concerned with their organization's performance, but they're not the only group that evaluates organizational effectiveness. Customers and clients make effectiveness judgments when they choose to do business with one firm rather than another. Security analysts, potential investors, potential lenders, and suppliers (especially those extending credit terms) also have to make effectiveness evaluations. In government, decisions as to which departments get budget increases or cuts are essentially effectiveness determinations. Even employees and potential employees evaluate an organization's effectiveness. When you decide to accept or reject a job offer from an organization, you undoubtedly consider effectiveness factors.

The facts above support the idea that managers should be concerned with controlling in order to maintain or improve their organization's overall effectiveness. But there is no singular measure of an organization's effectiveness. Productivity, efficiency, profit, morale, quality of output, flexibility, stability, and employee absenteeism are criteria that undoubtedly have an important bearing on an organization's overall effectiveness.[12] None, however, is synonymous with organizational effectiveness.[13] An organization's effectiveness can be assessed by any of three basic approaches.

organizational goals approach
Appraising an organization's effectiveness according to whether it accomplishes its goals.

The Organizational Goals Approach   The **organizational goals approach** states that an organization's effectiveness is appraised in terms of the accomplishment of ends rather than means.[14] It is the bottom line that counts. Popular organizational goals criteria include profit maximization, students educated per dollar, bringing the enemy to surrender, winning the basketball game, and restoring patients to good health. On the assumption that organizations are deliberately created to achieve one or more specified goals, the organizational goals approach makes a great deal of sense.

The problem with goals in the organization was elaborated upon in Chapter 7. Do we use official goals or actual goals? Whose goals? Short-term or long-term? Since organizations have multiple goals, how should they be ranked in importance? These problems are not insurmountable. If managers are willing to confront the complexities inherent in the organizational goals approach, they can obtain reasonably valid information for assessing an organization's effectiveness. However, it has been argued that there is more to organizational effectiveness than identifying and measuring specific ends. When managers give their sole attention to ends, they are likely to overlook the long-term health of the organization. An alternative is the systems approach.

The Systems Approach   We introduced the systems framework in Chapter 2. It was used to describe the organization as an entity that acquires inputs, engages in transformation processes, and generates outputs. Consistent with the systems perspective, it can be said that an organization should be judged on its ability to acquire inputs, process these inputs, channel the outputs, and maintain stability and balance. Outputs are the ends, whereas acquisition of inputs and processing efficiencies are means. If an organization is to survive over the long term, it must remain adaptive and healthy. The **systems approach to organizational effectiveness** focuses on those factors—means and ends—that can and do affect survival.[15]

systems approach to organizational effectiveness
Appraising an organization's effectiveness in terms of both means and ends.

The relevant criteria in the systems approach include market share, stability of earnings, employee absenteeism and turnover rates, growth in research and development expenditures, level of interunit conflicts, degree of employee satisfaction, and clarity of internal communications. Notice that the systems approach emphasizes factors that are important to the long-term health and survival of the organization but may not be critical in the short term. Research and development expenditures, for instance, are an investment in the future. Management can cut costs here and immediately increase profits or reduce losses. But the effect of this action will reduce the organization's viability in later years.

The major advantage to the systems approach is that it discourages management from looking for immediate results at the expense of future successes. They are less likely to make decisions that trade off the organization's long-term health and survival for goals that will make them look good in the near term. Another advantage of the systems approach is its applicability where goals are either very vague or defy measurement. Managers of public organizations, for instance, frequently use "ability to acquire budget increases" as a measure of effectiveness—that is, they substitute an input criterion for an output criterion.

strategic constituencies approach
Appraising an organization's effectiveness according to how well the organization satisfies the demands of its key constituencies.

The Strategic Constituencies Approach   The third approach proposes that an effective organization satisfies the demands of those constituencies in its environment from whom it requires support for its continued existence.[16] We call this the **strategic constituencies approach.**

Most public universities consider effectiveness in terms of acquiring students but feel that they need not be concerned with potential *employers* of their graduates. Why? Because these universities' survival does not depend on whether or not their graduates get jobs. Administrators in public universities devote considerable effort to wooing state legislators. Failure to win legislators' support is sure to have adverse effects on the budget of a public university. In contrast, a private university's effectiveness is hardly affected by whether or not it has a favorable relationship with the key people in the state capital. Administrators in private universities direct their energies to lobbying for increased federally subsidized student loans and to romancing alumni, wealthy philanthropists, and foundations who might donate money to their schools. These are constituencies who significantly determine whether private universities survive.

The strategic constituencies approach is just as applicable to business firms as it is to universities. A corporation with a very strong cash position, for instance, need not be concerned with the effectiveness criteria that bankers use. However, assume that the company you head has $200 million in bank loans coming due in the next quarter and that you will have to ask the consortium of banks with whom these loans were made to restructure this indebtedness because your firm can't meet this deadline. In such a situation, the criteria these bankers use to measure your organization's effectiveness will undoubtedly be the ones you will emphasize. To do otherwise would threaten your organization's survival. So the effective organization is defined as one that successfully identifies its critical constituencies—customers, government agencies, financial institutions, security analysts, labor unions, and so forth—and then satisfies their demands.

Notice the assumptions underlying the strategic constituencies approach. It assumes that an organization is faced with frequent and competing demands from a variety of interest groups. Because these interest groups are of unequal importance,

Goodyear Tire & Rubber's strategic constituencies include suppliers of critical petroleum products used in the tire-manufacturing process; officers of the United Rubber Workers Union; officials at banks where the company has sizable short-term loans; government regulatory agencies that grade tires and inspect facilities for safety violations; securities analysts at major brokerage firms who specialize in the tire-and-rubber industry; regional tire jobbers and distributors; and purchasing agents at General Motors, Mack Truck, and other vehicle manufacturers that are responsible for acquisition of tires.

effectiveness is determined by the organization's ability to identify its critical or strategic constituencies and to satisfy the demands they place upon the organization. Further, this approach assumes that managers pursue a number of goals and that the goals selected represent a response to those interest groups who control the resources necessary for the organization to survive.

While the strategic constituencies approach makes a lot of sense, it is not easy for managers to put into action. The task of separating the strategic constituencies from the larger environment is very difficult in practice. Because the environment changes rapidly, what was critical to the organization yesterday might not be so today. Even if the constituencies in the environment can be identified and are assumed to be relatively stable, what separates the "strategic" constituencies from the "almost strategic" constituencies? These problems are real for managers attempting to satisfy their strategic constituencies. Regardless of the difficulty of the task, it can pay big dividends. By using the strategic constituencies approach, managers decrease the likelihood that they might ignore or severely upset a group whose power could significantly hinder the organization's operations. If management knows whose support is necessary to the health of the organization, it can modify its preference ordering of goals to reflect the changing power relationships with its strategic constituencies.

MANAGERS WHO MADE A DIFFERENCE

Preston Smith at S-K-I Ltd.

Running ski resorts is no vacation nowadays. In 1980 there were 1100 ski area operators in the United States. In 1989 there were only half that many. Industry problems have included reduced growth because of the aging of the baby boomers, rapidly escalating costs for ski tickets and lodging, a number of mild winters in recent years, and the management challenge of keeping tabs on employees spread over several square miles of mountainside. One person who has weathered the industry's problems is Preston Smith, chief executive officer of S-K-I Ltd.[17] His firm operates popular Vermont ski areas at Killington and Mt. Snow, as well as Southern California's largest ski area at Bear Mountain.

Smith has invested heavily to develop special snow-making equipment that covers a lot more terrain than the average resort. "We've virtually eliminated our dependence on snow," says Smith. He has also devised a computerized control system that allows S-K-I's management to closely monitor operations, to quickly identify problems and to just as quickly move to correct problems. For example, he can rapidly identify changing demand patterns and shift workers to where they are needed.

Smith's actions have paid handsome dividends. By 1988 his S-K-I Ltd. had racked up record earnings for eight years running. In 1988 alone the price of his firm's stock increased 50 percent.

Photo courtesy of Preston Smith.

DESIGNING THE CONTROL SYSTEM

Let us look, finally, at how control systems are designed. Two questions are critical to developing such a system: What qualities should an effective system have? What contingency factors need to be considered in selecting the right control system?

Qualities of an Effective Control System

Effective control systems tend to have certain qualities in common. The importance of these qualities varies with the situation, but we can generalize that the following characteristics should make a control system more effective:

1. *Accuracy.* A control system that generates inaccurate information can result in management failing to take action when it should or responding to a problem that doesn't exist. An accurate control system is reliable and produces valid data.

2. *Timeliness.* Controls should call management's attention to variations in time to prevent serious infringement on a unit's performance. The best information has little value if it is dated. Therefore, an effective control system must provide timely information. The importance of minimizing surveillance lag is emphasized by the comments of one department manager in an insurance company: "My boss is particularly concerned that I keep my departmental duplicating costs within budget. That's fine, except that there is a four-month delay between the end of a month and my receipt of that month's expense summary report. By the time I get the first three or four reports and find I'm going over budget, two-thirds of the budget year is gone, and it's too late to correct it."

3. *Economy.* A control system must be economically reasonable to operate. Any system of control has to justify the benefits that it gives in relation to the costs it incurs. To minimize costs, management should try to impose the least amount of control that is necessary to produce the desired results. For instance, one accounting manager in a manufacturing firm believed that a number of the control reports his office generated were not being effectively used. To test his thesis, he instructed his staff to omit all control reports during one thirty-day period. A full 40 percent of the omissions received not even a query. For those 40 percent, he omitted the report for another month. A few complaints were registered, and these reports were then transmitted. The result was that, six months later, a quarter of the department's control reports had been eliminated.

4. *Flexibility.* Effective controls must be flexible enough to adjust to adverse change or to take advantage of new opportunities. Few organizations face environments so stable that there is no need for flexibility. Even highly mechanistic structures require controls that can be adjusted as times and conditions change.

5. *Understandability.* Controls that cannot be understood have no value. It is sometimes necessary, therefore, to substitute less complex controls for sophisticated devices. A control system that is difficult to understand can cause unnecessary mistakes, frustrates employees, and is eventually ignored.

6. *Reasonable criteria.* Control standards must be reasonable and attainable. If they are too high or unreasonable, they no longer motivate. Since most employees don't want to risk being labeled incompetent for telling superiors that they ask too much, employees may resort to unethical or illegal shortcuts. Controls should, therefore, enforce standards that are reasonable; they should challenge and stretch people to reach higher performance levels without being demotivating or encouraging deception.

7. *Strategic placement.* Management can't control everything that goes on in an organization. Even if it could, the benefits couldn't justify the costs. As a result, managers should place controls on those factors that are strategic to the organization's performance. Controls should cover the critical activities, operations, and events within the organization. That is, they should focus on where variations from standard are most likely to occur or where a variation would do the greatest harm. In a department where labor costs are $20,000 a month and postage costs are $50 a month, a 5 percent overrun in the former is more critical than a 20 percent overrun in the latter. Hence we should establish controls for labor and a critical dollar allocation, whereas postage expenses would not appear to be critical.

8. *Emphasis on the exception.* Since managers can't control all activities, they should place their strategic control devices where they can call attention only to the exceptions. An exception system ensures that a manager is not overwhelmed by information on variations from standard. For instance, if management policy gives supervisors the authority to give annual raises up to $200 a month, approve individual expenses up to $500, and make capital expenditures up to $5,000, then only deviations above these amounts require approval from higher levels of management. These checkpoints become controls that are part of the authority constraints and free higher levels of management from reviewing routine expenditures.

9. *Multiple criteria.* Managers and employees alike will seek to "look good" on the criteria that are controlled. If management controls by using a single measure such as unit profit, effort will be focused only on looking good on this standard. Multiple measures of performance decrease this narrow focus.

    Multiple criteria have a dual positive effect. Since they are more difficult to manipulate than a single measure, they can discourage efforts to merely look good. Additionally, since performance can rarely be objectively evaluated from a single indicator, multiple criteria make possible more accurate assessments of performance.

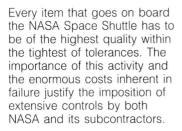

Every item that goes on board the NASA Space Shuttle has to be of the highest quality within the tightest of tolerances. The importance of this activity and the enormous costs inherent in failure justify the imposition of extensive controls by both NASA and its subcontractors.

10. *Corrective action.* An effective control system not only indicates when a significant deviation from standard occurs, but also suggests what action should be taken to correct the deviation. That is, it ought to both point out the problem and specify the solution. This is frequently accomplished by establishing *if-then guidelines;* for instance, *if* unit revenues drop more than 5 percent, *then* unit costs should be reduced by a similar amount.

Contingency Factors to Consider

While these generalizations about effective control systems provide good guidelines, their validity is influenced by situational factors. Let's look at a few key contingency variables you should keep in mind when choosing a control system appropriate to your situation. (See Table 18–3.)

Size of the Organization   Control systems should vary according to the size of the organization. A small business relies on informal and more personal control devices. Concurrent control through direct supervision is probably most cost efficient. As an organization increases in size, direct supervision is likely to be supported by an expanding formal system. Very large organizations rely on highly formalized and impersonal feedforward and feedback controls.

Position and Level in the Organization   The higher up in the organization a person is, the greater the need for a multiple set of control criteria. This reflects the increased ambiguity in measuring performance as a person moves up the hierarchy. Conversely, lower-level jobs have clearer definitions of performance, which allow for a more narrow interpretation of job performance. Controls should also be tailored to reflect a unit's goals. The criteria and measurement techniques used to evaluate the sales department are inappropriate for the engineering department. Flexibility requires that controls be adjusted both within and between units.

TABLE 18–3 Contingency Factors in the Design of Control Systems

Contingency Variable		Control Recommendations
Size of the organization	Small	Informal, personal, management by walking around
	Large	Formal, impersonal, extensive rules and regulations
Position and level	High	Many criteria
	Low	Few, easy-to-measure criteria
Degree of decentralization	High	Increase number and breadth of controls
	Low	Reduce number of controls
Organizational culture	Open and supportive	Informal, self-control
	Threatening	Formal, externally imposed controls
Importance of the activity	High	Elaborate, comprehensive controls
	Low	Loose, informal controls

Degree of Decentralization   The greater the degree of decentralization, the more managers need feedback on the performance of subordinate decision makers. Since managers who delegate authority are ultimately responsible for the actions of those to whom it is delegated, they will want proper assurance that their subordinates' decisions are both effective and efficient. If authority is centralized, feedback controls are not as essential.

Organizational Culture   The organizational culture may be one of trust, autonomy, and openness or one of fear and reprisal. In the former we can expect to find more informal, self-control measures, and in the latter, more externally imposed and formal control systems. As is the case with leadership styles, motivation techniques, degree of structuring, conflict management techniques, and the extent to which orga-

MANAGING FROM A GLOBAL PERSPECTIVE

Adjusting Controls for National Differences

Methods of controlling people and operations can be quite different in foreign countries. For the multinational corporation, managers of foreign operations tend to be less closely controlled by the head office, if for no other reason than that distance precludes direct controls. The head office of a multinational must rely on extensive formal reports to maintain control. But collecting data that are comparable between countries introduces problems for multinationals. A company's factory in Mexico might produce the same products as its factory in the United States. The Mexican factory, however, might be much more labor intensive than its counterpart in the United States (to take advantage of low labor costs in Mexico). If headquarters' executives were to control costs by, for example, calculating labor costs per unit or output per worker, the figures would not be comparable. Therefore distance creates a tendency to formalize controls, and technological differences often make control data uncomparable.

Technology's impact on control is most evident in comparing technologically advanced nations with more primitive countries. Organizations in technologically advanced nations such as the United States, Japan, Canada, Great Britain, Germany, and Australia use indirect control devices—particularly computer-related reports and analyses—in addition to standardized rules and direct supervision, to ensure that activities are going as planned. In Tanzania, Zambia, Lebanon, and other less advanced countries, direct supervision and highly centralized decision making are the basic means of control.

Constraints on managerial corrective action may also affect managers in foreign countries. For example, laws in some countries do not allow management the options of closing plants, laying off personnel, taking money out of the country, or bringing in a new management team from outside the country.

nization members participate in decision making, the type and extent of controls should be consistent with the organizational culture.

Importance of the Activity The importance of an activity influences whether and how it will be controlled. If control is costly and the repercussions from error small, the control system is not likely to be elaborated. However, if an error can be highly damaging to the organization, extensive controls are likely to be implemented, even if the cost is high.

SUMMARY

This summary is organized by the chapter-opening learning objectives found on page 563.

1. Control is the process of monitoring activities to ensure that they are being accomplished as planned and of correcting any significant deviations.

2. Control is important because it monitors whether objectives are being accomplished as planned and delegated authority is being abused.

3. The control process is made up of three steps: measuring actual performance, comparing actual performance against a standard, and managerial action.

4. If a performance is at variance with the standard, managers have three options: They can move to correct the performance, they can revise the standard, or they can conclude that the variance is not significant and do nothing.

5. There are three types of control: Feedforward control is future directed and prevents anticipated problems. Concurrent control takes place while an activity is in progress. Feedback control takes place after the activity.

6. Most control efforts are directed at one of these areas: people, finances, operations, information, or total organization performance.

7. The goals approach assesses effectiveness in terms of the accomplishment of ends. If the organization achieves its goals, it is effective. The systems approach assesses both means and ends. The systems approach is more comprehensive and takes a longer-term perspective than the goals approach.

8. The strategic constituencies approach requires the organization to satisfy the demands of those constituencies in the environment from whom the organization requires support for its continued existence. Management must identify its strategic constituencies, determine their effectiveness criteria, and then ensure that the organization satisfies these criteria.

9. An effective control system is accurate, timely, economical, flexible, and understandable. It uses reasonable criteria, has strategic placement, emphasizes the exception, uses multiple criteria, and suggests corrective action.

10. The key contingency variables that influence the design of a control system are organization size, managerial position and level, degree of decentralization, organizational culture, and importance of the activity.

REVIEW QUESTIONS

1. What is the role of control in management?
2. How are planning and control linked?

3. What are the steps in the control process?

4. Why is *what* is measured probably more crucial to the control process than *how* it is measured?

5. Name four methods managers can use to acquire information.

6. Are all deviations from standard relevant to a manager? Why or why not?

7. Contrast *immediate* and *basic* corrective action.

8. What are the advantages and disadvantages of feedback control?

9. How can management determine whether or not the organization is effective?

10. What does it mean when we say that control should "emphasize the exception"?

DISCUSSION QUESTIONS

1. "Basic corrective action is always preferable to immediate corrective action." Do you agree or disagree with this statement? Support your position.

2. Since a manager cannot control everything, what should guide his or her decision concerning what should be controlled?

3. "The more controls there are in an organization, the greater the likelihood that it will be effective." Do you agree or disagree with this statement? Discuss.

4. Using the strategic constituencies approach, what criteria would you expect the following organizations to emphasize:
   a. A local grocery store chain
   b. Mobil Oil
   c. The New York Public Library
   d. The U.S. Department of Defense

5. "For a business firm, the bottom line is profit. You don't need any other measure of effectiveness." Build an argument to support this statement. Then build an argument to refute this statement.

SELF-ASSESSMENT EXERCISE

How Willing Are You to Give Up Control?

Instructions: You can get a good idea of whether you are willing to give up enough control to be effective in delegating by responding to the following items. If you have limited work experience, base your answers on what you know about yourself and your personal beliefs. Indicate the extent to which you agree or disagree by circling the number following each statement.

	Strongly Agree				Strongly Disagree
1. I'd delegate more, but the jobs I delegate never seem to get done the way I want them to be done.	5	4	3	2	1
2. I don't feel I have the time to delegate properly.	5	4	3	2	1
3. I carefully check on subordinates' work without letting them know I'm doing it, so I can correct their mistakes if necessary before they cause too many problems.	5	4	3	2	1
4. I delegate the whole job—giving the opportunity for the subordinate to complete it without any of my involvement. Then I review the result.	5	4	3	2	1
5. When I have given clear instructions and the task isn't done right, I get upset.	5	4	3	2	1
6. I feel the staff lacks the commitment that I have. So any task I delegate won't get done as well as I'd do it.	5	4	3	2	1
7. I'd delegate more, but I feel I can do the task better than the person I might delegate it to.	5	4	3	2	1
8. I'd delegate more, but if the individual I delegate the task to does an incompetent job, I'll be severely criticized.	5	4	3	2	1
9. If I were to delegate a task, my job wouldn't be nearly as much fun.	5	4	3	2	1
10. When I delegate a task, I often find that the outcome is such that I end up doing the task over again myself.	5	4	3	2	1
11. I have not really found that delegation saves any time.	5	4	3	2	1
12. I delegate a task clearly and concisely, explaining exactly how it should be accomplished.	5	4	3	2	1

	Strongly Agree				Strongly Disagree
13. I can't delegate as much as I'd like to because my subordinates lack the necessary experience.	5	4	3	2	1
14. I feel that when I delegate I lose control.	5	4	3	2	1
15. I would delegate more but I'm pretty much a perfectionist.	5	4	3	2	1
16. I work longer hours than I should.	5	4	3	2	1
17. I can give subordinates the routine tasks, but I feel I must do nonroutine tasks myself.	5	4	3	2	1
18. My own boss expects me to keep very close to all details of my job.	5	4	3	2	1

Turn to page 677 for scoring directions and key.

CASE APPLICATION 18A

Chuck's Parking

If you were having a party in Hollywood or Beverly Hills, you would want to be sure the "name people" were there: Jack Nicholson, Madonna, Johnny Carson, Chuck Pick. Chuck Pick? Of course! You can't have a party without parking attendants, and Chuck Pick is *the* name in parking in southern California. Chuck's Parking employs more than 100 people, mostly part time, to park cars at the dozens of parties he handles in any given week. On a busy Saturday night, his service might be handling half a dozen parties simultaneously, with three to fifteen attendants working each.

Chuck's Parking is a big small business. It grosses nearly a million dollars a year. It is composed of two elements: parking for private parties and an ongoing contract to handle the parking concession at an exclusive country club. The country club requires two to three attendants, seven days a week. However, the bulk of Chuck's business is the private parties. He spends his days visiting the homes of the rich and famous, evaluating their driveways and parking facilities and then telling them how many attendants he will need to handle their get-together. A small party might require only three or four attendants, with a bill of $400 or so. However, it's not unusual for a large party to run up a $2,000 parking tab.

While the private parties and the country club concession both involve the parking of cars, the ways they generate revenues for Chuck are very different. The parties are done on a bid basis. Chuck estimates the number of attendants necessary to do the job right, he prices them out at so much an hour, and he gives the customer his total price. If the customer "buys" his service, he mails a bill for payment after the party. At the country club, Chuck's contract calls for him to pay the club a fixed monthly rent to operate his concession. His income is derived solely from the tips his attendants receive. So while he absolutely allows none of his attendants at private parties to accept tips, this is the only source of revenue for his country club operation.

Questions

1. Do Chuck's problems differ in the two operations? Explain.

2. Should he employ different controls for the two operations? If so, what controls?

3. For the country club, give examples of each type of control that Chuck might use, as follows:
   a. feedforward
   b. concurrent
   c. feedback

4. For the private parties, give examples of each type of control that Chuck might use, as follows:
   a. feedforward
   b. concurrent
   c. feedback

CASE APPLICATION 18B

The New Mayor

"I took office six weeks ago," the new mayor began, "and I'll be honest—I haven't the slightest idea of what is going on in this city. What surprises me the most, I guess, is that things *are* as bad as I'd been saying in my campaign speeches!"

The mayor of this community of 200,000 people continued, "I was a business executive for nearly thirty years. I know how things are supposed to be! And one thing I know for sure is that if you're gonna run an organization properly, you've got to have decent information on what's happening. That information just isn't here. For instance, I don't know how much of this year's budget each department has spent, and neither do they. Monthly expense reports are issued at least six months *after* the month ends! Can you believe it—getting a report on February's expenses in August? What can you do about it *then?* But that's the good news! The bad news is that there are no mechanisms in the system to tell me how well departments are performing. I don't know if waste collection is being done, never mind whether it's being done effectively and efficiently. The same goes for police and fire protection, snow removal, health care, recreational facilities, and so on. The only feedback I get is nasty phone calls when someone has a complaint. The problem is immense. I really don't know where to begin."

Questions

1. If you were the mayor, what questions would you be asking?
2. Describe the type of controls you would install if you were mayor.

19

INFORMATION CONTROL SYSTEMS

1. Define a management information system (MIS).
2. Differentiate between data and information.
3. Contrast the four directions in which communication can flow.
4. Identify five common communication networks.
5. Compare centralized and end-user systems.
6. Explain the value of networking.
7. Explain why more information is not always better.
8. Outline the key elements in designing an MIS.
9. Explain how an MIS can relate to an organization's strategy.
10. Describe how an MIS changes power relationships in an organization.
11. Identify ways in which MIS's are changing the supervisor's job.
12. Explain how MIS's are changing communication in organizations.

The thousands of cash registers in the 313 U.S. Toys "R" Us stores are all linked to the company's central computers at its New Jersey headquarters.[1] Each day, all information on every sale in every store is transmitted to these central computers. This system allows managers to know every morning exactly how many of each item was sold the day before. It also tells the manager how many have been sold in the year to date and in the prior year. Most reordering is done automatically by the computers without any communications by managers. This system allows Toys "R" Us to try out toys without committing to big orders in advance. It also provides managers with almost instantaneous information on what's hot and what's not.

You call Federal Express to pick up a package. The carrier arrives, fills out a form and sticks a bar-code label on the package, and then uses a portable device to read the bar code. This begins the package's odyssey through Federal Express's state-of-the-art information system.[2] Each time your package is transferred—from truck to clearing station to truck again to airplane to the central clearing hub in Memphis to another plane to destination clearing station to delivery truck to the final destination—its bar code is read, and that information is transmitted to Federal Express's central computer. This continuous-tracking information system helps Federal Express to process and deliver nearly 900,000 packages every day; 99.5 percent of them arrive at their destination by 10:30 A.M. the day after they are sent. Moreover, this system allows management to be able to tell a customer, at any time, precisely where his or her package is.

Tim Casey is a sales representative for Kawasaki Motors Corp. He sells bikes, moto-crossers, all-terrain vehicles, and jet skis to thirty-seven dealers in Oregon, Washington, and Alaska.[3] Kawasaki provides Casey and all of its other salespeople with eleven-pound laptop computers. His computer allows Casey to do things he could never do when the telephone and weekly reports were his basic control tools. Before laptops, "I'd call in to ask about a product and they'd tell me there are ten left," Casey remembers. "But in fact, eight of those would be on back order. So I'd sell ten and only be able to ship two." Now Casey taps into the mainframe computer at Kawasaki headquarters in southern California before he leaves his Seattle home. He scans inventory and orders. For customers on whom he plans to call that day, he checks which vehicles and parts are selling well. For slow-moving items he can review sales of other customers in his territory to see whether he can move these items to another dealer. Since every Kawasaki dealer has to provide the company with regular financial data, and that data is on the company's main computer, Casey can also use his laptop to closely monitor his dealers' financial condition. If there's a problem, Casey will be one of the first to know about it. Wasting time trying to sell to dealers whose orders won't be approved is now a thing of the past for Tim Casey.

Toys "R" Us computers identified early the popularity of Cabbage Patch Kids dolls, and management was able to reorder promptly. Therefore it had dolls to sell when its competitors were out of stock. These same computers also gave management an early warning that the Trivial Pursuit fad was fading, allowing the company to quickly work down its inventory.

As these cases illustrate, sophisticated information systems are changing the way organizations do business. In this chapter, we'll introduce the concept of management information systems, explain how they have evolved in organizations and what's entailed in designing an effective information system, and show the dramatic ways in which they are affecting the manager's job and changing organizational communication. As you'll see, technology is totally changing the way managers receive, use, and transmit information.

WHAT IS A MANAGEMENT INFORMATION SYSTEM?

management information systems (MIS)
A system that provides management with needed information on a regular basis.

While there is no universally agreed-upon definition for a **management information system (MIS),** we'll define the term as a system to provide management with needed information on a regular basis.[4] In theory, this system can be manual or computer based, although all current discussion, including ours, focuses on computer-supported applications. Table 19-1 provides the primary terminology you'll need for understanding the present uses of computers as decision and control tools in organizations.

The term *system* in MIS implies order, arrangement, and purpose. Further, an MIS focuses specifically on providing management with *information,* not merely *data.* These two points are important and require elaboration.

A library provides a good analogy. Although it can contain millions of volumes, a library doesn't do users much good if they can't *find* what they want *quickly.* That's why libraries spend a lot of time cataloging their collections and ensuring that volumes are returned to their proper locations. Organizations today are like well-stocked libraries. There is no scarcity of data. The scarcity is in the ability to process it so that the right information is available to the right person when he or she needs it.[5] A library is almost useless if it has the book you want, but you can't find it or takes a week to retrieve it from storage. An MIS, on the other hand, has organized data in some meaningful way and can access the information in a reasonable amount of time.

data
Raw, unanalyzed facts.

Data is raw, unanalyzed facts such as numbers, names, or quantities. But as data, these facts are relatively useless to managers.[6] When data is analyzed and processed, it becomes **information.** An MIS collects data and turns it into relevant information for managers to use. Figure 19-1 summarizes these observations.

information
Analyzed and processed data.

LINKING INFORMATION AND ORGANIZATIONAL COMMUNICATION

Management information systems are obviously closely linked with the topic of communication. In Chapter 16, we reviewed *interpersonal* communication, but there is still the important subject of *organizational* communication to consider. Before we discuss the evolution and current status of management information systems, let's review several key terms and concepts related to organizational communication. As you'll see by the end of this chapter, an MIS is an essential element in organizational communications, and computerization is significantly changing organizational communication practices.

FIGURE 19-1
MIS Makes Data Usable

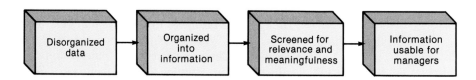

TABLE 19–1   Contemporary Computer Terminology

hardware   Physical equipment that performs input, output, processing, and storage functions.

software   A collective name for programs that instruct a computer on how to perform a particular task.

input devices   The means by which data and instructions are fed into a computer. The keyboard is the most common input device today.

output devices   The means by which a computer supplies information to a user. Monitors or video display terminals present output on a televisionlike screen. Printers produce a permanent output on paper.

central processing unit   The "brain" of a computer; it contains the main memory and controls the flow of operations.

peripheral device   Any hardware other than the central processing unit.

byte   One memory position that usually holds one alphabetic character or digit. A computer with a 128K memory can store approximately 128,000 characters.

megabyte   1,024,000 bytes.

disk   A form of storage that can be built into or attached to a computer.

modem   A device that links a computer to a telephone line and allows it to send and receive data from other computers.

Formal Versus Informal Communication

formal communication
Communication that follows the authority chain of command or that is necessary to do a job.

In Chapter 13, we differentiated between formal and informal groups. We can do the same with communication. **Formal communication** refers to communication that follows the authority chain of command or is part of the communications required to do one's job. When a boss makes a request of a subordinate, he or she is communicating formally, as does the employee who takes a problem to his or her superior.

A phone call to a friend in another department might get an answer to a question in five minutes. To get that same information through formal channels might require three levels of management and several days' time. Thus informal communication can act as a support system to the formal channels.

informal communication
Communication that is not approved by management and not defined by the structural hierarchy.

Formal communication also occurs when two shipping clerks must interact to coordinate a customer's order.

Informal communications arise to meet needs that are not satisfied by formal communication. These communications are not approved by management, and there is no predetermined structural hierarchy by which they are defined. However, the lack of management sanction does not mean that informal communications do not exist. Employees form friendships, and cliques develop. These in turn allow employees to fill in communication gaps within the formal channels. The informal communication system therefore serves two purposes. It permits employees to satisfy their need for social interaction. It can also improve an organization's performance by creating alternative, and frequently faster and more efficient, channels through which to communicate.

Direction of Communication Flow

Organizational communication can flow downward, upward, laterally, or diagonally. Let's look at each.

downward communication
Communication that flows from a manager down the authority hierarchy.

Downward   Any communication that flows from a manager down the authority hierarchy is a **downward communication.** When we think of managers communicating with subordinates, we usually think of a downward pattern. Downward communication is used to inform, direct, coordinate, and evaluate subordinates. When managers assign goals to subordinates, they are using downward communication. They are also using it when they provide subordinates with job descriptions, inform them of organizational policies and procedures, point out problems that need attention, or evaluate their performance. But downward communication doesn't have to involve oral or face-to-face contact. The sending of letters to employees' homes to advise them of the organization's new sick leave policy is also a downward communication.

upward communication
Communication that flows from below to higher-level managers.

Upward   Managers rely on those below them for information. Reports are sent upward in the authority hierarchy to inform higher management of progress toward goals and current problems. **Upward communication** keeps managers aware of how employees feel about their jobs, their co-workers, and the organization in general. Managers also rely on upward communication for ideas on how things can be improved.

The extent of upward communication, particularly that which is initiated at the lowest level, depends on the organizational culture. If management has created a climate of trust and respect, there is likely to be extensive use of participative decision making. There will be considerable upward communication as employees provide input to decisions. In a highly authoritarian environment, upward communication still takes place, but it is limited to the managerial ranks and to providing control information to upper management.

Some examples of upward communication include performance reports prepared by lower management for review by middle and upper management, suggestion boxes, employee attitude surveys, grievance procedures, superior-subordinate discussions, and informal "gripe" sessions in which employees have the opportunity to identify and discuss problems with their boss or representatives of upper management.

lateral communication
Communication among members of work groups, among managers, or among any horizontally equivalent personnel.

Lateral   Communication that takes place among members of the same work group, among members of work groups at the same level, among managers at the same level, or among any horizontally equivalent personnel is called **lateral communication.**

As implied in our discussion of formal and informal communication, horizontal communications are often necessary to save time and facilitate coordination. In some cases, these lateral relationships are formally sanctioned. In others, they are informally created to short-circuit the vertical hierarchy and expedite action. Lateral communications can, from management's viewpoint, be good or bad. Since strict adherence to the formal vertical structure for all communications can impede the efficient and accurate transfer of information, lateral communications can be beneficial. In such cases, they occur with the knowledge and support of superiors. However, they can create dysfunctional conflicts when the formal vertical channels are breached, when members go above or around their superiors to get things done, or when bosses find out that actions have been taken or decisions made without their knowledge.

diagonal communication
Communication that cuts across functions and levels in an organization.

Diagonal   **Diagonal communication** cuts across functions and levels in an organization. When a supervisor in the credit department communicates directly with a regional marketing manager, who is not only in a different department but also at a higher level in the organization, they are engaged in diagonal communication.

A major problem with this form of communication is that it departs from the normal chain of command. In the above example, the credit supervisor should notify his or her boss in order to avoid later surprises and to adhere to the chain of command. To minimize gaps, most diagonal communications also encompass a vertical communication to superiors or subordinates who have been bypassed.

Given the potential for problems, why would individuals resort to diagonal communication? The answer is efficiency and speed. In some situations, bypassing vertical and horizontal channels expedites action and prevents others from being used merely as conduits between senders and receivers.

Communication Networks

communication networks
Vertical and horizontal communication patterns.

The vertical and horizontal dimensions in organizational communications can be combined into a variety of patterns, or into what is referred to as **communication networks.** Most studies of communication networks have taken place in groups created in a laboratory setting. As a result, the research conclusions have limited application because of the artificial settings and the small groups used. Five common networks are shown in Figure 19-2; these are the chain, Y, wheel, circle, and all-channel networks. To treat the networks shown in the figure in an organizational context, let's assume that the organization has only five members.

Five Common Networks   Referring to Figure 19-2, the *chain network* represents a five-level vertical hierarchy in which communications can move only upward or downward. In an organization, this type of network would be found in direct-line authority relations with no deviations. For example, the payroll clerk reports to the payroll supervisor, who in turn reports to the general accounting manager, who reports to the plant controller, who reports to the plant manager. These five individuals would represent a chain network.

If we turn the Y *network* upside down, we can see two subordinates reporting to a manager, with two levels of authority above the manager. This is, in effect, a four-level hierarchy.

Looking at the *wheel diagram* as if we were standing above the network, we see that the wheel represents four subordinates who report to a manager. There is no interaction between the subordinates. All communications are channeled through the manager.

The *circle network* allows members to interact with adjoining members, but no further. It would represent a three-level hierarchy in which there is vertical communication between superiors and subordinates and lateral communication only at the lowest level.

FIGURE 19-2   Common Communication Networks

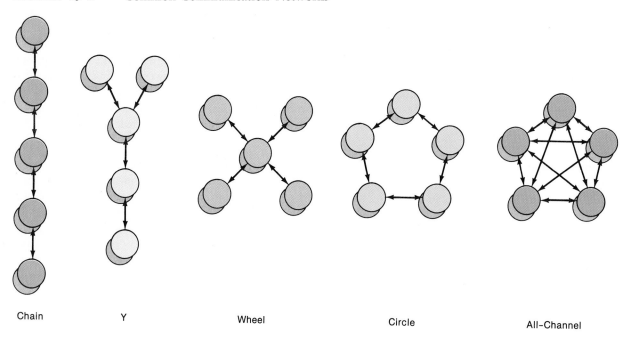

Chain   Y   Wheel   Circle   All-Channel

Finally, the *all-channel network* allows each of the members to communicate freely with the other four. Of the networks discussed, it is the least structured. There are no restrictions; all members are equal. This network is best illustrated by a committee in which no one member formally or informally assumes a dominant or take-charge position. All members are free to share their viewpoints.

Evaluation of Network Effectiveness   As a manager, which network should you use? The answer depends on your goal.

Table 19-2 summarizes the effectiveness of the various networks according to four criteria: speed, accuracy, the probability that a leader will emerge, and the level of morale among members. One observation is immediately apparent: No single network is best for all occasions. If speed is important, the wheel and all-channel networks are preferred. The chain, Y, and wheel score high on accuracy. The structure of the wheel facilitates the emergence of a leader. The circle and all-channel networks promote high employee satisfaction.

TABLE 19–2   Networks and Evaluation Criteria

	Networks				
Criteria	***Chain***	***Y***	***Wheel***	***Circle***	***All-Channel***
Speed	Moderate	Moderate	Fast	Slow	Fast
Accuracy	High	High	High	Low	Moderate
Emergence of leader	Moderate	Moderate	High	None	None
Morale	Moderate	Moderate	Low	High	High

Source: Adapted from Alex Bavelas and Dermot Barrett, "An Experimental Approach to Organizational Communication," *Personnel,* March 1951, p. 370.

grapevine

The informal communication network.

An Informal Network: The Grapevine   The previous discussion of networks emphasized formal communication patterns. Let's take a look at how communications travel along the informal network—more specifically, the well-known **grapevine.**

The grapevine is active in almost all organizations, and there appear to be patterns to this form of communication. Figure 19-3 illustrates four patterns that the grapevine can take. The *single strand* is the way in which most people view the grapevine. However, the evidence indicates that the *cluster* is the most popular pattern that grapevine communications take.[7] That is, a few people are active communicators on the grapevine. As a rule, only about 10 percent of the people in an organization act as liaisons who pass on information to more than one other person. Which individuals are active on the grapevine often depends on the message. A message that sparks the interest of an employee may stimulate him or her to tell someone else. However, another message that is perceived to be of lesser interest may never be transmitted further.

Can the grapevine be used to management's benefit? The answer is Yes. Given that only a small number of employees typically pass information to more than one other person, managers can analyze grapevine information and predict its flow. Certain messages are likely to follow predictable patterns. Managers might even consider using the grapevine informally to transmit information to specific individuals by "planting" messages with key people who are active on the grapevine and are likely to find a given message worth passing on.

Managers should not lose sight of the grapevine's value for identifying issues that employees consider important and that create anxiety among them. It acts as both a filter and feedback mechanism, picking up issues that employees consider relevant

FIGURE 19-3   Grapevine Patterns

Source: Keith Davis and John W. Newstrom, *Human Behavior at Work: Organizational Behavior,* 7th ed. (New York: McGraw-Hill, 1985), p. 317. Reproduced with permission.

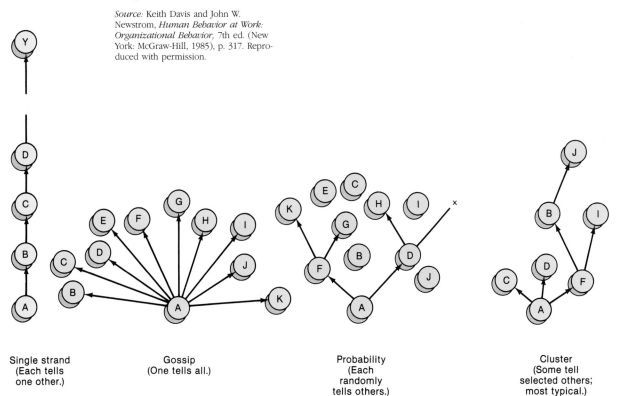

Single strand
(Each tells
one other.)

Gossip
(One tells all.)

Probability
(Each
randomly
tells others.)

Cluster
(Some tell
selected others;
most typical.)

IN PRACTICE

The Typical Manager's Day-to-Day Communications

Managers are often considered to be reflective planners, responding efficiently to a smooth, uninterrupted flow of messages. It's assumed that they carefully schedule their time to minimize interruptions and that they block out large segments of time to focus on high-priority activities. Studies of day-to-day managerial work find a very different reality. Diaries and observations of managerial activities reveal three interesting findings about communications.[8]

1. *Managers are busy.* The typical manager's day is made up of hundreds of separate incidents. The number of these incidents is usually greater at lower management levels. Instead of planning their days in great detail, managers react to events and people.
2. *Managerial work is fragmented.* Interruptions are frequent in managerial work, allowing little time to be devoted to any single activity. Tasks are completed quickly. Senior managers spend half their time on activities that require less than nine minutes.
3. *Managers rely on oral communication.* Managers spend most of their time communicating verbally on the telephone, in meetings, or in one-on-one personal contacts.

Taken together, these findings remind us that a manager's day-to-day communications are made up of literally dozens of brief encounters punctuated by constant interruptions. At any given moment, a manager might be reading correspondence, involved in a phone conversation, participating in a formal or informal meeting, taking an observational tour, or cornered in a hallway and forced to listen to a disgruntled subordinate. The effective manager learns to differentiate important messages from the unimportant and not let the constant disruptions deter him or her from the pursuit of paramount goals.

and planting messages that employees want passed on to upper management. For instance, the grapevine can tap employee concerns. If a rumor of a mass layoff is spreading along the grapevine and management knows the rumor to be totally false, the message still has meaning. It reflects the fears and concerns of employees and hence should not be ignored by management.

THE EVOLUTION OF MANAGEMENT INFORMATION SYSTEMS

MIS's have come a long way in the last four-plus decades. Most of this progress is a direct result of improvements in computing power. The trend has been toward smaller, faster, and cheaper technology. In 1946, there was one computer in the United States. It weighed 30 tons and had 18,000 vacuum tubes and 70,000 resistors. The computing power that in 1966 took a roomful of equipment and cost $15 million is available today on a $10 microprocessor chip that's only a quarter of an inch square.[9]

Table 19-3 describes the four-stage evolution of MIS. Beginning in 1954, it reflects extraordinary changes. In fact, only in stage four have MIS's reached their full potential as integrated and coordinated information systems.

Stage 1: Centralized Data Processing

The first computer was installed for a business application in 1954.[10] For all intents and purposes, that date marks the beginning of what is now MIS.

Until the mid-1960s, management information systems involved the processing of routine data for payroll, billing, accounting, and similar clerical functions. Because of its narrow focus, responsibility for overseeing an MIS tended to lie with an organization's financial controller's office.

Centralized data processing was characterized by **batch processing**—that is, transactions were stored and processed all at one time. This, of course, limited any MIS usage. Centralized data processing was fine for producing monthly accounting reports, but it was incapable of giving managers any current information on organizational activities. It wasn't until Stage 2 that organizations began to use **real-time processing,** which allowed data to be continually updated as transactions occurred.

Stage 2: Management-Focused Data Processing

The period between 1965 and 1979 saw centralized data processing expand by providing support information for management and operational activities. Information sys-

batch processing
Storing data and processing them all at the same time.

real-time processing
The continuous updating of data as transactions occur.

TABLE 19–3
The Evolution of Management Information Systems

Stage	Approximate Time Period	Description
1. Centralized data processing	1954–1964	Accounting and clerical applications
2. Management-focused data processing	1965–1979	Direct support for management and operational functions
3. Decentralized end-user computing	1980–1985	Personal computers under the direct control of users
4. Interactive networks	1986–	Linking of individual end-users

Large, centralized mainframe computers, like the one pictured, were the dominant management information systems from the mid-1960s until the late 1970s. During the 1980s, they were increasingly replaced by decentralized personal computers.

tems were now being designed specifically to help managers in diverse functions to make better decisions. Not only were managers in the accounting area involved with information control, but also managers in purchasing, personnel, marketing, engineering, research and development, and production and operations. In this second stage, separate data systems departments were created, and remote terminals were introduced.

By the mid-1960s, managers of every type had begun to see how computers could help them to do their jobs better and more efficiently. Computers could accumulate and analyze large quantities of data that could never be analyzed economically on a manual basis. Marketing executives, for instance, could now not only review weekly sales reports broken down by each salesperson, but also have those data analyzed by product groups. If the sales of a particular product line suddenly dropped, computer-generated information could alert management quickly and allow for rapid corrective action. This contrasts with information controls in Stage 1, when a similar report would have to be produced by a clerk or a group of clerks and might take a month or longer to complete. Thus Stage 2 marks the real beginning of *management* information systems.

The expanding role of computerized information control created the need for reorganization. As MIS became less an accounting control device and more a management tool, it needed to be separated from its accounting origins. In Stage 2, therefore, MIS units came into their own. Organizations created new departments with titles like Data Systems or Information Systems, run by MIS professionals. When managers in an organization had an information control problem, they now had a specific department to which they could go for a solution.

Finally, Stage 2 also saw the introduction of remote terminals that provided access to a computer's central processing unit from external locations. Remote terminals, for example, would allow a production supervisor to review and modify a production schedule by communicating directly with the central computer through a terminal on the production floor. Remote terminals not only made information more readily available, they also allowed managers who knew what information they needed to get it without going through the data systems department.

Stage 3: Decentralized End-User Computing

The next major breakthrough in MIS was the decentralization of information control. Centralized data processing was being rapidly replaced by decentralized systems in which part or all of the computer logic functions were performed outside the central computer. During Stage 3, managers became end-users, personal computers became overwhelmingly popular, managers found themselves enmeshed in software decisions, and data systems departments evolved into information support centers.

end-user
The person who uses information and assumes responsibility for its control.

When a manager becomes an **end-user,** he or she takes responsibility for information control.[11] It is no longer delegated to some other department or staff assistant. When managers became end-users, they had to become knowledgeable about their own needs and the systems that were available to meet those needs, and had to accept responsibility for their systems' failures. If they didn't have the information they wanted, there was no one to blame but themselves.

In Stage 3, whether they liked it or not, managers had to come face-to-face with computer technology and all that it could offer. Some were enthusiastic about the opportunity to bypass the data-processing technicians who spoke "computerese." Others, and they were the majority, resisted. Terrified of learning how to operate a personal computer, they continued to rely on others for their information needs. It's estimated that 45 percent of managers currently have hands-on access to a computer.[12] That still leaves more than half at a disadvantage. The important news is that the number of resisters is declining. While they may still fear having to use a computer, their contemporaries have accepted end-user computing and have a better information base from which to make more timely decisions. Managers who have overcome their fear have found that by developing their computer skills and by judiciously selecting the right software, they are able to get the exact information they want in literally seconds.

Table 19-4 describes the five types of personal computer software packages that are most relevant for managers. The packages a manager uses, of course, depend on what tasks he or she is trying to accomplish. For information control purposes, access to

Today's manager typically has her own desktop computer and accesses information without going through a data-systems department.

word processing
Software packages that allow users to write, change, edit, revise, delete, or print letters, reports, and manuscripts.

spreadsheets
Software packages that allow users to turn a computer's memory into a large worksheet in which data and formulas can be entered to perform a variety of calculations.

data base management
A computerized system that allows the user to organize, get at easily, and select and review a precise set of data from a larger base of data.

TABLE 19–4   Five Types of Personal Computer Software Packages

word processing   Allows the user to write, change, edit, revise, delete, or print letters, reports, and manuscripts. For example, a user can write a report and then correct it or update it without having to retype the whole thing.

spreadsheets   Allows a user to turn the computer's memory into a large worksheet in which data and formulas can be entered to perform a variety of calculations. The spreadsheet defines a structure and then allows the user to change a number within that structure to see how the change will affect other numbers. Permits managers to ask a series of what-if questions. For example, a manager could use a spreadsheet to see what effect a 5 percent increase in costs would have on monthly profitability.

data base management   Allows the user to organize, get at easily, and select and review a precise set of data from a larger base of data. A manager could use a data base for keeping an up-to-date record of each customer's purchases.

graphics   Allows the user to display (and often print) numerical findings in the form of charts or graphs. Managers can use these to present financial analyses, budgets, sales projections, and similar numerical data.

communication   Allows computers to communicate and transfer data to and from each other. Managers can use this software to transfer messages from their terminals to other managers' terminals, rather than use telephones to relay the same message.

Source: Based on James P. Morgan, "Software Buying: A New Purchasing Frontier," *Purchasing,* September 20, 1984, p. 71; and Lawrence J. Magid, "Software," *1988 Inc. Office Guide,* pp. 51–54.

data bases is going to be very important. For developing an annual budget, the spreadsheet becomes invaluable. The point to keep in mind is that managers who have an extensive library of software packages can make their computers *flexible.* They can use their hardware to the maximum extent. In minutes, for instance, they can change from "crunching numbers" on a spreadsheet to writing a perfectly prepared report based on those numbers, using a word-processing program.

A final outcome of Stage 3 has been the transformation of data systems departments into information support centers.[13] Rather than generating information for managers, they are helping managers become more effective end-users. For instance, they are advising managers on the availability of software, training them in using it, showing them how to access data base information from centralized mainframes, and overseeing user service hotlines. Thus as managers have become end-users, data-processing professionals have had to switch from *providing* managers with information to *helping* them get their own information.

Stage 4: Interactive Networks

The fourth and current stage of MIS development relies heavily on communication software packages to fully achieve the *systems* objective of MIS. In Stage 4, the emphasis is on creating and implementing mechanisms to integrate end-users. By means of an interactive network, a manager's computer can communicate with other computers.[14] This is opening up opportunities for electronic mail, teleconferencing, and interorganizational linkages.

Networking interconnects computer hardware. By networking, the user of a personal computer can communicate with other personal computers, turn the computer into a terminal and gain access to an organization's mainframe system, share the use of expensive printers, and tap into outside data bases.

The biggest computer network is also the oldest: our national telephone system. Run almost entirely by computers, it connects 100 million homes and businesses

networking
Linking computers so that they can communicate with each other.

through 1 billion circuit miles of wires, cables, microwave relays, and satellites.[15] Organizations are now installing networking systems, only on a smaller scale. To illustrate, Digital Equipment Corporation has designed a network system that integrates the company's 27,000 computers in twenty-six different countries.[16] Engineers in Israel, Japan, and the United States, for example, can collaborate on design work by exchanging memos, circuit diagrams, and even software. The network also facilitates open and flexible communication by allowing people to leapfrog levels in the organization. With this network, for instance, a DEC programmer in Australia can send a message directly to the corporate CEO in Massachusetts, essentially bypassing more than a half a dozen levels in the organization. Of course, key people in the hierarchy can still be kept informed by merely insuring that they receive "copies" of communications.

As we'll demonstrate later, networks are reshaping the manager's job. Electronic mail is lessening the manager's dependence on the telephone and traditional mail delivery service.[17] Electronic messages can be communicated in seconds, and if the receiver isn't at the terminal, there's no need for the sender to call back. Teleconferencing is reducing the need for travel. Group meetings can now take place among people thousands of miles apart. Telecommuting permits some employees, including managers, to do their jobs at home and connect to the workplace by means of a personal computer. (See Figure 19-4.) Networks are also enabling managers to monitor closely their subordinates' work. For employees who perform their tasks on a terminal, software packages are available that can summarize, in detail, each employee's hourly productivity, error rate, and the like.

We also shouldn't overlook the effect that networks are having on interorganizational communications.[18] They are making it possible for an organization's computers to interact with computers in other organizations. The computers at General Motors, for example, are also linked to those of primary suppliers and major dealers. These

FIGURE 19-4
The Telecommuting
Workplace

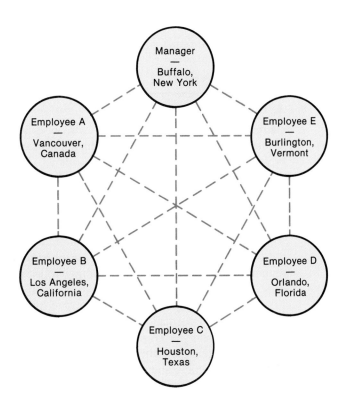

linkages are dramatically cutting paperwork and speeding up communications. Inter-organizational networks are also widening the scope of data base management. If you want to know what other companies are doing in regard to strategic planning, for instance, you can get your answer through a computer search of outside data bases. Companies like Dow Jones and Mead Corporation have developed extensive data bases that are available on a fee basis. Just as college students are researching their term papers by means of data base searches at a library instead of manually going through periodical indexes or journals, managers can now tap into a multitude of data bases without leaving the office.

The Next Stage: Expert Systems?

What will the next stage of development of MIS be? We're certain to see more personal computers, more end-users, and a much larger maze of interlocking grids linking them together. This, in turn, will reshape the way offices look and work.

expert systems
Software programs that encode the relevant experience of a human expert.

Maybe one of the most far-reaching MIS developments will be the application of artificial intelligence to managerial decision making.[19] These **expert systems** use software programs to encode the relevant experience of a human expert and allow a system to act like that expert in analyzing and solving unstructured problems.[20] Managerial expertise in handling complex decisions is a natural candidate for such systems.

The essence of expert systems is that they (1) use specialized knowledge about a particular problem area rather than general knowledge that would apply to all problems, (2) use qualitative reasoning rather than numerical calculations, and (3) perform at a level of competence that is higher than that of nonexpert humans.[21] In the not-too-distant future, we might see computers making unstructured decisions that were previously made by middle- and upper-level managers. A program that can model the reasoning and judgment of a marketing executive's mind, with its eighteen years of formal education and twenty years of experience (or those of senior-level managers in all key functional areas) can make that expertise available to others who are considerably less knowledgeable.

DEBUNKING A FEW MYTHS ABOUT MIS

There is no shortage of myths and misconceptions about management information systems. In this section, we want to challenge three widely circulated myths: (1) formal MIS's will replace other information sources, (2) more information is always better, and (3) managers need the latest technology available.

The Replacement Myth

Sophisticated, computer-based information systems have significantly improved the ability of managers to monitor and control organizational activities. But these formal systems *add to,* rather than *replace,* other sources of information for managerial controls. Meetings, chance encounters, one-on-one conversations, unscheduled walks around facilities, social activities, telephone calls, and the like continue to be important sources of information for managers.[22]

Verbal and personal communications are a very real part of every manager's job. As leaders, managers inevitably receive sizable quantities of rich information about how well things are going and what is or could be a problem. Often, such informal information will alert a manager more quickly to a potential problem than can any formal

MANAGERS WHO MADE A DIFFERENCE

John McCormack at Visible Changes, Inc.

John McCormack runs a chain of sixteen hair salons that generate three to four times the per-unit sales volume of his competitors. The secret of McCormack's success? Computer control.[23]

Every employee's work performance is closely tracked at Visible Changes. Computers identify how many customers each employee handles, who sells perms and colors and who doesn't, dollar volume of shampoo and conditioners sold, and the like. Each Monday, the computer gives the haircutters reports about the number of customers they served and the number who requested them during the previous week. They also get a report on how they did for the same week the year before—and for each of the previous five years in the case of employees who have been with the firm that long.

Once a week, a computer list is posted in all the salons, for everyone to see, that ranks all 350 employees in the company. The top fifty are put into a green zone, and the bottom fifty are put into a red zone. McCormack believes that such recognition rewards high performers and motivates poor performers to get out of the red zone.

McCormack's system allows him and his management staff to quickly identify problem employees as well as slow-moving products. For instance, he can check to see which stylists have had to give free recuts in any given month because customers were displeased with the original cut. If this happens too often, McCormack provides the stylist with additional training.

McCormack's tightly controlled system isn't for everyone. He has approximately a 40 percent dropout rate among new stylists during the first month. Those who stay, however, are paid well. The average salaries of stylists who have been with Visible Changes for three or more years are twice the industry average.

MIS. An MIS is not necessarily a panacea. It has not and will not replace other, less formal means of gaining information about organizational activities.

The "More Is Better" Myth

The "more is better" myth has two themes. The first is that a greater quantity of information will lead to better decisions. The second is that managers need all the information they request. Neither statement holds up under close scrutiny.

An increased quantity of information might not improve decisions for at least three reasons: (1) the manager can become overwhelmed with information, (2) the value of any information depends on a lot more than just its quantity, and (3) a manager who has the relevant data might not understand how it fits together.

Too much information, even high-quality information, can hinder decision-making performance after some optimal point.[24] Why? Because of information overload. Up to a point, new information is beneficial, but decision makers can assimilate only so much information. Once that maximum point has been reached, additional information can actually decrease decision performance.

The value of information used in decision making is measured not only in quantity. *Quality* also needs to be considered. Is the information relevant, accurate, complete, reliable, and timely?[25] If it fails to meet these criteria, then more isn't necessarily better.

Regardless of the quantity and quality of information available, decision performance still depends on the decision maker's ability to understand a problem, what's causing it, and which solution is most preferred. This is particularly true of complex decision situations in which numerous variables have to be considered. Managers often have difficulty in understanding cause-effect relationships among these variables, and more information doesn't necessarily improve the decision. More and better information should lead to better decision performance only when managers can use it in a logical, meaningful way.

Even if these criteria are met, there is still another factor that shouldn't be ignored: cost! The "more is better" argument overlooks the reality that increased information comes at an increased cost. Any request for more information therefore needs to be assessed in cost-benefit terms. What marginal improvement in decision performance can be expected as a result of the additional cost? Is that marginal improvement worth the extra cost?

Many managers fall into the habit of searching continually for more information, but they don't always need the information they request. In many organizational cultures, failure carries a very high price. In such organizations, managers often request more information as a security defense. Even if the decision later proves faulty, they at least cannot be attacked on the grounds that they acted hastily or with inadequate data. Some individuals, of course, are inherently risk aversive. Regardless of their organization's culture, they have a tough time making important decisions. When placed in managerial positions, they search for more information in order to put off making tough decisions.

Information overload slows decision making, makes organizing of data difficult or impossible, and often requires that some critical information be excluded.

The "New Is Better" Myth

The last myth that we want to dispel assumes that an effective information system requires the latest in technology. While teleconferencing, voice-activated input devices, supercomputers with enormous memory capacities, paperless offices, and the like *might* improve managerial effectiveness in some situations, it's dangerous to assume that all technological improvements should be adopted.

Like most consumers, managers are not immune to fashion. As computers have become faster and more powerful and innovative peripherals and software have been developed, many managers assume that the newest technological breakthrough is best. That is often not the case. Managers often don't need the greater power, speed, or other advantages offered by a new system. Whether new is better depends on the user's needs and the cost of the improved technology. Moreover, improved technology almost always requires change. A new system requires managers to learn how to use it. Even "user-friendly" systems often require fifty or more hours before the user is fully up to speed. When managers often earn in excess of $50 an hour (including benefits), bringing a new system on-line just to have the latest technology is certain to be both costly and disruptive. Before managers jump to purchase the latest MIS technological innovation, they need to consider the full repercussions of the decision.

DESIGNING THE MIS

While there is no universally agreed-upon approach to designing a management information system, the following steps represent the key elements in putting an MIS together.

Analyze the Decision System

It's the decisions that managers make that should drive the design of any MIS. Therefore, the first step is to identify all the management decisions for which information is needed. This should encompass all the functions within the organization and every management level from first-level supervisor to the chief executive officer.

This step should also consider whether each decision is being made by the right person. Is it being made at the right level? By the right department? Failure to ask these questions can misdirect the entire MIS design. If the wrong people are making the decision before a sophisticated information system is put in place, and if the new system doesn't correct this flaw, then it will continue to provide the wrong information, only faster.

Analyze Information Requirements

Once the decisions are isolated, we need to know the exact information required to effectively make these decisions.

Information needs differ according to managerial function and managerial level in the organization. The information that a marketing manager needs differs from that required by a financial manager. Thus the MIS has to be tailored to meet the varying needs of different functional managers.

As Table 19-5 illustrates, a manager's information needs also vary by organizational level. Top-level managers are looking for environmental data and summary reports. At

TABLE 19–5   Matching Information Requirements with Managerial Level

Characteristics of Information	Lower Management	Middle Management	Top Management
Source	Largely internal ——————————————→		External
Scope	Well defined, narrow ————————————→		Very wide
Level of aggregation	Detailed —————————————————→		Aggregate
Time horizons	Historical ————————————————→		Future

Source: Based on G. Anthony Gorry and Michael S. Scott Morton, "A Framework for Management Information Systems," *Sloan Management Review,* Fall 1971, p. 59. Copyright © 1971 by the Sloan Management Review Association. All rights reserved.

the other extreme, lower-level supervisors want detailed reports of operating problems. The well-designed MIS must consider these diverse requirements if it is to satisfy the varied needs of managers.

Aggregate the Decisions

After each functional area and manager's needs have been identified, those that have the same or largely overlapping informational requirements should be located. Even though needs vary up and down and across the organization, redundancies often occur. Both sales and production executives, for example, may want feedback data on a given product's quality level. One, however, wants the feedback to ensure customer satisfaction, while the other wants it to control for variances in the production processes. By identifying these redundancies, management can create systems that contain the least amount of duplication and that group together similar decisions under a single manager.

Design Information Processing

In this step, internal technical specialists or outside consultants are utilized to develop the actual system for collecting, storing, transmitting, and retrieving information. A detailed flowchart of the desired system will be drawn up. It will include, among other things, sources and types of data, locations of users, and storage requirements. The precise hardware and software requirements will also be determined.

Before the system is implemented, it is carefully evaluated to ensure that it will do what management wants it to do. That is, the bottom-line test of an MIS's effectiveness is its ability to meet each manager's information needs. A design that meets all of most managers' needs or most of all managers' needs will not provide the optimum amount and quality of information for the organization as a whole. Changes can improve the effectiveness of such designs.

IMPLEMENTING THE MIS

Once the design has been resolved, it needs to be implemented. The implementation phase should begin with pretesting the system and conclude with building in regular evaluations in the system. The following points highlight concerns that need to be addressed during the implementation phase.

ETHICAL DILEMMAS IN MANAGEMENT

When Do Information Control Systems Interfere With an Employee's Right to Privacy?

Do employees give up all their rights to privacy when they accept paid employment? Most people would answer with a resounding No! But present technology does dramatically increase management's access to information and can result in stepping over the line to what may become an invasion of an employee's privacy.[26] Let's take an example from the airline industry, although the practice we'll describe is certainly not isolated to airlines.

Supervisors at one particular airline have access to computer records that show how long each reservation clerk spends on each call and how much time passes before he or she picks up the next call. Workers earn negative points for such infractions as repeatedly spending more than an average 109 seconds handling a call and taking more than twelve minutes for restroom visits beyond the one hour a day allocated for lunch and coffee breaks. Employees who collect too many negative points can lose their jobs.

Has this airline's management overstepped the bounds of fair and reasonable control of its employees? Some might argue that this system merely performs more accurately and unobtrusively what used to be done imprecisely and obtrusively by a supervisor who directly hovered over his or her reservation clerks. Others, however, might describe such information control systems as the realization of some undesirable *Brave New World* with "Big Brother" (in this case—management) watching over you.

Do information control systems that provide minute details of an employee's daily activities unduly invade that employee's privacy? What do *you* think?

Pretest the System Before Installation

Flaws found before an information system is installed are much easier and less costly to fix than when the system is in place and people have begun to depend on it. If a full pretest is not feasible, then management should consider introducing the new system in parallel with the old. By running two systems side by side for a short period of time, bugs or omissions in the new system can be identified and corrected with minimal disturbances to the organization's operations.

Prepare Users with Proper Training

No matter how well a system is designed, if users aren't aware of its full capabilities and don't know how to obtain those capabilities, it will never achieve its full potential. Therefore, the budget of any new MIS installation must cover time and money for training users. Even the brightest and most competent managers will require some training if they are going to be able to make full use of a new system.

Prepare for Resistance

People tend to resist changes that appear threatening to them. A sizable body of research indicates that the introduction of computer-based information systems can be highly threatening.[27] Some people have difficulty adapting to the introduction of any new technology. Some also fear being unable to learn the new system. Many are threatened by the new system's potential for reducing their power and status in the organization, changing interpersonal relationships, or lessening their job security.

Get Users Involved

One of the most effective ways of neutralizing resistance to an MIS is to have those who will be affected by the system participate fully in its design and implementation.[28] Participation will familiarize users with the system before they have to use it, increase their commitment to it because they were involved in its creation, and lessen the likelihood that their needs will be overlooked.

Check for Security

As information systems become decentralized, there is a critical need to ensure that unauthorized individuals do not gain access to valuable or privileged information. When information was centralized at a single source, only a few people could tap into important data bases such as production schedules, customer records, inventory accounts, credit data, and employee files. Today, however, such data bases are much more vulnerable to unauthorized access. The solution is to ensure that adequate security measures are included in the system. Access to the place where hardware is located should be controlled. Software should be locked up when not in use. A system should also have impossible-to-guess passwords or codes for gaining access, require users to identify themselves once into the system, and impose strict controls over telephone access.

Build in Regular Reviews

The information that a manager needed last year is not necessarily the same that he or she needs today. As customers, suppliers, government regulations, and other environmental factors change, so too will the informational needs of managers. Implementation should be viewed as the beginning of an onging process. If an information system is to be valuable to managers over time, it must be regularly evaluated and modified to adapt to the changing needs of its users.

USING INFORMATION SYSTEMS TO GAIN A COMPETITIVE ADVANTAGE

As we discussed in Chapter 8, managers seek to develop organizationwide strategies that will give them an advantage over their competition. We talked about gaining a competitive advantage through strategies such as being the cost-leader in a given market or by carefully differentiating your product from that of the competition. In recent years, managers at a number of organizations have come to the realization that information systems can be used as a tool to give their firms a competitive advantage.[29] For example, take a look at American Airlines and Mrs. Fields Cookies.

For decades, American Airlines' SABRE system was programmed so that American's flight information received more display screen prominence than competitors' flights. This provided American with a clear competitive advantage over its rivals when travel agents selected flights for clients.

American Airlines developed a reservation system called SABRE in the 1960s. Its state-of-the-art capability at the time allowed it to get an early foothold in travel agencies. Today, 14,000 travel agencies keep up with some 45 million different fares of 281 airlines by subscribing to American's SABRE system.[30] SABRE not only brings in some $134 million a year in profits for American, but it also has allowed American to control the display of flight information that travel agents see.

Mrs. Fields Cookies has nearly 500 stores in thirty-seven states. Rather than going the franchising route, all these stores are owned by Debbi and Randy Fields and run out of their headquarters in Utah. Mrs. Fields has created a market niche by selling fresh, warm chocolate chip cookies, and the firm has used its management information system to exploit and sustain its competitive advantage.[31]

The typical employee at a Mrs. Fields store is young and inexperienced. How can such employees be expected to know when, for example, to bake batches of cookies or how large each batch should be to ensure that cookies are always warm while, at the same time, minimizing stockouts? Randy Fields has created software for store personnel that does these calculations for them. The program on each store's computer asks a set of questions each day, after which past sales data is analyzed and a detailed, hour-by-hour sales goal schedule is created for that day. A store manager then merely has to punch in hourly data on sales, and the program tells the manager precisely how many batches of cookie dough to make for every variety of cookie and exactly when to make them. This system allows Mrs. Fields to offer fresher cookies than most of its competitors, even those whose owners are present on site.

These two examples illustrate the potential that an MIS provides managers for gaining and sustaining a competitive advantage, but they only scratch the surface. Several book publishers are using information systems to link authors, editors, designers, production, and warehousing personnel to get books into print and into stores faster than the competition. Some paint manufacturers are developing interorganizational networks with industrial users in order to better serve their customers' needs. As you'll remember from the opening of this chapter, firms like Toys "R" Us

MANAGING FROM A GLOBAL PERSPECTIVE

Networking the World

An Exxon executive in Dallas wants to redirect one of the company's tankers that's somewhere in the Persian Gulf. Fifteen years ago this would probably have been done by telephone. Today, this can be accomplished via networked computers. Without leaving his desk, the executive in Dallas can send his communique directly to the ship's captain and get an immediate response. The executive can even make a hard copy of the communique for the record in case any future questions arise.

A Sony executive in Japan is concerned about the inventory of Sony Watchman mini-televisions in Canada. Is there enough product in the company's Vancouver and Toronto warehouses to meet retailers' needs over the next three months? Fifteen years ago, that type of question might have taken two days and half a dozen phone calls to answer. Not anymore! Because Sony's computers are networked to communicate with each other, tapping a few buttons on the executive's keyboard can immediately give the executive access to the inventory records at both Canadian warehouses. Today, the question about the status of Watchmans in Canada can be answered in two or three minutes.

As these examples illustrate, the networking of computers has important implications for management control in global organizations. Managers can now monitor activities halfway around the world with the speed and accuracy that were once available only through direct personal observation.

and Federal Express are using information systems to gain a competitive advantage over rivals in terms of product offerings and providing on-time deliveries.

In an increasingly competitive environment, success depends on gaining and sustaining a strategic advantage over rivals. Such advantages are hard to achieve and even harder to maintain. The creative use of an organization's information system provides managers with another tool for differentiating its products and services from those of its competitors.

HOW MIS IS CHANGING THE MANAGER'S JOB

No discussion of management information systems would be complete without assessing their impact on the manager's job. In this section, we'll touch on several of the key areas that are changing as a result of computer-based MIS's.

Hands-On Involvement

A few years ago, managers could avoid computers by claiming, "I don't have to know how to use computers. I can hire people to do that for me." Those days are gone, or close to it!

Today's younger managers, exposed to computers in college or even high school, feel at home in front of a keyboard. If anything, they have swung to the other extreme: they have become dependent on their computers and feel threatened when access is limited. By the mid-1990s, these individuals—nurtured on computers from their teenage years—will fill many lower- and middle-level managerial positions in organizations. Senior managers who refuse to learn their systems and take advantage of their MIS's capabilities will find it increasingly difficult to perform as effectively as their peers. Over time, managers will have no choice: Either they will become active, "hands-on" users, or they won't survive.

How will hands-on use change what managers do? Among other things, they'll spend less time on the phone, traveling to conferences, and waiting for subordinates to provide progress reports. They'll be using networks for electronic mail, videoconferencing, and closely monitoring organizational activities.

Decision-Making Capability

Since managers rely on information to make decisions and since a sophisticated MIS significantly alters the quantity and quality of information, as well as the speed with which it can be obtained, you come to the natural conclusion that an effective MIS will improve management's decision-making capability.[32]

The effect will be seen in ascertaining the need for a decision, in the development and evaluation of alternatives, and in the final selection of the best alternative. On-line, real-time systems allow managers to identify problems almost as they occur. Gone are the long delays between the appearance of a serious discrepancy and a manager's ability to find out about it. Data base management programs allow managers to look things up or get to the facts without either going to other people or digging through piles of paper. This reduces a manager's dependence on others for data and makes fact gathering far more efficient. Today's manager can identify alternatives quickly, evaluate those alternatives by using a spreadsheet program and posing a series of what-if questions based on financial data, and finally select the best alternative on the basis of answers to those questions.

Organization Design

Sophisticated information systems are reshaping organizations. The most evident change is that organizations are becoming flatter and more organic.[33]

Managers can handle more subordinates. Why? Because computer control substitutes for personal supervision. As a result, there are wider spans of control and fewer levels in the organization. The need for staff support is also reduced with an MIS. As was noted previously, hands-on involvement allows managers to tap information directly and makes large staff support groups redundant. Both forces—wider spans and reduced staff—lead to flatter organizations.

One of the more interesting phenomena created by sophisticated information systems is that they have allowed management to make organizations more organic without any loss in control.[34] As was noted in Chapter 10, management prefers bureaucracy because it facilitates control. But there's more than one way to skin a cat. Management can lessen formalization and become more decentralized—thus making their organizations more organic—without giving up control. In this case, an MIS substitutes computer control for rules and decision discretion. Computer technology rapidly apprises top managers of the consequences of any decision and allows them to take corrective action if the decision is not to their liking. There's the appearance of decentralization without any commensurate loss of control.

William Smithburg, CEO at Quaker Oats, has had an executive information system, designed to meet his exacting needs, on his desk since the early 1980s. He uses it for environmental scanning as well as for control purposes. He now has direct access to financial information without having to pick up the phone and call his controller. He also now has direct access to agricultural information that will influence Quaker Oats' costs for raw materials.

Power

Information is power. Anything that changes the access to scarce and important information is going to change power relationships within an organization.[35]

An MIS changes the status hierarchy in an organization. Middle managers have less status because they carry less clout. They no longer serve as the vital link between operations and the executive suite. Similarly, staff units have less prestige because senior managers no longer depend on them for evaluation and advice.

Centralized computer departments, which were extremely influential units in organizations during the 1970s, have had their role modified and their power reduced.[36] Reconstituted as information support centers, they no longer control access to data bases.

In aggregate, probably the most important effect that computer-based control systems have had on the power structure has been to tighten the hand of top management. In earlier years, top management regularly depended on lower-level managers to feed information upward. Because information was filtered and "enhanced," managers knew what their subordinates wanted them to know. End-user systems have put the power of information into top management's hands by giving them direct access to data.

The Supervisor's Job

A great deal of attention has been focused on how MIS's are changing the supervisor's job. While some observers propose that supervisors may become extinct,[37] it's unlikely that computers will replace first-line supervisors.[38] But MIS's are certainly reducing the supervisor's role as an on-site control mechanism.

It has been noted that, in the production area, computerization erodes supervision in four ways: (1) it allows operatives to be machine paced, (2) it provides automatic feedback and analyses of production performance information, (3) it undermines the skill superiority that supervisors have over operatives, and (4) it expands the autonomy of operatives.[39] For instance, the Pontiac division of General Motors now operates an engine assembly plant with approximately 100 workers and only two supervisors.[40] Before it was automated, the line needed about twice as many workers and about a dozen supervisors. Computer-controlled equipment allowed the span of control to be expanded from approximately seventeen to fifty.

The office supervisor's role is similarly being reshaped by automation. The supervisor can oversee a large number of workers performing their jobs on video-display monitors. The office supervisor no longer has to directly observe his or her employees to monitor their work. That function can be accomplished by software programs that aggregate each employee's productivity statistics and that the supervisor can access at the touch of a finger.

Computers and automation will not eliminate the need for supervisors. They will still be needed to help employees set goals, to provide leadership, and to offer problem-solving skills. However, organizations will need far fewer supervisors than in the past.

ORGANIZATIONAL COMMUNICATION: AN MIS UPDATE

Earlier in this chapter we presented the basics of organizational communication. But improvements in information technology—specifically, progress made in MIS's that has enhanced our ability to gather, synthesize, organize, monitor, and disseminate information—are significantly changing the way communication takes place in organizations.[41] The following discussion provides an MIS update to our earlier discussion of organizational communication.

Patterns of Communication Flow Will Change

Traditional discussions of organizational communication focused on upward and downward communication. The primary flow of formal communication was vertical. The MIS, however, permits more lateral and diagonal communication on a formal basis.

Employees using intraorganizational networks can get their work done more efficiently by jumping levels in the organization and avoiding the cumbersomeness of "going through channels." The direct accessing of data, rather than the traditional sequential passing of data up and down the hierarchy, also decreases the historical problem of distortion and filtering of information. The breaking down of sequential communication patterns allows managers to formally monitor information across the organization that previously was limited to informal channels like the grapevine.

Communication Overload Should Be Lessened

Overload occurs when an individual can't process information as rapidly as it is received. Because information systems can scan, filter, process, maintain, and distribute information, overload should be reduced. For instance, a sales manager needn't spend hours looking through dozens of reports and thousands of statistics—many of them irrelevant—to analyze why sales in a certain region have declined. A sophisticated management information system can do most of that in a few seconds and provide the sales manager with specific answers.

Face-to-Face Communication Will Take on a More Symbolic Role

Sophisticated information systems obviate the need for many communications that previously had to be done face-to-face. Managers can get timely, accurate information without being at the site of the action. However, this won't make face-to-face communication extinct. Rather, such communication will have a different purpose. Managers no longer need to meet with subordinates, peers, or superiors in person to be effective in their jobs. Face-to-face communication will still be practiced, but it will be important for its symbolic significance.

As a case in point, the head of Exxon was widely criticized in the spring of 1989 for not going to Alaska after one of the company's ships, the *Exxon Valdez,* ran aground and spilled millions of barrels of oil into Prince William Sound. His presence wasn't needed to manage the oil spill—he was able to communicate with Exxon personnel in Alaska via telecommunications—but his decision to stay in New York was viewed by many as a lack of concern. Managers will still need to visit company offices and go down to the shop floor to talk with employees about their problems because such behaviors are expected of caring managers, although these actions will contribute little to any objective measure of "better communications."

SUMMARY

This summary is organized by the chapter-opening learning objectives found on page 591.

1. A management information system (MIS) refers to a manual or computer-based system that provides management with needed information on a regular basis.

2. Data is raw, unanalyzed facts. Information is data that has been analyzed and processed.

3. Downward communication flows from a manager down the authority hierarchy. Upward communication flows from below to higher-level managers. Lateral communication takes place among members of work groups, among managers, or among any horizontally equivalent personnel. Diagonal communication cuts across functions and levels in an organization.

4. Five common communication networks are the chain, Y, wheel, circle, and all-channel networks.

5. Centralized systems are controlled by MIS departments. In contrast, an end-user system is controlled by the actual user.

6. The major value of networking is that it allows personal computers to be linked to peripherals and mainframes and provides access to outside data bases.

7. More information is not always better information; instead, it can overwhelm managers. Managers need to know how additional information fits into the whole decision framework.

8. Designing an MIS requires analyzing the decision system, analyzing information requirements, aggregating the decisions, and developing the actual information-processing capability.

9. MIS relates to an organization's strategy by its ability to provide a means for gaining a competitive advantage. Such advantages over rivals are hard to come by and even more difficult to sustain once obtained. The creative use of an organization's information system provides managers with a tool for differentiating its products and services from that of its competitors.

10. MIS's change power relationships because they change the access to scarce and important information.

11. MIS's are reshaping the supervisor's job by replacing the supervisor's on-site control responsibilities with computer-controlled equipment. The average supervisor's span of control will be significantly expanded, so organizations will need fewer supervisory positions.

12. MIS is increasing the flow of horizontal formal communications, lessening information overload, and making face-to-face communication more a symbolic gesture than a necessary requirement for effective communication.

REVIEW QUESTIONS

1. What does the term *system* in management information system imply?
2. Do managers want data or information? Explain.
3. Contrast communication networks in terms of effectiveness.
4. How can managers "manage" the grapevine?
5. What characterizes Stage 1 in the evolution of an MIS? Stage 2? Stage 3? Stage 4?
6. Contrast batch and real-time processing.
7. How is the executive's office likely to be different by the year 2000?
8. How do the information requirements of a supervisor and a senior executive differ?
9. How are MIS's changing the manager's job?
10. Explain how formal communications can move horizontally as well as vertically.

DISCUSSION QUESTIONS

1. Information is a resource just like land, labor, or capital. But it differs from these resources in some ways. Name some of these ways.
2. How can a manager's decision performance *decline* as a result of information overload?
3. Relate the MIS to organizational communication.
4. "One of the groups that is most resistant to computers is top management." Do you agree or disagree? Discuss.
5. How might an MIS change the typical manager's day-to-day communications described in this chapter's "In Practice" feature?

SELF-ASSESSMENT EXERCISE

Are You Computerphobic?

Instructions: The following test was designed to measure your anxiety about using computers. For each question, circle the answer that most closely reflects your opinion.

> 1 = Strongly disagree
> 2 = Disagree
> 3 = Uncertain
> 4 = Agree
> 5 = Strongly agree

1. I feel insecure about my ability to interpret a computer printout.	1	2	3	4	5
2. I look forward to using a computer on my job.	1	2	3	4	5
3. I do not think I would be able to learn a computer programming language.	1	2	3	4	5
4. The challenge of learning about computers is exciting.	1	2	3	4	5
5. I am confident that I can learn computer skills.	1	2	3	4	5
6. Anyone can learn to use a computer if they are patient and motivated.	1	2	3	4	5
7. Learning to operate computers is like learning any new skill—the more you practice, the better you become.	1	2	3	4	5
8. I am afraid that if I begin to use computers I will become dependent upon them and lose some of my reasoning skills.	1	2	3	4	5
9. I am sure that with time and practice I will be as comfortable working with computers as I am in working with a typewriter.	1	2	3	4	5
10. I feel that I will be able to keep up with the advances happening in the computer field.	1	2	3	4	5
11. I dislike working with machines that are smarter than I am.	1	2	3	4	5
12. I feel apprehensive about using computers.	1	2	3	4	5
13. I have difficulty in understanding the technical aspects of computers.	1	2	3	4	5
14. It scares me to think that I could cause the computer to destroy a large amount of information by hitting the wrong key.	1	2	3	4	5
15. I hesitate to use a computer for fear of making mistakes that I cannot correct.	1	2	3	4	5
16. You have to be a genius to understand all the special keys contained on most computer terminals.	1	2	3	4	5

17. If given the opportunity, I would like to learn about and use computers.   1   2   3   4   5

18. I have avoided computers because they are unfamiliar and somewhat intimidating to me.   1   2   3   4   5

19. I feel computers are necessary tools in both educational and work settings.   1   2   3   4   5

Turn to page 677 for scoring directions and key.

Source: Robert K. Heinssen, Jr., Carol R. Glass, and Luanne A. Knight, "Assessing Computer Anxiety: Development and Validation of the Computer Anxiety Rating Scale," *Computers in Human Behavior,* 1987, pp. 49–59. Copyright 1987, Pergamon Press, Inc. With permission.

CASE APPLICATION 19A

K mart

Since taking the job of CEO at K mart in 1987, Joseph Antonini has been trying to fix the discount chain's image as a merchandiser of schlock.[42] He is refurbishing old stores and introducing upscale goods. To retain his core clientele of serious bargain hunters, he has slashed prices on 8,000 basic items.

All this is in line with Antonini's five-year plan to turn K mart around. Meanwhile, as he attempts to overtake Sears as America's top retailer, Antonini has to look over his shoulder and keep a close eye on hard-charging Wal-Mart. Wal-Mart is fast outstripping K mart in squeezing more pretax earnings out of its real estate, which is one way that retailers measure their profitability. The faltering pace of Antonini's strategy also shows up in other numbers: Profits for the first half of 1989 were down nearly 16 percent. This followed a year when the company made $803 million, a 16 percent *increase* from the year before.

Some security analysts believe that Antonini should sell operations that do not fit, such as Waldenbooks, even though this Number 2 bookseller is very profitable. As for his core business, too many K mart stores still look sloppy, and a poor distribution system often results in outlets running out of merchandise while that merchandise languishes in warehouses.

This sort of thing rarely happens at Wal-Mart. Its computer technology, which allows headquarters staff and store employees to talk to one another on TV via satellite, enables the chain to keep an up-to-the-minute account of its inventory. Antonini recognizes his need for a better computer system and has been installing one, scheduled to be on-line in late 1990. This system will not only help move goods more efficiently but also save approximately $76 million a year in operating costs. In the interim, K mart's reputation has continued to sink, and consumers have been finding other places to shop.

There is another reason for K mart's problem: Antonini hates bad news. Says one insider, "There is no one to tell him things are going wrong. The culture here is to tell the chairman what he wants to hear." Adds another, "Things are sliding over his head because he isn't focusing all his energies on the competition."

Questions

1. Describe K mart's past strategy.
2. Describe its new strategy.
3. How has Wal-Mart gained a competitive advantage over K mart by using an MIS?
4. Do you think K mart's new computer system will change Antonini's job? Explain.

CASE APPLICATION 19B

The Management Edge

Ask managers to describe their most frequent or troublesome problems and they'll most often describe *people* problems. Imagine the delight, then, when managers learn about *The Management Edge,* an expert-system software package that tells them how to handle specific behavioral problems with co-workers and subordinates.[43]

Users first respond to nearly 100 questions with "agree" or "disagree" answers. These allow the computer to develop a personality profile of the user. Next, when the user has a problem with a specific person, he or she completes a set of questions that describe the person and the work environment. These data are then loaded into the computer, which searches through a huge store of "rules" that have been derived from experts and existing research. The result is a report giving the user specific pointers on how best to handle the targeted individual.

One user of *The Management Edge* is Gary Chapman, a manager for an electronic parts manufacturer in New York. Chapman thinks the program is great. For instance, the program told him that a co-worker, whose irritating habits he had chalked up to overenthusiasm, belongs to that troublesome class of individuals who don't recognize other people's responsibilities and obligations. The report admonished Chapman, "you too easily forgive those things. On the second or third occasion, point your view out to him, then go about your business"—advice that Chapman followed with good results.

Questions

1. What are the advantages of *The Management Edge?* What are its limitations?

2. How much confidence would you put in a program like *The Management Edge?*

3. Will expert systems like *The Management Edge* replace formal education? Experienced managers?

4. By the year 2000, will most managers be using an information system like *The Management Edge?* Explain.

20

OPERATIONS
MANAGEMENT

In the mid-1970s, America was going wild over motorcycles.[1] Harley-Davidson, then owned by AMF Corp., responded by nearly tripling production to 75,000 units annually over a four-year period. Along with this growth, however, came problems. Engineering and design of Harleys had become dated, and quality had deteriorated so much that more than half the cycles coming off the assembly line had missing parts, and dealers had to fix them before they could be sold.

In 1973, Harley had 75 percent of the super-heavyweight market. By 1980, its market share had plummeted to less than 25 percent. AMF was fast losing confidence in Harley and sold the company in 1981 to a group of Harley executives.

Harley's new owner-managers introduced a number of new products, redesigned and updated their basic product line, and greatly improved the company's marketing programs. However, none of these actions would have meant much if Harley hadn't dramatically revised its production and operations practices. The new managers visited Honda's assembly plant in Marysville, Ohio and realized what they were up against. In response, they initiated a number of changes on Harley's production floor. A new inventory system was introduced that eliminated the mountains of costly inventory parts. Management redesigned the entire production system, closely involving the employees in planning and working out the details. Workers were taught statistical techniques for monitoring and controlling the quality of their own work. Harley's management even worked with its suppliers—as has long been done by Japanese manufacturers—to help them adopt the same efficiency and quality-improvement techniques that Harley had instituted in its plants.

Harley's management has succeeded in pulling off one of America's most celebrated turnarounds. On the verge of bankruptcy in the early 1980s, by 1990 Harley again controlled nearly 50 percent of the super-heavyweight market. The company lost $25 million in 1982, but it earned profits of $27 million in 1988.

In the early 1980s, Harleys leaked oil, vibrated badly, and couldn't match the performance of the flawlessly built Japanese bikes. Hard-core Harley enthusiasts were willing to tolerate these inconveniences, but newcomers had no such devotion and bought Japanese bikes. Not so today. Harley is back and prospering, largely because of significantly improved products.

This chapter focuses on the importance of efficiency, productivity, and controls in the operations side of the organization. Managers who thoughtfully develop well-designed physical facilities, operating systems, and tight controls—as Harley-Davidson's managers have done—will be the survivors in the increasingly competitive global economy. They'll be able to produce higher-quality products and services at prices that meet or beat those of their rivals.

OPERATIONS MANAGEMENT AND THE TRANSFORMATION PROCESS

operations management
The design, operation, and control of the transformation process that converts resources into finished goods and services.

Operations management refers to the design, operation, and control of the transformation process that converts resources like labor and raw materials into finished goods and services. Remember that every organization produces something. Unfortunately, however, this is often overlooked except in obvious cases such as in the manufacturing of motorcycles or automobiles. But hospitals produce medical services, air-

FIGURE 20–1
The Operations System

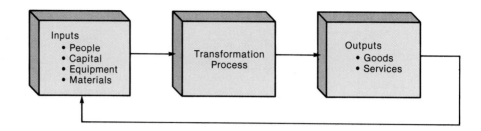

lines produce a transportation service that moves people from one location to another, the armed forces produce defense capabilities, and the list goes on. Take a university as a specific illustration. University administrators bring together instructors, books, academic journals, audio-visual material, and similar resources to transform "unenlightened" students into educated and skilled individuals.

Figure 20–1 portrays, in a very simplified fashion, the fact that every organization has an operations system that creates value by transforming inputs into outputs. The system takes inputs—people, capital, equipment, materials—and transforms them into desired finished goods and services. Thus the transformation process is as relevant to service organizations as to those in manufacturing.

Just as every organization produces something, every unit in an organization also produces something. Marketing, finance, research and development, personnel, and accounting convert inputs into outputs such as sales, increased market shares, high rates of return on capital, new and innovative products, productive and satisfied employees, and accounting reports. As a manager, you need to be familiar with operations management concepts—regardless of the area in which you manage—in order to achieve your objectives more efficiently.

MANAGING PRODUCTIVITY

productivity
The overall output of goods and services produced, divided by the inputs needed to generate that output.

Improving productivity has become a major goal in virtually every organization. By **productivity,** we mean the overall output of goods or services produced, divided by the inputs needed to generate that output. For countries, higher productivity generates "costless growth."[2] Employees can receive higher wages and company profits can increase without causing inflation. For individual organizations, increased productivity means a more competitive cost structure and the ability to offer more competitive prices.

Comparisons of growth rates in manufacturing productivity between the United States and Japan explain a good deal of Japan's prosperity. For instance, between 1979 and 1986, U.S. productivity increased at an annual rate of 2.8 percent. Japan's productivity during the same period grew at an annual rate of 5.5 percent. In the first half of the 1980s, Japan, Britain, France, and Italy were among the many nations whose growth in manufacturing productivity exceeded that of the United States.[3]

How can organizations improve their productivity? Productivity is a composite of people and operations variables. To improve productivity, management needs to focus on both.

On the people side, techniques discussed in previous chapters should be considered. Participative decision making, management by objectives, team-based work groups, and equitable pay systems are examples of people-oriented approaches toward productivity improvement. Management consultant and quality expert W.

TABLE 20-1
Deming's Fourteen Points for Improving Management's Productivity

1. Plan for the long-term future, not for the next month or next year.

2. Never be complacent concerning the quality of your product.

3. Establish statistical control over your production processes and require your suppliers to do so as well.

4. Deal with the fewest number of suppliers—the best ones, of course.

5. Find out whether your problems are confined to particular parts of the production process or stem from the overall process itself.

6. Train workers for the job that you are asking them to perform.

7. Raise the quality of your line supervisors.

8. Drive out fear.

9. Encourage departments to work closely together rather than to concentrate on departmental or divisional distinctions.

10. Do not be sucked into adopting strictly numerical goals, including the widely popular formula of "zero defect."

11. Require your workers to do quality work, not just to be at their stations from 9 to 5.

12. Train your employees to understand statistical methods.

13. Train your employees in new skills as the need arises.

14. Make top managers responsible for implementing these principles.

Source: W. Edwards Deming, "Improvement of Quality and Productivity Through Action by Management," *National Productivity Review,* Winter 1981–82, pp. 12–22. With permission. Copyright 1981 by Executive Enterprises, Inc., 22 West 21st St., New York, NY 10010-6904. All rights reserved.

Edwards Deming—consistent with his views that managers, not workers, are the primary source of increased productivity—outlined fourteen points for improving management's productivity. They are listed in Table 20–1.

A close look at Table 20–1 reveals that Deming understands the interplay of people and operations. High productivity cannot come solely from good "people" management. The truly effective organization will maximize productivity by successfully integrating people into the overall operations system. This can explain, for instance, why in one recent year alone, U.S. companies spent $17 billion on computers and new process-control equipment.[4] Increased capital investment will make facilities more modern and efficient. It also explains why so many organizations have laid off employees and shrunk in size in recent years. These organizations aspire to get more output per labor hour—that is, to increase their productivity.

In this chapter, we'll demonstrate that factors such as size and layout of operating facilities, capacity utilization, inventory usage, and maintenance controls are important determinants of an organization's overall productivity performance.

A CHALLENGE FOR THE 1990S: APPLYING OPERATIONS MANAGEMENT CONCEPTS TO SERVICE ORGANIZATIONS

manufacturing organizations
Organizations that produce physical goods like steel, automobiles, textiles, and farm machinery.

For the first half of this century, **manufacturing organizations**—that is, organizations that produce physical goods like steel, automobiles, textiles, and farm machinery—dominated most advanced industrialized nations. Today, in the United

IN PRACTICE

Revival of U.S. Manufacturing

In the mid-1980s, many world business observers concluded that the United States had lost its competitive advantages in world manufacturing.[5] Most of the blame was laid on high U.S. labor costs. Rarely did a week go by during the early 1980s that the business press wasn't reporting another U.S. plant closing and its jobs being exported to Taiwan, Singapore, South Korea, Brazil, or some other foreign location where labor costs were low.

The recent news is that U.S. manufacturing has bounced back from those bleak days.[6] A devalued dollar has been an obvious help. Furthermore, U.S. management has made significant strides in enhancing U.S. labor productivity by cutting layers of fat from their organizations, implementing improved cost controls, and focusing on quality. Between 1985 and 1987, U.S. manufacturing productivity improved 6.6 percent, well ahead of countries such as Canada (1.5 percent), West Germany (3.0 percent), and Japan (5.8 percent).[7] This revival of U.S. manufacturing is no better illustrated than in the steel industry.

Between 1982 and 1986, U.S. steelmakers lost $12 billion,[8] but managers responded to the challenge. The industry closed 400 outdated plants, drastically cut the size of its work force, and spent $7 billion on computer-controlled blast furnaces, continuous casters, and other high-tech systems. These measures cut the cost of producing and delivering a ton of steel by 20 percent, and in 1988, the industry racked up profits of $2 billion.[9] Bethlehem Steel, as a case in point, did about 25 percent less in sales in 1988 than it did in 1981, but with 60 percent fewer employees. It now uses only four hours of labor to make a ton of steel rather than the previous eight hours. Sales dollars were down 25 percent, but profits were up nearly 100 percent.[10] That's improved productivity!

---

service organizations
Organizations that produce non-physical outputs like educational, medical, and transportation services that are intangible, can't be stored in inventory, and incorporate the customer or client in the actual production process.

deindustrialization
The conversion of an economy from dominance by manufacturing to dominance by service-oriented businesses.

States, Canada, Australia, and Western Europe, **service organizations** dominate. They produce nonphysical outputs such as educational, medical, and transportation services that are intangible, can't be stored in inventory, and incorporate the customer or client in the actual production process.

Deindustrialization is taking place among advanced economies. Blue-collar jobs in manufacturing are being replaced by jobs in the service sector. The manufacturing firms that survive are becoming smaller and leaner. The bulk of new jobs are being created in services—from janitors to fast-food servers to computer repairers and programmers to accountants and physicians.

A major challenge for management in a deindustrialized society will be to increase productivity. It's a lot tougher to improve productivity in a service organization than in manufacturing because fewer factors are under management's control. College administrators, for example, have few options for improving instructional productiv-

Sleep Inn is proving that significant productivity gains can be achieved in service firms. It employs 13 percent fewer people than comparably sized no-frills hotels. It was designed with the mind set of an industrial engineer laying out an assembly line. Among some of its features: the laundry room is almost completely automated; closets have no doors for maids to open and shut; and the shower stalls are round, eliminating corners that collect dust.

ity. Faculty members can teach more classes per term or larger classes. Both result in a greater number of students being "processed." Teaching assistants, audio-visual aids, and computer-scored tests can make it easier to handle more students, but these efficiency measures are quickly exhausted. This explains, to a large extent, why college tuition fees have regularly outpaced inflation.[11] For managers and administrators in colleges, hospitals, airlines, government agencies, and all the other service sector organizations, a major challenge for the 1990s will be creatively transferring to service organizations the operations concepts and techniques that worked in manufacturing.

STRATEGIC OPERATIONS MANAGEMENT

Modern manufacturing was born three-quarters of a century ago in the United States, primarily in Detroit's automobile factories. The success U.S. manufacturers experienced during World War II led executives of manufacturing firms to believe that the troublesome problems of production had been conquered. These executives directed their attention to other areas such as finance and marketing. From the late 1940s through the mid-1970s, manufacturing activities were slighted. With only the occasional exception (such as the aerospace industry), top management gave manufacturing little attention, managers "on the way up" avoided it, and market leadership dwindled.

Meanwhile, with U.S. executives neglecting the production side of their business, managers in Japan, West Germany, and other countries took the opportunity to develop modern, computer-assisted facilities that fully integrated manufacturing operations into strategic planning decisions. The competition's success realigned world manufacturing leadership. For example, U.S. manufacturers found that foreign goods were being made not only more cheaply but also better. By the late 1970s, U.S. manufacturers were facing a true crisis, and a good percentage of them responded.[12] They invested heavily in improving manufacturing technology, increased the authority of manufacturing executives, and began incorporating existing and future production requirements into the organization's overall strategic plan. Today, successful manufacturers are taking a top-down approach to operations and implementing comprehensive manufacturing planning systems.

Harvard University professor Wickham Skinner has been urging a "manufacturing focus" to strategy for a number of years.[13] He argued that too many important production decisions had been relegated to lower-level managers. Production needed to be managed from the top down, rather than from the bottom up. The organization's overall strategy should directly reflect its manufacturing capabilities and limitations and should include operations objectives and strategies. He pointed out, for example, that each organization's operations strategy needed to be unique and reflect the inherent trade-offs in any production process. Cost reduction and quality enhancement often work against each other. So, too, do short delivery times and limited inventory levels. Since there is no single "most efficient way" to produce things, top management needs to identify and emphasize its competitive advantage in operations. Some organizations are competing on the more traditional basis of low prices achieved through cost reduction. Others are competing on the basis of quality, reliable delivery, warranties, short lead times, customer service, rapid product introduction, or flexible capacity.

As we noted, Skinner's appeals have been heeded. The manufacturing organizations that expect to compete successfully in world markets are incorporating operations decisions in their strategic plans and returning manufacturing executives to a place of prominence in the organization's power structure.[14]

PLANNING OPERATIONS

As we've noted in several places throughout this book, planning must precede control. Therefore, before we can introduce operations-management control techniques, we need to review a few of the more important decisions related to planning operations.

Four key decisions—capacity, location, process, and layout—provide the long-term strategic direction for operations planning. They determine the proper size of an operating system, where the physical facilities should be located, the best methods for transforming inputs into outputs, and the most efficient layout of equipment and work stations. Once these decisions have been made, three short-term decisions—the aggregate plan, the master schedule, and a material requirements plan—need to be established. These provide the tactical plans for the operating system. In this section, we'll review each of these seven types of planning decisions. (See Figure 20–2.)

Capacity Planning

Assume that you have decided to go into the boat-building business. On the basis of your analysis of the market and other environmental factors (see Chapter 8), you believe there is a market for a premium-quality 28-foot sailboat. You know *what* you want to produce. What's the next step? You need to determine *how* many boats you expect to build. This, in turn, will determine the proper size of your plant and other facility-planning issues. When managers assess their operating system's capabilities for

FIGURE 20–2
Planning Operations

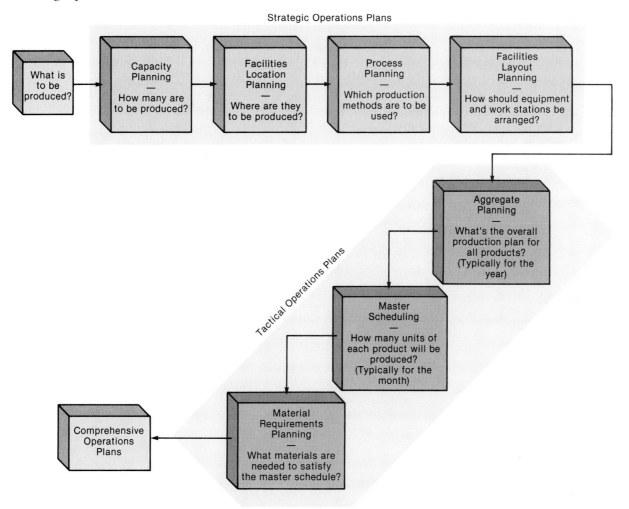

capacity planning
Assessing an operating system's ability to produce a desired number of output units for each type of product during a given time period.

producing a desired number of output units for each type of product anticipated during a given time period, they are engaged in **capacity planning.**[15]

Capacity planning begins by taking the forecasts of sales demand (see Chapter 9) and converting them into capacity requirements. If you produce only one type of boat, plan to sell the boats for an average of $50,000 each, and anticipate generating sales of $2.5 million during the first year, your physical capacity requirements need to handle fifty boats. This calculation is obviously much more complex if you're producing dozens of different products.

If your organization is already established, you compare this forecast against your existing production capacity. Then you can determine whether you'll need to add to or subtract from your existing capacity. Keep in mind that you don't have to be in a manufacturing business to use capacity planning. The following steps are just as relevant for determining the number of beds needed in a hospital or the maximum number of meals that a Burger King can serve.

Once you have converted the forecast into physical capacity requirements, you will be able to develop a set of alternative capacity plans that will meet the requirements.

MANAGING FROM A GLOBAL PERSPECTIVE

Global Operations Strategy

Japanese firms like Sony and Panasonic could never produce the quality electronic products they do at the prices at which they sell them if they sold their products only in Japan. Why? Because the Japanese home market is very small. These companies are able to justify the investments they make in research, technology, and quality design only because they enjoy the economies of selling their products worldwide.

In the global marketplace, the place where goods are manufactured, the amount to be produced, and similar production and operations decisions must consider international comparative advantages.[16] Because of rapidly rising labor costs in Japan, Sony has moved some of its low-skill, labor-intensive manufacturing operations to Taiwan. The need for creative design skills encouraged Mazda executives to locate a design center in Southern California. The rise of the yen in relation to the dollar motivated Honda to set up manufacturing plants in Ohio. Low-interest loans by the Irish government led California-based semiconductor equipment manufacturer Western Digital Corporation to open a new plant in Ireland.

Global organizations no longer produce their goods in one country and then ship them around the world. Companies like Ford, Procter & Gamble, and Royal Dutch Shell have manufacturing operations in countries throughout the world. They design products for world markets and use worldwide production and distribution systems, as well as vertical integration, to gain economies of scale. But many other benefits can accrue from pursuing a global operations strategy. Take, as examples, the ability to prolong life cycles and the benefits that can result from exploiting the volatility of economic factors. Companies can prolong product life cycles by manufacturing in developing nations. A tire retread manufacturer may face a declining market in the United States or Canada but a rapidly growing market in Latin American countries. Global firms can enjoy fluctuations of exchange rates, inflation rates, and similar volatile factors that provide advantages precisely because they do fluctuate, if the firms know how to benefit from the ups and downs. Firms that can accurately forecast economic fluctuations and adjust their manufacturing decisions accordingly, can outperform nonglobal organizations as well as global firms that forecast poorly or operate under the assumption of economic stability.

You will often have to make some modifications—that is, you will have to expand or reduce capacity. In the long term, you can alter the size of your operation significantly and permanently by buying new equipment or selling off existing facilities. In the short term, however, you're forced to make more temporary modifications. You can add an extra shift, increase overtime, or reduce work hours; temporarily shut down operations; or subcontract work out to other organizations. If you manufacture a product that can be stored (like sailboats), you can build inventories during slack periods to be used when demand exceeds capacity.

The building of this Reynolds Metals plant in Washington State is a clear response to low energy costs. Aluminum reduction mills require a great deal of energy, and Washington has cheap hydroelectric power.

facilities location planning
The design and location of an operations facility.

Facilities Location Planning

When you determine the need for additional capacity, you must design and choose a facility. This process is called **facilities location planning.** Where you choose to locate will depend on which factors have the greatest impact on total production and distribution costs. These include availability of labor skills, labor costs, energy costs, proximity to suppliers or customers, and the like. Rarely are all these factors of equal importance. The kind of business you're in typically dictates your critical contingencies, which then dictate—to a large degree—the optimum location.

The need for skilled technical specialists has led an increasing number of high-tech firms to locate in the Boston area. The area's high concentration of colleges and universities makes it easier for firms who require computer, engineering, and research skills to find and hold onto such people. Similarly, it's not by chance that many manufacturers whose conversion processes are labor intensive have moved their manufacturing facilities overseas to places like Taiwan and South Korea. When labor costs are a critical contingency, organizations will locate their facilities where wage rates are low. Tire manufacturers chose their original locations in northern Ohio in order to be close to their major customers, the automobile manufacturers in Detroit. When customer convenience is critical, as it is for many retail outlets, the location decision is often dictated by concerns like proximity to a highway or walking traffic.

What contingencies are going to be critical in your sailboat business? You'll need employees with boat-building skills, and they're most likely to be plentiful in places like New England, Florida, and southern California. Shipping costs of the final product are likely to be a major expenditure, so to keep your prices competitive, you might need to locate close to your customers. That again suggests the East, West, or Gulf coasts or possibly the Great Lakes. Weather might be a further factor. It might be less expensive to build boats outside in warm-weather climates than indoors during winter in the northeast. If labor availability, shipping costs, and weather are your critical contingencies, you still have a great deal of latitude in your location decision. After you choose a region, you still must select a community and a specific site.

Process Planning

process planning
Determining how a product or service will be produced.

In **process planning,** management determines how a product or service will be produced. Process planning encompasses evaluating the available production methods and selecting the set that will best achieve the operating objectives.

For any given production process, whether in manufacturing or the service sector, there are always alternative conversion methods. Designing a restaurant, for instance, allows a number of process choices: to-inventory fast food (as served at McDonald's), limited-option fast food (as served at Burger King or Wendy's), cafeteria-style delivery, drive-in take out, a no-option fixed menu, and complex meals prepared to order. Key questions that ultimately determine how an organization's products or services will be produced include: Will the technology be routine or nonroutine? What degree of automation will be utilized? Should the system be developed to maximize efficiency or flexibility? How should the product or service flow through the operations system?[17]

In our sailboat-manufacturing example, the boats could be made by an assembly-line process. If you decide to keep them highly standardized, you will find a routine transformation process to be most cost efficient. But if you want each boat to be made to order, you will require a different technology and a different set of production methods.

Process planning is complex. Deciding on the best combinations of processes in terms of costs, quality, labor efficiency, and similar considerations is difficult because the decisions are intertwined. A change in one element of the production process often has spillover effects on a number of other elements. As a result, the detailed planning is usually left to production and industrial engineers under the overall guidance of top management.

Facilities Layout Planning

facilities layout planning
Assessing and selecting among alternative layout options for equipment and work stations.

The final strategic decision in operations planning is to assess and select among alternative layout options for equipment and work stations. This is called **facilities layout planning.** The objective of layout planning is to find a physical arrangement that will best facilitate production efficiency and that is also appealing to employees. Table 20–2 offers some suggestions to guide plant layout decisions.

Layout planning begins by assessing space needs. Space has to be provided for work areas, tools and equipment, storage, maintenance facilities, rest rooms, offices,

TABLE 20–2   Guidelines for a Good Plant Layout

1. Keep activities in a straight-line flow.
2. Minimize overall production time.
3. Minimize handling between operations.
4. Minimize handling distances.
5. Be adaptable to changing conditions.
6. Make activities progress from receiving toward shipping.
7. Make provisions for employee convenience, safety, and comfort.

Source: Based on Richard L. Francis and John A. White, *Facility Layout and Location: An Analytical Approach* (Englewood Cliffs, NJ: Prentice-Hall, 1974), pp. 33–34; and James A. Apple, *Plant Layout and Materials Handling,* 3rd ed. (New York: John Wiley, 1977), pp. 18–19.

CalComp makes plotters that print computer drawings. It has replaced its straight, long transfer line on the shop floor with a U-shaped assembly area. This improved communication and reduced the distance that work in progress travels as it is pushed from station to station on individual carts. This change was a major contributor to lowering production costs by 30 percent and inventory-handling costs by 65 percent.

process layout
Arranging manufacturing components together according to similarity of function.

product layout
Arranging manufacturing components according to the progressive steps by which a product is made.

fixed-position layout
A manufacturing layout in which the product stays in place while tools, equipment, and human skills are brought to it.

aggregate planning
Planning overall production activities and their associated operating resources.

lunch areas and cafeterias, waiting rooms, and even parking lots. Then, based on previous process plans, various layout configurations can be evaluated to determine how efficient each is for handling the work flow. To help make these decisions, a number of layout-planning devices are available, ranging from simple, scaled-to-size paper cutouts to sophisticated computer software programs that can manipulate hundreds of variables and print out alternative layout designs.[18]

There are basically three work-flow layouts.[19] The **process layout** arranges components (such as work centers, equipment, or departments) together according to similarity of function. Figure 20–3 illustrates the process layout at a medical clinic. In **product layout,** the components are arranged according to the progressive steps by which the product is made. Figure 20–4 illustrates a product layout in a plant that manufactures aluminum tubing. The third approach, the **fixed-position layout,** is used when, because of its size or bulk, the product remains at one location. The product stays in place, and tools, equipment, and human skills are brought to it. Sound stages on a movie lot or the manufacturing of airplanes illustrates the fixed-position layout. The building of your 28-foot sailboats is likely to use either a product or fixed-position layout.

Aggregate Planning

Once the strategic design decisions have been made, we move to the tactical operations decisions. The first of these deals with planning the overall production activities and their associated operating resources. This is called **aggregate planning** and often occupies a time frame of up to a year.

The aggregate plan provides a "big picture." On the basis of the demand forecast and capacity plan, the aggregate plan sets inventory levels and production rates and estimates the size of the total operation's labor force on a monthly basis for approximately the next twelve months. The focus is on *generalities,* not specifics. Families of

FIGURE 20-3

A Process Layout at a Medical Clinic

Source: From Everett E. Adam, Jr. and Ronald J. Ebert, *Production and Operations Management: Concepts, Models, and Behavior,* 4th ed. (Englewood Cliffs, NJ: Prentice Hall, 1989), p. 233. With permission.

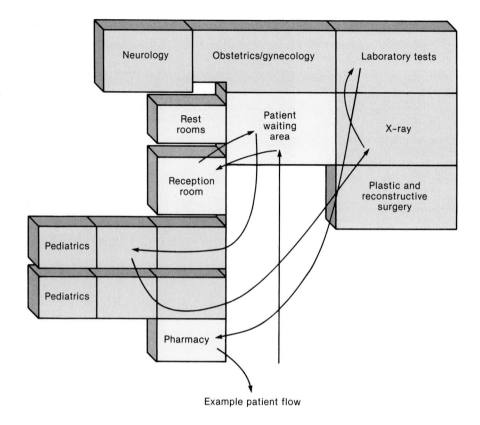

Example patient flow

items are considered, not individual items. A paint company's aggregate plan would look at the total number of gallons of house paint to be manufactured but avoid decisions about color or size of container. As such, the aggregate plan is particularly valuable to large operations that have a varied product line. As you'll see in the next section, for the small, one-product firm, such as the sailboat-manufacturing operation, the aggregate plan will look like the master schedule, only it will cover a longer time frame.

When completed, the aggregate plan often yields two basic decisions: the best overall production rate to adopt and the overall number of workers to be employed during each period in the planning horizon.[20]

Master Scheduling

master schedule

A schedule that specifies quantity and type of items to be produced; how, when, and where they should be produced; labor force levels; and inventory.

The **master schedule** is derived from the aggregate plan. It specifies the quantity and type of each item to be produced; how, when, and where they should be produced for the next day, week, or month; labor force levels; and inventory.

FIGURE 20-4

A Product Layout in an Aluminum Tubing Plant

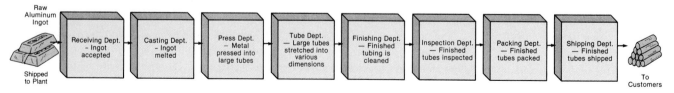

FIGURE 20–5

Developing a Master Schedule from an Aggregate Plan

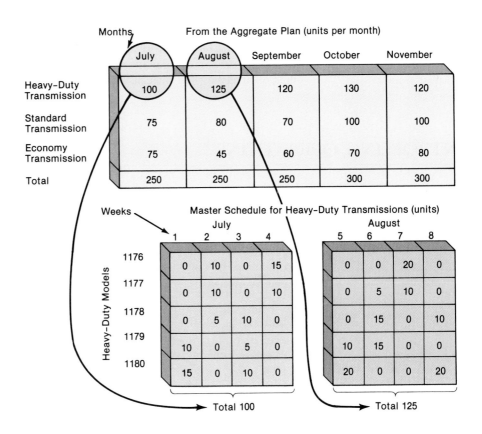

The first requirement of master scheduling is *disaggregation*—that is, breaking the aggregate plan down into detailed operational plans for each of the products or services the organization produces.[21] After that, these plans need to be scheduled against one another in a master schedule.

Figure 20–5 depicts a master schedule for a manufacturer of automobile transmissions. The top portion of the figure informs lower-level managers (through the aggregate plan) that top management has authorized the capacity, inventory, and people to produce 100 heavy-duty transmissions in July, 125 in August, and so forth. The lower part of the figure illustrates a master schedule. For example, it shows how lower-level managers consider the July production for 100 heavy-duty transmissions and determine which models to make. Not only do they determine what specific models to make each week, they also state how many. During the first week of July, for instance, ten units of Model 1179 and fifteen units of Model 1180 will be assembled.

material requirements planning (MRP)

A system that dissects products into the materials and parts necessary for purchasing, inventorying, and priority-planning purposes.

Material Requirements Planning

After the specific products have been decided upon, each should be dissected to determine the precise materials and parts that it requires. **Material requirements planning (MRP)** is a system that uses this data for purchasing, inventorying, and priority-planning purposes.

With the assistance of a computer, product design specifications can be used to identify all the materials and parts necessary to produce the product. By merging this information with computerized inventory records, management will know the quantities of each part in inventory and when each is likely to be used up. When lead times and safety stock requirements are established and entered into the computer, MRP ensures that the right materials are available when needed.

CONTROLLING OPERATIONS

Once the operating system has been designed and implemented, its key elements must be monitored. The following discussion offers guidance for controlling costs, purchasing, maintenance, and quality.

Cost Control

An automobile industry analyst has compared the U.S. and Japanese approaches to cost control: "The Japanese regard cost control as something you wake up every morning and do. Americans have always thought of it as a project. You cut costs 20 percent and say: 'Whew! That's over.' We can't afford to think that way anymore."[22]

U.S. managers have often treated cost control as an occasional crusade that is initiated by, and under the control of, the accounting staff. Accountants establish cost standards per unit, and if deviations occur, management looks for the cause. Have material prices increased? Is labor being used efficiently? Do employees need additional training? However, as the previous quote implies, cost control needs to play a central part in the design of an operating system, and it needs to be a continuing concern of every manager.

Many organizations have adopted the cost-center approach to controlling costs. Work areas, departments, or plants are identified as distinct **cost centers,** and their managers are held responsible for their units' cost performance. Any unit's total costs are made up of two types of costs: direct and indirect. **Direct costs** are costs incurred in proportion to the output of a particular good or service. Labor and materials typically fall into this category. On the other hand, **indirect costs** are largely unaffected by changes in output. Insurance expenses and the salaries of staff personnel are examples of typical indirect costs. This direct-indirect distinction is important. While cost-center managers are held responsible for all direct costs in their units, indirect costs are not necessarily within their control. However, because all costs are controllable at some level in the organization, top managers should identify where the control lies and hold lower managers accountable for costs under their control.[23]

Purchasing Control

It has been said that human beings *are* what they eat. Metaphorically, the same applies to organizations. Their processes and outputs depend on the inputs they "eat." It's difficult to make quality products out of inferior inputs. Highly skilled leather workers need quality cowhides if they are going to produce high-quality wallets. Gas station operators depend on a regular and dependable inflow of certain octane-rated gasolines from their suppliers in order to meet their customers' demands. If the gas isn't there, they can't sell it. If the gasoline is below the specified octane rating, customers may be dissatisfied and take their business somewhere else. Management must therefore monitor the delivery, performance, quality, quantity, and price of inputs from

cost center
A unit in which managers are held responsible for all associated costs.

direct costs
Costs incurred in proportion to the output of a particular good or service.

indirect costs
Costs that are largely unaffected by changes in output.

suppliers. Purchasing control seeks to ensure availability, acceptable quality, continued reliable sources, and, at the same time, reduced costs.[24]

What can managers do to facilitate control of inputs? They need to gather information on the dates that supplies arrive and their condition on arrival. They need to gather data about the quality of supplies and their compatibility with operations processes. Finally, they need to obtain data on supplier price performance. Are the prices of the delivered goods the same as those quoted when the order was placed?

This information can be used to rate suppliers, identify problem suppliers, and guide management in choosing future suppliers. Trends can be detected. Suppliers can be evaluated, for instance, on responsiveness, service, reliability, and competitiveness.

Building Close Links with Suppliers   A rapidly growing trend in manufacturing is turning suppliers into partners.[25] Instead of using ten or twelve vendors and forcing them to compete against each other to gain the firm's business, manufacturers are using only two or three vendors and working closely with them to improve efficiency and quality.

Motorola, for instance, sends its design-and-manufacturing engineers to suppliers to help with any problem.[26] Other firms now routinely send inspection teams to rate suppliers' operations. They're assessing these suppliers' manufacturing and delivery techniques, statistical process controls that identify causes of defects, and the ability of the suppliers to handle data electronically. Companies in the United States and around the world are doing what has long been a tradition in Japan—that is, they are developing long-term relationships with suppliers. As collaborators and partners, rather than adversaries, firms are finding that they can achieve better quality of inputs, fewer defects, and lower costs. Furthermore, when problems arise with suppliers, open communication channels facilitate quick resolutions.

Economic Order Quantity Model   One of the best-known techniques for mathematically deriving the optimum quantity for a purchase order is the **economic order quantity model (EOQ).** The EOQ model seeks to balance four costs involved in ordering and carrying inventory: the *purchase costs* (purchase price plus delivery charges less discounts); the *ordering costs* (paperwork, follow-up, inspection when the item arrives, and other processing costs); *carrying costs* (money tied up in inventory, storage, insurance, taxes, and so forth); and *stockout costs* (profits forgone from orders lost, the cost of reestablishing goodwill, and additional expenses incurred to expedite late shipments).

The objective of the EOQ model, as shown in Figure 20–6, is to minimize the total costs of two of these four costs—carrying costs and ordering costs. As the amount ordered gets larger and larger, average inventory increases and so do carrying costs. But placing larger orders means fewer orders and thus lowers ordering costs. For example, if annual demand for an inventory item is 26,000 units, and we order 500 each time, we will place 52 (26,000/500) orders per year. This gives us an average inventory of 250 (500/2) units. However, if the order quantity is increased to 2,000 units, there will be fewer orders placed, 13 (26,000/2,000), but the average inventory on hand will increase to 1,000 (2,000/2) units. Thus as holding costs go up, ordering costs go down, and vice versa. As depicted in Figure 20–6, the lowest total cost—and thus the most economic order quantity—is reached at the lowest point on the total cost curve. That is the point at which ordering cost equals carrying cost. It is called the *economic order quantity.*

To compute this optimal order quantity, you need the following data: forecasted demand for the item during the period (*D*), the cost of placing each order (*OC*), the value or purchase price of the item (*V*), and the carrying cost of maintaining the total

economic order quantity model (EOQ)

A technique for balancing purchases, ordering, carrying, and stockout costs to derive the optimum quantity for a purchase order.

FIGURE 20–6
Determining the Most
Economic Order Quantity

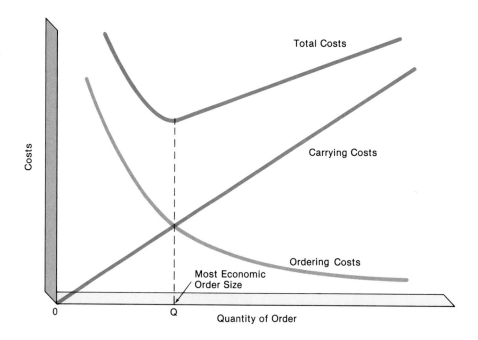

inventory, expressed as a percentage (*CC*). We can now present the standard EOQ formula and demonstrate its use:

$$EOQ = \sqrt{\frac{2 \times D \times OC}{V \times CC}}$$

As an example, Playback Electronics, a retailer of high-quality sound and video equipment, is trying to ascertain its economic order quantities. The item in question is a Century videotape recorder. The company forecasts sales of 4,000 units a year. Purchasing believes that the cost of each recorder will be $500. The accountants estimate the cost of placing an order for video players at $75 per order and annual insurance, taxes, and other carrying costs at 20 percent of the recorder's worth. Using the EOQ formula and the information above, we find

$$EOQ = \sqrt{\frac{2 \times 4,000 \times 75}{500 \times .20}}$$
$$= \sqrt{6,000}$$
$$= 77.46 \text{ units} \cong 78 \text{ units}$$

The inventory model suggests to Playback's management that it is most economic to order in quantities or lots of approximately 78 units; stated differently, they should order about 52 (4,000/78) times a year.

What would happen if the supplier of the video devices offered Playback a 5 percent discount on purchases if Playback buys in minimum quantities of 120 units? Should Playback's management now purchase in quantities of 78 or 120? Without the discount, and therefore ordering 78 each time, Playback's annual costs for this video player would be as follows:

$$\text{Purchase cost: } \$500 \times 4,000 \qquad\qquad = \qquad \$2,000,000$$

$$\text{Carrying cost: } \frac{78}{2} \times \$500 \times 0.20 \qquad = \qquad 3,900$$

$$\text{(average inventory units)} \times \text{(value of item)} \times \text{(percentage)}$$

$$\text{Ordering cost: } \quad 52 \qquad \times \qquad 75 \qquad\qquad = \qquad 3,900$$

$$\text{(number} \qquad\qquad \times \qquad \text{(cost to place order)}$$

of orders)

Total cost: $2,007,800

With the 5 percent discount for ordering 120 units, the item cost would be $475. The annual inventory costs would be as follows:

$$\text{Purchase cost:} \quad \$475 \times 4,000 \qquad = \qquad \$1,900,000$$

$$\text{Carrying cost:} \quad \frac{120}{2} \times 475 \times 0.20 \qquad = \qquad 5,700$$

$$\text{Ordering cost:} \quad \frac{4,000}{120} \times 75 \qquad = \qquad 2,500$$

$$\text{Total cost:} \qquad\qquad\qquad\qquad\qquad \$1,908,200$$

These computations suggest to Playback's management that it should take the 5 percent discount. Even though it has to stock larger quantities, the savings are almost $100,000 a year.

A word of caution should be added. The EOQ model assumes that demand and lead time are known and constant. If these conditions cannot be met, the model should not be used. For example, it generally should not be used for manufactured component inventory, since the components are taken out of stock all at once or in lumps or in lots, rather than at a constant rate. Does this mean that the EOQ model is useless when demand is variable? No. The model can still be of some use in demonstrating trade-offs in costs and the need to control lot sizes. Also there are more sophisticated lot-sizing models for handling lumpy demand and special situations.

fixed-point reordering system
A system that "flags" the fact that inventory needs to be replenished when it reaches a certain level.

Inventory Ordering Systems   In many checkbooks, after you use up about 95 percent of the checks, you find a reorder form included among the checks; it reminds you that it's time to reorder. This is an example of a **fixed-point reordering system.** At some preestablished point in the operations process, the system is designed to "flag" the fact that the inventory needs to be replenished. It is triggered when the inventory reaches a certain point or level.

The goal of a fixed-point reordering system is to minimize inventory carrying costs and to ensure a reasonable level of customer service (limiting the probability of an item running out—a *stockout*). Therefore the reorder point should be established to equate the time remaining before a stockout and the lead time to receive delivery of the reordered quantity. In such cases, the newly ordered items would arrive at the same time as the last item in inventory was used up. More realistically, management does not usually allow the inventory to fall below some safety stock level. (See Figure 20–7.) By using certain statistical procedures, one can set a reorder point at a level that gives an organization enough inventory to get through the lead-time period and some reasonable insurance against a stockout. This buffer, or safety, stock gives protection against greater usage than expected during the lead time or an unexpected delay in receiving the item.

As a simple example, in determining a check reorder point, let's assume that the lead time averages three weeks and we write about twenty checks a week. We would need sixty checks to get us through a "normal" reordering lead time. If we feel, on the

FIGURE 20–7
Inventory Cycle with Safety
Stock

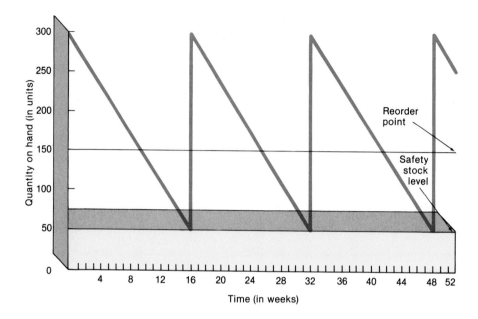

basis of past history, that a one-week safety stock would be sufficient to get us through most lead-time periods, the order should be placed when there are 80 (60 + 20) checks left. This is the reorder point. Another word of caution. The more safety stock, the less the risk of stockout. But the additional inventory will add to the carrying costs. Thus we again face a cost-benefit decision. At times it may be prudent (cost-wise) to run out of stock.

One of the most primitive but certainly effective uses of the fixed-point reordering system is to keep the item—for example, pens and duplicating paper in an office or boxes of shoes in a retail shoe store—in two separate containers. Inventory is drawn from one until it is empty. At that point, a reorder is placed, and items are drawn from the second container. If demand for an item has been estimated properly, the replacement order to replenish the stock should arrive before the second container is used up.

Another, more recent, version of the fixed-point reorder system relies on computer control. Sales are automatically recorded by a central computer that has been programmed to initiate a purchase order for an item when its inventory reaches some critical fixed point. A number of retail stores have such systems. The cash registers are actually computers, and each sale automatically adjusts the store's inventory record. When the inventory of an item hits the critical point, the computer tells management to reorder or, in some systems, actually prints out the purchase order requisition.

**fixed-interval reordering
system**

A system that uses time as the
determining factor for reviewing
and reordering inventory items.

Another common inventory system is the **fixed-interval reordering system.** The fixed-interval system uses time as the determining factor for inventory control. At a predetermined time—say, once a week or every ninety days—the inventory is counted, and an order is placed for the number of items necessary to bring the inventory back to the desired level. The desired level is established so that if demand and ordering lead time are average, consumption will draw the inventory down to zero (or some safety lead time can be added) just as the next order arrives. This system may have some transportation economies and quantity discount economies over the fixed-point system. For example, it may allow us to consolidate orders from one supplier if we review all the items we purchase from this source at the same time. This is not possible in the other system.

It might take a men's store three weeks to get an order for Levis 501 jeans filled by the manufacturer. If the store typically sells ten pairs of size 30-30 jeans a week, the store manager could set up two containers, keep thirty pairs of jeans in the second container, and initiate reorders whenever the first container is empty. This would be an application of the fixed-point reordering system.

In the 1800s, economist Vilfredo Pareto found that 80 percent of the wealth was controlled by only 20 percent of the population. College instructors typically find that a few students cause most of their problems, and students have probably similarly found that a few instructors cause most of their problems. This concept, the vital few and the trivial many, can be applied to inventory control.

It is not unusual for a company to have thousands of items in inventory. However, evidence indicates that roughly 10 percent of the items in most organizations' inventory account for 50 percent of the annual dollar inventory value. Another 20 percent of the items account for 30 percent of the value. The remaining 70 percent of the items appear to account for only 20 percent of the value. These have been labeled as A, B, and C categories, respectively. Thus we have the name **ABC system.** (See Figure 20–8.)

Cost-benefit analysis would justify that A items receive the tightest control, B items moderate control, and C items the least control. This can be accomplished because there are so few A items and they represent a large dollar investment. Similarly, there are so many C items, but so little dollar investment, that tight control would not be justified. A items, for example, might be monitored weekly, B items monthly, and C items quarterly, since they account for so little dollar value. Or C items might be controlled by using a simple form of order point.

ABC system

A priority system for monitoring inventory items.

Maintenance Control

To deliver goods or services in an efficient and effective manner requires operating systems with high equipment utilization and a minimum amount of downtime. Therefore managers need to be concerned with maintenance control. The importance of maintenance control, however, depends on the process technology used. For example, if a standardized assembly-line process breaks down, it can affect hundreds of

FIGURE 20–8
Example of an ABC Inventory
System

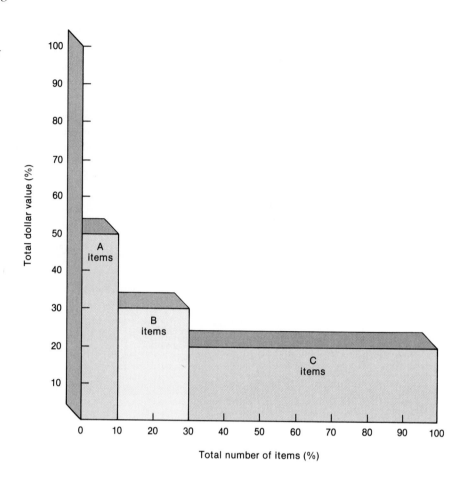

employees. On an automobile or dishwasher assembly line, it's not unusual for a serious breakdown on one machine to bring an entire plant to a halt. In contrast, most systems using more general-purpose and redundant processes have less interdependency between activities, so a machine breakdown is likely to have less of an impact. Nevertheless, an equipment breakdown—like an inventory stockout—may mean higher costs, delayed deliveries, or lost sales.

There are three approaches to maintenance control.[27] **Preventive maintenance** is performed before a breakdown occurs. **Remedial maintenance** is a complete overhaul, replacement, or repair of the equipment when it breaks down. **Conditional maintenance** refers to overhaul or repair in response to an inspection and measurement of the equipment's state. When American Airlines tears down its planes' engines every 1,000 hours, it is engaging in preventive maintenance. When it inspects the planes' tires every twenty-four hours and changes them when conditions warrant it, it is performing conditional maintenance. Finally, if American Airlines' operations policy is to repair lavatory equipment on board its planes only after the equipment breaks down, then it is using remedial maintenance practices.

The American Airlines example points out that the type of maintenance control depends on the costs of a breakdown. The greater the cost in terms of money, time, liability, and goodwill, the greater the benefits from preventive maintenance. That is, the benefits can justify the costs.

Maintenance control should also be considered in the design of equipment. If downtime is highly inconvenient or costly, reliability can be increased by designing redundancy into the equipment. Nuclear power plants, for example, have elaborate backup systems built in. Similarly, equipment can be designed to facilitate fast or

preventive maintenance
Maintenance performed before a breakdown occurs.

remedial maintenance
Maintenance that calls for the overhaul, replacement, or repair of equipment when it breaks down.

conditional maintenance
Maintenance that calls for an overhaul or repair in response to an inspection.

low-cost maintenance. Equipment that has fewer parts has fewer things to go wrong. High-failure items can also be placed in locations that are easily accessible or in independent modular units that can be quickly removed and replaced. Cable television operators follow these guidelines. Breakdowns infuriate customers, so when they occur, management wants to be able to correct them quickly. Speed is facilitated by centralizing equipment in easy-access locations and making extensive use of modular units. If a piece of equipment fails, the whole module of which it is a part can be pulled or replaced in just a few minutes. Television service is resumed rapidly, and the pulled modular unit can be taken to the shop and repaired without time pressures.

Quality Control

With the possible exception of controlling costs, achieving high quality has become the primary focus of today's managers. In this section, we want to consider how managers can control quality.

When we refer to *quality control,* we mean monitoring quality—weight, strength, consistency, color, taste, reliability, finish, or any one of a myriad of quality characteristics—to ensure that it meets some preestablished standard. Quality should be designed into the product and the manufacturing processes. Quality control will probably be needed at one or more points beginning with the receipt of inputs. It will continue with work in process and all steps up to the final product. Assessments at intermediate stages of the transformation process are typically part of quality control. Early detection of a defective part or process can save the cost of further work on the item.

In imposing quality control, managers should begin by asking whether they expect to examine 100 percent of the items or whether a sample can be used. The inspection of each and every item makes sense if the cost of continuous evaluation is very low or if the consequences of a statistical error are very high (such as a drug used in open-heart surgery). Statistical samples are usually less costly and sometimes are the only viable option. For example, if the quality test destroys the product—as happens with bombs or flash bulbs—then sampling has to be utilized.

There are two categories of statistical quality control procedures: acceptance sampling and process control. **Acceptance sampling** refers to the evaluation of purchased or manufactured materials or products that already exist. A sample is taken, then the decision to accept or reject the whole lot is based on a calculation of sample risk error. **Process control** refers to sampling items during the transformation process to see whether the transformation process itself is under control. For example, a process control procedure at Coca-Cola would be able to pick up that a bottling machine was out of adjustment because it was filling twenty-six-ounce bottles with only twenty-three ounces of soda. Managers could then stop the process and readjust the machine.

A final consideration in quality control relates to whether the test is done by examining attributes or variables. The inspection and classification of items as acceptable or unacceptable is called **attribute sampling.** This is the way paint color and potato chips are evaluated. An inspector compares the items against some standard and rates their quality as acceptable or not acceptable. In contrast, **variable sampling** involves taking a measurement to determine how much an item varies from the standard. It involves a range rather than a dichotomy. Management typically identifies the standard and an acceptable deviation. Any sample that measures within the range is accepted, and those outside are rejected. Inland Steel might test some steel bar to see whether the average breaking strength is between 120 and 140 pounds per square inch. If it is not, the cause is investigated, and corrective action is initiated.

acceptance sampling
A quality control procedure in which a sample is taken and a decision to accept or reject a whole lot is based on a calculation of sample risk error.

process control
A quality control procedure in which sampling is done during the transformation process to determine whether the process itself is under control.

attribute sampling
A quality control technique that classifies items as acceptable or unacceptable on the basis of some variable.

variable sampling
A quality control technique in which a measurement is taken to determine how much an item varies from the standard.

CURRENT ISSUES IN OPERATIONS MANAGEMENT

Capitalizing on new technology! Managing quality! Reducing inventories! Utilizing flexibility and speed as competitive advantages! These issues are currently focuses of management's renewed interest in manufacturing productivity. In this section, we review each of them, since managers consider them to be essential for making products and services competitive in world markets.

Technology and Product Development

Today's competitive marketplace has put tremendous pressure on manufacturers to deliver products with high quality and low cost and to significantly reduce time to market. Even if you have the proverbial "better mousetrap," customers won't be beating a path to your door if your competitor develops a mousetrap that is almost as good but is in stores a year to two ahead of yours. The two key ingredients to successfully accelerating the product-development process are an organizational commitment to improving the development cycle and investment in the technology to make it happen.[28]

computer-integrated manu-facturing (CIM)

Combines the organizations strategic business plan and manufacturing plan with state-of-the-art computer applications.

One of the most effective tools that manufacturers have in meeting the time-to-market challenge is **computer-integrated manufacturing (CIM).** This brings together the organization's strategic business plan and manufacturing plan with state-of-the-art computer applications.[29] The technologies of computer-aided design (CAD) and computer-aided manufacturing (CAM) are typically the basis for CIM.

CAD has essentially made manual drafting obsolete. Using computers to visually display graphics, CAD enables engineers to develop new product designs in about half the time required for manual drafting. Eagle Engine Manufacturing, for instance, used its CAD system to design a new race-car engine in nine months instead of the traditional two-plus years.[30]

CAM relies on computers to guide and control the manufacturing process. Numerically controlled programs can direct machines to cut patterns, shape parts, assemble units, and perform other complicated tasks.

In the not-too-distant future, CIM will permit the entire manufacturing process to be viewed as a continuum. Every step—from order entry to order shipping—will be expressed as data and be computerized. It will allow management to respond rapidly to changing markets. It will give firms the ability to test hundreds of design changes in hours rather than months and then provide the flexibility to efficiently produce multiple variations of products in lot sizes as small as one or two. When manufacturing is computer-integrated, for example, it is no longer necessary to stop the assembly line and spend valuable time changing dies and equipment in order to produce a new or nonstandard product. A single change in the computer program—which can be done in seconds—immediately realigns the manufacturing process.

Managing Quality

The story is told of a Japanese company that received a parts order from a U.S. firm. The purchase requisition stated that the 1,000 parts were to be 95 percent defect-free. A few weeks later, the U.S. firm received the shipment of parts. In the packing crate was the following note: "Enclosed are the 950 defect-free parts. The remaining 50 defective parts requested will be shipped shortly."

What's the message in this story? It says that the Japanese take quality seriously. They don't expect to build products with defects. Only in the past ten years or so have U.S. manufacturers come to realize that the quest for quality is a never-ending endeavor and that even 99.9 percent defect-free is not good enough. Remember that

Lockheed Corporation's Calfab sheet-metal facility slashed design and production time by 96 percent in just two days by using computer-integrated manufacturing.

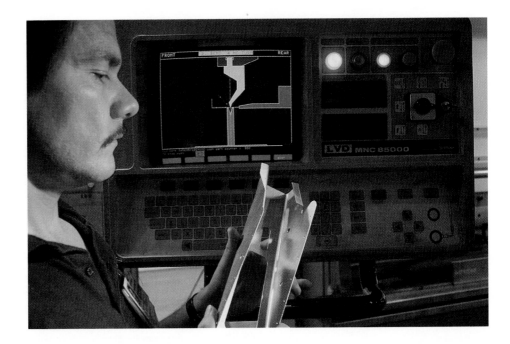

99.9 percent defect-free still means two unsafe landings *per day* at Chicago's O'Hare International Airport, 16,000 pieces of mail lost by the U.S. Postal Service *every hour*, and 22,000 checks deducted from the wrong bank accounts *each hour*.[31] These numbers vividly illustrate why quality matters and why a zero-defects policy makes a lot of sense.

In the 1950s and 1960s, "Made in the U.S.A." stood for the best that industry could turn out. But much of U.S. management got cocky and lazy. By the early 1980s, when consumers thought about quality products, they thought about goods made in places like Japan and West Germany. But U.S. management got the message during the 1980s. A 1987 survey of top executives showed that the task of improving service quality and product quality was the most critical challenge facing companies. Quality improvement was even rated ahead of such issues as productivity, product liability, government regulations, and labor relations.[32]

Florida Power & Light Co. has found that quality pays. For instance, its meter readers were found to be making one error for every 2,000 meter reads. By replacing dial meters with digital meters, it has reduced the error rate to one in every 150,000 reads.

Is All the Investment in Automation Justified?

A number of years ago, the president of the United Automobile Workers union was being given a tour of a new, highly automated General Motors factory. Managers pointed out the advantages of robots and how the plant could produce the same number of cars as a traditional plant but with fewer than 20 percent of the workers. Managers continually remarked with pride how much more efficient the robots were than human workers. Finally, in frustration, the UAW executive asked his tour guides, "How many cars do robots buy?"

This incident addresses an ethical dilemma associated with new technology. Automation frequently puts people out of jobs. Motorola, for instance, is automating its plants that produce cellular telephones.[33] Its conventional, nonautomated manufacturing plants require at least 300 to 400 workers to produce 1,000 units per week. The new automated plants can produce 3,700 units weekly with only 70 employees!

The factory of the future might well be made up of a multitude of robots with only a handful of engineers and technicians to run the place. Traditional skilled, blue-collar manufacturing jobs will be gone. But are people-free plants desirable? They cost billions of dollars to construct. In 1987, U.S. firms spent $15.5 billion on factory automation. Such expenditures are expected to reach nearly $25 billion by 1992.[34] Yet this outlay for improved technology hasn't necessarily resulted in lower costs, higher quality, or greater productivity for all its purchasers. General Motors, as a case in point, spent $50 billion between 1980 and 1987 on capital investment for robots, lasers, computers, and the like—enough to have bought Toyota and Nissan and had a few spare billions left over. Meanwhile, during this *same* period, GM's break-even point *rose* 30 percent.[35]

Are high-tech manufacturing plants, full of robotics and other state-of-the-art automated equipment, being constructed to improve competitive capabilities? If the answer is Yes, then what is the cost to society of the employees whose jobs are lost? It is also possible that a large part of the enthusiasm for automated plants is unjustified. Managers might simply want to appear "forward thinking." By creating automated plants, management makes itself look competent and effective.

Is the spending of all these billions of dollars for automation justified? Are some workers being displaced by robots for reasons that have more to do with appearances, fad, and fashion than economic efficiencies? What do *you* think?

U.S. managers are now accepting the responsibility for past failures and taking bold steps to improve the quality of their products and services.[36] They are redesigning operating systems to build quality into the manufacturing process, and they are educating workers to discard the long-held belief that occasional errors are normal and acceptable. For example, all of Xerox's 100,000 employees have completed at least

FIGURE 20–9
How a Typical Quality Circle
Operates

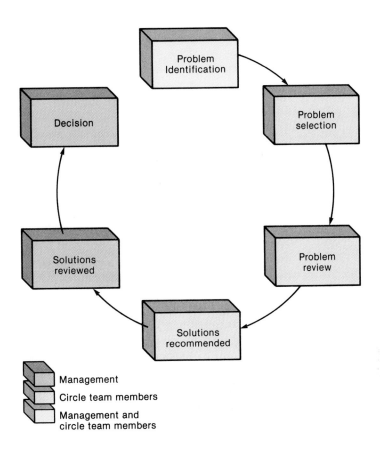

Management
Circle team members
Management and
circle team members

forty-eight hours of training that is designed to teach workers to think of everyone whom their work affects—co-workers as well as ultimate purchasers of copy machines—as a customer to please.[37] Eastman Kodak, which also makes copying machines, has eliminated product inspectors in its copier-manufacturing plants, has made each worker responsible for quality before passing work on to the next stage, and has reduced product defects by 90 percent.[38]

Management is also tapping into workers' expertise by creating quality circles. Originally conceived in the United States and exported to Japan in the 1950s, quality circles have been imported back to the United States, in no small part because of their contribution toward Japan's success in making low-cost quality products.

Quality circles are work groups of eight to ten employees and supervisors who share an area of responsibility.[39] They meet regularly (typically once a week on company time and on company premises) to discuss their quality problems, investigate causes of the problems, recommend solutions, and take corrective actions. They assume responsibility for solving quality problems, and they generate and evaluate their own feedback. Management usually makes the final decision about the implementation of recommended solutions. Of course, no one assumes that employees have an inherent ability to analyze and solve quality problems. Therefore part of the quality circle concept includes teaching participating employees group communication skills, various quality strategies, and measurement and problem analysis techniques. Figure 20–9 describes a typical quality circle process.

Quality circles have been widely adopted in recent years. One estimate indicates that over 90 percent of *Fortune* 500 companies now have them.[40] Some of these companies have literally dozens of quality circles. For instance, General Electric has

quality circles
Work groups that meet regularly to discuss, investigate, and correct quality problems.

MANAGERS WHO MADE A DIFFERENCE

■

■

Tom Gelb at Harley-Davidson

This chapter opened with a description of how Harley-Davidson became profitable by improving its productivity and quality. The man who deserves much of the credit for Harley's resurrection is Tom Gelb, senior vice president for manufacturing operations.[41]

Gelb was part of the management team that took over Harley-Davidson with its 1981 leveraged buyout. As head of manufacturing operations, he faced the challenge of improving productivity and quality. He had little money for investing in much-needed new production equipment, so he had to upgrade operations on the cheap. In place of new equipment, he borrowed production and quality techniques from the Japanese. He led a change in Harley's organizational culture from one that treated employees as merely hired hands to one in which employees were to be respected and take an active role in the decision-making process.

Gelb has transformed Harley-Davidson's manufacturing operations into one of the most efficient and competitive in the industry. It now takes only three days instead of thirty to build a Harley motorcycle frame, and production per employee has increased more than 50 percent. Dealers and customers, too, welcome the high-quality products that Gelb's manufacturing team has been able to produce.

Photo courtesy of Tom Gelb.

more than 1,000 at plants across the United States.[42] Are they a fad or a permanent addition to U.S. industry? While it's too early to draw any definitive conclusions, where quality circles have been properly introduced and supported, they appear to provide real improvements in quality and productivity.[43]

Reducing Inventories

A major portion of many companies' assets is tied up in inventories. Most *Fortune* 500 manufacturing firms maintain inventories valued literally in the *billions* of dollars. IBM, as a case in point, recently reported its inventory assets at $9,565,000,000![44] Firms that can significantly cut their inventories of raw materials and of in-process and finished goods can reduce costs and improve their efficiency.

This fact has not been lost on management. In recent years, U.S. managers have been seeking ways to better manage inventories.[45] On the output side, they have been improving the information link between internal manufacturing schedules and forecasted customer demand. Marketing personnel are being increasingly relied on to provide accurate, up-to-date information on future sales. This is then being coordinated with operating systems data to get a better match between what is produced and what the customers want. Manufacturing resource planning systems are particularly well suited to this function. On the input side, they have been experimenting with another technique widely used in Japan: **just-in-time (JIT) inventory systems.**[46]

just-in-time (JIT) inventory system
A system in which inventory items arrive at the time they are needed in the production process instead of being stored in stock.

In Japan, JIT systems are called **kanban.** The derivation of the word gets to the essence of the just-in-time concept. *Kanban* is Japanese for "card" or "sign." Japanese suppliers ship parts to manufacturers in containers, each of which has a card, or *kanban,* slipped into a side pocket. When a production worker opens a container, he or she takes out the card and sends it back to the supplier. That initiates the shipping of a second container of parts that, ideally, reaches the production worker just as the last part is being used up in the first container. The ultimate goal of a JIT inventory system is to eliminate raw material inventories by precisely coordinating production and supply deliveries. When the system works as designed, it results in a number of positive benefits for a manufacturer: reduced inventories, reduced setup time, better work flow, shorter manufacturing time, less space consumption, and even higher quality. Of course, suppliers must be found who can be depended on to deliver quality materials on time. Since there are no inventories, there is no slack in the system to absorb defective materials or delays in shipment.

An illustration of JIT's benefits can be seen at Walgreen Laboratories, a manufacturer of health and beauty products for the Walgreen drugstore chain.[47] The firm calculated the cost of carrying and managing its inventory at about 25 percent of its total inventory costs. By introducing JIT, it cut its inventory levels by about $8 million. Of course, these benefits required additional work on the part of Walgreen's management. For instance, to allow its suppliers to plan their own production schedules, Walgreen had to project its supply needs six months in advance and commit itself to firm delivery dates weeks ahead of time.

A JIT system isn't for every manufacturer.[48] It requires that suppliers be located in close proximity to the manufacturer's production facility and that suppliers be capable of providing consistently defect-free materials. Such a system also requires reliable transportation links between suppliers and manufacturer; efficient receiving, handling, and distribution of materials; and precisely tuned production planning. Where these conditions can be met, JIT can help management to reduce inventory costs.

kanban
The Japanese name for a just-in-time inventory system.

Flexibility as a Competitive Advantage

In today's changing world of business, firms that can't adjust rapidly won't survive. This is putting a premium on developing manufacturing flexibility.[49] As a result, many organizations are developing flexible manufacturing systems.[50]

They look like something out of a science-fiction movie in which remote-controlled carts deliver a basic casting to a computerized machining center. With robots positioning and repositioning the casting, the machining center calls upon its hundreds of tools to perform varying operations that turn the casting into a finished part. Completed parts, each a bit different from the others, are finished at a rate of one every ninety seconds. Neither skilled machinists nor conventional machine tools are used. Nor are there any costly delays for changing dies or tools in this factory. A single machine can make dozens or even hundreds of different parts in any order management wants.

The unique characteristic of **flexible manufacturing systems** is that by integrating computer-aided design, engineering, and manufacturing, they can produce low-volume, custom products at a cost comparable to what had been possible only through mass production. Flexible manufacturing systems are repealing the laws of economies of scale. Management no longer has to mass produce thousands of identical products to achieve low per-unit production costs. With a flexible manufacturing system, when management wants to produce a new part, it doesn't change machines—it just changes the computer program.

Some automated plants can build a wide variety of flawless products and switch from one product to another on cue from a central computer. John Deere, for instance, has a $1.5 billion automated factory that can turn out ten basic tractor models

flexible manufacturing systems
Systems in which custom-made products can be mass produced by means of computer-aided design, engineering, and manufacturing.

with as many as 3,000 options without plant shutdowns for retooling. These new flexible factories are also proving to be cost effective. IBM's automated plant in Austin, Texas can produce a laptop computer in less than two minutes without the help of a single worker. Compared to a conventional system, IBM's management has found the new plant to be 75 percent more efficient.[51]

Speed as a Competitive Advantage

For years we have heard that, on the highway, speed kills. Managers are now learning that the same principle works in business: Speed kills, only this time it's the competition's speed.[52] By quickly developing, making, and distributing products and services, organizations can gain a competitive advantage. Just as customers may select one organization over another because its products or services are less expensive, uniquely designed, or of superior quality, customers also choose organizations because they can get the product or service they want fast. In essence, Domino's has created a billion-dollar business by using speed as a competitive advantage, guaranteeing delivery of its pizzas in thirty minutes or less.

A number of companies have made incredible improvements in the time it takes them to design and produce their products.[53] AT&T used to need two years to design a new phone. Now it does the job in one year. Motorola used to turn out electronic pagers three weeks after the factory got the order. Now this process takes two *hours*. General Electric used to take three weeks after an order to deliver a custom-made industrial circuit breaker box. They've cut that down to three *days*. These firms and many others are cutting red tape, flattening their organization structures, adding cross-functional teams, redesigning their distribution chains, and using CIM and flexible manufacturing systems to speed up their operations and put increased pressure on their competitors.

SUMMARY

This summary is organized by the chapter-opening learning objectives found on page 625.

1. Operations management refers to the design, operations, and control of the transformation process that converts resources like labor and raw materials into finished goods and services.

2. U.S. managers are increasingly concerned with improving productivity. How people are integrated into the overall operations system determines how productive an organization will be. Factors such as the size and layout of operating facilities, capacity utilization, inventory usage, and maintenance controls are operations management concepts that have a critical bearing on overall productivity.

3. A manufacturing focus to strategy pushes important production decisions to the top of the organization. It recognizes that an organization's overall strategy should directly reflect its manufacturing capabilities and limitations and should include operations objectives and strategies.

4. Four key decisions—capacity, location, process, and layout—provide the long-term, strategic direction for operations planning. They determine the proper size of an operating system, the location of physical facilities, the best methods for transforming inputs into outputs, and the most efficient layout of equipment and work stations.

5. The three decisions that make up the tactical operations plans are the aggregate plan, the master schedule, and the material requirements plan.

6. The economic order quantity model balances the costs of ordering and carrying inventory. To calculate the optimal order quantity, you need to know the forecasted demand for an item during a specific period, the cost of placing each order, the value or purchase price of the item, and the carrying cost of maintaining the total inventory.

7. Alternative inventory ordering systems include fixed-point reordering, fixed-interval reordering, and the ABC system.

8. Quality circles are work groups composed of employees and supervisors that meet regularly to discuss quality problems, investigate causes of the problems, recommend solutions, and take corrective actions.

9. Just-in-time inventory systems seek to reduce inventories, reduce setup time, improve work flow, cut manufacturing time, reduce space consumption, and raise the quality of production. However, they require precise coordination; if this is lacking, they can threaten the smooth, continuous operation of a production system.

10. A flexible manufacturing system can give an organization a competitive advantage by allowing it to produce a wider variety of products, at a lower cost, and in considerably less time than the competition.

REVIEW QUESTIONS

1. "Operations management is part of every manager's job." Explain.
2. What has caused the recent interest in raising productivity?
3. What is the role of critical contingencies in facilities location planning?
4. Contrast process, product, and fixed-position layouts.
5. How is cost control transferred from accountants to managers?
6. What information do you need to calculate the economic order quantity?
7. What is the ABC system? Why is it a contingency approach to inventory control?
8. How do CAD and CAM speed the product-development process?
9. Explain how quality circles can improve product quality.
10. What conditions are necessary for a JIT system to be effective?

DISCUSSION QUESTIONS

1. Demonstrate how capacity, facilities location, process, and facilities layout planning concepts can apply to a service organization.
2. Discuss the relationship between an organization's strategy, its competitive situation, and its transformation processes.
3. "Just-in-time inventory systems are merely an excuse for large companies to pass their inventory costs down to their smaller suppliers." Do you agree or disagree? Discuss.
4. Discuss the operations management techniques used in the United States that have been influenced by Japanese practices.
5. "The fastest road to the top today in a manufacturing organization is through the production function." Do you agree or disagree? Discuss.

SELF-ASSESSMENT EXERCISE

Are You Technically Oriented?

Instructions: Some people tend to be left-brain dominant, while others are right-brain dominant. Studies suggest that left-brain people are more technically oriented. That is, they solve problems systematically, work best with sequential ideas, and like to solve problems logically. This is in contrast to right-brain people, who are intuitive problem solvers. The following questions are designed to provide feedback on your preference for left- or right-brain thinking. Answer each as accurately as you can. It is a forced-choice test, so choose the option you like best (or dislike least), but remember to answer each one.

1. When you solve problems, your basic approach is:
   a. logical, rational
   b. intuitive

2. If you were to write books, you would prefer to write:
   a. fiction
   b. nonfiction

3. When you read, you read for:
   a. main ideas
   b. specific facts and details

4. What kind of stories do you most like to read:
   a. realistic
   b. fantasy

5. When you study or read:
   a. you listen to music on the radio
   b. you must have silence

6. You prefer to learn:
   a. through ordering and planning
   b. through free exploration

7. You prefer to organize things:
   a. sequentially
   b. in terms of relationships

8. Which of these statements best describes you:
   a. almost no mood changes
   b. frequent mood changes

9. Do you enjoy clowning around?
   a. yes
   b. no

10. You would describe yourself as:
    a. generally conforming
    b. generally nonconforming

11. Are you absentminded?
    a. frequently
    b. virtually never

12. What types of assignments do you like best?
    a. well structured
    b. open ended

13. Which is most preferable to you?
    a. producing ideas
    b. drawing conclusions

14. Which is the most fun for you?
    a. dreaming
    b. planning realistically

15. Which of these would be most exciting for you?
    a. inventing something new
    b. improving on something already in existence

16. What type of stories do you prefer?
    a. action
    b. mystery

17. Which do you like best?
    a. cats
    b. dogs

18. What do you like best?
    a. creating stories
    b. analyzing stories

19. Do you think better:
    a. sitting up straight
    b. lying down

20. Which would you prefer to be?
    a. a music composer
    b. a music critic

21. Could you be hypnotized?
    a. yes, quite easily
    b. no, I don't think so

22. Which would you prefer to do?
    a. ballet dancing
    b. interpretative impromptu dancing

23. Which are you best at?
    a. recalling names and dates
    b. recalling where things were in a room or picture

24. When it comes to getting instructions, which do you prefer?
    a. verbal instructions
    b. demonstration

25. When getting verbal instructions, how do you generally feel?
    a. restless
    b. attentive

Turn to page 677 for scoring directions and key.

Source: From Steven Altman, Enzo Valenzi, and Richard M. Hodgetts, *Organizational Behavior: Theory and Practice* (Orlando, FL: Harcourt Brace Jovanovich, Inc), pp. 514–17. Copyright © 1985 of Harcourt Brace Jovanovich, Inc. With permission.

CASE APPLICATION 20A

Motorola

Motorola, like so many U.S. firms recently, has been borrowing many of the best Japanese manufacturing methods, refining them, and applying them to produce first-rate products.[54] For example, the superfast robotic production line Motorola created in its Boynton Beach, Florida plant to make pagers incorporates assembly methods developed by Seiko and Honda.

Robert Galvin, Motorola's CEO, has some extremely ambitious goals for his firm. He seeks to make things right the first time every time—to work better, faster, and cheaper. If all goes according to plan, by 1991, Motorola's pagers, modems, radios, cellular phones, and semiconductors will be 100 times better than they were in 1987. The goal for 1992 is 3.4 defects per million or 99.9997% perfect.

To achieve this goal, Galvin and his managers have automated factories, knocked down workplace barriers, and instituted a vast retraining program for all 102,000 employees. A few specifics include the following:

- Motorola is designing products that are easier to manufacture. Design and production engineers work together from day one.
- The company is spending $50 million or nearly 3 percent of its annual payroll budget on training employees. This covers everything from basic English and math skills to how to inspect and maintain their own machines.
- Employees are rewarded for making things right. Nearly everyone participates in a bonus plan, and an employee's bonuses are directly affected by the quality of his or her work.
- The company has demanded that suppliers meet its standards and has dumped those that haven't. In six years, for instance, Motorola's communications group cut its number of suppliers from 5,000 to 1,600; it eventually expects to lower that number to only 400.

So far, these changes have been working. In 1989, Motorola was the only major U.S. survivor in the paging business, and its products were so good that they ranked among the top sellers even in Japan. Motorola's mobile two-way radios dominated the world market. In the rapidly growing cellular telephone industry, the company was Number 1 worldwide. In 1988, Motorola received a national award for attaining "preeminent quality leadership." In that same year, the company's revenues and profits hit $8.3 billion and $445 million, respectively, which were both company records.

Questions

1. Contrast Motorola's approach to improving operations with Deming's fourteen-point program.
2. Why do you think the quality program hasn't resulted in Motorola's becoming the high-cost producer in each of its markets and in a reduction in the company's economic performance?
3. If you were Galvin, how could you carry Motorola's quality campaign to non-manufacturing entities such as sales, marketing, and purchasing?

CASE APPLICATION 20B

Caterpillar Inc.

Caterpillar's business of building farm and construction equipment collapsed after the 1982 recession.[55] Farmers had no money to buy new equipment, and the market for the company's highly profitable $500,000 monster tractors, which are used for earth moving, had dried up with the decline in highway building. Between 1982 and 1984, Caterpillar lost almost $1 billion. The company shut down old plants, slashed its payroll by 30 percent, and restructured its product lineup. Always known for its high standards of quality, Caterpillar's management decided to focus on smaller machines such as farm tractors and backhoe loaders, but in this market it faced slim profit margins and fierce competition. In 1986, management decided that further drastic action was needed if Caterpillar was to remain the world leader in earth-moving equipment. Komatsu, its prime Japanese competitor, already had a network of high-tech plants. To match and then exceed Komatsu's production capabilities, Caterpillar's management committed to a $1.8 billion plant modernization program.

Caterpillar dismantled its antiquated and costly production operation and installed a speedy, flexible manufacturing system. The company installed an electronic information network to link its thirty plants, its suppliers, and its dealers. Plants were reworked to include the latest computer-integrated equipment. For instance, computers can adjust machine tools within seconds to meet the specs on any new order.

Results to date have been mixed. By 1989, the time it takes to fill orders for machinery parts had been slashed by as much as 60 percent at some plants, and companywide inventory levels had been cut in half. By early 1993, when the conversion is scheduled to be fully completed, Caterpillar's management hopes to cut total manufacturing costs by 20 percent, or $1.5 billion a year. In the meantime, the conversion is well behind schedule and some $330 million over budget. The company earned record profits of $616 million in 1988, but earnings were flat in 1989. Wall Street was disappointed by these results, having expected continued increases in profit. Never very tolerant of long-term payoffs, Wall Street responded to the flat earnings by keeping Caterpillar's stock significantly below the stocks of other heavy-equipment manufacturers.

Questions

1. Describe how Caterpillar integrated its corporate and manufacturing strategies.

2. Was Caterpillar taking a risky, long-term gamble?

3. Management had other choices in 1986 besides spending nearly $2 billion to modernize its plants. What do you think these choices were? Do you think the choice it made was the correct one? Why or why not?

Paper Plane Corporation

PURPOSE

1. To integrate the management functions.
2. To specifically apply planning and control concepts to improve organizational performance.

REQUIRED KNOWLEDGE

1. Planning, organizing, and controlling concepts.

TIME REQUIRED

Approximately one hour.

INSTRUCTIONS

Unlimited groups of six participants each are used in this exercise. These groups may be directed simultaneously in the same room. Each person should have assembly instructions (Figure VI–1) and a summary sheet, plus ample stacks of paper (8½ by 11 inches). The physical setting should be a room that is large enough that individual groups of six can work without interference from other groups. A working space should be provided for each group.

- The participants are doing an exercise in production methodology.
- Each group must work independently of the other groups.
- Each group will choose a manager and an inspector, and the remaining participants will be employees.

- The objective is to make paper airplanes in the most profitable manner possible.
- The facilitator will give the signal to start. This is a ten-minute, timed event utilizing competition among the groups.
- After the first round, each group should report its production and profits to the entire group. Each group reports the manner in which it planned, organized, and controlled for the production of the paper airplanes.
- This same procedure is followed for as many rounds as there is time.

Your group is the complete work force for Paper Plane Corporation. Established in 1943, Paper Plane has led the market in paper plane production. Currently under new management, the company is contracting to make aircraft for the U.S. Air Force. You must establish a plan and organization to produce these aircraft. You must make your contract with the Air Force under the following conditions:

1. The Air Force will pay $20,000 per airplane.
2. The aircraft must pass a strict inspection.
3. A penalty of $25,000 per airplane will be subtracted for failure to meet the production requirements.
4. Labor and other overhead will be computed at $300,000.
5. Cost of materials will be $3,000 per bid plane. If you bid for ten but make only eight, you must pay the cost of materials for those you failed to make or that did not pass inspection.

FIGURE VI–1
Paper Plane Corporation: Data Sheet

Instructions for aircraft assembly

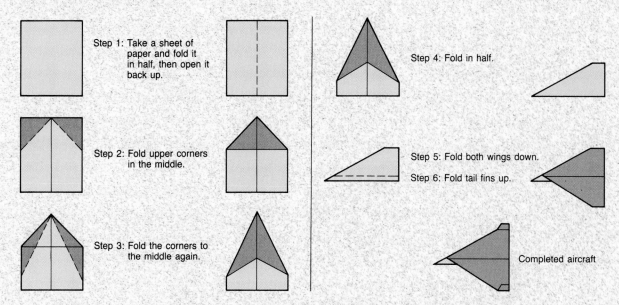

Step 1: Take a sheet of paper and fold it in half, then open it back up.

Step 2: Fold upper corners in the middle.

Step 3: Fold the corners to the middle again.

Step 4: Fold in half.

Step 5: Fold both wings down.

Step 6: Fold tail fins up.

Completed aircraft

Summary Sheet

Round 1:
Bid: _____ Aircraft @ $20,000.00 per aircraft
= _____
Results: _____ Aircraft @ $20,000.00 per
aircraft = _____
Less: $300,000.00 overhead
_____ × $3,000 cost of raw materials
_____ × $25,000 penalty
Profit: _____

Round 2:
Bid: _____ Aircraft @ $20,000.00 per aircraft
= _____
Results: _____ Aircraft @ $20,000.00 per
aircraft = _____
Less: $300,000.00 overhead
_____ × $3,000 cost of raw materials
_____ × $25,000 penalty
Profit: _____

Round 3:
Bid: _____ Aircraft @ $20,000.00 per aircraft
= _____
Results: _____ Aircraft @ $20,000.00 per
aircraft = _____
Less: $300,000.00 overhead
_____ × $30,000 cost of raw materials
_____ × $25,000 penalty
Profit: _____

Source: Based on an exercise in James H. Donnelly, Jr., James L. Gibson, and John M. Ivancevich, *Fundamentals of Management,* 6th ed. (Plano, Texas: Business Publications, Inc., 1987), pp. 231–34. With permission.

Osborne Computer: Trying for Rapid Growth Without Controls

Only rarely may a new firm hit the jackpot: a meteoric rise surpassing even the most optimistic expectations of founders and investors. In the heady excitement of great growth, anything seems possible. It is tantalizing to think that such an enterprise is invincible to competition. Alas, such stars can sometimes come tumbling back to earth, and reality. Perhaps no better example can be found in modern business annals than the almost vertical rise and collapse of Osborne Computer Corporation. Founded in 1981, the business was booming at a $100 million clip—in barely eighteen months. But on September 14, 1983, the company sought protection from creditors under Chapter 11 of the Bankruptcy Code.

ADAM OSBORNE

Adam Osborne was born in Thailand, the son of a British professor, and spent his earliest years in India. His parents were disciples of a maharishi, although Osborne was educated in Catholic schools. He was later sent to Britain for schooling, and in 1961, at the age of 22, he moved to the United States. He obtained a Ph.D. in chemical engineering at the University of Delaware and then worked for Shell Development Company in California.

Osborne and Shell soon parted company; the bureaucratic structure frustrated him. He became interested in computers, and in 1970 he set up his own computer consulting company. The market for personal computers had begun to mushroom in the mid-1970s,

and he emerged as a guru. He wrote a computer column, "From the Fountainhead," for *Interface Age*, and he began making speeches and building a reputation. He wrote a book, *Introduction to Microcomputers*, geared to the mass market, but it was turned down by a publisher. Osborne published it himself, and it sold 300,000 copies. By 1975, his publishing company had put out some forty books on microcomputers, nearly a dozen of which he had written himself. In 1979, he sold his publishing company to McGraw-Hill but agreed to stay as a consultant through May 1982.

Osborne was thus in a position to take full advantage of the growth of the microcomputer industry. But he had also angered many in the industry by his stinging criticisms and bold assertions. In particular, he spoke out sharply against the pricing strategies of the personal computer manufacturers, contending that they were ignoring the mass market by constantly raising prices with every new feature added.

Osborne himself came to be the subject of some of the most colorful copy in the industry. Tall and energetic, he possessed a strong British accent to go along with his volubility, his charm, and his supreme confidence. He seemed to epitomize the new breed of entrepreneurs that were drawn to the epicenter of the new high-tech industry, the so-called Silicon Valley in California.

Early in 1981, Osborne put his criticisms and assertions to the test. To a chorus of skeptics he announced plans to manufacture and market a new personal computer, one priced well below the competition. His first machines were ready for shipping by that July, and before long the skeptics were running for the hills. Now Osborne could prove that he was a doer and not merely a talker.

INDUSTRY BACKGROUND

In the early 1970s, computers ranged from small units to the very large, with prices reaching limits only affordable to well-heeled firms. The industry was dominated by one company, IBM, which held 70 percent of the market. All the other firms in the industry were scrambling for small shares. IBM seemed to have an unassailable advantage because it had the resources for the heaviest marketing expenditures in the industry as well as the best research and development. The firm with the masterful lead in a rapidly growing industry has ever-increasing resources over its lesser competitors, which can hardly hope to catch up and, it seems, must be content to chip away at the periphery of the total market.

The computer industry had been characterized by rapid technological changes since the early 1960s. By the early 1970s, however, the new technology being introduced generally involved peripheral accessories and not further major changes in main units.

Before the advent of microelectronics technology, which makes smaller parts possible, computers were very costly and complicated. It was not economically feasible for one person to interact with one computer. The processing power at that time existed only in a central data processing installation; for those who could not afford to have their own computer, time-sharing services were available.

The minicomputer industry began in 1974, when a few small firms began using memory chips to produce do-it-yourself-kit computer systems for as little as $400. These proved to be popular, and other companies began to build microcomputers designed for the affluent hobbyist and small-business owner.

In 1975, microcomputer and small-business computer shipments went over the $1 billion mark. As the mainframe market began to mature, the microcomputer industry was starting its rocketing ascent. In 1975, the first personal computer reached the market.

Personal computers can be defined as easy-to-use desktop machines that are microprocessor based, have their own power supply, and are priced below $10,000. With various software packages, these computers can be customized to serve the needs of businesses and a variety of professionals such as accountants, financial analysts, scientists, and educators, as well as sophisticated individuals at home. It should be noted that the minicomputer had grown up without IBM, the company that had dominated mainframe computers and had accounted for two-thirds of all computer revenues in the mid-1970s. And one of the great success stories of the century had occurred with personal computers. Apple Computer had been started in a family garage on $1,300 in capital in 1976. By 1982, sales had reached $583 million, and Steven Jobs, a college dropout who was the co-founder at age 21, had become one of the richest people in America with a net worth exceeding $225 million.[1]

Portable computers are a subset of personal computers, being, as the name implies, lightweight and relatively easy to carry. Actually, three categories of portable computers are recognized by the industry: (1) hand-held computers; (2) portable, which have a small display screen, limited memory, and weigh between 10 and 20 pounds; and (3) transportable, which have bigger screens and memories, and weigh more than 20 pounds. Osborne Computer was in the third group.

THE OSBORNE STRATEGY

Osborne had discerned a significant niche in the portable computer market: "I saw a truck-size hole in the industry, and I plugged it," he said.[2] He hired Lee Felsenstein, a former Berkeley radical, to design a powerful unit that weighed only 24 pounds and could be placed in a briefcase small enough to fit under an airline seat. It was the first portable business computer (other portable computers were far less sophisticated). And it sold for $1,795, which was hundreds of dollars less than other business-oriented computers and half the price of an Apple. Osborne was able to sell for this price because he ran a low-overhead operation. For example, he hired Georgette Psaris, then 25, and made her vice president of sales and marketing. But her office was in a chilly former warehouse. He was able to achieve economies of scale and also capitalized on the declining prices of semiconductor parts. The computers were assembled from standard industry components. The display screen was small, only five inches across, and there was no color graphics capability. Osborne himself admitted, "The Osborne 1 had no technology of consequence. We made the purchasing decision convenient by bundling hardware and needed software in one price."[3]

To cut costs on software, Osborne employed no programmers, a drastic departure from the practice of other personal computer makers. Instead, he relied entirely on independent software companies to provide programs written in the popular programming languages. To reduce software costs still further, Osborne gave some software suppliers equity in the company. The result was that Osborne was able to provide almost

$1,500 worth of software packages as part of the $1,795 system price.

Osborne had a flair for showmanship. One of his first triumphs was at the 1981 West Coast Computer Fair in San Francisco. In place of the rather ordinary booths and displays of the other computer makers, he spent a substantial part of his venture capital to build a plexiglas booth that towered toward the ceiling. The Osborne company logo, the "Flying O," dominated the show.

He believed that mass distribution was a key to success. By 1982, he had signed an agreement with Computerland, the largest computer retailer. This extended Osborne's distribution by doubling in one swoop the number of retail stores carrying his computer. The Osborne 1 was proving to be a hot item, with sales hitting $10 million by the end of 1981, the first year of operation, although the first computer had not even been shipped until July. By the end of 1982, after only eighteen months of operation, annual sales were soaring to $100 million. Predictions were that "most of the Osborne management team would be millionaires by the time they're 40 or even 30."[4] And the bare-bones operating style had been forsaken.

By 1983, some 750 retail outlets were stocking the company's portables: the Computerland chain, Xerox's retail stores, Sears's business centers, and department stores such as Macy's. Early in 1983, 150 office equipment dealers with experience in selling the most advanced copiers were also added, enabling Osborne to reach small- and medium-sized businesses.

In summary, Osborne was certainly not the originator of the portable computer, but he was the first to sell such computers in mass quantities. And he expanded the market greatly: every key person in a data-processing department and every manager behind a desk became a sales target.

MARCHING INTO 1983

By early 1983, Osborne, under pressure from his investors, began to loosen his grip on the company. It was felt that the growing operation—it already had 800 employees—required professional managers, which Osborne and his early hirees were not. Osborne was an entrepreneur, not an administrator, and the two abilities were quite different. To protect the company's front-running position (estimated at an 80 to 90 percent market share), Robert Jaunich, II, president of Consolidated Foods, was hired to head up Osborne Computer as president and chief executive officer. Adam Osborne moved up to chairman. Jaunich had turned down offers from Apple and Atari because he felt that these firms would not give him enough control. He also sacrificed

a $1 million incentive to remain at Consolidated Foods. So he must have felt strongly that the opportunities and the potential of Osborne far surpassed those of his other options.

Jaunich moved quickly to decentralize the management structure. Georgette Psaris, vice president of marketing, was moved into a newly created position as vice president of strategic planning. She was replaced by Joseph Roebuck, lured from Apple Computer, where he had been marketing director. Fred Brown, the director of sales for Osborne, was elevated to vice president of sales; and David Lorenzen, a consultant for Osborne, was made director of marketing services, with responsibility for dealer-support programs.

The distribution strategy that Adam Osborne believed to be one of the strengths of the venture was refined. The computer store outlets were continued, but some alternative channels were instituted. A major addition was an affiliation with Harris Corporation's computer systems division, which would act as a national distributor for contacting major firms. Harris was a $1.7 billion minicomputer firm that had in its computer systems division some seventy salespeople and 1,200 support personnel, including systems analysts. To protect Osborne's smaller clients, Harris agreed to handle only large orders of fifty units and over.

Brown, vice president of sales, targeted United Press International (UPI), the news service, in order to sell Osborne portables as personal workstations to its 1,000-subscriber newspapers. He also began to explore other distribution possibilities, including independent sales organizations, airlines, and hotel chains.

As competitors started to enter the portable market and offer cheaper and fancier machines than the Osborne 1, the firm began readying itself to broaden its product line. An even cheaper version of the Osborne 1, the Vixen, was prepared. And an Executive 1 was unveiled in the spring of 1983, with an Executive 2 planned for late summer; these offered more storage capacity and larger screens than Osborne 1. The Executive 1 could serve as a terminal to communicate with a mainframe, enabling users to work with larger data bases and handle more complicated jobs. This was to have a $2,495 price tag with some $2,000 worth of software, including word processing, an electronic spreadsheet, and data base management. The Executive 2, at $3,195, was to be promoted as compatible with IBM's hot-selling personal computer, the IBM PC.

In 1982, Osborne spent $3.5 million on advertising. This included $1.5 million in consumer magazines, $500,000 on television spots, and $1.5 million in business publications. Plans were laid to continue heavy advertising to reinforce product differentiation. The sales force was also being expanded to keep pace with the growing firm. An eight-person sales force was to be expanded to thirty or forty, permitting more specialized selling. Instead of selling to all types of customers, sales specialists would concentrate on either retail or non-retail accounts. Brown explained this rationale: "Retailers . . . need help on such things as point-of-sale displays to stimulate the guy who comes in off the street. Dealers call on purchasing and data-processing departments and need advice on direct mail campaigns."[5]

The sky seemed to be the limit. Osborne was predicting revenues of $300 million for 1983. And when he made one of his frequent trips abroad, he was received by ambassadors and prime ministers, most of whom wanted stock in his company. He was the head of the fastest-growing company Silicon Valley had ever seen—even faster than Apple.

PREMONITION

The first premonition of trouble came to Adam Osborne on April 26, 1983. He was giving a seminar in Colorado when he received a call. "Over the weekend considerable losses were discovered," he was told. "That's not possible," he is reported to have said.[6]

The news that earlier profit figures had been in error was particularly ominous because of its timing. A public stock offering had been planned on April 29. This was designed to raise about $50 million, and would make the top executives of Osborne rich. How would news of losses instead of profits affect the stock offering? Adam Osborne had to wonder.

Actually, in the few days Adam had been away from the office, the bad news had been building up. In the first two months of the fourth fiscal quarter (the fiscal year ended in February 1983), pretax profits had been reported to be running $300,000 ahead of company projections; and in February, the company had racked up an all-time high in shipments—all these with supposedly very high profit margins. Projections had been that profits in February would be in the neighborhood of $750,000 for that month alone, and the future had seemed euphorically bright.

But the heady optimism was to disappear emphatically. By late March, the results for February showed, instead of the profit, a loss of more than $600,000, reflecting charges against new facilities as well as very heavy promotional spending. For the entire fiscal year, a loss of $1.5 million was incurred, despite revenues of slightly more than $100 million.

The worst was yet to come. On April 21, Jaunich, the CEO, had learned that later data showed that the company would have a $1.5 million loss for the February quarter and a $4 million loss for the full year. The chief reasons seemed to be excessive inventories of old stock

that the company did not even realize it had, liabilities in software contracts, and the need for greater bad debt and warranty reserves. Jaunich still planned to file for the stock offering, although the attractiveness of the company's stock was rapidly diminishing.

Unbelievably, worse was to come. On April 24, Jaunich was informed that the losses would be even greater: $5 million for the quarter and $8 million for the year, owing to further unrecorded liabilities and more inventory problems.

That same day Jaunich decided to scrap the offering, despite heavy pressure to find another underwriter to bring the stock to market. Now every report blackened the situation further. The final report for the year showed a loss of more than $12 million. Heavy losses continued over the next months, as further adjustments in inventories and reserves became necessary. Adam Osborne's house of cards was on the verge of collapse.

Osborne had had no trouble attracting seed money from venture capitalists before—indeed, venture capital firms had been clamoring to participate. But now that the company's earnings problems had come to light, such funding was drying up. A few investors still had hopes, and Osborne found another $11 million in June. But an additional $20 million, which the company considered necessary to speed a needed competitive product from drawing board to market, could not be found.

BLACK FRIDAY

Sporadic employee layoffs had been occurring since late spring as the company desperately tried to improve its cash flow. But the climax came on Friday, September 16. On the previous Tuesday, the company had filed for protection from creditor lawsuits under Chapter 11 of the Federal Bankruptcy Code. The company filed its petition after three creditors had filed two lawsuits saying Osborne owed them a total of $4.7 million. Osborne's petition stated that it owed secured and unsecured creditors about $45 million, while its assets were $40 million.

Osborne's employees had to expect the worst when a meeting was abruptly called in the company cafeteria. They soberly listened as top management announced that more than 300, about 80 percent of the company staff still remaining, were to be immediately "furloughed." Final paychecks were issued, and the workers were given two hours to empty their desks and vacate the company offices.

News of the company's Chapter 11 filing and near-total shutdown shocked the industry, although Osborne's recently sagging sales and the consequent need for cash were well known. The company had made strenuous efforts to raise money, especially after

July shipments had turned soft, and the banks were pressing it to improve its shrinking capital base. But venture capitalists were fleeing the industry as a serious shakeout got underway not only for Osborne, but for other personal computer firms as well. The market was just not able to support some 150 microcomputer companies.

POSTMORTEM

Internal Factors

Adam Osborne was an entrepreneur, not a professional manager. Perhaps this accounted for most of the problems that befell his company. The entrepreneur is often incompatible with the manager, who must necessarily be engrossed with the nitty-gritty of details and day-to-day controls over operations. Osborne had never managed more than fifty people, but the organization had grown twenty times larger. He had operated according to a "fire-fighting" perspective: he never planned in advance and dealt with problems as they arose. "I had no professional training whatsoever in finance or business management," Osborne admitted.[7]

Osborne's board of directors and the venture capitalists who had contributed mightily to the fledgling enterprise exerted sufficient pressure to persuade Adam Osborne to step aside and turn over operating responsibilities to a professional manager, Robert Jaunich, early in 1983. But this was apparently too late to rectify the damage that had already been done. It is tempting to speculate on what might have happened had such measures been taken six months earlier.

Some of the mistakes are inexcusable from the standpoint of any prudently run operation. But perhaps they can be explained as a result of the heady excitement that can accompany geometrically rising sales and the euphoria that clouds rational judgments and expectations. Other mistakes can be credited to simple miscalculations—of which any firm could be guilty—as to the impact of competitors of all kinds, and particularly the rapidity with which the awesome IBM entered the market and dominated it.

Lack of controls was the most obvious failing of the company. It had no efficient means of monitoring inventories of finished products. Consequently, managers did not know how much inventory they had. They did not know how much they were spending or needed to spend. Information management was sorely lacking—and this in a company whose product was primarily geared to aiding information management. Although rapid growth can be accompanied by growing pains and difficulty in keeping abreast of booming operations, in Osborne's case the lack was abysmal and accounted for supposed profits suddenly being revealed as devastating losses. Other examples of incompetence were unrecorded liabilities, with some bills never handed over to the accounting department; no reserves established for the shutdown of a New Jersey plant that was producing computers with a 40 percent failure rate; and insufficient funds set aside to pay for a new European headquarters on Lake Geneva in Switzerland.

Lack of controls permitted expenses to run rampant. "Everybody was trying to buy anything they wanted," said one former Osborne employee.[8] When Jaunich finally took over the managerial reins, he clamped down hard on expenses, but it was too late.

By spring of 1983, miscalculations had reduced cash flow to a trickle. Osborne had planned to introduce a new computer, the Executive, but he made the grievous mistake of announcing it too soon. Although the Executive was not supposed to compete against the original Osborne 1, many dealers saw it as doing just that. Upon learning of the new machine in April, many canceled their orders for the Osborne 1. This in itself necessitated heavy inventory write-offs, as the Osborne was not planned to be phased out. Compounding the problems, the Executive was delayed and not ready for initial shipments until May. Consequently, April was a month with practically no sales.

Another major mistake was failing to realize just how quickly competitors could react and counter a successful strategy in this volatile industry, how quickly a competitive advantage—the low price, portability, and bundling of software—could be matched by competitors and even improved upon.

Other companies, notably Kaypro and Compaq, entered the market with low-priced computers and at least as much bundled software. But the biggest impact was that of IBM. Its personal computer was introduced in late 1981, and it quickly became the industry standard against which other competitors were judged. And Osborne turned out to be slow in adopting IBM's state-of-the-art technology. Furthermore, Osborne was slow to come up with a model that was compatible with the IBM personal computer at home or in the office. Scores of other computer companies jumped to produce IBM-compatible computers, while Osborne lagged. Suddenly, its product was not selling; hardly a year after coming to market, the formerly popular Osborne computer with its tiny screen was practically obsolete.

One new product developed by Osborne was obsolete before it was even introduced. The Vixen was originally scheduled to be introduced in December 1982. It was a cheaper version of the Osborne 1 and ten pounds lighter. But a poorly designed circuitboard caused production delays, and the project was finally scrapped as company resources were at last redirected to the Executive model, an IBM-compatible unit with a larger screen. But the Osborne production delays and the speed with which IBM took over the personal computer market were tough to cope with.

External Factors

The environment for personal computer makers was rapidly becoming unhealthy by 1983. A major shakeout for the more than 150 small manufacturers in this industry had been inevitable. A major reason for the proliferation of firms had been a tidal wave of venture capital. Early winners like Apple Computer had dazzled investors and led to the perception of a "can't lose" industry. It became almost too easy to start a new computer company. "As a result, a whole series of 'me-too' companies have been started. They are developing products that do not have a unique feature or competitive advantage. They don't stand a chance," one venture capitalist said.[9] Only the strongest firms were likely to survive. Yet, because of its size and its head start, Osborne should have been one of the survivors.

As demand by businesses and consumers alike for small computers was rapidly increasing, so was cutthroat competition. Price cutting and shrinking profit margins were inevitable. And certainly, dealers' shelves could hardly accommodate more than a few brands.

The first presentiment of worsening problems for the industry came early in 1983, when three big manufacturers of low-priced home computers, Atari, Texas Instruments, and Mattel, reported first-half losses totaling more than half a billion dollars. Makers of higher-priced computers tried to disassociate themselves from this low-end calamitous environment. But other well-known companies such as Victor Technologies, Fortune Systems, and Vector Graphics all reported shocking losses for the second quarter. Even Apple Computer saw its stock price sink nearly 34 points between June and September of 1983.

Indicative of the price cutting going on, Texas Instruments' (TI) 99/4A home computer, which sold for $525 when introduced in 1981, was retailing for $100 by early 1983. Yet each 99/4A cost about $80 in parts and labor, to which TI's overhead expenses, dealer profits, and marketing costs had to be added.[10]

Other computer makers were struggling desperately to revamp their production and marketing efforts. For example, Vector Graphic, after losing $1.7 million in the second quarter of 1983, obtained a new $7 million line of credit to help it tailor its computers to specialty markets such as accounting systems for farmers.[11]

Now the problems of the industry had dried up venture capital. Osborne was partly the victim of an external situation over which it had no control. The external factors were unforgiving of its internal mistakes.

QUESTIONS

1. Of what value is a portable business computer to a typical manager?
2. What factors accounted for the surge of competition in the portable computer field? Should these have been anticipated by a prudent executive?
3. In what ways does this case reveal the importance of the linkage between planning and control?
4. What kind of controls would you have advised Osborne to set up to prevent its debacle?
5. Did Osborne Computer have any unique strengths that could have enabled it to survive in this hotly competitive industry?
6. If you had been called in as a consultant to Osborne Computer in March of 1983, what advice would you have given Jaunich?

Source: Adapted from Robert F. Hartley, *Management Mistakes*, 2nd ed. (John Wiley & Sons, 1986), pp. 215–28. Copyright © 1986 by John Wiley & Sons, Inc. Reprinted by permission of John Wiley & Sons, Inc.

1. For more details of the Apple success story, see Robert F. Hartley, *Marketing Successes* (New York: John Wiley, 1985), pp. 200–13.
2. "Osborne: From Brags to Riches," *Business Week*, February 22, 1982, p. 86.
3. "Osborne Bytes the Distribution Bullet," *Sales & Marketing Management*, July 4, 1983, p. 34.
4. Steve Fishman, "Facing Up to Failure," *Success*, November 1984, p. 48.
5. "Osborne Bytes the Distribution Bullet," p. 36.
6. Steve Fishman, "Facing Up to Failure," p. 51.
7. Jaye Scholl, "Osborne's Back Byting," *Barron's*, July 26, 1984, p. 26.
8. "Shaken Osborne Computer Seeking Suitor in the Face of Possible Failure," *Wall Street Journal*, September 12, 1983, p. 35.
9. "Trouble in Computer Land," *Newsweek*, September 26, 1983, p. 73.
10. "Behind the Shakeout in Personal Computers," *U.S. News & World Report*, June 27, 1983, pp. 59–60.
11. "Trouble in Computer Land," p. 73.

SCORING KEYS FOR SELF-ASSESSMENT EXERCISES

Chapter 1: How Do You (or Would You) Rate as a Manager?

Section	SCORE 10	20	30	40	50	60	70	80	90	100
Management Style										
Planning										
Information/ Communication										
Time Management										
Delegation										
TOTALS										

(Grand Total)_____ + 5 = _____(Composite Score)

Total your score. You might also want to mark the appropriate boxes in the chart above. You can draw a line connecting all the scores in the chart. The variations in the line will identify where improvement effort should be concentrated.

The composite score, which is the sum of each section total divided by 5, will give a more general evaluation of your performance as a manager. If your composite score is 80–100, your strengths should serve you well *if utilized*. A score of 60–80 suggests unbalanced skills that may retard your professional progress. A score of 50 or less suggests a wide area for improvement.

Chapter 2: Are You the Quantitative Type?

Using the ratings (one through four) that you assigned to each of the fifteen items, add up your points. You can assess your level of math anxiety by comparing your scores to the following:

> 15–25 points = Math secure
> 26–40 points = Math wary
> 41–45 points = Math shy
> 46–60 points = Math anxious

Business students tend to score low (relatively math secure) on this exercise. This is probably due, in part, to self-selection. The fact that accounting, finance, statistics, and other quantitative courses are requirements for degrees in business is likely to discourage individuals with high math anxiety to pursue these majors.

Chapter 3: What Kind of Organizational Culture Fits You Best?

For items 1, 3, 4, 5, 8, 9, and 10, score as follows:

> Strongly agree   = +2
> Agree   = +1
> Uncertain   = 0
> Disagree   = −1
> Strongly disagree = −2

For items 2, 6, and 7, reverse the score (Strongly agree = −2, and so on). Add up your total. Your score will fall somewhere between +20 and −20. Most business and public administration students score on the positive side of this scale.

What does your score mean? The higher your score (positive), the more comfortable you'll be in a formal, mechanistic, rule-oriented, and structured culture. This is synonymous with large corporations and government agencies. Negative scores indicate a preference for informal, organic, innovative, and flexible cultures that are more likely to be found in research units or small businesses.

Chapter 4: What Are Your Cultural Attitudes?

Sum up items 1 through 9 and divide by nine. This is your mean masculinity-femininity score. Sum up items 10 through 14 and divide by five. This is your mean individualism-collectivism score. Sum up items 15 through 19 and divide by five. This is your mean uncertainty avoidance score. Sum up items 20 through 25 and divide by six. This is your mean power distance score.

You can compare your scores with a sample of U.S. and Mexican students:

Dimension	U.S.	Mexico
Masculinity-femininity	2.78	2.75
Individualism-collectivism	2.19	3.33
Uncertainty avoidance	3.41	4.15
Power distance	1.86	2.22

Chapter 5: What's Your Ethical Orientation in Decision Making?

This questionnaire differentiates between two types of ethical orientations in decision making: formalists and utilitarian. Formalists most closely reflect the theory of justice. Utilitarians seek the greatest good for the greatest number. A brief description of each type indicates the following features:

Formalists emphasize conceptualization when they deliberate, see actions as right or wrong, focus on peace of mind and consistency, see issues in terms of "black-and-white" categories, and prefer social tradition and stability.

Utilitarians emphasize practicality when they deliberate, accept compromises when reason does not produce a consensus, focus on achieving good results, see answers in terms of "shades of grey," and seek social progress and change.

To score this instrument, give yourself one point for each answer marked A on questions 2, 4, 6, 8, 10, 12, and 14. Give yourself two points for each answer marked B on questions 1, 3, 5, 7, 9, 11, 13, and 15. Now add up your score. The range of scores is 15 (a "pure" formalist) to 30 (a "pure" utilitarian).

Did you score toward the formalist classification (below 22.5) or toward the utilitarian (above 22.5)?

Chapter 6: How Good Are You at Decision Making?

The most desirable response earns four points, the least desirable gets one point. Give yourself four points for Yes responses and one point for No responses to items 4, 9, and 11. Give yourself four points for No responses and one point for Yes responses to items 1, 2, 3, 5, 6, 7, 8, 10, and 12.

A score of 42 and above suggests a strong capacity for decision making. A score of 30–40 is average, while a score below 30 is below average.

Chapter 7: Are You a Good Planner?

According to the author of this questionnaire, the "perfect" planner would have answered: (1) Yes, (2) No, (3) Yes, (4) Yes, (5) Yes, (6) Yes, (7) Yes, and (8) No.

Chapter 8: Are You an Entrepreneur?

The scoring is weighted to determine your entrepreneurial profile. Score as follows:

1	2	3	4	5	16	17	18	19	20
a = 10	a = 10	a = 5	a = 10	a = 10	a = 0	a = 5	a = 2	a = 5	a = 8
b = 5	b = 7	b = 4	b = 5	b = 7	b = 10	b = 5	b = 10	b = 15	b = 10
c = 5	c = 0	c = 3	c = 0	c = 0	c = 3	c = 5	c = 0	c = 5	c = 0
d = 2		d = 0			d = 0	d = 5			d = 0
e = 0						e = 15			

6	7	8	9	10	21	22	23	24	25
a = 8	a = 15	a = 10	a = 2	a = 0	a = 0	a = 3	a = 0	a = 3	a = 10
b = 10	b = 2	b = 2	b = 3	b = 15	b = 15	b = 10	b = 10	b = 3	b = 2
c = 5	c = 0	c = 2	c = 10	c = 0		c = 0		c = 10	c = 0
d = 2	d = 0		d = 8	d = 0		d = 0			
			e = 4						

11	12	13	14	15	26				
a = 10	a = 0	a = 0	a = 0	a = 0	a = 8				
b = 5	b = 5	b = 10	b = 2	b = 10	b = 10				
c = 10	c = 10	c = 0	c = 10	c = 0	c = 15				
d = 5			d = 5	d = 3	d = 0				

Add up your total points. Based on responses by 2,500 people who have successfully launched small businesses, your score can be interpreted as follows:

235–285 points = Successful entrepreneur
200–234 points = Entrepreneur
185–199 points = Latent entrepreneur
170–184 points = Potential entrepreneur
155–169 points = Borderline entrepreneur
Below 155   = Hired hand

Chapter 9: Are You an Effective Time Manager?

Time management involves many different abilities: self-awareness, assertiveness, flexibility, prioritizing, organizing, and delegating. The items in this exercise tap these abilities. Although some characteristics might be considered to be positive attributes, those described are carried too far. Thus, all of these statements describe a person who lacks effective time management skills. Some comments:

Item 1: If you are often tired at the close of a day, this is an indication that something is wrong. Learn how to pace yourself, reserving some energy for the unexpected.

Item 2: It is not your responsibility to do others' work. Trying to be a superperson will decrease your effectiveness. Not only won't your own work get done, but you will eventually be resented for your efforts.

Item 3: You will actually increase your on-the-job effectiveness if you make sure to regularly schedule recreation and socializing with friends.

Item 4: Although consistency and firmness are definite attributes of a good worker, too much control implies rigidity.

Item 5: Being unable to discard items can be a symptom of poor time management.

Item 6: It's fine to concentrate on details—but not when it prevents you from having a perspective on the whole picture.

Item 7: By doing everything yourself, you generally limit what you can accomplish.

Chapter 10: Is a Management Career in a Large Organization Right for You?

Compute your score as follows: You get one point for a Strongly Disagree response, two points for Disagree, and so on up to five for a Strongly Agree answer. Add up your score for items 5 through 8. For items 1 through 4, you need to reverse the scoring table. That is, one becomes five, two becomes four, four becomes two, and five becomes one. Using the reverse scoring, add up your total for items 1 through 4 and combine that with the sum you obtained for items 5 through 8 to get your total score.

The results from this questionnaire are not precise predictors. In comparing your score against others, differences of a few points are probably insignificant. However, on the basis of research into leadership and motivation patterns of successful managers, we can say that the higher your score, the more likely you are to fit the role requirements of a managerial job in a large bureaucratic organization.

Chapter 11: Is an Enriched Job for You?

This exercise is designed to assess the degree to which you desire complex, challenging work. A high need for growth suggests that you are more likely to experience the desired psychological states in the job characteristics model when you have an enriched job.

This twelve-item questionnaire taps the degree to which you have a strong versus weak desire to obtain growth satisfaction from your work.

Each item on the questionnaire yields a score from 1 to 7 (that is, "Strongly prefer A" is scored 1; "Neutral" is scored 4; and "Strongly prefer B" is scored 7). To obtain your individual growth need strength score, average the twelve items as follows:

#1, #2, #7, #8, #11, #12 (direct scoring)
#3, #4, #5, #6, #9, #10 (reverse scoring)

Average scores for typical respondents are close to the midpoint of 4.0. Research indicates that if you score high on this measure, you will respond positively to an enriched job. Conversely, if you score low, you will tend *not* to find enriched jobs satisfying or motivating.

Chapter 12: What's the Right Career for You?

Score your responses by writing the number that corresponds to your response (SA = 4, A = 3, D = 2, SD = 1) to each question in the space next to the item number.

1 ___	2 ___	3 ___	4 ___	5 ___	6 ___
7 ___	8 ___	9 ___	10 ___	11 ___	12 ___
13 ___	14 ___	15 ___	16 ___	17 ___	18 ___
19 ___	20 ___	21 ___	22 ___	23 ___	24 ___
25 ___	26 ___	27 ___	28 ___	29 ___	30 ___
31 ___	32 ___	33 ___	34 ___	35 ___	36 ___
37 ___	38 ___	39 ___	40 ___	41 ___	42 ___
43 ___	44 ___				

Now obtain subscale scores by adding your scores on the items indicated and then divide by the number of items in the scale, as shown:

Technical competence	_____	÷ 6 = _____
	#1, 2, 27, 35, 38, 41	
Autonomy	_____	÷ 6 = _____
	#3, 18, 23, 36, 39, 40	
Service	_____	÷ 6 = _____
	#4, 21, 37, 42, 43, 44	
Identity	_____	÷ 5 = _____
	#7, 13, 20, 22, 26	
Variety	_____	÷ 6 = _____
	#5, 12, 14, 24, 31, 32	
Managerial competence	_____	÷ 6 = _____
	#6, 10, 11, 15, 25, 30	
Security	_____	÷ 5 = _____
	#8, 16, 17, 28, 33	
Creativity	_____	÷ 4 = _____
	#9, 19, 29, 34	

The preceding identifies your career anchors or "a syndrome of motives, values, and self-perceived competencies which function to guide and constrain an individual's career." Briefly, the eight career anchors mean the following:

- *Technical competence*. You organize your career around the challenge of the actual work you're doing.
- *Autonomy*. You value freedom and independence.
- *Service*. You're concerned with helping others or working on an important cause.
- *Identity*. You're concerned with status, prestige, and titles in your work.
- *Variety*. You seek an endless variety of new and different challenges.
- *Managerial competence*. You like to solve problems and want to lead and control others.
- *Security*. You want stability and career security.
- *Creativity*. You have a strong need to create something of your own.

The higher your score on a given anchor, the stronger your emphasis. You'll function best when your job fits with your career anchor. Lack of fit between anchor and a job can cause you to leave the organization or suffer excessive stress.

Ask yourself now: On which anchor did I receive the highest score? What jobs fit best with this anchor? You can use your analysis to help you select the right job and career for you.

Chapter 13: Who Controls Your Life?

This exercise is designed to measure your locus of control. Give yourself 1 point for each of the following selections: 1B, 2A, 3A, 4B, 5B, 6A, 7A, 8A, 9B, and 10A. Scores can be interpreted as follows:

     8–10 = High internal locus of control
      6–7 = Moderate internal locus of control
        5 = Mixed
      3–4 = Moderate external locus of control
      1–2 = High external locus of control

The higher your internal score, the more you believe that you control your own destiny. The higher your external score, the more you believe that what happens to you in your life is due to luck or chance.

Chapter 14: What Needs Are Most Important to You?

Place the values you gave A, B, C, D, and E for each question in the spaces provided in the scoring key. Notice that the letters are not always in the same place for each question. Then, add up each column and obtain a total score for each of the motivation levels.

Scoring Key						
Question 1		A	C	B	E	D
Question 2		A	B	D	C	E
Question 3		B	C	E	D	A
Question 4		E	A	C	B	D
Question 5		C	B	D	A	E
Question 6		B	C	A	E	D
Question 7		E	A	D	C	B
Question 8		B	C	A	E	D
Question 9		B	C	E	D	A
Question 10		B	D	C	E	A
TOTAL SCORE						
		I	II	III	IV	V
		MOTIVATION LEVELS				

The five motivation levels are as follows:

Level I   Physical needs
Level II   Safety needs
Level III Social needs
Level IV   Esteem needs
Level V   Self-actualization needs

Those levels that received the highest scores are the most important needs identified by you in your work. The lowest show those needs that have been relatively well satisfied or de-emphasized by you at this time.

Chapter 15: What Kind of Leader Are You?

To find your leadership style,

1. Circle the item numbers for items 8, 12, 17, 18, 19, 30, 34, and 35.
2. Write a "1" in front of the *circled items* to which you responded S (seldom) or N (never).
3. Write a "1" in front of *items not circled* to which you responded A (always) or F (frequently).
4. Circle the "1's" which you have written in front of the following items: 3, 5, 8, 10, 15, 18, 19, 22, 24, 26, 28, 30, 32, 34, and 35.
5. Count the circled "1's." This is your score for concern for people. Record the score.
6. Count the uncircled "1's." This is your score for concern for task. Record this number.
7. Now refer to the diagram. Find your score on the *concern for task* dimension on the left-hand arrow. Next, move to the right-hand arrow and find your score on the *concern for people* dimension. Draw a straight line that intersects the two scores. The point at which that line crosses the *shared leadership* arrow indicates your score on that dimension.

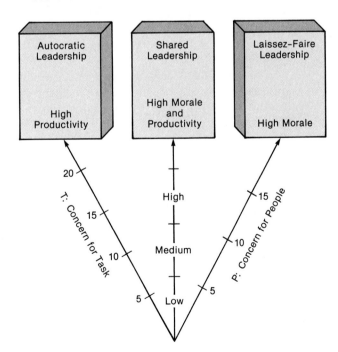

Chapter 16: What's Your Communication Style?

This questionnaire taps nine dimensions of communication style:

Dominant: The dominant communicator tends to take charge of social interactions.

Dramatic: The dramatic communicator manipulates and exaggerates stories, metaphors, rhythms, voice, and other stylistic devices to highlight or understate content.

Contentious: The contentious communicator is argumentative.

Animated: An animated communicator provides frequent and sustained eye contact, uses many facial expressions, and gestures often.

Impression leaving: The concept centers around whether the person is remembered because of the communicative stimuli that are projected.

Relaxed: This construct refers to whether the communicator is relaxed, tense, or anxious.

Attentive: In general, the attentive communicator makes sure that the other person knows that he is being listened to.

Open: Behavior associated with openness include activity that is characterized by being conversational, expansive, affable, convivial, gregarious, unreserved, somewhat frank, definately extoverted, and obviously approachable.

Friendly: Friendly ranges from simply being unhostile to deep intimacy.

To get your score for each item, give yourself +2 for strong agreement, +1 for agreement, −1 for disagreement, and −2 for strong disagreement. The only exception are items with an asterisk (*), which should be reversed. Total your scores for each dimension and divide by the number of items.

> Dominant = Items 25, 28, 31, 35, 41, 43
> Dramatic = Items 18, 22, 32, 33, 48
> Contentious = Items 10, 27, 30, 36, 37, 40, 42
> Animated = Items 17, 23, 44, 47
> Impression leaving = Items 4, 5, 12, 14, 45
> Relaxed = Items 1, 8*, 9, 15*, 16
> Attentive = Items 3, 11, 20, 39, 49
> Open = Items 21*, 24, 34, 50
> Friendly = Items 2, 6, 38, 46

The remaining items tap your total communication image. They are used for research purposes only and are not included in our discussion.

The higher your score for any dimension, the more that dimension characterizes your communication style.

Chapter 17: How Ready Are You for Managing in a Turbulent World?

Score four points for each A, three for each B, two for each C, one for each D, and zero for each E. Compute the total, divide by 24, and round to one decimal place.

While the results are not intended to be more than suggestive, the higher your score, the more comfortable you seem to be with change. The test's author suggests analyzing scores as if they were grade point averages. In this way, a 4.0 average is an A, a 2.0 is a C, and scores below 1.0 flunk.

Using replies from nearly 500 MBA students and young managers, the range of scores was found to be narrow—between 1.0 and 2.2. The average score was between 1.5 and 1.6—a D+/C− sort of grade!

Chapter 18: How Willing Are You to Give Up Control?

Add up your total score for the eighteen items. Your score can be interpreted as follows:

72–90 points = Ineffective delegation
54–71 points = Delegation habits need substantial improvement
36–53 points = You still have room to improve
18–35 points = Superior delegation

Chapter 19: Are You Computerphobic?

To get your score, add up your circled responses to questions 1, 3, 8, 11, 12, 13, 14, 15, 16, and 18. For the other nine questions, reverse your score. That is, if you circled 5, give yourself one point. If you circled 4, give yourself two points, and so on. Now tally up your total score.

The possible range of scores is 19 to 95. The higher your score, the greater your computer anxiety. As a point of reference, 270 students in an introductory psychology class (with an average age of 19), scored a mean of 43.58.

Chapter 20: Are You Technically Oriented?

Compare your responses to the key below. Circle your response to each and then add up the total of circled responses in each column.

	I	II		I	II
1.	b	a	14.	a	b
2.	a	b	15.	a	b
3.	a	b	16.	b	a
4.	b	a	17.	a	b
5.	a	b	18.	a	b
6.	b	a	19.	b	a
7.	b	a	20.	b	a
8.	b	a	21.	a	b
9.	a	b	22.	b	a
10.	b	a	23.	b	a
11.	a	b	24.	b	a
12.	b	a	25.	a	b
13.	a	b		TOTAL __ __	

Column I measures your perceived preference for using right-brain functions; Column II measures your perceived preference for using left-brain functions. A high score in Column II suggests that you're technically oriented. You may, for example, be more effective in the planning and operations activities of management than in the intuitive, creative, or human relations aspects of management.

NOTES

Chapter 1

1. Henri Fayol, *Industrial and General Administration* (Paris: Dunod, 1916).

2. Harold Koontz and Cyril O'Donnell, *Principles of Management: An Analysis of Managerial Functions* (New York: McGraw-Hill, 1955).

3. For a comprehensive review of this question, see Colin P. Hales, "What Do Managers Do? A Critical Review of the Evidence," *Journal of Management Studies,* January 1986, pp. 88–115.

4. Henry Mintzberg, *The Nature of Managerial Work* (New York: Harper & Row, 1973).

5. See, for example, Larry D. Alexander, "The Effect Level in the Hierarchy and Functional Area Have on the Extent Mintzberg's Roles Are Required by Managerial Jobs," *Academy of Management Proceedings* (San Francisco, 1979), pp. 186–89; Alan W. Lau and Cynthia M. Pavett, "The Nature of Managerial Work: A Comparison of Public and Private Sector Managers," *Group and Organization Studies,* December 1980, pp. 453–66; Morgan W. McCall, Jr., and C. A. Segrist, *In Pursuit of the Manager's Job: Building on Mintzberg,* Technical Report No. 14 (Greensboro, N.C.: Center for Creative Leadership, 1980); Cynthia M. Pavett and Alan W. Lau, "Managerial Work: The Influence of Hierarchical Level and Functional Specialty," *Academy of Management Journal,* March 1983, pp. 170–77; Hales, "What Do Managers Do? A Critical Review of the Evidence;" and Allen I. Kraut, Patricia R. Pedigo, D. Douglas McKenna, and Marvin D. Dunnette, "The Role of the Manager: What's Really Important in Different Management Jobs," *Academy of Management Executive,* November 1989, pp. 286–93.

6. Pavett and Lau, "Managerial Work: The Influence of Hierarchical Level and Functional Specialty."

7. Stephen J. Carroll and Dennis A. Gillen, "Are the Classical Management Functions Useful in Describing Managerial Work?," *Academy of Management Review,* January 1987, p. 48.

8. See, for example, Harold Koontz, "Commentary on the Management Theory Jungle—Nearly Two Decades Later," in Harold Koontz, Cyril O'Donnell, and Heintz Weihrich (eds.), *Management: A Book of Readings,* 6th ed. (New York: McGraw-Hill, 1984), pp. 10–14; and Stephen J. Carroll and Dennis A. Gillen, "Are the Classical Management Functions Useful in Describing Managerial Work?," pp. 38–51.

9. Ibid.; and Peter Allan, "Managers at Work: A Large-Scale Study of the Managerial Job in New York City Government," *Academy of Management Journal,* September 1981, pp. 613–19.

10. Fred Luthans, Stuart A. Rosenkrantz, and Harry W. Hennessey, "What Do Successful Managers Really Do? An Observation Study of Managerial Activities," *The Journal of Applied Behavioral Science,* Vol. 21, No. 3, 1985, pp. 255–70; Fred Luthans, "Successful Vs. Effective Real Managers," *Academy of Management Executive,* May 1988, pp. 127–32; Fred Luthans, Richard M. Hodgetts, and Stuart A. Rosenkrantz, *Real Managers* (Cambridge, Mass.: Ballinger Publishing, 1988); and Fred Luthans, Dianne H. B. Welsh, and Lewis A. Taylor III, "A Descriptive Model of Managerial Effectiveness," *Group & Organization Studies,* June 1988, pp. 148–62.

11. See, for example, James W. Driscoll, Gary Cowger, and Robert Egan, "Private Managers and Public Myths—Public Managers and Private Myths," *Sloan Management Review,* Fall 1979, pp. 53–57; David Rogers, "Managing in the Public and Private Sectors: Similarities and Differences," *Management Review,* May 1981, pp. 48–54; Graham Allison, "Public and Private Management: Are They Fundamentally Alike in All Unimportant Respects?," in F. S. Lane (ed.), *Current Issues in Public Administration,* 2nd ed. (New York: St. Martin's Press, 1982); Douglas Yates, Jr., *The Politics of Management* (San Francisco: Jossey-Bass, 1985), pp. 12–39; J. Norman Baldwin, "Public vs. Private: Not That Different, Not That Consequential," *Public Personnel Management,* Summer 1987, pp. 181–91; and Hal G. Rainey, "Public Management: Recent Research on the Political Context and Managerial Roles, Structures, and Behaviors," *Journal of Management,* June 1989, pp. 229–50.

12. See, for example, William A. Nowlin, "Factors That Motivate Public and Private Sector Managers: A Comparison," *Public Personnel Management Journal,* Fall 1982, pp. 224–27.

13. Based on Jay Finegan, "Four-Star Management," *INC.,* January 1987, pp. 42–51.

14. U.S. Small Business Administration, *The State of Small Business: A Report of the President* (Washington, D.C.: GPO, 1986), p. x; "As Exports Rise, Big Companies Rev Up Hiring," *Business Week,* April 11, 1988, p. 91; and "The 1990 Guide to Small Business," *U.S. News & World Report,* October 23, 1989.

15. Joseph G. P. Paolillo, "The Manager's Self-Assessments of Managerial Roles: Small vs. Large Firms," *American Journal of Small Business,* January–March 1984, pp. 58–64.

16. See, for example, Gérald d'Amboise and Marie Muldowney, "Management Theory for Small Business: Attempts and Requirements," *Academy of Management Review,* April 1988, pp. 226–40.

17. Cited in "Sweat at the Top," *Forbes,* June 30, 1986, p. 9.

18. Joani Nelson-Horchler, "The Top Man Gets Richer," *Industry Week,* June 6, 1988, p. 51.

19. Based on Michael A. Verespej, "Who Can Argue With His Results?," *Industry Week,* June 6, 1988, pp. 57–60; "American Airlines' Jet Purchases to Modernize Fleet," *St. Louis Post-Dispatch,* February 7, 1989, p. 6C; "American Aims for the Sky," *Business Week,* February 20, 1989, pp. 54–58; Richard Woodbury, "How the New No. 1 Got There," *Time,* May 15, 1989, p. 57; "The Best and the Brassiest," *U.S. News & World Report,* October 23, 1989, pp. 52–54; and "Look Out, Europe, Here He Comes," *Forbes,* January 5, 1990, p. 205.

Chapter 2

1. Claude S. George, Jr., *The History of Management Thought,* 2nd ed. (Englewood Cliffs, N.J.: Prentice-Hall, 1972), p. 4.

2. Exodus 18:17–23.

3. Frederick W. Taylor, *Principles of Scientific Management* (New York: Harper and Brothers, 1911), p. 44.

4. See, for example, Frank B. Gilbreth, *Motion Study* (New York: D. Van Nostrand, 1911); and Frank B. Gilbreth and Lillian M. Gilbreth, *Fatigue Study* (New York: Sturgis and Walton Co., 1916).

5. Henri Fayol, *Industrial and General Administration* (Paris: Dunod, 1916).

6. Max Weber, *The Theory of Social and Economic Organizations,* ed. Talcott Parsons, trans. A. M. Henderson and Talcott Parsons (New York: Free Press, 1947).

7. Reported in *Business Week,* October 21, 1988, p. 28.

8. W. Jack Duncan, *Great Ideas in Management* (San Francisco: Jossey-Bass, 1989), p. 137.

9. Robert A. Owen, *A New View of Society* (New York: E. Bliss and White, 1825).

10. Mary Parker Follett, *The New State: Group Organization the Solution of Popular Government* (London: Longmans, Green and Co., 1918).

11. Chester Barnard, *The Functions of the Executive* (Cambridge, Mass.: Harvard University Press, 1938).

12. Elton Mayo, *The Human Problems of an Industrial Civilization* (New York: Macmillan, 1933); and Fritz J. Roethlisberger and William J. Dickson, *Management and the Worker* (Cambridge, Mass.: Harvard University Press, 1939).

13. See, for example, Alex Carey, "The Hawthorne Studies: A Radical Criticism," *American Sociological Review,* June 1967, pp. 403–16; Richard H. Franke and James Kaul, "The Hawthorne Experiments: First Statistical Interpretations," *American Sociological Review,* October 1978, pp. 623–43; Berkeley Rice, "The Hawthorne Defect: Persistence of a Flawed Theory," *Psychology Today,* February 1982, pp. 70–74; and Jeffrey A. Sonnenfeld, "Shedding Light on the Hawthorne Studies," *Journal of Occupational Behavior,* April 1985, pp. 111–30.

14. Dale Carnegie, *How to Win Friends and Influence People* (New York: Simon & Schuster, 1936).

15. Daniel A. Wren, *The Evolution of Management Thought,* 3rd ed. (New York: John Wiley & Sons, 1987), p. 422.

16. Abraham Maslow, *Motivation and Personality* (New York: Harper & Row, 1954).

17. Douglas McGregor, *The Human Side of Enterprise* (New York: McGraw-Hill, 1960).

18. Daniel A. Wren, *The Evolution of Management Thought,* p. 127.

19. Lyndall Urwick, *The Elements of Administration* (New York: Harper & Row, 1944).

20. Harold Koontz, "The Management Theory Jungle," *Journal of the Academy of Management,* December 1961, pp. 174–88.

21. Harold Koontz, ed., *Toward a Unified Theory of Management* (New York: McGraw-Hill, 1964).

22. Kenyon B. DeGreene, *Sociotechnical Systems: Factors in Analysis, Design and Management* (Englewood Cliffs, N.J.: Prentice-Hall, 1973), p. 13.

23. See, for example, Louis W. Fry and Deborah A. Smith, "Congruence, Contingency, and Theory Building," *Academy of Management Review,* January 1987, pp. 117–32.

24. This box is based on "When Managers Are Owners," *Time,* November 7, 1988, p. 99.

25. See, for instance, W. Edwards Deming, *Quality, Productivity and Competitive Position* (Cambridge, Mass.: MIT Center for Advanced Engineering Study, 1982).

26. William G. Ouchi, *Theory Z: How American Business Can Meet the Japanese Challenge* (Reading, Mass.: Addison-Wesley, 1981).

27. Rosabeth Moss Kanter, *The Change Masters: Innovation for Productivity in the American Corporation* (New York: Simon & Schuster, 1983).

28. Tom Peters, *Thriving on Chaos* (New York: Alfred Knopf, 1988).

29. Based on Norm Alster, "What Flexible Workers Can Do," *Fortune,* February 13, 1989, p. 62.

Chapter 3

1. "J & J Will Pay Dearly to Cure Tylenol," *Business Week,* November 29, 1982; and "A Hard Decision to Swallow," *Time,* March 3, 1986, p. 59.

2. For insights into the symbolic view, see Jeffrey Pfeffer, "Management as Symbolic Action: The Creation and Maintenance of Organizational Paradigms," in L. L. Cummings and B. M. Staw (eds.), *Research in Organizational Behavior,* Vol. 3 (Greenwich, Conn.: JAI Press, 1981), pp. 1–52; Donald C. Hambrick and Sidney Finkelstein, "Managerial Discretion: A Bridge Between Polar Views of Organizational Outcomes," in L. L. Cummings and B. M. Staw (eds.), *Research in Organizational Behavior,* Vol. 9 (Greenwich, Conn.: JAI Press, 1987), pp. 369–406; John A. Byrne, "The Limits of Power," *Business Week,* October 23, 1987, pp. 33–35; and James R. Meindl and Sanford B. Ehrlich, "The Romance of Leadership and the Evaluation of Organizational Performance," *Academy of Management Journal,* March 1987, pp. 91–109.

3. Jeffrey Pfeffer, "Management as Symbolic Action: The Creation and Maintenance of Organizational Paradigms."

4. Linda Smircich, "Concepts of Culture and Organizational Analysis," *Administrative Science Quarterly,* September 1983, p. 339.

5. Alice M. Sapienza, "Believing Is Seeing: How Culture Influences the Decisions Top Managers Make," in Ralph H. Kilmann et al. (eds.), *Gaining Control of the Corporate Culture* (San Francisco: Jossey-Bass, 1985), p. 68.

6. Ibid., p. 67.

7. Ibid.

8. Based on George G. Gordon and W. M. Cummins, *Managing Management Climate* (Lexington, Mass.: Lexington Books, 1979); and Chris A. Betts and Susan M. Halfhill, "Organization Culture: Theory, Definitions, and Dimensions," paper presented at the National American Institute of Decision Sciences' Conference; Las Vegas, Nevada, November 1985.

9. Donald C. Hambrick and Sidney Finkelstein, "Managerial Discretion: A Bridge Between Polar Views of Organizational Outcomes," pp. 384–85.

10. Edgar H. Schein, "The Role of the Founder in Creating Organizational Culture," *Organizational Dynamics,* Summer 1983, pp. 13–28.

11. Edgar H. Schein, *Organizational Culture and Leadership* (San Francisco: Jossey-Bass, 1985), pp. 314–15.

12. This theme is explored in Anna Cifelli, "Rolling Back the Freedom to Manage," *Fortune,* January 9, 1984, pp. 90–94.

13. Robert H. Miles, *Macro Organizational Behavior* (Santa Monica, Calif.: Goodyear Publishing, 1980), p. 195.

14. Timothy S. Mescon and George S. Vozikis, "Federal Regulation—What Are the Costs?," *Business,* January–March 1982, pp. 33–39.

15. See, for instance, Marisa Manley, "Charges and Discharges," *INC.,* March 1988, pp. 124–28; Larry Reibstein, "Firms Find It Tougher to Dismiss Employees for Off-Duty Conduct," *Wall Street Journal,* March 29, 1988, p. 31; and Ralph King, Jr., "Fair—To Whom?," *Forbes,* November, 28, 1988, pp. 116–24.

16. "The Aftershocks of $20 Oil," *Business Week,* February 3, 1986, p. 28.

17. See Davita Silfen Glasberg and Michael Schwartz, "Ownership and Control of Corporations," in Ralph H. Turner and James F. Short, Jr. (eds.), *Annual Review of Sociology,* Vol. 9 (Palo Alto, Calif.: Annual Reviews, 1983), p. 320.

18. "Business Week/Harris Executive Poll," *Business Week,* October 23, 1987, p. 28.

19. Based on "Guardian of the Long-Term," *Forbes,* April 4, 1988, p. 128.

Chapter 4

1. Shawn Tully, "Nestlé Shows How to Gobble Markets," *Fortune,* January 16, 1989, pp. 74–78.

2. Kenichi Ohmae, "Managing in a Borderless World," *Harvard Business Review,* May–June 1989, pp. 152–61.

3. "Honda's Coupe is a Coup," *Fortune,* May 9, 1988, p. 6.

4. (1) Venezuela, (2) Canada, (3) Japan (Sony), (4) United States (Chrysler), (5) United States, (6) Japan (Bridgestone), (7) Italy (Banca Commerciale), (8) West Germany, (9) Britain (Maxwell Communication), (10) Britain (BAT Industries), (11) West Germany (Continental), and (12) Britain (Grand Metropolitan).

5. Nancy Adler, *International Dimensions of Organizational Behavior* (Boston: Kent Publishing, 1986), p. 5.

6. See D. A. Ricks, M. Y. C. Fu, and J. S. Arpas, *International Business Blunders* (Columbus, Ohio: Grid, 1974); Amanda Bennett, "American Culture Is Often a Puzzle for Foreign Managers in the U.S.," *Wall Street Journal,* February 12, 1986, p. 29; and Charles F. Valentine, "Blunders Abroad," *Nation's Business,* March 1989, p. 54.

7. World Bank, *World Development Report: 1986* (Washington, D.C., 1986); and "International 150," *Business Week,* April 18, 1986, p. 290.

8. Rone Tempest, "No Magic in These Kingdoms," *Los Angeles Times,* October 21, 1989, pp. 1, 17, and 18.

9. See, for example, "Reshaping Europe: 1992 and Beyond," *Business Week,* December 12, 1988, pp. 48–51; Philip Revzin, "Europe Will Become Economic Superpower as Barriers Crumble," *Wall Street Journal,* December 29, 1988, p. 1; John S. McClehahen, "Europe 1992; The Challenge to U.S.," *Industry Week,* April 3, 1989, pp. 78–85; and David Mitchell, "1992: The Implications for Management," *Long Range Planning,* February 1989, pp. 32–40.

10. Chuck Hawkins and William J. Holstein, "The North American Shakeout Arrives Ahead of Schedule," *Business Week,* April 17, 1989, pp. 34–35.

11. See, for example, "The Rise of Gringo Capitalism," *Newsweek,* January 5, 1987, pp. 40–41; Janice Castro, "Yankee! Welcome to Mexico!" *Time,* June 1, 1987, p. 51; and "The Magnet of Growth in Mexico's North," *Business Week,* June 6, 1988, pp. 48–50.

12. "The Rise of Gringo Capitalism," p. 40.

13. Based on "The Rise of Gringo Capitalism"; and "The Magnet of Growth in Mexico's North."

14. See, for instance, "Reinventing Europe," *U.S. News & World Report,* November 27, 1989, pp. 39–43; "The Shape of Europe to Come," *Business Week,* November 27, 1989, pp. 60–64; "Toward a New Era of Possibilities," *Fortune,* December 4, 1989, p. 10; and Richard I. Kirkland, Jr., "Who Gains From the New Europe," *Fortune,* December 18, 1989, pp. 83–88.

15. This section is based on Christopher J. Chipello, "Foreign Rivals Imperil U.S. Firms' Leadership in the Service Sector," *Wall Street Journal,* March 21, 1988, pp. 1 and 11.

16. This section is based on "Mr. Smith Goes Global," *Business Week,* February 13, 1989, pp. 66–72.

17. See, for example, Geert Hofstede, *Culture's Consequences: International Differences in Work-Related Values* (Beverly Hills, Calif.: Sage Publications, 1980), pp. 25–26.

18. See Nancy J. Adler, *International Dimensions of Organizational Behavior,* pp. 46–48.

19. Geert Hofstede, *Culture's Consequences: International Differences in Work-Related Values;* and Geert Hofstede, "The Cultural Relativity of Organizational Practices and Theories," *Journal of International Business Studies,* Fall 1983, pp. 75–89.

20. Geert Hofstede, "The Cultural Relativity of Organizational Practices and Theories," p. 85.

21. Based on Carol Kennedy, "Planning Global Strategies for 3M," *Long Range Planning,* February 1989, pp. 9–17.

Chapter 5

1. See Frederick D. Sturdivant, *Business and Society: A Managerial Approach,* 3rd ed. (Homewood, Ill.: Richard D. Irwin, 1985), pp. 43–44; Robert Johnson, "Fast-Food Chains Draw Criticism for Marketing Fare as Nutritional," *Wall Street Journal,* April 6, 1987, p. 27; and Kenneth Sheets, "Products Under Fire," *U.S. News & World Report,* April 16, 1990, p. 44.

2. Archie B. Carroll, "A Three-Dimensional Conceptual Model of Corporate Performance," *Academy of Management Review,* October 1979, p. 499.

3. Milton Friedman, *Capitalism and Freedom* (Chicago: University of Chicago Press, 1962); and "The Social Responsibility of Business Is to Increase Its Profits," *New York Times Magazine,* September 13, 1970, p. 33.

4. Saul W. Gellerman, "Why 'Good' Managers Make Bad Ethical Choices," *Harvard Business Review,* July–August 1986, p. 89.

5. Ibid., p. 86.

6. Steven L. Wartick and Philip L. Cochran, "The Evolution of the Corporate Social Performance Model," *Academy of Management Review,* October 1985, p. 760.

7. This section is based on R. Joseph Monsen, Jr., "The Social Attitudes of Management," in Joseph M. McGuire (ed.), *Contemporary Management: Issues and Views* (Englewood Cliffs, N.J.: Prentice-Hall, 1974), p. 616; and Keith Davis and William C. Frederick, *Business and Society: Management, Public Policy, Ethics,* 5th ed. (New York: McGraw-Hill, 1984), pp. 28–41.

8. See, for example, Rogene A. Buchholz, *Essentials of Public Policy for Management,* 2nd ed. (Englewood Cliffs, N.J.: Prentice Hall, 1990).

9. See S. Prakash Sethi, "A Conceptual Framework for Environmental Analysis of Social Issues and Evaluation of Business Response Patterns," *Academy of Management Review,* January 1979, pp. 68–74.

10. William C. Frederick, "From CSR1 to CSR2: The Maturing of Business and Society Thought," Working Paper No. 279, Graduate School of Business, University of Pittsburg, 1978.

11. Steven L. Wartick and Philip L. Cochran, "The Evolution of the Corporate Social Performance Model," p. 763.

12. Ibid., p. 762.

13. Ibid.

14. Frederick D. Sturdivant, *Business and Society: A Managerial Approach,* p. 5.

15. James E. Post, *Corporate Behavior and Social Change* (Reston, Va.: Reston, 1978).

16. Milton R. Moskowitz, "Company Performance Roundup," *Business and Society Review,* Spring 1986, pp. 125–28.

17. See, for instance, Jeanne M. Logsdon and David R. Palmer, "Issues Management and Ethics," *Journal of Business Ethics,* March 1988, pp. 191–98.

18. Robert H. Miles, *Managing the Corporate Social Environment: A Grounded Theory* (Englewood Cliffs, N.J.: Prentice-Hall, 1987), pp. 134–35.

19. See, for instance, Philip Cochran and Robert A. Wood, "Corporate Social Responsibility and Financial Performance," *Academy of Management Journal,* March 1984, pp. 42–56; and Kenneth Aupperle, Archie B. Carroll, and John D. Hatfield, "An Empirical Examination of the Relationship Between Corporate Social Responsibility and Profitability," *Academy of Management Journal,* June 1985, pp. 446–63.

20. See Arieh A. Ullmann, "Data in Search of a Theory: A Critical Examination of the Relationships Among Social Performance, Social Disclosure, and Economic Performance of U.S. Firms," *Academy of Management Review,* July 1985, pp. 540–57; and Richard E. Wokutch and Barbara A. Spencer, "Corporate Saints

and Sinners: The Effects of Philanthropic and Illegal Activity on Organizational Performance," *California Management Review,* Winter 1987, pp. 62–77.

21. Philip Cochran and Robert A. Wood, "Corporate Social Responsibility and Financial Performance."

22. See Joanne Rockness and Paul F. Williams, "A Descriptive Study of Social Responsibility Mutual Funds," *Accounting, Organizations and Society,* Spring 1988, pp. 397–411.

23. Charles W. Stevens, "Socially Aware Investing Turns Profitable," *Wall Street Journal,* July 29, 1988, p. 23.

24. Walter F. Abbott and R. Joseph Monsen, "On the Measurement of Corporate Social Responsibility: Self-Report Disclosure as a Method of Measuring Social Involvement," *Academy of Management Journal,* September 1979, p. 514.

25. See "Marketing: Cause-Related Marketing," *Wall Street Journal,* February 19, 1987, p. 29; Brian Bremner, "A New Sales Pitch: The Environment," *Business Week,* July 24, 1989, p. 50; and Joshua Levine, "I Gave at the Supermarket," *Forbes,* December 25, 1989, pp. 138–40.

26. Kathleen K. Wiegner, "A Cause on Every Carton," *Forbes,* November 18, 1985, pp. 248–49; Monci Jo Williams, "How to Cash in on Do-Good Pitches," *Fortune,* June 9, 1986, pp. 71–80; and Zachary Schiller, "Doing Well by Doing Good," *Business Week,* December 5, 1988, pp. 53–57.

27. Kathleen K. Wiegner, "A Cause on Every Carton," p. 248.

28. Ibid.

29. Monci Jo Williams, "How to Cash in on Do-Good Pitches," p. 72.

30. Ibid., p. 80.

31. Zachary Schiller, "Doing Well by Doing Good," p. 53.

32. Louis W. Fry, Gerald D. Keim, and Roger E. Meiners, "Corporate Contributions: Altruistic or For-Profit?" *Academy of Management Journal,* March 1982, pp. 94–106; and Timothy S. Mescon and Donn J. Tilson, "Corporate Philanthropy: A Strategic Approach to the Bottom-Line," *California Management Review,* Winter 1987, pp. 49–61.

33. Zachary Schiller, "Doing Well by Doing Good," p. 57.

34. "Laura Scher: Doing Good Business Helps Good Causes," *Business Week,* October 26, 1987, p. 76.

35. This section has been influenced by Kimberly B. Boal and Newman Peery, "The Cognitive Structure of Corporate Social Responsibility," *Journal of Management,* Fall–Winter 1985, pp. 71–82.

36. Archie B. Carroll, *Social Responsibility of Management* (Chicago: Science Research Associates, 1984), p. 13.

37. Keith Davis and William C. Frederick, *Business and Society,* p. 76.

38. Frederick D. Sturdivant, *Business and Society,* p. 128.

39. Gerald F. Cavanagh, Dennis J. Moberg, and Manuel Valasquez, "The Ethics of Organizational Politics," *Academy of Management Journal,* June 1981, pp. 363–74. See F. Neil Brady, "Rules for Making Exceptions to Rules," *Academy of Management Review,* July 1987, pp. 436–44 for an argument that the theory of justice is redundant with the prior two theories.

40. Gerald F. Cavanagh, Dennis J. Moberg, and Manuel Valasquez, "The Ethics of Organizational Politics."

41. David J. Fritzsche and Helmut Becker, "Linking Management Behavior to Ethical Philosophy—An Empirical Investigation," *Academy of Management Journal,* March 1984, pp. 166–75.

42. This section is based on Mary Shepard Thibodeaux and James Donald Powell, "Exploitation: Ethical Problems of Organizational Power," *SAM Advanced Management Journal,* Spring 1985, pp. 42–44; and Linda Klebe Trevino, "Ethical Decision Making in Organizations: A Person-Situation Interactionist Model," *Academy of Management Review,* July 1986, pp. 601–17.

43. John H. Barnett and Marvin J. Karson, "Personal Values and Business Decisions: An Exploratory Investigation," *Journal of Business Ethics,* July 1987, pp. 371–82.

44. Barry Z. Posner and William H. Schmidt, "Values and the American Manager: An Update," *California Management Review,* Spring 1984, pp. 202–16.

45. Bart Victor and John B. Cullen, "The Organizational Bases of Ethical Work Climates," *Administrative Science Quarterly,* March 1988, pp. 101–25.

46. Saul W. Gellerman, "Why 'Good' Managers Make Bad Ethical Choices."

47. George Getschow, "Some Middle Managers Cut Corners to Achieve Corporate Goals," *Wall Street Journal,* November 8, 1979, p. 1.

48. Michael Davis, "Working with Your Company's Code of Ethics," *Management Solutions,* June 1988, pp. 5–10; and Amanda Bennett, "Ethics Codes Spread Despite Skepticism," *Wall Street Journal,* July 15, 1988, p. 13.

49. Paul Richter, "Big Business Puts Ethics in Spotlight," *Los Angeles Times,* June 19, 1986, p. 29.

50. Fred R. David, "An Empirical Study of Codes of Business Ethics: A Strategic Perspective," paper presented at the 48th Annual Academy of Management Conference, Anaheim, California, August 1988.

51. Rick Wartzman, "Nature or Nurture? Study Blames Ethical Lapses on Corporate Goals," *Wall Street Journal,* October 9, 1987, p. 27.

52. Ibid.

53. D. R. Cressey and C. A. Moore, "Managerial Values and Corporate Codes of Ethics," *California Management Review,* Summer 1983, p. 71.

54. Laura Nash, "Ethics Without the Sermon," *Harvard Business Review,* November–December 1981, p. 81.

55. "Ethics: Part of the Game at Citicorp," *Fortune,* October 26, 1987, p. 12.

56. R. Ricklefs, "Executives and General Public Say Ethical Behavior is Declining in U.S.," *Wall Street Journal,* October 31, 1983, p. 33.

57. See, for instance, Archie B. Carroll, *Social Responsibility of Management,* p. 14.

58. Alan L. Otten, "Ethics on the Job: Companies Alert Employees to Potential Dilemmas," *Wall Street Journal,* July 14, 1986, p. 19.

59. Based on Erik Larson, "Forever Young," *INC.,* July 1988, pp. 50–62.

Chapter 6

1. Based on John H. Taylor, "Risk Taker," *Forbes,* November 14, 1988, p. 108.

2. William Pounds, "The Process of Problem Finding," *Industrial Management Review,* Fall 1969, pp. 1–19.

3. Roger J. Volkema, "Problem Formulation: Its Portrayal in the Texts," *Organizational Behavior Teaching Review,* Vol. 11, No. 3, 1986–87, pp. 113–26.

4. Morgan W. McCall, Jr., and Robert E. Kaplan, *Whatever It Takes: Decision Makers at Work* (Englewood Cliffs, N.J.: Prentice-Hall, 1985), pp. 36–38.

5. Herbert A. Simon, *The New Science of Management Decision* (New York: Harper & Row, 1960), p. 1.

6. See Graham T. Allison, *Essence of Decision: Explaining the Cuban Missile Crisis* (Boston: Little, Brown, 1971), p. 30; and Herbert A. Simon, "Rationality in Psychology and Economics," *The Journal of Business,* October 1986, pp. 209–24.

7. See, for example, Milton Moskowitz, "Uprooting the Corporation," *Los Angeles Times,* October 1, 1989, p. IV-3.

8. Fremont A. Shull, Jr., André L. Delbecq, and Larry L. Cummings, *Organizational Decision Making* (New York: McGraw-Hill, 1970), p. 151.

9. A few of the more enlightening of these would include: Michael D. Cohen, James G. March, and Johan P. Olsen, "A Garbage Can Model of Organizational Choice," *Administrative Science Quarterly,* March 1972, pp. 1–25; Henry Mintzberg, Duru Raisinghani, and André Théorêt, "The Structure of 'Unstructured' Decision Processes," *Administrative Science Quarterly,* June 1976, pp. 246–75; Karl E. Weick, *The Social Psychology of Organizing,* rev. ed. (Reading, Mass.: Addison-Wesley, 1979); Anna Grandori, "A Prescriptive Contingency View of Organizational Decision Making," *Administrative Science Quarterly,* June 1984, pp. 192–209; and Paul C. Nutt, "Types of Organizational Decision Processes," *Administrative Science Quarterly,* September 1984, pp. 414–50.

10. Herbert A. Simon, "Information-Processing Models of Cognition," in M. R. Rosenzweig and L. W. Porter, eds., *Annual Review of Psychology,* Vol. 30 (Palo Alto, Calif.: Annual Reviews, 1979), pp. 363–96.

11. Paul A. Anderson, "Decision Making by Objection and the Cuban Missile Crisis," *Administrative Science Quarterly,* June 1983, p. 217.

12. See Stephen P. Robbins, *Organizational Behavior: Concepts, Controversies, and Applications,* 4th ed. (Englewood Cliffs, N.J.: Prentice-Hall, 1989), pp. 89–92.

13. Leonard R. Sayles in McCall and Kaplan, *Whatever It Takes: Decision Makers at Work,* p. x.

14. McCall and Kaplan, p. 27.

15. Charles A. O'Reilly, III, "Variations in Decision Makers' Use of Information Sources: The Impact of Quality and Accessibility of Information," *Academy of Management Journal,* December 1982, pp. 756–71.

16. Paul C. Nutt, "Types of Organizational Decision Processes."

17. Glen White, "Escalating Commitment to a Course of Action: A Reinterpretation," *Academy of Management Review,* April 1986, pp. 311–21.

18. Graham T. Allison, *Essence of Decision: Explaining the Cuban Missile Crisis,* p. 79.

19. Ibid., p. 175.

20. Ibid., p. 176.

21. Jeffrey Pfeffer, *Power in Organizations* (Marshfield, Mass.: Pitman Publishing, 1981).

22. Daniel Katz and Robert L. Kahn, *The Social Psychology of Organizations,* 2nd ed. (New York: John Wiley, 1978), p. 501.

23. Charles E. Lindholm, "The Science of 'Muddling Through,'" *Public Administration Review,* Spring 1959, pp. 79–88.

24. See, for example, James G. March, "Footnotes to Organizational Change," *Administrative Science Quarterly,* December 1981, pp. 563–77.

25. James G. March, "Decision-Making Perspective: Decisions in Organizations and Theories of Choice," in Andrew H. Van de Ven and William F. Joyce (eds.), *Perspectives on Organization Design and Behavior* (New York: Wiley-Interscience, 1981), pp. 232–33.

26. Neil McK. Agnew and John L. Brown, "Bounded Rationality: Fallible Decisions in Unbounded Decision Space," *Behavioral Science,* July 1986, pp. 148–61.

27. Based on "Taking Charge," *Black Enterprise,* August 1989, pp. 49–50.

28. "This Meeting Will Come to Order," *Time,* December 6, 1985.

29. Timothy W. Costello and Sheldon S. Zalkind, eds., *Psychology in Administration: A Research Orientation* (Englewood Cliffs, N.J.: Prentice-Hall, 1963), pp. 429–30.

30. Fremont A. Shull, André L. Delbecq, and Larry L. Cummings, *Organizational Decision Making,* p. 151.

31. Irving L. Janis, *Victims of Groupthink* (Boston: Houghton Mifflin, 1972).

32. A. F. Osborn, *Applied Imagination: Principles and Procedures of Creative Thinking* (New York: Scribners, 1941).

33. The following discussion is based on André L. Delbecq, A. H. Van de Ven, and D. H. Gustafson, *Group Techniques for Program Planning: A Guide to Nominal and Delphi Processes* (Glenview, Ill.: Scott, Foresman, 1975).

34. This box is substantially based on Ellen F. Jackofsky, John W. Slocum, Jr., and Sara J. McQuaid, "Cultural Values and the CEO: Alluring Companions?," *Academy of Management Executive,* February 1988, pp. 39–49.

35. Based on John Heins, "After Cost Cuts, What?," *Forbes,* May 1, 1989, p. 46.

36. See Ken Wells and Charles McCoy, "How Unpreparedness Turned the Alaska Spill into Ecological Debacle," *Wall Street Journal,* April 3, 1989, p. 1; George J. Church, "The Big Spill," *Time,* April 10, 1989, pp. 211–13; and "Getting Ready for Exxon Vs. Practically Everybody," *Business Week,* September 25, 1989, pp. 190–94.

Chapter 7

1. See "The Greenhouse Effect: What Will It Mean," *Fortune,* July 4, 1988, pp. 104–105; and "When the Rivers Go Dry and the Ice Caps Melt . . . ," *Business Week,* February 13, 1989, pp. 95–98.

2. See, for example, John A. Pearce II, K. Keith Robbins, and Richard B. Robinson, Jr., "The Impact of Grand Strategy and Planning Formality on Financial Performance," *Strategic Management Journal,* March–April 1987, pp. 125–34; Lawrence C. Rhyne, "Contrasting Planning Systems in High, Medium, and Low Performance Companies," *Journal of Management Studies,* July 1987, pp. 363–85; Richard Brahm and Charles B. Brahm, "Formal Planning and Organizational Performance: Assessing Emerging Empirical Research Trends," paper presented at the National Academy of Management Conference, New Orleans, August 1987; and John A. Pearce II, Elizabeth B. Freeman, and Richard B. Robinson, Jr., "The Tenuous Link Between Formal Strategic Planning and Financial Performance," *Academy of Management Review,* October 1987, pp. 658–75.

3. Russell Ackoff, "A Concept of Corporate Planning," *Long Range Planning,* September 1970, p. 3.

4. Several of these factors were suggested by J. Scott Armstrong, "The Value of Formal Planning for Strategic Decisions: Review of Empirical Research," *Strategic Management Journal,* July–September 1982, pp. 197–211; and Rudi K. Bresser and Ronald C. Bishop, "Dysfunctional Effects of Formal Planning: Two Theoretical Explanations," *Academy of Management Review,* October 1983, pp. 588–99.

5. Richard F. Vancil, "The Accuracy of Long-Range Planning," *Harvard Business Review,* September–October 1970, p. 99.

6. Rick Molz, "How Leaders Use Goals," *Long Range Planning,* October 1987, p. 91.

7. Y. K. Shetty, "New Look at Corporate Goals," *California Management Review,* Winter 1979, pp. 71–79.

8. "Icahn Threatens to Dismantle TWA," *San Diego Union,* March 3, 1986, p. A1.

9. Charles K. Warriner, "The Problem of Organizational Purpose," *Sociological Quarterly,* Spring 1965, p. 140.

10. Ibid.

11. Ibid.

12. Richard M. Cyert and James G. March, *A Behavioral Theory of the Firm* (Englewood Cliffs, N.J.: Prentice-Hall, 1963).

13. Francis D. Tuggle, *Organizational Processes* (Arlington Heights, Ill.: AHM Publishing, 1978), p. 108.

14. The concept is generally attributed to Peter F. Drucker, *The Practice of Management* (New York: Harper & Row, 1954).

15. See, for example, Edwin A. Locke, "Toward a Theory of Task Motivation and Incentives," *Organizational Behavior and Human Performance,* May 1968, pp. 157–89; Edwin A. Locke, Karyl N. Shaw, Lise M. Saari, and Gary P. Latham, "Goal Setting and Task Performance: 1969–1980," *Psychological Bulletin,* July 1981, pp. 125–52; Mark E. Tubbs, "Goal Setting: A Meta-Analytic Examination of the Empirical Evidence," *Journal of Applied Psychology,* August 1986, pp. 474–83; and Anthony J. Mento, R. P. Steel, and R. J. Karren, "A Meta-Analytic Study of the Effects of Goal Setting on Task Performance: 1966–1984," *Organizational Behavior and Human Decision Processes,* February 1987, pp. 52–83.

16. See, for example, Gary P. Latham and Lise M. Saari, "The Effects of Holding Goal Difficulty Constant on Assigned and Participatively Set Goals," *Academy of Management Journal,* March 1979, pp. 163–68; Miriam Erez, P. Christopher Earley, and Charles L. Hulin, "The Impact of Participation on Goal Acceptance and Performance: A Two-Step Model," *Academy of Management Journal,* March 1985, pp. 50–66; and Gary P. Latham, Miriam Erez, and Edwin A. Locke, "Resolving Scientific Disputes by the Joint Design of Crucial Experiments by the Antagonists: Application to the Erez-Latham Dispute Regarding Participation in Goal Setting," *Journal of Applied Psychology,* November 1988, pp. 753–72.

17. Based on Daniel Machalaba, "Transit Manager Shows New York Subway Isn't Beyond Redemption," *Wall Street Journal,* October 14, 1988, pp. A1 and A6.

18. Gary P. Latham, Terence R. Mitchell, and Dennis L. Dossett, "Importance of Participative Goal Setting and Anticipated Rewards on Goal Difficulty and Job Performance," *Journal of Applied Psychology,* April 1978, pp. 163–71.

19. Jack N. Kondrasuk, "Studies in MBO Effectiveness," *Academy of Management Review,* July 1981, pp. 419–31.

20. J. C. Aplin, Jr., and P. P. Schoderbek, "MBO: Requisites for Success in the Public Sector," *Human Resource Management,* Summer 1976, pp. 30–36.

Chapter 8

1. Based on Stephen Koepp, "Do You Believe in Magic?," *Time,* April 25, 1988, pp. 66–73; and Christopher Knowlton, "How Disney Keeps the Magic Going," *Fortune,* December 4, 1989, pp. 111–32.

2. See, for example, Larry J. Rosenberg and Charles D. Schewe, "Strategic Planning: Fulfilling the Promise," *Business Horizons,* July–August 1985, pp. 54–62; and Walter Kiechel III, "Corporate Strategy for the 1990s," *Fortune,* February 29, 1988, pp. 34–42.

3. "How Academia Is Taking Lessons from Business," *Business Week,* August 27, 1984, pp. 58–60.

4. Based on "Shades of Geneen at Emerson Electric," *Fortune,* May 22, 1989, p. 39.

5. William K. Hall, "SBUs: Hot, New Topic in Management of Diversification," *Business Horizons,* February 1978, p. 17.

6. See Susan E. Jackson and Jane E. Dutton, "Discerning Threats and Opportunities," *Administrative Science Quarterly,* September 1988, pp. 370–87.

7. See, for example, Jay B. Barney, "Organizational Culture: Can It Be a Source of Sustained Competitive Advantage?," *Academy of Management Review,* July 1986, pp. 656–65; Christian Scholz, "Corporate Culture and Strategy—The Problem of Strategic Fit," *Long Range Planning,* August 1987, pp. 78–87; and Sebastian Green, "Understanding Corporate Culture and Its Relation to Strategy," *International Studies of Management and Organization,* Summer 1988, pp. 6–28.

8. See William F. Glueck, *Business Policy: Strategy Formulation and Management Action,* 2nd ed. (New York: McGraw-Hill, 1976), pp. 120–47; John A. Pearce II, "Selecting Among Alternative Grand Strategies," *California Management Review,* Spring 1982, pp. 23–31; and Theodore T. Herbert and Helen Deresky, "Generic Strategies: An Empirical Investigation of Typology Validity and Strategy Content," *Strategic Management Journal,* March–April 1987, pp. 135–47.

9. "How to Be Happy in One Act," *Fortune,* December 19, 1988, p. 119.

10. See, for example, Kathryn Rudie Harrigan, *Strategies for Declining Businesses* (Lexington, Mass.: Lexington, 1980); Leonard Greenhalgh, "Maintaining Organizational Effectiveness During Organizational Retrenchment," *The Journal of Applied Behavioral Science,* Vol. 18, No. 2, 1982, pp. 155–70; Kim Cameron, "Strategic Responses to Conditions of Decline," *Journal of Higher Education,* July–August 1983, pp. 359–80; Larry Hirschhorn and Associates, *Cutting Back* (San Francisco: Jossey-Bass, 1983); V. V. Murray and T. D. Jick, "Taking Stock of Organizational Decline Management: Some Issues and Illustrations from an Empirical Study," *Journal of Management,* Fall–Winter 1985, pp. 111–23; Cynthia Hardy, "Strategies for Retrenchment: Reconciling Individual and Organizational Needs," *Canadian Journal of Administrative Sciences,* December 1986, pp. 275–89; Kim S. Cameron, Myung U. Kim, and David A. Whetten, "Organizational Effects of Decline and Turbulence," *Administrative Science Quarterly,* June 1987, pp. 222–40; and Donald C. Hambrick and Richard A. D'Aveni, "Large Corporate Failures as Downward Spirals," *Administrative Science Quarterly,* March 1988, pp. 1–23.

11. Phillipe Haspeslagh, "Portfolio Planning: Uses and Limits," *Harvard Business Review,* January–February 1982, pp. 58–73.

12. *Perspective on Experience* (Boston: Boston Consulting Group, 1970).

13. Donald C. Hambrick, Ian C. MacMillan, and Diana L. Day, "Strategic Attributes and Performance in the BCG Matrix: A PIMS-Based Analysis of Industrial Product Businesses," *Academy of Management Journal,* September 1982, pp. 510–31; H. Kurt Christensen, Arnold C. Cooper, and Cornelis A. DeKluyver, "The Dog Business: A Re-Examination," *Business Horizons,* November–December 1982, pp. 12–18; William Baldwin, "The Market Share Myth," *Forbes,* March 14, 1983, pp. 109–15; Richard A. Bettis and William K. Hall, "The Business Portfolio Approach—Where It Falls Down in Practice," *Long Range Planning,* April 1983, pp. 95–104; and Jaclyn Fierman, "How to Make Money in Mature Markets," *Fortune,* November 25, 1985, pp. 47–53.

14. See, for example, James Leontiades, "Going Global—Global Strategies vs. National Strategies," *Long Range Planning,* December 1986, pp. 96–104; Sumantra Ghoshal, "Global Strategy: An Organizing Framework," *Strategic Management Journal,* September–October 1987, pp. 425–40; Richard I. Kirkland, Jr., "Entering a New Age of Boundless Competition," *Fortune,* March 14, 1988, pp. 40–48; and Jeremy Main, "How to Go Global—And Why," *Fortune,* August 28, 1989, pp. 70–76.

15. See, for example, Kathryn Rudie Harrigan, "Strategic Alliances: Their New Role in Global Competition," *Columbia Journal of World Business,* Summer 1987, pp. 67–69; Louis Kraar, "Your Rivals Can Be Your Allies," *Fortune,* March 27, 1989, pp. 66–76; and Bryan Borys and David B. Jemison, "Hybrid Arrangements as Strategic Alliances: Theoretical Issues in Organizational Combinations," *Academy of Management Review,* April 1989, pp. 234–49.

16. See Raymond E. Miles and Charles C. Snow, *Organizational Strategy, Structure, and Process* (New York: McGraw-Hill, 1978); and Donald C. Hambrick, "Some Tests of the Effectiveness and Functional Attributes of Miles and Snow's Strategic Types," *Academy of Management Journal,* March 1983, pp. 5–26.

17. See, for example, Michael E. Porter, *Competitive Strategy: Techniques for Analyzing Industries and Competitors* (New York: Free Press, 1980); Michael E. Porter, *Competitive Advantage: Creating and Sustaining Superior Performance* (New York: Free Press, 1985); Gregory G. Dess and Peter S. Davis, "Porter's (1980) Generic Strategies as Determinants of Strategic Group Membership and Organizational Performance," *Academy of Management Journal,* September 1984, pp. 467–88; Gregory G. Dess and Peter S. Davis, "Porter's (1980) Generic Strategies and Performance: An Empirical Examination with American Data—Part I: Testing Porter," *Organization Studies,* No. 1, 1986, pp. 37–55; Gregory G. Dess and Peter S. Davis, "Porter's (1980) Generic Strategies and Performance: An Empirical Examination with American Data—Part II: Performance Implications," *Organization Studies,* No. 3, 1986, pp. 255–61; Michael E. Porter, "From Competitive Advantage to Corporate Strategy," *Harvard Business Review,* May–June 1987, pp. 43–59; Alan I. Murray, "A Contingency View of Porter's 'Generic Strategies,'" *Academy of Management Review,* July 1988, pp. 390–400; and Charles W. L. Hill, "Differentiation Versus Low Cost or Differentiation and Low Cost: A Contingency Framework," *Academy of Management Review,* July 1988, pp. 401–12.

18. Danny Miller and Jean-Marie Toulouse, "Strategy, Structure, CEO Personality and Performance in Small Firms," *American Journal of Small Business,* Winter 1986, pp. 47–62.

19. John G. Burch, *Entrepreneurship* (New York: John Wiley, 1986), p. 4.

20. See, for instance, Thomas M. Begley and David P. Boyd, "A Comparison of Entrepreneurs and Managers of Small Business Firms," *Journal of Management,* Spring 1987, pp. 99–108.

21. Peter F. Drucker, *Innovation and Entrepreneurship* (New York: Harper & Row, 1985).

22. Gifford Pinchot III, *Intrapreneuring: Or, Why You Don't Have to Leave the Corporation to Become an Entrepreneur* (New York: Harper & Row, 1985).

23. Karl H. Vesper, *New Venture Strategies* (Englewood Cliffs, N.J.: Prentice-Hall, 1980), p. 14.

24. John A. Hornaday, "Research About Living Entrepreneurs," in Calvin A. Kent, Donald L. Sexton, and Karl H. Vesper (eds.), *Encyclopedia of Entrepreneurship* (Englewood Cliffs, N.J.: Prentice-Hall, 1982), p. 28.

25. Robert H. Brockhaus, Sr., "The Psychology of the Entrepreneur," in Calvin A. Kent, Donald L. Sexton, and Karl H. Vesper (eds.), *Encyclopedia of Entrepreneurship,* pp. 41–49.

26. Howard H. Stevenson and David E. Gumpert, "The Heart of Entrepreneurship," *Harvard Business Review,* March–April 1985, pp. 85–94.

27. Executive Office of the President, *The State of Small Business* (Washington, D.C.: GPO, 1983), pp. 70–71.

28. Based on James E. Ellis, "Beyond Bunnies: Rewriting the Playboy Philosophy," *Business Week,* November 14, 1988, pp. 89–90.

29. Based on Lucien Rhodes, "Piano Man," *INC.,* January 1987, pp. 52–56; and Leslie Brokaw, "Sour Notes," *INC.,* January 1990, p. 25.

Chapter 9

1. Based on "This Video 'Game' Is Saving Manufacturers Millions," *Business Week,* August 17, 1987, pp. 82–84.

2. Mark Robichaux, "'Competitor Intelligence': A Grapevine to Rivals' Secrets," *Wall Street Journal,* April 12, 1989, p. B2.

3. John Diffenbach, "Corporate Environmental Analysis in Large U.S. Corporations," *Long Range Planning,* June 1983, pp. 107–16; Subhash C. Jain, "Environmental Scanning in U.S. Corporations," *Long Range Planning,* April 1984, pp. 117–28; Leonard M. Fuld, *Monitoring the Competition* (New York: John Wiley & Sons, 1988); and Elmer H. Burack and Nicholas J. Mathys, "Environmental Scanning Improves Strategic Planning," *Personnel Administrator,* April 1989, pp. 82–87.

4. William L. Renfro and James L. Morrison, "Detecting Signals of Change," *The Futurist,* August 1984, p. 49.

5. Mark Robichaux, "'Competitor Intelligence': A Grapevine to Rivals' Secrets"; and Subhash C. Jain, *Marketing Planning and Strategy* (Cincinnati: Southwestern Publishing, 1985), pp. 165–69.

6. Mark Robichaux, "'Competitor Intelligence': A Grapevine to Rivals' Secrets."

7. Robert E. Linneman and Harold E. Klein, "Using Scenarios in Strategic Decision Making," *Business Horizons,* January–February 1985, pp. 64–74.

8. This section is based on Essam Mahmoud, "Accuracy in Forecasting: A Survey," *Journal of Forecasting,* Vol. 3, No. 2, 1984, pp. 139–59; Reed Moyer, "The Futility of Forecasting," *Long Range Planning,* February 1984, pp. 65–72; and Ronald Bailey, "Them That Can, Do, Them That Can't, Forecast," *Forbes,* December 26, 1988, pp. 94–100.

9. Leonard Merewitz and Stephen H. Sosnick, *The Budget's New Clothes: A Critique of Planning-Programming-Budgeting and Benefit-Cost Analysis* (Chicago: Markham, 1971), pp. 239–71.

10. James C. Weatherbee and John R. Montanari, "Zero-Base Budgeting in the Planning Process," *Strategic Management Journal,* January–March 1981, pp. 1–14.

11. R. D. Behn, *Policy Termination: A Survey of the Current Literature and an Agenda for Future Research* (Washington, D.C.: Ford Foundation, 1977).

12. Peter A. Pyhrr, "Zero-Base Budgeting," *Harvard Business Review,* November–December 1970, pp. 111–18.

13. Virendra S. Sherlekar and Burton V. Dean, "An Evaluation of the Initial Year of Zero-Base Budgeting in the Federal Government," *Management Science,* August 1980, pp. 750–72.

14. John V. Pearson and Ray J. Michael, "Zero-Base Budgeting: A Technique for Planned Organizational Decline," *Long Range Planning,* June 1981, pp. 68–76.

15. See Harold E. Fearon, William A. Ruch, Vincent G. Reuter, C. David Wieters, and Ross R. Reck, *Fundamentals of Production/Operations Management,* 3rd ed. (St. Paul, Minn.: West Publishing, 1986), p. 97.

16. For a discussion of software and application to a project for restructuring a large retail chain, see Paul A. Strassmann, "The Best-Laid Plans," *INC.,* October 1988, pp. 135–38.

17. See, for example, Sarah Stiansen, "Breaking Even," *Success,* November 1988, p. 16.

18. Stephen E. Barndt and Davis W. Carvey, *Essentials of Operations Management* (Englewood Cliffs, N.J.: Prentice-Hall, 1982), p. 134.

19. David A. Whetten and Kim S. Cameron, *Developing Management Skills* (Glenview, Ill.: Scott, Foresman, 1984), p. 106.

20. Peter F. Drucker, *The Effective Executive* (New York: Harper & Row, 1967), pp. 47–51.

21. Ross A. Webber, *To Be a Manager* (Homewood, Ill.: Richard D. Irwin, 1981), p. 373.

22. For a more detailed discussion of these time-management suggestions, see R. A. Mackenzie, *The Time Trap* (New York: McGraw-Hill, 1975); R. A. Webber, *Time Is Money* (New York: Free Press, 1980); and M. E. Haynes, *Practical Time Management: How to Make the Most of Your Most Perishable Resource* (Tulsa, Okla.: Penn Well Books, 1985).

23. Adapted from Charles N. Greene, Everett E. Adam, Jr., and Ronald J. Ebert, *Management for Effective Performance* (Englewood Cliffs, N.J.: Prentice-Hall, 1985), pp. 736–37. With permission.

24. From Gareth Morgan, *Creative Organization Theory: A Resource Book* (Newbury Park, Calif.: Sage Publishing, 1989), p. 330. With permission.

Chapter 10

1. Based on Eric Morgenthaler, "Herb Tea's Pioneer: From Hippie Origins to $16 Million a Year," *Wall Street Journal,* May 7, 1981, p. 1; "Kraft Is Celestial Seasonings' Cup of Tea," *Business Week,* July 28, 1986, p. 73; and "Why Celestial Seasonings Wasn't Kraft's Cup of Tea," *Business Week,* May 8, 1989, p. 76.

2. Stephen P. Robbins, *Organization Theory: Structure, Design, and Applications,* 3rd ed. (Englewood Cliffs, N.J.: Prentice-Hall, 1990), Chapter 4.

3. See, for instance, Brian S. Moskal, "Supervisors, Begone!," *Industry Week,* June 20, 1988, p. 32; and Gregory A. Patterson, "Auto Assembly Lines Enter a New Era," *Wall Street Journal,* December 28, 1988, p. A2.

4. The matrix organization is an obvious example of an organization design that breaks the unity of command. See, for instance, David I. Cleland, ed., *Matrix Management Systems Handbook* (New York: Van Nostrand Reinhold, 1984); and Erik W. Larson and David H. Gobeli, "Matrix Management: Contradictions and Insights," *California Management Review,* Summer 1987, pp. 126–38.

5. See, for instance, David Kipnis, *The Powerholders* (Chicago: University of Chicago Press, 1976); Jeffrey Pfeffer, *Power in Organizations* (Marshfield, Mass.: Pitman Publishing, 1981); Henry Mintzberg, *Power In and Around Organizations* (Englewood Cliffs, N.J.: Prentice-Hall, 1983); and David W. Ewing, *"Do It My Way or You're Fired": Employee Rights and the Changing Role of Management Prerogatives* (New York: John Wiley, 1983).

6. See John R. P. French, Jr. and Bertram Raven, "The Bases of Social Power," in Dorwin Cartwright and A. F. Zander (eds.), *Group Dynamics: Research and Theory* (New York: Harper & Row, Pub., 1960), pp. 607–23; Philip M. Podsakoff and Chester A. Schriesheim, "Field Studies of French and Raven's Bases of Power: Critique, Reanalysis, and Suggestions for Future Research," *Psychological Bulletin,* May 1985, pp. 387–411; Ramesh K. Shukla, "Influence of Power Bases in Organizational Decision Making: A Contingency Model," *Decision Sciences,* July 1982, pp. 450–70; and Dean E. Frost and Anthony J. Stahelski, "The Systematic Measurement of French and Raven's Bases of Social Power in Workgroups," *Journal of Applied Social Psychology,* April 1988, pp. 375–89.

7. Steven N. Brenner and Earl A. Molander, "Is the Ethics of Business Changing?," *Harvard Business Review,* January–February 1977, pp. 57–71.

8. Herbert C. Kelman and Lee H. Lawrence, "American Response to the Trial of Lt. William L. Calley," *Psychology Today,* June 1972, pp. 41–45, 78–81.

9. Based on Sharon R. King, "At the Crossroads," *Black Enterprise,* August 1988, pp. 45–51.

10. Lyndall Urwick, *The Elements of Administration* (New York: Harper & Row, 1944), pp. 52–53.

11. Quoted in Jim Braham, "Money Talks," *Industry Week,* April 17, 1989, p. 23.

12. John S. McClenahen, "Managing More People in the '90s" *Industry Week,* March 20, 1989, p. 30.

13. David Van Fleet, "Span of Management Research and Issues," *Academy of Management Journal,* September 1983, pp. 546–52.

14. John H. Sheridan, "Sizing Up Corporate Staffs," *Industry Week,* November 21, 1988, p. 47.

15. Tom Burns and G. M. Stalker, *The Management of Innovation* (London: Taristock, 1961).

16. Alfred D. Chandler, Jr., *Strategy and Structure: Chapters in the History of the Industrial Enterprise* (Cambridge, Mass.: MIT Press, 1962).

17. See, for instance, Raymond E. Miles and Charles C. Snow, *Organizational Strategy, Structure, and Process* (New York: McGraw-Hill, 1978); and Danny Miller, "The Structure and Environmental Correlates of Business Strategy," *Strategic Management Journal,* January–February 1987, pp. 55–76.

18. See, for instance, Peter M. Blau and Richard A. Schoenherr, *The Structure of Organizations* (New York: Basic Books, 1971); D. S. Pugh, "The Aston Program of Research: Retrospect and Prospect," in A. H. Van de Ven and W. F. Joyce (eds.), *Perspectives on Organization Design and Behavior* (New York: John Wiley, 1981), pp. 135–66; and R. Z. Gooding and J. A. Wagner III, "A Meta-Analytic Review of the Relationship Between Size and Performance: The Productivity and Efficiency of Organizations and Their Subunits," *Administrative Science Quarterly,* December 1985, pp. 462–81.

19. See, for instance, Rod Willis, "What's Happening to America's Middle Managers?," *Management Review,* January 1987, pp. 24–30; Tom Peters, *Thriving on Chaos* (New York: Knopf, 1988), pp. 17–20; Mark B. Roman, "Lean and Mean Inc.," *Success,* December 1988, pp. 40–41; and John A. Byrne, "Is Your Company Too Big?," *Business Week,* March 27, 1989, pp. 84–94.

20. Joan Woodward, *Industrial Organization: Theory and Practice* (London: Oxford University Press, 1965).

21. Charles Perrow, *Organizational Analysis: A Sociological Perspective* (Belmont, Calif.: Wadsworth, 1970).

22. Donald Gerwin, "Relationships Between Structure and Technology," in P. C. Nystrom and W. H. Starbuck (eds.), *Handbook of Organizational Design,* Vol. 2 (New York: Oxford University Press, 1981), pp. 3–38; and Denise M. Rousseau and R. A. Cooke, "Technology and Structure: The Concrete, Abstract, and Activity Systems of Organizations," *Journal of Management,* Fall–Winter 1984, pp. 345–61.

23. See Stephen P. Robbins, *Organization Theory: Structure, Design, and Applications,* pp. 210–32.

24. See, for example, "GM Faces Reality," *Business Week,* May 9, 1988, pp. 114–22; and Alex Taylor III, "The Tasks Facing General Motors," *Fortune,* March 13, 1989, pp. 52–59.

25. Geert Hofstede, "Motivation, Leadership, and Organization: Do American Theories Apply Abroad?," *Organizational Dynamics,* Summer 1980, p. 60.

26. Based on Buck Brown, "How the Cookie Crumbled at Mrs. Fields," *Wall Street Journal,* January 26, 1989, p. B1.

Chapter 11

1. See, for instance, Howard S. Schwartz, "On the Psychodynamics of Organizational Disaster: The Case of the Space Shuttle Challenger," *Columbia Journal of World Business,* Spring 1987, pp. 59–67; Robert Marx, Charles Stubbart, Virginia Traub, and Michael Cavanaugh, "The NASA Space Shuttle Disaster: A Case Study," *Journal of Management Case Studies,* Winter 1987, pp. 300–18; and Judith H. Dobrzynski, "Morton Thiokol: Reflections on the Shuttle Disaster," *Business Week,* March 14, 1988, pp. 82–91.

2. U.S. Department of Labor, Bureau of Labor Statistics, *Employment and Wages,* First Quarter, 1983 (Springfield, Va.: National Technical Information Service, 1986), pp. 520–21.

3. Henry Mintzberg, *Structure in Fives: Designing Effective Organizations* (Englewood Cliffs, N.J.: Prentice-Hall, 1983), p. 157.

4. See, for instance, Jay Galbraith, "Matrix Organization Designs: How to Combine Functional and Project Forms," *Business Horizons,* February 1971, pp. 29–40; and Lawton R. Burns, "Matrix Management in Hospitals: Testing Theories of Structure and Development," *Administrative Science Quarterly,* September 1989, pp. 349–68.

5. See, for example, "And Now, the Post-Industrial Corporation," *Business Week,* March 3, 1986, pp. 64–71; and Raymond E. Miles and Charles C. Snow, "Organizations: New Concepts for New Forms," *California Management Review,* Spring 1986, pp. 62–73.

6. Sumantra Ghoshal, "Global Strategy: An Organizing Framework," *Strategic Management Journal,* September–October, 1987, pp. 425–40.

7. Ibid.

8. William J. Altier, "Task Forces: An Effective Management Tool," *Sloan Management Review,* Spring 1986, pp. 69–76.

9. Henry Mintzberg, *Structure in Fives: Designing Effective Organizations,* p. 159.

10. See, for example, Ricky W. Griffin, "Toward an Integrated Theory of Task Design," in L. L. Cummings and Barry M. Staw (eds.), *Research in Organizational Behavior,* Vol. 9, (Greenwich, Conn.: JAI Press, 1987), pp. 79–120; and Michael Campion, "Interdisciplinary Approaches to Job Design: A Constructive Replication with Extensions," *Journal of Applied Psychology,* August 1988, pp. 467–81.

11. Martin J. Gannon, Brian A. Poole, and Robert E. Prangley, "Involuntary Job Rotation and Work Behavior," *Personnel Journal,* June 1972, pp. 446–48.

12. Described in Tom Peters, *Thriving on Chaos* (New York, Knopf, 1988), pp. 290–91.

13. J. Richard Hackman, G. R. Oldham, R. Janson, and K. Purdy, "A New Strategy for Job Enrichment," *California Management Review,* Summer 1975, pp. 57–71.

14. See, for example, J. R. Hackman and G. R. Oldham, *Work Redesign* (Reading, Mass.: Addison-Wesley, 1980); and John B. Miner, *Theories of Organizational Behavior* (Hinsdale, Ill: Dryden Press, 1980), pp. 231–66.

15. Toby D. Wall, Nigel J. Kemp, Paul L. R. Jackson, and Chris W. Clegg, "Outcomes of Autonomous Work-groups: A Long-Term Field Experiment," *Academy of Management Journal,* June 1986, pp. 280–304.

16. Donald B. Thompson, "Everybody's a Boss," *Industry Week,* February 23, 1987, pp. 16–17.

17. J. Richard Hackman and Greg R. Oldham, "Development of the Job Diagnostic Survey," *Journal of Applied Psychology,* April 1975, pp. 159–170.

18. J. Richard Hackman, "Work Design," in J. Richard Hackman and J. Lloyd Suttle (eds.), *Improving Life at Work* (Glenview, Ill.: Scott, Foresman, 1977), p. 129.

19. General support for the JCM is reported in Yitzhak Fried and Gerald R. Ferris, "The Validity of the Job Characteristics Model: A Review and Meta-Analysis," *Personnel Psychology,* Summer 1987, pp. 287–322.

20. J. Richard Hackman, "Work Design," pp. 136–40.

21. See, for instance, Randall B. Dunham, Jon L. Pierce, and Maria B. Castañeda, "Alternative Work Sched-ules: Two Field Quasi-Experiments," *Personnel Psychology,* Summer 1987, pp. 215–42.

22. Dan Olson and Arthur P. Brief, "The Impact of Alternative Workweeks," *Personnel,* January–February 1978, p. 73.

23. John M. Ivancevich and Herbert L. Lyon, "The Shortened Workweek: A Field Experiment," *Journal of Applied Psychology,* February 1977, pp. 34–37.

24. See, for example, Jay S. Kim and A. F. Campagna, "Effects of Flextime on Employee Attendance and Performance: A Field Experiment," *Academy of Management Journal,* December 1981, pp. 729–41; and David R. Ralston, William P. Anthony, and David J. Gustafson, "Employees May Love Flextime, But What Does It Do to the Organization's Productivity?," *Journal of Applied Psychology,* May 1985, pp. 272–79.

25. For a review of misconceptions surrounding flextime, see M. Ronald Buckley, Diane C. Kicza, and Nancy Crane, "A Note on the Effectiveness of Flextime as an Organizational Intervention," *Public Personnel Management,* Fall 1987, pp. 259–67.

26. Edward G. Thomas, "Flextime Doubles in a Decade," *Management World,* April–May 1987, p. 19.

27. "Flextime Pros and Cons," *Boardroom Reports,* March 1, 1989, p. 15.

28. Ibid.

29. Edward G. Thomas, "Flextime Doubles in a Decade"; and Patricia Amend, "Workers Get a Share of the Action: Job Sharing Splits Hours," *USA Today,* April 27, 1989, p. 9B.

30. See, for example, "The 'Just In Time' Worker," *U.S. News & World Report,* November 23, 1987, pp. 45–46; Jack L. Simonetti, Nich Nykodym, and Louella M. Sell, "Temporary Employees: A Permanent Boon?" *Personnel,* August 1988, pp. 50–56; Michael A. Verespej, "Part-Time Workers: No Temporary Phenomenon," *Industry Week,* April 3, 1989, pp. 13–18; "Contingent Work Force is Growing Rapidly," *Wall Street Journal,* May 2, 1989, p. B1; and "Taking Stock of the Flexible Work Force," *Business Week,* July 24, 1989, p. 12.

31. David Kirkpatrick, "Smart New Ways to Use Temps," *Fortune,* February 15, 1988, p. 110.

32. "The Disposable Employee Is Becoming a Fact of Corporate Life," *Business Week,* December 15, 1986, pp. 52–56.

33. "Contingent Work Force Is Growing Rapidly."

34. "The Disposable Employee Is Becoming a Fact of Corporate Life," p. 52.

35. Ibid.

36. See, for example, Steve Shirley, "A Company Without Offices," *Harvard Business Review,* January–February 1986, pp. 127–36; C. A. Hamilton, "Telecommuting," *Personnel Journal,* April 1987, pp. 91–101; and Donald C. Bacon, "Look Who's Working at Home," *Nation's Business,* October 1989, pp. 20–31.

Chapter 12

1. Based on William J. Hampton, "How Does Japan Inc. Pick Its American Workers?," *Business Week,* October 3, 1988, pp. 84–88.

2. See, for example, Steve Weiner, "Sears' Costly Win in a Hiring Suit," *Wall Street Journal,* March 18, 1986, p. 21.

3. See Aric Press and Ann McDaniel, "Mixed Signal in Court," *Newsweek,* June 2, 1986, p. 65; Paula Dwyer, "The Blow to Affirmative Action May Not Hurt That Much," *Business Week,* July 3, 1989, p. 61; and Stuart Bompey, "Employment Rules Revolution," *Boardroom Reports,* August 1, 1989, p. 1.

4. Elmer H. Burack, "Corporate Business and Human Resource Planning Practices: Strategic Issues and Concerns," *Organizational Dynamics,* Summer 1986, pp. 73–87.

5. Thomas J. Bergmann and M. S. Taylor, "College Recruitment: What Attracts Students to Organizations?" *Personnel,* May–June 1984, pp. 34–46.

6. Judith R. Gordon, *Human Resource Management: A Practical Approach* (Boston: Allyn and Bacon, 1986), p. 170.

7. See, for example, Leonard Greenhalgh, Anne T. Lawrence, and Robert I. Sutton, "Determinants of Work Force Reduction Strategies in Declining Organizations," *Academy of Management Review,* April 1988, pp. 241–54.

8. Based on "Help Wanted," *Business Week,* August 10, 1987, pp. 48–53; Anthony Ramirez, "Making Better Use of Older Workers," *Fortune,* January 30, 1989, pp. 179–87; and Dyan Machan, "Cultivating the Gray," *Forbes,* September 4, 1989, pp. 126–28.

9. This story was directly influenced by a similar example in Arthur Sloane, *Personnel: Managing Human Resources* (Englewood Cliffs, N.J.: Prentice-Hall, 1983), p. 127.

10. James J. Asher, "The Biographical Item: Can It Be Improved?" *Personnel Psychology,* Summer 1972, p. 266.

11. George W. England, *Development and Use of Weighted Application Blanks,* rev. ed. (Minneapolis: Industrial Relations Center, University of Minnesota, 1971).

12. John Aberth, "Pre-Employment Testing Is Losing Favor," *Personnel Journal,* September 1986, pp. 96–104.

13. The validity of written tests as predictors of job performance is an area of considerable controversy. See, for instance, Frank L. Schmidt and John E. Hunter, "Employment Testing: Old Theories and New Research Findings," *American Psychologist,* October 1981, pp. 1128–37; John E. Hunter and Ronda F. Hunter, "Validity and Utility of Alternative Predictors of Job Performance," *Psychological Bulletin,* January 1984, pp. 72–98; and L. S. Gottfredson, ed., "The g Factor in Employment," *Journal of Vocational Behavior,* December 1986, pp. 293–450.

14. Edwin E. Ghiselli, "The Validity of Aptitude Tests in Personnel Selection," *Personnel Psychology,* Winter 1973, p. 475.

15. G. Grimsley and H. F. Jarrett, "The Relation of Managerial Achievement to Test Measures Obtained in the Employment Situation: Methodology and Results," *Personnel Psychology,* Spring 1973, pp. 31–48; and Abraham K. Korman, "The Prediction of Managerial Performance: A Review," *Personnel Psychology,* Summer 1968, pp. 295–322.

16. I. T. Robertson and R. S. Kandola, "Work Sample Tests: Validity, Adverse Impact, and Applicant Reaction," *Journal of Occupational Psychology,* Vol. 55, No. 3, 1982, pp. 171–83.

17. See, for example, B. B. Gaugler, D. B. Rosenthal, G. C. Thornton, III, and C. Bentson, "Meta-Analysis of Assessment Center Validity," *Journal of Applied Psychology,* August 1987, pp. 493–511; and Richard Klimoski and Mary Brickner, "Why Do Assessment Centers Work? The Puzzle of Assessment Center Validity," *Personnel Psychology,* Summer 1987, pp. 243–60.

18. Richard D. Arvey and James E. Campion, "The Employment Interview: A Summary and Review of Recent Research," *Personnel Psychology,* Summer 1982, pp. 281–322.

19. Marvin D. Dunnette and Bernard M. Bass, "Behavioral Scientists and Personnel Management," *Industrial Relations,* May 1963, p. 117.

20. See, for instance, Eugene C. Mayfield in Neal Schmitt, "Social and Situational Determinants of Interview Decisions: Implications for Employment Interview," *Personnel Psychology,* Spring 1976, p. 81; Richard D. Arvey and James E. Campion, "The Employment Interview: A Summary and Review of Recent Research"; Milton D. Hakel, "Employment Interview," in K. M. Rowland and G. R. Ferris (eds.), *Personnel Management: New Perspectives* (Boston: Allyn and Bacon, 1982), pp. 129–55; and Edward C. Webster, *The Employment Interview: A Social Judgment Process* (Schomberg, Ontario: S.I.P. Publications, 1982).

21. T. J. Hanson and J. C. Balestreri-Spero, "An Alternative to Interviews," *Personnel Journal,* February 1985, pp. 114–23.

22. David A. DeCenzo and Stephen P. Robbins, *Personnel/Human Resource Management,* 3rd ed. (Englewood Cliffs, N.J.: Prentice-Hall, 1988), pp. 197–98.

23. See Irwin L. Goldstein, "The Application Blank: How Honest Are the Responses?" *Journal of Applied Psychology,* October 1971, pp. 491–92; and Winifred Yu, "Firms Tighten Résumé Checks of Applicants," *Wall Street Journal,* August 20, 1985, p. 27.

24. James Mosel and Howard Goheen, "Validity of the Employment Recommendation Questionnaire in Personnel Selection," *Personnel Psychology,* Winter 1958, pp. 481–90; and Rufus C. Browning, "Validity of Reference Ratings from Previous Employers," *Personnel Psychology,* Autumn 1968, pp. 389–93.

25. Cited in "If You Can't Say Something Nice . . . ," *Wall Street Journal,* March 4, 1988, p. 25.

26. Eugene C. Mayfield in Neal Schmitt, "Social and Situational Determinants of Interview Decisions: Implications for Employment Interview."

27. Cited in "Resumé Falsehoods," *Boardroom Reports,* May 1, 1989, p. 15.

28. Cited in "The Five Factors That Make for Airline Accidents," *Fortune,* May 22, 1989, p. 80.

29. Based on "A Personnel Chief Slams the Brakes on High Turnover," *Business Month,* August 1989, p. 76.

30. "Corporate Training Has Itself Become Big Business," *Wall Street Journal,* August 5, 1986, p. 1.

31. See, for example, David A. DeCenzo and Stephen P. Robbins, *Personnel/Human Resource Management,* pp. 365–72.

32. BARS have not been without critics. See, for example, Luis R. Gomez-Mejia, "Evaluating Employee Performance: Does the Appraisal Instrument Make a Difference?" *Journal of Organizational Behavior Management,* Winter 1988, pp. 155–71.

33. Ronald J. Burke, "Why Performance Appraisal Systems Fail," *Personnel Administration,* June 1972, pp. 32–40.

34. Donald E. Super and Douglas T. Hall, "Career Development: Exploration and Planning," in Mark R. Rosenzweig and Lyman W. Porter (eds.), *Annual Review of Psychology,* Vol. 29 (Palo Alto, Calif.: Annual Reviews, 1978), p. 334.

35. See, for instance, Elmer H. Burack, "The Sphinx's Riddle: Life and Career Cycles," *Training and Development Journal,* April 1984, pp. 53–61; and Douglas T. Hall and Associates, *Career Development in Organizations* (San Francisco: Jossey-Bass, 1986).

36. James A. Breaugh, "Realistic Job Previews: A Critical Appraisal and Future Research Directions," *Academy of Management Review,* October 1983, pp. 612–19; and Steven L. Premack and John P. Wanous, "A Meta-Analysis of Realistic Job Preview Experiments," *Journal of Applied Psychology,* November 1985, pp. 706–19.

37. Alan N. Schoonmaker, *Executive Career Strategy* (New York: American Management Association, 1971); Andrew J. DuBrin, *Fundamentals of Organizational Behavior: An Applied Perspective,* 2nd ed. (Elmsford, N.Y.: Pergamon Press, 1978), Chapter 5; and Eugene E. Jennings, "Success Chess," *Management of Personnel Quarterly,* Fall 1980, pp. 2–8.

38. Charles Perrow, *Complex Organizations: A Critical Essay* (Glenview, Ill.: Scott, Foresman, 1972), p. 43.

39. Stephen C. Bushardt, Roy N. Moore, and Sukumar C. Debnath, "Picking the Right Person for Your Mentor," *S.A.M. Advanced Management Journal,* Summer 1982, pp. 46–51; and Ellen A. Fagenson, "The Power of a Mentor," *Group and Organization Studies,* June 1988, pp. 182–94.

40. Cynthia D. Fisher, "Current and Recurrent Challenges in HRM," *Journal of Management,* June 1989, p. 161.

41. Mark E. Mendenhall, E. Dunbar, and Gary R. Oddou, "Expatriate Selection, Training, and Career-Pathing: A Review and Critique," *Human Resource Management,* Spring 1987, pp. 331–45.

42. Vladimir Pucik and J. H. Katz, "Information, Control, and Human Resource Management in Multinational Firms," *Human Resource Management,* Spring 1986, pp. 121–32.

43. See, for example, Michael A. Verespej, "Partnership in the Trenches," *Industry Week,* October 17, 1988, pp. 56–64; and "Unions and Management Are in a Family Way," *U.S. News & World Report,* June 12, 1989, p. 24.

44. Cited in Carol Hymowitz, "One Firm's Bid to Keep Blacks, Women," *Wall Street Journal,* February 16, 1989, p. B1.

45. Ibid.

46. Selwyn Feinstein, "Women and Minority Workers in Business Find a Mentor Can Be a Rare Commodity," *Wall Street Journal,* November 10, 1987, p. 37.

47. *Employment and Training Report of the President, 1980* (Washington, D.C.: Government Printing Office, 1980), p. 244; and U.S. Department of Labor, Bureau of Labor Statistics, *Employment and Earnings,* January 1989.

48. Kenneth E. Newgren, C. E. Kellogg, and William Gardner, "Corporate Responses to Dual-Career Couples: A Decade of Transformation," *Akron Business and Economic Review,* Summer 1988, p. 85.

49. Ibid, pp. 85–96.

50. Ibid., p. 89.

51. Ibid., p. 94.

52. Ibid., p. 92.

53. See, for instance, David E. Terpstra and Douglas R. Baker, "Outcomes of Sexual Harassment Charges," *Academy of Management Journal,* March 1988, pp. 185–94; "Hands Off at the Office," *U.S. News & World Report,* August 1, 1988, pp. 56–58; Gretchen Morgenson, "Watch That Leer, Stifle That Joke," *Forbes,* May 15, 1989, pp. 69–72; and Kenneth M. York, "Defining Sexual Harassment in Workplaces: A Policy—Capturing Approach," *Academy of Management Journal,* December 1989, pp. 830–50.

54. See, for instance, Peggy Simpson, "If the Wage System Doesn't Work, Fix It," *Working Woman,* October 1985, pp. 118–21; and "Comparable Worth: It's Already Happening," *Business Week,* April 28, 1986, pp. 52–56.

55. *Women, Work, and Wages: Equal Pay for Jobs of Equal Value* (Washington, D.C.: National Academy of Sciences Committee on Occupational Classification and Analysis, 1981).

56. Marsha Katz, Helen Lavan, and Maura Sendelbach Malloy, "Comparable Worth: Analysis of Cases and Implications for Human Resource Management," *Compensation and Benefits Review,* May–June 1986, pp. 26–38.

Chapter 13

1. Leon Festinger, *A Theory of Cognitive Dissonance* (Stanford, Calif.: Stanford University Press, 1957).

2. Arthur H. Brayfield and Walter H. Crockett, "Employee Attitudes and Employee Performance," *Psychological Bulletin,* September 1955, pp. 415–22; and Robert L. Kahn, "Productivity and Job Satisfaction," *Personnel Psychology,* Autumn 1960, pp. 275–87.

3. See, for example, Victor H. Vroom, *Work and Motivation* (New York: John Wiley, 1964), pp. 184–85.

4. Edward E. Lawler III and Lyman W. Porter, "The Effect of Performance on Job Satisfaction," *Industrial Relations,* October 1967, pp. 466–80.

5. Julian B. Rotter, "Generalized Expectancies for Internal Versus External Control of Reinforcement," *Psychological Monographs,* vol. 80, no. 609 (1966).

6. See, for instance, Dennis W. Organ and Charles N. Greene, "Role Ambiguity, Locus of Control, and Work Satisfaction," *Journal of Applied Psychology,* February 1974, pp. 101–2; and Terence R. Mitchell, Charles M. Smyser, and Stan E. Weed, "Locus of Control: Supervision and Work Satisfaction," *Academy of Management Journal,* September 1975, pp. 623–31.

7. T. Adorno et al., *The Authoritarian Personality* (New York: Harper & Brothers, 1950).

8. Harrison Gough, "Personality and Personality Assessment," in Marvin D. Dunnette (ed.), *Handbook of Industrial and Organizational Psychology* (Skokie, Ill.: Rand McNally, 1976), p. 579.

9. R. G. Vleeming, "Machiavellianism: A Preliminary Review," *Psychological Reports,* February 1979, pp. 295–310.

10. R. N. Taylor and M. D. Dunnette, "Influence of Dogmatism, Risk-Taking Propensity, and Intelligence on Decision-Making Strategies for a Sample of Industrial Managers," *Journal of Applied Psychology,* August 1974, pp. 420–23.

11. Based on Jim Braham, "No, You *Don't* Manage Everyone the Same," *Industry Week,* February 6, 1989, pp. 28–35.

12. Edward L. Thorndike, *Educational Psychology: The Psychology of Learning,* Vol. 2 (New York: Columbia University, 1913); and B. F. Skinner, *Beyond Freedom and Dignity* (New York: Knopf, 1971).

13. This section is based on the work of J. T. Gullahorn and J. E. Gullahorn, "An Extension of the U-Curve Hypothesis," *Journal of Social Sciences,* January 1963, pp. 34–47.

14. See, for example, Edwin A. Locke, "The Nature and Causes of Job Satisfaction," in Marvin D. Dunnette (ed.), *Handbook of Industrial and Organizational Psychology,* pp. 1297–1350; and Peter W. Hom, Ralph Katerberg, Jr., and Charles L. Hulin, "Comparative Examination of Three Approaches to the Prediction of Turnover," *Journal of Applied Psychology,* June 1979, pp. 280–90.

15. Steven Kerr, "On the Folly of Rewarding *A,* While Hoping for *B,*" *Academy of Management Journal,* December 1975, pp. 769–83.

16. Leonard R. Sayles, "Work Group Behavior and the Larger Organization," in Conrad Arensburg et al. (eds.), *Research in Industrial Relations* (New York: Harper & Row, 1957), pp. 131–45.

17. Bruce W. Tuckman and Mary Ann C. Jensen, "Stages of Small-Group Development Revisited," *Group and Organizational Studies,* Vol. 2, No. 3, 1977, pp. 419–27.

18. Linda N. Jewell and H. J. Reitz, *Group Effectiveness in Organizations* (Glenview, Ill.: Scott, Foresman, 1981).

19. See, for example, L. Berkowitz, "Group Standards, Cohesiveness, and Productivity," *Human Relations,* November 1954, pp. 509–19.

20. Stanley E. Seashore, *Group Cohesiveness in the Industrial Work Group* (Ann Arbor: University of Michigan, Survey Research Center, 1954).

21. This model is substantially based on the work of Paul S. Goodman, E. Ravlin, and M. Schminke, "Understanding Groups in Organizations," in L. L. Cummings and B. M. Staw (eds.), *Research in Organizational Behavior,* Vol. 9 (Greenwich, Conn.: JAI Press, 1987), pp. 124–28; and J. Richard Hackman, "The Design of Work Teams," in J. W. Lorsch (ed.), *Handbook of Organizational Behavior* (Englewood Cliffs, N.J.: Prentice-Hall, 1987), pp. 315–42.

22. Fred Friedlander, "The Ecology of Work Groups," in J. W. Lorsch (ed.), *Handbook of Organizational Behavior,* pp. 301–14.

23. Marvin E. Shaw, *Contemporary Topics in Social Psychology* (Morristown, N.J.: General Learning Press, 1976), pp. 350–51.

24. See, for example, J. Richard Hackman and C. G. Morris, "Group Tasks, Group Interaction Process and Group Performance Effectiveness: A Review and Proposed Integration," in L. Berkowitz (ed.), *Advances in Experimental Social Psychology* (New York: Academic Press, 1975), pp. 45–99.

25. Based on Marc Bassin, "Teamwork at General Foods: New & Improved," *Personnel Journal,* May 1988, pp. 62–70; John Hoerr, "Is Teamwork a Management Plot? Mostly Not," *Business Week,* February 20, 1989, p. 70; and John Hoerr, "The Payoff from Teamwork," *Business Week,* July 10, 1989, pp. 56–62.

26. Jay Galbraith, *Organizational Design* (Reading, Mass.: Addison-Wesley, 1977).

27. Based on John Hoerr, "Benefits for the Back Office, Too," *Business Week,* July 10, 1989, p. 59.

Chapter 14

1. See Kenneth A. Kovach, "What Motivates Employees? Workers and Supervisors Give Different Answers," *Business Horizons,* September–October 1987, pp. 58–65.

2. Ralph Katerberg and Gary J. Blau, "An Examination of Level and Direction of Effort and Job Performance," *Academy of Management Journal,* June 1983, pp. 249–57.

3. See Stanley J. Modic, "Is Anyone Loyal Anymore?," *Industry Week,* September 7, 1987, pp. 75–82; and John H. Sheridan, "'Loyalty Crisis': Just a Myth?," *Industry Week,* June 5, 1989, pp. 47–50.

4. Abraham Maslow, *Motivation and Personality* (New York: Harper & Row, 1954).

5. See, for example, Edward E. Lawler, III, and J. Lloyd Suttle, "A Causal Correlational Test of the Need Hierarchy Concept," *Organizational Behavior and Human Performance,* April 1972, pp. 265–87; and Douglas T. Hall and Khalil E. Nongaim,"An Examination of Maslow's Need Hierarchy in an Organizational Setting," *Organizational Behavior and Human Performance,* February 1968, pp. 12–35.

6. Abraham K. Korman, Jeffrey H. Greenhaus, and Irwin J. Badin, "Personnel Attitudes and Motivation," in Mark R. Rosenzweig and Lyman W. Porter (eds.), *Annual Review of Psychology* (Palo Alto, Calif.: Annual Reviews, 1977), p. 178.

7. Ibid., p. 179.

8. M. A. Wahba and L. G. Bridwell, "Maslow Reconsidered: A Review of Research on the Need Hierarchy Theory," *Organizational Behavior and Human Performance,* vol. 15 (1976), pp. 212–40.

9. Douglas McGregor, *The Human Side of Enterprise* (New York: McGraw-Hill, 1960).

10. Frederick Herzberg, Bernard Mausner, and Barbara Snyderman, *The Motivation to Work* (New York: John Wiley, 1959); and Frederick Herzberg, *The Managerial Choice: To Be Efficient or to be Human,* rev. ed. (Salt Lake City: Olympus, 1982).

11. See, for instance, Michael E. Gordon, Norman M. Pryor, and Bob V. Harris, "An Examination of Scaling Bias in Herzberg's Theory of Job Satisfaction," *Organizational Behavior and Human Performance,* February 1974, pp. 106–21; Edwin A. Locke and Roman J. Whiting, "Sources of Satisfaction and Dissatisfaction Among Solid Waste Management Employees," *Journal of Applied Psychology,* April 1974, pp. 145–56; and John B. Miner, *Theories of Organizational Behavior* (Hinsdale, Ill.: Dryden Press, 1980), pp. 76–105.

12. David C. McClelland, *The Achieving Society* (New York: Van Nostrand Reinhold, 1961); John W. Atkinson and Joel O. Raynor, *Motivation and Achievement* (Washington, D.C.: Winston, 1974); and David C. McClelland, *Power: The Inner Experience* (New York: Irvington, 1975).

13. David C. McClelland, *The Achieving Society.*

14. David C. McClelland and David G. Winter, *Motivating Economic Achievement* (New York: Free Press, 1969).

15. David C. McClelland, *Power: The Inner Experience;* David C. McClelland and David H. Burnham, "Power Is the Great Motivator," *Harvard Business Review,* March–April 1976, pp. 100–10.

16. "McClelland: An Advocate of Power," *International Management,* July 1975, pp. 27–29.

17. David Miron and David C. McClelland, "The Impact of Achievement Motivation Training on Small Businesses," *California Management Review,* Summer 1979, pp. 13–28.

18. James C. Naylor and Daniel R. Ilgen, "Goal Setting: A Theoretical Analysis of a Motivational Technique," in B. M. Staw and L. L. Cummings (eds.), *Research in Organizational Behavior,* Vol. 6 (Greenwich, Conn.: JAI Press, 1984), pp. 95–140.

19. John B. Miner, *Theories of Organizational Behavior,* p. 65.

20. B. F. Skinner, *Science and Human Behavior* (New York: Free Press, 1953); and B. F. Skinner, *Beyond Freedom and Dignity* (New York: Knopf, 1972).

21. Fred Luthans and Robert Kreitner, *Organizational Behavior Modification and Beyond: An Operant and Social Learning Approach* (Glenview, Ill.: Scott, Foresman, 1985).

22. The same data, for instance, can be interpreted in either goal-setting or reinforcement terms, as shown in Edwin A. Locke, "Latham vs. Komaki: A Tale of Two Paradigms," *Journal of Applied Psychology,* February 1980, pp. 16–23.

23. J. Stacey Adams, "Inequity in Social Exchanges," in Leonard Berkowitz (ed.), *Advances in Experimental Social Psychology,* Vol. 2 (New York: Academic Press, 1965), pp. 267–300.

24. Paul S. Goodman, "An Examination of Referents Used in the Evaluation of Pay," *Organizational Behavior and Human Performance,* October 1974, pp. 170–95; Simcha Ronen, "Equity Perception in Multiple Comparisons: A Field Study," *Human Relations,* April 1986, pp. 333–46; and R. W. Scholl, E. A. Cooper, and J. F. McKenna, "Referent Selection in Determining Equity Perception: Differential Effects on Behavioral and Attitudinal Outcomes," *Personnel Psychology,* Spring 1987, pp. 113–27.

25. Paul S. Goodman and A. Friedman, "An Examination of Adams' Theory of Inequity," *Administrative Science Quarterly,* September 1971, pp. 271–88.

26. See, for example, Michael R. Carrell, "A Longitudinal Field Assessment of Employee Perceptions of Equitable Treatment," *Organizational Behavior and Human Performance,* February 1978, pp. 108–18; Robert G. Lord and Jeffrey A. Hohenfeld, "Longitudinal Field Assessment of Equity Effects on the Performance of Major League Baseball Players," *Journal of Applied Psychology,* February 1979, pp. 19–26; and John E. Dittrich and Michael R. Carrell, "Organizational Equity Perceptions, Employee Job Satisfaction, and Departmental Absence and Turnover Rates," *Organizational Behavior and Human Performance,* August 1979, pp. 29–40.

27. Paul S. Goodman, "Social Comparison Process in Organizations," in B. M. Staw and G. R. Salancik (eds.), *New Directions in Organizational Behavior* (Chicago: St. Clair, 1977), pp. 97–132.

28. See, for instance, Shane P. Premeaux, R. Wayne Mondy, and Art L. Bethke, "The Two-Tier Wage System," *Personnel Administrator,* November 1986, pp. 92–100.

29. Steven Flax, "Pay Cuts Before the Job Even Starts," *Fortune,* January 9, 1984, p. 75.

30. Aaron Bernstein, "Why Two-Tier Wage Scales Are Starting to Self-Destruct," *Business Week,* March 16, 1987, p. 41; and "Two-Tier Pay May Be Going Underground," *Business Week,* April 25, 1988, p. 16.

31. Victor H. Vroom, *Work and Motivation* (New York: John Wiley, 1964).

32. See, for example, Herbert G. Heneman, III, and Donald P. Schwab, "Evaluation of Research on Expectancy Theory Prediction of Employee Performance," *Psychological Bulletin,* July 1972, pp. 1–9; and Leon Reinharth and Mahmoud Wahba, "Expectancy Theory as a Predictor of Work Motivation, Effort Expenditure, and Job Performance," *Academy of Management Journal,* September 1975, pp. 502–37.

33. See, for example, Victor H. Vroom, "Organizational Choice: A Study of Pre-and-Postdecision Processes," *Organizational Behavior and Human Performance,* April 1966, pp. 212–25; and Lyman W. Porter and Edward E. Lawler, III, *Managerial Attitudes and Performance* (Homewood, Ill.: Richard D. Irwin, 1968).

34. Among academicians these three variables are typically referred to as *valence, instrumentality,* and *expectancy,* respectively.

35. This four-step discussion was adapted from K. F. Taylor, "A Valence-Expectancy Approach to Work Motivation," *Personnel Practice Bulletin,* June 1974, pp. 142–48.

36. Edwin A. Locke, "Personnel Attitudes and Motivation," in Mark R. Rosenzweig and Lyman W. Porter (eds.), *Annual Review of Psychology* (Palo Alto, Calif.: Annual Reviews, 1975), p. 459.

37. Geert Hofestede, "Motivation, Leadership, and Organizations: Do American Theories Apply Abroad?," *Organizational Dynamics,* Summer 1980, p. 55.

38. Adi Ignatius, "Now if Ms. Wong Insults a Customer, She Gets an Award," *Wall Street Journal,* January 24, 1989, p. 1.

39. Edwin A. Locke, D. B. Feren, V. M. McCaleb, K. N. Shaw, and A. T. Denny, "The Relative Effectiveness of Four Methods of Motivating Employee Performance," in K. D. Duncan, M. M. Gruneberg, and D. Wallis (eds.), *Changes in Working Life* (London: John Wiley, 1980), pp. 363–83.

40. Nancy J. Perry, "Here Come Richer, Riskier Pay Plans," *Fortune,* December 19, 1988, p. 51.

41. "Pay for Performance: Problems Persist, but Companies Plug Away," *Wall Street Journal,* February 19, 1988, p. 1.

42. Based on Anne R. Field, "Managing Creative People," *Success,* October 1988, pp. 85–87.

43. See Brian Bremner, "Among Restauranteurs, It's Dog Eat Dog," *Business Week,* January 9, 1989, p. 86; and Jolie Solomon, "Managers Focus on Low-Wage Workers," *Wall Street Journal,* May 9, 1989, p. B1.

44. Based on "Why This 'Obsolete' Company is a 'Great Place to Work'," *International Management,* April 1986, pp. 46–51; Bruce G. Posner, "Right From the Start," *INC.,* August 1988, pp. 95–96; and Gene Epstein, "Inspire Your Team," *Success,* October 1989, p. 12.

Chapter 15

1. Stratford P. Sherman, "Ted Turner: Back from the Brink," *Fortune,* July 7, 1986, pp. 25–31; and Scott Ticer, "Ted Turner," *The 1989 Business Week Top 1000,* p. 142.

2. Kate Ballen, "The No. 1 Leader is Petersen of Ford," *Fortune,* October 24, 1988, p. 69.

3. Kenneth Labich, "The Seven Keys to Business Leadership," *Fortune,* October 24, 1988, p. 58.

4. Bernard M. Bass, *Stogdill's Handbook of Leadership: A Survey of Theory and Research,* rev. ed. (New York: Free Press, 1981).

5. Ibid.

6. Based on "Sun Microsystems Turns On the Afterburners," *Business Week,* July 18, 1988, pp. 114–180.

7. Ralph M. Stogdill and Alvin E. Coons, eds., *Leader Behavior: Its Description and Measurement,* Research Monograph No. 88 (Columbus: Ohio State University, Bureau of Business Research, 1951). For an updated literature review of the Ohio State research, see Steven Kerr, Chester A. Schriesheim, Charles J. Murphy, and Ralph M. Stogdill, "Toward a Contingency Theory of Leadership Based upon the Consideration and Initiating Structure Literature," *Organizational Behavior and Human Performance,* August 1974, pp. 62–82; and Bruce M. Fisher, "Consideration and Initiating Structure and Their Relationships with Leader Effectiveness: A Meta-Analysis," in F. Hoy (ed.), *Proceedings of the 48th Annual Academy of Management Conference,* Anaheim, Calif., 1988, pp. 201–05.

8. R. Kahn and D. Katz, "Leadership Practices in Relation to Productivity and Morale," in D. Cartwright and A. Zander (eds.), *Group Dynamics: Research and Theory,* 2nd ed. (Elmsford, N.Y.: Row, Paterson, 1960).

9. Robert R. Blake and Jane S. Mouton, *The Managerial Grid III* (Houston: Gulf Publishing, 1984).

10. L. L. Larson, J. G. Hunt, and R. N. Osborn, "The Great Hi-Hi Leader Behavior Myth: A Lesson from Occam's Razor," *Academy of Management Journal,* December 1976, pp. 628–41; and Paul C. Nystrom, "Managers and the Hi-Hi Leader Myth," *Academy of Management Journal,* June 1978, pp. 325–31.

11. See, for example, the three styles—autocratic, participative, and laissez-faire—proposed by Kurt Lewin and Ronald Lippitt, "An Experimental Approach to the Study of Autocracy and Democracy: A Preliminary Note," *Sociometry,* no. 1, (1938), 292–380; or the 3-D Theory proposed by William J. Reddin, *Managerial Effectiveness* (New York: McGraw-Hill, 1970).

12. Jeffrey C. Barrow, "The Variables of Leadership: A Review and Conceptual Framework," *Academy of Management Review,* April 1977, pp. 231–51.

13. Fred E. Fiedler, *A Theory of Leadership Effectiveness* (New York: McGraw-Hill, 1967).

14. Lawrence H. Peters, D. D. Hartke, and J. T. Pholmann, "Fiedler's Contingency Theory of Leadership: An Application of the Meta-Analysis Procedures of Schmidt and Hunter," *Psychological Bulletin,* March 1985, pp. 274–85.

15. Ibid.

16. See, for instance, Robert W. Rice, "Psychometric Properties of the Esteem for the Least Preferred Co-worker (LPC) Scale," *Academy of Management Review,* January 1978, pp. 106–18; and Chester A. Schriesheim, B. D. Bannister, and W. H. Money, "Psychometric Properties of the LPC Scale: An Extension of Rice's Review," *Academy of Management Review,* April 1979, pp. 287–90.

17. See Edgar H. Schein, *Organizational Psychology,* 3rd ed. (Englewood Cliffs, N.J.: Prentice-Hall, 1980), pp. 116–17; and Boris Kabanoff, "A Critique of Leader Match and Its Implications for Leadership Research," *Personnel Psychology,* Winter 1981, pp. 749–64.

18. Paul Hersey and Kenneth H. Blanchard, "So You Want to Know Your Leadership Style?," *Training and Development Journal,* February 1974, pp. 1–15; and Paul Hersey and Kenneth H. Blanchard, *Management of Organizational Behavior: Utilizing Human Resources,* 4th ed. (Englewood Cliffs, N.J.: Prentice-Hall, 1982), pp. 150–61.

19. Paul Hersey and Kenneth H. Blanchard, *Management of Organizational Behavior: Utilizing Human Resources,* p. 171.

20. Paul Hersey and Kenneth H. Blanchard, "Grid Principles and Situationalism: Both! A Response to Blake and Mouton," *Group and Organization Studies,* June 1982, pp. 207–10.

21. R. K. Hambleton and R. Gumpert, "The Validity of Hersey and Blanchard's Theory of Leader Effectiveness," *Group and Organization Studies,* June 1982, pp. 225–42; Claude L. Graeff, "The Situational Leadership Theory: A Critical View," *Academy of Management Review,* April 1983, pp. 285–91; Warren Blank, John R. Weitzel, and Stephen G. Green, "Situational Leadership Theory: A Test of Underlying Assumptions," paper presented at the National Academy of Management Conference, Chicago, August 1986; and Robert P. Vecchio, "Situational Leadership Theory: An Examination of a Prescriptive Theory," *Journal of Applied Psychology,* August 1987, pp. 444–51.

22. Robert P. Vecchio, "Situational Leadership Theory: An Examination of a Prescriptive Theory."

23. Robert J. House, "A Path-Goal Theory of Leader Effectiveness," *Administrative Science Quarterly,* September 1971, pp. 321–38; Robert J. House and Terence R. Mitchell, "Path-Goal Theory of Leadership," *Journal of Contemporary Business,* Autumn 1974, p. 86; and Robert J. House, "Retrospective Comment," in Louis E. Boone and Donald D. Bowen (eds.), *The Great Writings in Management and Organizational Behavior,* 2nd ed. (New York: Random House, 1987), pp. 354–64.

24. Julie Indrik, "Path-Goal Theory of Leadership: A Meta-Analysis," paper presented at the National Academy of Management Conference, Chicago, August 1986.

25. Victor H. Vroom and Phillip W. Yetton, *Leadership and Decision-Making* (Pittsburgh: University of Pittsburgh Press, 1973).

26. From Victor H. Vroom, "A New Look at Managerial Decision Making," *Organizational Dynamics,* Spring 1973, pp. 66–80. With permission.

27. See, for instance, R. H. G. Field, "A Test of the Vroom-Yetton Normative Model of Leadership," *Journal of Applied Psychology,* October 1982, pp. 523–32; and Carrie R. Leana, "Power Relinquishment Versus Power Sharing: Theoretical Clarification and Empirical Comparison of Delegation and Participation," *Journal of Applied Psychology,* May 1987, pp. 228–33.

28. Steven Kerr and John M. Jermier, "Substitutes for Leadership: Their Meaning and Measurement," *Organizational Behavior and Human Performance,* December 1978, pp. 375–403; Jon P. Howell and Peter W. Dorfman, "Substitutes for Leadership: Test of a Construct," *Academy of Management Journal,* December 1981, pp. 714–28; Peter W. Howard and William F. Joyce, "Substitutes for Leadership: A Statistical Refinement," paper presented at the 42nd Annual Academy of Management Conference; New York, August 1982; and Jon P. Howell, Peter W. Dorfman, and Steven Kerr, "Leadership and Substitutes for Leadership," *Journal of Applied Behavioral Science,* vol. 22, no. 1, 1986, pp. 29–46.

29. Victor H. Vroom and Arthur G. Jago, *The New Leadership: Managing Participation in Organizations* (Englewood Cliffs, N.J.: Prentice-Hall, 1988). See especially Chapter 8.

30. Based on Jonathan Weber, "Workplace Democracy More Talk Than Action," *Los Angeles Times,* July 25, 1989, p. IV-5.

31. Bernard M. Bass, *Leadership and Performance Beyond Expectations* (New York: Free Press, 1985); and Karl W. Kuhnert and Philip Lewis, "Transactional and Transformational Leadership: A Constructive/Developmental Analysis," *Academy of Management Review,* October 1987, pp. 648–57.

32. Geert Hofstede, "Motivation, Leadership, and Organization: Do American Theories Apply Abroad?" *Organizational Dynamics,* Summer 1980, p. 57.

33. See Jay A. Conger and Rabindra N. Kanungo, "Toward a Behavioral Theory of Charismatic Leadership in Organizational Settings," *Academy of Management Review,* October 1987, pp. 637–47; and Jay A. Conger, Rabindra N. Kanungo, and Associates, *Charismatic Leadership: The Elusive Factor in Organizational Effectiveness* (San Francisco: Jossey-Bass, 1988).

34. B. J. Smith, *An Initial Test of a Theory of Charismatic Leadership Based on Responses of Subordinates.* Ph.D. Thesis, University of Toronto, 1982.

35. Jon P. Howell, "A Laboratory Study of Charismatic Leadership," paper presented at the National Academy of Management Conference; San Diego, Calif., 1985.

36. Robert J. House, "A 1976 Theory of Charismatic Leadership," in J. G. Hunt and L. L. Larson (eds.), *Leadership: The Cutting Edge* (Carbondale, Ill.: Southern Illinois University Press, 1977), pp. 189–207.

37. Dyan Machan, "The Charisma Merchants," *Forbes,* January 23, 1989, pp. 100–101; and "Charisma Is Costly in the Executive Suite," *Wall Street Journal,* March 21, 1989, p. 1.

38. Laurence I. Barrett, "Going Home a Winner," *Time,* January 23, 1989, pp. 14–18.

39. "Yankee Doodle Manager," *Time,* July 7, 1986, pp. 12–16.

40. This and the following quotes came from Gloria Borger, "The Year of Living Timorously," *U.S. News & World Report,* November 13, 1989, pp. 26–27; and "How to Rule Without a Big Shtick," *U.S. News & World Report,* February 5, 1990, p. 10.

Chapter 16

1. Cited in *Business Month,* April 1989, p. 40.

2. See, for example, "The Battle of the B-Schools Is Getting Bloodier," March 24, 1986, pp. 61–70; and Anthony P. Carnevale, Leila J. Gainer, Ann S. Meltzer, and Shari L. Holland, "Workplace Basics: The Skills Employers Want," *Training and Development Journal,* October 1988, pp. 22–30.

3. Sandra A. Waddock, "Educating Managers for the Future Not the Past," in William A. Ward and Eugene G. Gomolka (eds.), *Managing for Improved Performance: Proceedings of the Eastern Academy of Management;* Portland, Maine, May 1989, pp. 71–73.

4. Lyman W. Porter and Lawrence E. McKibbin, *Future of Management Education and Development: Drift or Thrust into the 21st Century?* (New York: McGraw-Hill, 1988).

5. Charlotte Olmstead Kursh, "The Benefits of Poor Communication," *Psychoanalytic Review,* Summer–Fall 1971, pp. 189–208.

6. David K. Berlo, *The Process of Communication* (New York: Holt, Rinehart, & Winston, 1960), pp. 30–32.

7. Ibid., p. 54.

8. Ibid., p. 103.

9. Albert Mehrabian, "Communication Without Words," *Psychology Today,* September 1968, pp. 53–55.

10. Abraham K. Korman, "A Cause of Communication Failure," *Personnel Administration,* September 1960, pp. 17–21; and C. H. Weaver, "The Quantification of the Frame of Reference in Labor Management Communication," *Journal of Applied Psychology,* February 1958, pp. 1–19.

11. Based on Shoukry D. Saleh, "Relational Orientation and Organizational Functioning: A Cross-Cultural Perspective," *Canadian Journal of Administrative Sciences,* September 1987, pp. 276–93.

12. Jesus Sanchez, "The Art of Deal Making," *Los Angeles Times,* February 15, 1988, Part IV, p. 3.

13. See, for instance, Stephen P. Robbins, *Training in InterPersonal Skills: TIPS for Managing People at Work* (Englewood Cliffs, N.J.: Prentice-Hall, 1989), pp. 5–6.

14. Robert J. Graham, "Understanding the Benefits of Poor Communication," *Interfaces,* June 1981, pp. 80–82.

15. Carl R. Rogers and Richard E. Farson, *Active Listening* (Chicago: Industrial Relations Center of the University of Chicago, 1976).

16. Stephen P. Robbins, *Training in InterPersonal Skills: TIPS for Managing People at Work,* pp. 31–34.

17. Phillip L. Hunsaker and Anthony J. Alessandra, *The Art of Managing People* (Englewood Cliffs, N.J.: Prentice-Hall, 1980), p. 123.

18. Cynthia Fisher, "Transmission of Positive and Negative Feedback to Subordinates: A Laboratory Investigation," *Journal of Applied Psychology,* October 1979, pp. 533–40.

19. Daniel Ilgen, Cynthia D. Fisher, and M. Susan Taylor, "Consequences of Individual Feedback on Behavior in Organizations," *Journal of Applied Psychology,* August 1979, pp. 349–71.

20. Fernando Bartolome, "Teaching About Whether to Give Negative Feedback," *The Organizational Behavior Teaching Review,* vol. 9, no. 2, 1986–87, pp. 95–104.

21. Keith Halperin, C. R. Synder, Randee J. Shenkel, and B. Kent Houston, "Effect of Source Status and Message Favorability on Acceptance of Personality Feedback," *Journal of Applied Psychology,* February 1976, pp. 85–88.

22. Cyril R. Mill, "Feedback: The Art of Giving and Receiving Help," in Larry Porter and Cyril R. Mill (eds.), *The Reading Book for Human Relations Training* (Bethel, Maine: NTL Institute for Applied Behavioral Science, 1976), pp. 18–19.

23. Ibid.

24. Ibid.

25. Ibid.

26. Kathleen S. Verderber and Rudolph F. Verderber, *Inter-Act: Using Interpersonal Communication Skills,* 4th ed. (Belmont, Calif.: Wadsworth, 1986).

27. Lyle E. Bourne, Jr. and C. Victor Bunderson, "Effects Delay of Information Feedback and Length of Post-Feedback Interval on Concept Identification," *Journal of Experimental Psychology,* January 1963, pp. 1–5.

28. Cyril R. Mill, "Feedback: The Art of Giving and Receiving Help," pp. 18–19.

29. Kathleen S. Verderber and Rudolph F. Verderber, *Inter-Act: Using Interpersonal Communication Skills.*

30. Carrie R. Leana, "Predictors and Consequences of Delegation," *Academy of Management Journal,* December 1986, pp. 754–74.

31. Lawrence L. Steinmetz, *The Art and Skill of Delegation* (Reading, Mass.: Addison-Wesley, 1976).

32. Charles D. Pringle, "Seven Reasons Why Managers Don't Delegate," *Management Solutions,* November 1986, pp. 26–30.

33. Stephen P. Robbins, *Training in InterPersonal Skills: TIPS for Managing People at Work,* pp. 133–35.

34. Richard D. Arvey and Allen P. Jones, "The Use of Discipline in Organizational Settings," in L. L. Cummings and Barry M. Staw (eds.), *Research in Organizational Behavior,* Vol. 7 (Greenwich, Conn.: JAI Press, 1985), pp. 367–408.

35. Based on *U.S. News & World Report,* January 16, 1989, pp. 48–49.

36. David A. DeCenzo and Stephen P. Robbins, *Personnel/Human Resource Management,* 3rd ed. (Englewood Cliffs, N.J.: Prentice-Hall, 1988), pp. 478–82.

37. Bureau of National Affairs, *Employee Conduct and Discipline,* Personnel Policies Forum, Survey No. 102 (Washington, D.C.: Bureau of National Affairs), August 1973.

38. Ibid.

39. Douglas McGregor, "Hot Stove Rules of Discipline," in George Strauss and Leonard Sayles (eds.), *Personnel: The Human Problems of Management* (Englewood Cliffs, N.J.: Prentice-Hall, 1967).

40. Stephen P. Robbins, *Training in InterPersonal Skills: TIPS for Managing People at Work,* pp. 111–14.

41. Joseph Seltzer, "Discipline with a Clear Sense of Purpose," *Management Solutions,* February 1987, pp. 32–37.

42. Kenneth W. Thomas and Warren H. Schmidt, "A Survey of Managerial Interests With Respect to Conflict," *Academy of Management Journal,* June 1976, pp. 315–18.

43. Ibid.

44. J. Graves, "Successful Management and Organizational Mugging," in J. Papp (ed.), *New Directions in Human Resource Management* (Englewood Cliffs, N.J.: Prentice-Hall, 1978).

45. This section is adapted from Stephen P. Robbins, *Managing Organizational Conflict: A Nontraditional Approach* (Englewood Cliffs, N.J.: Prentice-Hall, 1974), pp. 11–14.

46. Ralph H. Kilmann and Kenneth W. Thomas, "Developing a Forced-Choice Measure of Conflict Handling Behavior: The MODE Instrument," *Educational and Psychological Measurement,* Summer 1977, pp. 309–25.

47. Leonard Greenhalgh, "Managing Conflict," *Sloan Management Review,* Summer 1986, pp. 45–51.

48. Stephen P. Robbins, *Managing Organizational Conflict: A Nontraditional Approach,* pp. 31–55.

49. Charlotte O. Kursh, "The Benefits of Poor Communication," *The Psychoanalytic Review,* Summer–Fall 1971, pp. 189–208.

50. Kenneth W. Thomas, "Conflict and Conflict Management," in Marvin Dunnette (ed.), *Handbook of Industrial and Organizational Psychology* (Chicago: Rand McNally, 1976), pp. 889–935.

51. See, for instance, Dean Tjosvold and David W. Johnson, *Productive Conflict Management: Perspectives for Organizations* (New York: Irvington Publishers, 1983).

52. Stephen P. Robbins, *Managing Organizational Conflict: A Nontraditional Approach,* pp. 78–89.

53. Based on an exercise in Stephen P. Robbins, *Training in InterPersonal Skills: TIPS for Managing People at Work,* pp. 138–39.

Chapter 17

1. Based on Andrew Kupfer, "Bob Allen Rattles the Cages at AT&T," *Fortune,* June 19, 1989, pp. 58–66; and "Bob Allen Is Turning AT&T into a Live Wire," *Business Week,* November 6, 1989, pp. 140–52.

2. The idea for these metaphors came from Peter B. Vaill, *Managing as a Performing Art: New Ideas for a World of Chaotic Change* (San Francisco: Jossey-Bass, 1989).

3. Kurt Lewin, *Field Theory in Social Science* (New York: Harper & Row, 1951).

4. See, for instance, Tom Peters, *Thriving on Chaos* (New York: Alfred A. Knopf, 1987).

5. Daniel M. Kehrer, "The Miracle of Theory Q," *Business Month,* September 1989, pp. 45–49.

6. Ibid., p. 47.

7. Tom Peters, *Thriving on Chaos,* p. 3.

8. Ibid.

9. See, for example, Barry M. Staw, "Counterforces to Change," in Paul S. Goodman, and Associates, (eds.), *Change in Organizations* (San Francisco, Calif.: Jossey-Bass Publishers, 1982), pp. 87–121.

10. John P. Kotter and Leonard A. Schlesinger, "Choosing Strategies for Change," *Harvard Business Review,* March–April 1979, pp. 107–109.

11. Ibid., pp. 106–14.

12. See, for example, Wendell L. French and Cecil H. Bell, Jr., *Organization Development: Behavioral Science Interventions for Organization Improvement,* 4th ed. (Englewood Cliffs, N.J.: Prentice-Hall, 1990).

13. P. B. Smith, "Controlled Studies of the Outcome of Sensitivity Training," *Psychological Bulletin,* July 1975, pp. 597–622.

14. John P. Campbell and Marvin D. Dunnette, "Effectiveness of T-Group Experience in Managerial Training and Development," *Psychological Bulletin,* August 1968, pp. 73–104.

15. Morton A. Lieberman, Irvin D. Yalom, and Matthew B. Miles, *Encounter Groups: First Facts* (New York: Basic Books, 1973); and Carl A. Bramlette and Jeffrey H. Tucker, "Encounter Groups: Positive Change or Deterioration? More Data and a Partial Replication," *Human Relations,* April 1981, pp. 303–14.

16. Edgar H. Schein, *Process Consultation: Its Role in Organizational Development* (Reading, Mass.: Addison-Wesley, 1969), p. 9.

17. See Thomas H. Fitzgerald, "Can Change in Organizational Culture Really Be Managed?," *Organizational Dynamics,* Autumn 1988, pp. 5–15; and Brian Dumaine, "Creating A New Company Culture," *Fortune,* January 15, 1990, pp. 127–31.

18. See, for example, Ralph H. Kilmann, Mary J. Saxton, and Roy Serpa, eds., *Gaining Control of the Corporate Culture* (San Francisco: Jossey-Bass, 1985); and Donald C. Hambrick and Sidney Finkelstein, "Managerial Discretion: A Bridge Between Polar Views of Organizational Outcomes," in L. L. Cummings and B. M. Staw (eds.), *Research in Organizational Behavior,* Vol. 9 (Greenwich, Conn.: JAI Press, 1987), p. 384.

19. Michael Albert, "Assessing Cultural Change Needs," *Training and Development Journal,* May 1985, pp. 94–98.

20. Kenneth Labich, "The Innovators," *Fortune,* June 6, 1988, p. 49.

21. Russell Mitchell, "Masters of Innovation," *Business Week,* April 10, 1989, p. 58.

22. These definitions are based on Teresa M. Amabile, "A Model of Creativity and Innovation in Organizations," in B. M. Staw and L. L. Cummings (eds.), *Research in Organizational Behavior,* Vol. 10 (Greenwich, Conn.: JAI Press, 1988), p. 126.

23. Amanda Bennett, "SAS's Nice Guy Is Aiming to Finish First," *Wall Street Journal,* March 2, 1989, p. B8; and "The Art of Loving," *Inc.,* May 1989, pp. 35–46.

24. See, for example, Teresa M. Amabile, "The Social Psychology of Creativity: A Componential Conceptualization," *Journal of Personality and Social Psychology,* August 1983, pp. 357–76.

25. Anne Anastasi and C. E. Schaefer, "Note on the Concepts of Creativity and Intelligence," *Journal of Creative Behavior,* Second Quarter 1971, pp. 113–16.

26. See, for instance, Teresa M. Amabile, "A Model of Creativity and Innovation in Organizations," p. 147; Michael Tushman and David Nadler, "Organizing for Innovation," *California Management Review,* Spring 1986, pp. 74–92; Rosabeth Moss Kanter, "When a Thousand Flowers Bloom: Structural, Collective, and Social Conditions for Innovation in Organization," in B. M. Staw and L. L. Cummings (eds.), *Research in Organizational Behavior,* Vol. 10, pp. 169–211; and Gareth Morgan, "Endangered Species: New Ideas," *Business Month,* April 1989, pp. 75–77.

27. See William J. J. Gordon, *Synectics* (New York: Harper & Row, 1961); and Bryan W. Mattimore, "Breakthroughs: Creatively Destroying the Barriers to Business Innovation," *Success,* November 1988, pp. 44–51.

28. William J. J. Gordon, *Synectics,* p. 34.

29. For a review of the material on organizational retrenchment, see Kim S. Cameron, Robert I. Sutton, and David A. Whetten, *Readings in Organizational Decline* (Cambridge, Mass: Ballinger Publishing, 1988); and William Weitzel and Ellen Jonsson, "Decline in Organizations: A Literature Integration and Extension," *Administrative Science Quarterly,* March 1989, pp. 91–109.

30. These suggestions are derived from Ronald Lippitt and Gordon Lippitt, "Humane Downsizing: Organizational Renewal Versus Organizational Depression," *S.A.M. Advanced Management Journal,* Summer 1984, pp. 15–21; Lee Tom Perry, "Least-Cost Alternatives to Layoffs in Declining Industries," *Organizational Dynamics,* Spring 1986, pp. 48–61; Cynthia Hardy, "Strategies for Retrenchment: Reconciling Individual and Organizational Needs," *Canadian Journal of Administrative Sciences,* December 1986, pp. 275–89; and George E. L. Barbee, "Downsizing with Dignity: Easing the Pain of Employee Layoffs," *Business and Society Review,* Spring 1987, pp. 31–34.

31. Adapted from Randall S. Schuler, "Definition and Conceptualization of Stress in Organizations," *Organizational Behavior and Human Performance,* April 1980, p. 189.

32. Ibid., p. 191.

33. "Stress and Boredom," *Behavior Today,* August 1975, pp. 22–25.

34. Robert L. Kahn, B. N. Wolfe, R. P. Quinn, and J. D. Snock, *Organizational Stress: Studies in Role Conflict and Ambiguity* (New York: John Wiley, 1964).

35. Thomas H. Holmes and Minoru Masuda, "Life Change and Illness Susceptibility," in J. P. Scott and E. C. Senay, (eds.), *Separation and Depression,* Publication No. 94 (Washington, D.C.: American Association for the Advancement of Science, 1973), pp. 176–79.

36. Arthur P. Brief, Randall S. Schuler, and Mary Van Sell, *Managing Job Stress* (Boston: Little, Brown, 1981), pp. 94–98.

37. See, for instance, Meyer Friedman and Ray H. Rosenman, *Type A Behavior and Your Heart* (New York: Knopf, 1974); and Muhammad Jamal, "Type A Behavior and Job Performance: Some Suggestive Findings," *Journal of Human Stress,* Summer 1985, pp. 60–68.

38. Randall S. Schuler, "Definition and Conceptualization of Stress in Organizations," pp. 200–205.

39. Terry A. Beehr and John E. Newman, "Job Stress, Employee Health, and Organizational Effectiveness: A Facet Analysis, Model, and Literature Review," *Personnel Psychology,* Winter 1978, pp. 665–99.

40. Ibid., p. 687.

41. Susan E. Jackson, "Participation in Decision Making as a Strategy for Reducing Job-Related Strain," *Journal of Applied Psychology,* February 1983, pp. 3–19.

42. See Randall S. Schuler, "Time Management: A Stress Management Technique," *Personnel Journal,* December 1979, pp. 851–55; and M. E. Haynes, *Practical Time Management: How to Make the Most of Your Most Perishable Resource* (Tulsa, Okla.: Penn Well Books, 1985).

43. Nealia S. Bruning and David R. Frew, "Effects of Exercise, Relaxation, and Management Skills Training on Physiological Stress Indicators: A Field Experiment," *Journal of Applied Psychology,* November 1987, pp. 515–21.

44. Based on Brian O'Reilly, "Apple Computer's Risky Revolution," *Fortune,* May 8, 1989, pp. 75–83.

45. Based on William M. Bulkeley, "Wang, Bogged Down by Debt, Could Face Loss of Independence," *Wall Street Journal,* July 14, 1989, p. 1; and "Wang Will Eliminate 2,000 Jobs By the First of the Year," *Los Angeles Times,* November 10, 1989, p. D1.

Chapter 18

1. Rick Wartzman and Andy Pasztor, "Stealth Bomber's First Flight Is Greeted with Cheers and the National Anthem," *Wall Street Journal,* July 18, 1989, p. C27.

2. Cited in "Cost Bombshells," *Time,* July 25, 1983, p. 16.

3. Kenneth A. Merchant, "The Control Function of Management," *Sloan Management Review,* Summer 1982, pp. 43–55.

4. Eric Flamholtz, "Organizational Control Systems as a Managerial Tool," *California Management Review,* Winter 1979, p. 55.

5. Steven Kerr, "On the Folly of Rewarding *A,* While Hoping for *B,*" *Academy of Management Journal,* December 1975, pp. 769–83.

6. Harold Koontz and Robert W. Bradspies, "Managing Through Feedforward Control," *Business Horizons,* June 1972, pp. 25–36.

7. William H. Newman, *Constructive Control: Design and Use of Control Systems* (Englewood Cliffs, N.J.: Prentice-Hall, 1975), p. 33.

8. Cited in Archie B. Carroll, "In Search of the Moral Manager," *Business Horizons,* March–April 1987, p. 7.

9. Andy Zipser, "How Pressure to Raise Sales Led MiniScribe to Falsify Numbers," *Wall Street Journal,* September 11, 1989, p. 1.

10. Edward E. Lawler III and John Grant Rhode, *Information and Control in Organizations* (Santa Monica, Calif.: Goodyear, 1976), p. 108.

11. James D. Thompson, *Organizations in Action* (New York: McGraw-Hill, 1967), p. 124.

12. John P. Campbell, "On the Nature of Organizational Effectiveness," in Paul S. Goodman, J. M. Pennings, and Associates (eds.), *New Perspectives on Organizational Effectiveness* (San Francisco: Jossey-Bass, 1977), pp. 36–41.

13. Arie Y. Lewin and John W. Minton, "Determining Organizational Effectiveness: Another Look, and an Agenda for Research," *Management Science,* May 1986, pp. 514–38.

14. Stephen Strasser, J. D. Eveland, Gaylord Cummins, O. Lynn Deniston, and John H. Romani, "Conceptualizing the Goal and System Models of Organizational Effectiveness—Implications for Comparative Evaluation Research," *Journal of Management Studies,* July 1981, pp. 321–40.

15. Ibid.

16. Jeffrey Pfeffer and Gerald Salancik, *The External Control of Organizations* (New York: Harper & Row, 1978).

17. Based on "Preston Smith: The High-Tech Way to Success on the Slopes," *Business Week,* December 5, 1988, p. 64.

Chapter 19

1. Subrata N. Chakravarty, "Will Toys 'B' Great?," *Forbes,* February 22, 1988, p. 38.

2. Larry Reibstein, "Federal Express Faces Challenges to Its Grip on Overnight Delivery," *Wall Street Journal,* January 8, 1988, p. 1.

3. Dan Gutman, "Super Laptop," *Success,* June 1989, p. 18.

4. John T. Small and William B. Lee, "In Search of an MIS," *MSU Business Topics,* Autumn 1975, pp. 47–55.

5. Herbert A. Simon, *Administrative Behavior,* 3rd ed. (New York: Free Press, 1976), p. 294.

6. John C. Carter and Fred N. Silverman, "Establishing an MIS," *Journal of Systems Management,* January 1980, p. 15.

7. Keith Davis, "Management Communication and the Grapevine," *Harvard Business Review,* September–October 1953, pp. 43–49; and Harold Sutton and Lyman W. Porter, "A Study of the Grapevine in a Governmental Organization," *Personnel Psychology,* Summer 1968, pp. 223–30.

8. See, for example, Henry Mintzberg, *The Nature of Managerial Work* (New York: Harper & Row, 1973); Jack William Jones and Raymond McLeod, Jr., "The Structure of Executive Information Systems: An Exploratory Analysis," *Decision Sciences,* Spring 1986, pp. 220–46; and Fred Luthans and Janet K. Larsen, "How Managers Really Communicate," *Human Relations,* February 1986, pp. 161–78.

9. See W. David Gardner and Joseph Kelly, "Technology: A Price/Performance Game," *Dun's Review,* August 1981, pp. 66–68; and "Computers: The New Look," *Business Week,* November 30, 1987, pp. 112–23.

10. John T. Small and William B. Lee, "In Search of an MIS."

11. See Steven A. Stanton, "End-User Computing: Power to the People," *Journal of Information Systems Management,* Summer 1988, pp. 79–81; and Glen L. Boyer and Dale McKinnon, "End-User Computing Is Here to Stay," *Supervisory Management,* October 1989, pp. 17–22.

12. Cited in *1988 Inc. Office Guide,* p. 76.

13. George F. Kimmerling, "Gaining Firm Ground," *Training and Development Journal,* March 1986, pp. 22–25.

14. See, for example, Ronald M. Lockin, "Choosing a Data Communications Network," *Journal of Business Strategy,* Winter 1986, pp. 14–26.

15. "Networking the Nation," *Time,* June 16, 1986, p. 38.

16. "How the Leader in Networking Practices What It Preaches," *Business Week,* May 16, 1988, p. 96.

17. "Electronic Mail: Neither Rain, Nor Sleet, Nor Software . . . ," *Business Week,* February 20, 1989, p. 36; and "Neither Rain, Nor Sleet, Nor Computer Glitches . . . ," *Business Week,* May 8, 1989, pp. 135–37.

18. See, for example, "An Electronic Pipeline That's Changing the Way America Does Business," *Business Week,* August 3, 1987, pp. 80–82; and Therese R. Walter, "Network Interference," *Industry Week,* May 2, 1988, pp. 43–45.

19. See, for example, Hugh J. Watson and Robert I. Mann, "Expert Systems: Past, Present, and Future," *Journal of Information Systems Management,* Fall 1988, pp. 39–46; and Eugene Linden, "Putting Knowledge to Work," *Time,* March 28, 1988, pp. 60–63.

20. See, for example, Fred L. Luconi, Thomas W. Malone, and Michael S. Scott Morton, "Expert Systems: The Next Challenge for Managers," *Sloan Management Review,* Summer 1986, pp. 3–14; and Beth Enslow, "The Payoff from Expert Systems," *Across The Board,* January–February 1989, pp. 54–58.

21. Fred L. Luconi, Thomas W. Malone, and Michael S. Scott Morton, "Expert Systems: The Next Challenge for Managers," p. 4.

22. "Technology and Managing People," *1988 Inc. Office Guide,* pp. 48–49.

23. Jack William Jones and Raymond McLeod, Jr., "The Structure of Executive Information Systems: An Exploratory Analysis," *Decision Sciences,* Spring 1986, pp. 220–46.

24. Charles A. O'Reilly, III, "Individuals and Information Overload in Organizations: Is More Necessarily Better?" *Academy of Management Journal,* December 1980, pp. 684–96.

25. Robert W. Zmud, "An Empirical Investigation of the Dimensionality of the Concept of Information," *Decision Sciences,* April 1978, pp. 187–95.

26. See, for instance, "Privacy," *Business Week,* March 28, 1988, pp. 61–68; and "Is Nothing Private?," *Business Week,* September 4, 1989, pp. 74–81.

27. See, for example, G. W. Dickson and John K. Simmons, "The Behavioral Side of MIS," *Business Horizons,* August 1970, pp. 59–71; Craig Brod, "Managing Technostress: Optimizing the Use of Computer Technology," *Personnel Journal,* October 1982, p. 754; and Sara Kiesler, Jane Siegel, and Timothy W. McGuire, "Social Psychological Aspects of Computer-Mediated Communication," *American Psychologist,* January 1985, pp. 14–19.

28. Blake Ives and Margrethe H. Olson, "User Involvement and MIS Success: A Review of Research," *Management Science,* May 1984, pp. 586–603.

29. See, for instance, John C. Henderson and Michael E. Treacy, "Managing End-User Computing for Competitive Advantage," *Sloan Management Review,* Winter 1986, pp. 3–14.

30. Thomas McCarroll, "Big Eagles and Sitting Ducks," *Time,* May 15, 1989, p. 54.

31. Tom Richman, "Mrs. Fields' Secret Ingredient," *Inc.,* October 1987, pp. 65–72.

32. See, for instance, Susan M. Gelfond, "The Computer Age Dawns in the Corner Office," *Business Week,* June 27, 1988, pp. 84–86; Therese R. Welter, "Tools at the Top," *Industry Week,* November 21, 1988, pp. 41–45; Lou Wallis, "Power Computing at the Top," *Across the Board,* January–February 1989, pp. 42–51; Jeremy Main, "At Last, Software CEOs Can Use," *Fortune,* March 13, 1989, pp. 77–83; and Stephen W. Quickel, "Management Joins the Computer Age," *Business Month,* May 1989, pp. 42–46.

33. Lynda M. Applegate, James I. Cash, Jr., and D. Quinn Mills, "Information Technology and Tomorrow's Manager," *Harvard Business Review,* November–December 1988, pp. 128–36.

34. Stephen P. Robbins, *Organization Theory: Structure, Design, and Applications,* 2nd ed. (Englewood Cliffs, N.J.: Prentice-Hall, 1987), pp. 399–400.

35. See, for example, Jane C. Linder, "Computers, Corporate Culture, and Change," *Personnel Journal,* September 1985, pp. 49–55; and William L. Gardner and John R. Schermerhorn, Jr., "Computer Networks and the Changing Nature of Managerial Work," *Public Productivity Review,* Fall 1989.

36. Michael Newman and David Rosenberg, "Systems Analysts and the Politics of Organizational Control," *Omega,* vol. 13, no. 5 (1985), pp. 393–406.

37. "Automation Could Make the Factory Foreman Extinct," *Business Week,* March 31, 1986, p. 73; and "The Boss That Never Blinks," *Time,* July 28, 1986, pp. 46–47.

38. Patrick Dawson and Ian McLoughlin, "Computer Technology and the Redefinition of Supervision: A Study of the Effects of Computerization on Railway Freight Supervisors," *Journal of Management Studies,* January 1986, pp. 116–31.

39. D. Buchanan and D. Boddy, eds., *Organisations in the Computer Age* (Aldershot, England: Gower, 1983), p. 249.

40. "Automation Could Make the Factory Foreman Extinct."

41. This section is based on Richard C. Huseman and Edward W. Miles, "Organizational Communication in the Information Age: Implications of Computer-Based Systems," *Journal of Management,* Summer 1988, pp. 181–204.

42. Based on Faye Rice, "Why K Mart Has Stalled," *Fortune,* October 9, 1989, p. 79.

43. Based on Abby Solomon, "Electronic Advisers," *Inc.,* March 1984, pp. 131–32.

Chapter 20

1. Peter C. Reid, "How Harley Beat Back the Japanese," *Fortune,* September 25, 1989, pp. 155–64.

2. "The Productivity Paradox," *Business Week,* June 6, 1988, p. 101.

3. Ibid., p. 102.

4. Ibid., p. 100.

5. See, for instance, Steven C. Wheelwright, "Restoring the Competitive Edge in U.S. Manufacturing," *California Management Review,* Spring 1985, pp. 26–42.

6. Alex Taylor III, "The U.S. Gets Back in Fighting Shape," *Fortune,* April 24, 1989, pp. 42–48.

7. William H. Miller, "U.S. Manufacturing on Whose Turf?," *Industry Week,* September 5, 1988, p. 57.

8. See John Hillkirk, "Modernizing Cuts Costs, Raises Quality," *USA Today,* January 6, 1988, p. B1; and Clare Ansberry, "Steel Industry Is on the Verge of David vs. Goliath Test," *Wall Street Journal,* October 17, 1989, p. A10.

9. Christine Gorman, "Big Steel Is Red Hot Again," *Time,* February 13, 1989, p. 61.

10. Gregory L. Miles, "Forging the New Bethlehem," *Business Week,* June 5, 1989, pp. 108–10.

11. Jean Evangelauf, "Tuition Seen Likely to Outpace Inflation for 9th Straight Year," *The Chronicle of Higher Education,* March 1, 1989, p. 1.

12. "Manufacturing Is in Flower," *Time,* March 26, 1984, pp. 50–52.

13. See Wickham Skinner, "Manufacturing—Missing Link in Corporate Strategy," *Harvard Business Review,* May–June 1969, pp. 136–45; and Wickham Skinner, *Manufacturing in the Corporate Strategy* (New York: John Wiley, 1978).

14. See, for example, "Manufacturing Is in Flower"; and "Business Refocuses on the Factory Floor," *Business Week,* February 2, 1981, p. 91.

15. See Martin K. Starr, "Global Production and Operations Strategy," *Columbia Journal of World Business,* Winter 1984, pp. 17–22; and Everett E. Adam, Jr. and Paul M. Swamidass, "Assessing Operations Management from a Strategic Perspective," *Journal of Management,* June 1989, pp. 194–95.

16. See Everett E. Adam, Jr. and Ronald J. Ebert, *Production and Operations Management: Concepts, Models, and Behavior,* 4th ed. (Englewood Cliffs, N.J.: Prentice-Hall, 1989), p. 150.

17. Richard B. Chase and Nicholas J. Aquilano, *Production and Operations Management: A Life-Cycle Approach,* 3rd ed. (Homewood, Ill.: Irwin, 1981), pp. 34–41.

18. Everett E. Adam, Jr., and Ronald J. Ebert, *Production and Operations Management: Concepts, Models, and Behavior,* p. 235.

19. Ibid., pp. 231–33.

20. Ibid., pp. 341–44.

21. Ibid., p. 340.

22. Cited in *Fortune,* October 28, 1985, p. 47.

23. Stephen E. Barndt and Davis W. Carvey, *Essentials of Operations Management* (Englewood Cliffs, N.J.: Prentice-Hall, 1982), p. 112.

24. Ibid., p. 93.

25. Joel Dreyfuss, "Shaping Up Your Suppliers," *Fortune,* April 10, 1989, pp. 116–22; and Thomas M. Rohan, "Supplier-Customer Links Multiplying," *Industry Week,* April 17, 1989, p. 20.

26. Thomas M. Rohan, "Supplier-Customer Links Multiplying."

27. Richard B. Chase and Nicholas J. Aquilano, *Production and Operations Management: A Life-Cycle Approach,* pp. 551–52.

28. John Teresko, "Speeding the Product Development Cycle," *Industry Week,* July 18, 1988, pp. 40–41.

29. John Teresko, Mark Goldstein, and William Pat Patterson, "Linking the Pieces of CIM," *Industry Week,* March 23, 1987, p. 40.

30. John Teresko, "Speeding the Product Development Cycle," p. 41.

31. "It's Here, It's Now," *Forbes,* July 25, 1988, p. 192.

32. Ibid.

33. William J. Hampton and James R. Norman, "General Motors: What Went Wrong," *Business Week,* March 16, 1987, pp. 102–10; and James B. Teece, "GM's Bumpy Ride on the Long Road Back," *Business Week,* February 13, 1989, pp. 74–78.

34. Cited in "Why 99.9% Just Won't Do," *Inc.,* April 1989, p. 26.

35. Cindy Skrzychi, "Making Quality a Priority," *Washington Post,* October 11, 1987.

36. See, for instance, Christopher Knowlton, "What America Makes Best," *Fortune,* March 28, 1988, pp. 40–43; Joel Dreyfuss, "Victories in the Quality Crusade," *Fortune,* October 10, 1988, pp. 80–88; and "The U.S. and Quality: A New Culture," *Industry Week,* April 17, 1989, pp. 43–55.

37. Jim Schachter, "People Power at Xerox," *Los Angeles Times,* December 8, 1987, p. 1 (part IV).

38. Otis Port, "The Push for Quality," *Business Week,* June 8, 1987, p. 133.

39. See, for instance, Philip Thompson, *Quality Circles: How to Make Them Work in America* (New York: AMACOM, 1982); and Ricky W. Griffin, "Consequences of Quality Circles in an Industrial Environment," *Academy of Management Journal,* June 1988, pp. 338–58.

40. Cited in Edward E. Lawler, III, and Susan A. Mohrman, "Quality Circles After the Fad," *Harvard Business Review,* January–February 1985, p. 66.

41. Jeremy Main, "The Trouble with Managing Japanese-Style," *Fortune,* April 2, 1984, p. 51.

42. See, for instance, Merle O'Donnell and Robert J. O'Donnell, "Quality Circles: The Latest Fad or a Real Winner?" *Business Horizons,* May–June 1984, pp. 48–52.

43. Tom Murray, "Tom Gelb: VP, Manufacturing," *Business Month,* September 1989, p. 31.

44. IBM, *1988 Annual Report,* p. 35.

45. Vivian Brownstein, "The War on Inventories Is Real This Time," *Fortune,* June 11, 1984, pp. 20–24.

46. See, for instance, Arjan T. Sadhwani and Mostafa H. Sarhan, "Putting JIT Manufacturing Systems to Work," *Business,* April–June 1987, pp. 30–37; Lad Kuzela, "Efficiency—Just in Time," *Industry Week,* May 2, 1988, p. 63; and Ernest H. Hall, Jr., "Just-In-Time Management: A Critical Assessment," *Academy of Management Executive,* November 1989, pp. 315–18.

47. Steven P. Galante, "Distributors Bow to Demands of 'Just-In-Time' Delivery," *Wall Street Journal,* June 30, 1986, p. 25.

48. Dexter Hutchins, "Having a Hard Time with Just-In-Time," *Fortune,* June 9, 1986, pp. 64–66.

49. Patricia L. Nemetz and Louis W. Fry, "Flexible Manufacturing Organizations: Implications for Strategy Formulation and Organization Design," *Academy of Management Review,* October 1988, pp. 627–38; and Arnaud De Meyer et al., "Flexibility: The Next Competitive Battle the Manufacturing Futures Survey," *Strategic Management Journal,* March–April 1989, pp. 135–44.

50. See, for example, Richard L. Engwall, "Flexible Manufacturing System Pays off for Both Westinghouse and the Air Force," *Industrial Engineering,* November 1986, pp. 41–49.

51. "Factories That Turn Nuts into Bolts," *U.S. News & World Report,* July 14, 1986, p. 44.

52. George Stalk, Jr., "Time—The Next Source of Competitive Advantage," *Harvard Business Review,* July–August 1988, pp. 41–51; Brian Dumaine, "How Managers Can Succeed Through Speed," *Fortune,* February 13, 1989, pp. 54–59; and Tom Peters, "Speed Becomes a 'Leading Edge,'" *Industry Week,* June 19, 1989, p. 12.

53. Brian Dumaine, "How Managers Can Succeed Through Speed."

54. Based on Ronald Henkoff, "What Motorola Learns from Japan," *Fortune,* April 24, 1989, pp. 157–68; and Mark Stuart Gill, "Stalking Six Sigma," *Business Month,* January 1990, pp. 42–46.

55. Based on Brian Bremner, "Can Caterpillar Inch Its Way Back to Heftier Profits?," *Business Week,* September 25, 1989, pp. 75–78.

GLOSSARY

●

The number in parentheses following each
term indicates the chapter in which the term
is defined.

ABC system (20) A priority system for monitoring inventory items.

acceptance sampling (20) A quality control procedure in which a sample is taken and a decision to accept or reject a whole lot is based on a calculation of sample risk error.

acceptance view of authority (2) The theory that authority comes from the willingness of subordinates to accept it.

accommodation (16) Resolving conflicts by placing another's need and concerns above one's own.

active listening (16) Listening for full meaning without making premature judgments or interpretations.

activities (9) The time or resources required to progress from one event to another in a PERT network.

adaptive strategy (5) Responding to a changing social environment after the fact.

adjourning (13) The final stage in group development for temporary groups, characterized by concern with wrapping-up activities rather than task performance.

affirmative action program (12) Programs that enhance the organizational status of members of protected groups.

aggregate planning (20) Planning overall production activities and their associated operating resources.

analyzers (8) A business-level strategy that seeks to minimize risk by following competitors' innovations but only after they have proven successful.

assessment centers (12) Places in which job candidates undergo performance simulation tests that evaluate their managerial potential.

assumed similarity (13) The belief that others are like oneself.

attitudes (13) Evaluative statements concerning objects, people, or events.

attribute sampling (20) A quality control technique that classifies items as either acceptable or unacceptable on the basis of some variable.

authoritarianism (13) A measure of a person's belief that there should be status and power differences among people in organizations.

authority (10) The rights inherent in a managerial position to give orders and expect the orders to be obeyed.

autonomous work team (11) A vertically integrated team that is given almost complete autonomy in determining how a task will be done.

autonomy (11) The degree to which a job provides substantial freedom, independence, and discretion to an individual in scheduling and carrying out his or her work.

avoidance (16) Withdrawal from or suppression of conflict.

basic corrective action (18) Determining how and why performance has deviated and correcting the source of the deviation.

batch processing (19) A data-processing procedure in which transactions are stored and processed all at one time.

BCG matrix (8) Strategy tool to guide resource allocation decisions based on market share and growth of SBUs.

behavior (13) The observable actions of people.

behaviorally anchored rating scales (BARS) (12) A performance appraisal technique in which an evaluator rates employees on specific job behaviors derived from performance dimensions.

behavioral science theorists (2) Psychologists and sociologists who relied on the scientific method for the study of organizational behavior.

behavioral theories (15) Theories that try to identify behaviors that differentiate effective from ineffective leaders.

body language (16) Gestures, facial configurations, and other movements of the body that convey meaning.

bona fide occupational qualification (BFOQ) (12) A criterion such as sex, age, or national origin may be used as a basis for hiring if it can be clearly demonstrated to be job related.

bounded rationality (6) Behavior that is rational within the parameters of a simplified model that captures the essential features of a problem.

brainstorming (6) An idea-generating process that encourages alternatives while withholding criticism.

break-even analysis (9) A technique for identifying the point at which total revenue is just sufficient to cover total costs.

budget (9) A numerical plan.

bureaucracy (2) A form of organization marked by division of labor, hierarchy, rules and regulations, and impersonal relationships.

business-level strategy (8) Seeks to determine how a corporation should compete in each of its businesses.

byte (19) A computer memory position that can usually hold one alphabetic character or digit.

capacity planning (20) Assessing an operating system's capabilities for producing a desired number of output units for each type of product anticipated during a given time period.

capital expenditure budget (9) Budget that forecasts investments in property, buildings, and major equipment.

career (12) The sequence of positions occupied by a person during the course of a lifetime.

cash budget (9) A budget that forecasts how much cash an organization will have on hand and how much it will need to meet expenses.

cash cows (8) Products that demonstrate low growth but have a high market share.

cause-related marketing (5) Social actions that are directly motivated by profits.

centralization (10) The concentration of decision-making authority in upper management.

central processing unit (19) The "brain" of the computer; contains the main memory and controls the flow of operations.

certainty (6) A situation in which a manager can make accurate decisions because the outcome from every alternative is known.

chain of command (10) The flow of authority from the top to the bottom of an organization.

change (17) An alteration in people, structure, or technology.

change agents (17) People who act as catalysts and manage the change process.

channel (16) The medium by which a message travels.

classical theorists (2) A group that includes writers on scientific management and general administrative theory.

classical view (5) The view that management's only social responsibility is to maximize profits.

closed systems (2) Systems that neither are influenced by nor interact with their environment.

code of ethics (5) A formal statement of an organization's primary values and the ethical rules it expects its employees to follow.

coercive power (10) Power that depends on fear.

collaboration (16) Resolving conflict by seeking a solution advantageous to all parties.

collective bargaining (12) A process for negotiating a union contract and for administering the contract after it has been negotiated.

collectivism (4) A cultural dimension in which people expect others in their group to look after them and protect them when they are in trouble.

combination strategy (8) A corporate-level strategy that pursues two or more of the following strategies—stability, growth, or retrenchment—simultaneously.

command group (13) A group composed of subordinates who report directly to a given manager.

commitment concept (7) Plans should extend just far enough to see through current commitments.

committee structure (11) A temporary or permanent structure that brings together a range of individuals from across functional lines to deal with problems.

communication (16) The transference and understanding of meaning.

communication networks (19) Vertical and horizontal communication patterns.

communication process (16) The seven steps by which meaning is transmitted and understood.

comparable worth (12) The doctrine that jobs that are equal in value to the organization should be equally compensated.

competitor intelligence (9) Environmental scanning activity that seeks to identify who competitors are, what they're doing, and how their actions will affect the focus organization.

complexity (10) The amount of differentiation in an organization.

compressed workweek (11) A workweek comprised of four ten-hour days.

compromise (16) A solution to conflict in which each party gives up something of value.

computer-integrated manufacturing (CIM) (20) Combines the organization's strategic business plan and manufacturing plan with state-of-the-art computer applications.

concurrent control (18) Control that takes place while an activity is in progress.

conditional maintenance (20) Maintenance that calls for an overhaul or repair in response to an inspection.

conflict (16) Perceived incompatible differences that result in some form of interference or opposition.

consideration (15) The extent to which a person has job relationships characterized by mutual trust, respect for subordinates' ideas, and regard for their feelings.

contingency approach (2) The development of situational variables that moderate "if X, then Y" statements of causation.

contingent workers (11) Temporary and part-time workers who supplement an organization's permanent work force.

continuous reinforcement schedule (14) A schedule that reinforces a desired behavior each and every time it is demonstrated.

control (18) The process of monitoring activities to ensure that they are being accomplished as planned and the correcting of any significant deviations.

controlling (1) Monitoring activities to ensure that they are being accomplished as planned and correcting any significant deviations.

control process (18) The process of measuring actual performance, comparing actual performance against a standard, and taking managerial action to correct significant deviations or inadequate standards.

corporate-level strategy (8) Seeks to determine what businesses a corporation should be in.

cost center (20) A unit in which managers are held responsible for all associated costs.

cost-leadership strategy (8) The strategy an organization follows when it wants to be the lowest-cost producer in its industry.

creativity (17) The ability to combine ideas in a unique way or to make unusual associations among ideas.

critical incidents (12) A performance appraisal technique in which an evaluator lists key behaviors that separate effective from ineffective job performance.

critical path (9) The longest sequence of activities in a PERT network.

culture shock (13) Confusion, disorientation, and emotional upheaval caused by immersion in a new culture.

cumulative learning curve (8) The assumption that when a business increases the amount of product manufactured, the per-unit cost of the product will decrease.

customer departmentalization (10) Grouping activities on the basis of common customers.

data (19) Raw, unanalyzed facts.

data base management (19) A computerized system that allows the user to organize, get at easily, and select and review a precise set of data from a larger base of data.

decentralization (10) The handing down of -decision-making authority to lower levels in an organization.

decision criteria (6) Criteria that define what is relevant in a decision.

decisional roles (1) Management roles that include those of entrepreneur, disturbance handler, resource allocator, and negotiator.

decision-making process (6) A set of eight steps that include formulating a problem, selecting an alternative, and evaluating the decision's effectiveness.

decoding (16) Retranslating a sender's message.

decruitment (12) Techniques for reducing the labor supply within an organization.

defenders (8) A business-level strategy that seeks stability by producing only a limited set of products directed at a narrow segment of the total potential market.

deindustrialization (20) The conversion of an economy from dominance by manufacturing to dominance by service businesses.

delegation (16) The assignment of authority and responsibility to another person to carry out specific activities.

Delphi technique (6) A group decision-making technique in which members never meet face to face.

devil's advocate (16) A person who purposely presents arguments that run counter to those proposed by the majority or against current practices.

diagonal communication (19) Communication that cuts across functions and levels in an organization.

differentiation strategy (6) The strategy an organization follows when it wants to be unique in its industry along some dimensions that are widely valued by buyers.

direct costs (20) Manufacturing costs incurred in proportion to the output of a particular good or service.

directional plans (7) Flexible plans that identify general guidelines.

discipline (16) Actions taken by a manager to enforce the organization's standards and regulations.

discretionary time (9) The part of a manager's time that is controllable.

disk (19) A form of storage that can be built into or attached to a computer.

dissonance (13) Inconsistencies among attitudes or between attitudes and behavior.

distinctive competence (8) The unique skills and resources that determine the organization's competitive weapons.

divisional structure (11) An organization structure made up of autonomous, self-contained units.

division of labor (2) The breakdown of jobs into narrow, repetitive tasks.

dogs (8) Products that demonstrate low growth and low market share.

downward communication (19) Any communication that flows from a manager down the authority hierarchy.

dual-career couples (12) Couples in which both partners have a professional, managerial, or administrative occupation.

dysfunctional conflicts (16) Conflicts that prevent an organization from achieving its goals.

economic order quantity model (EOQ) (20) A technique for balancing purchases, ordering, carrying, and stockout costs to derive the optimum quantity for a purchase order.

effectiveness (1) Goal attainment.

efficiency (1) The relationship between inputs and outputs; seeks to minimize resource costs.

ego strength (5) A personality characteristic that measures the strength of one's convictions.

electronic mail (16) Instantaneous transmission of written messages on computers that are linked together.

encoding (16) Converting a message into symbols.

end-user (19) In information systems, the person who uses the information and assumes responsibility for its control.

entrepreneurship (8) Undertaking ventures, pursuing opportunities, innovating, and starting businesses.

environment (3) Outside institutions or forces that affect the organization's performance.

environmental complexity (3) The number of components in an organization's environment and the extent of an organization's knowledge about its environmental components.

environmental scanning (9) The screening of large amounts of information to detect emerging trends and to create a set of scenarios.

environmental uncertainty (3) The degree of change and complexity in an organization's environment.

equity theory (14) The theory that an employee compares his or her job's inputs-outcomes ratio to that of relevant others and then behaves so as to correct any inequity.

escalation of commitment (6) An increased commitment to a previous decision in spite of negative information.

esteem needs (14) In Maslow's hierarchy, internal factors such as self-respect, autonomy, and achievement and external factors such as status, recognition, and attention.

ethics (5) The rules or principles that define right and wrong conduct.

European Community (EC) (4) The 320 million people living in the following twelve countries: Belgium, Denmark, France, Greece, Ireland, Italy, Luxembourg, Netherlands, Portugal, Spain, the United Kingdom, and West Germany.

events (9) End points that represent the completion of major activities in a PERT network.

expectancy theory (14) The theory that the strength of a tendency to act in a certain way depends on the strength of the expectation that the act will be followed by a given outcome and on the attractiveness of that outcome to the individual.

expense budget (9) Budget that lists the primary activities undertaken by a unit and that allocates a dollar amount to each.

expert power (10) Power based on one's expertise, special skill, or knowledge.

expert systems (19) Software programs that encode the relevant experience of a human expert.

facilities layout planning (20) Assessing and selecting among alternative layout options for equipment and work stations.

facilities location planning (20) The design and selection of an operations facility.

feedback (11) The degree to which carrying out the work activities required by a job results in an individual's obtaining direct and clear information about the effectiveness of his or her performance.

feedback control (18) Control imposed after an action has taken place.

feedforward control (18) Control that prevents anticipated problems.

femininity (4) A cultural dimension that describes societies that emphasize relationships, concern for others, and the overall quality of life.

Fiedler contingency model (15) The theory that effective group performance depends upon the proper match between a leader's style of interacting with subordinates and the degree to which the situation gives control and influence to the leader.

filtering (16) The deliberate manipulation of information to make it appear more favorable to the receiver.

first-line managers (1) Supervisors; the lowest level of management.

fixed budget (9) Budget that assumes a fixed level of sales or production.

fixed-interval reordering system (20) An inventory system that uses time as the determining factor for reviewing and reordering inventory items.

fixed-point reordering system (20) An inventory system that "flags" the fact that the inventory needs to be replenished when it reaches a certain point or level.

fixed-position layout (20) A manufacturing layout in which the product stays in place while tools, equipment, and human skills are brought to it.

flexible manufacturing system (20) A system in which "custom-made" products can be mass produced by means of computer-aided design, engineering, and manufacturing facilities.

flexible work hours (flextime) (11) A scheduling system in which employees are required to work a number of hours a week but are free, within certain limits, to vary the hours of work.

focus strategy (8) The strategy a company follows when it seeks a cost or differentiation advantage in a narrow segment.

forcing (16) Resolving conflict through the use of formal authority.

forecasts (9) Predictions of future outcomes.

formal communication (19) Communication that follows the authority chain of command or that is necessary for performing a job.

formalization (10) The degree to which an organization relies on rules and procedures to direct the behavior of employees.

forming (13) The first stage in group development, characterized by a great deal of uncertainty.

friendship group (13) A group that develops because members have one or more characteristics in common.

functional conflicts (16) Conflicts that support the goals of the organization.

functional departmentalization (10) Grouping activities by functions performed.

functional-level strategy (8) Seeks to determine how to support the business-level strategy.

functional structure (11) A design that groups similar or related occupational specialties together.

Gantt chart (2) A graphic bar chart that shows the relationship between work planned and completed on one axis and time elapsed on the other.

general administrative theorists (2) Writers who developed general theories of what managers do and what constitutes good management practice.

general environment (3) Everything outside an organization.

geographic departmentalization (10) The grouping of activities on the basis of territory.

global strategies (8) The search for competitive advantages outside an organization's domestic borders.

goal-setting theory (14) Specific goals increase performance, and difficult goals, when accepted, result in higher performance than easy goals.

grapevine (19) The informal communication network.

graphic rating scales (12) A performance appraisal technique that requires an evaluator to rate a set of performance factors on an incremental scale.

group (13) Two or more interacting and interdependent individuals who come together to achieve particular objectives.

group cohesiveness (13) The degree to which members of a group are attracted to one another and share the group's goals.

group order ranking (12) A performance appraisal technique that groups employees into ordered classifications.

groupthink (6) The withholding by group members of different views in order to appear in agreement.

growth strategy (8) A corporate-level strategy that seeks to increase the level of the organization's operations. This typically includes increasing revenues, employees, and/or market share.

halo effect (13) A general impression of an individual based on a single characteristic.

hardware (19) Physical equipment that performs input, output, processing, and storage functions.

Hawthorne studies (2) A series of studies during the 1920s and 1930s that provided new insights into group norms and behavior.

hierarchy of needs theory (14) Five human needs identified by Abraham Maslow: physiological, safety, social, esteem, and self-actualization. As each need is substantially satisfied, the next need becomes dominant.

higher-order needs (14) According to Maslow, social, esteem, and self-actualization needs.

high-high leader (15) A leader who is high in both initiating structure and consideration.

"hot stove" rule (16) Discipline should immediately follow an infraction, provide ample warning, be consistent, and be impersonal.

human relations movement (2) The belief, for the most part unsubstantiated by research, that a satisfied worker will be productive.

human relations view of conflict (16) The view that conflict is a natural and inevitable outcome in any organization.

human resource management process (12) Activities necessary for staffing the organization and sustaining high employee performance.

human resource planning (12) The process by which management ensures that it has the right personnel who are capable of completing those tasks that help the organization reach its objectives.

human resources approach (2) The study of management that focuses on human behavior.

hygiene factors (14) Factors that, if present, eliminate dissatisfaction.

ill-structured problems (6) New problems in which information is ambiguous or incomplete.

immediate corrective action (18) Correcting an activity right now in order to get things back on track.

implementation (6) Conveying a decision to those affected and getting their commitment to it.

incremental budget (9) Budget that allocates funds to departments according to allocations in the previous period.

indirect costs (20) Manufacturing costs that are largely unaffected by changes in output.

individualism (4) A cultural dimension in which people are supposed to look after their own interests and those of their immediate family.

individual ranking (12) A performance appraisal technique that ranks employees in order from highest to lowest.

Industrial Revolution (2) The advent of machine power, mass production, and efficient transportation.

informal communication (19) Communication that is not approved by management and not defined by any predetermined structural hierarchy.

information (19) Analyzed and processed data.

informational roles (1) Roles that include monitoring, disseminating, and spokesperson activities.

initiating structure (15) The extent to which a leader defines and structures his or her role and those of subordinates to attain goals.

innovation (17) The process of taking a creative idea and turning it into a useful product, service, or method of operation.

input devices (19) The means by which data and instructions are fed into the computer.

integrated work team (11) A group that accomplishes many tasks by making specific assignments to members and rotating jobs among members as the tasks require.

interactionist view of conflict (16) The view that some conflict is absolutely necessary for an organization or units within an organization to perform effectively.

interactive strategy (5) Anticipating environmental change and adapting a firm's actions to it.

interest group (13) A group of people who affiliate to attain a specific objective with which each is concerned.

intergroup development (17) The process of changing the attitudes, stereotypes, and perceptions that members of work groups have about each other.

intermittent reinforcement schedule (14) A schedule in which reinforcement is given only often enough to make a behavior worth repeating.

interpersonal communication (16) Communication between two or more people in which the parties are treated as individuals rather than objects.

interpersonal roles (1) Roles that include figurehead, leadership, and liaison activities.

intrapreneurship (8) The creation of entrepreneurial spirit in a large organization.

intuition (13) Gut feelings and interpretations based on personal experience.

job analysis (12) An assessment that defines the jobs in an organization and the behaviors that are necessary to perform these jobs.

job characteristics model (11) A framework for analyzing and designing jobs; it identifies five primary job characteristics, their interrelationships, and their impact on outcome variables.

job depth (11) Allowing employees greater control over their work by expanding it vertically.

job description (12) A written statement of what a jobholder does, how it is done, and why it is done.

job design (11) The way in which tasks are combined to form complete jobs.

job enlargement (11) The horizontal expansion of a job; an increase in job scope.

job enrichment (11) Vertical expansion of a job by adding planning and evaluating responsibilities.

job evaluation (12) A procedure that ranks all the jobs in an organization according to criteria such as knowledge and skills, mental demands, responsibility, and working conditions.

job involvement (13) The degree to which an employee identifies with his or her job, actively participates in it, and considers his or her performance important to his or her sense of self-worth.

job rotation (11) Lateral job transfers.

job satisfaction (13) An employee's general attitude toward his or her job.

job scope (11) The number of different operations required in a job and the frequency with which the job cycle is repeated.

job sharing (11) The practice of having two or more people split a traditional forty-hour-a-week job.

job specification (12) A statement of the minimum acceptable qualifications that an incumbent must possess to perform a given job successfully.

just-in-time (JIT) inventory system (20) A system in which inventory items arrive at the time they are needed in the production process instead of being stored in stock.

kanban (20) The Japanese name for just-in-time inventory systems.

labor-management relations (12) The formal interactions between unions and an organization's management.

labor union (12) An organization that represents workers and seeks to protect and promote their interests through collective bargaining.

lateral communication (19) Communication among members of the work groups, among managers, or among any horizontally equivalent personnel.

law of effect (13) The principle that behavior is a function of its consequences.

leader-member relations (15) The degree of confidence, trust, and respect subordinates have in their leader.

leader-participation model (15) A theory of leadership that provides a sequential set of rules that should be followed to determine the form and amount of participation in decision making in different situations.

leaders (15) Those who are able to influence others and who possess managerial authority.

leading (1) Includes motivating subordinates, directing others, selecting the most effective communication channels, and resolving conflicts.

learning (13) Any relatively permanent change in behavior that occurs as a result of experience.

least-preferred co-worker (LPC) questionnaire (15) A questionnaire that purports to measure whether a person is task or relationship oriented.

legitimate power (10) Power based on a person's position in the formal hierarchy.

life cycle of the organization (7) Four stages that organizations go through: formation, growth, maturity, and decline.

linear programming (9) A mathematical technique that solves resource allocation problems.

line authority (10) The authority that entitles a manager to direct the work of a subordinate.

load chart (9) A modified Gantt chart that schedules capacity by work stations.

locus of control (5) A personality attribute that measures the degree to which people believe they are masters of their own fate.

long-term plans (7) Plans that extend beyond five years.

lower-order needs (14) Physiological and safety needs.

Machiavellianism (13) A measure of the degree to which people are pragmatic, maintain emotional distance, and believe that ends justify means.

management (1) The process of getting activities completed efficiently with and through other people.

management by objectives (MBO) (7) A system in which subordinates jointly determine specific performance objectives with their superiors, progress toward objectives is periodically reviewed, and rewards are allocated on the basis of this progress.

management functions (1) Planning, organizing, leading, and controlling.

management information system (19) A system that provides management with needed information on a regular basis.

management roles (1) Behavior attributable to a manager's job or position.

managerial grid (15) A two-dimensional graphic portrayal of leadership based on concerns for people and for production.

managers (1) The individuals in an organization who direct the activities of other people.

manufacturing organizations (20) Organizations that produce physical goods such as steel, automobiles, textiles, and farm machinery.

maquiladoras (4) Non-Mexican companies operating assembly plants along the Mexican side of the U.S.-Mexican border from Texas to California.

marginal analysis (9) A planning technique that assesses the incremental costs or revenues in a particular decision.

masculinity (4) A cultural dimension that describes a society that emphasizes assertiveness and the acquisition of money and material things.

mass production (10) Large-batch manufacturing.

master schedule (20) A manufacturing schedule that specifies the quantity and type of each item to be produced; how, when, and where it should be produced for the next day, week, or month; labor force levels; and inventory.

material requirements planning (MRP) (20) A manufacturing system that dissects products into the precise materials and parts necessary for purchasing, inventorying, and priority-planning purposes.

matrix structure (11) A structural design that assigns specialists from functional departments to work on one or more projects that are led by a project manager.

maturity (15) The ability and willingness of people to take responsibility for directing their own behavior.

mechanistic organization (bureaucracy) (10) A structure that scores high on complexity, formalization, and centralization.

megabyte (19) A computer memory position that holds 1,024,000 bytes.

mentor (12) A person who sponsors or supports another employee who is lower in the organization.

message (16) A purpose to be conveyed.

mission (8) The purpose of an organization.

modeling (13) Learning that occurs from observing others and copying their behavior.

modem (19) A device that links a computer to a telephone line and allows computers to send and receive data from other computers.

motivation (14) The willingness to exert high levels of effort to reach organizational goals, conditioned by the effort's ability to satisfy some individual need.

motivation-hygiene theory (14) The theory that intrinsic factors are related to job satisfaction, while extrinsic factors are associated with dissatisfaction.

motivators (14) Factors that, if present, increase job satisfaction.

multinational corporation (4) A company that maintains significant operations in two or more countries simultaneously.

multiperson comparison (12) A performance appraisal technique in which individuals are compared to one another.

national culture (4) The attitudes and perspectives shared by individuals from a specific country that shape their behavior and the way they see the world.

need (14) An internal state that makes certain outcomes appear attractive.

need for achievement (14) The drive to excel, to achieve in relation to a set of standards, to strive to succeed.

need for affiliation (14) The desire for friendly and close interpersonal relationships.

need for power (14) The need to make others behave in a way that they would not have behaved otherwise.

networking (19) Linking computers so that they can communicate with each other.

network structure (11) A small central organization that relies on other organizations to perform its basic business functions on a contract basis.

noise (16) Disturbances that interfere with the transmission of a message.

nominal group technique (6) A group decision-making technique in which members are present but operate independently.

nonprogrammed decisions (6) Unique decisions that require a custom-made solution.

nonverbal communication (16) Communication conveyed without words.

norming (13) The third stage of group development, characterized by the formation of close relationships and cohesiveness.

norms (13) Acceptable standards shared by a group's members.

objectives (7) Desired outcomes for individuals, groups, or entire organizations.

omnipotent view of management (3) The view that managers are directly responsible for an organization's success or failure.

open systems (2) Dynamic systems that interact with and respond to their environment.

operational plans (7) Plans that specify the details of how overall objectives are to be achieved.

operations management (20) The design, operation, and control of the transformation process that converts resources like labor and raw materials into finished goods and services.

operatives (1) People who work directly on some job or task and have no responsibility for overseeing the work of others.

organic organization (adhocracy) (10) A structure that scores low on complexity, formalization, and centralization.

organization (1) A systematic arrangement of people to accomplish some specific purpose.

organizational behavior (13) The study of the actions of people at work.

organizational commitment (13) An employee's orientation toward an organization in terms of his or her loyalty to, identification with, and involvement in the organization.

organizational culture (3) A system of shared meaning.

organizational development (OD) (17) Techniques to change people and the quality of interpersonal work relationships.

organizational goals approach (18) Appraising an organization's effectiveness in terms of how it accomplishes its goals.

organization design (10) The construction or changing of an organization's structure.

organization structure (10) The degree of complexity, formalization, and centralization in an organization.

organizing (1) Determining what tasks are to be done, who is to do them, how the tasks are to be grouped, who reports to whom, and where decisions are to be made.

orientation (12) The introduction of a new employee into his or her job and the organization.

output devices (19) The means by which a computer supplies information to a user.

paired comparison (12) A performance appraisal approach in which each employee is compared to every other employee in a comparison group and rated as either the superior or weaker member of the pair.

paraphrasing (16) Restating what a speaker has said but in your own words.

parochialism (4) A selfish, narrow outlook on the world; an inability to recognize differences between people.

path-goal theory (15) The theory that a leader's behavior is acceptable to subordinates insofar as they view it as a source of either immediate or future satisfaction.

perception (13) A process by which individuals organize and interpret their sensory impressions in order to give meaning to their environment.

performance appraisal (12) A process of evaluating an individual's work performance in order to make an objective personnel decision.

performing (13) The fourth stage in group development, when the group is fully functional.

peripheral device (19) In a computer, any hardware other than the central processing unit.

personality (13) A combination of psychological traits that classifies a person.

PERT network (9) A flowchartlike diagram that depicts the sequence of activities needed to complete a project and the time or cost associated with each activity.

physiological needs (14) Basic hunger, thirst, shelter, and sexual needs.

planning (1) Includes defining goals, establishing strategy, and developing plans to coordinate activities.

Planning-Programming-Budgeting-System (PPBS) (9) Program budget that combines budgeting with management by objectives and allocates funds for the achievement of specific objectives.

policy (6) A guide that establishes parameters for making decisions.

position power (15) The degree of influence a leader has over power variables such as hiring, firing, discipline, promotions, and salary increases.

power (10) An individual's capacity to influence decisions.

power distance (4) A cultural measure of the extent to which a society accepts the unequal distribution of power in institutions and organizations.

preventive maintenance (20) Maintenance performed before a breakdown occurs.

principles of management (2) Universal truths of management that can be taught.

proactive strategy (5) The manipulation of a firm's social environment in ways that will work to the firm's advantage.

probability theory (9) The use of statistics to analyze past predictable patterns and to reduce risk in future plans.

problem (6) A discrepancy between an existing and a desired state of affairs.

problem analyzability (10) The type of search procedures employees follow in responding to exceptions.

problem solving (16) The resolution of conflict through face-to-face confrontation of opposing parties.

procedure (6) A series of interrelated sequential steps that can be used to respond to a structured problem.

process approach (2) Management performs the four functions of planning, organizing, leading, and controlling.

process consultation (17) Help given by an outside consultant to a manager in perceiving, understanding, and acting upon the process events.

process control (20) A quality control procedure in which sampling is done during the transformation process to determine whether the process itself is under control.

process departmentalization (10) Grouping activities on the basis of product or customer flow.

process layout (20) Arranging manufacturing components together according to similarity of function.

process planning (20) Determining how a product or service will be produced.

process production (10) Continuous-process manufacturing.

product departmentalization (10) Grouping activities by product line.

productivity (20) The overall output of goods and services produced, divided by the inputs needed to generate that output.

product layout (20) Arranging manufacturing components according to the progressive steps by which a product is made.

professional managers (2) Managers who have no significant ownership in their organization.

profit budget (9) Budget that combines revenue and expense budgets into one.

program budget (9) Budget that allocates funds to activities needed to achieve a specific objective.

Program Evaluation and Review Technique (PERT) (9) A technique for scheduling complicated projects with hundreds or thousands of activities, some of which are interdependent.

programmed decision (6) A repetitive decision that can be handled by a routine approach.

prospectors (8) A business-level strategy that seeks innovation by finding and exploiting new product and market opportunities.

qualitative forecasting (9) Uses the judgment and opinions of knowledgeable individuals to predict future outcomes.

quality circles (20) Work groups of eight to ten employees and supervisors who meet regularly to discuss, investigate, and correct quality problems.

quantitative approach (2) The use of mathematical statistics to improve decision making.

quantitative forecasting (9) Applies a set of mathematical rules to a series of past data to predict future outcomes.

question marks (8) Products that demonstrate high growth but low market share.

queuing theory (9) A technique that balances the cost of having a waiting line against the cost of service to maintain that line.

range of variation (18) The acceptable parameters of variance between actual performance and the standard.

rational (6) Describes choices that are consistent and value-maximizing within specified constraints.

reactors (8) A business-level strategy that characterizes inconsistent and unstable decision patterns.

realistic job preview (12) Exposing job candidates to negative as well as positive information about a job and an organization.

real objectives (7) Objectives that an organization is actually pursuing, as defined by the actions of its members.

real-time processing (19) A data-processing procedure in which data are continually updated as transactions occur.

recruitment (12) The process of locating, identifying, and attracting capable applicants.

referent power (10) Power based on identification with a person who has desirable resources or personal traits.

referents (14) The persons, systems, or selves against which individuals compare themselves to assess equity.

reinforcement theory (14) An individual's purposes direct his or her actions; behavior is a function of its consequences.

reinforcer (14) Any consequence that, when immediately following a response, increases the probability that the behavior will be repeated.

reliability (12) The ability of a selection device to measure the same thing consistently.

remedial maintenance (20) Maintenance that calls for the complete overhaul, replacement, or repair of equipment when it breaks down.

response time (9) Uncontrollable time spent responding to requests, demands, and problems initiated by others.

responsibility (10) An obligation to perform.

retrenchment strategy (8) A corporate-level strategy that seeks to reduce the size or diversity of an organization's operations.

revenue budget (7) Budget that projects future sales.

revenue forecasting (9) Predicting future revenues.

reward power (10) Power based on the ability to distribute anything that others may value.

rights view of ethics (5) Decisions are concerned with respecting and protecting basic rights of individuals.

risk (6) Those conditions in which the decision maker has to estimate the likelihood of certain outcomes.

risk propensity (13) A measure of a person's willingness to take chances.

role (13) A set of behavior patterns expected of someone occupying a given position in a social unit.

rule (6) An explicit statement that tells managers what they ought or ought not to do.

safety needs (14) According to Maslow, a person's need for security and protection from physical and emotional harm.

satisficing (6) Acceptance of solutions that are "good enough."

scenario (9) An internally consistent view of what the future is likely to be.

scheduling (9) A listing of necessary activities, their order of accomplishment, who is to do each, and time of completion.

scientific management (2) The use of the scientific method to define the "one best way" for a job to be done.

selection process (12) The process of screening job applicants to ensure that the most appropriate candidates are hired.

selectivity (13) The process by which people assimilate what they observe by choosing certain bits and pieces, depending on their interests, background, experience, and attitudes.

self-actualization need (14) According to Maslow, a person's drive to become what he or she is capable of becoming.

sensitivity training (17) A method of changing behavior through unstructured group interaction.

service organizations (20) Organizations that produce nonphysical outputs like educational, medical, and transportation services that are intangible, can't be stored in inventory, and incorporate the customer or client in the actual production process.

sexual harassment (12) Behavior marked by sexually suggestive remarks, unwanted touching and sexual advances, requests for sexual favors, or other verbal and physical conduct of a sexual nature.

shaping (13) Learning that takes place in graduated steps.

short-term plans (7) Plans that cover less than one year.

simple structure (11) An organization that is low in complexity and formalization, but high in centralization.

simulation (9) A model of a real-world phenomenon that contains one or more variables that can be manipulated in order to assess their impact.

situational leadership theory (15) A contingency theory that focuses on the followers' maturity.

skill variety (11) The degree to which a job includes a variety of activities that call for a number of different skills and talents.

small business (1) An independently owned and operated profit-seeking enterprise that has fewer than 100 employees, has annual sales of less than $5 million, and offers its product or service in a limited geographical area.

smoothing (16) The process of playing down differences between individuals or groups while emphasizing common interests.

social issues management (5) Identifying, analyzing, and responding to issues in order to minimize surprises and enforce social policies that benefit the firm.

social needs (14) According to Maslow, a person's needs for affection, belongingness, acceptance, and friendship.

social obligation (5) The obligation of a business to meet its economic and legal responsibilities.

social responsibility (5) A social obligation, beyond that required by the law and economics, for a business firm to pursue long-term goals that are good for society.

social responsiveness (5) The capacity of a firm to respond to social pressures.

socioeconomic view (5) The view that management's responsibility goes well beyond making profits to include protecting and improving society's welfare.

software (19) A collective name for programs that instruct a computer on how to perform a particular task.

span of control (10) The number of subordinates a manager can direct efficiently and effectively.

specific environment (3) The part of the environment that is directly relevant to the achievement of an organization's goals.

specific plans (7) Clearly defined plans that leave no room for interpretation.

spreadsheets (19) Software packages that allow users to turn a computer's memory into a large worksheet in which data and formulas can be entered to perform a variety of calculations.

stability strategy (8) A corporate-level strategy characterized by an absence of significant change.

staff authority (10) Authority that supports, assists, and advises holders of line authority.

stakeholders (5) Any constituency in an organization's environment that is affected by the organization's decisions and policies.

stars (8) Products that demonstrate high growth and high market share.

stated objectives (7) Official statements of what an organization says—and what it wants various publics to believe—are its objectives.

status (13) A prestige grading, position, or rank within a group.

stereotyping (13) Judging a person on the basis of one's perception of the group to which the person belongs.

storming (13) The second stage of group development, characterized by intragroup conflict.

strategic alliances (8) Joint partnerships between two or more firms to gain a competitive advantage in a market.

strategic business unit (SBU) (8) A single business or collection of related businesses that is independent and formulates its own strategy.

strategic constituencies approach (18) Appraising an organization's effectiveness according to how well the organization satisfies the demands of its key constituencies.

strategic management process (8) A nine-step process encompassing strategic planning, implementation, and evaluation.

strategic plans (7) Plans that are organizationwide, establish overall objectives, and position an organization in terms of its environment.

stress (17) A dynamic condition in which an individual is confronted with an opportunity, constraint, or demand related to what he or she desires and for which the outcome is perceived to be both uncertain and important.

strong cultures (3) Organizations in which the key values are intensely held and widely shared.

stuck in the middle (8) Descriptive of organizations that cannot compete through cost-leadership, differentiation, or focus strategies.

superordinate goals (16) Common goals that two or more conflicting parties desire and that cannot be reached without the cooperation of those involved.

survey feedback (17) A technique for assessing the attitudes, identifying discrepancies in them, and resolving the differences by using survey information in feedback groups.

symbolic view of management (3) The view that management has only a limited effect on substantive organizational outcomes owing to the large number of factors outside of management's control; however, management greatly influences symbolic outcomes.

synectics (17) A method for fitting together different and irrelevant elements to arrive at new solutions to problems.

systematic study (13) Study conducted in an objective and rigorous manner.

systems approach to management (2) A theory that considers an organization to be a set of interrelated and interdependent parts that depends on its environment for survival.

systems approach to organizational effectiveness (18) Appraising an organization's effectiveness in terms of both means and ends.

task force structure (11) A temporary structure created to accomplish a specific, well-defined, and complex task that requires the involvement of personnel from a number of organizational subunits.

task group (13) A group of people who work together to complete a job task.

task identity (11) The degree to which a job requires completion of a whole and identifiable piece of work.

task significance (11) The degree to which a job has a substantial impact on the lives or work of other people.

task structure (15) The degree to which job assignments are procedurized.

task variability (10) The number of exceptions individuals encounter in their work.

team building (17) Having members of work teams interact with one another to learn how each member thinks and works.

technological forecasting (9) Predicting changes in technology and when new technologies are likely to be economically feasible.

technology (8) The means by which an organization converts inputs into outputs.

telecommuting (11) The linking by computer and modem of workers at home with co-workers and management at an office.

theory of justice view of ethics (5) Decision makers seek to impose and enforce rules fairly and impartially.

Theory X (14) The assumption that employees dislike work, are lazy, seek to avoid responsibility, and must be coerced to perform.

Theory Y (14) The assumption that employees like work, seek responsibility, and can exercise self-direction.

therbligs (2) A classification scheme for labeling seventeen basic hand motions.

three-needs theory (14) The theory that the three major motives in work are the needs for achievement, power, and affiliation.

time management (9) A method for scheduling personal time effectively.

traditional objective setting (7) Objectives are set at the top and then broken down into subgoals for each level in an organization. The top imposes its standards on everyone below.

traditional view of authority (2) The view that authority comes from above.

traditional view of conflict (16) The view that all conflict is bad and must be avoided.

trait theories (15) Theories that try to isolate characteristics that differentiate leaders from nonleaders.

transactional leaders (15) Leaders who guide or motivate their followers in the direction of established goals by clarifying role and task requirements.

transformational/charismatic leaders (15) Leaders who inspire followers to transcend their own self-interests for the good of the organization and who are capable of having a profound and extraordinary effect on their followers.

two-tier pay system (14) A system in which new employees are hired at a significantly lower wage than that paid to people already employed in the same job.

Type A behavior (17) Behavior characterized by a chronic sense of time urgency and an overly competitive drive.

Type B behavior (17) Behavior characterized by relaxed, easygoing, noncompetitive attitudes.

ultimate responsibility (10) Responsibility that must be retained by the person who has delegated authority.

uncertainty (6) A situation in which a decision maker has neither certainty nor reasonable probability estimates available.

uncertainty avoidance (4) A cultural measure of the degree to which people tolerate risk and unconventional behavior.

unit production (10) The production of items in units or small batches.

unity of command (10) The principle that a subordinate should have one and only one superior to whom he or she is directly responsible.

upward communication (19) Any communication that flows from subordinates or lower-level managers to higher-level managers.

utilitarian view of ethics (5) Decisions are made solely on the basis of their outcomes or consequences.

validity (12) The proven relationship that exists between a selection device and some relevant criterion.

values (5) Basic convictions about what is right and wrong.

variable budget (9) Budget that takes into account those costs that vary with volume.

variable sampling (20) A quality control technique in which an actual measurement is taken to determine how much an item varies from the standard.

verbal intonation (16) An emphasis given to words or phrases that conveys meaning.

well-structured problems (6) Straightforward, familiar, easily defined problems.

whistleblowing (3) Reporting unethical practices by your employer to outsiders such as the press, government agencies, or public interest groups.

word processing (19) Software packages that allow users to write, change, edit, revise, delete, or print letters, reports, and manuscripts.

work sampling (12) A personnel selection device in which job applicants are presented with a miniature replica of a job and allowed to perform a task or set of tasks that are central to the job.

work teams (11) Groups of individuals that cooperate in completing a set of tasks.

written essay (12) A performance appraisal technique in which the evaluator writes a narrative describing an employee's strengths, weaknesses, past performance, and potential and then makes suggestions for improvement.

zero-base budgeting (9) A system in which budget requests start from scratch, regardless of previous appropriations.

ACKNOWLEDGMENT OF ILLUSTRATIONS

•

Chapter 1

1 The Seattle Art Museum, Eugene Fuller Memorial Collection **2** Courtesy of Sarah Lawrence College **6** Joseph Nettis/Photo Researchers **8** Eric Kahan/Leo de Wys **13** Top: Arnold C. Hinton/Monkmeyer Press; Bottom: Charles Gupton/Stock, Boston **17** Spencer Grant/Leo de Wys **18** John S. Abbott, Onyx

Chapter 2

27 Farrell Grehan/Photo Researchers **28** Courtesy of Honeywell **31** Farrell Grehan/Photo Researchers **37** AP/Wide World Photos **42** Courtesy of Western Electric **53** Richard Sobol **54** Courtesy of the Tom Peters Group, photo by Jamie Tanaka

Chapter 3

67 M. Schneps/The Image Bank **68** Mitch Kezar/Black Star **70** Teri Stratford **75** Jim Knowles/Picture Group **78** Jan Irish/Leo de Wys **83** Stacy Pick/Stock, Boston **84** Dan Ford Connolly/Picture Group

Chapter 4

93 Milton Glaser Inc. **97** Ken Straiton/The Stock Market **98** Arthur Meyerson **101** Cary Wolinsky/Stock, Boston **102** Peter Menzel/Stock, Boston **104** John Lei/Stock, Boston **106** Jeff Klein/Gamma-Liaison

Chapter 5

117 William Cone **118** Rick Friedman/Black Star **120** Edwards/Gamma-Liaison **125** @ 1989 Hallmark Cards, Inc. **129** Courtesy of Ben & Jerry's Homemade Inc./Photo by Teri Stratford **137** Brad Bower/Picture Group **138** Courtesy of Butler Manufacturing Company **141** Courtesy of Ocean Spray Cranberries, Inc.

Chapter 6

151 Pete Saloutos/The Stock Market **152** Phil Huber/Black Star **156** Kevin Horan/Picture Group **173** David Pollack/The Stock Market **173** Gabe Palmer/The Stock Market **175** Courtesy of Hewlett-Packard

Chapter 7

190 Courtesy of Weyerhauser **195** Michael Patrick/Picture Group **200** Lawrence Migdale/Photo Researchers **205** Diana Walker/Gamma-Liaison

Chapter 8

215 C. Russell Wood/Taurus Photo **216** Courtesy The Disney Store **221** Courtesy of Black & Decker **223** Courtesy of Chrysler Corp. **225** Joe McNally/Wheeler Pictures **227** Courtesy of WD-40 Co. **232** Marc PoKempner **234** Van Bucher/Photo Researchers **238** Courtesy of Norman Pattiz

Chapter 9

245 Tony Duffy/Allsport **246** Michael L. Abramson **249** Courtesy Dialog Information Services Inc. **261** @ Computer Associates International, Inc. **265** Audrey Gottlieb/Monkmeyer Press **266** Courtesy American Airlines

Chapter 10

283 Stephanie Burgher **284** Courtesy Celestial Seasonings **287** Courtesy Cessna Aircraft Company **288** Courtesy Aid Association for Lutherans **304** Courtesy 3M **306** Allen Green/Photo Researchers

Chapter 11

313 Courtesy of King James Cast Coat **314** Mike Brown/Gamma-Liaison **321** Peter Menzel/Stock, Boston **326** Kevin Horan/The Picture Group **329** Courtesy GM Corporation **332** Courtesy General Motors **333** B. Edelhast/Gamma-Liaison **340** Courtesy Hewlett Packard

Chapter 12

349 Superstock **350** Peter Yates/Picture Group **355** Dawson Jones/Stock, Boston **359** Leo de Wys Inc./Comnet **365** Bob Daemmrich/Stock, Boston **368** Flip Schulke/Black Star **370** Charles Moore/Black Star **380** Bill Nation/Sygma

Chapter 13

397 Bernard Asset/Agence Vandystadt/Photo Researchers
398 Gail Greig/Monkmeyer Press **403** Left: Courtesy Dean Witter; Right: Tom Tracy/The Stock Market **406** Spencer Grant/Monkmeyer Press **411** Pedro Coll/The Stock Market **415** Joseph Nettis/Stock, Boston **416** David Valdex/The White House

Chapter 14

425 Focus on Sports **426** Brownie Harris/The Stock Market **428** Barry O'Rourke/The Stock Market **436** Courtesy Consolidated Freightways **441** Rhoda Sidney/Monkmeyer **445** Timothy White/Onyx **448** Kevin Horan/Picture Group

Chapter 15

457 Mark C. Schwartz **458** Christopher Cunningham/Gamma-Liaison **467** Courtesy United Way **470** Gabe Palmer/The Stock Market **475** Jerry Howard/Stock, Boston **478** Courtesy Mary Kay Cosmetics

Chapter 16

487 Photo by Andrzej Dudzinski; 1988 Annual Report cover for Time, Inc. **488** John Hillery/Black Star **493** Courtesy Apple Computer, Inc. **501** Jon Feingersh/Stock, Boston **510** John Coletti/Stock, Boston **514** Courtesy Compaq Computer Corporation **518** Courtesy Hewlett Packard

Chapter 17

528 Berenholtz/The Stock Market **535** Gabe Palmer/The Stock Market **541** Teri Stratford **545** Robert Holmgren **550** Charles Feil/Stock, Boston

Chapter 18

563 Bob Krist Photography **564** Courtesy United States Air Force **566** Courtesy Mattel Toys **568** Gabe Palmer/The Stock Market **578** Courtesy Goodyear Tire & Rubber Company **581** NASA

Chapter 19

591 Comstock **592** Teri Stratford **595** Courtesy IBM **602** Courtesy ETA Systems **603** Courtesy IBM **608** Gabe Palmer/The Stock Market **613** Sepp Seitz/Woodfin Camp & Associates **616** Courtesy Quaker Oats Company

Chapter 20

625 The Regis Collection, Minneapolis, MN **626** Spencer Grant/Monkmeyer Press **631** Courtesy Quality International **635** Courtesy Reynolds Metals Company **637** Alan Levenson **645** Courtesy Levi Strauss & Company **649** Top: David Strick/Onyx; Bottom: Red Morgan

NAME INDEX

●

ORGANIZATION INDEX

•

SUBJECT INDEX

•

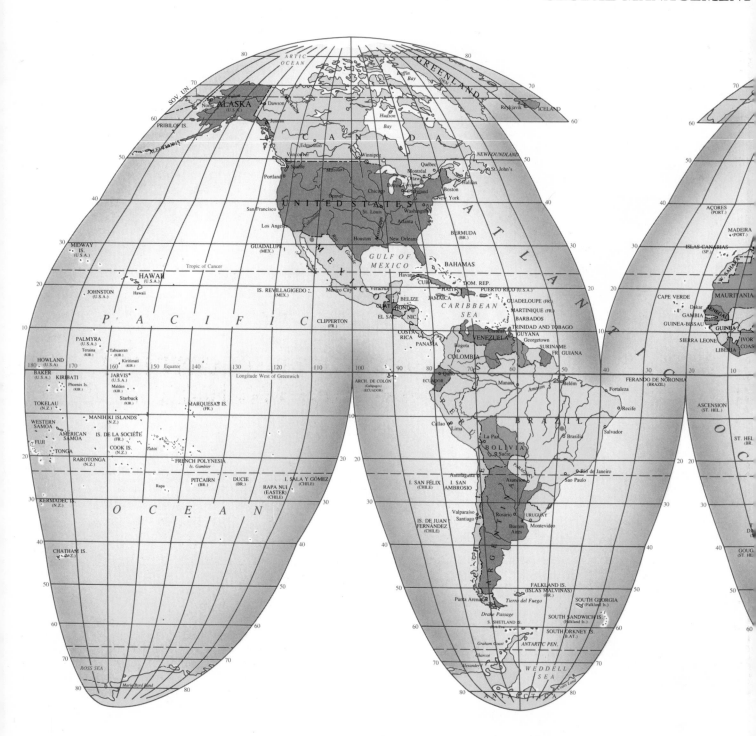

● Indicates countries about which the text provides international management applications in cases and/or boxes.